14.09.2024
To Glen — a wonderful
With admiration M

RENÉE HOUSTON

SPIRIT OF THE IRRESISTIBLES

By Miranda Brooke

Tempest Time

First published in 2016
By Tempest Time – London WC1

Copyright: main text © Miranda Brooke, 2016

Quoted text is in several instances acknowledged to be under copyright and is used in each case with the owner's permission.

Unless otherwise stated, all photographs are privately owned.

All rights reserved. No part of this publication may be reproduced, stored in a retrieval system, or transmitted, in any form, or by any means, electronic, mechanical, photocopying, recording or otherwise, without the prior permission of the publisher and copyright holder.

Miranda Brooke hereby asserts the moral right to be identified as the author of this work.

A catalogue record for this book is available from the British Library.

ISBN 978-1-5262-0636-7

Printed and bound in Great Britain by imprintDigital.com

To My Parents
John and Katherine

Acknowledgments

I offer sincere thanks to the families of Renée Houston, Patrick de Lacy Aherne, Donald Stewart, Terry Long, Billie Houston, James Alan Rennie and Shirley Houston. Without the time, support, and guidance given to me by individual family members and their generosity in making treasured photographs available, this project would have been impossible.

I would like to acknowledge the following, many of whom are stage folk, whose support was invaluable and whose knowledge of theatre history or memories relating to Renée's theatrical career has helped me tell an accurate history: Bob Bain, Sue Barbour, Jean Bayless, Helen Beardsley, Patsy Blower, Geoff Bowden, Judith Bowers, Peter Bowles, Wyn Calvin, Gary Chapman, Cyril Chresta, Gail Clarkson, Joyce Critchley, Giles Davies, Dabber Davis, Ken Dodd, Lawrence Douglas, Vivyan Ellacott, Janina Faye, Fenella Fielding, John Fisher, Joan Hall, Gordon Irving, Dame Vera Lynn, Bill Maynard, Thea McIntyre, Richard O'Callaghan, Brian O'Gorman, Matthew Lloyd, Robin Hawdon, Michael Gaunt, The Grand Order of Lady Ratlings, The Grand Order of Water Rats, Barry and Joan Grantham, Simon McKay, Eric Midwinter, Lee Montague, Richard Moore, Ann Raitt, Malcolm Rudland, Staff at Sands Film Studios, Edward Thomas, Tilly Tremayne, Elizabeth Seal, Michael Slater, Effie Star, Peter Waterman.

My search for memories of Renée during her film career and my efforts to enhance my understanding of cinema history has been helped by the assistance of the following kind individuals: Polly Baber, Kevin Brownlow, Petula Clark, Pauline Collins, Kenneth Cope, David Cleveland, Vera Day, Edward De Souza, Jean Diamond, Charles Drazin, Tony Fletcher, Rufus Frampton, Alex Gleason, Melvyn Hayes, Annabelle Heath, Lorna Henderson, Amanda Huntley, Malcolm Knight, Mike Lang, Family of late J. Lewis, Paul Matthew St Pierre, Brian McFarlane, Virginia McKenna, Juliet Mills, Patrick Moules, Piers and Hilary Murray Hill, Grahame Newnham, Margaret Nolan, Leonard Pearson, Greg Philip, Jacki Piper, A.Richardson, Dame Barbara Windsor, Marjorie Yates.

Likewise, in seeking memories and information regarding Renée Houston's television and radio career I would like to express my gratitude to the BBC for kindly allowing me to use copyright material and thank the following people who kindly responded to my enquiries: Jane Asher, Geoffrey Davies, Denise Coffey, Bernard Cribbins, Harry Enfield, Robert Gillespie, Bettine Le Beau, Baroness Heyhoe-Flint, Andrew Foster, Jonathan Lynn, Aimi MacDonald, Rita Merkelis, Sir Roger Moore, Mavis Nicholson, Nicholas Parsons, Paul Sarony, Norma Shepherd, Linda Taylor (BBC Scotland), David Wickes, Brian Willey, Barry Wilsher.

These people helped me on a practical level, with a part of research, welcomed enquiries or provided me a window into a time and place: Beryl Allingham, Joanna Bogle, Liam Fair, Suzanne Frate, Tony Freed, Sam Gates, Mélanie Gregoire-Conlon, Derek Hall, Peter Harvey, Alan Haynes, Wendy Hughes, Ivy

Keats, Mike Keats, Gráinne Madden, John Marsh, Barry May at THE BARON, John McCuin, Janet and Hugh Muir, Mary Newman, Richard Pearson, Renée's neighbours in Walton-on-Thames, Josephine Siedlecka, Peter Stone, Charlie Street, Ivy Tillson, Tony Aherne's neighbours, Sam Wall, Carolyn Wickware, Margaret Whittle, Christina Zandona.

I would like to extend my wholehearted gratitude to the following individuals, archives and libraries: Sister Mary Anthony (Archive for Our Lady and St Francis), Staff at the BFI Reuben Library, The British Library and British Newspaper Library for its generosity and support, Victor Bristoll (British Library), The BMHS, Grant Buttars (Research Collections, University of Edinburgh), The CAA, Sybil Cavanagh (West Lothian Local History Library, Linlithgow), Valerie Crosby (Haringey Archives), David Cutler (Reuters Archive), Zoe Darani (Lambeth Archives), Jonny Davies (BFI), Claire Devine (Perth & Kinross Council Archive), Helen Fisher(Cadbury Research Library), Tom Foty (Downhold Wire), Kay Foubister (Scottish Screen Archive), Dawn Galer (Redbridge Museum), Catherine Gerbrands (THE STAGE), Michelle Gibbs (Elmbridge Borough Council), Amy Graham (Kingston Upon Thames Archive), Jenny Hammerton (AP Archive), Catherine Hardman (Parliamentary Archives), Alan Harrison (Crosby Library), Hornsey Historical Society, Richard Jeffs and Kate Lees (Adelphi Films), Mike Johnson (Wintermute Society), Haley Jenkins (Weybridge Society), Andy Linehan (British Library), Brian Loudon (Festival Theatre, Edinburgh), Allison Martin (ITV GE), Claire McKendrick (Scottish Theatre Archive), Staff at The Mitchell Library, Glasgow, Vicky Mitchell (BBC), Massimo Moretti (STUDIOCANAL FILMS Ltd), Gillian Morgan (Crosby Library), Gudrun Muller (NPG), Staff at the National Archives at Kew, Staff at The National Library of Scotland, Staff at The National Portrait Gallery, Rebecca Nielsen (Barts Health NHS Trust Archives), Kathleen Dickson (BFI), John Oliver (BFI curators), Hazel Ogilvie (Harrow Archives), Margaret Peat - George Heriot's School, Liza Penn-Thomas (Richard Burton Archives), Jo Peet (Nottinghamshire County Council), Hugh Petrie (Local Studies, Barnet), Kate Poynton (Spotlight), Vic Pratt (BFI Curators), Hannah Ratford (BBC Written Archives), Josette Reeves (University of Liverpool Library), Ian Ross (at Crich Tramway Village), Neil Sayer (Lancashire Archives), Susan Scott (Savoy Archive), Sue Shickle (Holborn Community Association), Kimberley Smith (Archives - Kensington Central Library), Peter Snell (British Lion), Steve Tollervey (BFI), Staff at the Victoria and Albert Museum Theatre & Performance Archive, Simon Vaughan (Alexandra Palace Television Society), Louise Watling (Churchill Archives), Staff at Westminster Reference Library, Sian Williams (South Wales Miners' Library).

To all those whose permission to make use of copyright material is formally acknowledged, I would express my personal thanks. In a few cases where it hasn't been possible to trace representatives I ask to be forgiven, and hope to be informed so I can correct this in the future.

CONTENTS

			Page
Chapter 1	Everything in an Act	1902 – 1980	1
Chapter 2	The Last Petticoat Line	1965 – 1976	20
Chapter 3	The First Petticoat Line	1880 – 1915	38
Chapter 4	Little Mother in a Theatrical Family	1908 – 1918	51
Chapter 5	Early Training	1916 – 1919	62
Chapter 6	More Pitfalls and Pantomimes	1919 – 1925	72
Chapter 7	Lucky Number	1925 – 1927	93
Chapter 8	Identities to Play With	1910 – 1928	116
Chapter 9	The Artiste at his Work	1924 – 1930	140
Chapter 10	London and Everywhere by Storm	1926 – 1936	163
Chapter 11	The Love and Loves of the Houstons	1925 – 1938	177
Chapter 12	Enduring Loves	1920 – 1930	210
Chapter 13	Film Star of the 1930s	1932 – 1937	226
Chapter 14	Star of Musical Comedy	1935 – 1938	264
Chapter 15	Kidnapped	1936 – 1938	282
Chapter 16	Who's Your Love?	1936 – 1940	304
Chapter 17	Tough Glamour	1940 – 1945	342
Chapter 18	Variety's Sweethearts	1945 – 1949	373
Chapter 19	Milestones between Past and Future	1949 – 1952	397
Chapter 20	Driving Me Potty	1951 – 1954	415
Chapter 21	You Can Take It From Me	1954 – 1959	438
Chapter 22	Time and Tide	1958 – 1961	466
Chapter 23	Playing Mature	1961 – 1965	488
Chapter 24	It's Over Let It Go	1965 – 1970	510
Chapter 25	Punishing the Shop Steward	1970 – 1974	534
Chapter 26	Back to the Old Caravan	1974 – 1980	546
Chapter 27	Final Thoughts	1901 – 2016	558
	Notes and Credits		564
	Index		579

Chapter 1   Everything In An Act

Radio Four, October 1974. *That* panel game – the *all women* one where they discuss letters received from members of the public. The final letter wishes to know what gives each panellist her greatest simple pleasure.

Anthea Askey:	Cooking Sunday lunch and children saying poems.
Mary Stocks:	Waking in the morning and not having to get up.
Katie Boyle:	The sunset and the dawn. Long country walks.
	Leafy green trees... Dewdrops and roses...
	Putting a shine on dirty brass...
Anona Winn:	Renée dear, the last word?
Renée Houston:	Well... My greatest simple pleasure
	(pauses, and looks triumphantly around)
	is when this programme's finished and I can go to the ladies!'[1]

No wonder! They had been sitting in the Playhouse Theatre recording *Petticoat Line* well over an hour. It was typical of Renée Houston to capture the mood, lift the spirits or lower the tone with her infectious humour and gruff Scots accent. For sizeable stretches between January 1965 and January 1976 she was the show's unpredictable voice and it only took a little patter for people to take her to their hearts. She died on Saturday February 9, 1980 and television and radio shows in coming decades never witnessed her warmth, wit and thorny spirit. In her day she had no hesitations about saying what she thought, and if she was pulled up for it her inquisitor at least got shredded in the process, and there was some relief in that.

Her zest for life was saucy and game, and her belief in family values strong. She sounded like an old reactionary with her comments about young women of today leading men astray and the need to bring back chastity belts, but all of that needn't be taken literally. The middlebrow, middle class audience screamed with laughter because of the way Renée told it. She delivered a line like no other, and it wasn't necessarily in jest. Those forceful opinions could be directed at others and she would find herself living with the consequences. Painfully, for her son Tony, his introverted personality and his having a same sex partner brought him under fire, and a battle of wills between son and mother ensued. To ordinary fans however, she was so funny that agreeing or disagreeing didn't matter.

Who was that old bird beating seven bells out of her strike-leading son in the *Carry On* film? And what about before? Those with an interest in yesteryear's variety theatre and radio are a knowledgeable minority. Ask about Renée and they perk up instantly as if they've been included in a heavily guarded secret. To a generation of British comedians now legends themselves, she was held in high regard. Bob Monkhouse went to see Renée in one of her shows and said 'Jesus, she's quick!'

Today's internet-fed generation knows the Houston Sisters because of You Tube. Archive junkies, and I include myself in that group, have a taste of the Houston Sisters as they appeared in 1933 in a film called 'Radio Parade'. They're odd and a tiny bit embarrassing to modern eyes used to seeing a narrower range of identities in the world of showbiz: a cute dark-haired lassie and the other with gruff voice, boyish looks and blond Eton-cropped hair in dapper old-fashioned clothes. The accents are no different to the loons and quines you overhear on the 19 Bus heading home from Glasgow's city centre. Who's the strange boy? That's *Bill*, and the girl is Renée. *Bill* is definitely a girl and is Renée's sister, and in their time, they were two of Britain's best-loved personalities of the stage. The clip features a slick performance. You laugh forgetting eighty years have passed since then.

In 1936 at the BBC, writer Nerina Shute sat behind a nice-looking head of yellow hair, very short, very smooth. She wondered who the boy was and why he peroxided his hair, then discovered it wasn't a boy. It was a girl who came up to her with a radiant smile and started talking. The voice was exactly like a man's voice. Extraordinary. Charming. It was Billie Houston. Billie knew what Nerina was thinking.

Billie:	Isn't my voice terrible? Did you ever hear anything like it?
	Of course it's all right on the stage, very useful.
	But in real life it's a nuisance, and that's a fact.
Nerina:	Well, I like it. It's terribly distinctive.
Billie:	It's terrible. When I'm in evening dress. People look at me and wince. And it's been like this ever since I was a child.
	As a little girl with golden curls I sounded like a sergeant major with a sore throat!'[2]

Shutting down your laptop, you ask if anyone remembers Renée and Billie. Nonagenarian friends, if you have any, have a half-memory or two to share. These are precious and a truer anthem of the past compared to You Tube. With Renée you go way back – long ago to when comics like Ted Ray, Charlie Chester and Tommy Trinder would say 'Watch out – she'll skin you to death.' Bob Hope saw her and exclaimed 'Hey - That Tommy Trinder'd better be careful!' The all male top-lining act - the *Crazy Gang* chose not to work with Miss Houston and be outshone.

It emerges she was once one of Britain's brightest stars. Sprightly and elf-like in the 20s, her magic continued in 30s film musicals. She was your comic oddball. Absolutely tiny she was, bobbing along with her Clara Bow curls. The early films languish in film vaults. Some are in fragments like Adrian Brunel's masterpiece 'Variety' and John Argyle's 'Happy Days Are Here Again.' Some elude the British Film Institute's archive. Renée and Billie suffer from a sketchy visual record as a result. In the early sound era Renée was Britain's unsung female Chaplin in films like 'Their Night Out' (1933) and after that was a youthful Peter Pan, thriving most in unscripted territories. Changing herself into a strikingly beautiful woman, she went on to combine wit and glamour in such perfect proportions that she's the closest we ever got to having our own Lucille Ball. Highly sexed, Renée immediately became the focus of all eyes when she appeared on stage or elsewhere.

The Houston Sisters never officially split but from February 1936 onwards their engagements were separate, and people wondered why. That year ended with the gloom surrounding the abdication of King Edward VIII and some wished to return to happier days, just as thirty-five years later people thought about happier days before the break-up of the Beatles. Hopes the Houston Sisters would re-group came to nothing. Billie wrote a detective novel and forged new stage partnerships then faded from public view. Renée's career in musical comedy reached a zenith but her successes were mixed with frustrations, and for a while a spectral figure in a sinister pantomime seemed to punish her for losing the sister act.

Life had barely started for Renée Houston. In 1936 she began a thirty-year partnership with Donald Stewart, keeping that pantomime *hooded claw* figure at bay and acquiring new popularity. Donald was an American whose love for Britain and for Renée kept him here, when he would without question have succeeded in Hollywood given his looks and talent. His mother selflessly accepted his choice and the distance separating her while Renée gained a younger man's devotion. In a new act - *Variety's Sweethearts* - Donald's rich-voiced composure punctuated their friendly and hilarious contrapuntal singing matches such as 'St Louis versus Glasgow.' Donald was a genius in his own right for comic understatement and a source of strength and unselfish love. They had several successes in London's West End – individually and together - their voices clear and resounding in an age when the spoken word reigned supreme. Houston and Stewart survived all life threw at them: landmines, rockets, shrapnel and tax demands. Don died far too early, in 1966.

As well as thousands of theatrical appearances, Renée made at least forty-seven feature films, appeared in several film shorts and news items, and made at least seventy TV appearances. She was on countless radio broadcasts, produced a handful of gramophone recordings, gave about fifty press interviews and put her name to one book. Billie, Renée, and Donald are no different from countless pre-television stars whose glory days have been overshadowed by later stars whose film and TV appearances preserve them. Much of Renée's radio and television output appears to have been wiped. Her radio show *Petticoat Line* is largely unobtainable at the time of writing.

The main reason she's off the radar is because she neither became an international star, nor won an award for her work in theatre, film and television. There was no OBE or DBE, or dedication in the actors' church in Covent Garden, but she was a Catholic Woman of the Year in 1970. She could have *made it* internationally. Between her twenties and late fifties she was getting offers from America for Broadway and films. She was sought out for a film with Spencer Tracy and Frank Sinatra in 1959. For different reasons she turned them down: Sometimes the offer wasn't generous enough or commitments here prevented her going. She made it to the sixty years of show business mark in the mid 70s, when many of today's beloved performers were getting established. People campaign to keep the memory alive of others like Gracie Fields and quite right too. Recreating Renée's life is what's needed - so sunken in the sands is she, like Cleopatra's palace. She was once a great British star. Isn't that enough reason to remember her?

I discovered Renée only recently. Born on Thursday July 24, 1902, she was long before my time and died when I was only very young, but she appeals to me even though many timeless comediennes have appeared since. Renée's voice is closest to one in my head when I've retreated to a secret humorist world lacking courage to be so outspoken. Her voice helps me send up the world, shatteringly enough that I feel better for it. And how the world needs a sending up and cheering up. Something was special about Miss Houston and it wasn't just the talent she possessed.

Society and the way we have been entertained has changed a lot, especially if you glimpse it through the lens of someone whose career stretched all the way from 1916 to 1976. Renée's a 'way in' – an eccentric lady piloting the barge down that river of change, enhancing the journey, connecting the old world of the music hall with the familiar entertainment scene of my own lifetime. At any stage of her career in show business, elements of the 'Houston brand' were present. Recognizable was the ability to adlib in the 'live' environment of theatre and radio. If you saw the Houston Sisters back in 1929 you lived that fleeting moment, travelling vicariously, feeling their triumphs.

The comic stuff you got with Renée included physical comedy or the playing out of rivalries with her on-stage partner. You might witness an unleashing of whatever Freud's *Id* stage is, or a raucous lowering of tone. You saw her sweetly self-deprecating when happy, or fired up into a sarcastic fever pitch in the throes of quarrel. She didn't 'know her place' – an important characteristic favourably received by our grandmothers sitting in audiences across the land. Then came the misunderstandings, crosstalk, and burlesques of the rich and famous. Sometimes Renée might lord it over members of the public as compère or embarrass someone least expecting it. No idea was off limits as material, although much of it had to be *suggested*. She had guts too - a quality that turns up time and again in her story.

Beware people sitting out in front! Perhaps the most exciting thing about seeing her was when she tackled people in the audience and you couldn't be sure where the jollity would lead. You still see it happen today in pantomimes or at stand-up comedy. Renée out-talked anyone strong enough to take her on. Back in the 30s she conceded she met her match with a woman in Sunderland: 'I thought I was hot with repartee but that darling old soul had me skinned to death,'[3] she noted, impressed she had been outdone. Alan Aherne, who thought his mother a genius, witnessed her fearlessly deal with hecklers in the halls of the 40s. He recalled unsettling yells from someone high up in the gods in a 6d seat, who met everything she said with a 'Get off!' and 'Put a sock in it!' as well as other boorish banalities. Renée got more assured, stunning the hall with gathering energy. 'Bring your big foot down then, son, and I'll put a sock in it' was how she confronted the lout and her returns were threatening enough to silence him. If you catch one of her old movies, you're bound to observe how well she holds your attention, extracting the funniest elements out of a line. In 'Old Bill And Son', her *Stella* character floats across the floor in the military concert scene, flirting with soldiers she's there to entertain. Looking for a musician among them, a cheeky soldier offers to help:

Stella:	Do you play?
Soldier:	I play the 'armonica.
Stella:	Och - no you doorn't. One toot and yoo-r 'oot![4]

The variety theatre in these far off days could be something of a Sunday at Hyde Park Corner. Comics were critics or opinion-formers albeit within bounds. They tended to be patriotic but sometimes couldn't help crashing in with their opinion, especially if patriotism was twisted by unfair propaganda or a scurrilous press report. It was just like Renée to give a member of the audience her guineas-worth.

One example was the issue of Gracie Fields 'shame' for being married to 'enemy alien' Monty Banks – the Italian film director. Monty didn't want to be interned or stuck on a ship, forced to chart perilous waters bound for an internment camp. This was June 1940 and Italy had entered the war on Germany's side. Churchill had encouraged an atmosphere of suspicion with his 'Collar the lot!' statement about supposed Fifth Columnists. Gracie said 'If they intern Monty, they intern me with him,'[5] and she and Monty left for Canada, then the USA. For the last five years *Our Gracie* had been the best thing since sliced bread and now press reports were implying Gracie had deserted her country. Renée hated to see people turning on her and wasn't having any of it. Without a flinch, she responded to the rotten jeers mentioning Miss Fields, leaving a theatre slashed and silenced and the jeerer chucked out. Atmosphere was restored with the usual Houston send up. Soon the two-faced members of the audience were laughing at the expense of something or someone else. Flowers of gratitude arrived - sent by the Rochdale superstar in exile. For Alan, who witnessed the frightening episode, the big box of liqueur chocolates from Gracie was how the episode never got to be forgotten. The Glaswegian Rottweiler had growled. Gracie and Monty toured and raised money for the British war effort all the time they were abroad, taking no wages for themselves.

Wyn Calvin, Vice-President of the British Music Hall Society and Water Rat is of the generation that learned the fundamentals of theatre in *Twice Nightly Variety*. He appeared with Renée in a touring revue - one of the *principals* or *No. 1 tours*. It went to Edinburgh, Glasgow, and Plymouth. This was before she stopped touring in the 50s. Whether it was variety or weekly Rep, the tradition was for younger artistes to develop their voice. On Tuesdays a man would walk round to the back of the stalls, judging anyone lacking projection, yelling 'Are you keeping it a secret?'

He told me Renée had trained her voice so well it travelled to the back row of the circle. Tessie O'Shea was another lady artist whose voice had the same impact. Of course, the clubs took over from the variety theatres as the place to see comedians in the 70s and 80s, and comics played to the tables in front with the overall performance becoming smaller. Performers of Renée's generation also tended towards aggressively large movements - too big for television and requiring a toning down. Miss H first dabbled in television in the early days as one of Professor Baird's variety guinea pigs at Crystal Palace, and did her first TV in April 1937. Boy could that voice tell a story! Albert Mackie, commenting on Scotland's greats in 1973 theorized that Renée's 'ability to amuse was derived from the old Glasgow linguistic contrast. She could talk awfully posh Kelvinside or Mayfair or lapse into her broader accent.'[6]

When Renée was a young comedienne, variety was the nation's most popular form of entertainment. Her act with Billie says something about what people found funny in the age of George V. Strangely it isn't so different to today. They played to packed Empires, Palaces and Hippodromes across the country, touring with an energy few business people today could sustain. Playbills added the words *'The Irresistibles'* as bill matter and Renée believed in her irresistibility – where men were concerned. She possessed an element of self-deprecation for most of her Houston Sisters years. Early on, she was an eccentric wallflower in the Nellie Wallace vein. Nellie is someone we never hear of now - the girl whose soldier never took her out in the light, because she was best in the *gloaming*. Nellie's looks were awkward and her behaviour eccentric. The joke was her self-delusion about her attractiveness to men. Renée's parents used to tease her calling her 'Nellie Wallace.' Yet, both comediennes sent up the topic of female attractiveness and being 'on the market' for love. For all her flirting and exuberance, Renée didn't have what they used to call 'it' – not early on. The funny thing was, Miss Houston's beauty developed and she seemed to grow more beautiful and seductive as the years went on.

The Houston Sisters were roguish, impromptu and a type of alternative comedy in their time. 'A Riot with the Houston Sisters' was how these little *Glesca keelies* were sometimes billed. Appearing by Royal Command at the Alhambra Theatre London, on Thursday May 27, 1926, they scored with a 'new Susie song' - Leslie Sarony's 'Susie Was A Real Wild Child'[7] - a hymn to naughty children, with choruses about mama's rich relations calling by only for *Susie* to blab the nasty things her dad had said about them. What a terror!

Believe me, I knew Susie, I knew Susie. Susie Was A REAL Wild Child!'[8]

Many a crooner covered it, Eddie Cantor-like: eyes rolled up to heaven, but the Sisters did it with a true coming home quality.[9] Driving everyone crazy was Houston territory.

Gramophone record of 'Susie Was A Real Wild Child' – The Houston Sisters. ACO label, September 1926
(Photo: Author's Collection)

Beware young men standing in the wings! Actor Richard O'Callaghan remembered Renée as a strong and feisty woman with a resounding Scots accent, entering her seventies at the time of the film 'Carry On At Your Convenience' but he didn't share any scenes with her. His mother Patricia Hayes had worked with Ted Ray in the *Ray's a Laugh* show on the radio, and with Renée in *Rock-A-Bye Sailor* at the Phoenix Theatre in 1962. Patricia told her son an extraordinary story she'd heard from Ted Ray about Renée that went back to an evening in the variety theatre when they were on the same bill, and it shows how totally uninhibited she was. Waiting in the wings Ted stood beside Renée and asked her 'What time is it?' Totally serious, taking her breast out of her dress, she looked down at the nipple and said 'I make it about a quarter to eight'. Quite the little rule-breaker the young Miss Houston was - if it meant a good gag AND the joy of seeing a young man blush to high heaven.

In their stage act Renée was most frequently *Bill*'s kid sister, despite being older by four years in reality. She was sweet-voiced and inquisitive but fiendishly impudent at the end of the turn. *Bill* was gruff-voiced, very Scottish and matter-of-fact. At the beginning Renée's stage character brimmed with the exuberance of a child wild with curiosity and irrepressibility. How those watching from the gallery loved to see her entrance! She didn't so much as *walk* as bob up and down constantly like the lightest ping-pong ball. She weighed less than seven stone. Her feet forever seemed to be dancing and her curly mop shook as she followed *Bill* - a boy scout with an air of authority. With her dander up, Renée would take raking strides across the stage then do something madcap such as running out into the audience, chattering to delighted members of the public.[10] Sometimes the Houstons were girlfriend and boyfriend and other times just partners in crime. It's down to variety theatre's amazing lack of reality that role and scenario shifted without the slightest care. Try straightening out the gangly lack of refinement of these irresponsible youngsters? No chance.

Sometimes, as the curtains went up, you might glimpse them on stage lulled into apparent slumber by a nurse. As soon as *nursie* has tiptoed off, up get the terrible infants and proceed to imitate *Pa* and *Ma* at a cabaret.[11] Seen in their wee nursery there's a shock value to the idea of infants behaving like a couple of moderns. The stage design makes an illusion of the children's size, with a towering sofa or chair so big the kiddies require all sorts of physical feats to climb them. There's *Bill* pushing his sister off and Renée falling and exposing her knickers. The illusion is an old theatrical device but with the two Houstons scrambling over the furniture it's new. Sixty years later we're in hysterics watching Harry Enfield and Kathy Burke in the *Harry and Lulu* sketches - toddlers more diabolical. When I asked what had inspired the sets for these Harry Enfield told me his idea came from Laurel and Hardy and suggested their idea might have been swiped from Renée and Billie. The 30s film is 'Brats' and Stan and Ollie's shrunken selves look so 'wrong 'against the sets it's hilarious just for that. Did impresario Sir Oswald Stoll really have three sets of outsize furniture specially built at the London Coliseum, each appearing at the turn of a revolving stage? The playwright and promoter of Scottish Arts, Tom Gallacher refers to this in a dramatic work he wrote about Renée? Few images of their sets have survived.

Occasionally, in sketches, the Sisters contrived against another character but mostly it was Renée versus *Bill* – the miniature *Clara Bow* doing her utmost to annoy the sensible dour blonde *boy*. In one sense they projected an ideal version of a relationship: so close that insults didn't matter. In Renée, mischief was willful and obvious with *Bill* rationalizing and keeping control until his patience was tried. If you have an older brother who has tolerated your subversive antics with patience and forbearance as you try to grab his interest by shocking him, then you are Renée and he is poor *Bill*. Writers in the theatrical press described the mounting tension of the Houston's 'wee quarrel'. In one 'Renée skirmishes around Billy while he sturdily employs 'stonewall tactics.'[12] It's surprising just how much column space was devoted to their trials and tribulations. How they would report the game of redskins and cowboys afoot that saw *Bill* eager to lose his sister's company!

Even national newspapers would inform us how, in spite of *Bill*'s pleas and threats, Renée was stubbornly insisting on staying put. And so followed an 'extraordinarily clever study of a child struggling against the fear of being left alone.'[13] Little did they know that expressing the 'supernatural terrors of childhood' was a Houston specialty. Some manic quality allowed Renée to keep us gripped. She mirrored fake confidence and human denial like no other. *Bill*'s tactics got crueller and a columnist who witnessed the squabbles in 1927 reported: 'She shall be left alone in the dark – at the mercy of mice and ghosts.' *Bill* strides away and Renée laughs 'at the idea she was afraid.' She's gabbling and laughing more and more, but unconvincingly so. She tries to deny she's afraid 'until every man Jack of us wants to rush forward with a box of night-lights.'[14] In spite of her provocations Renée was a dab hand at getting sympathy - on and off the stage.

A 'domestic quarrel' was central to the repertoire and grew out of the squabbles with *Bill*. A musical sketch from the Thirties begins with a poignant song by Renée. *'Nicky'* is her 'six weeks married and no sign of a

Everything in an Act

quarrel' betrothed, about to shatter all with his piano playing. *Nicky* finishes shaving, begins tinkling on the keys, and as Renée puts breakfast on the table the couple pride themselves on being 'too modern' to argue. Soon little irritations disturb the bliss. Accusations lead to a near breakdown of marital harmony. The central object restoring peace for Renée and *Nicky* is '*mumma's little bird . . . love love in fetters and chains.*' That's the canary in a cage she speaks to after her opening song. The dialogue in the sketch is fast-interspaced and quickly comes to the boil:

Renée: Oh Nicky, nobody's ever said anything like that to me before, darling.
Don't play the piano when I'm talking to you. Do you really mean it?
Never mind the sailor shirt. Nicky sweet, (tinkling gets louder)
Nick - I've said don't do it.
DON'T DO IT! (loud)- it's most aggravating please!(smashes on piano)
Nicky: Who are you bullying? You would lose your temper, wouldn't you!
Renée: Haven't I got reason to? Well my mother was right - now that I come to look at you she was right. You watch him, she said. You'll find him out – the long-jawed villain.
Nicky: Is that so! Well I quit. I can only expect this from a common chorus girl.
Renée: Chorus girl yes, but common? Common! You!
You think that because you've given me this lousy dump to live in, you've done something for me.[15]

It gets petty with the question of who owns which possession right down to the tea cloth. Then it emerges that the canary was given to both of them:

Nicky: If he's so crazy about you why does he start whistling when I come up the stairs at night?
Renée: What do you want him to do, bark and wag his tale?
Nicky: Now let's be fair. You want your freedom and I want mine.
Renée: That's obvious.
Nicky: So let's give him his - open the window.
Renée: That suits me - yes it does. (starts to cry)
Put the window down. Put the window down I tell you!
Oh it's terrible - you can have him. I've changed my mind.
Nicky: Oh no, he likes you. You must have him.
Renée: Oh no, he's fond of you too. He does whistle when you come upstairs everyday night.
Nicky: Oh no, you must have him. He likes us both.[16]

There's compactness in this lead up to a crisis and Renée's ability to squeeze out the comedy is astonishing. Renée made a gramophone record[17] of the sketch in February 1936 with her husband Patrick de Lacy Aherne voicing the role of '*Nicky*' in an accent that sounds very 'London' although he was born and bred in the West Midlands.

The romantic couple's quarrel saw countless variations, and became one of the most polished routines in the business in the hands of Renée and

9

Donald Stewart, who became her third husband in 1948. They combined elegantly barbed dialogue and a foundation that was tuneful, albeit with interruptions. A typical skit involved Donald in the role of 'producer' writing an adaption of *Forever Amber*, trying to persuade Renée to go 'legit' whilst she has other ideas. He might sing a heartfelt song like 'You're breaking my heart' with Renée making an attempt at ballet so valiant it diverts the audience from the pathos. With his patience forfeited, the inevitable quarrel ensues until they reach a compromise. With Billie it had been more dagger-like with arguments often not resolved, whereas Donald could offer hope of resolution with Renée sometimes melting in submissiveness.

She could accompany fast-paced comic delivery with a swash-buckling physicality worthy of a Stewart Grainger at full mettle, fire-breathing at the same time. Sir Carol Reed's film 'A Girl Must Live' (1939) places Renée in an unforgettable girl-fight that has to be cinema's best. The latent violence touches a nerve but never do you see the physically frightening more redeemed by hilarious verbal onslaught. Similarly, Renée packs the punches in a priceless film from Frank Launder and Sidney Gilliat: the patriotically themed 'Two Thousand Women' (1944). Something about her voice and Scots identity made her earthy and human. She stood out a mile at a time when actresses had to present themselves as such ladies.

Renée stayed well within the bounds of decency if the all-seeing and all-knowing Sir Oswald Stoll, owner of the London Coliseum, was watching. Nevertheless, a dangerous streak of commonness ran through the Houston Sisters: their naughty antics rescued by youth and femininity. You couldn't resist Renée whether you were Joe Bloggs or Queen Mary. She was a dab hand at Max Miller-like innuendo but this side of her came later. In the 20s and until the mid 30s, she might be good for a prank but she was seldom coarse. Tom Gallacher tells us that Renée and Billie were among the favoured few for whom Queen Mary would remove her white gloves when clapping. Under less scrutiny, Renée could revert to gags of the salty sort. When you have years of experience providing seaside entertainment you raise or lower the barometer of suggestiveness to suit an audience effortlessly.

Vesta Tilley as 'Algy the Masher'   (Photo: Author's collection)

Vesta Tilley - international male impersonator - dubbed by Punch as *The London Idol* and still treading the boards when Renée and Billie were starting their double-act, was the ultimate provider of witty, inoffensive and studied male characterization. She would have stood for none of Renée's salty humour. If Billie was the modern Vesta, then *Algy the Masher* was now bravely deflecting one browbeating after another by his appalling innuendo-prone little 'wife'. How things had changed! From the 40s onwards Renée's act featured cheekier dialogues and this segued into the body of humour that future dialogues grew out of - those of Norman Hudis et al: the kind that flourished in the 60s and 70s in the 'Carry On' movies. That was before tastes changed and all that too went out of the window, at the dawn of Punk and the new wave in comedy.

The strong visual appeal of the Houston Sisters made them palatable. The moral misgivings of a less attractive couple of kids might have offended the holier than thou. The 20s was a great age for mad-looking dollies. Adrienne's toyshop in Paris turned out beauties whilst OXO dolls and the bisque-headed type that now grace antiques magazines were truly popular. The doll-maker of the bisque-headed ones must somehow have appropriated the look of the Sisters, or vice versa. This fashion direction arrived at the same time. A 'nursery' look was in vogue. Not only did women look doll-like but baby talk was all the rage. Boys named '*Teddy*', girls named '*Baby*', *Toy soldiers* and cross-talking kids were acceptable then. Kiddie acts were plentiful in the theatre. You could understand why any motif of regeneration held a place in the psyche then, with the Great War and all its horrors still so recent.

The effect on stage of the Houston Sisters appealed to children. Thea McIntyre and her sister Anne were taken to see Renée and Billie at the Pavilion Theatre, Glasgow, around 1933 or 1934. She was barely eight years old, and remembers the Houstons starting with a song. They did a dance and followed this with banter. Thea told me Renée and Billie were enjoyable to watch and the single most appealing thing to her was the fact that on stage she saw a little girl and a little boy. When her local Brownies organized a concert Thea devised a routine based what she had witnessed at the Pavilion, and this was the impetus for Thea and Anne to go into the business - their mother masterminding their development into 'The Hislop Sisters.'[18] At first they intentionally resembled the Houstons, with Thea playing the girl and Anne, the boy. They look amazing in a photo wearing their Toy Drum Major outfits, beating small drums and standing on a large drum – really an orange box. When Anne wanted to wear dresses they altered their act. Becoming professional in 1938 they travelled the British Isles and toured with ENSA from 1942-1946. Later on in Thea's long career she was on the *Les Dawson Show* rib tickling the nation as one of the *Roly Polys*. Still youthful and charming as ever Thea wows with a song and instructs a dance routine.

Renée's specialty was holding forth a line of crosstalk, responding to questions with unexpected answers and mining of the workings of her

Houston brain – strange territory at times. Something restored order and led into song. I've transcribed a little Houston Sisters dialogue from the 1935 film 'Variety - The Romance of the Music Halls' directed by Adrian Brunel where Renée and Billie are seen on a bare stage: a close representation of their real act in the theatre. *Bill* is Renée's *producer cum fiancé* in the sketch. *Bill* wants to put on 'a real legitimate play' giving a reluctant Renée the part of a village belle. She launches into it with the worst line in raunchy dance:

Billie:	No, No, No! Renée! Listen darling. I said a village Belle.
Renée:	Oh yeah but you don't know what a tough village you've landed in.
Renée:	And I'm the quietest babe in town.
Billie:	Now listen. Do it artistic. Oh yes. Classical.
Renée:	Oh sort of toujours politesse. (sings 'toujours toujours la politesse')
Billie:	Oh minus the song!
Renée:	Oh my je suis but you're a blinkin' mess… Still I'll do my best. I know what you want and you're going to get it.
Renée:	Can I have some classical music please, Horace? (to conductor) (Dances artistically to classical music)
Billie:	Beautiful darling, beautiful! Now that really is perfect.
Billie:	No, No, No, No!!!
Billie:	Just a minute? (a loud dissonant noise of 'clap' 'clap' 'clap')
Billie:	Yeah, we heard it the first time …
Renée:	Someone was applauding and I hadn't finished.
Billie:	It was yer legs that were rattling, dear.
Renée:	Oh yes, rattling good pair of legs.[19]

Only fragments remain of Brunel's film. The story is about a variety theatre through decades of change and features 'behind the scenes life.' In the Sisters' speech are non-sequitors and malaprops and the art of coming back to something 'placed'. Misunderstandings and their consequences make for funny and cheeky sketches like this sample from the 'Radio Parade' sketch.

Billie:	Listen darling, there's something else I've decided. In future I'm doing my single act.
Renée:	Bill, I've always wanted to see you do a single act.
Billie:	You have, have you?
Renée:	Now let me see you - Pull down your jumper and begin.
Billie:	Now leave me alone.
Renée:	Now what are you going to do?
Billie:	I'm a ventriloquist.
Renée:	A whatuquist?
Billie:	I said a ventriloquist.
Renée:	Oh don't worry, I'm a Presbyterian, don't let that worry you, we'll get on very well.
Billie:	You mean to tell me you don't know what a vent is?
Renée:	One of the things in the new houses to let the air in and out.[20]

Symbolizing criminal lawyer *Billy Flynn*'s manipulative methods, the 2002 film 'Chicago' has him in one sequence with puppet *Roxie Hart* on his knee, copying the Houstons' vent act in 'Radio Parade.' Old footage truly inspires!

Early routines of Renée and Donald's stage partnership included embarrassments with Donald ridiculed for his attempts to be as Caledonian.[21] Before Donald arrived she used to win little victories over *Bill*. It also became de rigueur for the conductor of the orchestra to be coaxed into taking her part often against a partner, or to find his worthy self the butt of her joke. Bandleaders braved themselves for the likely moment of embarrassment with Renée and some of these priceless moments survive on film. In another part of 'Variety', Horace Sheldon, leading the orchestra, is roped into the quarrel and the sketch twice features very risqué jokes. Billie delivers the scenario – a 'picture' of them *married six weeks* and finding out Renée's been led astray.

Billie: Little did he know that a villain lurked in the background.
Renée: In the background! No . , . in the foreground.
Look at him! (Looks at Horace Sheldon – Horace looks up)
Billie: Don't be silly. Horace is no good as a villain.
Renée: He hasn't been up to your dressing room for a cup of tea –
I can see that!
Billie: Now get off and I'll tell you then.
Renée: Tha' suits me.
Renée: Horace! Oi! – (winks) (Horace silently put his finger to his lips)
Billie: I said get off.
Renée: Now what do you think I'm doing?
Billie: Off the stage!
Renée: Alright Horace (very Mae West) if you don't want to follow me,
you don't know what you're missing.[22]

The fragment is a record of how Renée and Billie typically operated as laughter-maker and 'feed'. They filled our imaginations with fast-moving scenarios, building the interest then releasing the energy. There was plenty of scope for Renée's stockpile of comic voices. Horace gets brought in a later on as we hear about *Bill*'s estrangement from his baby's mother, whom he's surprised to learn is Josephine Baker:

Billie: Even yet I can't believe it's true.
If it wasn't for my child, I'd commit suicide.
Renée: Daddy Daddy! (Shirley Temple voice)
Billie: Why Baby?
Renée: Daddy I've been looking for you.
Billie: Have you my love?
Renée: Been out in all pubs and I couldn't find you, and so Horace there . . .
(Horace raises his elbow)
Billie: Nicely nicely . . . (nudge and wink) (changes the subject)[23]

When the Sisters were to appear before King George V and Queen Mary, her family ordered Renée to avert from making eye contact with royalty. In the dressing room after the performance Billie declared 'the King has the kindest smile I have ever seen.' Then came a stink about why Billie could look at the King and Renée couldn't. Her sister had to admit that 'knowing you as we do, we were afraid you might speak to them.'[24] Renée had, after all, and not long before, started up a line of patter with a man in a balcony seat with his arm in a sling: 'That'll teach you not to bite your nails, my lad', she teased him, not realizing, apparently, that it was the Prince of Wales who had injured his arm after falling off a horse. The performance before King George was actually the first time parts of a Royal Performance were broadcast to the nation by the BBC, and the Houstons were one of only three acts selected to go on air. The broadcast has not survived. A solemn-voiced announcer supplied commentary and filled the gaps between turns, telling us about Dick Henderson's small bowler hat, or Robb Wilton's brand of confused officialdom. The Houston Sisters were in the second act, and Renée was provocative as ever, addressing the conductor in the pit as 'George' in more than familiar terms. It was her husband George Balharrie carrying the baton, although few knew this. It led to misinterpretation, especially with friends and family in Scotland. Listening to the radio they exclaimed with pride 'See how Renée has got on - she calls the King 'George!'[25] First in a line of conductors to meet Renée's jibes with a look of forbearance, Mr Balharrie played his part, allowing the Sisters to be more irresistible than ever.

Renée had the same cheek with Sir Henry Wood who, with his eighty-strong symphony orchestra, returned to the London Coliseum[26] in early 1930 conducting Wagner's 'Song from the Rhine Daughters.' Sir Henry was full of praise for Sir Oswald Stoll's fine music hall, for Stoll himself, and for the Coliseum's superb lighting. On final call, the Clyde Maiden suddenly swathed the velvet curtain round her waist behaving as if someone from behind was pulling at it. With yells of 'Oh Sir Henry *do* contain yourself!' she led the audience on. Then one night, to surprise her, Sir Henry did actually seize her from behind the curtain, only to carry her off in front of the Coliseum audience. Such a great scout he was, Renée recalled, looking back.

You didn't have to pay close attention to a Houston Sisters sketch although engagement paid off through attentively following the quick fire jokes and clever dialogue. Sometimes you still needed imagination to fathom out that unfolding 'quarrel' between Renée and *Bill*. The maximum was achieved in the most concise timeframe. Still, the act appeared funny in a nonsense way - lively and absurd - not trying to be smart and erudite.

In 1920s Britain the term 'burlesque' meant a parody or send-up of anything ripe for a laugh that the audience could share in. Among provincial and metropolitan audiences mitochondria were out on deck: a pulse – sparking the funny bones of the future – the same that shook with laughter at sketches by French and Saunders years later. Those Houston Sisters did burlesque after burlesque. There were send-ups of *Cinderella* and the *Three*

Bears, and anything to do with childhood. At the Coliseum, in which they were often in highbrow company, the sisters would be their rude and satirical little selves. Returning from a party where Renée has done nothing but howl and eat, she suddenly demonstrates a new taste for classic contemporary dance. Billie is persuaded to be *Anton Dolin* while Renée assumed the grace of *Nemchinova*. Having done their worst with Diaghilev's Russian Ballet they feel confident to introduce their own terpsichorean creation - *Clogwallop* - atonal in setting and calling for the loan of George's boots.[27] George had no choice but to oblige. The real Dolin and Nemchinova were frequently sharing the very same bill.

The Sisters sent up people who made films, like Garbo, Shirley Temple and Tallulah Bankhead, and parodied new crazes or contemporary events. Almost thirty years later in *Cockles and Champagne*, at London's Saville Theatre, Renée was getting laughs burlesquing the Hollywood actress whose casting call with producer, ingénue and leading man has explosive dynamics. In a scene *Queens of Sport*, in the company of Donald Stewart and Fenella Fielding, Renée introduced a 'hunting woman' persona. A few years before, in *Sauce Tartare* at the Cambridge Theatre, she jibed at the Cold War and the MI5 and one burlesque - her *Deanna of the Dairies* – was enough to make the Daily Mail declare 'The show would have been worth seeing if only for her delicious stage-struck dairy girl selling milk by day and stopping amateur shows by night, but it clicked from the start.'[28]

A little stage anarchy suited them. Witness Billie and Renée rehearsing a *play within a play* at the Hackney Empire in 1929 with unpredictable results: the Sisters as thespians, with the great music hall star Billy Bennett butting in on the sketch. How will they ever become legitimate at this rate? In the halls, having another star butt in on your act was a *time-honoured brand*, to use a phrase beloved of Chinese food packaging. The Sisters were notorious at it. Why not see them in a rattling good send up of the music hall itself! This happened same year, same Billy Bennett - but at the Holborn Empire. In their all-star *Night of Old Time Music Hall*, for the last turn the leading players did a version of Fred Karno's *Mumming Birds* sketch. Bennett - world famous for 'She was poor but she was honest' played the inebriated and disruptive swell - the one Chaplin was famed for. Billie was the saucy boy high in the box, Fred Lewis was a stagey Dickens impersonator and Renée was a classical vocalist and ballerina.[29] Even in the real old days these sketches weren't as *Old Time* as you would think, but cutting send ups. Tamer nostalgia-themed variety nights were, of course, revived by Don Ross et al, and have been ever since.

In programmes for obscure 50s variety shows, you discover the forgotten impact of Renée and Donald on small theatres or Butlins holiday camps, in shows like *Renée Houston Discoveries* - on the road in 1956 - stopping twice at Inverness after a week at Dingwall's Town Hall. 'Scotland's Ambassadress to England'[30] was compère, and her audience interaction and repartee was one Cilla Black and others would have found inspirational. Constant jokes at the audience's expense came with every prize distributed at swift-moving shows such as *Alive and Stripping* at Woolwich Empire. Their act followed a *model Derby Day* provided by Percival's dogs, with Bob and Rita Rema's balancing act on the bill. Renée was fond of 'chattering in asides to the audience' and at this time, the parlous financial position they found themselves in meant bread and butter jobs were accepted with good grace. Patter came fast and loose, and they were at ease with the public in these mingles, forgetting radio and TV producers or executives.

'Riotous' was an adjective used to describe the antics of the Houston Sisters. Ever wanted to smash up your office in joyful abandon and stick a litter basket over your boss's head? I think the best way to illustrate this side of the Sisters is to refer to their unexpected scene in 'Blighty' – a silent film from 1927 directed by Adrian Brunel. Told that the long 1914-18 war is over, the film shows people going mad with joy. Brunel injected a slice of vaudeville in the right place, having a pair of comediennes defeat pomposity in a nice way. Working at the Ministry of Information's Cinematograph Department, set up in 1917 to advise the War Office on film production, Brunel had himself, hated 'stupid Departmental methods.' He risked getting into trouble writing scurrilous skits concerning Ministry methods in the Department's newspaper.

In the hands of these diabolical imps drama was also taken down from its lofty heights to a level best described as 'Saturday night Shettleston'. How Renée loved it when the act preceding or following the Houstons offered scope for one of her ripe comments! She ran in crying out 'A thousand times goodnight!' in broad Glasgow, having the audience in fits as the Coliseum's revolving stage hadn't quite spun *'The Balcony scene from Romeo & Juliet'* away from view, happily sending up *Romeo*'s line.

This was the week of June 6, 1926 when John Gielgud and Gwen Ffrangcon-Davies were top-liners - presenting a Shakespeare playlet to music hall audiences. Compared to the Regent, formerly the Euston Palace of Varieties where the full play had seen a revival in 1924, the two thespians were paid well by Sir Oswald that fortnight. It was worth putting up with Stoll's 'pink and cardboard-looking' marble balcony that made Gwen look like she was standing in the bath.[31] To tone down the blossom pink bath, Miss Ffrangcon-Davies changed to a darker wig for the second week instead of the golden one she had on the week before. Theatre entertainment was fantastically varied then, with audiences carried away by the dancing of Anton Dolin and Phyllis Bedells.[32] And who could forget the act following the Sisters: a twenty stone saxophonist: *'Robins with his walking music store'*!

A modern appetite for that vein of juvenile delinquency exists although it's all too real now with TV shows like *Geordie Shore*. In the 20s, voluble patter of young women if the accent was Home Counties, was a torturous prospect, but a Scots accent passed. A columnist mused that a 'willful perversity of the young' summed up the spirit of the Houston Sisters.[33] He places them in the tradition of Burns whose *'Address to the Unco Guid or Rigidly Righteous'* criticized narrow-minded and excessively religiosity and epitomized the youth of Scotland's ease in defying sacrosanctity. It's amazing that their broad Glaswegian should suddenly become the *cat's meow*! As The Era newspaper puts it: 'though the Houston Sisters may describe Scotch as 'not a language but a beverage it has long been something a music hall audience wants to hear as well as swallow, and Will Fyffe's brand of the spoken kind is well above proof...'[34] Renée and Billie's act sampled vernacular with a few words requiring translation to bring non-Scots up to speed. Not all knew *Bill*'s *'wee but and ben'* was his humble house recreated on stage. When common little Renée caused a scene outside it, the meaning became obvious.

Variety stage, broadcasting, gramophone discs, Silent Films, Talkies: the Houston Sisters conquered each. Success followed, but so did unexpected pitfalls. Renée triumphed in musical comedy – having one of the biggest West End hits of 1935 and continued in variety for the next two decades in a double act with Donald Stewart, whose looks and wit complimented hers. As an older performer Renée became radio's gruffest voice. I wonder why the type of truly outspoken older entertainer of Renée's ilk is now rare? Once, it reassured us, offering us a kind of catharsis.

Her witticisms stay in your mind, as do her stories. Her ghost written memoir 'Don't Fence Me In' published by Pan in paperback, had the misfortune to come out at a time when nostalgic respect for variety's glory days was on the wane. Young and fashionable folk were finding traditional variety embarrassing. Time has moved on, and in the second decade of the 21st Century, interest in the period seems to revive as the *Downton Abbey* generation has succeeded the *Upstairs Downstairs* generation.

Tom Gallacher (by kind permission of Heroes Centre)

Tom Gallacher, born in 1934, known for his play *Mr Joyce is Leaving Paris*, wrote *Renée Houston Rehearses Her Life*. It's a play within a play with the fictional Renée directing a musical production about her life and members of the cast staging a mutiny against the stubborn, irascible old veteran. The play was never performed although it was published. Timing was a reason. I don't find it extraordinary in the least that our Renée inspired a play.

Some people have an unpleasant memory of Renée they wish to forget, and some, frankly, couldn't stand her. She made them know she was the star. She told people what she thought of them and was known to cut up rusty like no other. After being at the receiving end of her acid tongue some personalities of the entertainment world were turned off. On a few occasions her argumentativeness and threatening manner led to ugly scenes. This really was the effect of alcoholism – a tragic flaw. She often took the moral high ground after an outburst. She would sometimes say she wished she knew what it was she did – or didn't do, about apparent mistakes and estrangements. She was 'innocent' - she'd have you know. Having said that, she bravely stood her ground and didn't skirt around issues. Pushover she was not, and if it meant her material or her due fee were compromised, or if her lifestyle met with complaints, someone had gone too far.

Gone is that theatrical milieu of acid tongues, histrionic rages and putdowns backstage. Renée was a *Margo Channing* of that world. Confronting her about her behaviour might get you a wallop over the head, as Sir Peter Hall found out. Dignified performers like Jessie Matthews fell victim to Renée's *cruelty* campaign, and comedians like Chic Murray got a panning. Showdowns with management were spectacular public affairs, and producer meetings could be scorched by her dragon-like tendencies. The grapevine says it happened a lot, if the grapevine is worth believing.

Friends in high places came in handy. Renée could always rely on a friend to get her out of a mess. Fabulous at getting away with it, she was! All that said, the truth is plain that significantly more friends than enemies existed. Judging by my conversations with many from the theatrical profession who knew her, she was loved and admired. All in all, she never ceased to be irrepressible or irresistible. You've got to see the funny side . . . Was it a case of the world of music hall colliding with the legitimate theatre, with Renée Houston, emerging from the explosion?

Theatre played a big part in the life of her parents, her siblings, three husbands and her wider family. Her four children - two of whom were impetuously and mysteriously adopted - saw the pressures of this lifestyle on their mother and rebelled against it. There's much more to her story than the anecdotes Miss Houston used to tell, and the big question that seems to hang in the air when you read Renée's memoir 'Don't Fence Me In' is why can someone so lovable be so alone? She writes on page 157, two pages before the end: 'Two of my sons have vanished beyond my ken. The other, Alan, lives 6000 miles away in Hollywood, and my daughter Terry-Jo is also in the States.'[35] There's a sense she's begging for an explanation to that question. Is it a cry for help? It's been a 'journey' finding out why. What if the onus placed on the performer is overwhelming, when a whole life has been spent in the theatre? Ironically, the very parts she was playing seemed to blend into real life and vice versa. There's a flaw to Renée's character that caused her loneliness - faintly suggested in the title 'Don't Fence Me In.' Tom Gallacher gets at Renée's *neglect* of Billie in later life as a key to her problems, but this is misdiagnosed, and I put forward my own answers later.

Characters abound in this history. There were three Houston Sisters, including the talented Shirley - living to some extent in the shadow of her two older sisters. There was a talented Houston brother and lots of husbands. Renée is the main protagonist, but her family story, the times she lived through and the industry she worked in, are all important threads in interpreting her life. She's a human sort you sympathize with. Harmony comes most often - dysfunction and alcoholism other times. With the latter she had a personal struggle and during her last years tried to keep this in check. As a private individual she is elusive, and my understanding is limited but there are conclusions I draw based on the varied accounts of her I have listened to. Love, laughter and survival are at the heart of this story.

During her sixty years in entertainment there was a period of basking in the limelight followed by a brave and tough struggle to keep working that many actors share and can understand. It's a rags-to-riches fairytale if you consider the experience of Renée and Billie's granddad as an immigrant worker in Glasgow. Billie lived with mounting debts in later years. In Renée's case, everything went back to rags for a decade and they lived in the shadow of bailiffs. Despite making an insane amount of money in their golden years, Renée had no handle on money and the taxman was on her back for almost half a century. Somehow she managed to be gay and happy regardless. 'Do you have any standing orders?' she might have been asked. 'No ducks - just standing ovations' would have been a likely reply.

In this day and age lifelong theatrical apprenticeships are very rare and magical success stories are few. Impresarios are risk-averse where productions are concerned. Individuals not cushioned by privilege, whose self-belief alone propels them might recognize something of themselves in this story's heroes. Carefree and careless was our Renée, who came up from humble beginnings and went through a long apprenticeship to enjoy a few golden years with the world at her fingertips. In a notoriously precarious business, she survived rock bottom partly because of her talent, and partly because she had one of the best things in life - the love of those around her.

Before I bring to a close the longest introduction in the world, I want to say that many people inside and outside the profession remember Renée's big heart and helping hand. She had the gift of fun and on stage or in a studio was everyone's dear old aunt – the image most of the young actors or directors who worked with her still retain. As a young woman she was always surrounded by family, friends and well wishers. They crowded her dressing rooms. As a result there'd be no chair to sit on and when Renée's lunch arrived – a cup of tea and a boiled egg – she'd sit on the floor to eat it without a word of complaint. Getting her alone was impossible in those days. Contrast that with her latter years when she was a lone figure capable of isolating people. It was a reversal of the boiled egg on the floor at any rate. For those Houston Sisters love and anger lingered never far from the surface. They had started a little too early in the game of show business. At times they could be infuriating. It's about never being alone, putting your family first, having an open door always, encouraging others, and never believing something is impossible. The Glasgow spirit was indefatigable as was the Glasgow constitution strong.

Chapter 2   The Last Petticoat Line

November was an old month, 1974 an old year, but when another day came, the newest things seemed most important. Never did she sleep beyond seven O'clock - not like in her prime when she would rise in the afternoon. Now, too eager for life outside her window, ears and eyes were sensitive to a distant call or feet stepping along the gravel path. When you're lonely you listen hard. Voices intrigued her, especially those of Jean's children braving the morning chill for school – poor wee chittering mites. Renée Houston's front door looked on to a picture postcard garden with a giant magnolia tree between her home and the main house. That tree collected mysterious secrets and playful angels in its luscious foliage. Renée's hand trembled as she opened the door of her ground floor flat: the rearmost apartment of one of the most attractive and quietest lanes you will find in Walton-on-Thames's Oatlands quarter. En route to Renée's door, two doors back from Jean's, you might think for a minute you are in a little lane in a northern village and imagine the other buildings to be a farrier and a dairy. I can understand why Renée's granddaughter Tavy used the word 'cottage' to describe her grandmother's home.

The Oatlands Drive home is part of the former mansion of an army brigadier and stockbroker[1] and retains a country hamlet feel, even if the modernist houses and concrete thoroughfares of 70s Walton are just a short distance away. When the Surrey stockbroker abided here Renée was living with her children and stage partner Donald Stewart in a mansion called *'Green Trees'* in Buckinghamshire, then at the height of her wealth. The two mansions have a strange similarity: *'Green Trees'* was sliced into two after Renée left, and *'Brighthampton'* was sliced into more pieces, and when Renée and Donald moved here, their conversion was the stockbroker's former squash court. Such is the 'slicing effect' of fate. A lot had happened to the family in the thirty years since *'Green Trees'* and her daughter Terry, and youngest son Alan now lived in the United States. Alan's family travelled long distance when Renée turned seventy when a party was held for her. It had been several years since he last visited his mum and it was Tavy's first meeting with her grandmother.

Renée adored kids. They had the knack of separating from her but they couldn't forget her. Had she been born in later times she might have tried making films for kids - her directorial debut perhaps echoing Lionel Jeffries' in 'The Railway Children.' It was natural to Renée to place herself in the right setting, to grasp what gave a scene its essential power and what tugged on the heartstrings. For her 1972 reunion Renée stood - a lone cinematic figure on the grass outside her cottage – patiently waiting. The taxi arrived and little Tavy emerged. Renée's arms were outstretched and loving. Thinking about that greeting brings tears to Tavy's eyes over forty years later.

Jean's daughter was pleading with her mother that November morning to let her go to the pictures. In the Oatlands hamlet, she and her brother paid less attention to the lady in the corner flat whose welcoming nature was taken for granted. Renée never forgot the time the two Hutchings kids from upstairs attended a church service at their school, taking their mum along. The mums had posies made by their kids. The preacher asked if there were any mums not there anyone would like a posy for, and the kids each got one for Renée. Donald laughed at his wife's fondness for these kids, who were free to run in and out of their home at any time. Their closest pals were the Bowleys and Mrs Robertshaw who sometimes looked after the budgies. Even those who moved away, like the Tarrants and the Showlers, kept in touch, and took the trouble to write. Renée's front door was always open. An inner door beyond the hallway was closed to keep out draughts. Her early morning door-opening ritual was a familiar event.

She was a part of nature, breathing in fresh air, or on sunny days sitting outside on a stool inviting laughter. She offered approval of wee Paul McCartney and *Wings*, told the kids she enjoyed the latest by *Hot Chocolate*, or considered lovely Olivia Newton John to have a future. Many an evening before dusk she walked around the communal grounds scattering bread for the birds. Maureen Cleave, who came to do an interview with her for the Evening Standard, observed the fondness Renée had for these wee little things that grew feathers but didn't emigrate.[2] At least *they* relied on her.

Donald used to grow roses either side of the rear windows of the 'veranda' that looked out onto another large lawn, and his rosebushes lined the outdoors patio.[3] After he died, this part of the house remained a shed and Renée let her neighbours have free use of it to store their geraniums during the winter months. It gave her an opportunity to chat to them. They, in turn, learned no end of things about her eventful life and were much entertained. She was an open, giving and vulnerable character and they looked out for her when they could. They were fond of her. The truth about Renée was easy to see. She wasn't one to disguise the frailties. Regrettably, there'd been a couple of times they had to come to her aid after she had fallen in the bushes - out for the count - but it wasn't a big deal. They knew she had this problem.

Renée was a serene presence watching her friend Jean slowly walk her daughter to the gate and kiss her. 'It's like my Mama used to do,' she thought, remembering how it was to have someone care for her. Inside the flat she lit a cigarette and raised a glass to her husband. 'Here's tae us!' They drank their last toast shortly before he died on March 1, 1966 - a date etched on her heart. She kept the glass from which he had taken his last sip. Donald's picture was on the mantelpiece - a reminder for her to say her prayers. Eight years on from her loss Father Madden, her parish priest, urged her to settle down but she told him she couldn't. She felt that she had aged tremendously. She compared the aftermath of her loss to a disease'[4] in her interview with Maureen Cleave. These nights and days were spent alone, apart from Jimfy - also bereaved and feeling his age - which was fourteen. He had to be roused out of silence to meet Renée's quips with a twitter. Jimfy surprised her with things he would suddenly say – and he was such a small little thing. He used to jump up to the side of the cage to kiss her. That budgie cage was next to her as she sat in the sun outside her door.

Her next-door neighbour's son, visiting his gran, saw a different neighbour. It wasn't the invisible old lady shuffling around, but a curious figure in a black cloak and wide brimmed black hat – looking like the figure on the Sandeman Vintage Port label. That's the way he described Renée to his mother. Miss H, who appreciated cheek, would have loved the joke. On the radio she used to say she thought teenagers were wonderful and that Britain was best. The black-cloaked figure was her *'film star'* self - emerging from taxis, escorted between Walton and Surbiton station care of the BBC after a day's filming. Monday was her regular recording day. She looked forward to it – drinks in the dressing room, and the thrill of being before adoring members of the public. It would take twenty-five minutes for her to walk to Walton station. She was very slow and usually used buses and taxis. She boarded the train for Waterloo, and took one stop on the underground to Charing Cross. Getting on and off was awful with that frightening gap between train and platform. She didn't dare look down.

A little verbal sparring on the radio is a pleasant distraction. You're afraid to leave the room in case you miss the next witty rejoinder or acerbic comment. Letters from members of the public provided the basis for discussion on *Petticoat Line* - last heard forty years ago on Radio Four. A ten-year run was decent going and twelve series too: each episode signalled by a catchy bit of easy listening that brought up an image of fairies *Flora*, *Fauna* and *Merryweather* going into battle over what colour your curtains should be. The music was 'Fluter's Holiday' by Bert Kaempfert who had composed 'Strangers In The Night.'

In 1974 there was a revival of interest in Renée Houston and journalists in print, radio and television helped re-introduce her to those who only knew the gruff lady baritone voice. She was a regular on *Petticoat Line* - the radio panel-show made up exclusively of female panellists then in its eleventh series. She brought a lot of joy to listeners as its resident voice of bombastic commonsense. Nicholas Parsons believes Renée was truly rediscovered later on in life. I like the comments of Wyn Calvin - veteran of variety and pantomime, who quoted Shakespeare's *King Richard the Second*: his thoughts of Renée summed up by the line *'Small showers last long, but sudden storms are short.'* Renée was a small shower that lasted a long time – a career boosted as a result of this radio show.

Renée's voice was once described as 'a slice of Maryhill spread over with Mayfair'! The gravel suited her. If a voice could be a whisky that warmed the heart, hers was of the most aged quality. Her career in the old days of radio and films wasn't exactly celebrated in the 70s or even remembered. Once *one of the five English rosebuds - until the bloom wore off* - to quote a line from one of her earlier films, she now stereotyped thorny Scotch thistledom. On television she had played feisty old hags or eccentric landladies. Generations had sprung up who hadn't witnessed her rosebud youth and the hilarious masquerade that was. Her latest fans were listeners of *Petticoat Line*, accustomed to her lion-like tones. The show was a radio forerunner of today's *Loose Women*, with Renée's surprising comments being the 'loosest' that producers of the time would allow. Everything remained very much in the bounds of respectability then.

In the obituary he wrote for Renée, Ian Messiter, famous for initiating *Just a minute*, tells us: 'When we were looking for a woman to sum up the down-to-earth attitude of the good British housewife for *Petticoat Line* we turned to Renée. She impressed all the panel at her interview . . . She was the commonsense but seldom the logic.'[5] Similarly Anona Winn, the authoritative, witty, and cool-headed chairwoman of *Petticoat Line*, told Robin Russell how, in 1964, Renée had the audience laughing at the time the show was first piloted, telling everyone a beautifully captioned story about being ill in bed with a cold, dressed in one of Donald's old cardigans. Donald apparently came in and said to her 'D'you know darling you look lovelier than the day I married you.' Renée cried out to the audience 'I didn't even have me teeth in.' She liked to bring the people around her in. She complemented and enhanced the panel lineup, even with eminent guests present. There weren't many female personalities in the public eye then who could personify the British housewife AND tell a story like this.

A memo exchange between producers Bobby Jaye and Trafford Whitelock in mid 1965 tells us Renée was just a name on a list of recommended guests, along with Cilla Black and Dora Bryan. Neither Dora nor Cilla were ever guests. Fourteen broadcasts, a two-month gap in transmission and a repeat followed, and Renée was still not officially 'resident'. Then, in September 1966 the BBC confirmed 'only Anona and Renée will be heard regularly.'[6]

Ian Messiter, co-creator of *Petticoat Line,* was often present at recordings, as he was on *Just a Minute*.[7] He had once worked for Alastair Cooke before assisting producers at the BBC's Variety department. By 1974 he had created *Many a Slip, False Evidence* - with Gilbert Harding, and *Forecast* - a broadcast for scouts and guides. Ian had worked with Renée in 1951 on his very first panel game *One Minute Please* – a precursor to his best-known programme. Frank Muir and Dennis Norden were famous for bringing the house down on that show. Ian was proud of *Petticoat Line* and he had a cosy working relationship with Anona. Both were creative lights of the BBC's Light Entertainment department. They designed *Petticoat* together, and with producer John Bridges clustered in the Playhouse's upstairs staff canteen – a cheerless place. It was only a few hours before the show was recorded that they decided which topics to include for discussion, having a flip through letters from listeners. They also devised the all-male equivalent to *Petticoat Line* – a show called *Be Reasonable* that started transmission in 1968, chaired by Michael Smee. Its guests included footballer Danny Blanchflower, jazzman Humphrey Lyttelton, and Lieutenant Colonel Sammy Lohan.

Anona Winn was a veteran - successful in musical comedy, variety, radio, TV and films - just like Renée. In her earliest days she hadn't struggled to the same degree as her old Scottish friend. Born to English parents in Australia, Anona had sung with Dame Nellie Melba, toured with Ada Reeve, made her debut in broadcasting, and been a journalist – and that was before she left Australia. She came to England in 1928 appearing in *Hit The Deck* at the London Hippodrome with Stanley Holloway. Once her soprano voice was very familiar on the airwaves. She had appeared at the annual radio exhibition that the Radio Manufacturers' Association used to hold at Olympia in west London over the summer months. People checked out the latest wireless receivers at *'Radiolympia'* and variety stars broadcast from there. Anona would find herself on the same bill as the Houston Sisters in the early 30s. By the mid 60s she was extremely well respected at the BBC, having through the years helped many a broadcaster develop his or her microphone tricks. Her accent was the flawless BBC type, and she drew on both her international experience and her family's no-nonsense Yorkshire roots in her tactful chairing of *Petticoat Line*. Her dedication went without saying and over the ten years she never missed a single show.

Anona Winn with Tommy Mansfield's dog Juno. (By kind permission of The Queen Alexandra Hospital Home)

Ian Messiter
(Author's Collection)

October 7, 1974 between 12.45 and 2 pm is one example of a pre-recording of *Petticoat Line* – part of the autumn season. Transmission was a week later so this episode went out on Wednesday 16 October at 18.15 with a repeat on Friday 18 at 12.27. John Bridges initially walked on stage to welcome everyone. He was a former Grenadier Guards sergeant and Dunkirk survivor, and in his BBC career had worked on Dylan Thomas's legendary *Under Milk Wood* broadcast. He was *Petticoat Line*'s last producer having followed Trafford Whitelock, Alastair Scott-Johnston, Christopher Serle, John Cassels and Bobby Jaye. That day's audience included a party of blind people from Merton - their transport arranged by the social service, and a group outing of staff from the Psychiatric Unit of St Mary's Hospital, Paddington.

The two resident ladies of *'The Line'* were immaculately turned out: Anona at sixty-seven typified a lady of the British Empire in tinted glasses, white gloves, prints and black hat with white ribbon. Renée, by contrast wore the urban chic of a Tartan trilby and light fur wrap. Sheila Tracy, a well-loved voice on the radio in the 60s was *Petticoat Line*'s announcer - a role previously occupied by Angela Buckland. Sheila was the first woman to read the news on Radio and a TV host of *A Spoonful of Sugar*, which took celebrities to surprise hospital residents, and earlier in her career had played the trombone with *Ivy Benson's All Girl Band*. Sheila's beautifully modulated voice began the pre-recording: 'And now the programme in which listeners letters are subjected to the feminine point of view - it's called Petticoat Line.'

Tickets to join the studio audience were purchased from the Ticket Unit at Broadcasting House and long queues formed outside London's Playhouse Theatre on Northumberland Avenue. The three guest panellists came on one by one and took their seats before Anona and Renée - aged seventy-two - made their appearance. Journalist Molly Parkin was a witness that day and noted how, in Renée's case, her entrance was met with waves of loving warmth.[8] On stage, the ladies sat behind a desk on which the only objects were microphones and pots of African violets placed here and there to give a decorous, feminine setting. Anona had a bell for restoring order and a banner hung from her desk facing the audience. On it was *'Petticoat Line'* in large curly lettering - a 60s and 70s evocation of Victoriana: a statement in itself.

Petticoat Line received a phenomenal number of letters from men as well as women, so Anona et al must have had help narrowing down the selection in advance of the canteen chat. Usually, an organized approach was followed, saving certain topics for guests best suited to answer. They would have a medical person on the panel when letters were about health.[9] Some letters never made it to *'The Line'* like those from 'notorious cranks' such as a Captain MacMichael who had been badgering the BBC for years with all kinds of complaints. Because he waged a campaign against the use of animals by performing showmen, he was incensed after one of the 'team' on a December 1966 broadcast was 'insistent that kindness and not cruelty was the mainspring in performing animal 'training.'[10] This sounds rather like Renée talking about the *speciality acts* she knew during her variety career: acts she held in great respect. Using animals for scientific research was a different matter and she railed against the idea. Renée's sister-in-law, a vegetarian, tuning in that day to 'something called *Petticoat*' wrote to her aunt about how 'Lady Barnett was all for vivisection being a doctor, and good old Renée put her right in her place. Congratulated her on this.'[11]

In the letters Messiter was quick to spot talking points: "The Most Extraordinary Person I Ever Met" was his classic *Just A Minute* opener of choice. The questions originating from *Petticoat Line's* postbag covered a wide range of subjects. Similar letters had been openers on an earlier peak-time panel show from the 1940s – *The Brain's Trust* – *Petticoat Line's* direct ancestor. Now the feminine viewpoint regarding conundrums and moral dilemmas would be heard. In October 1974, the 'canteen trio' found one sent by a woman who had just fallen down the stairs, one asking 'How does the team define intelligence?' Another letter asked 'How does *Petticoat Line* make a good gravy?' Anona's view was that when people are in a white-hot rage the first thing they reach for is a pen! Controversial topics were not ignored. Gentle questions started proceedings for the first few minutes: the stickiest time of the recording. With the tapes rolling Anona read out a letter in her authoritative voice and soon gratification came in the form of a familiar gravelly Glaswegian voice:

> Anona: (reading letter from listener) I was eating in a restaurant when I found a large caterpillar in my lettuce. What would the team have done in the same embarrassing situation?
> Renée: I'd ask for seconds and make the two run races on the tablecloth.
> Anthea: You know, it happened to me on my honeymoon.
> Renée: I jolly well hope it did![12]

Anona would read a letter from a lady on behalf of her clever, attractive twenty-four year-old daughter – unmarried – with apparently no interest in boys because they lack ambition. Renée's view was that if the girl was twenty-four and unmarried, she wasn't half as clever as her mother was making out. Everyone clapped. Curiously, Renée added that when she was that age she was looking for a nice man with warm feet in winter. A man wrote in, seeking the panel's views on apologizing. Anona highlighted that in a recent TV interview John Wayne revealed he never apologized. Sounds in the auditorium made it clear the audience didn't approve of that.

> Katie Boyle: I think to apologize shows tremendous strength of character. (applause)
> Renée: John Wayne is a gorgeous piece of homework. Even if he whooped me right up the skirt he needs never apologize! (Screams from audience)[13]

Juno Alexander, older sister of Conservative politician Norman St John Stevas, was a *Petticoat Line* panellist twenty-seven times. She had lived a very eventful life during the war, had been an actress, and was now a campaigner. She got behind causes like human rights and support for the homeless. Another guest was Pat Jacob, then chair of the National Federation of Women's Institutes for England and Wales. Pat told the panel how the WI advised government committees, helping people take part in their communities. The word 'Institute' gets inside of Renée Houston's mind:

> Renée: It reminds me of a story of an old dear up in front of a judge.
> The poor darling was 85 – up for soliciting.
> 'I'm 85 m'lord,' she said, and the judge said:
> 'I don't understand. How can you be up for soliciting?'
> 'It's a long story, judge,' she said. 'I'm trying to help a friend. '
> 'I'm a substitute for a prostitute who's destitute in an institute.'
> Pat J: Marvellous story. Not sure it relates to the Women's Institutes.
> I wish I had your gift for storytelling.[14]

Anona and Juno weren't strangers themselves to the WI being regular speakers on different subjects at venues around the country. The NFWI is politically sound, Anona tells listeners. Renée then offers her own public speaking experience into the rounds:

Renée: I'm not an intellectual speaker like you two, but I was invited to Margate the other week to one of the ladies dos, and there were 105 of them. They were wonderful. They were nervous about me for saying things about liking men.[15]

Anona follows this with something about Renée probably not knowing where she was, which is an example of the subtle bitchiness delivered to Renée by the chair that can be detected if you listen carefully. Anona sometimes would put Renée back on track with the topic. In *Petticoat Line's* first year the BBC commissioned an audience research report. A sample of listeners was polled to judge reactions. Several people in the poll disliked having only women panellists, finding their comments rather spiteful. The majority, however, found it entertaining.[16] This report, produced in November 1966, also reveals that 'answers were in general too flippant and that the speakers gave the impression they did not know whether or not they were meant to answer seriously.' Missing the point and speaking about irrelevant things was also considered a failing by the survey. I've no doubt Renée missed the point a lot, although her utterances were probably so surprising the digression was forgivable. People I've spoken to who listened to the show tell me they often found the speakers dogmatic and it was never about the subject itself, just the prowess of people like Renée at adlib. *Petticoat Line* seemed patronizing to some, too genteel or jolly hockey sticks to others but at least Renée's presence served as an amusing counter.

Anona, as chair of the panel, came across as very correct and a little distant and headmistress-like but Renée was always 'one of us.' These are Rachael Heyhoe-Flint's recollections when I asked her about her six *Petticoat Line* shows between 1972 and 1974 - a time when she was getting a profile as England's Women's Cricket captain. Rachael tells me that Renée and Anona were chalk and cheese and that Renée got away with saying things nobody else would because she delivered them in such a funny way – even if, by today's standards, it wasn't much in terms of being rude or provocative.

Speaking to a member of Renée's family, it would appear that there were plenty of times in the ten-year history of Petticoat Line when the relationship between Renée and the 'canteen trio' was stormy. Apparently, Renée's dealings with Ian Messiter and the production team were temperamental, even acid-like. There was a side to her that cared little for professional consequences.

Telling producers what she thought of them was a dangerous thing. In this story Renée tore Messiter off a strip in front of BBC executives. He didn't forgive her and came extremely close to firing her from the show. It was actually Renée's brother-in-law, Paul Eve, who intervened and this changed the situation. Anona's family had known Paul's family back in Australia in her journalist days. Paul asked Anona to fight Renée's corner and persuade them to keep her. Anona talked Ian Messiter into this. All this happened barely within a year of *Petticoat Line*'s arrival. By the time ten or eleven series had elapsed, the 'chalk and cheese' contrast between Renée and Anona was more pronounced. 'Anona Winn *hated* her,' says my family source.

I'm unsure what to make of this story because from a listener's perspective, the panellists appear to make *Petticoat Line's* atmosphere bright and amiable. I like to believe that relationships backstage were good and if there were fights they managed to forgive and forget. Bettine Le Beau recalled that during the pre-recordings and time spent at the theatre in general the mood was bright and happy. Everyone liked each other and one panellist regularly gave everyone honey as she used to keep bees. Anona speaks warmly of Renée in a 1973 radio broadcast looking back on Renée's life. In the same programme Renée says a nice thing about Anona that she 'has same quality that Billie and Donald had,' and that 'Anona lets me get so far and knows when to come in. If she didn't the fire brigade would come in!'

With her white hair pulled back from her face, eighty-three year-old Baroness Stocks was a guest panellist that day in early October 1974. She was an eminent campaigner and humanist, used to serving on various official government committees often as the only woman. Years earlier Mary Stocks, along with her friend Marie Stopes, had furthered the birth control movement. She had supported women's suffrage, opposed restrictive dress for women, and been a campaigner for family allowances. Katie Boyle, then forty-eight, was famous for presenting the Eurovision Song Contest and had done it four times running. Sweden had won that April with '*Waterloo*' performed by an attractive foursome called ABBA. Anthea Askey, aged forty-one, was the other guest - a familiar name and a star in her own right from the *Dickie Henderson Half-hour* and films. Anthea had known Renée a long time. The dressing rooms were downstairs at the Playhouse and prior to the recording Molly Parkin came to get a few words from the programme's stars. She took Renée and Anthea unawares, discovering that the usual form was to have a tongue-loosening tipple beforehand.[17] Molly didn't heed Renée's request that she avoid mentioning this in her article.

Left:
Baroness Stocks
(Courtesy of
The New Humanist)

Centre:
Katie Boyle
(Author's Collection)

Right:
Pat Jacob
(By kind permission
of the NFWI archive)

An episode of Petticoat Line from 18th November 1969.
Left to right: actress Hy Hazel (then starring in *Fiddler on The Roof*), actress Jill Adams, Renée Houston and singer and actress Roberta Rex (Author's Collection)

Some panellists represented the young like Cathy McGowan who, aged twenty, went from a job in a television office to presenting *Ready Steady Go* because her style epitomized the 'typical teenager.' Cathy's eye-catching clobber came in for pertinent questions during her two *Petticoat Line* visits. 'I always wear what I like', said Cathy 'I never consciously promote anything or dress just for effect.' Her one secret ambition, she confessed, was 'to own a spotted dog with a smashing gold collar to parade at the hairdressers.'[19] The dialogue between Cathy and women like Anona and Florence Desmond might have echoed that between granddaughters and puzzled grandmothers. Renée seemed to cross generations, and seemed more in her element, especially with younger women from the performing arts.

The essence of *Petticoat Line* was similar to that of *One Minute Please*. Back in 1952, Messiter had pointed out that players mustn't take the game seriously. *Petticoat Line* too was to be light-hearted. Guests who were fast and freewheeling in their comments were welcome – more so than those who were erudite and serious. *Petticoat Line* usually was thirty minutes long, sometimes a little less. It wasn't long enough for a number of speakers to make many serious comments. You had to be to the point.

It wasn't the easiest series to be a panellist on, as is the case with *Just A Minute* today. Listening to the latter, I feel for new players: some daunted when forced to think fast. Bettine le Beau, who appeared in nineteen *Petticoat Line* shows, is vivacious as ever. Her childhood was traumatic and she was lucky to be smuggled out of a Nazi concentration camp and hidden with a French family. Later, she was in a Bond movie and did TV with Benny Hill. I asked Bettine about coping when you had no warning about the topic you had to speak about, with *Petticoat Line* unscripted and unrehearsed. How did you come up with cogent responses in the time available? Bettine said that in the pre-recording several younger actresses stumbled with 'Err, Err...' so much that the producer always let the show run on at least fifteen minutes extra in order to edit out the excessive *'Erring.'* Apparently, just one time only, when Fanny Cradock was on, there was a landmark episode with no *'Erring'* whatsoever. Miriam Karlin complained to the producer about having no warning of the topic, miffed that Anona and Renée had some forewarning of the topics. Bettine didn't mind and felt comfortable making mistakes, joking her way out of it. Her amusing technique was to improvise around the subject with a *'Confucius says...'*

Serious subjects cropped up, producing sincere answers or uncertainty among panellists. It's true they wondered whether to react seriously or circumvent with an entertaining witticism. No one attempted to tackle the world's problems. Giving a 'talking point' airtime was more important than wishing to analyze what was difficult and real. The receipt of offensive letters might be a topic. Religion was sometimes discussed without any fear. Anything could drift into the discussion and there were occasional references by panellists to international issues. The audience research report mentions that some questions were thought too serious for entertainment. This indicates they *were* trying to be serious sometimes. Radio lent itself well to the panel show and, on occasions, an edge-of-the-seat atmosphere existed. Mostly though, it was a light-hearted show and generally the panel failed hands down in providing a decent response even to the simplest of questions. Anona Winn was upfront about this. Frequently, at the end of a programme, she would say with sincerity 'We haven't solved anything but we've given opinions, made you laugh and made people think.'[18]

Women were becoming more 'vocal' than ever before - a major change in broadcasting, since for decades it was the opinions of men that had most commonly been heard. Merely *having an opinion* was 'to be encouraged' in this changing feminine landscape. It was still something relatively 'new' - unbelievable to conceive now in today's 'rent a gob' world in which we're sated with noisy opinions on TV, radio and Internet. Unlike *Woman's Hour*, the personal opinions of the guests of *Petticoat Line* emerged as they tackled a subject head on. The *Petticoat* allowed the airing of different opinions but it entertained an audience unlikely to be troubled by the same issues we find contentious today. In the 60s and 70s you could probably be less guarded with some opinions compared to now. Also voicing an unpopular opinion wasn't a matter of outrage. It wasn't like today with celebrities facing a media backlash or finding themselves subject to a hate campaign on social media. In the 60s and 70s it was things like bad manners that were likely to be strongly criticized. It was an unspoken rule that radio voices should never be coarse. Few upset the applecart and dared venture outside the bounds of decency. When people were offended this prompted a polite but 'to the point' letter to the BBC. The Sixties might have been swinging but a general culture of respect, innocence and calmness prevailed in broadcasting. Trust in the BBC, as an institution, was also unquestioned then.

Frequently the opinions expressed were about bland things. We were satisfied to discuss housekeeping and hear how Renée boiled her linen in a zinc bucket on top of the stove. How much she admired the Queen or was devoted to her late darling husband Donald were typical 'views' and there was advice from Miss H to budgie owners. The interchange and repartee between the panellists gave the show its edge. Of course, Renée was just one of a team providing fun. The guffaws heard from the auditorium of the Playhouse said it all. We laugh more when we're in jolly company. For those at home it was catching. They forgot themselves too, happy to go along with the joke that had suddenly sprung from the most commonplace source.

Modern TV equivalents of *Petticoat Line* such as *The View* in America and *Loose Women* in the UK find it impossible to avoid political and contentious issues. The concept of the topical talk show obviously works well in the present day on TV when you consider *Loose Women* is now in its twentieth series but there are underlying things that have changed with the transfer of a show like this from radio to television. Comparing *Loose Women* with *Petticoat Line* makes me think that the spoken word mattered more in the 60s and 70s than today. It was heard only, and therefore had to be witty or at least reasonably intelligent. TV enables the form to be extended by visual feats, such as Denise Welch attempting to break a world record by dressing a semi-naked fireman. It's hilariously funny and I like the panellists but if today's *Loose Women* were forced to make people laugh on the radio, without TV cameras making their frowns, cackles and other visually interactive behaviour such a highlight, I would tune in regularly. Calling a panel member a 'bitch' to their face is an acceptable way to get a laugh now, which would have been unforgivably crude before. Today's panellists talk about a far greater range of subjects than in the 70s like women using sex toys. We've shed the old restraint and the things you hear are probably less intelligent-sounding on the whole. All the same, I appreciate the warmth of the current *Loose Women* regulars and a recent episode when they let their kids embarrass them on live TV, then embarrassing their kids in return, was fantastic viewing. Of all of the *Petticoat Line* panellists, Renée would be the one you could lift off the 60s and 70s shelf and place among today's *Loose Women*. She would have had no trouble 'keeping her end up' as she used to say, and today's ladies would meet their match.

Evidence indicates that *Petticoat Line's* guests were drawn from a wider set of professions than *Loose Women* - which uses panellists from the entertainment and journalism industries. With its spectrum of backgrounds and professions *Petticoat Line* appealed to the listeners' intelligence. Older women had more of a say, as did women from the top ranks. All this added to the show's popularity. Listeners numbered one million at the beginning of 1967[20] rising to two million in 1974.[21] Women who were genuine trailblazers featured in its lineup. Shirley Becke, a policewoman who had bravely fought crime in the vice-ridden West End and Soho of the 50s before rising to be the first woman commander in the Metropolitan Police, was on the panel twice. Christian Howard - part of the movement for the Ordination of Women was on the panel once. There were journalists like Romany Bain - admired for 'putting Renée in her place!' Some had changed the face of TV such as Nan Winton - the first woman to read the news on the BBC. Barbara Blake Makeda - the first black woman TV journalist in Britain, who later became a filmmaker and novelist, was on *Petticoat Line* twelve times.

Margaret Powell, whose experiences as a domestic servant in the 1920s became subject-matter in several of her books, was a well-loved guest who made her first appearance on *Petticoat Line* in November 1969. Her traditional London Cockney accent contrasted with the posh voices, and Anona joked how, with the success of her latest book, Margaret had finally got her nose onto the top landing. Anona reads one of the questions:

Anona: Mrs Kay of Streatham writes to say she is a woman of sixty and spent ten years in domestic service. I wonder if the young of today who turn their noses up at this kind of work are really any happier?
Margaret: I wish I'd got there earlier. Anytime when you are young, you are happy.
Renée: I'm only 3 years off seventy and I'm still young and enjoying myself.
Margaret: It's not in proportion to a more affluent life.
What I mean is they are not happier for it.
I had a miserable life – hardly ever any free time, but - you see, it was impossible to be miserable.
You are happy BECAUSE you are young.[22]

Left:
Margaret Powell
(Courtesy of
The Argus)

Centre:
Barbara Blake Makeda
(with Eamonn Andrews)

Right:
Barbara Cartland
(Author's Collection)

Margaret is lively and amusing, and cheerful about the fact that society in general had become more affluent. The only time she had time to herself in those early days was her weekday evening from 4.30 pm to 9.30 pm, and at the same time on Sundays. She talks about how people in modern domestic roles have the red carpet laid down and how the climate of opinion has changed with mothers welcomed into domestic service whether married or unmarried. Girls in Margaret's day, by contrast, got the sack if they became pregnant and would even be refused a reference. This prompts a wonderful story from Renée that has the panel and audience screaming:

Renée: During the war we needed help and we arranged to have a daily to come in as a live in. So I interviewed this one for it, told her about the role and she said: 'Ow'll think about it.'(Renée does Cockney accent)
She asked me 'What do you like?' I said tea in the morning.
So the next morning she comes in with the tea, and says to me -
'There you are. Ow does it feel to be like a lady?'
As if I'd never had it in my life! I caught the poor thing standing up and bending over while doing the floor. After I'd been down on my knees ten minutes she said: 'Ow, you've missed a bit over there.'[23]

There were capable ladies from the House of Lords like socialist peer Baroness Summerskill who had helped prepare the way for the National Health Service and would often be seen in the press giving her staunch views opposing the noble art of boxing. Margaret Thatcher was on *Petticoat Line* twice. In 1969, she contrasted with enormously popular Daily Mirror 'sob-sister' Marjorie Proops. In 1970 Mrs Thatcher was alongside Andrée Melly - famous for her work in British films and TV.

Joy Adamson devoted years to raising money for wildlife. Many were notable in the world of sport. Sheila Van Damm's 'good sensible replies' made her a well-liked member of the panel as evidence in the BBC's Audience Research Report testifies. She was famous in the field of competitive driving, winning the *Coupe des Dames* before retiring and carrying on the running of the Windmill Theatre she had inherited from her father in 1956. Of course many talented actresses graced the panel too, like Diana Dors, bubbly Beryl Reid, Sheila Hancock, and Jane Asher.

Left:
Lady Isobel Barnett

Centre:
Beryl Reid

Right:
Renée Houston

(Photos: Author's collection)

Some commentators who mention *Petticoat Line* in books about radio history say it could be patronizing to listeners, especially since several of the guests had posh accents. At least they were accepting of others and themselves. The need to pretend that everyone is from some classless common denominator didn't exist then and you didn't get privileged people changing their accents to appear unstuffy. You needn't feel any guilt in being a former "Deb of the Year" turned TV panellist. On the whole you were admired for it. The Countess of Dartmouth exemplified a role model of this type. She was on the show twice, taking time off from the environmental planning job she did for Westminster City Council. She became familiar to royal watchers later on as Raine Spencer, stepmother to Diana Princess of Wales. Her mother, Barbara Cartland, was on the show five times.

Just because *Petticoat Line* is a fossil representing the culture of politeness we had in the 70s, it didn't mean heated conversation never occurred. Under Anona's chairwomanship, a respectful atmosphere was enforced. The backchat might be catty but restraint was upheld. War, if it existed in the *Petticoat Line* universe, broke out when comments passed between the panellists had an acid undertone. When interviewed by Molly Parkin, Ian Messiter confessed that they sometimes invited guests who loathed each other, telling her he daren't name names. Anona could always be relied on to ring her bell and restore order. He stressed that they did not censor the show. There was never a single occasion of four-letter words being used. The worst occasion was when Renée called something a '*bloody* nuisance.' They didn't edit this out. On hearing Renée's 'favourite word,' the elegant, witty Isobel Barnett, doyenne of the panel game, and twenty-three times panellist on *Petticoat Line*, chided her. The event made the newspapers and some listeners complained. 'Really Renée - you don't have to use that word!' she said. To this Renée replied 'I do darling . . . it's me. I'm just a cross between Alf Garnett and Isobel Garnett.'[24] The waving of Anona's white-gloved hand failed to command authority on this occasion. That said, Renée played a positive part in peace-keeping at times: brilliant as she was at preventing things getting too tense and serious by stepping in and setting the audience laughing. Ian Messiter called this taking the curse out of the situation.[25]

The 'permissive society' – one in which the law in relation to sexual morals plays a minimum role, was a subject frequently debated in the early 70s. The phrase was used first by Pope Pius XII. If a panellist on *Petticoat Line* was in favour of permissiveness friction was likely, given the traditional stance of the chair and anchorwoman. The older panellists had many opinions in common with Mary Whitehouse, secretary of VALA - the National Viewers and Listeners Association, who was on *Petticoat Line* in February 1972, along with fellow guests Beryl Reid and Isobel Barnett. Mrs Whitehouse was at this time ready to fight against the tide-race of immorality sweeping through our society and *Petticoat Line* was an opportunity for her to deliver her views. She opposed the legal reforms ushered in during the late 60s and was anxious there should be no repeal of the pornography laws. She was 100% behind the idea that violence on TV can create a violent society and wary about the power of producers and the manipulation tactics of TV broadcasters to sway opinion. She had never forgiven the BBC for screening the film 'Up the Junction' shortly before the Abortion Law Reform Bill was introduced to parliament in 1967. The thorny anchorwoman of *Petticoat Line* was to some extent on her wavelength, concerned more about the permissive society than the economic situation.

Still, Renée never beat to anyone's drum. Her typical treatment of the topic was to make it absurd and amusing, as a 1973 episode reveals when the panel discuss the wearing of seatbelts:

Renée: As a matter of fact - there isn't anything that'd be worse in this world for me, cause I'm an awful claustrophobic, as to be shut in into anything. I won't wear those belts! It's alright for the people who can suffer it. I'd rather sit in the back seat with my feet against the seat.
But mind you, I will say one thing, Nonni - that I think it should be compulsory that we ALL wear chastity belts.[26]

In 1975 the panel discussed a letter about what to do if a male dinner guest starts boasting about his successes with women. Renée initially takes the man's side for his efforts to bring spark to the conversation then says he's a cad. Anona is wondrous about Renée's sudden change in opinion and possible misunderstanding of the question. Pat Jacob makes a comment about how we should hear the other side's opinion. Young actress Aimi MacDonald says that she'd rather hear a man talk about his success than a woman. She admits to being interested when a man talks about it.

Aimi: I find sex very seldom comes up. People have to say 'let's talk about sex.'
Renée: Well. When you get to my age, Aimi, all you can do is talk about it!
Juno: I think the really sexy fella can find a little enthusiasm for his missus after a few years.
Renée: I wish I could get his address.
Renée: Juno. This reminds me of the story of a lassie who went on a cruise. Soon after she met her friend on the street who had travelled with her. She was pushing a pram with a baby in it at the time.
The friend asked her if it was the cruise? 'No,' she said, 'the captain's!'
Juno: Very good, well done!
Anona: I had a feeling it would end up like this.[27]

Anona reads a letter from Mrs Hunt of Guildford referring to a comment by Monica Dickens that 'American women are now more relaxed than thirty years ago because there is no longer any stigma attached to divorce, or living with a man you're not married to. Is this a recipe for happiness?' Beryl Reid talks about New York where she opened in *The Killing of Sister George*. She remembers how New York women seemed 'gripped at the knickers' and particularly tough with their men 'We're not going to see that play' a woman said to her husband, knowing he wanted to see it. Beryl admits that there's been a 'slackening of loyalty' inside marriage. She points out that her Scottish upbringing tells her it's too slack but it's better than in the past when daughters would get thrown out on the street for having a baby.

Renée: As a matter of fact I don't agree with promiscuity at all if circumstances permit. Ma wee Beryl was right. Get a good man! There's nothing better than if you've remained faithful.[28]

Renée, who led the field in outspokenness, received the most fan mail. She used to joke that some of the 'blasphemous' things she came out with on *Petticoat Line* would get her arrested. In the audience research report, comments from listeners such as 'she carries this programme - the love, compassion, good common sense, wit and wisdom she gives out seems to be boundless,'[29] reflect her personal contribution. Rita Merkelis, a young psychotherapist who made twelve appearances on *Petticoat Line* between 1968 and November 1975 gave me this short recollection of Renée: 'She was a plain-speaking, funny, warm person, with no pretensions and a lot of guts. She was a wonderful foil for Anona Winn on that programme. Renée would get straight to the point. I think she felt I was supportive. I always relate to Glaswegians. But I did not know her, away from that show. I remember her fondly.' Rachael Heyhoe-Flint, a panellist in 1972, was, at the time a young and practical-minded woman from the Midlands. She was unfamiliar with London. The broadcasting environment was new and a little nerve-wracking especially before the broadcast went out. Pacing up and down the corridor, Renée would suddenly appear from the door of her dressing room at the Playhouse, chatting away in her Scottish burr, telling Rachael she'd only be more nervous walking back and forth. She always put her at ease, and seemed so calm and experienced. There was also the lovely warm smell of Scotch that emanated from Renée's dressing room. Renée left a lasting impression on Rachael on account of her warmth and spirit.

The first of thirteen transmissions in the twelfth series of Radio Four's *Petticoat Line* began on Wednesday October 29, 1975 in the 6.15pm slot with a regular shortened repeat on Fridays at 12.27pm. Isobel Barnett, Janet Hitchman - who had just written a biography of Dorothy L Sayers[30] and Beryl Reid were guests. It was difficult getting up to the Playhouse for Renée and it was a blessing when her nephew Anton accompanied her. It's shocking to hear about how much booze was needed somedays to propel her out of her home and up to the studio. If she did get up there alone, the return journey was easier through the assistance of her loyal fan Esmé who hadn't missed a show in ten years. After the recording Esmé took Renée to Waterloo and put her on her train, before going to Chingford where she lived with her husband Bill. In the last programme of this series, on January 23, 1976, Janet Hitchman was on again, along with Isobel and Beryl, but none could be described as good angels where Renée was concerned.

When each series of *Petticoat Line* ended there was a gap of between six and ten months before it returned. In March, Radio Four Controller, Clare Lawson Dick, thought about ways to improve production suggesting Ted Taylor as a possible successor to John Bridges[31] and in May, Madeau Stewart, the well-connected archivist and expert on early music was proposed. Having a woman producer was a 'good publicity angle'. There was a decision to remove Ian and Anona's last minute flipping through listeners' letters and have new guests like Bridget Bardot (by then a voice in conservation) and Shirley Temple. They were *possibles* for the twelfth series.

Then, on June 16, Clare was writing both to Ian and Anona to break the news that the *Petticoat* was to end. She explained that the decision had been a difficult one and that BBC Light Entertainment had looked at ways of updating the formula. The powers that be had concluded that the programme's 'coach party trade' appeal was something they wanted to redesign. It meant a change to the 'broad humour' as represented by the salty exchanges between Renée and Anona: these often being 'nothing to do with the subject under discussion.'[32] Ian Messiter replied to Clare accepting the decision, even though he had hoped a re-hash had been possible. He adds that 'Given time, Anona and Renée will be glad they have bowed out from the top rather than be replaced, which would have been an almost an unendurable humiliation.'[33] With tact, Anona thanked Clare for her support and encouragement during the '10 happy years the petticoat has flown from the line,' while expressing that she didn't share the view that the show had passed its 'popularity peak' when feedback she had received in speaking engagements around the country indicated quite to the contrary. She admitted, of course, that those who came out in the show's favour were middle-aged and preponderantly middle class.[34] It's only forty years since this radio show was on the air but the *Petticoat Line* view of life seems distant – something that makes me feel sad.

Interestingly, a strange letter from Janet Hitchman exists in the BBC archive files dated October 1976, criticizing the decision to axe the show mainly because it was the 'only source of income to Renée Houston. She is now well into her seventies and although I could not stand her, has given years of service to the radio and should not be left to social security alone.'[35] Funny that the interests of one you can't stand should prompt you to write a letter. Janet didn't know that Renée was, in fact, in receipt of a pension.

So it came to an end: the Wednesday 6.15 pm slot taken over by *Oh, Get On With It* with Kenneth Williams, Miriam Margolyes and Lance Percival: new, witty and cutting. The new blood did not want to do it the way it used to be done. Renée deeply felt the loss of what had been her purpose. She didn't stay in touch with anyone from *Petticoat Line*. She looked to herself to survive the blow, keeping a cheery demeanour. She chose a theatrical production with an upcoming provincial tour. *Get back on the road* had so long been the answer. Her mind flashed back to the young Renée Houston and thirsty audiences needing to be entertained. Meantime the *guid-willie waught of whisky* arrived before bedtime, and the hope of awakening to a child's voice in the distance so she could remember the earth was turning.

Chapter 3   The First Petticoat Line

> *When I am really lonely I like to remember Friday Nights at home when my Granny used to wash my hair and dried my head against her body. My poor wee nose was nearly rubbed off with the bones in her corsets.*[1]

Renée was four when she was having her nose pummelled to the sound of Daddy's booming voice talking about men having to attend sermons on the braes because they watched doggies running circles. Her world was the picnic field of flowers sloping down to trees to hide behind - a wee ride away. Carntyne was its name: a village in Glasgow's East End. She thought neither of the city's beating heart nor something called time living in the wee 'wag at the wa' Granny's eye seldom ignored. She wanted to be the fairy doll in the shop window a few doors from their tenement. People came to see it. She never forgot the day the fairy's wax face melted under the heat of a light.

It was Granny Houston she saw most and whose Christian name she shared. They said Granny was old but she always looked young. Her clothes were frayed but chic on her rounded frame. One of the cleverest people for miles, Granny could reduce someone to shreds or be self-ridiculing at will. Born Catherine Murphy in Dalry in Ayrshire in 1850, her lineage was 'aristocratic on the wrong side of the bed.' In Ireland, Granny's mother had been in service with a titled family. She had caught the eye of the master of the house. Soon after, that lady moved from Ireland to Scotland to have Granny. She had no contact with the Murphys - at least for while.

Granny had a *silver spoon* quality. She downplayed it but that only fed the magic. Why else would they nickname her the *Duchess* when she was a young woman? Her young life had been harsh and so easily could have mirrored her own mother's. Sent out as a maid to a farmer's house, Granny only attracted the eye of the farmer's psychotic daughter who would slap her hard across the face daily to vent her spleen. How long poor Granny coped is uncertain, but she confronted her attacker. That's courage, although some say Granny became a tyrant herself. She left service and worked at a bleach-works. Every respectable window in Victoria's reign had lace and Ayrshire had several towns where it was bleached in industrial proportions. The *Duchess* worked at one of these. She was a popular figure with storytelling skills and a deadpan delivery. Such were the Houston genes. Or weren't they? Did Granny bring up her sister's illegitimate daughter as her own? That wean was Lizzi, born in March 1875, different in character and raised that she might enjoy the better things in her life. That story seems to be a fable, especially as Granny's looks run in the family.

The *Duchess* married a Scot called John Houston and there were Houston relatives on his side. Their house was in what was the Eastmuir enumeration district of Shettleston. Number 3 Squairs Court was in a part of town characterized by proud little businesses, a Roman Catholic school and a pub. In the 1891 census William Murphy lives with them, possibly Granny's brother or nephew. Listed as a 'bleacher' by trade, Granny was quick to spot a blemish, and was so sure of her own sense of chic to tell at a glance what was wrong with the toilet of a woman, especially one who thought she was well dressed. Granny was down to earth, on the side of fairness, and would tell you life was about taking chances. Renée would say 'If you ever meet Granny Houston don't try to put on too much 'side.' If you dare to do so her gimlet eye will bear straight through you and as like or not she'll say 'There's some foolish folk in the world' in the loudest whisper. She rose in the morning, made her perfect bed, had breakfast, and did her rosary. At her last home *'Green Trees,'* her challenge was to go up one flight of stairs every day.

The thing a visitor from London immediately appreciates about Glasgow is its smaller scale. It's possible to start at the Broomielaw, head east along the Clyde on the north side, detouring via the Cathedral, then cross the hidden Molendinar Burn - sacred to St Mungo, before you pass Tennants Brewery on Duke Street. You've reached Dennistoun by then. Go east along the desolate highway until Celtic's football stadium and the Emirates Centre are in sight. Head further and you're in the vicinity of Tollcross Park and you can cut up to Carntyne and Shettleston. Your feet will be tired now. You will have seen buildings interesting and heinous. The architecture of Glasgow has great civil buildings, futuristic developments on the Clyde and Georgian wonders in Park Circus and Kelvingrove. Areas where ordinary folk lived have come off badly in the thrust for modernity we've seen in the last seventy years or so. Town planners of the 60s and 70s had high hopes but came close to murdering the character that many of Glasgow's districts once had. Thousands of tenements like the one where my Dad was born, where dark red brick had soaked up time and memories, were wiped away in an instance - unnecessarily it seems. Several still exist but not in a quantity to re-imagine Glasgow's suburban streets quite as they were early in the last century. I might as well take out a very old vintage toy from its original packaging: a collection of small heavy metal and wood pieces - to arrange my own town. In some places a trace of brickwork and a good imagination restore to life the city little Renée and her family saw day upon day.

The Square, Johnstone (Courtesy Peter Harvey)

Having said all that, Renée was born in Johnstone, now a half hour's train journey from Glasgow Central where Houston Square is: the large square at the town's heart that brings with it the feel of a proud market town. A landowning family called Houston helped build the town and had a fine house in the area, 'Easter Cochrane', later known as Johnstone Castle. Their lands were sold off and the last laird died in 1931. Parts of the town have the Houston name but a connection to Granny's husband is speculative.

Renée's first two years were spent a long distance from where the train station is. Irish immigrants had for two generations congregated on this side of town, having flocked to Johnstone's metal tool factories and mills. The industrialization of Johnstone in the middle of the previous century had caused a meteoric rise in population 'not exceeded in the annals of Scotland,' and the town was a hugger-mugger of factories and cheap dwellings. It wasn't the nicest place to live by a long stretch. Efforts to beautify the town didn't happen until after the First World War. Having said that, the countryside just outside the town was beautiful. The family lived at 55 Grahame Street, a few doors away from St Margarets - a pretty and atmospheric Catholic church built to the designs of Pugin Junior.[2] The Johnstone Directory reveals that there were an astonishing four confectioners in Grahame Street! It was obviously important to sweeten the load in 1904. I saw a pub called *The Hagg Bar*. I thought of the tavern her 'licensed victualler' father Jimmie Gribbin helped run with his older siblings John and Eliza. Yes, Gribbins worked as a family unit early on, if good business was to be had. Help was at hand for Lizzi. In Johnstone thirteen year-old Mary Ann McCabe stayed with them assisting with the kids.

A raucous atmosphere with shouts and clinking beer glasses was hardly apparent when I arrived in this part of Johnstone, braving the rain under my umbrella with its four broken prongs. But long ago this was the all too human world Renée emerged into: of crowded rooms, heavy glasses and sorrows sunk. Suddenly downstairs would vibrate with energy as punters with frightening laughter filled the bars. Those spirit salesmen and spirit waitresses took customer orders completely unperturbed.

Jimmie Gribbin's youth was a period when the unskilled Irish Catholics of Clydeside struggled to get work. In the shipyards they got a break only if the person dispensing employment was a Catholic, as Jimmy Reid tells us, recalling his father's attempt at dock-working and the religious bigotry of the time.[3] Your prospects worsened during times of slump. Grafting as an iron ship builder and making parts in a factory were jobs Jimmie Gribbin tried.[4] Jimmie's father had come from Ireland to work the mines of North Lanarkshire, and when he met a beautiful girl from Greenock - the port town famous for sugar, herrings and shipbuilding, he married her. They moved first to Stevenston near Saltcoats, then to Airdrie, the market town of New Monkland, eleven miles from Glasgow. Another move took them to Shettleston, close by Carntyne, in the late 1880s.

Jimmie got to know Lizzi Houston at the age of twelve or thirteen: the two of them confirmed into the Catholic Church at the same time.[5] Lizzi's family had recently settled in the Shettleston area having moved from Dalry in Ayrshire. Like his brother John - two years his senior - Jimmie became a miner around seventeen years of age. Lads usually took up mining aged fourteen, and were paid 1s, 8.5d per day at the pithead and almost double this if they went down the pit. Men lived in fear, as getting buried alive was a reality with safety precautions few and far between. You used initiative, got out and did something else if you could. Jimmie Gribbin travelled during his stint as a miner. The Gray family who controlled the pits in Shettleston[6] had stopped operation owing to floods no amount of steam pumping could remedy. Happily for little Renée, Carntyne reverted to a farming village, its gravel pits and airshafts reminders of the erstwhile colliery.

One of Jimmie's near contemporaries was John Wheatley, whose father left Waterford in Ireland to work as a miner in Lanarkshire. John too, became a miner, switching to printing and journalism. Roman Catholic and deeply conscious of the suffering of others, he led the rent strikes in Glasgow in 1915. Wheatley, whose pamphlets included 'Miners, Mines and Misery' (1909), was a true pioneer, sitting in Glasgow's city council before being elected to the House of Commons in 1922 as MP for Shettleston. Harry Lauder sang in the mines he worked in and was encouraged by his colleagues to try his luck in the local halls. At Glasgow's Scotia Music Hall, Stockwell Street South, he was discovered and quit the mines. When fame came to Lauder he was an inspiration to anyone who had been in the pits and dreamed of better things. Jimmie's employment in the mines was brief, and money and the lack of actual mining work near Glasgow prompted the interlude in Johnstone. At St Paul's Catholic Chapel, Shettleston on April 13, 1898, he married Lizzi just before going to Johnstone. Jimmie would ideally have stayed in Shettleston, having family networks here. On January 29, 1899 came a little boy, whom they named Jim, of course.

Jimmie moved from the mines to being a publican: a pathway that took initiative on his part. He put his natural performing talents to good use and there was money in it. People turned up to hear this young man sing, play musical instruments, and recite sketches he'd written. His commanding voice was also an asset when it came to clearing stragglers at the evening's end. Jimmie did this type of work for at least four years, meeting men from a range of professions and local men of influence. If news is breaking, a publican is hottest on its trail and his powers of persuasion can serve him well, getting him out of fixes and projecting him into new social circles. His job initially included possession of a pony and cart but something disastrous happened, as Renée's brother, the writer James Alan Rennie, recollects: 'A strange man came to the house, gave father some gold sovereigns and then drove off with our gig and Prince'[7] went the story. They had to leave their home presumably one in Johnstone. The wine-selling part of the business fell through. The cart would have been vital to it. It doesn't appear to have been so serious though, as Jimmie continued as a merchant. Around 1905 the family returned to Carntyne, where the Gribbin family were nearby, and they were back forever with Granny Houston. Jimmie might well have moved from publican to politician as John Wheatley did, but in some ways his own career choice mirrored Wheatley when it came to influence.

Marriage to Lizzi Houston was the key to the flowering of Jim's artistic ambitions and career change. Renée said that from their teenage years until they married, they met each week at the local amateur dramatic society. What they held highest were achievements connected to performance and music. Friends acted as advisors, supporters, and critics. Open-mouthed children were the circle's adoring public. Lizzi, famous locally for her auburn hair and glorious soprano, won every singing competition she entered, amassing gold medals. Dedication counted in this intelligentsia. Jimmie, according to his daughter, appointed himself a dramatic coach, lording it over adults with theatrical personalities as infectious as the diseases in the Lightburn hospital. This was the structure they gazed upon at the far side of the sunny meadow, after feasting on picnics following open-air rehearsals. Writer AJ Cronin worked as the Lightburn's superintendent after the Great War and drew upon the experience for characters in his 'Dr Finlay's Casebook.' Famously televised, Renée acted in the series fifty years later. Talent contests had been all the rage since the 1890s and Jimmie's drama coaching is likely to have been connected to the local shows and pub recitals he staged, many showcasing Lizzi. Then they became full-time pros.

Jimmie and Lizzi became busy people, boarding trains at Carntyne station that sped into Queen Street on matters of importance. They lived close to the railway. Today, land to the north side of the railway line has escaped heavy development and rows of dark four-storey tenements, in the street bordering the railway line north of the High Street, have views from their upper floors that stretch for miles. They could see the distinctive chimney pots of Barlinnie Prison from the kitchen window of their top floor 'hoos' – a view Daddy Jimmie made much of when someone visited. It was a decade after *Charging Thunder* - Lakota Sioux from Buffalo Bill Cody's *Wild West show* was among that prison's inmates. He was in for assaulting a showman. Cody's troupe left a legacy on the area, when a local Dennistoun gang took the name 'The Redskins' – a saga that impressed Jim Junior.

Tenements and view, Shettleston, 2015 (Miranda Brooke)

Granny took responsibility for young Jim and Renée whilst her daughter and son-in-law were absent. From an early age Renée was sent out to town for 'messages'. To her mind's eye, Farmer Murdoch - whom she regularly called upon wheeling her tiny chariot to receive a milk supply, and her Granny were the town's VIPS. Glasgow's sweeping streets stretched north and south, from the eastern fringes of the great merchant city to the Firth. The rain stopped and the cobbles of every street gleamed with happiness. Shettleston's lush green tramcars slid between tenement rows - lower decks filled with women and children, men on the upper levels.

Their tenement made of red-brownish stone that glowed when rain followed sun was recently built. It hadn't acquired a blackening from soot. Almost 70% of Glasgow families before the Great War lived in tall tenements each typically with twelve 'houses' (flats if you are a southerner) and it didn't matter what class or religion you were because people happily got on. Conditions were cramped and damp and some houses had seven to eight people in two rooms. Jim tells us that they were among the first tenants in their new 'red sandstone' and that Shettleston had been 'a small place where a doctor, miner and MP lived next door to each other on a first floor tenement landing.' He adds that its quiet character was being lost day by day. At their home 'up several stairs' lived a railway worker, a pharmacist, a glass blower, an engineer, and shopkeeper – each with their respective families. It was a respectable place. You knew everyone in the 'close' or passageway and kept the place tidy, showing a master sense of organization and fitting all manner of things into your 'house'. Beds formed the bulk of the furniture: folded flat by the wall or folding up into chairs. Parents slept in the 'hole in the wall bed' in the kitchen, swishing a curtain across the recess for privacy.

Jimmie Gribbin observed the *couthy* comedy about him. He and Lizzi discussed his new plan. He had already tried his luck as a compère and master of ceremonies, exploiting his confident presence and commanding voice. His contacts might be called upon to open a few doors. Cleverness had delivered him from the mines. He could furnish his own material in a stage act, and he had the guts to depend upon himself. With newcomers achieving public renown in the music hall, you were more likely to try your luck in 1909 than ever before. This was a time of growth, not decay. In the decade just passed, beautiful grand theatres had been built everywhere. The success stories were real and overruled *doubting Thomases* whose belief was that it wasn't worth the fluctuations in work and likely exploitation. In their proud tenement, built when Edward and George were monarchs, the Gribbins were the only resident theatricals. They were never back with the rent.

The variety business then, was a vast enterprise with the biggest syndicates run by Moss Empires, De Frece, Oswald Stoll, and Frank McNaghton. The syndicates were at times rivals or combined to stop clever artistes playing them off against each other. 1910 had seen Stoll break away from Moss - a move that led to him becoming chairman of thirteen companies covering some of the most prestigious theatres in the South East, Leicester and Manchester: their combined value amounting to £1,944,890.00 in 1917.[8] There was always a risk of experiencing less than decent terms and conditions and poor pay, especially if you were starting out in variety. You could be transferred from one hall to another without your consent. However, a Variety Artistes Federation (VAF) came into being in 1906, through the brave actions of Joe O'Gorman – *Irish and Proud of It*, and others, to help safeguard the interests of pros. The next year, small but significant victories were won by artistes during the 'Music Hall War' in terms of the amount of commission agents took, payment, and the limiting of the *barring clause* that had prevented you appearing in nearby localities for strict lengths of time. With a degree of protection from exploitation in place, the circuits and combines offered the performer up to six months work per year.

The earliest comic sketch featuring Renée's parents I've found evidence for is entitled *Coming home from the Club* presented at Forfar Pavilion on September 25, 1911 and Lizzi is featured separately on the bill as a soprano. Their act was initially billed as *'The Gribbens'* or *'the Gribben Trio'* with George Arnott (described in notices as an 'eccentric comedian'). Arnott went solo a little later. Austin Kerr, possibly from the provisioning merchant family in Main Street, Shettleston, was another who played in Jimmie's comic company. In the latter part of 1911, the *Trio* was on the George Urie Scott tour. Long before he ran Glasgow's Empress Theatre, GU Scott built up an empire of modest-looking picture palaces in southwest and east end Glasgow: the Annfield Electric in Gallowgate and several in Falkirk and Hawick. Soon, cine-variety houses were everywhere. Right close to where Jimmie and Lizzi lived was Scott's Electric Cinema in Denbeck Street, previously a wire works, and the Palaceum in Hill Street. GU Scott needed acts and was, around this time, giving exclusive booking rights to Fred Collins's theatrical agency, so it's possible the Gribbins were on their books.

Picture-variety houses were noisy places. Children congregated in the cheapest area downstairs in three halfpence seats, receiving a pelting of orange peelings delivered from the better off kids in gallery seats. You arrived an hour before the film began to hear variety acts, suffering the howls of babies and screams then the film ran and the piano rolled. Being silents, auditorium noise mattered far less. Gripping serials kept you coming back. Cinema exerted its phenomenal influence in unexpected ways. In Birmingham in 1911, film was already showing its social conscience and cinema was blamed for school strikes after it caused struggling mothers to demand that both school fees and the use of canes be abolished.[9] Via a newsreel Glaswegians watched events close to home such as of the 11,000 striking employees at the Singer Sewing Machine Factory, Clydebank. The eternal grinders were upset with increased workloads and decreased wages. The crusade mounted by Lloyd George to get his people's budget into law was anxiously followed. A few years later, crowds lined up outside cinemas to find out about war breaking out in Europe. News and features were sides of a whole entertainment experience: film just one 'turn' in the variety.

In February 1912, Jimmie shed the *'Gribben'* name – an Irish one originating from County Down and Armagh. It was passed over in favour of

'*Houston*' - of English origin and a synonym of '*MacQuiston*'- numerous in Ulster. Thereafter, his act was called *James Houston and Company* with Lizzi and Jimmie now known as *Mr and Mrs Houston* both on and off stage. Some years previously lived a James Houston (1828-1892) - a transatlantic traveller and great Burns enthusiast who also did comic roles. For this new *James Houston* the name was not a coincidence, and Jimmie saw himself as poet, comic, and Burns exponent. The old theatrical trick was applied when Charles Olden, a Wigan comic, was named[10] Ted Ray after a golfer, giving new life to a name from a not far off consciousness. Jimmie travelled on the circuit with his *Trio* and by February 1913 was playing the Empires of Glasgow and Edinburgh, then Leeds City Varieties earning £15 to £20 a week for theatres like this - a huge sum – equivalent to over £1000 now. He had his first London dates in November that year.

For Jimmie, he valued quickness and wit, and never believed that what he and Lizzi did was any way less skillful than actors who trod the legitimate stage. He was proud of the class act he and Lizzi had created. *James Houston and Company* developed about seven domestic style sitcoms, each with a flexible plot. A couch or table placed at the stage's centre line symbolized their act. They weren't trying to be sophisticated. The craft of the performer mattered even more so than having up to date material. The formula was successful and the same sketch was taken around the country. By 1919, comedy-loving audiences had developed a fondness for *James Houston* sketches and never criticized them for being repetitive, which is surprising. Their reviews were glowing. One of their sketches, *The Best Man,* was even 'acknowledged to be the Scotch sketch of the century.' It was about a man who arrives home from work, met by his sister who keeps house for him. She tells him the news that his friend's wedding takes place that very day. He hurries with his tea and, helped by his sister, changes into his best clothes. That proves to be no light task and when he's finally ready, the bridegroom arrives to tell him the wedding is on the following day.

The Encore wrote of the brilliance of James Houston and Company when they appeared at The Euston in 1915. That paper's artist 'SIC' captured a moment from *The Best Man* in one of his brilliant pen drawings. (By kind permission of The British Library)

This plain little scenario was Jimmie's biggest hit, one they played around the country. The same audiences saw it as years went by. When they played Burnley, papers reported 'the comedy is not lacking in humour and the piece is enlivened by three Scotch songs rendered by the *sister* in excellent style.'[11]

I was fascinated to read a second review when they did the turn at Burnley's Empire Music Hall, that compared the chief character of *The Best Man* to the comic and histrionic gallant of *Much Ado About Nothing* who performs for others using witty hyperbole to express his feelings. It describes James Houston's playlet as 'the troubles of a *would be Benedict*,'[12] insisting that his friends prepare for a wedding after he's anticipated it by a day.

Jimmie's personality towered. He was the one up to no good, playing an eccentric version of his real self. Lizzi was an ideal feed, getting laughs by her cool funny responses to Jimmie's lines. She adlibbed when the situation arose, and Jimmie had to be quick. 'Why is it that all Scots jokes are about men - never Scotswomen?' Renée Houston got asked in 1927. She replied with a serious expression 'Scots women are no joke'[13] saying no more. The female in a Scotch comedy was formidable, judging from Renée's comment. To be billed as 'the latest Scotch comedy' says a lot about the era's fondness for national identities, and somehow Jimmie and Lizzi wore the mantle of *premier* Scotch comedy couple. A modest and thrifty king and queen they were, but the pearls they threw at swine were lustrous. They splashed out on a few publicity photos. Jimmie looks a beau in his boater and Lizzie wears her Regency hat with dignity.

Living in tenements could be relied upon to spark endless jokes, and the second most popular playlet in the Houston Company repertoire - entitled *The Flittin,* was a powerful sketch. Its theme was an order to quit for being 'back with the rent' but owing to the 'intoxicated condition of the male tenant and his bosom companion, the wife's effects are cruelly ill-used, until the removal of a picture reveals the hiding place of a lost 'nest-egg.' Of course this removes the necessity of flitting, re-establishing 'the comforts of their ain wee hoose.'[14] A plot about being back with the rent registered big in cities where hated bailiffs were met by gangs of women who showered them in flour, wet clothes and other missiles. A bell was rung to warn everybody. Tenants had long been dodging letters attempting to force them into paying a year's rent upfront. 25,000 households refused to pay rent.[15] Evictions were common and desperation explained why rent money was withheld. When rents increased at the beginning of the First World War, strikes followed and shipyard workers came out to support the rent strikers. William Weir, in charge of Scottish industrial production, brought in American workers and paid them more. Yet local workers had built a record 757,000 tons of vessel in 1913,[16] adding considerably to civil defence and the government risked alienating public opinion if they evicted them. A Rent Restriction Act freezing rents at pre-war levels came out of those strikes.

Everyone who came to see *The Flittin* enjoyed the jokes despite the unease. Scottish life at its most humdrum was mocked. Washing days, as fans of *Scotch comedy* could appreciate, gave much scope for new quips. This was the world where kids in the backcourt *dreeped* themselves from the boundary walls whilst women took turns to use the washhouse, never letting a boiler of water go to waste at the end of a day's washing if someone with a stream of nappies to clean could benefit. That was if you had a good water supply. If you didn't, it was the local 'steamie' attached to the public baths you went to. There was currency in the arguments flaring up if someone lit a fire in the backcourt. The strict rota for cleaning shared facilities was a resource. It did happen too, that mutually antagonistic 'stair neighbours' in different parts of the building, unexpectedly became buddies in a *tenement war*. All these were ripe for exploitation in the latest twist of *The Flittin*.

During the Great War, practically every music hall was kept open. There was more willingness to get work in the profession than jobs would allow. An article in The Era mentioned how over a thousand actors applied for engagements in one touring company that required nine characters only for a play. War played 'havoc with the chances of employment in theatres and music halls.'[17] Manipulative theatre managers hoped to draw in more punters with schemes for mid-week *split programmes*. Such interference meant a shorter lifespan where material was concerned, with performers having to change digs every three nights.[18] If that wasn't bad enough, just as the world needed entertainment, the government began Entertainment Tax to help the war effort.[19] Thankfully, the Variety Artists Federation (VAF) fought the corner of disadvantaged artistes. Being a performer wasn't easy but business frequently would turn out better than was expected.

Established before the war, home defence came via the 'Territorials' or British Army volunteer reserve, nicknamed "Saturday Night Soldiers" as it was a part-time vocation. These men were not obliged to serve overseas. If they did, the wearing of an *Imperial Service Brooch* signified it. Many lads joined overseas battalions thinking the war would be over by Christmas. They expected a kind of summer camp or an easy way to escape jobs they didn't like.[20] In August 1914 orders were issued to separate the *home service* men from the seventy battalions who had volunteered to go overseas.

With this as context, *James Houston and Company* perfected a new satire, taking the Burnsian name *Fireside Sodgers*. 'Full of pawky humour,' the theme was topical with references to the Territorials. It had sparkling humour and witty repartee. A notice testifies how the 'magnificent vocalism of the lady member of the company adds considerably to the enjoyment of the audience.'[21] They performed *Sodgers* at Motherwell's Empire Electric Theatre on May 22, 1914, getting second main billing to Jack Lorimer, the popular Scotch Comedian whose son, Max Wall, would appear in many a theatre with their daughters. Just two years later, during an air raid, a cast iron bed frame came between Max and death. Lizzi's fine soprano voice helped rally the audience's spirit. This was a time when music hall songstresses bade you do your duty and join the nation's fight against Kaiser Bill. *James Houston and Company*'s act never got caught up in such fervour and, if anything, would have taken snipes at one or more government lines. Scotland had been on the verge of Home Rule in spring 1914. A devolution bill had two readings in the Commons, supported by a Liberal Party that held

80% of seats north of the border. As war continued, devolution was put on the backburner.

May and June 1915 saw James Houston's Company play the Argyle Birkenhead and several London houses like Collins Music Hall and the Metropolitan, Edgware Road - the same time Marie Lloyd was at Tottenham Palace. Jimmie took part in *Tag Day* on June 4 - an event involving two hundred and fifty artistes including Charles Coborn and Elsie Janis collecting money for *Mr Stoll's War Seal Foundation for Disabled Soldiers,* the *Music Hall Ladies Guild* and the *Variety Artists Benevolent Fund.* Theatre manages allowed collections to take place at theatres whilst patches of fields and London flower shops were ransacked for forget-me-nots sold on by 240 lady volunteers. £438 was raised.[22] Jimmie gave valuable service as a steward. He continued to make friends with useful people, beginning his association with the VAF. In 1916 he tried unsuccessfully to get on the executive committee for Scotland's VAF and was finally elected to its advisory committee in February 1921. Until 1924 he was a regular at meetings at the Central Halls in Glasgow's Bath Street. The committee members were active in pantomime and theatre worlds - people his daughters would work with: JW Bowie, and Bert Bendon, of Power and Bendon.

At Collins Music Hall Jimmie and Lizzie were on the same bill as *Buffallo Bill,* now at the end of his career, for the week of June 7, 1915. Next they were at Euston's Palace of Varieties that used to face St Pancras Station before 1960s planners saw fit to demolish it and put a brutalist construction in its place. There, the top-lining act Jimmie and Lizzi supported was *In the Clouds* –a 'sensational Egyptian military aerodrama' with lots of palm trees and pyramids on stage, typifying the atmospheric 'spectaculars' music halls staged then, but with a militaristic edge. Set in Egypt where the British Army is operating against the *Unspeakable Turk*, the audience witnessed a dance in an Arab sheikh's tent, a mid-air aircraft fight between hero and villain, and no end of anti-aircraft special effects and searchlights.[23]

Jimmie's Company had decent standing, whilst bottom liners competed to get an engagement from all-powerful agents. For unknown London comics, turning up at pubs, like The York Arms at Waterloo Bridge Road and York Road, helped, as these were 'labour exchanges.' Mr and Mrs Houston got to know several big music hall stars of their day. Performers were full of admiration for each other's work. Marie Lloyd was apparently a great friend of Lizzi's - surprising, given the latter's genteel nature. 'Aunt Marie we called her,' Renée explained, proceeding to tell her funny story about Marie's experiences of *turn working* in London – one that illustrates how artistes coped with stressful travel. *Aunt Marie* had to be in Tottenham or Edmonton by a certain time. Trundling along in her hansom cab, she wondered if traffic would ease up. In her ladylike voice, she called to the driver 'Oh Cabbie, do hurry up,' getting the reply, 'I'm doing my best Miss Marie.' This happened a couple of times and time was getting on, with precious little progress made. Losing the posh accent, *Aunt Marie* stuck her head out 'Oh, for goodness sake.' As the pace became even slower, she totally lost it, hysterically yelling out the window 'Kick it up the arse!' which only received the neutral response: 'I'm saving that for Ludgate Hill, Miss Marie.'

Marie Lloyd (Author's collection)

Half of Scotland's male population under forty-five served in the Great War. A high level of Scots infantrymen fought in the Battle of Loos in October 1915. Throughout the conflict 147,609 Scots died. Scotland had just a tenth of the UK's population, but its soldiers made up a fifth of Britain's war dead. Jimmie's son added four years to his age and joined the Royal Field Artillery. He was proud to receive his first wound after just one month. He was back cowering in ditches in France and Flanders, getting hit in the head in October 1918. Jim recovered after being paralyzed down his left side with shrapnel embedded in his upper abdomen and lower chest. He was never completely fit. While some argued that Catholics reserved allegiance to a foreign power, every boy in a photograph of a play put on at Jim's school in 1912 perished.[24]

Since the Nineteenth century, being 'Scotch' was something to trade on in the halls. Forgotten names like The Real McKay, Wullie Durkin, Sammy Shields, Jolly Jock Welsh, and Daisy Taylor had 'Scots comedian' or 'Scotch Wandering minstrel' on their bill matter. It extended into the animal world with *'Duncan's Scotch Collies'* apparently internationally famous. Still, times came when you hid your 'Scotchness' and were content to be nameless on the bill. One such time was when Bransby Williams came to Dublin's Theatre Royal between July 27 and August 3, 1914. Some years before, this 'Irving of the Music halls' had appeared before King Edward VII and toured the United States. He was old enough to have heard Gladstone speak and interpreted Dickens characters like *Micawber, Uriah Heep, Bill Sykes and Fagin* as well as ones of his own making like *'Regency Buck'* or *'Waxworks night watchman.'*

One month into the war, Jimmie and Lizzi were troopers within Williams' 'Powerful Company of Vaudeville Stars.' It may have been two years before the Easter Rising, but the city wasn't a safe place that Sunday July 26 when Jimmie, his wife and two daughters settled into their lodgings. That morning 900 German rifles and 20,000 rounds of ammunition had been smuggled into the mainland from German tugboats off Howth and police tried in vain to disarm the Irish volunteers - recipients of these weapons. Gun running activities existed on both sides. The one to aid those wishing for Home Rule was a response to a shipment of 35,000 German rifles, which the Ulster Volunteers had received the previous April.[25] A regiment - the King's Own Scottish Borderers - put up with a brutal stoning from crowds loyal to the Volunteers. That evening three civilians including a woman were killed when shots were fired at Bachelor's Walk, in the vicinity of the metal bridge near Liffey Street, with many more injured with bayonets.[26] Renée's 1974 memoir has her family caught up in events, running like the wind in savage crossfire, and taking refuge in a pub. A week later, an inquest concluded that two dozen civilians, many of them women and girls, threw bottles and stones at the soldiers, provoking firing, although no order had been given to fire.

Renée had first mentioned these events in 1936, recalling how 'no one Scottish dared show his face.' It was why her parents' names were kept off the bill in case a demonstration was mounted against them. The two sisters were kept close by in the Theatre Royal's dressing room on the south side of the Liffey. In the days following the shooting there was still a lot of ferment. As they journeyed to Mrs Dalby's boarding house at 12 Eden Quay, they were forced to take a long detour to avoid the bridge where the trouble had been. A nerve-racked Lizzi feigned an Irish brogue as people spoke to her. She warned her daughters to avoid speaking Scots at all costs. That was easier said, and eight year-old Billie risked giving the game away: 'Mother – where are oor digs?' she said, and 'Mother – Hoo far hae we tae go noo?'[27] Nothing untoward happened, thankfully. Had people found out they were Scottish, before they left Dublin on August 3, things might have been different.

In these tumultuous times the weekly wage earned by *James Houston and Company* was in the region of £25 when business was good, so Renée's parents were comfortably off. To their observant nine year-old daughter they set the standard for graft. She never witnessed them shirk from frantic touring and they went on with the show whatever the obstacle. Lizzi was happy by her husband's side. Such close professional companionship for husbands and wives is rare in the 21st Century. How far they let someone admit to a weakness or give them the space they desired is another matter. They always had people around to help cater to their demands.

Chapter 4   Little Mother in a Theatrical Family

'Yoo gaun play,' said the friend. She slid the peever encouragingly across the stone step. Afterwards they went inside and set off the music boxes on the sideboard. They hid, hoping to surprise the next person entering the room. Another friend arrived and they carefully opened a drawer revealing the stereoscope with the red velvet eyepiece. One of them unfolded its wooden handle, holding it in one hand and looking into the lens, whilst another decided which card to insert on the wire rack in front of the eyepiece. Adjusting it made the two images merge into one. The naughty card of Camille Clifford Mammy complained about, owing to the lowness of the lady's décolletage, caused deafening screams - enough to produce a skelping if they weren't careful. Daddy Jimmie arrived one day not only with a Pathéphone but discs and a catalogue. It was a proud talking point that Renée and her brother thrived on, and the scamps of the neighbourhood wished to visit their house of secrets.

When Renée's sister Billie was born on Saturday April 28, 1906, the family lived at 27 Salisbury Place, Shettleston. Back from the railway and bordering Tollcross Park, these dwellings predated the surge in tenement construction that had accompanied the building of the Coatbridge to Glasgow railway. Now vanished, the house was one of smart red brick similar to those in Hillview and Edrom Street: solid-looking two-storey homes with romantic names like *'Corra Lynn'* and *'Vesta Lynn'*. The British Empire beyond Parkhead had yet to be experienced by the Gribbin kids. They were in the good end of town although *'Hell Square'*[1]- a danger zone of ruffians - wasn't far. Soon, Jimmie and Lizzi's weans, including Billie aged two, were absorbed into their theatrical doings - hauled into a local production of *East Lynne* in which Lizzi played the tragic heroine. In a heart-rending scene with her baby next to her in a crib, Lizzi began wringing her hands crying out in deepest pain: 'Dead, Dead, and not a soul to help me!' But that wean could not contain herself with this realistic display of emotion: 'Mammy a'm not dead!' wailed a deep little voice from inside the crib.

Mammy was special. Her eldest daughter, sensitive to colour, observed her dressing for a ball, her red hair piled high on top of her head, Edwardian style, with a scarlet felt opera coat over her evening dress. The storybook lady disappeared weeks on end with Daddy. Lizzi and Jimmie's absences provided a measure of freedom for the kids but Mammy wrote home every day. Then that lady reappeared in rustling silk with a smell of heliotrope filling the room. 'She was 'a beautiful creature, enviably serene' Renée later recalled. From Lizzi she learned the fabulous entrance and strove to emulate her singing. Lizzi possessed the finest voice of them all and her 'Ave Maria' brought tears to people's eyes. She exercised her voice regularly and maintained it, piercing an egg and drinking its raw contents. Singing was cherished then,[2] and was prevalent in girls' education, long before modern times saw its erosion from the curriculum. A song was ever-present in their home and the tatty little pedal harmonium Lizzi played meant the 'house' was alive with the sound of music. Crisp and comic Gilbert and Sullivan numbers nobody liked were rehearsed, and light opera ruled.

Renée mother provided her with an image of how her life might take shape but she differed in temperament. Mammy was a quieter character who, although fond of her profession, never cared to be conspicuous offstage. Billie Houston was closer to her in this respect. Renée, when she later recalled her childhood, made gentle jokes at her mothers' expense. There was the time the family fronted a revue with a company of players. Travelling by tramcar, everyone was addressing Lizzi as 'Mammy'. An old lady remarked 'My, Missus, you've got an awful big crowd 'o' wains!' Renée tells us her mother was very embarrassed. 'My mother's dignity was a great source of amusement to all of us.'[3] All the same Lizzi was resolute in her self-belief. She had no time for ballet school, drama school or anything else, encouraging budding performers to learn on the job. She did everything instinctively and had never received any formal training.[4] Lizzi relied on what she had, and it was pretty good. You either had it or you hadn't.

Salisbury Place may have suited Lizzi but the family didn't reside there long. They always found themselves back living in Granny's tenement. In between theatrical engagements, Lizzi did what she could in the cramped home. She was a fair seamstress and might cheerily carry ashes from the coal fire down to the backcourt middens but she wasn't your typical Shettleston housewife. When she boiled dishcloths or lit fires, she was acting the role. Granny saved the day. With her Ayrshire know-how about washing and drying clothes, the *Duchess* was their secret weapon. A polished and well turned-out look counted a great deal in the trade.

Renée's relationship with her father was one of argument and joviality. From the cradle each of us responds to applause and encouraging words. As eldest daughter of a man known in the business for showmanship and verbal absurdities, Renée was at the receiving end of frighteningly fast wit and the parental 'last word' became the cue for her own. She needed to parry a finer stroke. A war of words between them was typical before any plan transpired. When his daughters were starting out in the halls and picture houses, he would make his point loud and clear when he lectured his eldest daughter prior to an engagement: 'Don't ye forget we have played at all these places and we want to go back again. Behave yourselves!' Renée told this to interviewer Robin Russell[5] and there's a sense of resentment in her voice. She found she had to look to herself both for justification and for taking initiative. Daddy Jimmie's loud bark or belief in his superior leadership might unsettle some, but not his eldest daughter, who had the real upper hand, having seen his weaknesses. From early on she was apt to be his protector. He knew his eldest daughter was full of surprises, liable to do the most ridiculous things but these he took in his stride. All the time was this façade of him being this 'strict disciplinarian.' Even when she and Billie were young women, Renée tells us of Daddy 'treating us as he always did like two very small children.'[6] It was a game. Still, he was the essential part of her, and as so many of us find, our parents' love for each other and their resourcefulness is a 'blueprint' for survival, buried deep and drawn upon when needed most.

St Mark's School, and views bordering Tollcross Park, 2015 (Miranda Brooke)

Buildings shook and bells rang out of time, and it was nothing short of exciting when, on December 14, 1910, Glasgow had a small earthquake. Renée could not ignore a possible religious resonance to the event. She whispered her fears to her brother and together they said a prayer. Jim cried, believing that he was to blame. The Catholic infants school, where the girls spent their first years, was St Mark's where Renée decided she could help Mammy by being a good singer herself. In their kinderspiel everyone remarked how quick she was at learning lines or the words of a song, and Mr Connelly, her teacher, was so pleased with her he awarded her with a lovely book. Her parents took note, after witnessing little Rena in the school play. She wasn't quite as bad as they thought. St Mark's then stood alone in a field - a short walk away via a dusty path. At the time of writing it stands derelict and boarded up.

Little Billie, or Cissie as she was, loved to sing. Scarcely had 'I Love a Lassie' been on the turntable than Billie began giving authentic impressions of Scotland's superstar, Harry Lauder. She held a tune perfectly and there was no question about her talent. This was 1911 and word got around about this talented little person - a source of pride where her parents were concerned. A nice bit of song and dance might strike a note with the scions of influence promenading around Glasgow for the *International Exhibition* – if you were very lucky. The talent radar got wheeled out a lot between May and November that year. One day, a friend asked Jimmie if one of the Houston kids might perform before assembled council members. The City Hall's tradition of Saturday night concerts had been established in 1854 by the Glasgow Abstainers' Union, its core of 'Covenanters' reflecting the beliefs of the Scotland's strictest Presbyterian body. These concerts were to keep folk out of the pubs. That's why they didn't finish until 11 pm. Much to Renée's relief she didn't have to perform. She lived in fear of the talent radar at this time. The same couldn't be said for her sister.

Jimmie was on the cusp of breaking into a career in the halls, and displaying his talented offspring was a form of self-promotion. Billie's 'discovery' preceded his own. It was at one of the 'City Hall bursts' that Billie Houston made her first public appearance standing on the platform late one Saturday evening in little kilt, hat, and stick, singing the Lauder song. She not only impressed all present with her lack of fear, but proved she had an unbelievable voice for a kid her age. Remarkably, nobody made much noise about the issue of five year-olds being too young to be up at that late hour.

Prodigies are still stunning auditoriums. There's Kaitlyn Maher, a four year-old singer from *America's Got Talent* and five year-old Heavenly Joy performing at the *Unstoppable* gala at the Century City Hyatt. Little Connie Talbot, not much older, has had an album released. Shirley Temple is, of course, the most famous child star. Precociousness has long held a fascination, and, for parents, can be an obsession.

A few months later, at a similar City Hall 'Councillors' Concert', Billie made her second public appearance. This time onlookers saw a different side of her. Waiting in the green room she heard the compère announce they would next hear a song by 'Baby Gribbin'. That was too much, and her iron will was invoked. She told her father she would not go on after that '*Baby*' insult. 'I am Miss Cissie Gribbin,' she insisted. This was granted, but facing the sizeable crowd, she froze again as the pianist started to play the opening bars of her song. Stubbornly, she waited with a closed mouth. In the room that years before had witnessed speeches by Dickens, Disraeli and Gladstone, came twitters of laughter. Mammy took over on the piano. Billie had a sensitive ear and the pianist had been playing her precious music in too high a key. With that technicality dealt with, Billie proceeded to be the hit of the evening.

In those early days it was Billie, not Renée who was earmarked to make something of her talent. There are huge similarities to the young Vesta Tilley: starting at eight years old, with an ever-present father seeing the little performance she made in front of the mirror, donning a man's top hat and cape, as very bankable. Billie's skills at male impersonation saw their greatest development, according to her brother, in her mimicry of all his movements. Jim junior was a strapping six-footer, a dab hand in the boxing ring, who overcame his war injury by running with the local Harriers. Eight years his junior, Billie was a brave little fighter, and self-appointed guardian to Renée if any unfairness befell her older sister. Given Billie's earnest and brave character, she would have faced a foreign legion. How wounding it was when Renée, in her crueller moments, mocked this earnest little *Fountleroy*.

Many children played games like 'shops' in the backyard, or 'wee heiders' on rainy days running in and out of the close, getting on the adults' nerves. The age where kids ruled the streets and yards was a lot less neurotic than the present. Loitering adults were few, as most couldn't afford the leisure. They tended to be targets themselves. There was no lack of 'life' to inspire savage wits among the imaginative kids. One was the seemingly weak-looking Renée, who appeared out of nowhere like a terrifying spectre holding you in her grasp with a pointed look in her eyes whilst words were muttered beneath that mobile upper lip. As her brother recalls, that petite ten-year old was fascinating to watch as she reproduced imaginary showdowns between two local ladies. There were shifts in energy as she went from 'brooding thoughtfully or creeping mouse-like about the house,' to being the ballerina, or sometimes mimicking that shrew of a neighbour. Jim felt she was 'so unpredictable that dullness could not exist while she was around.'[7] Without a doubt, she was what the type of comedian Little Tich had in mind when he used to say 'comedians are born, not made.'

Yet a sense of injustice took root in childhood. It started with her being 'second' to Jim: Lizzi's favourite. Such things drove her sarcasm. At times, her parents presented themselves as her enemies. Then, her little pale face spent long periods seething in the shade, and this is why everything - the beetle on the wall, the dirty sponge in a bucket, the neighbour with airs and graces - could get her dander up, finding expression in a new secret rage. It was funnier each time but also sad. She occasionally built a wall around herself but nevertheless seems never to have been without friends.

The endless hours of childhood are an ocean, and games filling these hours are sometimes the stuff of brilliance. Many of us have larked around with a sibling and been proper little showstoppers, only to grow out of the fantasies. Generally, nobody wants to remember, and the flights of fancy and ridiculous heights reached as young children become a source of embarrassment as adults. Renée and Billie, of course, maintained their flights of fancy. Renée always had power over her two younger sisters and they doted on her, valuing the silly games. Even as adults, only a 'lead in' was required, and they were re-living some ancient situation with original naturalness. Some early private games were repackaged. Daddy and Mammy had an old rocking chair. No one could part with it for love nor money. That heap of junk, Renée explained, was 'as dear to us as the most priceless antique in the world. Many a mile of desert prairie have Billie and I ridden, on the arms of that antique rocking chair.'[8] Mammy often suggested having the arms upholstered, but every time she mentioned it, her daughters talked her out of it, so important was it to preserve those memories.

During school holidays an unsophisticated version of the sisters' double act developed when they accompanied their parents to towns in Scotland. Left to run free, while Jimmie and Lizzi were pre-occupied with business, the girls discovered scenes of imprisonment, mercy, and death. Castles like Alloa, in Clackmannanshire, had the best scenery. This one had a 15th century medieval tower - a backdrop for a damsel and her knight. Roaming like the two perils in Beryl Bainbridge's 'Harriet Said' they frightened the living daylights out of one of Alloa's more restrained visitors. Books were always at hand, like Frank Richard's 'Greyfriars School' series, and the girls extracted a plotline from school stories by Angela Brazil, where rebellious hoydens, careless as to their appearance got into scrapes, demure girls exchanged confidences by the cabbage patch, and continental girls aroused suspicion.[9]

At home, on the mantelpiece were two photos: one of the Pope and one of Celtic Football Club's centreforward. Heroes were as important then as now. Aged six, Billie prided herself on being a 'fellow,' even talking of becoming a railway engine driver or a professional footballer.[10] Her handsome brother, over six foot, was back from the army. He couldn't believe the way his kid sister copied his walk, voice, and manner. Billie was no stranger to Fitba' in the playground or on the street. In fact she was 'the star of the boys' football games,' and made 'mincemeat'[11] of anyone who crossed her.

It helped to show a bit of brawn then. Bunches of youths, some with those adult misfits who hung around them, were a common sight in industrialized towns. It was typical for their slang to be injected into the local culture.[12] Shettleston had its share of street games of 'pitch and toss' by young gamblers who developed into little syndicates. Local policemen would eventually try to crush these would-be gangsters. Whilst the Band of Hope, with its temperance message, was a presence in many towns, it was smoking and gambling, not drinking, that was considered the number one social ill among young people of this era.[13]

A lad growing up in Glasgow's East End would do well to learn how to deliver a deadly left hook. Jim had had a few lessons in self-defense when he was tiny in Johnstone. You could be picked on just for being a Catholic and the memoir of Unionist Jimmy Reid tells us that religious bigotry was the scourge of Clydeside. That taunting *'are you a Billy or a Dan?'*[14] might lead to roughing up. Being a sportsman, a member of the Boy's Brigade or part of a running team helped build a boy's confidence and forge common ground with other boys. For Jim, he had the tyranny of the Catholic brotherhood to put up with as well as small boys. There was a time when Jim was heard expressing ideas about deserving to be flayed or caned. It's the mindset that comes from listening too long to adults highlighting your guilt. It caused Lizzi to get very down in the dumps thinking of the harrowing ordeal Jim had gone through at school at the hands of certain priests promoting their ideas about discipline or worse. With other lads Jim found sanity in *The Loobs* - a secret club with a mission 'to be against all meanness,' and survive the harsher experiences that growing up in Glasgow presented. The 'Loobs' significance was enough for Jim to dedicate his first book 'Riddle of Rainbow Mountain' to them when he was a bestselling author in the 30s.

Renée and Billie suffered some degree of meanness inflicted by their religious teachers but nothing as awful as Jim's punishments. Renée used to get a slap on the knuckles from the nuns from time to time and told the son of a colleague from variety about how pupils in her school would get instructed to go to the local hardware shop to buy a cane and bring it back to the school. She made sure to drop the cane down the drain and decided to put up with the 'double walloping' this brought.[15]

Catholic schools in Glasgow were run by orders like the Franciscans and the Marists, whose influence on the community was significant. Brother Walfrid's founding of Celtic Football Club in 1888 is a lasting legacy of the Marist Brotherhood. The Franciscan Sisters at Renée's school kept their French culture alive. Invited from France to the parish of St Mary's in the Calton by the Bishop, they were primarily a teaching institution with a mission to form in their pupils 'hearts of virtue.' Our Lady and St Francis

School was at 58-60 Charlotte St, at the edge of Glasgow Green. It was then one of the smartest streets in the city lined by classical villas in the Robert Adam style. The villa at 52 Charlotte Street is the only reminder of that elegance. A document kindly provided to me by the school's archivist, reveals that when Our Lady and St Francis School celebrated its Silver Jubilee a decade before Renée joined, it was a very small school. When not mentioning the need for exercise classes to improve the 'carriage of the girls,' school logbooks for 1915 and 1916 point to the sheer lack of space. It saw little structural expansion until the 1920s.

Back in 1900 an inspector's report indicates a curriculum 'somewhat narrow at present but no complaint can be made of the quality of the instruction.' By 1912, when Renée was making her morning trek to school, girls' education had risen to a standard higher than at any time previously.[16] The nuns, with their *Scottish Franciscan* identity, maintained their reputation for giving girls an excellent standard in French. Not all the teachers were nuns and at least three male teachers taught at her school in 1916.[17] Shortly before Renée joined, the school had gained a museum of stuffed birds, a small aquarium, a cooking range for cookery classes, and botany was added as a science subject.[18] Clay and cardboard modelling and even cane weaving were established lessons, and a modern typewriter was acquired for the fifth and sixth form. Clay modelling was something Renée maintained as a hobby later in life. Her love of reading and interest in history is likely to have been shaped here, and her artistic gifts did not go unnoticed. Once, receiving praise for her calligraphy, she wept in class. Presided over by Mother Jerome Gordon at this time, the school took contributions from parents, and Renée's parents had the means to pay.

Views of Charlotte Street, Glasgow, 2015 (Miranda Brooke)

A logbook mentions the school plays performed in January 1915, one for the Archbishop of Glasgow, followed by two public performances for the benefit of the Belgians, raising £26. Senior pupils took part in *Dances of the olden times*, and there were two French sketches: *Isabelle de Lisle* and *Reine des Fees,* as well as cantata singing. A year later, during Renée's final months at the school, the Archbishop was back, giving prizes at another fund-raising performance, this time for the benefit of soldiers and sailors and raising £34.[19] There's no doubt the future Miss Houston was part of these school plays. Singing was highly valued and the nuns took pride in girls with acting talent. They called her *Katerina*, a name she never liked, preferring the diminutive *Rina* or *Rena* and ultimately the French-sounding 'Renée'.

The little *Greek Thompson*-looking building facing the street at the north end of Charlotte Street was there during Renée's schooldays, without its current sign *'Glasgow's oldest chippie 1884.'* Fish and chips was, of course, one of her favourite meals. In later years the school was a girls' comprehensive, and 1950s pupils enjoyed annual trips to Millport and boat-trips down the Clyde. Several 1980s pupils enjoyed a special audience with Pope John Paul II and drama students staged *Oliver* and *Cinderella*. Charlotte Street's surroundings have subsequently dramatically changed. Its 1954 structure remains - a listed building, but the area is less vibrant. Despite a campaign by former pupils to save the school, it closed in 1989. It is remembered in blogs by former schoolmates for the character it gave the area, for the girls' famous chocolate brown uniforms, and for certain sinister teachers with a fondness for the belt.

Back in 1912, home-life was starting to be characterized either by freedom from supervision or by travel: rare privileges that Renée and Billie's peers weren't as lucky to experience. Granny was there in the absence of 'the Houston Company'. No one could call her a killjoy. If their parents' engagements weren't too far, Rena and Cissie could take a privileged peek from the wings. At the ages of twelve and ten, they were fine judges of situation comedy, sensitive to its twists and turns. They saw the pure and upright character Mammy played in *The Flittin,* and the way she held the audience's sympathy as she strove to reform the hopelessly renegade character Daddy played.

The girls also had their own experience of treading the boards. The first time they were on stage together was at Greenock Hippodrome. The availability of recordings of Irving Berlin's 'Everybody's Doing It Now' helps date this to 1913. At West Blackhall Street, Jimmie and Lizzi shared the bill with 'The Darky Ragtime Octette.' The eight performers, described as *America's Foremost Ragtime Octette* were on tour and would play the Palace, Lincolnshire in the week starting November 28, 1913.[20] The Octette had enjoyed success in London in shows like *Hitchy Koo* and *Waiting for the Robert E. Lee*. One of their harmonious songs from 1912 was 'My little lovin' sugar babe.'[21] For one week Greenock held a talent-spotting competition each evening[22] and Lizzi rehearsed Renée and Billie's harmonies for 'That Mesmerizing Mendelssohn Tune' –a popular ragtime song. The time came to step in front of that living, breathing and cursing audience. All in a dither, and racked by stage fright, Renée couldn't utter a word and quickly started to sob. 'Daddy, take me off. Take me off please!' Ashamed, she fled, but Billie remained alone on the stage, looking at Daddy with a steady gaze.

She was barely seven, and again she showed pluck, carrying on alone and winning first prize. She was asked to appear for a few extra days by special request of the management, billed as *'Miss Cissie Johnstone of Port Glasgow.'* The name Houston was dropped so it wouldn't seem she got the prize unfairly. This time she sang 'Everybody's doing it', from the Leicester Square musical the previous year. It had the line: 'It's a bear, it's a bear! Where?

There!' A little joke was arranged that when the seven year old said the word *there* she pointed to a large gentleman in the Octette seated near the proscenium. He would rise up and scowl. The audience loved it.

You can cross the Clyde from the east via the Calton, and Bridgeton Cross where today, the Olympia Theatre of Varieties has been revamped as a boxing circuit and a Mediatheque. St Andrew's Suspension Bridge - built to let East End workers cross to Hutcheson town and the Gorbals - takes you to the south side, and along Ballater Street, at the junction of Moffat Street, a monstrous brewing plant awaits you on the site of what was once a proud civic building - St Mungo Halls - where Renée and her kid sister came to perform solo turns, a bit of clog dancing, and duets like 'Top of the Morning' or 'Molly Molloy'. They were two little ragtimers: Renée, in her Tartan coat, was self-conscious but still knocked 'em dead with her solo rendering of that amusing little classic *'O' Brien is tying to learn to talk Hawaiian.'* What it was to walk along a populous street and shine brighter than the brightest star! Others in the Gorbals came home to cry, but she was born for comedy. In recent times a mysterious fire took away St Mungo Halls leaving the coast clear for industrial development and change. And here, a faint murmuring of a child's song, a ukulele or glimpse of a Tartan coat captures your heart - if you could only hear it through the traffic.

With clog dancing in the bag, and ragtime a cinch, a pantomime for Shettleston's 1914-15 season was the next challenge for Glasgow's youngest theatre producer. Little Miss H had already led a company that included a bunch of Scots-Italian chums, charging ha'penny admission for a show at the tenement's washhouse on a Saturday evening – the night no one used it. They sought a new venue with scope for special effects and ambitious technical innovations. The Houstons made a discovery of Jeanette Binkz, one of 8000 Belgian Refugees in the city. The refugee committee, in association with The City of Glasgow Corporation welcomed refugees in the city in the months following the invasion of Belgium by Kaiser Bill's army. Some were placed in the city while others lived and worked on farms in Strathaven.

Little Jeanette changed her name to Scots-sounding Mabel Nairn but the name 'Cousin Binkie' stuck after the Houston Sisters christened their puppy like friend. Binkie and Renée's international exchange was long-term, perfect to help her polish up her French. Every bit as plucky as her country, Binkie loved a good joke and she got absorbed in *The Magic Ruby* - the latest 'Carntyne Production.'[23] Two hole-in-the-wall beds in the Houstons' kitchen proved to be ideal theatrical spaces. Granny was impressed beyond measure by the ingenious use of recessed beds, bells, lights and lampstands. They transformed a pulley for drying clothes into a drop curtain, made costumes from crepe de chine and satin mammy had sent them, as well as producing crayoned playbills and distributing these in the neighbourhood. Daddy's gramophone provided music, and a horsehair couch, pushed to the front area, extended space for the lead players to venture into to the audience.

Granny ensured these artistes wouldn't get the bird, and presided over the box office, whilst a little cousin of the Gribbins' worked electrical lights and machinery. On opening night the kitchen crowded with street kids. This 'continuous variety' stipulated an audience limited to how many could squeeze into the kitchen at any one time. Renée, as *Nellie O'Neal* - adopted daughter of *Major Bangs V.C* remained cool and professional. Billie, in a set of real boys' braces, was *Harry the young Highlander* - in love with *Nellie* but too poor for the major. A wicked spirit has nabbed the ruby of the *Rajahs of Rajahpore*, and *Harry* bravely searches for it in the darkest caves assisted by *Electra* - fairy goddess of light – a comical role for Binkie. He gains command over the *Imps of Darkness*, recovers the ruby and finds himself not only the toast of *Rajahpore*, but able to marry *Nellie* and enjoy untold riches. It was a resounding success and despite the smashed bed boards, company and producer were pleased with the result.

To leave home just when you reach twelve to tour as part of a musical quintette, away for long periods, can't have been easy for Billie, however serious she was about developing her musical abilities. A trusted friend of Lizzi and Jimmie headed a troupe of five young musicians and needed to replace a boy. An offer to coach the little girl, whose City Hall fame was fresh in people's minds, was put to them and her parents agreed. She'd be practicing music daily and her foray into the commonsense world of the pro would be useful. She lacked a genteel quality. A music apprenticeship, affording a little 'finishing' for her younger daughter appealed to Lizzi who packed her off, remembering the independent little spirit so disinterested in her looks, who never fastened her hair properly with a ribbon. As a child Billie's hair reached her knees, and when all the girls wore wreaths in their hair and a veil for St Mark's School's May procession, the parish priest wouldn't let Billie have a veil, hating to see that lovely hair covered. Billie didn't appear to have reservations about leaving home. The minimum school leaving age had just been raised to fourteen so there was a loose agreement for her to attend school in the towns they happened to be playing.

Albert Whelan and Wee Georgie Wood played the Empire, Gateshead in February 1918 - on one of the weeks Billie's instrumentalist act was on the bill. Albert Whelan came on with cloak, gloves, top hat and cane. Thirty years Billie's senior, he was born in Melbourne, arriving in Britain when the century began. He was the first to use a signature tune to open his act, often whistling it. In the 20s, he introduced Americans to the song 'Show Me the Way to Go Home'. Billie popped her head round the door of his dressing room one night, proclaiming she could do his act. Whelan asked her to do it for the benefit of his group of friends. Grabbing his hat, gloves and stick, Billie gave a word-perfect performance and they were dumbstruck. Everyone knew after that there was great potential in that quiet little lady in the quintette. She played the banjulele, ukulele, and guitar and sang as the tour lengthened into months.

Little Mother in a Theatrical Family

Albert Whelan (Author's Collection)

Meanwhile, at the old Electric Theatre in Shakespeare Street, Dumfries, somebody called 'On in five minutes Houston Company!' and a stagehand carried on the furniture. Two boys pushed on a tall flat on which the backcloth was hung. Clever perspective in brown and black suggested a tenement interior and a daub of white paint in an upper part, light in a cramped room. A sock was warming in front of a fireplace with two silhouette pictures crooked on the wall. In came Jimmie, with his preamble: new each time: a burnt frying pan today, a man fixing the wind-up bell and a glow in the dark canary yesterday. Enter Lizzi, unable to accomplish any domestic task, setting up their dysfunction. Jimmie discusses the merits of a tea bag or shouts about his packed lunch mistaken for an engineer's tools. Finding his missus's cat in his seat, Jimmie tosses it up into the air. A little while later, there's a ring on the door and a third character enters. 'Is this your cat, madam?' asks the bonneted old crone carrying the dead moggie. She gives the couple a piece of her mind. The pernickety old woman was Renée Houston. An extra part was written into *The Flittin* for her *widow* part.

In spring 1918 Billie wrote to say she was coming home. What Lizzi experienced when she opened the door was absolute shock. This wasn't the infant she had once boasted of to her neighbours. All Billie's lovely fair hair had been brutally hacked off and swished back over her head in an absurd way. The twelve year old grinned, oblivious to the impression she was making. Lizzi's striken looks, worthy of an Elenora Duse, would sum up the memory of this homecoming. Jimmie was happy to see Billie packed off to join Renée in Rothesay, safely away from Lizzi whose despair got him down. Renée was overjoyed to see her.

Chapter 5   Early Training

Illusion appealed to Renée, and she was convincing enough a chameleon to be 'taken for her own daughter' backstage at Bridgeton's Olympia in April 1916. The engagement prompted The Daily Record to refer to the growing demand for Scots sketches, stating that this was 'one of happiest.' A similar thing happened when they put on *The Flittin* at Bo'ness Hippodrome. She played two roles here: widow and wife. Calling in by day to see if there were any letters for her Daddy and Mammy, she met proprietor, Louis D. Dickson. Curious about the Houston company, he asked her who was the mature actress who played the widow carrying the cat's carcass (not a real moggie, I should add). 'Well. I'll be jiggered' cried Dickson in disbelief, when she told him. That night in their dressing room, he presented her with the first floral tribute and basket of fruit she ever received. He swore she'd go far.

James Houston and Co. travelled from Scotland to London for some important engagements.[1] The Daylight Saving Bill had been carried by parliament and the clock advanced one hour in the summer months. Into that brighter world Renée's youngest sister Shirley was born - in the dressing room of the Metropolitan Theatre, Edgware Road, apparently as the Zeppelin guns sounded up ahead. Jim was forty-two and Liz forty-one, and the baby wasn't planned. Their eldest daughter's help as understudy was relied on as soon as they knew Shirley was coming. Her move from convent to music hall was no chance happening. She wasn't in tow to help with nursing babes even if she did used to claim 'I had to play the part of a wee old woman in real life as well as on the stage.'[2] It came more natural to Renée to drink up Shirley's evaporated milk. Her help was practical nonetheless. She claims she made 'every stitch of clothing Shirley wore as a kiddie.'

View of the Bridgeton Olympia
(Miranda Brooke)

The Kingston Empire, early 20th Century
(Author's Collection)

The look and feel of the theatre impressed Renée. She liked the old Empire at Kingston, with its shimmering gold and white interior, blue and gold seats and lush curtains. She shared the bill with an illusionist, burlesque comedians, dancers, and actors. In the afternoons, a film ran called 'What I saw in Russia,' accompanied by a talk by a war correspondent.[3] She had seen performers many times but hadn't been so close to backstage life. Now, at fourteen, her theatrical calling was fast in coming. Lizzi had gone back to the stage too soon after having Shirley. 'The first day I deputized for Mammy I was petrified,' she wrote, 'but a week later I was telling all the other folks on the stage what to do!'[4] It's an early example both of Renée's professionalism, and of her outspokenness. She was to prove an asset to James Houston's company, and would go all over the country with *The Flittin,* playing Lizzi's part frequently. Apparently the public was none the wiser.

Exactly when she ceased turning up as old ladies or deputizing isn't clear. Renée's life story saw different versions but each one was told with charm. Her parents and grandmother were alive when she wrote early versions of her path to fame, so she may have emphasized the role they played. Her generation always put a positive spin on their autobiographies. Bad bits didn't exist. Showman Sam Kelly spotted her in her parents' act and asked if he could whisk her off to entertain holidaymakers in Rothesay. Her folks, of course, were fine with this, and she spent her first summer there in 1916. Kelly was a taskmaster but made sure she received training in dance. She lived with him and his sisters, citing these girls as the ones who turned her from gawky girl into sophisticated artiste.[5] Early versions of her story credit her start in seaside entertainment to the actions of someone else. Later versions place Renée in a controlling role: bravely calling up agent WR Galt or sometimes Jimmy McQueen – impressing the latter because of her London appearance. One artiste then, dancer Billy Cameron, claims Galt only saw the 'high heid yins' at the top of the bill, and seeing him was like getting 'an audience with the Pope.'[6] Choreographer May Moxon, however, credits Galt with helping her after she injured her leg in a car accident.[7]

Renée went from old woman to *little Peter* or *'Pierrot'* in white silk costume. White ruffles represent the snow in which a little child lay outside Heaven's gates before St Peter finds him. Black pompoms symbolize the dirty marks on his clothing – his breaking of a promise not to play with other kids. Worse still, the poor thing is excluded from Paradise forevermore hence the tear falling from his eye. Almost every entertainer around this time was part of a 'Pierrot' troupe. Names like 'The Moonbeams', 'Blue Follies', 'Queer Quakers', 'Portland's Pierrots for Little People', 'Tweenies', 'Society Idols', 'Scarlet Cloakes', 'Watteaus', 'Whimsicals' and 'Royal Pierrots' each express the gentle happiness of those distant summers. It was the age of the concert party - a little remembered time before wireless and gramophone were widespread, but one when railways provided excellent transport for holiday-makers, musicians and entertainers moving between bustling seaside resorts and spas.

In this day and age with all the fears and worries people have, we've forgotten about the Pierrot shows and the quality of the music once found at our seaside places. Music was rife then - in assembly halls, bandstands, church halls, thé dansants, musical soirees, and picture palaces. Llandudno in north Wales had a distinguished resident orchestra and there were 'all year' orchestras in Bournmouth, Folkestone, and Worthing. Gustav Holst played trombone on Brighton pier, Harrogate had a municipal orchestra and Scarborough possessed a renowned spa orchestra and a troupe of Pierrots organized by Will Catlin. These resorts later adapted to changing tastes and a Pavilion orchestra might find itself in rivalry with a variety theatre or dance hall along the front.[8] Nevertheless, for several years it was a thriving scene. Scotland understandably had less of a winter season but Saltcoats and Rothesay attracted major talent. With positions regularly advertised in The Era and other theatrical papers, musicians did good business. Smart ones like Douglas Wilcox rose to become musical director of the King's Theatre, Edinburgh. A professional concert party artiste might even have his or her own 'Thalia diary' containing handy checking tables to help ascertain the value of the house, percentage tables, and places to list your accounts.

Audiences at these resorts wanted something light-hearted so programmes varied between musical comedy sketches and classical music. Many entertainers who came up this route became huge stars in the mid 20th Century. These include Jack Warner, Mona Washbourne, Naunton Wayne, Arthur Askey, and Richard Murdoch in England, and Tommy Lorne, Will Fyffe, Jimmy Logan, Stanley Baxter, Duncan Macrae, Andy Stewart, Moira Anderson, Rikki Fulton, and the brilliant Jack Milroy in Scotland.

In the early period, the absence of a permanent sheltered platform saw the need for the concert party troupe to 'pitch' a portable stage on the sand and entertain an audience with their backs to the sea. In these breezy conditions, you saw comedy, farce, and tragedy performed. Then one of the team, a 'bottler' went into the audience to collect money. On the sands at Girwan, Molly Weir was one of the children the bottler came to, but she was too poor to contribute. How glamorous and prosperous the pierrots seemed, all the same![9] For some troupes, real life was grim, with poor takings and three to a bucket using the same dirty water to remove makeup. Will Fyffe's father ran a penny geggie - a wooden theatre. They assembled one on South Inch, close to the Tay not knowing it was prone to flooding. Whilst taking down the set in storm conditions, the geggie's roof was torn off and the whole thing came afloat with Will hanging on to the wood. He floated down river and began to despair until providence shone[10] and he survived to become a star of variety, panto, and films.

It's hard to imagine the island of Bute having outdoor entertainers in silky costumes putting on concert parties to big crowds because the weather can change so. Also, the modern equivalent of paw, ma and weans take their buckets and spades to warmer climates. The Scottish islands are more likely to be filled with wiry hikers wearing the latest outdoor clothing labels. Holiday entertainers are still going strong and often feature brilliant dancers and fair singers. They often seem to be Russian, called Olga or Nastia and are usually at least seven foot tall. At least they have been when I've travelled to resorts in Turkey, Morocco and Egypt to experience a week of sun and inventive sunburn such as the forty lashes on the back variety. The holiday entertainers are flat when it comes to repartee and deliver it in cringe-worthy English with a Euro accent. What these scantily clad artistes do well is wow us with renditions of songs from *Cabaret* or Queen compilations. They are beloved of children who pose with them after the show as their parents take photos, and provide a nice thing to watch as you relax and finish off a day spent doing absolutely nothing.

Bandstand and Bay, Rothesay, early 20th Century (Author's collection)

Renée was one of the top holiday entertainers of her day, and she might be *Pierrot* one day and back to *wee old woman* the next, with other costume changes in between. Silent film footage from 1918 in the Scottish Screen Archive shows the Rothesay Entertainers in a trailer advertising their forthcoming revue. It was sent to the Galashiels Pavilion, owned by Fyfe and Fyfe (the company set up in 1890 by Robert and Isaac Fyfe) and was possibly filmed in April and May in advance of the season. Almost a century later, the personality of these players still comes across. They link arms and do a chorus kick in unison before the camera decides to focus on each entertainer's grimace or shy smile. From a music hall historian's point of view it's an incredible record. We see tomboyish Billie Houston, looking older than her twelve years and elf-like Renée Houston, unsophisticated but dainty. You see the uniforms of the male artists, which were *air force blue* with a letter 'F' on their caps. Most of the ladies of the Fyfe and Fyfe Company are in Chinese-inspired outfits - possibly taking a cue from *Chu Chin Chow*, the musical comedy loosely based on the tale of Ali Baba.

Each member of the company pulls faces at the camera, beginning with Charlie Kemble, then JW Bowie - from a famous family of actor-singers, then Sylvia Watt, who pulls a lot of faces. Sylvia has a look of Susan Boyle about her. She would often be kilted up, playing Scots girl parts. We next see Fred Davis, the ventriloquist, then Doris Duncan, who just laughs, then slim and pretty Laura Richardson, then Billie, then Renée, then Myra Fyfe, the boss's daughter. Alec Main does a salute, then producer Julian Ross - shorter and important looking with a little star on his hat - is declaring something. Finally we see Isaac Fyfe, hatless and in casual clothes – squinting and smoking a cigar. Julian puts his hat on Isaac as a prank.

The *Madeira of Scotland* has a pretty seafront, church steeple, promenade curving across to Skeoch wood, and hills rising to the distance. Fyfe & Fyfe presented their touring show in late summer in a permanent bandstand with a dome on the wide esplanade. Sailing boats in the bay, steam ships ready to berth and passers by at the waterfront created a backdrop. There were afternoon and evening shows on weekdays, three shows on Saturdays and midnight shows. It cost about 6d to sit and children were half price. Rothesay was to Glasgow rather like what Margate was to London although cultured man and working man alike holidayed in Bute. Any holiday was a dream come true for kids, ecstatic to be 'gaun doon th'watter' to salty air and sand. Simple pleasures counted to these cheerful folk, and as Finlay Hart, born in 1901, put it, 'People might have been living in poverty-stricken conditions but we didn't realize it was poverty.'[11] The ten days of the Glasgow Fair at the end of July proved a deliverance. The Fyfe and Fyfe comics made observations about which competing steamer would reach the island first, about steamers weighted down with greedy passengers, about folk changed by the elements between Broomielaw and disembarking. Numerous were the jokes about landladies.

Charlie Kemble was the biggest star in seaside entertainment with the longest career – all down to his monumental talent. Maybe it was being a fruit salesman loudly selling his wares in the Gorbals, that bred his famous extempore *'Fal al a diddle al a day'* song with ever-changing impromptu vocals, referencing people in the audience least expecting it. Usually anyone wearing a particularly silly hat or outfit would be the target and wouldn't they get to know it! He had a 'sixth sense' about what would go down well with an audience, and any comic angle could be explored in the verses which ended with a *'Fal al a diddle al a day'*. Little soubrette Renée, arriving for her second summer in 1917 - no longer with Kelly but with Fyfe and Fyfe, was a comic for Charlie to nurse. He was her first stage partner. Her adlibbing skills were honed improvising with Charlie. She credited him for giving her chances in the sketches they did together, and summed him up as 'a man worth knowing and a friend to go down in the book of memories.'[12] She was even quick enough to invent her own *'Fal al a diddle,'* song one 'topsy turvy' night when everyone swapped roles with somebody else for the night. Her impersonation of Kemble was a smash. Her fellow entertainers were suspended in disbelief at how well she could adlib. Charlie said to her after that 'That's yer last! You'll no' go on again for that!' Not wishing for the tide of appreciation to stop, there was no limit to what this Shettleston girl could do. Renée didn't hold back. She added inventive words to popular songs, creating new moods and receiving new laughs of her own making.

The three years at Rothesay were the happiest in her young life. She didn't take work seriously. She never had to do the type of dreary job girls her age were doing. She was a local celebrity who had a measure of independence.

Restraint in girls was still encouraged then but the term 'flapper' was beginning to appear – to some a derogatory term. Sensible girls directed their energies into being capable Girl Guides whilst young Miss Houston wasn't sensible at all. Social commentators like Lady Baden Powell, who promoted the Guides, wrote about these flappers and how familiarity with freedom might make a girl blasé: 'She means no harm by her frivolity at first, but she soon grows wise in exploiting herself. One finds her aiding nature by eyebrow pencil and lip-salve, powder-puff and rouge-pot, at an age when such things should not exist for her.'[13]

Renée was never supposed to be roaming but practicing new numbers assiduously and observing fellow entertainers. When Julian Ross kept tabs on her, she'd say, 'Julian, let me go bathing today and I promise to get a new song ready for tonight,' then constantly break this vow. He was apparently such a dear he didn't challenge her – even if everyone knew she was spending the time enjoying walks with admirers through Skeoch Woods. 'I knew all the nice places,' she later confessed, admitting there was 'a new boyfriend every week.' Some among the early beaux of this champion flirt were serious enough to offer her engagement rings, but Renée changed her ring with each new invasion of holidaymakers. Julian tried to keep a paternal eye on her and would suddenly appear from the bushes when she and her *fiancé* least expected it. Oh, it was all very innocent, she would recall. A love of pranks spoiled these romances. Never mind.

She took the demands of the work in her stride. The schedule Jimmy Logan experienced at Rothesay seasons a decade later was tough. With a demand for fresh material to satisfy the changing programme over a fifteen-week period, Logan mentions the struggle to get things ready. The only available time to prepare was between twice nightly performances. Renée did a long season but never spoke of being under pressure, although she'd get homesick for Granny, who was minding Shirley back in Glasgow. For the 1918 season Billie was there. *James Houston and Company,* meanwhile, was making a killing in Motherwell and provincial English towns.

The relationship with Fyfe & Fyfe, gave five summers of work, and Renée and Billie took absences then returned for seasons and also toured with Julian, Charlie et al, on the circuit of theatres Fyfe & Fyfe controlled.[14] Anyone working in the business knows the irregular nature of work, taking an engagement for a period somewhere, experiencing a gap, then taking an engagement somewhere else. At Rothesay you made useful contacts for future bookings. Negotiating your terms was a side to the business Renée and Billie lacked experience in. For ages they were forced either to wait for opportunities or scuttle back into James Houston's company. They got some experience doing variety turns in cine-variety houses and traditional theatres where Daddy Jimmie and Mammy were featured. You would see Renée separately billed in a theatre in Fife as 'Rena Gribben- *Comedienne and Dancer'*, alongside '*Hiawatha and his Squaw Minnehaha, not counting the*

Dogs.' This particular stint featured *'the most astounding Chimpanzees ever presented to the Public.'*[15] It was probably the time when Billie famously placed a chimpanzee's paw in the hand of an unknowing Renée. Another bill featured Billie as 'Cissy Gribben - *Little Irish Male Impersonator*' among novelty jugglers at the Picture House, Falkirk.[16] The Sisters hated performing in cine-variety. It meant standing and watching the picture at the sides of the stage before you did your act, and by the time you went on you couldn't move your neck - it was dreadful.

The term 'revue' has its own meaning in the UK - one that's different to France. The craze began around 1913 with exciting musical shows with a quirky theme, comedy sketches, instrumentals, novelty acts, and big closing numbers using all the cast becoming common. It was a development on music hall inasmuch as artistes could be 'free singers' in contrast to having 'individual singers' like Marie Lloyd, Eugene Stratton, and Dan Leno singing their own songs exclusively. 'My Old Man,' for instance, was a ballad sung by Leno. Revues were a haven for those who criticized the practice of 'swollen-salaried variety stars' getting all the breaks at the expense of smaller salaried variety folk. Revue offered more of a chance of employment. These companies seldom carried less than thirty people and The Era's 'On the road' column argues that but for the revue, large numbers of clever 'pros' and other hard workers would have faced starvation.[17] It was easier to be with a good company than make it on your own. You had an environment to develop plus scope to be creative. The revue always meant touring so diehards could boast of all the cities they had played. It was regular work, if the production didn't fold.

The names of artistes who toured in revue in the teens and 20s and hit the big time are endless. Fred Karno's classic revue company helped Charlie Chaplin and his brother Sidney. Gracie Fields joined *Yes, I think so* in 1915: the beginning of a collaboration with its principal comedian Archie Pitt, which led to *Mr Tower of London* at the Alhambra in 1923. In 1919 Albert de Courville of Moss Empires brought the Original Dixieland Jazz band over for *Joy Bells*. Joe O'Gorman presented his revue *Round the Town* in 1924. Nellie Wallace triumphed in a burlesque *Whirl of the World* that same year. Further into the 20s *Cochran's* revue, *One Dam Thing After Another*, and *Blackbirds* became the stuff of legend. The genre survived as the century grew older, when Danny La Rue delighted with *Forces in Petticoats* - an all-male revue.

Renée, between the age of seventeen and nineteen, was in search of the break that every fledgling entertainer wishes for. Finding parts as a revue artiste was the natural step. These shows were similar to those staged by Fyfe and Fyfe and she could earn decent money outside of Rothesay's season. The Stage Year Book for 1917 tells us that 'Revue, like the war, is still with us, but bids fair to last rather longer than the war,'[18] and reported that revue was going strong in London, whilst in the provinces it had waned. In late 1919 The Era's 'On the Road' column lists shows on tour in the 'revue' category, with new ones added each week, all with bright and snappy sounding names. Opportunities to break into revue in Scotland were vast, but some might break a career rather than make it. Success depended on the revue's controlling impresario.

Renée had been independent at Rothesay so braving extended periods away from home was easy. Apart from Granny, where was home anyway? She had been used to her parents disappearing since she was ten. Her brother was trying his luck as a merchant seaman, intent on seeing the world. Her sister was moving in a different direction with music and male impersonation. In Renée's account of her path to fame published in 1936, she tells us how Lizzi eyed touring revues with suspicion and was against her joining one owing to the startling amount of freedom that this would allow her. Then, someone in a revue in whom her mother had faith, promised to keep an eye on Renée, so Lizzi conceded to the will of her seventeen year old.

I question Lizzi's fears since the Houston parents were always keen their children take opportunities whatever the odds. She didn't mind Billie being away from home for massive amounts of time. One other reason why Lizzi might have been glad her daughter was outside of Glasgow just then was because the immediate post war climate was one of turmoil. George Square had seen 60,000 men and women rallying in the hope that better conditions for workers and a forty-hour week might be granted. Never mind the peace negotiations in far off Paris - what about the downtrodden? On 31st January 1919 the Red Flag was raised in Glasgow. Was it a new Bolshevik revolution? Many Conservatives and obedient types wondered if madness and guillotines might replace fitba and chip shops. Tanks and soldiers were sent in to occupy the area immediately. Leaders like Manny Shinwell and John McLain were sent to jail for inciting the riot, and there was an atmosphere of tension in the city for some time afterwards.

Against this atmosphere of turbulence, the revue *Hooray! We're Here* lived up to its positive sounding name. The Falkirk Herald tells us it was a Teddy Grant presentation, praising Haydn Halstead's first class direction.[19] Reading the notices, there's a sense it was pulled off by a young ensemble after a hard slog. Nobody minded that. *Hooray* linked five scenes, including the set of a musical comedy, the scene of a crime, a railway station, a scene in India and one in a sultan's harem so artistic sets were called for. An actress called Hazel Glade was *Betty* - '*revue star,*' while Joe Poynton - *acrobatic comedian*, played a waiter and amateur detective. Madge Aubrey was a 'saucy barmaid,' baritone Dennis J Hawkes played another role and there's a curious mention of 'famous raggedy dogs' being part of the ensemble. A press report mentions that 'Miss Rena Gribben, as *Betty's* friend, is distinctly good. She sings well and dances much better.' The same paper draws attention to the titillating aspects of the revue, adding, for instance, that 'Hazel Glade sings with delightful unction . . . in a fetching manner,' pointing out Miss Glade's 'personal attractions' and that the chorus, 'while they do not sing with much power, make themselves attractive by their posing and actions.'[20]

Hooray! We're Here: Renée Houston, Joe Poynton, the Seann Triubhas
Stars on the variety circuit: Georgie Wood, Nellie Wallace, Coram and Jerry, Will Hay.
(My Thanks to Westminster Records Library)

It was full of laughs, glamour and glitz. Grant and Glade had earlier been a comic double act and this show was his showcase for dazzling Hazel. Scots music care of the Stewart Tartan Pipers featured strongly, and a number of highland dances were woven in. Renée loved the atmosphere backstage. It was during this tour she made friends with dancer Ella Hempseed, daughter of a former police sergeant in Edinburgh, who seems to have been not in the least bit law abiding. She thrived on walking in and out of danger and living off the tale she could tell thereafter. She and Renée were inseparable, forever laughing, and Renée writes in 1936 that people in the street used to think they were mad.[21] Information about Ella (who used different surnames, including 'Reed' and 'Pearson') is scarce but she and Miss Houston were still friends in the 1950s. When Ella did the Fling or the *Seann Triubhas*, Renée called it 'poetry in motion' and others commented how 'Miss Ella Reid, in Irish jig and hornpipe dancing, is exceedingly graceful and full of charm.'[22]

Renée was in this revue throughout her seventeenth year, and it started off bright and sparkly in Falkirk on November 29, 1919, travelling to Hull, Derby, Chesterfield, and Stockport, up to mid May 1920. Renée later explained that early on the small independent management company had trouble in securing dates.[23] They lacked a big name producer and were going it alone with their tour manager lacking force. To use a bit of artiste's terminology *Hooray! We're Here* started as a 'number 2' tour descending to 'number 3' with towns played like Long Eaton, Ilkeston, Burslem, and Cannock, later going to 'number 4' as places became more out of the way. Rather like Drake's Golden Hind, venturing in unexpected waters around a coast that was not yet California, *Hooray* drifted to South Wales's furthest most reaches, miles from home. This was the setting of one of Renée's stories of appearing for miners in a small company in Merthyr Tydfil, Tredegar, Port Talbot, Aberystwyth, Abertillery, and Aberavon. In her 1974 book and interview with Mavis Nicholson she recalls the time at Ogmore Vale when she had to be up at 6 am for the miners coming off the backshift. This made her want to go to sleep for hours on end between performances. She sang 'Somewhere in Somebody's Eyes' with a large baritone - who must have been Dennis J Hawkes - falling asleep in his arms after the first verse.[24] On reaching Oswestry, on July 5, 1920, the revue had got very tatty.

Some piece of gossip filtered its way to Lizzi who sent Jim to Greenock Hippodrome to spy on her daughter. Known for its rough beery audiences, this theatre was at its most rowdy the time Jim witnessed *Hooray!* The Hippodrome was struggling and would close for good in 1923. Jim was

Early Training

ordered to take his sister home but Renée persuaded her mother to wait a couple of weeks, leaving the company in Wales. Looking at the show's run, this was definitely more than a couple of weeks. Finally, before it folded, the prodigal made an ignoble return to Shettleston, evincing stares and nudges among her parents' respectable neighbours.

Left: Shettleston Cross, Glasgow - early 20th Century (Author's Collection)
Right: Product to dye hair blonde (early 1920s) (Author's Collection)

She had dyed her hair blonde and must have been naïve to follow a beauty tip about cutting her long eyelashes. Dyes weren't as moisture-rich then as they are now. Her hair was burnt to the roots, and she looked 'like a skinned rabbit.' She climbed the stairs of the tenement. Lizzi, still recovering from Billie's transformation, met her with a withering look that would have floored Goliath. Daddy exploded crying out: 'Whit hae ye done to yer heid? Where's ma wean's eyelashes?'[25] Her mother was equally appalled at Renée's financial ignorance. After consenting to Renée's plan to go on tour Lizzi kitted her out with a wicker basket of costumes apparently costing £60 – a fortune then and a gesture that confirms the family's spending power. Renée came back without it: 'What I didn't give away I sold in order to pay my digs,' she explained. Some money went on travelling expenses. She was proud of the £6 she earned a week with the revue but she hadn't saved a farthing and was broke. She admitted she frittered away money buying 'the little things that mean a lot to a woman.' It was an inglorious outcome but her experience was formative and life was, after all, an adventure. She would continue playing with the revue form: in 1935 virtually as an impresario herself and in the 50s as the life and soul.

Chapter 6   More Pitfalls and Pantomimes

When these two get going there's no stopping them.[1]

That freckle-face with blown about hair in the advertising film experienced 'life in the raw' during her 1920 tour only to return back where she had begun. It wasn't so long before that Will Fyffe had been at rock bottom following a few highs. Proof that the struggle was worth it, he went on to make it big, coming home to deliver the anthem 'I Belong to Glasgow' at the Pavilion Theatre. When Fyffe turned up at Rothesay and wanted a word, Renée listened up. They took a walk by the bay and he, like a moonlit soothsayer commanding elemental forces, decried 'If you remain the nice girl that you are now, and behave like your father and mother, you are going to be a great star. I know this a silly thing to say to a wee lassie but I think you are one of the greatest artists I have ever seen.' She begged him not to go on.

Will Fyffe (Author's Collection)   Steamers at the Broomielaw (Author's Collection)

Well, you shouldn't let compliments like this go to your head, but who can help it. 'You're far too good for this. You should be in London,' a voice said as she primped in front of the cracked mirror in the dressing room of the Annfield Halls at 609 Gallowgate. At the Queens Theatre, Watson Street - where they said low jokes escaped the Lord Chancellor's interference because he could not understand the language, her pride returned after the humiliation suffered after *Hooray! We're Here.* Granny Houston was still a supporter and confidante. Grounded by Lizzi, Renée practiced toe dancing, which helped on the occasion she and Billie deputized for their parents. Occurring between August and December 1920 this particular engagement would be significant. It saw the formation of the Houston Sisters.

The story goes something like this: Mama and Papa, are struck down with flu and are on the verge of cancelling a date at Airdrie Hippodrome. Renée suggests to Daddy that she and Billie do a double act and go on in their place. After some hesitation Jimmie agrees and she calls Mr Loudon the manager, who says, 'Well we've got to fill the gap anyway, you might as well come up.' It's a convenient journey up the railway line from Glasgow, and they work out what to do en route. Billie and Renée know one song only 'Let the Rest of the World Go By,' and the manager suggests they perform a piano act. Billie, in green satin trousers and a tussore silk shirt sits on top of an upright piano, whilst Renée sits on the stool, managing the keys with one hand. They sing, and all of a sudden the piano collapses and Billie hurts her botty on falling.

Receiving heaps of applause, Mr Loudon says to the girls 'Can ye do tha' again the next hoose?' How they 'broke into the business' underwent much experiment in its telling over the years. It varied with every interview. Renée indicated to veteran BBC presenter Robin Russell that she and Billie combined forces straight after Rothesay. Earlier stories such as her 1936 memoir say it followed *Hooray* with toe dancing but sans collapsing piano. She twists her ankle on stage and looks agonized as she tries to keep going. Dragging her injured foot, she forgets her lines, apologizing to their pianist Miss Loudon - the manager's daughter. Mistaking all this for comedy, the audience shrieks with laughter. In a 1925 interview, the piano story isn't in Airdrie, but in a small mining town at a picture variety theatre. One thing is certain - any story told by Renée Houston is much better than the truth.

In 1920 and 21, she and Billie barely had an act, and that's the reality. The girls thought to combine forces for a while but it didn't look set to last. A first engagement took them to Armadale, a little town between Glasgow and Edinburgh, and the manager here, who worked a shift in the pits, was to be their pianist. The sisters hadn't estimated what would work with a bunch of miners, and when Renée chose a little French song with lots of *'Oui Oui'*, the coalminers looked on in horror. One dissatisfied punter threw a potato and almost killed her. They looked like a couple of sheep when the manager came up to them disgusted, and told it to them plain:

Manager: I cannae understand it. You two can't do anything. Look you, wean!' Can you play the piano?
Billie: Oh aye.

Billie was made to be the accompanist at the picture palace and since she could only play 'Pale Hands I Love You,' bashing this out for the length of the picture, stopping for breath now and then, the audience sighed at the repetition, but there were no potatoes. Renée, meanwhile, was forbidden from performing and consigned to the box office. That was fatal. She was never very good with money, and while they did terrific business, the box office saw none of it as she let everyone in for free. This story is a bit suspect. The miner's institute in Armadale didn't open until 1925 so this could have happened at Armadale's recently opened Star Theatre - one that boasted splendid electric lighting. A little before or after the Houston Sisters' visit it witnessed the death of one half of a sister act. An escapology-linked tragedy in a water tank caused the death of one of Lancashire's Sisters Billington. The Houstons' cine-variety offering might have been at the Picturedrome, part of the chain owned by the Green family, or even at the shabby Empire Palace Theatre, on Armadale's George Street. Its owner, Mickey Burns, invented the 'caterpillar' track for tanks in the First World War.[2]

Billie did a number of solo dates as a male impersonator, going under the name of Cissie Benson, distancing her act from the Houston Company, perhaps to save her parents' embarrassment. At Fyfe & Fyfe's Pavilion in Galashiels, there was a boy on the same bill called Robbie Graham. Billed as *the small boy with the big voice*, next to Billie, the two looked similar. If Robbie hadn't worn a kilt, nobody could have told them apart. Renée did a couple of weeks as a single act in Dublin and then Belfast, negotiated through a contact from Rothesay. She remembered Granny's lack of tact as she saw her off the Broomielaw: 'Have you got your warm woolly draws on? – Ooh, she gave us such a showing up!'

The Dublin engagement was only memorable for a dramatic fall she had on stage crashing into the footlights. She felt afterwards like she had been run over by a steamroller. A glorious summer's day at the beach led to sunstroke and a headache. On stage blackouts were rare for Renée and her injury sounds bad – perhaps having a long-term impact. She went to Belfast next and worked alone. Then Billie turned up, singing the chorus to Renée's songs from the side of the stage in her beautiful tenor's voice. Without bothering to tell the management, they decided to go on as a double-act thereafter, and all was well, with a joint weekly salary of £10.

Next, came an engagement at Glasgow's Lyceum at Govan Road and McKechnie Street on October 24, 1920 in a lineup featuring Hamilton Conrad's Pigeons, The Two Californians, comics 'Fame and Fortune', and dancers 'Melville and Meta'. They were billed below Hamilton Conrad's Pigeons but at least that week the venue wasn't providing the dreaded cine-variety. Rena Gribben and Cissie Benson used the opportunity to show off their fine voices singing ragtime. They weren't selling themselves intentionally as a comedy double act. They were not yet the 'Houstons' they became – and didn't trade on their patter. But who's to say they didn't come alive in front of that auditorium decorated in blue, pink and lilac. Interestingly, Hamilton Conrad and his Pigeons would fly by - nine years later sharing a stage with the Sisters at London's Coliseum.

Most performers underwent a long period working up their act. People close to the variety world tell me this, emphasizing that it's very difficult to do a variety act. For Renée and Billie's turn, the roles of laughter-maker and feed found a natural footing. They would introduce themselves with a jibe at each other, before going into a song. Such is the evolution that spawned Punch and Judy, Naughton and Gold (fellow Glaswegians with the record of longest, unbroken partnership in the history of British music hall), Harry Lauder and Neil Kenyon, or the pantomime pairing of Will Fyffe and Harry Gordon. Sisterhood contained enough trust and friendship to say anything to each other, with secret in-jokes plentiful enough that clever new material didn't always have to be relied on. Morecambe and Wise, similarly, never had a pretence of novelty and, as Dennis Potter said of them, they could 'salvage material from a yellowing stock of back numbers of Dandy and Beano' and do not 'deliver their lines as resuscitate them.'[3] All kinds of memory banks existed for plundering. Perhaps it was an Irish inheritance of enjoying a debate. Eric Midwinter makes a thoughtful point concerning Eric and Ernie,

More Pitfalls and Pantomimes

saying their 'verbal and physical ping-pong' was 'characteristic of an age when there was much debate going on.'[3] Patter is a barometer of the times.

Who would have thought that these two ragtime songbirds would find themselves boon companions of *Boy Blue* – son of *Old Mother Hubbard*, with the likes of *Old King Cole, Matilda - Queen of Hearts*, and *Tommy Tucker* for company? Some little bird told Renée and Billie that Pete Davis was looking for acts for a pantomime he'd written and produced. Pete had been a child performer starting in Edinburgh as a boy tap dancer. He partnered Jackie Goodfellow in a Jewish double-act and did the rounds at the Panopticon on Trongate, experiencing its rowdiest matinee on Tuesdays at 4 pm where peltings were common. He led a concert party in Flanders during the First World War, knew the business inside and out, and went on to represent top names in the business.

The girls jumped at the chance and went and introduced themselves. Renée left an impression on Pete he'd never forget: 'Right from the very beginning I was impressed with this fantastic girl Renée Houston. No matter what you gave her to say, she knew the right way to say it, and the way to get the laugh out of it.'[4] That meeting was in November 1921! Thrilled to be engaged, Renée and Billie were working with May Dalziel, Jimmy Logan's mother - a year older than Renée.[5] They weren't cast as the two fairies who come to the aid of *Bo-Peep*. Instead press reports tell us that in *Boy Blue,* Cissie Benson and Renee Gribben played *Jack* and *Jill*. Billie was yet to take the name 'Bill'. Pete's *Super pantomime for 1922,* travelling to Fife, Motherwell, and Falkirk was a milestone for the Houstons. Their stage antics throughout the run brought to their minds days of mucking around in castles when they were kids. *Boy Blue* helped fix their little boy and girl identities and 'tumbling down' quality. Pete recalled they got laughs even though their scene had no particular gags in it. When I read the words 'Don't miss the *Pogo* scene'[6] on the faded advertisement, I think to myself this is Renée and Billie territory. Pogo competitions were also arranged for members of the audience: obviously a riot with adults and children alike. Was Pogo eradicated by health and safety, or is it still alive and well?

Booked together didn't necessarily mean a double turn. What happened next was unexpected. After the pantomime the sisters did a revue for Pete. Their brother Jim, on shore leave in Glasgow, witnessed his little sisters doing a week at Glasgow's Pavilion – surely the first time they ever played in a prestigious house. According to Jim, they began in separate spots on the bill but one scene had them playing opposite each other in which there was a short bit of patter. The managing director liked what he saw, paid off Pete Davis, and requested the sisters work their magic in a permanent double turn from the next night onwards. With barely any time to plan anything, and no piano to fall off, this was frightening. They hadn't asked to be a comic duo.

Left to right: Airdrie Hippodrome, Hallcraig Street, site of the Queen's Theatre Watson Street, Glasgow Pavilion Renfield Street (Author's Collection)

When the orchestra was about to strike up their introductory music the next evening, Billie panicked. She wailed in desperation 'What are we going to say or do when we get out there?' All Renée could say apparently, was 'How do I know, until I see what the audience is like? Come on we'll finish this argument on the stage.'[7] Finishing an argument on stage is an advantageous technique and the *little quarrel*, with asides to the audience, became the modus operandi that defined the Houston Sisters. They did the Pavilion proud. This proves that her years at Rothesay had left her completely unafraid of audiences. She knew how to dominate them even at this early stage. There was no time for Renée or Billie to wonder what to do next. Soon, *Jack* and *Jill* were whisked up by winged monkeys and taken to a wizard. In his presence they fell under his magic and became willing slaves. The sun shone bright that February afternoon in 1922 when she walked out of the Unity Agency at 96 Renfield Street, having met Mr Cummings.

Johnnie Cummings - the 'Wizard of the North' deserved the title. One of the biggest revue magnates in Scotland, his career began in Kilmarnock in 1903 when he got the lease for the Palace Theatre of Varieties. He was sensitive to all the latest trends and brought bawdy, earthy entertainment to Kilmarnock, competing with the rival King's Theatre. He scored a long running hit in 1916 with *Risk It*. His show *Is that a fact* billed as 'the Original Scotch comedy' did well in 1921. His latest production *See You Later* was praised for its 'up-to-date humour and music, and while a revue, was thought to have all the 'best qualities of a first-class musical comedy in its construction.'[8] It continued for fifteen months, attracting a changing cast with names drawn from the cream of Scottish and North Country talent. Dave Westwood was longest in the cast. For substantial periods Bret Harte, Dan Young, Jack Clifford, Charles Clare, Lilian Gordon and Ray Cardle joined him. Glamour and glitz were care of the *Eight Sunshine Girls* who were a ready-made bunch of madcap girlfriends for the Shettleston girls, sharing digs and train calls and making the experience a non-stop hoot.

Renée would look back and say: 'Johnnie gave us our first starring parts, and probably did as much as anybody to set us on the road to fame.'[9] He saw their potential. One thing stipulated from the start was that the name 'Cissie' be ditched, making Billie use Billie Benson for *See You Later*. The ubiquitous pair that sang a duet in each scene got good mention for the harmonious blending of their voices and the catchy airs of their songs. Reviewers spoke of the 'hearty welcome' this 'new and original concoction of mirth and melody' received with its seven 'fast and furious' scenes. The girls' best items were *'Travelling'*, *'All by Myself'*, *'I'm laughing at you'*, and *'Ain't we got fun'*. That last song number should have come with a government health warning, as Renée's memoir from 1936 indicates.

They were singing it at the Empire Theatre, South Shields - the sixth stopping place on a twenty-strong itinerary. All the chorus girls came in at the end of the song, joined hands for a huge circle, swinging round briskly to the last few bars of the song. One night some of the girls swung too vigorously causing others to lose their grip and Billie went sailing into the orchestra. 'Talk about the daring young man on the flying trapeze,' Renée quipped, adding that Billie 'has now become so expert at the job that she can almost pick the place to land on, . . . Personally, if I were a conductor, and she were on the bill, I'd insure myself against her acrobatics.'[10] The job required such dedication and they put up with these knocks, although Billie would later suffer miserably for them in later years. *See You Later* played two weeks in London on April 24 1922 at the Euston Palace, where the sisters made people laugh in a sketch called *My Little Bimbo,* and on May 1, 1922 at the Metropolitan. Their father was their chaperone in London, and having brought his own acts to these same theatres, he was well known at each to the staff.

One of the London dates provides the Houston Sisters' earliest surviving press interview, and it was *Proscenius* - famed theatre critic of The Era, who spoke to them. Asked her age, Renée removed two years, and talked about their unrehearsed dances. Their Spanish dance, a frequent feature of their act in the later 1920s and 30s was already present in their repertoire in 1922 which I find striking. 'We 'faked' it so successfully,' a proud Renée told *Proscenius*. The critic was impressed by a personality which 'gets over' every time. He writes that they gave a 'right-down rattling good performance' and tells readers it would be more 'to the liking of a West End audience than to most of those in the suburbs or the provinces.' It was only four years since the Representation of the People Act had given the vote to less than half the female population in the UK but *Proscenius* argued that one of the more refreshing outcomes of that so-called emancipation of women, was that it has 'given us the attractive and well-dressed girl who does not mind distorting both face and figure into a thing of fun.'[11]

The sisters were grateful to *Proscenius,* and in an interview for The Era four years later, Renée comments how that same paper 'discovered our ability.' In 1922 the sisters were in no hurry to take up early engagements in the capital. They stayed loyal to Cummings because they were happy. Backing and strategy sustained this revue: factors lacking in *Hooray!* Even when they joined *See You Later* it was fully booked up to April 1923. It was placed among all the major theatrical tour listings and Cummings had plenty of technicians to support the performers, as well as his own production department for scenery and stage effects.

Leaving the 'Met', *See You Later* moved to Nottingham where they played the Empire on August 28, 1922, the same time actor Matheson Lang headed the cast of *The Wondering Jew* at the Theatre Royal next door.[12] Renée never grew tired of telling the story of how they got into trouble and were sent home when she knowingly sent part of a foreign gun-toting act to the Theatre Royal after he asked her which theatre he was due at. Lang's performance was thus disturbed by blanks being fired in the auditorium. She got sent home for this apparently, but was back in a few days to appear at South Shields. Reaching Gloucester's Hippodrome in November 1922, *See You Later* was raved about for its beautiful staging.

Palace Theatre, Kilmarnock | Pete Davis | Dan Young | Tommy Lorne | Matheson Lang
(Author's Collection)

For those two wide-eyed kids it was fertile territory. They learned what worked and what didn't. 'Pa Cummings' was as sweet a wizard as could be hoped, and it was a family atmosphere as Pa's twin sons Billy and Johnny were ever present. The girls had a fun time with these boys who escorted them around in their motorcars. Both girls developed crushes on them, although Renée tells us these were one-sided. William Cummings Jnr returned as lessee in Kilmarnock in 1953, reintroducing the name 'Palace Theatre' in the place his father had first begun his enterprise. By Christmas 1922, the company changed to pantomime format, staging *Robinson Crusoe* at theatres in Scotland and northern towns. The pantomime saw Billie as *Lieutenant Pop*. Dan Young and Eugene Fields playing *Billy* and *Mrs Crusoe*, and Renée as *Polly Perkins*. Dan Young would go on to feature in a number of Mancunian Films, often with Frank Randle. Several members of the cast of *See You Later* were utilized: the temporary change making financial sense. It had super reviews. Then, from March until late June 1923 *See You Later* played several houses including Manchester's King's Theatre, Leeds Hippodrome, and the Aberdeen Palace.

Pa Cummings and Pete Davis were just a few of Scotland's clever impresarios. Fred Collins had a hit in 1920 with his a populist reworking of *Mother Goose*, the pantomime made for Dan Leno years earlier. Harry McKelvie took over the Royal Princess in the Gorbals in 1922. Stewart Cruickshank directed the King's in Edinburgh and Harry Lee produced pantomimes and revues: among them *Ole King Cole*, *Hooch-Aye*, *Froth* and *Kee-Hoy*. A craze for pantomimes was taking hold. The Wylie-Tate Company in the mid 20s typically produced four different ones at one time. Julian Wylie, whom composer Vivian Ellis described as 'the funniest man I have ever met,' was a pantomime 'King.' To him, a pantomime had to combine a

More Pitfalls and Pantomimes

'fairytale touch' with modern innovations. Star performers were showcased, whilst others got their start in these pantomimes.

Of Scotland's female performers, the one everyone went to see then was Dora Lindsay. She used to work with Bret Harte in an act dubbed *'the Greatest of all Scotch comedy duos.'* Lindsay and Harte were contemporaries of Renée's parents. Harte, slim and elegant and photographed with a pipe, was a brilliant 'feed' and master of timing. He affected a high-pitched 'Kelvinsider' accent and together they did 'super revues' such as *It's a Walk Over* before Dora starred in *Mother Goose* at the Pavilion, singing 'Meet me at the Shell,' all about Glasgow's Central Station. Dora was hailed 'Scotland's greatest comedienne' and headed into an international career.

Renée's youthful brand of cheek did not go unnoticed among the crowd that represented the cream of Scottish talent, but some, like Lindsay and Harte, weren't laughing. Renée told Robin Russell that at that time 'there was no question of a girl comedian being allowed in' at all. The fact that there was a wee lassie with the cheek to go on 'sort of irritated them.'[13] Dora's cold-shouldering of the young upstart probably started before Bret worked with Renée on *See You Later*. Lessons in tact were needed in a profession where egos required a careful side step. Renée's words about the difficulty of being 'allowed in' suggests Scotland had a pecking order among its 'stars' and theatrical inner circles weren't easy to penetrate. Despite all the pantomimes the Houston Sisters did between 1922 and 1925 they were never mentioned in the Sunday Chronicle's *Pantomime Annual* and didn't look set to break through any time soon.

The long apprenticeship with Pa Cumming's company did not prevent a parting after summer 1923, and it's a mystery why they broke off, especially since the next offer the Houston Sisters got wasn't much to speak of. Perhaps it was the body found under the bed in the digs in Manchester, that rainy night, when Renée, Billie and the girls from the show shared a room. The girls learnt that this was the landlady's husband, prior to his interment the next day.[14] For a couple of months Renée and Billie did *'Vaudeville Tit-bits'* in Aberdeen and at the Princess Theatre, Dundee where they supported the main act - a playlet dramatizing the WW Jacob's story *The Monkey's Paw*. Cold nights, corpses and devilish wishes were enough to make the Sisters jump into a Harry Lee show. They spent the first few weeks of December 1923 in Lee's revival of *Froth*, a lively revue full of Scotch humour, at the Glasgow Pavilion. Tommy Lorne was the principal comedian. Lorne, sacked from a steel company after being caught tap dancing on night shift, was a rapid-fire comic who wore a kilt, glengarry bonnet, high collar and bootlace tie. He made his debut at the Royal Princess in 1920 and McKelvie never forgave Lorne when the comic dropped him to work at the Glasgow Pavilion, and meanly extracted compensation from Lorne's new employer. Lorne frequently worked with Bret Harte.

After *Froth*, the Sisters opened at the Victoria, Dundee in *Jack and Jill* alongside Billy Rejane as the *Demon King* and the hilarious Maie Wynne as *Prince Bountiful*. The panto went to Glasgow Pavilion, Edinburgh's Pringles Palace, the Opera House Fife, the Hamilton Hippodrome, La Scala Electric Theatre – Edinburgh, and the Palace, Aberdeen. A couple of weeks before the pantomime closed Renée and Billie curiously attended a pageant entitled *'Motley of Youth, fashion and beauty'* organized by the Grand Order of the Eastern Star's Isla Chapter at Victoria Hall in Coupar Angus, the quiet Perthshire town. Were they there as a consequence of Jimmie's masonic connections? Was it to judge a talent contest or be judged in their musically inspired costumes? Billie went as an Indian squaw so a newspaper report tells us. I can't see her as a *Minnehaha* and I expect she came as *Hiawatha* and was misinterpreted. The story set to music by Coleridge-Taylor was a recent phenomenon at London's Royal Albert Hall. Renée came as *Elsie Maynard* from Gilbert and Sullivan's *Yeomen of the Guard* so the audience might have been in for some soprano singing. Given the girls' costumes, was it a last ditch desire to escape being typecast as the nursery rhyme fetchers of the pail?

Notices indicated people liked seeing the boy and girl pair. As *Jack* and *Jill*, their solos and duets were thought 'captivating.' At this stage the Sisters were still very rooted in Glasgow. Renée would say to Robin Russell years later that 'We never seemed to go far over the border without getting homesick.' For their next move, they either didn't opt for an impresario, or it was a lean period. March to late October 1924 represented the toughest months they would experience plying their trade.

In the *Topsy Turvy* revuette Renée had a hand in running a show. A family conference (or to be more exact, an argument between Renée and Jimmie with others butting in) started the idea. The concept was viable, given the success revues were having. At least they could rely on a core team of reliable individuals. *James Houston and Company* was scaling back the act. Jimmie and Lizzi last worked on the halls in late 1922 and early 1923 with their comic sketch *The Loony Lodger*.[15] A new direction for Jimmie, now fifty, was no bad thing. They had no concept of retiring despite health issues. Managing others, and making the most of networks was something Jimmie - the publican-cum-showman with VAF connections - did well.

Daddy thundered 'Where am I going to get scenery?' His eldest daughter said 'I'll see to that.' Renée excelled with artistic ideas, and could re-work ideas from *Hooray* and *See You Later* with fabulous results. With a sewing machine she knocked up shapes in canvas and other materials to serve as backdrops and helped paint these. She created costumes for the company, although her trousers won no prizes in garment technology. In the dress rehearsal the boys couldn't sit down in their pants and when they opened their show in Greenock (a town that features a lot in early Houston fact and legend) one of their comics got very excited, sat down, and couldn't get up again. All the dramatic ups and downs of this period would one day become

More Pitfalls and Pantomimes

the subject of a feature film, sadly one that hasn't survived. Eight year-old Shirley was left in Granny's care, with occasional visits from Lizzi - rather sad for her, as years before, Renée and Billie at least had each other for company. Lizzi was with the revue as often as possible but only behind the scenes. Jimmie shared top billing with his daughters. They assembled a fine cast of pals both young and old. Back from her latest escapade, and into the lineup was Renée's friend and international woman of mystery, Ella Pearson, to mesmerize all with her wild Scottish dance. The cast included comedian Harold Carlyle, Lilly Hunter, Charles Clare, Bert Douglas, Charles Smart, Cara and Doro Machaela, Harry Chapman, David Holden, Bert Poole and George Balharrie - as noted by The Stage, August 21, 1924, at the time *James Houston and Co* presented *Topsy Turvy* - a bright new revue at the Gaiety Theatre, Houghton-Le-Spring.

That last name in *Topsy Turvy's* lineup was a quiet red-haired young man, slightly built, but tall compared to Renée. He wore a little moustache, had twinkling eyes, and a dapper dress sense - favouring ties in a tartan plaid. He met the sisters in March 1924 when they were doing a couple of picture variety appearances at Johnstone's Pavilion - owned then by the Green family. This was the only time Renée performed in Johnstone, although it was her birthplace.

The only son of Alexander Balharrie - mercantile clerk, and Isabella Nicol, George Balharrie was born on February 1, 1903 in Edinburgh. His primary education was at Bruntsfield School – where actor Alastair Sim went, possibly at the same time. George had led a happy young life, showing interest in music, before he was orphaned at eight - his aunt becoming his guardian thenceforth. He entered Heriot's School in October 1912 as a '*Foundationer*'[16] then, gaining his Intermediate certificate, he trained to be a chemist with Laird & Sons, a local firm, whilst attending classes at Heriot-Watt Technical College. For some years he was the organist at a large church in Edinburgh. Music provided consolation and sometimes camaraderie when he performed with others. He decided to leave a safe career and go it alone in the performing arts. At nineteen, he toured England with *The Imperial Scots*, an all-tartan concert party led by Jock Downes and featuring Jock's soprano sister. Almost a year later, in July 1923, whilst *See You Later* was at its height, George was at Leas Pavilion in his own revue, with a different team demonstrating as much dexterity in his playing of Zez Confrey tunes as he would the likes of Beethoven and Bach: 'Mr George Balharrie is a very talented pianist, his rendering of 'The Kitten on the Keys' being highly acceptable' went one notice.[17]

On May 19, 1924 the Houston family played Glasgow's Old Metropole - the low-rise theatre in Stockwell Street South, near Victoria Bridge, (previously the Scotia, where Harry Lauder went to the weekly go-as-you-please nights). The effect of the Houston Sisters and a fresh company of actors on the same stage as Jimmie was rivetingly novel. A reporter noted that that the revue was well set, with catchy music. Jimmie took the 'revuette' from Glasgow to the North of England. It's curious why they went out of Scotland, where they couldn't rely on loyal audiences. Timing was a likely reason, with other shows on the road having booked up the theatres on the valuable circuits.

The family's lifestyle at this point wasn't unlike that of Violet Godfrey Carr, niece of popular entertainer Teddy Knox. Her indomitable mother's revuette toured towns in the north at the same time. It was an on-the-road life with equipment and costumes packed in wicker baskets on the back of a truck. In Violet's case they had a portable theatre with unfolding sidewalls of polished mahogany, portable naphthalene footlights all under a canvas roof held up by ropes. The troupe's arrival in a town caused a stir and the idea was to stay as long as possible in one place.[18] It wasn't easy to sustain a company of players in all weathers and in out of the way locations. The Houstons got themselves a lorry with a tarpaulin top, carrying their theatre with them and probably dressed at the side of a stage, removing makeup using lard, followed by lavender water to take away the smell.

The *Topsy Turvy* revue played at Whitehaven but early on ran into financial difficulties. Renée tells us that the bookings were in small venues, where attendance was so low it didn't raise enough for salaries. One venue was the Gem Theatre in Haltwhistle, where the audience was 'two little boys and an orange.'[19] They also appeared at Hetton-le-hole, Seaham harbour, and at West Stanley's Victoria Theatre. This was the original colliery town before East and West Stanley merged. In these towns, the trick used for hastening success was to meet miners after a show, and buy them all a drink so word spread around that the players were a good bunch. It tended to produce good attendance. Violet Godfrey Carr's mother did all this, despite being a teetotaler. Letting miners who wanted to come on stage, sing, or do a turn, was also a way to ensure a good house.

There was always the risk that your revue might not suit the miners' taste. As GS Melvin wrote 'If people cannot have a laugh . . .They prefer to stay away. They don't come to see the scenery or beautiful dresses.'[20] Jimmie bought a round of drinks here and there and they adapted the show with opportunities for miners to do a turn in *Topsy Turvy,* and offered prizes. The downside was not turning a profit, given these added outgoings. According to Renée 'We hit bad times and the Houstons crawled' with only enough to pay for their digs every week only. After appearing at Spennymoor, Daddy Jimmie informed everyone they did not have the train fayre to their next engagement in Jarrow. He was thinking of pulling out. The local stage manager at the theatre, who liked them, suggested they buy the motor lorry from his friend. With a comedian at the wheel, equipment piled high, and everyone holding on for dear life, they reached Jarrow, where they played a week, and there they achieved success. They went on to play Blyth, Consett and Crook before the tour stopped for a week at the Gaiety Theatre, Houghton-Le-Spring on August 24. Even after covering all their costs they actually had made a profit of £110.00[21] – a fortune!

The eight-month experience was enjoyable from Renée's perspective, because she was in a community. She often took pride in succeeding against the odds, although strangely, not when alone. She liked to have people around her including family. Both girls didn't want that sociable summer to end - so happy were they with the countless impromptu picnics and swimming parties for all involved in *Topsy Turvy*. An offer came in for Renée and Billie to be in Tommy Lorne's pantomime opening at the Pavilion in Glasgow followed by a tour. There were tears because the party would be breaking up. What would happen to all the friends they had got used to seeing. The sisters considered turning down the offer. Jimmie, however, told them they had to take this one.

Tom, Tom the Piper's Son, would break all British records for long runs, extending a month beyond its pantomime forecast of eight weeks. Whenever Tommy Lorne headed the cast that was expected. There were twelve scenes, many beautifully-lit, and Lorne had the audience in fits with his facial expressions alone especially in two of these: *The Fire Station* and *The Tenement House*. Tenement gags were popular as ever. The lavish pantomime was written and produced by Edward Marris with Howard Croft as musical director. The prettiest scenes were *The Village of Berry*, *The Pier at Roth Port*, *Clock Store* with its effective costumes, and *Donald's Reception*. Ouida Macdermott, no stranger to the Pavilion, played dashing principal boy *Donald* and 'California Here I come' was among the numbers this lively lassie belted out. 'Juvenile turns' Renée and Billie, as *Primrose* and *Petlet*, were thought the 'best items in the piece,' according to the Aberdeen Journal. They came into their own during the *Pier at Roth Port*. It might just as well have been an autobiographical scene given their Rothesay years. Their singing of 'Charleston Cabin' received an encore every time, and the number became all the rage in Glasgow as people went out and bought the music. *Tom Tom* had something for everyone but Tommy Lorne carried it. He would live another ten years, dying at the height of his success.

At this point Renée and Billie's double-act was five years old. They had stayed within a pattern of summer seasons, pantomime and revue. It's quite a leap to go from the comfort of a revue to have everything resting on your shoulders as an independent centripetal force on stage. The Sisters knew the impact they made and realized the enthusiastic reception of an audience was enough to sustain them. They still needed to firm up practicalities such as whom to count on to support their professional variety act.

Two days before *Tom, Tom* closed, on Thursday February 19th 1925, Catherina Rita Gribbin and George Alexander Joseph Balharrie were married at Bath Street's Sheriff Court, skipping back to the theatre for the matinee. The sheriff needed to ask George to speak up more than once, so shy and hesitant this young fellow was, especially with Renée happy to do much of the talking. 'Do you take this woman to be your lawful wedded wife?' the Sheriff asked George. 'Oh yes he does!' Renée cut in. They were the same age

– twenty-two, with Renée six months older. One of the witnesses at this secret marriage came from Hillhead – possibly George's neighbour.

Back at the theatre, the 'not so secret' marriage gave Tommy Lorne scope for suitable 'gags' that went into the pantomime to the delight of the audience, who applauded the couple's joy or embarrassment. Miss Houston received a tremendous ovation standing quietly on the Pavilion's stage. She was overwhelmed by the surge of adulation. Afterwards, George, Billie and co. had a party in her dressing room. Renée's closest friends were baffled by the marriage. The story Renée told in 1936 was she that she proposed to George after he told her one day he didn't know what he would do if she went away. In that account he laughed self-effacingly when she suggested marriage, but she was serious. She couldn't bear the thought of him being on his own and took him down to the registry office despite his arguments.

This was the delicate boy who'd bought Renée a pair of stockings, leaving them on her dressing room table one night when *Topsy Turvy* played West Stanley and the revue was at its lowest point. His telltale blushes gave him away, and of course he denied being the one who left the gift. It had rained all that miserable week and Renée was going about stocking-less, not wanting to pay for such an expense. She'd met George in town a day or so previously and he looked troubled when she had a coughing fit. 'Oh, I hate stockings,' was her reply, when he earnestly asked her why she wasn't wearing any. George's gesture made her confess: 'I was so touched by his thoughtfulness that I became his friend for life.' George had seen the highs, but had also been there when they played empty houses and went hungry. He was close to all the family and this counted for a lot. They'd known each other a little under a year when they married. It was a spiritual closeness - two kids leaning on each other, as thick as thieves. He might have been quiet but he was sharp and capable of sarcasm. He was also business-like and kept her on her toes. His approval was important to her. She had a power over him and it sounds like Renée's influence, when placid George casually revealed to his aunt 'I'm getting married today,'[22] and walked out the door, the day of their appointment at Bath Street.

At the time they married, in February 1925, the fear George had about future loneliness was well founded. Renée was leaving town completely within months. *Tom Tom* was the real vehicle that sped The Houston Sisters to success. This prompted an invitation, via the Sisters' new Glasgow agent Harry Kenyon, to appear at the Argyle Theatre, Birkenhead two months hence. Every variety entertainer wishing to make it big saw this theatre, on the Wirral Peninsula, as a talisman. If you played here and made a success of it, as Harry Lauder had, news of your discovery was telegraphed to all the leading music hall managements in London. The influence of Dennis J. Clarke, who had been the Argyle's owner-manager since he was eighteen, was noteworthy. He remained a key figure for forty-five years, respected for the encouragement he gave so many hopefuls. He was also quick to respond to every innovation. The Argyle showed colour films before anyone did, in 1897, and demonstrated one of the earliest gramophones in 1898.

Before *Tom Tom*'s curtain finally came down George watched his Renée bathe in glory. He had seen 1924 change into 1925 with the two Houston Sisters rubbing shoulders with the high and mighty at the *Actors Association Dance* at Berkeley Street's Palais de Danse, and heard of the wannabes waiting outside Green's Playhouse when the sisters attended the *Glasgow Cinema Ball*. Its midnight fancy dress parade and glamorous stars always made it a big event, turning people's heads.

In later years Renée would refer to 'Poor George' making out she wanted the Houstons to be his surrogate family. But how much did he need compassion? Despite the loneliness he'd faced early in life, he'd worked hard and his own efforts were receiving praise. He had an invitation to work in Bert Bendon's syndicate. He didn't compose but he could command an orchestra. He understood musical comedy and how to set up her act. He was willing to make Renée his priority and was prepared to be the stooge the Houston Sisters needed, doing everything from managing the score sheets to booking travel. He wasn't part of *Tom Tom* but he spent this time on the look out for new numbers to showcase her talent. He was also Renée's steadfast fan. From Miss H's point of view, she wanted to be a star and he could be valuable to her. There weren't many others queuing up to offer the same. The two of them seem to have been focused on their careers and what their joint efforts might achieve. They didn't think of future concerns – like sorting out the mess if either partner wanted to get out down the line. This was bold considering that in those days you just didn't get divorced.

Renée's son and other members of the family believe the marriage was a way of ensuring her parents couldn't refuse to let George live under their roof. If that were the case Lizzi must have been thinking ahead to the practicalities of her daughter touring with George, and to the time when the family would share a big house together. She can't have been thinking of there and then because living under their current roof at 671 Shettleston Road[23] would have been a very crowded arrangement – almost impossible. Renée would say 'my Mammy wouldn't take him in as a lodger,' but there was no room for a lodger. I'm sure Granny Houston, all the same, would have found some corner for George to pitch in, with a clever little bed that pulled out from an ancient chest of drawers. George also wasn't destitute, as some of the stories imply. Either Renée continued to stay with her parents, or George returned to 19 Havelock Street where he lived with his aunt, near Glasgow University. It's possible the young married couple lived together at the latter address - a much nicer home, spacious enough for a grand piano with plenty of light.

Renée and George anticipated touring in variety and each needed the other to be close at hand. They married morally, in order to work alongside each other, to travel together and share accommodation without having to worry about humbug created by convention. The idea of an unmarried young man and woman living together aroused strong emotions. It was a different world then: one that's changed enormously, making such a marriage meaningless nowadays. George and Renée's marriage was not unlike that between George Burns and first wife Hannah Siegel, one of his dance partners. That only happened because her family would not let them go on tour unless they married and their marriage was never consummated. But while Burns and Hannah divorced at the end of their tour, George and Renée's marriage curiously lasted seven years.

The Balharrie marriage has echoes of Gracie Fields' marriage to Archie Pitt being one of 'investment', although George had nothing of Archie's drive as an impresario and was the same age as Renée. Even though a marriage had taken place, Renée and Billie usually shared a room when touring – perhaps not always though. It's interesting that the requirement to 'marry for moral reasons' only really applied for those who had 'come of age.' Billie, by contrast, had toured in the company of a number of men as a teenager. Perhaps George Balharrie was happy to act as chaperone to both sisters.

Archie Pitt and Gracie Fields enjoying a game of snooker
(My thanks to the family of J. Lewis)

After their visit to the registry office, Renée told a story about how the guilty couple had to face her parents. She suddenly got the 'breeze up,' pushing George up the stairs in front of her to explain all to Lizzi who stood in her best 'Lady Macbeth' attitude as the account unfolded. Jimmie's laughter broke the ice and they came around to the 'marriage' of the half-witted pair. There were few complaints from her parents and they knew, of course, it wasn't George's doing. 'Poor wee souls . . . we'll have to make the most of it,' said Lizzi, after the tears, 'And to think it's your wedding and I haven't even a present for you,' was all she could think of saying. On the fireplace lay one of the unclaimed prizes from the talent shows for *Topsy Turvy,* put on for the miners in the north of England. It was a heavy 20s style black marble alarm clock nobody liked. Lizzi handed it to the doleful George, it ticking all the while, making enough noise to awaken all the dead in the neighbourhood. It was a comic absurd moment Renée never forget.

More Pitfalls and Pantomimes

I've wondered if the reason for the *few complaints* from her parents might be because *they* told her to marry George because it was a good opportunity and therefore good 'business.' If the Sisters' act was going to work they desperately needed music and also needed security. Security is all the more necessary for an act coming from nowhere. The help of trusted men was crucial then for women in show business. It's possible that Renée's story about asking him to marry her is a fabrication. He might just as well have initiated it with her having to fall in and accept him. Doing something to meet expectations can stoke the fires of rebellion in later years. This might be why she couldn't care less for humbug in the next two decades when she laughingly hammed it up with her stage husband (Donald Stewart) and talked with pride about her real husband (Pat Aherne) and vice versa.

In a Sunday Post interview given three days after the marriage, there's a photo of the neat little couple, his arm stiffly around her. The copy supplied to the reporter has Billie Houston chiming into the conversation, recalling an undignified incident that happened during George and Renée's 'courtship'. Posing for a photo in a shallow river in the north of England, George slipped and Billie was able to take a photo at that opportune moment. There is also the story of how at Johnstone, Renée and George fell in love at a séance, holding hands. This was when one girl, due to join *Topsy Turvy*, was scaring everyone with her exploits as an amateur spiritualist. At the end of the interview, asked about her plans, Renée sweetly says 'I should like to be in the same show as George.' Reading this, I ask if Renée and George really did love each other, and if the relationship was more than innocent.

She had had a traditional Catholic upbringing, and marriage and divorce are usually major considerations, especially when marrying a non-Catholic. Renée brought two children into the marriage by adoption and the 'marriage' to George lasted those seven years. Years later, Renée denied she and George were in love, although tellingly, in her 1936 memoir, she revealed they were both lonely and had been through the mill together. In her 1974 interview with Mavis Nicholson, she admitted George liked her.[24]

So, it was an unconsummated marriage with them never sharing a bedroom, as Miss Houston's story goes. Unless they were happy to wait until their marriage was annulled, you'd think, for curiosity's sake, they'd have got closer. Marriage then, was the only way youngsters might understand the mystery of the unopened rose, so to speak. The vast majority of young people were innocent in the 20s, nothing like their modern equivalents. As one of Renée's chorus girl contemporaries put it, you never knew what the word 'f---' meant until you were married. It was also a total fallacy that people in the theatre were any less innocent than the majority of people.

If health issues ruled out sex or if he was impotent, the couple coped with it. I'm cautious regarding suggestions – like those of Tom Gallacher in his 1974 play *Renée Houston Rehearses Her Life - A Musical Play in Two Acts* - that George was gay, even if a *hand me down* recollection from Elana Aherne

87

seems to indicate that George was uninterested in women. Recalling George, whom she met in the 30s, Elana mentioned to her son that there seemed to be no real love between him and Renée. He might equally have been a shy personality who outwardly came across as cold.

A reference dating from the 30s has Miss H saying she benefited from George's kind-hearted and almost feminine understanding, referring to how he consoled her in her lonely moments, assuring her 'Mr Right will come along.'[25] Renée sometimes would say 'I'm glad I did what I did for him' which has a ring about it that indicates she was protecting him. In those days there wasn't the language we have now to refer to a person's sexuality. Of course ignorant comments were common. Renée's comment might equally refer to how George benefitted professionally by being associated with her.

I think of a careless promise whispered at Glasgow Cross as they listened to the bells 'ring in' 1925: a promise that turned to a reality in a prankish way, with Renée enjoying the shock value of a madcap action. She wanted to satisfy a burning desire for *possession* at the beginning. It wasn't unlike the almost *divine* calling she had to satisfy later on in adopting kids. She and George might have felt something for each other, waking up only to realize it was nothing, deciding afterwards to stay together for the sake of friendship. They remained good friends, and it's touching that Renée stood by him in and out of the marriage. I believe wholeheartedly that Renée had compassion for him, but I believe very little of what she later said about the nature of their relationship.

He might have brought her disappointment but he was loyal to her, carrying out duties, hen-pecked for much of it, with Renée free to be the biggest flirt in the world within that 'arrangement'. He never broke away, and after they divorced, lived at her parents' home as a fully paid up *Houston*. Even in the late 30s, with Pat Aherne her husband and Donald Stewart on the scene as Miss Houston's stage partner, George was still there: a lonely figure, though he had a couple of girlfriends. George died in Pat's arms and how much Renée grieved is unknown. Of the quiet man whose gift of stockings helped at a time she was being put through the mill, she said 'it was the little thought behind the gift that counted.' She never forgot a friend.

The next show entitled 'Bright Spots'- described as 'some sense interrupted by nonsense' had them work alongside Jimmie's friend Bert Bendon – *'One of the Scots Wha Hae'* - the draw of the show, as well as its producer. Bendon was known for his silly cap or Glengarry hat, tartan trews and 'silly boy' pantomime parts. It was George Balharrie's biggest collaboration with Renée so far, and a chance to display his prowess in a large revue. The revue featured Dorothy Langley, Mabel Mack, Betty Robb, and the Eight Ritchie girls. There were ten 'illuminations' including 'The Bright Spots Club', 'A Wild and Woolly Spot', and 'An Oriental Spot'. It played a few weeks at Aberdeen's Tivoli before going to Edinburgh for the end of March 1925. The Houston Sisters appeared in nine out of ten scenes and a reporter remarked how 'Burlesque is the keynote,' and that 'George

More Pitfalls and Pantomimes

Balharrie, as musical director, keeps his forces well in hand, and under his direction... the revue dovetails in neatly and smoothly.'[26]

The Houston Sisters' first appearance at the Argyle Theatre, Birkenhead, where Ella Shields first sung her 'Burlington Bertie from Bow,' was on April 5, 1925. Renée wasn't going to leave it all to Dennis Clarke and his telegraph machine to decide when the Sisters' assault on London was due. At Birkenhead, Renée noted the London address of agent George Barclay: Boylands Oak, Brixton Hill. She faked a letter recommending the Houstons to his talent office. This paid off because an advert in the Stage on May 7, 1925 confirms that Barclay was their sole representative at this early date. Though the sisters had yet to meet him, he was safe in Renée's books, given that the digits of his house number '241' added up to 7, a good omen. Numerology was vital for each of the Houston sisters - Billie and Shirley unusually preferring 13 to be their lucky number.

An opportunity came about at Birkenhead on April 5 when Wilkie Bard, the headline act, failed to appear. The Stage tells us: 'Wilkie Bard is announced this week but through a motor accident he missed the first house on Monday.' A forgotten name now, in 1919 Bard was *'England's greatest genius of laughter,'* delighting fans both sides of the Atlantic. He had appeared by Royal Command more times than any living artist. David Lloyd George said: "I never so worried during the war that Wilkie Bard couldn't make me laugh and forget Flanders for a while.'[27] Covering for his absence, the Houstons extended their act using free adlibs. They were a hit, and earned house points from Denny Clarke for their professionalism. 'Last night my name was Wilkie Bard - now it's just barred' was actually back the next night to give the audience characterizations they loved like 'Scrubwoman', or the fruity 'I Want to Sing in Opera'.

Left to right:
Wilkie Bard, Power and Bendon with Burt Bendon on right (Westminster Reference Library) Frank Tinney (Author's Sketch) and The Argyle, Birkenhead (Author's Collection)

The Sisters carried on travelling on different tour circuits. Jim surprised them with a visit for their second appearance at Birkenhead, having returned from Portland, Maine to Liverpool. He was waiting on board the train at Lime Street about to leave for Glasgow when an advert in the newspaper of the man opposite him said the Houstons were at the Argyle. Jim immediately leapt out of the train and went to see his little sisters who greeted him with hugs in the dressing room. What he found was applause so overwhelming, he felt sorry for the 'top of the bill' act following the Houstons.

89

That was Frank Tinney – known as *'the Funbeam'* - a small, often black-faced comedian, who had been in the Ziegfeld Follies of 1913 before making England his base. He was a master of the corny joke and known for his banter with the conductor in the pit: an ideal means for making an impact, and something the eagle-eyed Renée absorbed. There was euphoria the next day when George took over the conductor's stool for the Sisters' opening music. It was truly memorable. Renée later wrote that just at this time, she and Billie began to believe in themselves. 'People say that is fatal, but I think . . . you have to believe 'I am the one who matters - The whole show depends on my performance. It is the only way to stardom.'[28] Ads for the Houston Sisters, so frequent in the press between May and December 1925 indicate George Barclay's strategy to get big houses in provincial centres, ensuring word of mouth marketing that translated into return visits, all before the Houston Sisters were going to break London.

The Sisters were committed to Scottish engagements at Ayr Pavilion in early June, and at Harry Kemp's La Scala, in Saltcoats, in July and August. There was no George in late June when he stayed on with Bendon's 'BB Productions' *What's Yours* - a revue at the Tivoli, Hull. It was fortuitous for Harry Kemp, another legendary impresario, that he had booked the Houston Sisters some time before they had become famous celebrities. Kemp secured talented Scottish performers for summer seasons at his Ayrshire coast venues from 1922 until the 50s. He did lucrative business. Kemp's concert party was important enough to advertise months in advance. Pete Davis was producing it, and a version had toured the north of England before opening at La Scala on July 19, 1925. *Scotch Broth – A Revue of Speed, Spice and Sparkle*, would feature The Houston Sisters, Maie Wynne, Billy Howard, Pete Davis, Dave Bruce, Betty Maldwyn, Dave Willis, George Balharrie and Louie Freeman's Orchestra.

Watching another of those flickering soundless films at the Scottish Screen Archive, you travel back to 1925 and immediately, as you watch the young lads crowd the Saltcoats lido, bobbing up and down, you've visited somewhere in your deep consciousness where sheer happiness prevails. Not only the sense of mirth present in the faces of the holidaymakers in this little clip picks you up. You can almost smell the water! Then, lo and behold, it's none other than Miss Houston, or should I say Mrs Balharrie, wearing a 1920s black shift dress, hat and beads. She's animated although you can't see her close-up. Surrounded by onlookers she tries out the crazy golf putting, capturing a ball from a scrum and then takes part in many physical activities that get the crowd cheering. It's like watching a Chaplin silent! Running in a race, she holds on to her cloche. In another scene, surrounded by children, she's entertaining a baby in a pram. Men and women do some putting and one of the golfers looks like Billie. The film deteriorates but you can make out the charabancs carrying Renée, Billie, Dave Willis and the rest of the *Scotch Broth* entertainers, dressed in their classic Pierrot outfits.

More Pitfalls and Pantomimes

It's hard to believe that the work was in reality quite demanding. The entire programme changed every three days throughout its fourteen-week season, partly on account of fact that they were playing mostly to local audiences and partly because Kemp believed that only the best was good enough. In a BBC Scotland Spotlight interview Pete Davis gave to Robin Russell shortly before he died, he remarked 'you can imagine the lengths comedians had to go to, to find material.'[29] Nevertheless, the atmosphere was, by all accounts, happy, and when Renée looked back she would describe Kemp as a 'marvellous man' or tell you that you 'couldn't get a fellow who knew the business better than Pete.' Nobody made a secret of the fact that several times she erupted into a rage, quit, or was given notice to go by Pete. Somehow, she would forget to go, or he would forget he'd sacked her. He tried to worry her saying that Harry Kemp would sue her, and she couldn't stop laughing at the idea of placid Harry ever doing this. The Kemp-Davis-Houston formula was revived for summer seasons in the 1930s.

Harry Kemp's "Scotch Broth" Entertainers La Scala, Saltcoats, July 1925

Dave Willis is next to Renée Houston with Billie behind her. Maie Wynne and Renée sit either side of Pete Davis. Harry Kemp is at the centre in the back row with Billy Howard, Dave Bruce and Betty Maldwyn. The man behind Pete might be George Balharrie. (By kind permission of North Ayrshire Heritage Centre)

Asked by Robin Russell about Scottish entertainers she worked with in these early days, Renée described Davy Willis as 'a great little comedian and such a charming man. That's always gone a long way with me. You could be a great comic but if you weren't kind, I had no time for you.' Earlier she declared that 'Nothing seemed to worry Dave Willis - he was one of the best-natured souls.'[30] Sporting that little moustache - a Willis trademark - people always thought his Hitler was the real Mackay: dictatorial frown, *Chancellorian* moustache, and lock of hair flapping in the breeze. Even Charlie Chaplin was said to credit Willis as one of the best comics in Britain. He was the son of a butcher from Glasgow's New City Road - a natural at suggesting something funny on stage with the merest gesture. His first comedy films in the 30s caused some to wonder if there was room for two Chaplins on the screen. At the time of Munich crisis, Willis's comic impressions of Hitler were so successful and talked about, that the Germans complained to the British Foreign Office. At this time, they sent Renée's friend Lord Inverclyde to advise Willis to stop.[31] Magic acts were a big part of Willis's family, his brother being *The Great Claud - spoof magician*. That struck a chord with Renée who had been a magician's assistant at fourteen.

She had learned a few tricks from that illusionist at Kingston Empire and held onto the skills. When her son brought a boy home from school interested in magic tricks, Renée amazed them by whipping a tablecloth off a table without disturbing any of the objects above.

The sketches produced by Pete Davis didn't just feature Renée and Billie, but also Shirley - their nine year-old sister. She had been sent on a long holiday in Saltcoats by her parents only to find herself written into short sketches featuring one of Dave Willis's three sons. Pete Davis tried to get the kids involved in *Scotch Broth* but finding the two youngsters for a rehearsal was another matter. Usually, everyone had to go out on a search – only to discover them up to their necks in sand. Poor Shirley! It sounds like she thought she might actually be just allowed to behave like a normal kid on holiday. Sadly, wherever there's a Houston, there's an act to be roped into. In one of Shirley's sketches, she had to act as if she'd been poisoned and her dying scene was so authentic she caused women in the audience to sob. Shirley proved to be such a natural she caused George Balharrie to predict in 1925 that she would soon make her own way in show business.

Renée and Billie were a success in *Scotch Broth* and in a relatively short period had amassed a veritable library of sketches. When they went to London they owed Pete a debt as all the material he had forced them to find lasted them three years. After Saltcoats, the sisters were keener than ever to storm London, no longer afraid of going independent of a familiar company.

Chapter 7   Lucky Number

Seven jets of light splinter out gloriously beneath the turning illuminated globe, the whole effect like a crown blurring through the night skyline. London's smog only increases the ambience surrounding the stately Coliseum, St Martin's Lane. Nearer to street-level the names of tonight's variety acts glow white overhead. 'Will we play there?' asked Billie that October's night in 1925 when they were new to London. 'Yes hen, we will,' affirmed Renée, counting. Yet their first Coliseum appearance was not until January 18, 1926, over three months after their arrival in London.

Coliseum by night   London Music Hall   Toy Drum Major Score
                           (Author's Collection)

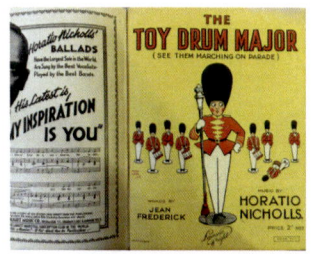

Renée's entertaining tale has Daddy Jimmie giving her firm instructions to come home on the Sunday directly after their first week at Shoreditch. Discovering they've been given top billing at the Coliseum the next week, there's no going back for her. 'You'll cop it when father hears about this,' Billie warns her, and telephoning home, Daddy declares he's going to give her a good spanking. Quite the reverse was the reality. They were sacrificial lambs tested by their manager at a succession of venues: in London's East End, then Belfast again, then Manchester with Robb Wilton and Van Dock - the military-attired Italian cartoonist, then Cardiff alongside Harry Tate, then Exeter, London, Birmingham and finally London again. In Belfast the sisters shared billing with their cousin Charlie Wincot who, with the *Avalos*, wowed all with an act involving a giant xylophone. On the same bill *Sylvestre the Sunshade Maker* offered Belfast uncanny atmospherics.

The Houston Sisters played the London Music Hall October 4 to 12, 1925 and included in their act the ventriloquist skit that had made the audience howl in their *'Pier'* scene in *Tom Tom* a year earlier. At the London it was especially funny as they followed a regular ventriloquist - Benson Gray, in the lineup. People loved their vent act. Renée's dummy would later sing songs like 'When I met Sally down in our alley,' and we would see *Bill* putting the 'croos-eyed' dummy on *his* knee on the cinema screen in 1933. That week at the London, the audience got the Brothers Walsh, the Junes, Laura Little's Six Spotlights, and Hart & O'Brian. The latter, popular enough to place custom ads in the papers, did their comic courtroom routine.

George Barclay, or 'the Guv' as everyone called him, wanted to see how these Scots girls got on with a London audience. George O' Shea used the name 'Barclay' as part of the comic duo Barclay and Perkins - *Brewers of Fun*[1] before giving up his own music hall career to manage Gertie Gitana and most of all, that of his wife, Kate Carney - popular cockney comedienne. They were a down-to-earth pair: Barclay as Cockney as they come, and Kate, red-haired and dumpy figured. She famously used to say 'I know the London working girl - I ought to. I was one.' Perhaps a little bit of the Cockney couple rubbed off on Renée who did a neat Old Kent Road accent. Jim Houston describes the Guv as small, slim and dapper, with a close-cropped moustache, checked suit and a soft grey hat, often flanked by talent scouts, Pa Wade and Bert Nolan. Jim recalled that irrespective of company present Barclay could always 'use swear words in ordinary conversation without giving offence at the same time.'[2] The Guv and Kate never got above themselves, despite having an eleven-bedroom home on Brixton Hill, racehorses and expensive cars. Their welcoming nature boosted the creative powers of the young blood they took under their wing such as the Houston Sisters and Ted Ray.

The London Music Hall, or Shoreditch Empire, seated over a thousand and was managed by Fred Peel. Kate Carney sang and gave out prizes here on competition nights on Fridays. It was also a 'try out' venue for young acts. Bransby Williams made his first London appearance here in 1896, and Leslie Sarony was a hopeful at its monthly matinee for amateurs. Some acts died quick and as Sarony put it to interviewer Stephen Dixon, 'they used to give you the bird and the stagehands used to hook 'em off, round the neck.'[3] The nearby Pavilion Theatre at 191 Whitechapel Road, dubbed in its Edwardian heyday as the *'Drury Lane of the East,'* by far drew the biggest audience from the Jewish East End[4] but the London had many Jewish patrons too, and the Sisters were apparently a big hit with them. Their brother Jim tells us how, in the 'Hogarthian atmosphere,' the 'audience rose to their feet' – quite a turnaround considering that when they first came on it was 'puzzled stares' all round. Renée went after that audience who were daring her to make them laugh – 'a challenge she could not refuse.'[5] Returning to the Jewish quarter a second week on December 21, 1925, Renée loved to say how she cracked a joke or two in Yiddish causing some people to believe they were Scottish Jewesses. Gifts began appearing at the stage door including delicious ghuvelti fish. 'I thought this could make you poor children happy being so far away from home,' said a dear old Jewish lady, apparently convinced the two *Irresistibles* must be representatives of her people. Unable to spoil such a pleasant little scene, Renée felt bad afterwards for taking the fish.

The London Music Hall used to stand at 95-99 Shoreditch High Street on a curve in the road where the Ace Hotel is now. Gone is that old façade lit by glass braziers. Even though London's *engaged district* caters for creatives and renegade artists from around the world today, they're a different sort to those who once received prizes from Kate Carney. At the Ace Hotel you'd have to major in necromancy to summon up Billie and Renée standing on a pair of drums or Leslie Sarony singing massive songs of the day like 'I Caught Two Cods Cuddling' or 'I Found a Hard-Boiled Egg in My Love-nest.' It's a paean to stylish living: all hip magazine stuff with pale wood and Sixties-style furniture. Recent website bloggers write how Ace's:

staff are über cool, but still friendly, in their specially designed John Smedley knitwear and Converse trainers. Most were helpful: check-in staff were particularly pleasant, but marks were lost for the very slow service at dinner – my starter of soup took 20 minutes to arrive – although the waiter did apologize for this.

The hotel is undoubtedly hip . . . two gallery spaces decked out with folksy Scottish tapestries and bespoke bicycles on offer. Ace also has a 'concept store' feel: hotel-branded items are sold at the check-in desk.

I might have gone gaga in my Houston Sisters world, finding descriptions of the hotel's 52 square metre rooms screamingly funny:

'WiFi, sexy oak table for dining or work, a Rega record player + selection of vinyl, acoustic Martin Guitar, Revo radio with Ace-curated radio stations, in-room safe and flatscreen TV, plus a well-stocked minibar keeping you ready to take all comers.'

I wish furniture didn't have to be so sexy nowadays. I imagine a modern Houston Sisters sketch entitled *'A friend's Shoreditch apartment.'* I can't help but imagine the Sisters haunting the *Deluxe Double* for a laugh, using vinyls for frisbies, and raiding its minibar stocked with Monster Munch crisps, Pot Noodles, other assorted snacks, and condom.

The Stage reported that 'Shoreditch audiences are making much this week of the two clever young Scottish ladies,' mentioning the 'strikingly boyish voice' of Billie, that they began with a duet in the baby style, before singing 'Let it Rain' and 'Toy Drum Major.' Either George Balharrie or Billie chose the music for the act. Looking at the turnaround from score publication to stage performance they were hot off the mark. There was a huge market for sheet music and the possibilities of promotion by a headline act meant that the theatrical press devoted pages to the latest sensational song sure to be swiped off the shelves by the public. The social impact the music score market had on people's lives was immense. There were pianos in homes across the country and people were only too ready to sing along to the latest ripping little fox trot. A daily fix of melodies could be enjoyed anywhere. These tunes were in the pubs, in the theatres, banged out by accompanists at picture houses as soundtracks for silent movies, and played again as we danced cheek to cheek. Composer Lawrence Wright, or to use his other name, Horatio Nichols, turned out hit after hit. He also founded 'Melody Maker'. Even if you can't tell a treble clef from your armpit, you can lose yourself looking at the dreamy imagery on the front covers of these scores. In the 1980s other kids had posters on their walls of real people. My Woolworths frames featured old Valses and Fox Trots my mum had acquired in an auction job lot: covers graced by ample-bosomed ladies so swooning they might have been drug-laden.

Lawrence Wright's 'Toy Drum Major: See them Marching On Parade' had just appeared around May 14, 1925. The artwork by cartoonist Fred Low has a set of Busby-topped toy soldiers, some with little drums or trumpets, some fallen, on a bold yellow background. This image alone seems to have got into the psyche, flashing across your screen in a short sequence from 'Singing in the Rain' or a costume dance featuring Shirley Temple and Bill Robinson. It's very old and 'The Drum Major' grew out of early minstrelsy.[6]

Variety artists competed to be first to be associated with a new song, as you can tell reading the 'Song Notes' column in The Stage. This reported on who was scoring with which composer's popular tune. Less than a week after 'Toy Drum Major' came out, the writer for this column told his readers that a letter was received from the Houstons saying they were using 'Toy Drum Major' to great success, during their first Birkenhead week. In November 1925, when the Sisters were at the Ardwick Green Empire Manchester, the columnist pointed out how the sisters were first to score with it. This shows the mutual promotion between performer and composer, and hints at agent George Barclay's publicity plan for the run up to the girls' 'assault' on London. Soon full-page adverts by music publisher Keith Prowse & Co. Ltd displayed large photos of the Sisters - such was their selling factor.

How artists use a song from a score is another matter. For Renée and Billie, their *Parade of the Toy Soldiers* was a 'nursery' burlesque that closed their show. 'Their paint and glue, they'll be on review, with the toy - drum - major' – went the line, but imagine it with a jazz step added for good measure. No video preserves the routine but agent Pete Davis, who witnessed it, tells us 'this finale was the limit.' To glimpse them on parade there's a single photograph only and not a contemporary one, being from the pressbook of an autobiographical film the Sisters made in 1936 utilizing the routine. I heard a snatch of a song that Renée sings, in her coloratura voice, telling how you 'put your first foot forward' and 'shake your shoulders gladly in rhythm.' I thought of the film's *Parade* scene alternating this with Wright's forthright little number that had played a part in their London success.

How can I sell the star factor of long ago variety stars to people nowadays? In the 20s, Renée and Billie's youth, striking looks and funny routines were an antidote to staleness. For five years an obscure act, they scintillated in the limelight for ten solid years. Then a short run of reunions followed a fifteen-year gap. Theirs was the skill of making comedy out of what seemed like little material: a private exchange thrust open to public view. There was a lot of 'cheek' and a sense they were getting away with it. The stuff they said could be suggestive but was mostly innocent. The charming thing was their intimacy and quick-fire clever nonsense. All her life Renée had been a talented wordsmith and rhymer who loved experimenting with speech. With giant pixie ears, usually unseen, she was an acute listener stealing phrases to tamper with, and putting them to use in unpredictable situations. She tested these utterances unashamedly and was the possessor of a convoluted brain that suited zany sketches very much in the Gracie Allen mould.

Lucky Number

Once they had a couple of good numbers the Houston Sisters only had to be themselves to a large extent. It was never properly rehearsed, often not even discussed. Billie admitted to BBC producer and executive Howard Thomas that the Houston Sisters never wrote a word of their act together. They chose the songs, roughly worked out the situations, and left the rest to their native wit.[7] It takes real comediennes to do that. Alan Aherne recalls his father saying how shocked he was to discover, whilst driving Renée and Billie to engagements in the early 30s, they were working out their evening's act in the back of the car. Billie would say 'What shall we do?' and Renée would suggest 'Ill say this, you say that' and everything was kept lose in format so they could just improvise on stage. Their performance was never spoiled from being too 'studied'. Listening at the wheel, Pat was downright worried for them. Just as then, people today regard stand-up as fearful.

This contrasts with the line 'Nothing comes to an artist without thought. He has got to think, and think hard,' as GS Melvin said. The Houstons' thoughts stemmed from long before. Under the lights, they were mostly concerned about time. The plentiful gags, each depending on an economical tag, came fast and loose. It was a tight little act that didn't overrun.

The sources of their material came out of everyday situations. Harry Kemp tells us how Renée was in a Glasgow tramcar and an old lady beside her asked if the tram 'wid be gaun ower the Jamaica Bridge.' 'If it disna,' replied Miss Houston, 'there'll be a terrible splash.' They were natural observers of the idiocies of life. True, their jokes were mostly tame ones, but language was the key ingredient and they adored a nice little play upon words.

Always, the dynamic was the quarrel between the two of them. It was a battle of the sexes played out by *children*: a silly thing between a boy and girl. This distance provided scope for ripe comments on 'adult' issues left hanging at the level of suggestion. No 'grudge' about society peppered their act though. There was *Bill* annoyed at Renée's irreverence regarding tradition or for her flirting. It wouldn't have worked if the sisters were allies and there was never any 'sisters are doing it for themselves' quality to their behaviour. They weren't 'sisters' on stage. The little quarrel had supremacy.

They could achieve anything if they had each other, feeding upon each other's confidence. A fine rapport between two individuals and the power of friendship goes a long way, and we've been blessed with comedy double acts drawn from real sisters and real brothers over the years with the O'Gorman brothers - Dave and Joe, the Marx brothers, and Mike and Bernie Winters being a few examples. It's not a large list. Every double act has a bond of mutual love - sibling, marital, or otherwise. George Burns and Gracie Allen are possibly one of the greatest results of the workings of comedy where a marriage is the basis of closeness, scintillating throughout their thirty-eight wedded years.

Gracie Allen worked in a similar way to Renée. It was about sending yourself up. Renée and Gracie were experts and had no worries about doing this. Dabber Davis told me that a lot of comediennes did not like sending themselves up in this way. In the case of Bebe Daniels whose act with Ben Lyon was also enduring, Bebe would get 'back on the line.'

The Houstons' act was about exchange and neither sister felt at ease as a single act. If Renée ever worked alone, there was a conductor or an interviewer to be the 'feed'. She said in a report in 1937 that she improvised on stage on the spur of the moment to such a pitch that people working with her required a sort of *sixth sense*. She says her sister Billie had it, and Donald Stewart had it very strongly developed. A partner had to judge when exactly to hang back and let her drop in the line she had just thought of. Donald was an excellent straight man. He would start to do something and she would come in to make it funny. Of course, Donald was a first-rate singer too.

Renée used to say she got her skill at ad-libbing from her mother. This is probably why she managed for the most part to keep it clean. In the 30s Howard Thomas admired how she worked at the BBC. Whilst nobody knew what she would come out with on the air they considered her the least person of all to want to offend anyone, knowing her audience consisted of whole families.[8] That trust was less watertight in later decades. Renée was made for a theatrical career by virtue of the fact that by fourteen she was a natural at speechmaking, and could memorize lines incredibly fast. This alone didn't make her unique. She would often say her main talent was the ability to jump in with just the right word at the right time, something that wasn't as utilized on the radio as it could have been, but eventually found a permanent place in *Petticoat Line,* serving her until this show finished in 1976. Anona Winn said that when the show started in 1965, they needed the gaiety that comes out of a really professional woman comedienne, and Renée was the one. Speaking to Robin Russell in an interview, Anona described in almost poetic terms how her colleague worked: 'She's got a Scottish attitude to life, to problems, and she leavens the lump, she brings the spark, she brings the absurdity in when we're getting a little bit 'deed' in.'[9]

To return to those early days in London, the sisters made a first visit to the Victoria Palace on December 28, 1925 and clearly caught the fancy of the house. For their first visit to Charles Gulliver's Holborn Empire on November 23, with Georgie Wood and Dolly Harmer in the lineup, a notice in The Stage mentions how their quarrel in 'comical Scottish baby talk might be quickened up.' Like other theatre top dogs, Gulliver had links to the British film industry as it was then. Two months later, scientifically minded Cyril Elwell presented the 'first complete demonstration in Europe of the synchronized talking motion pictures shown by the De Forest Phonofilm Company Ltd' at Holborn. The chosen 'sound-on-film' was 'Till the Bells Ring' - a comedy routine by Graham Moffatt - a Scottish actor who had a smash hit in *Bunty Pulls the Strings* at the Haymarket Theatre. The Houston Sisters would make their own Phonofilm the following year.

Unknown to London just a short while before, the Sisters' child-like faces were now splashed on the front page of The Performer at the end of 1925.

Renée, George, Billie, and Jim felt the same mixture of curiosity, excitement and fear that anyone who lives in the capital for a length of time acquires. Somewhere homely to stay makes a difference. Arriving at King' Cross that first gloomy morning, their taxi took them to Dalston and the sordid-looking houses splattered with rain and mud proved to be a sprawl more marked than Glasgow. The taxi pulled up outside their digs and Renée read the number of the house 124 - thrilled because '1'2'4' were lucky, adding up to 7. 'We're quids in here,' she said to her sister, and naturally enough, the jolliest welcoming soul met them. Her real name was Emma but they called her Dulcie. As Cockney as they came, she never said anything that wasn't worthwhile and witty. ''Ave you bought me an haggis?' Dulcie blurted out, 'because if you 'ave you can eat it yourselves!' Billie thought they might be moving in with Nell Gwynne, but their landlady's heart of gold shone. She would run herself off her feet searching for digs for any poor artiste she couldn't accommodate, like the troupe of Chinese acrobats she traipsed out in the rain for. Returning soaked to the skin, she laughed and winked at Billie with a 'Blimey, it must 'ave been raining!'

The distance between their digs and the Shoreditch Empire was minor. A short tram ride was possible but it was easily walked. They stayed at Dalston all the time they were not touring before the family established a home at the end of March 1926. Dulcie was a 'mother' to both girls and George. When the sisters did late night cabaret she waited up until 3 am so that they got a hot supper. A couple of years later when they played the Hackney Empire she came to see them each night arraigned in a new dress and hat. George and Billie's husband met her at the stage door with a kiss and she would accuse them of flirting with her. At the Alexandra Theatre Stoke Newington, in early 1935, Dulcie turned up glammed to the nines yet again but the next day saw the Shettleston girls grief-stricken, discovering their beloved ex-landlady had been knocked down by a motorcar outside the theatre.

In the early days in London her parents came to visit. Renée described how Daddy Jimmie, looking out of the window of a cab at the names *'Renée and Billie Houston'* up in lights at the Coliseum, exclaimed 'Gawd Hen, w'hav ye done?' A similar story has Renée and her sister getting off the tram at Covent Garden and standing like waifs marvelling at the white letters, although the lights weren't on at the time. In reality no tram took you direct to Covent Garden in early 1926. They would have taken tram number 81 from Dalston to Theobalds Road for an afternoon trek to the West End. 8 minus 1 is the magic number for one crazy about numerology. Renée said 'if I pass a bus and it has the number 7 in it, adds up to 7 or is divisible by 7, I am lucky for the rest of the day.'[10] The number 7 tram at the time took you from Chingford Market to Victoria and Albert Docks, and our mystery-minded variety star must have given that trip a miss. How they glided through the vast unknown metropolis, getting off at Theobalds Road, before the interesting walk to St Martin's Lane through Holborn and Covent Garden! It wasn't long before they were urban sophisticates: Billie mastering routes through the capital in scout fashion, and Renée chewing gum and checking the shop-windows for ideas to spend her dough on.

In 1925 and 1926 some longed for a more modern-looking London and pitied poor 'Rima' - the controversial memorial in Hyde Park sculpted by Epstein - that got desecrated daily with paint and litter. Deviations in the landscape were seldom apparent. All the same it must have been sensational walking through London at the apex of its Edwardian grandeur with formality the governing force: baroque palaces in city centres and the unbroken lines of mansions in the suburbs. Looking up at each spectacular elevation from under your hat was awe-inspiring, if not dizzying. A sense of obedience had been drummed into each passer by and London's streets were a sea of grey. Anything different had a place – on the halls was one place - but certainly not in the open. It was a time when you were expected to say the right thing in many situations, or at least speak in the King's English. Regional accents were an oddity down south and by a lucky quirk, helped make the Houston girls special. Bubbling over with fun and chatter, Renée and Billie charmed not only members of the crew backstage at the Coliseum, but housewives, shop folk and taxi drivers. Many people thought Renée was half her age. At this time her enthusiasm was so immense it could be embarrassing. She wanted to tell the world she had arrived.

Clothes were formal and you seldom saw anything similar to the dishevelled-looking lines and forgiving stretchiness typical of London fashion nowadays. On the one hand, the sway that formality held over appearance was constraining, but on the other, clothing equalled flirtation on a grand scale. Next to our age of scantiness the way folk covered up during the first five decades of the 20th Century created a charge in energy nationwide. Greater sexual freedom has snubbed that out with today's low energy jeans and T-shirts quite a bore. 20s fashion tried to cry out against the sea of grey. The geometric patterns on facings might look crazy, but the little tube dresses on women could look ravishing if their figure allowed it. In the finest chic Sauchiehall Street had to offer and carrying some crisp air of the Highlands about her, Renée looked brighter and more interesting than many of the young women she passed as she and Billie bobbed up and down the streets. She wore her clothes well, liked a shock of colour, ditzy necklaces, and hats with little cherries falling from one side. Billie's florals sat awkwardly on her soft frame, but soon she emerged as the epitome of feminine chic with her understated sports dresses.

For stage outfits, it was no good looking like wooden heroines from 'The School Friend' with Sir Oswald Stoll to impress. Once they were regulars at London's Coliseum and Alhambra the 'look' of the Sisters became sharper, and their hair was subjected to the most advanced primping and waving technology would allow. Renée would claim she made many of their kids' clothes herself, like the velvet pants with criss cross straps Billie wore, and her little baby dresses that showed the back of her panties. Her dress typically had a huge Peter Pan collar and Billie's shirt and dungarees were often cut in coordinated gingham in vivid colours that seized attention. Their socks were the crispest white. At the beginning the Sisters were careful not to tamper with the way their trusted brand was packaged, although later on variation in style and pattern was ok. They harnessed the power of the singular and recognizable image, just as Chaplin made his *Tramp* iconic.

A simple note beneath their billing summed up their act: '*Renée: A precocious child, Billie: A fine little fellow, Conductor GA Balharrie*' and when they appeared they were met with cries of 'aaah' - strange given the fact Renée was in her mid-twenties. People believed they were real children and rushed to see them before they grew up.[11] Countless comments in reviews stand as evidence to this youthful illusion, most prevalent being the phrase 'clever youngsters' refering to the Houstons. Renée joked that callboys took them for a child act too, and that the taxman ignored them, believing they were too young to pay tax. A seemingly harmless old lady called *Auntie* got into their dressing room at the Coliseum, telling the stage doorkeeper she was a friend. They found her touching at first with her bags of sweets and thoughts for their welfare. Then, as her visits became frequent and the presents became weirder, such as the tiny pinafore for Renée, *Auntie* proved a pain – especially the time she got Billie up on the dressing table and commenced to wash her knees. They had to break off. *Auntie* invited them to an afternoon tea party and oldest guest was no more than twelve. The Sisters took it in their stride. It might be pure coincidence, but perhaps the 'lady' Renée refers to in her ancient memoirs was PL Clark – a famous turn billed as *Auntie: a gate, a bike and a gamp*. Clark had done his turn since 1922, appearing with Marie Lloyd's company. He later appeared by Royal Command. If the sisters weren't aware of this and *Auntie* was one and the same, it's an odd affair all round: the Sisters' mistaken ages and identities on one hand, and the mistaken identity of *Auntie* on the other.

Notice for PL Clark "Auntie" (Artwork by author)

Renée never lost her girlish appearance or skinny legs. In a film the Sisters made, released in 1936, her shepherdess bonnet, ringlets and short dress puts me in mind of Lautrec's lithograph of May Belfort, who famously sang 'Daddy wouldn't buy me a bow-wow.'[12] Surprisingly, it wasn't until the time the sisters were in their revue *More Dam Things* in 1935 that they dropped the kiddy outfits with Renée doing her stuff in long flowing robes and Billie strutting about in the latest cut in men's evening wear. Renée's outfit for the film 'Variety' that same year is brash and a complete departure from her little girl image. Before then there were occasional opportunities for Renée to wear outlandish outfits, her costume with a distinct 'hiatus' in it being one.[13] As merits anyone with a passion for infinite variety, her hair adopted different shades at different times. Her son Alan told me that whilst his mother was a blonde for a movie she was making in the early 1930s, she needed to be a redhead for her cabaret appearance and instead of a using a hairdresser or high quality wig, improvised with a bottle of red ink.

Fellow variety acts from 1926 (Artworks by Author)

Left: Balliol and Merton

Centre: Radiana

Right: Gaston and Andre

When the Houston Sisters first played the Coliseum on January 18, 1926, the other acts billed included Robb Wilton in *The Magistrate*, Shistl's Wonderettes, Cecilia Loftus, and Radiana *'the electrical mystery'*. *The Honeymoon* - a playlet about a couple arriving at a hotel only to end up in a domestic quarrel followed the Houstons. The last spot was Cato Pallenberg's 'Merry-Making Bears' that rode bicycles, roller-skated and performed other tricks. Speaking of Lautrec, the Houston Sisters followed *A Fantastic Dream* performed by Loïe Fuller's Ballet Fatastique. She first created a sensation at the Folies Bergère with her serpentine *Danse du Lys* in 1892: swirling costumes dazzling under iridescent lighting. Her stage lighting had been inspired by the nuances of the rose window at Notre Dame falling on her handkerchief. She inspired evocations by American artist Joseph Cornell when he made his series of conceptual 'boxes'. Sadly, the use of electrical devices in her act had damaged Loïe's eyesight and, in huge dark glasses, she was a curious sight to the Glasgow girls. It wasn't the *fashionista* look we know today. An extra page enclosed in your evening's programme about *A Fantastic Dream* described how witches put children to sleep but their guardian angel hovers over them so when they dream they and are carried to the moon where creatures of steel and light meet them.

What naughty smiles must have come on people's faces when those earthbound children with Glaswegian accents came on the stage straight after. Renée and Billie's turn at the Coliseum caused The Performer[14] to opine that their 'rendering of the American rag 'Brown Eyes' and their original burlesque of the *'Toy Drum Major'* were their best items' and 'The Houston Sisters are all that the critics have said.'[15] The Stage concluded 'there can be little doubt that they have a bright future before them.'[16]

Perhaps in the Houston Sisters, Sir Oswald Stoll saw something of his mother, who long before had trod the boards as one of the three Hardcastle Sisters. In 1925 Stoll dedicated a monument to his mother Adelaide in a room off the lobby at the London Coliseum. Dublin-born, she had been a force in shaping his career. Talented and business-minded she travelled from Australia, remarried the owner of the Liverpool Parthenon, and on his death, ran this hall as well as others. By 1917 this modern equivalent of Tiberius and Livia Drusilla controlled over ten theatres in London: the Coliseum and the London Alhambra foremost in importance. They turned a healthy profit and legend has it that in a little room above the box office, Stoll would be watching and counting every customer issued with a receipt. He even had a curious little wooden balcony built for spying on the box office. He enjoyed nothing less than comparing his own figures with those the cashier had produced. He counted the pennies even putting signs up in every dressing room saying: 'Do not ask for complimentary tickets. If your friends won't pay to see you, who will?'

Renée and Billie were solid gold with their ability to draw crowds to that Roman-themed music hall with its fearful gilt charioteer ready to fly down from the gods. Its comfortable dressing rooms had *'SPQR'* on the carpets. There were classical key motif of friezes along the upper walls and benches had small sphinxes carved on their armrests. As you passed through its doors and saw the Romano-Edwardian mosaics of graceful muses on the lyre, lute or organ, it felt more than just a music hall and retained the ethic of 'improvement' by music, comedy and variety entertainment. The temple to the planetary gods by architect Frank Matcham had tremendous acoustics. People witnessed Bernhardt, arms extended, bleating out her *Phedre* with vocal rise and fall. That was after Stoll promised she would not be placed before or after any animal acts. Here, Stoll compèred the Royal Variety Performance in July 1919, with Elgar conducting. He genuinely loved ballet, helping the troubled Diaghilev troupe when they came here in 1918. The rake, perfect for ballet, is still considered superior to many theatres.

A colonnade sculpture at the base of one of the marble staircases - a sphinx-like creature with a handlebar moustache is a quirky dig on tee-totalling Sir Oswald. A deferential joke was ok but he was a shrewd operator, known to be strict with his performers, especially comedians. Renée said how in the 20s, they referred to the Coliseum as 'the Cathedral' and you wouldn't dare say a word out of place. Brash American Sophie Tucker, astonished to find her suggestive lyrics being cut, quipped: 'Mr Stoll, you shouldn't be the manager of a Vaudeville Theatre, you should be a bishop!'[17]

Nevertheless, he inspired loyalty among the leading stars. George Robey, for example, declined a higher offer of pay from Sir Alfred Butt, staying for another season at Stoll's Alhambra. Marie Lloyd never appeared at the London Coliseum, but she did accept an invitation from Stoll to appear in an *Old Time Music Hall* show at the Alhambra before she died in 1922. Stoll might have been a traditionalist but he didn't make enemies. He genuinely loved variety and any interesting act that stayed within the realm of decency. The Futurist Marinetti came in June 1914 with his *Noises* reflecting the rush and hurry of the world today and Layton and Johnstone, the talented black artistes brought syncopated singing to the Coliseum. Any song that appealed to the heart got Stoll's vote. He had written songs himself, and was said to have been in love with Vesta Tilley as a youth. Vesta, on her retirement at the

Coliseum in June 1922, received a book containing a million of her admirers' signatures: a tribute for all she had done for England.

The Coliseum by day, its auditorium and 'Stoll' staircase statue (Photos: Author's collection)

The Coliseum's technological innovations - a stage with steel cantilevers capable of a triple revolve and an interior railway powered off the tram system, heightened your expectations. Acquatic wonders inside a towering glass and gilt column beside the lift transfixed you as you ascended. The Coliseum was the first theatre in the city to have a modern electric lift and one of its salvaged gates is on display in a room in today's theatre. You took your seat and gazed at the cupola, and your 2¾ hours entertainment was second to none. You were immersed in music with the orchestra playing symphonies and oratorios in the intermission. There was tea afterwards, in the balcony tearooms, or on the bright and airy terrace, or in the roof garden.

The Houston Sisters returned a couple of weeks later causing The Billboard to report 'Houston Sisters Stop London Coliseum Program Dead' and that the two Scottish girls had 'jumped right into a stellar position.' After dates in Nottingham and Plymouth the Sisters were back at the Coliseum and took part in a charity night to raise money for the Wireless for Hospitals Fund. Billy Merson, Gillie Potter, and Elsie Carlisle were also among those who performed in this special Jewish appeal.

Cabaret appearances in London paid well and George Barclay got them a stream of these. On March 8, Renée and Billie made their debut in at the Cosmo Club at 33 Wardour Street. It hosted two performances at 9.15 pm and 11.15 pm. It had recently enjoyed an American night with club attendants got up as as New York policemen and pageboys as miniature 'Uncle Sams' or bootleggers. One of the two house bands specialized in Tango music and individual dancers graced the floor. The *'Hippodrome Eight'* were an attraction with their pony dance. Marie Lloyd Junior, performing some of her mother's best-known numbers, was another in the evening's lineup.

Back at the Coliseum the Houston Sisters first shared billing with Gracie Fields at a Variety Artists Benevolent Fund Gala on March 28, 1926, although they could have met prior to this. Interestingly, the top hat Dan Leno wore in his last appearance at the old Tivoli, and Dan's silver snuffbox, previously bought by Irving and later owned by Seymour Hicks, were among the items in a charity auction. Twenty-two years after Dan's death a talismanic status was attached to the possessions of this tragic star of whom they used to say if it rained: 'It's the angels crying with laughter at Dan.'

By March the Houston family was living in leafy West Kensington. The Encore, a witty theatrical weekly, asked jokingly if the Houstons had engaged Lyons to cater for their housewarming, believing every Scotch act attended. Binkie had come down to the Smoke to become their permanent dresser. The move was inevitable. Transport mattered to Jimmie. In Shettleston he was close to a station. From their new home - 43 Elsham Road - he could walk to the underground at Holland Park easily and there were many trams and buses. The house, at the junction of Holland Road and Lower Addison Gardens, was a safe bet for Renée in numerological terms, and suited a family of respectable theatrical entertainers. Always rented, never owned, it was their latest stopping place. When I trotted off to find the house, unaware of the house number change and becoming bewildered, I felt a surge of energy discovering a sentence scrawled on somebody's front wall in Holland Road. It said: 'Being happy makes you live longer' - a message from Miss Houston, perhaps? The Houston house still stands - an end house that lacks a garden, except for a large front terrace, and lacks off the road car parking. It's now number 29, and has since been converted into flats.

Elsham Road (Miranda Brooke)

You wonder if any tears were shed when maw and paw Houston sold up everything in Scotland. Practical-minded, their strongest tie was to their family and it mattered not if they found themselves in Scotland or England. Jimmie, for all his Scots comedy credentials, thought of himself as Irish. The Houston family had been frugal in terms of possessions. Suddenly money was talked about - multiplied on a scale nobody was used to. Lizzi was cautious and although the respectable neighbourhood appealed to her, she was modest about affluence and sentimental about her tatty pedal harmonium. This still outshone the brand new Bechstein piano the girls bought her: the £350 model that came with a delicious yellow lacquer finish. There was a car each for Jim and George - one a huge and gleaming Crossley Tourer, with room to seat all three Houston Sisters, Binkie and other friends, and there was enough material wealth to see the house quickly furnished and chic-looking with the latest in 1920s gadgets. The girls were earning at the least £600.00 per week - an astonishing sum equivalent to about

£15,000.00 today. They sampled the good things in life, brushing up against spending power's perilous nature.

Wasn't it intoxicating – all this earning potential? It might have been, but I can say decidedly that in the Houston home, you couldn't put a price on a good plate of porridge. 'We tried six cooks since settling down in London but none of them could make a good broth or anything resembling porridge,'[18] wrote Miss Houston, indicating that Lizzi was still 'parked' in the kitchen, fetching milk from their front terrace hole-in-the-ground, joined by Granny for tea in the basement kitchen. They were like nativity figurines around baby Trevor, the latest recruit to the family in his crib in the underbelly of that generously proportioned house. It was a smart alternative to Shettleston Road: its ground floor encased in white stucco. Nevertheless, it didn't take long for Renée and Billie to find fault, wishing for grander things as they got George to take the roadster the classier route via Holland Villas Road, taking in its stately mansions before he garaged the car. The nearby streets had a village feel and they were only ten minutes walk to Shepherd's Bush Green, handy for the Empire. It's curious to think of the Houstons uprooted from Glasgow and relocated in Shepherd's Bush and I've no doubt that feelings about the huge city were mixed.

They always got on with their job whatever stood in the way. They carried on in Dublin back in 1914, and when Glasgow city centre was awash with demonstrators in 1919. They knew they were blessed to have found success, and while sympathetic to others, didn't align themselves with any cause that might adversely affect business. The Sisters had returned fresh from engagements in Belfast and Blackpool when the General Strike happened and you would have had to be totally out of touch not to know the struggles facing the country's miners - a workforce numbering about a million.

The coal industry was the largest employer, with a league of caddish mine-owners at the top, resistant to providing better conditions and modern equipment, and threatening wage cuts and increases in working hours. In Glasgow in 1921, miners were silenced by machine gun carrying English marines and the British Army's Highland regiments maintained a policing presence. Blacklisting happened and emigration to distant New Zealand was the dread of rebel Scottish miners. A 'Black Watch,' guarding the pits during strikes, represented a law unto itself on different sides at different times.[19]

Prior to 1926, miners' strikes had been averted by government subsidies, but this went out the window when influential bankers persuaded Stanley Baldwin's Conservative government to go on the Gold Standard. Parity between the pound and the gold reserves was supposed to boost Britain's international trade position. Winston Churchill, then at the Exchequer, was featured in an early form of fake photo[20] with the Chancellor behind a grocer's shop counter where no one has the capacity to afford the prices. Churchill initially disliked the strategy of bankers such as Montague Norman who claimed the action would make money representative. JM Keynes was also strongly against it. Whatever good the Gold Standard did, it made exports expensive and upped the price of coal. To cope, mine-owners sought to reduce costs. Grinding deflation was the outcome and the National Government abandoned it in 1931.

On Tuesday May 4, 1926, the Trades Union Congress called a General Strike and railwaymen, transport workers, dockers, builders, iron, steel and utilities workers - amounting to a fifth of the adult male population - all stayed off work to support the miners. The printers joined so no newspapers were published. A special anti-strike newspaper, the 'British Gazette' was immediately circulated: caddish Henry 'Chips' Channon at the helm. The Prince of Wales, fearing Communists were behind the strike, lent his car and chauffeur to transport the 'British Gazette' to Wales. The strike bitterly divided opinion: the Roman Catholic Church declaring it 'a sin' and Labour leader Ramsey MacDonald refusing to support it. Oswald Mosley - a Keynesian, backed it, paying the costs of a 'Strike Bulletin' in Birmingham and donating £500 to the miners.[21] In South Wales, Nye Bevan distributed strike pay, and his future wife to be, Jennie Lee, organized provisions.

Men who worked that week faced angry-looking thugs at street corners in Elephant and Castle and New Cross, and jobbing theatricals commanded scant respect from these surly onlookers. If you drove cars during the ten days in May, you did so at your peril. Either you didn't dare or you went to the TUC headquarters at Eccleston Square to obtain a TUC permit. Lewis Casson, who later ran Equity, drove Socialist leaders to their meetings putting a permit on his car's windscreen. Casson and his wife Sybil Thorndike tried their best to carry on their production of 'St Joan.' They might lean towards Socialism but the strike was slaughtering them, as it did all West End players.[22] Foul-mouthed Eccleston Square officials refused Jim Houston's request, as the Houstons' rep, for a TUC permit and he would have thumped the official 'if London hadn't civilized his behaviour by then.'

That week the Houston Sisters were appearing conjointly at two or more theatres per night, including the Coliseum and the South London Palace of Varieties.[23] Getting nowhere at the TUC, Jim's big idea was to grab a large Coliseum playbill, paste it on the windscreen of his car and take a back street route, relying on the Sisters' appeal to ensure passage through the crowds. On a bright summer evening, they crossed Waterloo Bridge - their playbill as subtle as a brick through a window - and as they got down to Lambeth, the highway was blocked by hundreds of yobbish men and women. A missile bombardment was expected any moment and there were worrying shouts of 'Where's the Owston Sisters?' and 'There they are! That's em!'

Tensions rose but these highly paid economic migrants weren't dragged out of their conveyance. Nor did they have their limbs torn apart by an angry mob if this story is to be believed. The loudest voice in the throng of strikers roared out a gravelly 'Hello kids, wotcheer!' With this encouragement, irresistible Renée stuck her head out with a 'Ow are yer ducks? . . . Come and see us at Souf London!' With smiles all round from fans, the car drove safely through. It seems the muse of comedy with a common touch won over the muse of violence. Jim wrote of the 'transformation' from 'threatening mob into 'the most warm-hearted gathering in world.'[24] Their playbill tactics worked but apparently the trick produced awful results when copied by other pros. The strike ended within ten days: the miners starved into submission. Thousands of Londoners had to foot it to work in the days after the strike walking miles from the suburbs. The country returned to normal.

So where next for the Houston Sisters? The answer was to throw on a mantilla and Spanish shawl and present yourself to the public as a bouncing señorita with señor *Bill* - your tongue in cheek adorer. 'Picador', a Lawrence Wright number evocative of castanets and cloaked villains, was introduced into the act, parodying a current craze for Spanish shawls. They wired Lawrence Wright Music Co. with a 'Picador Huge Success Houston Sisters.' The Era wrote how, in this high falutin number, 'their flair for discovering the ludicrous romantic notions of today finds full scope,' and was played with 'serious intensity until their sense of humour overcame the effort.' Like delirious troubadours in a modern Al Khazar, they closed with this at the mighty Alhambra Theatre between May 17 and 21.

The London Alhambra (Author's Collection)

The London Alhambra stood where the Odeon Cinema currently stands in Leicester Square. Five gleaming domes each topped with a shining Tengrian crescent stood proud, arousing no other emotions other than mirth: emblematic as they were of creative expression. The crescents, there since 1857, turned graceful sideways glances away from the saucy French Can Can dancers of 1870 and the Thuringian giantess in silver cuirass. They were happy to let the young man in the flying trapeze be dashing, and to allow pioneering cinematographer Robert William Paul film variety acts in a little studio on the theatre's roof in the 1890s. It was a beautiful theatre. It had dark grilled woodwork alternating with sections of oriental tiles, with peaceful indoor fountains and alabaster columns predating Leighton House's zonana. Stoll acquired it in January 1916. Soon after, revues, Russian Ballet and smash hits like *The Bing Boys Are Here* were staged. In April 1922 Stoll returned it to thrice-daily variety and it enjoyed a decade of tremendous profitability. Performance times were 3.30 pm, 6.10 pm, 8.45 pm.

Renée and Billie's first visit to the Alhambra offered a chance for them to have a feel for the theatre, before returning for their Royal Command Performance in aid of the Variety Artistes Benevolent Fund on May 27, 1926. They also appeared at the Cosmo, their favourite cabaret venue, on May 23, giving their vocal chords a good old work out with 'Picador', 'Ukelele Baby', 'Smile all the While', 'Waited For You' and 'Wait til Tomorrow Night.'

On the morning of Thursday May 27, 1926, while sharp essences of lavender and violet filled the air at 43 Elsham Road, a mad Renée tore hell for imperial leather up to the bathroom only to find Billie, cool and detached as ever, giving Hamish Houston, the family's dark haired Scottie dog, a gorgeous bath. If everyone was going to the Royal Performance then Hamish was too, Billie said, oblivious to Renée's rage. 'That little pig has been at my bath salts again and hasn't left a drop,' screamed her sister so all Kensington could hear, and as she exploded Lizzi froze her with a 'Have you no sense of decency? Your language gets worse every day.' Ignoring her, Renée yelled 'I'll teach her a lesson' but Granny stopped her, preventing the bath salts war getting dirtier: 'Don't bother, ma bairn. Ye promised ye wid fix ma feather boa for me the nicht, and if ye get yersel' all excited ye'll no please the King.' All of a sudden their father appeared, sighing with sarcasm, 'The charming Houston Sisters at home,' and Hamish began shimmying, getting everyone wet in the process. Billie's next task was to tie a red, white and blue ribbon around Hamish's neck, which soon got chewed up.

Lizzi, Granny, ten year-old Shirley, and Daddy Jimmie decked themselves up to the nines, the latter resplendent in *Command socks*. Jim rushed in at 5.15 pm to tell Renée: 'You and Bill can leave it to me, all right - the new car is a pip! I can drive her great. I can even back out.' Billie met his keenness with a blank look. If you believe the stories, arrival at the Alhambra for the Royal Performance was not before a series of Mack Sennett-like traffic mishaps, as Jim escorted the Houston Sisters to Leicester Square.

A group of London theatre worthies stood in the Alhambra's foyer. The boxes, decorated with roses and carnations, were ready for the royals. The recent strike had threatened to disorganize the Performance but these men were calm and immaculate in their evening suits. The wife of the secretary of the VABF fund had worked the embroidery of the silk brocade outer covers encasing programmes presented to the royals. This performance would raise £3600 and Stoll didn't take a penny. Their Majesties, accompanied by Princess Mary and Viscount Lascelles were greeted by Stoll and took their seats, the audience standing. After the National Anthem, came an overture 'March Great Big David,' and the first of the twelve acts - the John Tiller girls

– followed, outfitted in Saxe-blue. The Queen was observed to enjoy Dick Henderson's chatter enormously. He sang 'A Little White Rose.' Then Robb Wilton, renowned for his facial by-play and expressive hand gestures, performed *The Magistrate*. Lillian Burgiss, wearing a Spanish shawl, sang 'Tomorrow Morning,' then Jack Hylton's band followed with a string of upbeat hits. Their encore number, 'Collegiate,' allowed the boys to introduce a burlesque of the schoolroom. During the interval the Alhambra orchestra under George M Saker's direction played Myddleton's *'Rose'*. Conn Kenna's *funny airman* act, complete with a hybrid aeroplane, opened the second act, and Carr and Parr did a novelty dance. Jack Carr had been in the Eight Lancashire Lads along with Charlie Chaplin.

Daddy Jimmie and the family had seats in the dress circle bang next door to the royal box, but Hamish's hopes were dashed when he was refused entrance. Hamish had adopted the girls after they played the Palace, Plymouth that February, following them to the station and leaping into the train with them. He loved Billie most of all. Daddy went backstage to deposit him in their dressing room. Undemonstrative as ever, he looked at his girls in their drum-major costumes saying: 'Now do your best, or I'll skelp the pair o' ye when ye get hame.' Renée started crying only to be reminded by cool-headed Billie to keep the act down to ten minutes only, 'or you'll get something to cry for.' The callboy rushed upstairs with a 'Come along Houston Sisters please,' and the girls began to quake.

Variety act into film: Left: Cartoon by Ernest Cralford, January 1926 (The British Library)
Right: Scene from the lost film 'Happy Days Are Here Again' (Aherne Family)

On stage the magical Bransby Williams got roars of applause for his impersonations of *Wilkins Micawber*, *Tony Weller* and *Dan'l Peggotty*. He was something of a good fairy to Renée and Billie. In Dublin in 1914, in the dressing room of the Theatre Royal Hippodrome, little Rina and Cissie had enacted a private drama before his eyes, unaware their antics were observed. 'They'll be stars yet or my name isn't Bransby Williams,' he had said to their parents. And here they were, twelve years later, following him at the Alhambra.

Before they were on, Renée stood at the wings invoking the aid of Saint Anthony, then caught *Bill* laughing at her, which seemed to sober her up a little. George played their opening music and she bounded on from stage right: rapid-fire in the midst of chattering. Billie followed from the rear of the stage. Queen Mary opened her programme – 'Now who are these two,' the gold tassel of its cover unfurling on her dove-grey gown. It read *'The Houston Sisters: Billie – a splendid little fellow, Renee – Billie's naughty playmate.'* Their effervescent sibling rivalry had Renée telling stories and goading Bill before they quickly went into their little 'Susie' number. *Bill*'s authority seemed to win the day and after *'Toy Drum Major,'* the applause for their little turn was so sustained that Billy Bennett's introductory music was still being played before it ceased. Rich Hayes, the 'Lazy Juggler,' closed the entertainment with his *Robinson Crusoe*-themed skit.

Afterwards, in their dressing room, Hamish went crazy when family and friends filled the room. Granny Houston's verdict counted most. 'Well Gran?' Renée asked with a look pleading for approval, but the *Duchess* looked at her with a faraway look in her eyes. All the magic for this former washerwoman came courtesy of the royal box, separated from them by just a balustrade: 'Well, my hen . . . little did I imagine when I was a wee lassie that some day I'd sit in company with the Queen,' she told her. Surely it was a coincidence that Granny was outfitted in a grey cloak lined with pink satin, exactly the same as the Queen. It was too much for Granny, for whom kings and queens were beings apart, holy in their significance. She made no comment regarding the two weans.

At the Scala, on the Ayrshire coast, on the night of the Command Performance, Harry Kemp rigged up loudspeakers with cut outs of the Sisters on stage. When Renée mentioned 'Saltcoats ' in her patter the crowd went mad, and when the Houstons visited two months later every inch of street space was packed with fans. The girls waved and Renée could be counted on as always for a speech. The Houston Sisters never forgot the loyal residents of these holiday towns, even if London was now home. They made an *Annual Scottish Visit* each year, usually in mid July, and played theatres at the invitation of Ben Popplewell, Harry Kemp and others.

These weeks offered the nearest thing to a holiday during the years 1926 to 1930. In London their schedule was manic with a bit of breathing space during provincial tours that were sadly never particularly long. London loved them, especially the Coliseum, the Alhambra and the Victoria Palace: first, second, and third in terms of the most appearances they made.

For the big London theatres each day's work meant two evening performances sometimes with a matinee. They often did 'turn working,' combining suburban theatres with central London engagements. If you add the midnight nightclub cabarets, the amount of appearances could rise to seven per day. It seems like nothing with each performance only fifteen to twenty-two minutes a time, totalling less than two hours in a day. However, they were endlessly producing their brand of vitality, arriving on time, dealing with management, dressing and waiting to go on. The hours of frantic car travel from one venue to another add up. Returning to the same place again on the same night wasn't unusual. Turn working would die out in the early 30s, surviving in those working in cine-variety a little longer. Busy schedules in London with interludes of provincial touring characterized the years of Renée and Billie's stage partnership. Jim Houston describes how his sisters were lucky if they got away with a sixteen-hour working day. They made light of the daily stress of leaping into action from the wings. They had the youth and manic energy to cope. A lifestyle of being forever 'on the go' has long-term repercussions. When are you ever settled? Family members tell me Renée and Billie's love of an audience sustained them.

Tracking the Sisters' movements using press reports and old programmes, I counted about two hundred and fifty separate theatre engagements for 1926-1930. Each booking varied between two and six days in duration. Of course these are only those theatre bookings I've found evidence for. The figure might be much higher. I counted seventy-four separate venues in this period but more could easily exist. The image below shows the quantity of bookings they had specific to each of their top ten theatres between 1926 and 1930. I based it on the amount of separate engagements at each of these 'top ten' venues I have found evidence for.

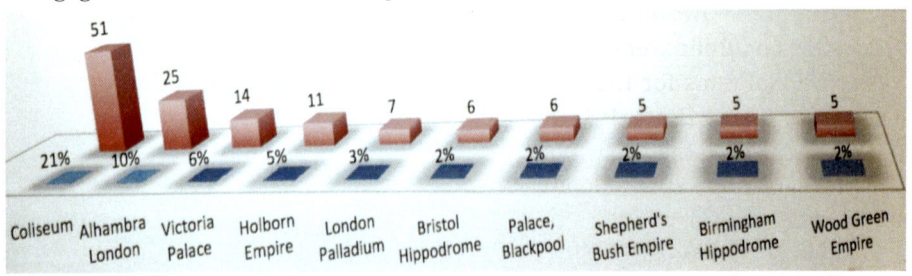

Houston Sisters number of bookings at 'top ten' theatres between 1926 and 1930 **(red)**
Appearances at this theatre between 1926 and 1930 as a percentage of ALL bookings **(blue)**

Quality counted, not the length of time on stage. The most tricky bit of all was being sure to deliver gags, songs and dances in a short and sweet time, leaving 'em laughing. Overrunning was looked at very badly by the turns that followed, and the manager might give you an unfavourable report.[25]

Speed characterized the modern world in 1926 – and with all these mad variety people on the road it was only prudent London should install its first traffic lights that year at Piccadilly. Roads were clearer in the evenings compared to now, although these vintage streets weren't safe given that the roads doubled as racetracks for *Bright Young Things* in the evenings. The denizens of Birdcage Walk were even privileged enough to catch a glimpse of thrill-seekers like Jim Houston racing cars alongside St James's Park.

In the 20s, Jim was considered something of a ne'er do well. Too much of the Houston Sisters' earnings that went to Lizzi got funnelled through to Jim. Some in the family say the proceeds were spent on wine, women and song. Renée's future husband Pat Aherne told his sons he'd seen Jim roll up a ten bob note - a lot of money in those days – setting light to it, simply to get a light for his cigar. Lizzi had taken to heart all her son had endured at school, blaming herself and excusing what Jim did, whatever it was. When favouritism blinded her to Jim's excesses, it hastened an alliance between the Sisters against Jim. For a while he was the butt of their jokes, and in moments of united sarcasm they would declare to each other he was living not only with them but 'off' them. Jim crumbled when luxuries and privilege came his way whereas living on his wits with no comforts had brought out his ingenious and visionary qualities. Born in very modest surroundings at 15 Buchanan Street, Johnstone, he couldn't hack the crowd-pleasing nature of performing. Recovering from war wounds, he made a few appearances in some of his family's shows but resisted such a career. He always listened to his conscience. In the 1921 coal strike he signed up with England's National Defense Force Battalion but quickly regretted it. Not wanting to be sent across the Irish Sea to kill Irishmen, he got himself a passage to Montreal where he worked in hostels, as a lumberjack, as a commercial artist and in dairy and cattle farms. In Fort Saskatchewan he toiled with a young American known as 'Yank' - a runaway student. Years later he met him again, when Captain Clark Gable of the US Eighth Army's Air Force patted him on the back at a showbiz party and said 'Remember me?'

Renée and Billie were used to being in front of the camera having been in promotional films for the Rothesay players and those made at Saltcoats to advertise *Scotch Broth*. In October 1926 they made a cinematic short in an installment of Pathé's long-running cine magazine series. When you visited the cinema in the 20s you were likely to see one of these shorts preceding or following the main feature. 'A Match Or Two - Two Little Tricks By The Houston Sisters' was the focus of 'Eve's Film Review' – the cinema short that might give you a mini-documentary, describe hobbies and jobs for women, or amuse with *Felix the Cat*, or *Sammy and Sausage*.[26] Several variety stars were invited to the Pathé Periodical Department's top floor studio in Wardour Street to be directed by Fred Watts, who also created the amusing inter-titles. In 'Eve's Film Review No.280', Billie does a couple of match tricks: one match sticks to one cup then the other, and one nozzles a coin when lit before it slowly leans upwards for 'The passionate kiss!' Renée, with hideous cupid bow lips is all gushing admiration whilst *Bill* is only interested in demonstrating, as that's what boys do. They provide little elements of their stage act, popping their heads through curtains smiling and full of beans, then entering the performing space. *Bill* swaggers and Renée hops around like a monkey to suggest their trademark personalities.

In 1955, part of the original 'A Match Or Two' short was included in a special film made by Pathé called 'This was Yesterday: a reminiscence of our times.' Produced by Howard Thomas and Terry Ashwood, images of 'our glamorous yesterdays' flickered on the screen to the commentary of Edward Ward: his distinctive voice well known to cinema audiences. For the showing, a crowd of celebrities including Janette Scott gathered in Oxford

Street. Renée wasn't present at this exercise in nostalgia. Howard Thomas, once been a great pal of hers, doesn't seem to have invited her.

The 'Eve's Film Review' short was widely distributed in cinemas, unlike the next one Renée and Billie made in December 1926. This was a De Forest Phonofilm and their film might only have been seen at one theatre - in Southsea, near Portsmouth. Seeing a Phonofilm was an entrancing experience limited to lucky folk who lived near a picture house rigged up with the equipment that made such exhibition possible. Only about thirty cinemas in Britain exhibited De Forest Phonofilms and had equipment necessary to do so. They were always located in the provinces and suburbs, never the centre – the reason for this being the 'distance' law that used to govern variety stars.[27] The Victoria Hall was a massive cinema that stood at the southern end of Commercial Road until 1960. As early as 1900, the hall was witnessing cinematic spectaculars. Entrepreneur Arthur Andrews had his early silent film 'Our Navy' booked here for a three-week run, with a running commentary delivered from the side of the screen by former Navy man Harry Coveney and proceeds going to a sailors' fund. In January 1927 the intriguingly named Nazi Jackson, sang 'Am I wasting my time on you' in his Phonofilm at Victoria Hall. I wonder if the Houstons, fresh from the *nursery* with their baby voices, made as big a hit with the nautical audience, or were they wasting their time too? When their film was exhibited, the local advert went: 'Enormous Attraction exclusive to the Victoria Hall - *The World Famous Music Hall Artistes who recently played at the Hippodrome, The Houston Sisters in De Forest Phonofilms, Films that Talk, Films That sing.*'[28] It supported 'Spanish Passion,' the main feature – 'a *Thrilling Story of Love and Hate'* starring Hungarian vamp Lya de Putti.

Their picture, simply entitled 'The Houston Sisters,' when projected on to the screen, looked square, not rectangular, and that was if all went well. 10% of the De Forest films didn't work when they were shown. Ideally, the moving images would be perfectly synchronized to the sound. Occasionally these didn't match up and one can imagine the titters if the crosstalk of Renée and Billie was out of synch. The equipment was standardized in 1928. One hundred and seventy miles to the west another Phonofilm mecca was at Millbay Drill hall, Prospect Place, Plymouth. It boasted the world's largest screen converted for the purpose of showing Phonofilms. The Savoy in Burnley was another, featuring De Forest films of the Radio Franks, John Henry and Blossom in their *Lady Godiva* skit, and Dick Henderson. The latter provoked much laughter singing about the 'Straight banana'

MB Schlesinger, owner of a UK cinema chain, had taken over the Phonofilm Company by agreement with Lee De Forest. It had four producers: George Cooper, CC Calvert, Thomas Bentley and Miles Mander. Vivian van Damm took over from WJ Eliott as general manager. Cyril Elwell was their technical man. In the preceding ten years, De Forest had taken the latest innovations in recording electrical waveforms from a microphone, using cells on one side of the surface of the film, translating them back into sound waves when the movie was projected. He developed the photoelectric cell, replacing selenium cells.[29] De Forest had gravitated towards this field in Berlin, where discoveries regarding the transference of sound waves onto film came through research into television. One camera recorded picture and sound, although some accounts talk about two simultaneous cameras powered by one motor, with one designed to 'photograph the sound waves'. The Phonofilm process influenced the move to the Talkies even though De Forest struggled, as many of the best inventors do, losing out in terms of commercial gain where Fox Movietone and RCA Photophone succeeded.

De Forest, who was Bebe Daniels' second cousin, had produced numerous short films throughout the 20s but is best known for his technical genius. He had pioneered the radiotelephone process, transmitting the first ship-to-shore messages in 1907, and had given us the audion – a three element vacuum tube sensitive to the detection of electric oscillations - basically the thingummybob all radio, telephone, radar, television, and early forms of computers used for amplifying their signals in the days before transistors.

The Phonofilm featuring the Houstons was made in a cramped studio at Cranmer Court, Clapham. The prints were developed in the ladies' loo as it offered the best water supply. When the Sisters came here, their director was twenty-six year-old Widgey Newman. He had recently joined the company as assistant director to Lee De Forest on 'Bleak House' (1926) and probably didn't take credit for 'The Houston Sisters.' His second film as principal director had Nervo and Knox performing their song 'The Love of Phtohtenese.'[30] Widgey directed two hundred sound-on-films, later forming his own production company with his wife Joan, a director in her own right, and specialized in films to do with sport and animals in the 30s.[31] Being a musical short, Renée and Billie performed songs, possibly their latest 'Susie' song, interwoven with a quarrel in a neat turn of about eight minutes. The date is a little early for Billie's sailor burlesque. They probably didn't know their little film was to be shown in a naval town. If they had, they might have done something suitably nautical.

Many of the hundred and fifty Phonofilms at the BFI record music hall performances. Sir Oswald Stoll had one of the biggest collections and allowed thirty-eight to be printed. Some were sold privately as 16 mm films. The Houston Phonofilm got re-released as 'Musical Medley No. 5' in December 1932: part of the six-part 'Musical Medleys' series. Some of the six parts have gone astray, including the one with Renée and Billie. I am waiting to find out if it might survive in a private collection. Since the original sound-on-film was barely shown, with the Victoria Hall having an exclusive on it, a copy of the original might also be languishing in an attic in Southsea.

Chapter 8   Identities to Play With

With talent and personality any comedy pairing works. It might be Pete and Dud, Eric and Ernie, or French and Saunders, or a man and a woman team like Burns and Allen. The Houston Sisters were a combination of comedy act, sister act, kiddy act, 'man' and woman team, and singing act. They contrasted well in looks and behaviour and had characters complex and unexpected.

Sisters who sing are ancient and modern, in every culture and continent: a tradition that in the last century travelled from variety theatre to Pop. America had the Boswell Sisters, Lennon Sisters, Pointer Sisters, Bangles, Heart and Dixie Chicks and you could start your list with the seven Sutherland Sisters who sang Scotch songs in Niagara County New York in the 1860s before finding the freak value of their Rapunzel length tresses a better money-spinner. Britain has boasted the Beverleys and the Nolans among its sisters of song. The American Trix Sisters, and the Australian Pounds Sisters graced London's West End in the early 1920s. In syncopated renditions and impeccable harmonization, Renée and Billie had expertise similar to their tuneful contemporaries: the Brox Sisters – Lorayne, Bobbie and Patricia, the forgotten Donovan Sisters - Jayne and Kathryn, or megastars of the future, that fabulous trio the Andrews Sisters - LaVerne, Maxine and Patty. Some sang and played instruments like the accordion: the Hyde Sisters and Langtry Sisters are two from 1933. The Norman Sisters, famous in 1927, could sing, play violin and dance, but there's no indication they were funny.

Many lady siblings trained in music, song, dance and patter have turned up since, scattered across the western hemisphere. They left a mark on Britain's culture, achieved international fame, and sang to us from radios, bringing us hope and joy during the Second World War, and through the big-band era. Some survived for decades, others no longer than a year. The majority worked hard on those harmonies and seamless performances. Nobody minded if it later emerged some sister acts weren't siblings, although the majority were sisters.

Kiddy acts aren't common, whether they are real kiddies or adults acting the parts. In Britain, Jimmy Clitheroe and Janette Krankee are two of the most famous - surprisingly long-lived. American vaudeville had notable kiddy acts: Louise Hovick and sister *Baby June* were *Just Kids.* They worked between 1918 and 1924 with Louise doing solo burlesque later on as Gypsy Rose Lee. Fanny Brice, although she worked alone most of the time, had an alter ego *Baby Snooks* who exchanged patter with sensible children like the young Judy Garland. There had been several little boy and girl acts in British variety but the Houstons paved the way for more. The juvenile-looking Hale Sisters, around 1928-1929, were a chip off the old block.

Sisters who cross-talked could already be found on the variety circuit. Might it be that *James Houston and Company* shared the bill with the Parsons family once famous in the North of England? The daddy of the family was Barnaby Parsons, a gifted humorist. Mother Eleanor was a contralto vocalist and there were seven little lasses as well as two lads. The lasses, active from 1911, were described as the first female cross patter comedy team[1] and might have inspired Renée and Billie.

Throughout the years of their fame, the Houston Sisters produced a comic act quite distinct from their closest rivals in the popularity stakes. Cockney kids Ethel Revnell and Gracie West *'the Long and the Short of it'* wore gingham dresses similar to the *Irresistibles* around the same time. However, in their case, endearing weirdness was remembered instead of childlike beauty. The East End team Elsie and Doris Waters, sisters of Jack Warner, cross-talked with ease but didn't quarrel. Renée and Billie's number one rival when they made it big in London was the young American duo Dollie and Billie, who could effortlessly turn out the perfect *boy* and *girl* in a nursery scene, sassy city girls next, then glamazons. An instant success after they appeared at the Chiswick Empire a week before Christmas 1919 you could be forgiven for confusing these two with the *Irresistibles* as you read about their 'delightful fooling . . . daring at times . . . carried off with joyous abandon,' and the decided freshness 'in their singing, dancing and patter.'[2] Dollie and Billie were decked out in feathers for the number 'Steppin in Society.' They pipped their Scots counterparts to the post with their hit record 'We Keep Them Guessing' and their silent film comedy 'We Women' directed by WP Kellino in 1925. These versatile flappers strayed far too close to the Houston patch to be trusted.

Left to right: Dollie and Billie, Right: Ella Shields, Walter de Frece and Vesta Tilley (Author's Collection)

Renée and Billie would have gladly expunged Dollie and Billie leaving them in variety's no man's land given half a chance. Perhaps they did, as the American duo disappeared following an appearance at the Coliseum in 1927. They might have been too sugary to last. It was the homegrown style and idiom that came so natural to Renée and Billie that touched the souls of audiences in the late 20s.

Sister acts are as varied and iridescent as the wings of butterflies. Some featured amazing acrobatic techniques such as the Austin Sisters, whose contortions created a stir at the Victoria Palace in 1927. There were dancing figurines like the Dolly Sisters with a reputation for glamour and for collecting admirers. Might the Houstons be compared to the Dale Sisters of 1933: *'an act with Progressive Ideas'*? Probably not, and neither did they have a string of pet dogs and monkeys to perform with, like the Johnny Sisters of 1935. The Houstons were dynamic. They could be a duo or a trio, when accompanied by Shirley, who incidentally did have a pet monkey.

Sisters who cross dress come from a long tradition, on both sides of the Atlantic. In the 1880s, one of the earliest to strike it big were the US-born Sisters Richmond who dressed in boys' clothes as they sang about the Richmond cigarette imported from America, or dispensed sugary tunes like 'My Nellie's Blue Eyes', or 'Pretty as a Butterfly.' May-Lilian, Carlotta, and Adèle: the three Levey Sisters, who appeared in 'Red Riding Hood' at the Princes Theatre Manchester, had been famous since the 1890s for doing their *march song* dressed in identical men's dinner suits.

Women wearing breeches is traditional to pantomime. In 1913 the Reeve Sisters: Mabel and Hester, younger sisters of internationally famous Ada Reeve, did their first panto at Leeds. Described as the 'little dainty boy and girl who sing so sweetly,' they were still successful six years on, dubbed 'the Ideal Boy and Girl' in *Dick Whittington*. Similarly *Boy Blue*, *Robinson Crusoe*, *Jack and Jill* and *Tom Tom* were part of the evolution of the Houstons whose dynamism made a writer look back at past sister acts and admit that they stood out: 'Admirer as I was of the Sisters Leamar, the Watson Sisters, three Sisters Hawthorne - *the Mashers*, or any of the others, I think that the Houston Sisters leave them in the far off shade.'[3]

Bill was the character Billie Houston created – one that had no peer. If other male impersonators were doing their stuff in the 20s and 30s, none were so acceptable. People sensed *Bill*'s intelligence, trustfulness and rationality. Bessie Bonehill - a male impersonator of the 1890s anticipated Billie, but her man about town seemed less trustful. *Bill*'s acceptance was enhanced by impeccable clobber. As Billie told a reporter 'My wardrobe includes lounge suits, evening dress, both dinner jacket and tails, sweaters, slacks, a wedding outfit complete with pearl grey waistcoat, stock and striped trousers, soldiers' uniforms, those of a private, an officer, full mess kit, sailor suits, Eton suits - Oh those Eton suits - I dread to think of the agonies endured by the youngsters who have to wear them.'[4] Renée joked about how conceited Billie was about her togs both on stage and off stage. Her sister would get sent an absurd amount of ties from fans including feminine ones. Someone sent her one with Scottie dogs on it to remind her of her own Scottie, causing her to remark: 'Have you ever seen a man wearing dogs all over his tie?' Times have changed, but back then, Billie understood authenticity, costume and lighting. She knew plain colour should not be too pale in case on stage it will look almost white. She knew a pattern that's too neat wouldn't show up at all.

With Vesta Tilley, Ella Shields, Hetty King and Billie Houston, gentlemanly chic was accompanied by gentlemanly behaviour. With both qualities scarcer nowadays, where does our current male impersonator go to channel them, or has she herself now appropriated them, needing no model? Where is the flawless English male dresser who was the best dressed in the world? This was a gentleman who was a slave to convention. In the 30s, such perfectly presented outward characteristics were still an almost sacred thing. A candid film on You Tube about Hetty King shows how the gentleman's wardrobe is

Identities to Play With

seen through the eyes of a male impersonator. It amounted to veneration in Hetty's case illustrating the values behind the clothes. At the time of Billie's greatest fame the internationally admired men she mirrored were the dashing Prince of Wales, who became her friend, and James John Walker, known as Jimmy Walker - Mayor of New York City 1926 to 1932, and a Democrat politician. Often seen in newspapers groomed to the limit in the latest in male chic, Walker was America's symbol of jazz age romanticism. While scandals of corruption and backhanders from businessmen surrounded him, he led men's fashion and was later portrayed in a film called 'Beau James' starring Bob Hope. Even in times of slump, the impeccable gentleman was a cult. Everything about him was founded on tradition. He wore a lounge-suit and a black felt hat to a function, and cutaway coat, sponge-bag trousers and topper to a garden party.

Images of Billie Houston in the early and mid 1930s (Author's Collection)

These clothes and the values '*Bill*' exemplified reflected an age in which the benchmarks for chic and beauty were harsher: when there was more attention to detail in clothes, and when a regal carriage, good posture and manners counted for more. Costuming was propelled into the realms of art and touched the deepest corners of the human psyche. The wearing of trousers by the classic male impersonator counted in terms of expressing breeding and civilization. Billie would hate the current American cult of the 'Drag King' in which impersonators hang out at comedy conventions, in San Francisco and elsewhere, competing with each other for the title of most aggressive persona or best facial hair. This was not the world of style that inspired Billie, who shared a tailor with the Prince of Wales.

A popular variety act absorbs qualities of the here and now. Times change and it can't work again, with so much tied to a time and a society. This shifting pattern happened with Vesta Tilley. The *London Idol* was the consummate male impersonator and was internationally famous. Ella Shields and Hetty King owed her a debt. Vesta's clothes were by Linney of Maddox street or from the Marquis of Angelsea's auctioned wardrobe. In starched 'olla boys' collar or top hat and tails she dressed with an 'ease and elegance no mere man ever aims to.'[5] After a visit to New York the dudes of

Broadway copied her pearl grey frock coat and silk hat. In the First World War her impersonation of the young Tommy 'combined pathos and patriotic appeal'[6] but Vesta and manager husband Walter de Frece 'realized it would not be possible to present the act as a living force in the post-war world' because of 'increased sophistication, and a wider knowledge of Freudian sophistication.'[7] An evolutionary cycle of male impersonation occurred, opening the stage up for Billie's sophistication, before extinction came.

Billie presented a fresh take on male impersonation for a modern audience. Vesta, Ella and Hetty did not cross into the Jazz Age and, whilst still famous, represent a distant time. Vesta had been a 'tightly rehearsed, non-spontaneous performer' in contrast to the jovial impromptu of the Houstons. Like Vesta, Billie presented favourable impressions of masculinity and the message transmitted about men was one of innocence. In the late Victorian age jibes were tender and full of humanity when Vesta sang of the 'pretensions of a poor little London chappie' in his humble place of work, 'saving up all his money for a week at Brighton where he can pass muster on the promenade as a masher.'[8] This was the skill of laughing *with* men, not *at* them. Despite her gruff voice Billie offered the gentlest parody of a young man and several notes in theatre programmes refer to *Bill* as 'pleasant-faced' or the 'beautiful blond boy'.

Everyone gladly accepted Billie as a boy. It was a deception everyone knew to be a deception. While the illusion required gesture, voice and a smart pair of trousers, nobody expected Billie to hide her woman's shape. This can be seen in the Pathé news footage from July 1932 at the Ace of Spades Roadhouse on Kingston Bypass. Billie's modern looking short coat hardly conceals her ample bust. Renée adds to the illusion of *Bill*'s maleness by her exaggerated femininity and baby voice.

Where *Bill* was famous for *his* fair hair, always short and elegantly combed, the most important thing in Vesta's theatrical make-up was her wig - a skullcap covered with short hair - that took an hour to fix. Twisting her own hair into tiny plaits and pinning these carefully around her head, this created the bulk that gave her head a masculine shape. Willie Clarkson, wigmaker and costumier to the stars, constructed it and in the last decade of his life he was a friend of Renée and Billie who visited his numerologically sound premises at 43 Wardour Street, where previous clients reputedly included Jack the Ripper, Ethel le Neve – mistress of Dr Crippen, and bright young intellectuals Horace de Vere Cole and Virginia Woolf.

Being Scottish and dour, *Bill* had a totally different personality to Vesta's *'Algy'* or other characters from her repertoire. In *Bill*'s case it was the same character every time audiences knew, admired, and sympathized with. Each year his male behaviour developed so that by 1935, when the Sisters were stars of Adrian Brunel's 'Variety', the level of perfection and attention to detail Billie instilled into the act is remarkable to see. She was at her peak in terms of mime and gesture, just as Vesta was before the Great War. Billie's naturalness and economy of movement amounted to genius. Little tricks of flicking ash, twitching a cuff and puffing a cigarette are a treat. She's the image of the Prince of Wales (soon to become King Edward VIII) with one hand elegantly placed in a pocket. She also says bucket-loads with her eyes. She can look disgusted but forgiving at the same time. She raises her eyes or looks aside in a manner impressively communicating her polite patience. It would be hard to see anyone do this with the same mastery. Visually, Billie was a studied genius at male impersonation in the 20s and 30s, channeling the spirit of the age into a peculiar and unique art form.

Billie was bang up to date for the radio age, and her singing voice was that of a velvet-voiced crooner in a sea of croonettes. Her singing contrasted with earlier male impersonators. Sara Maitland, in her book about Vesta, tells us she seldom used her speaking voice, going straight into ballads, and that Vesta never sang false bass, using her own treble.[9] At the Ace of Spades, Billie sings 'It's Great To Be In Love' - a hit for Ray Noble's orchestra in 1932 with Al Bowlly on vocals. It's so gravelly it's unhealthy. Thankfully, Billie's true singing voice wasn't like this. It was deep in timbre with a feminine edge, and snatches of it I've heard remind me of Barbara Dickson's beautiful rich contralto. I shudder at her use of the Louis Armstrong falsetto, something she would do, for the fun of it, as late as 1958. Along with her forty-a-day fag habit, this was just another thing poor Billie inflicted on herself, adding to her stack of health problems. She had to use an inhaler in order to breathe every day of her life from 1958 to 1972. So long had been spent over-extending her voice that, by the 1960s, her lungs had badly collapsed. In her prime some of the finest among Britain's musical establishment considered her voice to be a miracle. In late 1933 or 1934, the London Symphony Orchestra, conducted by Sir Henry Wood, performed with a solo baritone who would sing an aria from *Don Giovanni*. Billie Houston was that baritone. Sir Henry, an influential friend, suggested she would be ideal to sing the part for a performance at Kings Hall, Covent Garden, in the building where Evan's Supper Club used to stand.

Nellie Turner was a star of de Courville's *Zig-Zag* at London Hippodrome. She writes how the idea of women in trousers was still unacceptable in 1926 except on the stage: 'It is nice to wear trousers for a change. In pantomime, or on the stage, generally, is the only place a woman can legitimately wear the trousers without being in constant fear of being run in by police for masquerading as a man. It is nice to get your own back on the men!'[10] Her article concludes that 'the principal boy is always the hero': a comment that would have appealed to Billie Houston. Billie, in her day-to-day life, not only wore trousers but spoke like the next man.

Billie's voice was unique in the variety world - an unusual voice for a girl. 'There is nothing forced, unnatural or falsetto about it,' said Renée. 'Billie speaks just the same off the stage as on it. It is a blend of contralto and light baritone.'[11] Whereas Vesta Tilley's voice was female in essence, Billie's voice raised eyebrows especially combined with her cropped hair. It happened when she wasn't in stage clothes. It was impossible for some to detect she was a girl, and this led to piquant situations when she was mistaken for a female impersonator. In an interview back in 1925 Billie told a Scots reporter about a run in with the police in Greenock. 'A high official had seen our show,' she said, 'and the next day when Renée and I, both in our ordinary clothes, of course – were walking along the street, he stopped and said to me: "Do you know young man, that you can get into trouble for masquerading as a girl!" She added that he was serious, advising them in didactic terms, "It's all right for an advertisement, but you'd better not do it too often, I warn you." Billie tells the reporter that luckily other members of the company came along just then and were able to assure the officer that she really was a girl.[12] Writing in 1935, Renée pointed out 'Many a scrape that voice has got us into' and tells how her poor sister had 'found herself the subject of controversy in tube, train and tram.' Once, staying in digs, their landlady had a special aversion to men, taking lady boarders only. Entering the room when Billie was trying on a new suit, she looked as though she had seen an apparition. When Billie enquired what the matter was, she screamed 'Oot o' ma hoose. I'll no' have it. I winna ha'n any men in my establishment.' Too astonished to reply at first, Renée and Billie tried to explain but she would not listen. No amount of reasoning would alter the impression. Wearily, all four of their party collected their belongings and left.

   Once, the Houston Sisters played a theatre in the North of England a year or so prior to making it big in London. They shared a dressing room with two ladies. One of the ladies looked at *Bill* - sitting in her little velvet shorts, and said to Renée 'Do you mind asking your brother to retire while I change?' 'I'll ask him but I do not think he'll go,' replied Renée to the lady's surprise. Her next tactic was to ask *Bill* to leave directly. Sensing some fun, Billie replied in her manliest tone 'I don't see why I should. Nobody else asks me to leave while they are changing.' The lady started to boil into a rage: 'I don't care what anyone else does. I'm not changing while you're here. Go at once, or I'll fetch the manager.' *Bill* coolly lit a cigarette and shrugged at the threat. Before stalking out of the room the lady cried 'I don't know where you were brought up. You are the most impossible boy I've ever met in my life!' She returned with the manager who meekly tried to point out the truth: 'My dear! Don't you know who this is? This is Billie Houston, sister of Renée. Billie is a girl - just the same as Renée.' Things weren't pleasant after and a bad atmosphere entered that dressing room for the remainder of the night. Even press reporters were fooled, thinking *Bill* was a real boy, as the writings of one who witnessed *See You Later* testifies: 'They act and sing clearly and charmingly and the boy has a winning smile reminding one of an august personage so often seen on the screen.'[13]

   The male-sounding voice deceived onlookers despite the fact Billie was only 5 foot 1 inch tall. Renée, by the way, was 5 foot 4 inches. On stage height didn't matter and the theatrical illusion diminished only when they happened to stand next to someone tall, and *Bill* shrank to toy-like dimensions. The Houston Sisters soon got sick of the mistakes people would make about them, even though the infinite variety of mistakes was amusing. At the Coliseum, *Bill* was strutting along the stage with usual aplomb whilst a young couple sat near the stage. The man was trying to impress the woman and Lizzi Houston was seated near them. The man attempted to make out he knew the acts personally and stated chauvinistically to his girlfriend: 'They aren't sisters at all. They are really husband and wife.' In a voice loud enough for anyone to hear, Lizzi said 'If they are married to each other it is very strange, because they happen to be my daughters.'

Appearing in midnight cabaret at the Ace of Spades, Renée flirtatiously goads a disinterested *Bill*, pulling down a strap of her 30s bathing costume, hoping her pose for the cameraman will make *Bill* jealous. 'I hope that Pathé guy gets me when I'm looking cute,' she says. 'He'll wait up all night' quips Billie, eliciting much laughter. Billie was able to understate her performance as 'feed' to Renée's attention-grabbing character. Yet she could hold the floor with ripostes to her sister that were stinging. In a playful moment in one of their early interviews, Billie sums up her calling in life using a Wildean pun: 'Better be a 'he' than not a 'she' at all!' A little missile of retaliation came in Renée's sarcastic comment. 'Oh yes, Billie is a girl all right. *He*'s known to friends as *Cissie* for that is *his* name. We thought *Cissie* inappropriate for the work we do and we changed *his* name to Billie. Isn't she a nice boy?' Billie shuts her up with 'Stop that nonsense!'[14]

That audiences sustained acts like Renée and Billie for so long and let them craft their illusion to perfection is something worth pondering about. The Houston Sisters did nothing radical enough to appeal to somebody turning out a thesis in gender politics, and their song and dance brought no serious real-life issues into the comedy. The public wanted to laugh not cry. Man's role in relation to women was never questioned. Nevertheless, it was quarrelled over by Renée. Still, the Sisters fulfilled a need and were certainly unusual enough in their interplay that folk paid money to see them.

The Houston Sisters helped break new ground for women in their own way. They were part of the *'All Women Performance'* known as *'Eve's Week'* at the Victoria Palace between August 22 and 26, 1927, which according to The Performer, was the first time a London hall had composed such a bill. Produced by Jack Hayman, this 'Adamless Eden' hit the public's fancy and would be repeated for the next few summers. Present were Ella Shields, the Victoria Girls, dancer Myra Glen, and impersonator Ann Penn. Featuring in the *Eden* was American low comedy artist Dorothy Maughan, making her London debut, and the acrobatic Austin Sisters. The Sisters opened their act with Renée gagging anent the absence of men with enough doses of mock Cockney to make The Encore ask 'Who are the *Euston Sisters?*' They retired to big applause, the curtain fell, rose again, but the audience could still hear Renée and Billie arguing on stage. As the lights went up they realized it was only Ann Penn carrying on before she got to her other impersonations of Bea

Lillie and other famous women. The Four Falcory Sisters closed the show in a sensational high trapeze act that The Performer called 'a striking finish to a programme which was an unqualified triumph for the fair sex.'[15] Another critic observed that only in the case of the orchestra did we see 'Eve condescending to accept the help of Adam.' Ella's *Burlington Bertie* substituted, and Ann Penn put on Talbot O' Farrell's topper at a raffish tilt, and of course *Bill* donned the 'wee panties.' The Era at this time praised Billie for being so 'grave and reverend' a feed.

The voice came before the image, and Billie occasionally exploited the situation. In the 20s she seems to have had lots of fun with it as comments to reporters reveal. 'At dances I generally go in a dinner suit, and at the Glasgow Cinema Ball I was three times ordered off the floor because men can't dance together.' She added she was also 'ejected from the ladies' cloak-room.' In the same interview Billie takes pride in her deception, pointing out wistfully that 'It's always girls that fall in love with me, and I've got bundles of letters from love-sick girls all over the country. I've even known two girls in a company fall out over me till they discovered that I was one of their own sex.'[16] The problem of alarming levels of worship from females was one Billie shared with Vesta Tilly. My feeling is Billie enjoyed these gender games when she was young, even though family members tell me it is a mistake to believe Billie intentionally wanted to be androgynous.

Female cross-dressers might have believed she was breaking new ground for them, and you could forgive them for thinking they had a hero in Billie. However, she never really meant to make any statement about gender roles. The Houstons were popular because they represented a funny version of 'normality' – not a form of diversity. As Billie got older her stage persona became a legend. She preferred to remember the refined stagecraft of her act and had little time for anyone who employed cross-dressing for its own sake outside the theatre. She might admire marvellous technique, like that of Danny La Rue, but content mattered and I doubt the gags you hear in lesbian cabarets today would get her vote.

A typical press comment about male impersonation at the time might be that 'Hetty King gives us enjoyment because she imitates soldiers, sailors, tinkers and tailors, never ceasing to be a very charming woman.'[17] Peter Ackroyd might have had such comments in mind when he wrote that 'sexism is a major element in all forms of 'acceptable' transvestism' and that the female cross-dresser 'enhances the putative superiority of male culture.'[18] This observation might apply to 'Masher' type male impersonators like Fannie Leslie who seemed to validate the *jolly good boys* of the 19th Century, or Fanny Robina: an amusing mirror of male chauvinism. Hetty King's male impersonation was a more laddish and *rougher round the edges* type, in comparison to Billie's. Hetty - the last of the 'Mashers' - strutted alone on a stage. By contrast, Billie worked with Renée 99% of the time and the impact of their combined personalities created a different outcome. Whereas Hetty

Identities to Play With

King was a loner on stage – proud and never ridiculed, the Houston Sisters had the proud 'male' constantly challenged by the vain and neurotic female.

These male impersonators might have been patronizingly described as 'charming women' but the steadfastness, charm and honour they were impersonating has all but gone out the window in the 21st Century. Gone is the masculine refinement admired at the root of Billie's observation. For all the unfair double standards that existed and still exist, this must count as one *loss* in the modern rejection of a culture of 'male superiority.' Post Women's Lib we can't have Billie's type of male impersonation any more, perhaps because it shows men and paternalistic values in an honourable light, and this is considered too dreadful a thing to go back to.

There is nobody with Billie's skill for male impersonation now. For modern audiences her persona is cringe-worthy - a package less acceptable in today's formula-driven world than in what we like to think of as the *intolerant* 30s. The concept of 'maleness' piped out through the media in the 21st century has narrowed compared to the 30s. Now, society takes itself too seriously and male impersonation is the domain of males. There was a fashion in the gender-bending 80s for starkly suited women with cropped hair with Annie Lennox (an icon on and off the stage) epitomizing the look. The image was played for its shock-value and had a political message. The 80s trouser-suited fashionista was an angry rejection of the inoffensive light entertainment values Billie Houston stood for. There was no call for any lasting entertainment factor. 80s cropped hair and trouser-suits were passing things controlled by fashion, which has no soul: revived for a while in recent years and stubbed out again.

British male impersonation evolves in the 21st century in a non-theatrical way and moves into blurred territory. Outwardly feminine women work alongside male colleagues in tough boardrooms taking on gestures and behaviour we used to class as traditionally male. You might think the lower register voice has taken root with a move towards gender neutrality as you listen to the majority of women on television and radio. The higher register feminine voice seems to be thought unsuitable for informing us nowadays. Voices of TV and radio women veer between an insincere male pitch to share a laddish moment with a man, and a disingenuous feminine pitch if the situation arises.

If you stuck one of these women in an immaculate man's suit, put a cigarette in her hand with their other hand in a trouser pocket, you might have the rudiments of one half of a music hall act. Could they reproduce the refinements of a Billie Houston? To achieve such a thing, the bearing and psyche must be that of a young gentleman: upright in posture and character, with gestures commanding. Youthful, boyish, brother-like, virgin, idealistic, dour and stoic are adjectives to describe this persona. Authority and fairness are relevant. Add short hair, handsome visage and expressive eyes, and this completes a specification to give Dr Frankenstein. Someone mirroring Billie's approach would need to stay in pristine character with no chameleon-like crosses from male to female or gauche, laddish gestures. Such inconsistency wouldn't do in the music hall and would instantly *get the bird*.

There were blue innuendos from time to time, when Sir Oswald Stoll wasn't around. He wanted artistic and family-friendly entertainment. When Stoll wasn't hiring Renée and Billie they could be racy and do something provocative with the male and female dynamics. One cheekier Houston Sisters turn was *All Hands on Deck*. Introduced at Holborn Empire on March 24, 1930, the Sisters took their nautical item to Chiswick Empire, then the Coliseum, where both Renée and Billie were in masculine attire. What started as a burlesque of 'A Girl In Every Port' was developed to give *Bill* a new sexualized sailor identity flirting with 'girls of different nationalities, all amusingly hit off by Renée,' went The Stage.[19]

The *Irresistibles* fanned the sex war in their own way but their inconsequential battles had a comic relief quality in which neither sex gained superiority. Leicester Square Theatre saw the closing days of *All Hands on Deck* in 1933. It was the Sisters first visit to that seven-storey faience-clad building in the southwest corner of Leicester Square. It opened at the end of 1930 close by the faded Alhambra. Jack Buchanan had taken it over in 1933 with his Non-Stop Revels from 2 pm to midnight daily. It became the Odeon West End but after eighty-five years vanished from Leicester Square. When *All Hands on Deck* came here, the Sisters coped with the extra labour the trend for *continuous variety* required. At Holborn, a month earlier, in a stupendous lineup that included Naunton Wayne, Max Miller, and debonair pianist Hutch (Leslie Hutchinson), it had been far less gruelling.

Onstage Billie Houston was highlighting parts of her personality – the sensible, dour Scot. *Bill* was usually the one in the pair with whom sympathy lay. 'Billie's persona is not a pose,' her chatterbox sister would often say. Offstage, she was patient and down to earth but she had a side to her that wasn't dour. She was light-hearted and engaging. She was not an enigma. The producer Dabber Davis remembers Billie being great fun. Others tell me she was a softhearted feminine character who loved children and men.

Renée would say how 'The voice may be a bit unusual but *Bill*'s manliness ends there.' The studied boyishness contributed to her charm yet she was popular with the opposite sex, attracting clever men. She had three husbands - men who were very handsome. That Billie could be a genius at the craft of illusion on stage (nurturing a convincing masculine persona) and yet remain a charming feminine character off stage underlines the wonder of theatre. A French journalist was taken by Billie's beauty in 1929 writing how her large eyes were a 'spiritual china blue' and 'full of laughing grace,' so friendly that 'enemies melt in the presence of this urchin fair, with ruffled flaxen hair cut short, and her smile accentuating two charming dimples.' He writes of her voice, far too deep in register - a 'continual surprise with its rough inflections.'[20]

Identities to Play With

Billie made the best of nature's gift. It might have been odder had she tried to appear in a very feminine way. She trusted her instinct with a theatrical 'look' tailored expertly to her physique. From a young age she found it hard to accept any look that didn't suit her. I'm reminded of her stubbornness at the public appearance at the City Hall as a child star. You might think Billie a control freak in terms of perfectionism. In fact, she could be a trifle lazy - a quality targeted by Renée during impromptus on the stage. Having said that, when she left the stage, her view of her femininity met with certain exacting standards and her hair was the prime example. She coloured it herself and never changed her Eton-crop as the decades rolled by. She was uncomfortable if it grew a centimetre longer than her usual short crop.

The real Billie valued femininity and deportment. She sent her daughter to ballet classes considering it would be good for her. She dressed untheatrically in her private life. I used to imagine that her stage image forced Billie to suppress her girly and frivolous side. I was wrong. She was never fluffy and frivolous: qualities that were opposite to how she saw herself. She tells us: 'though I have been on the stage since I was a child of 10, and during that time I have never appeared in anything but men's or boy's clothes, I take a great interest in my feminine wardrobe in spite of that fact, or perhaps because of it. I am not, and never would be, the type to wear 'frilly' things. I prefer a heavy silk kimono to a lace negligee, a tailored frock to a ruffled organdie blouse, but apart from the sense of freedom that a pair of slacks gives you when you are taking a 'day off', I have no wish to emulate my stage appearances in my private life.'[21] Her daughter agrees that she steered clear of all artifice and anything frivolous. There is a picture of her in a satin negligee half-reclining on a sofa with her knees cheekily exposed. A caption reads 'Billie, off-duty, is as feminine in her love of 'pretties' as could be wished. She used to joke about the picture saying that this was one of her 'pretending' to be a girl.' Situations requiring *pretend* outfits were thankfully few. While she wore trousers as soon as these became fully acceptable for women in the 1930s, always preferring them to skirts in real life, she never cared to make any gender-bending statement, or draw attention to herself in her private life. She had a lifelong fear of the press.

In the late 20s she frequently wore fashionable tube dresses and sassy shoes, and looked slim and almost mannequin-like. In one photo from 1933 her large panda eyes, emphasized with masses of eyeliner, propel her out of the 30s, making her a dead ringer for a 60s model. She was happy with the way she looked. Family tell me that in the 60s there was an advertisement for Van Heusen shirts in a magazine - a classic type of man's shirt worn by a very pretty girl in the ad. This, more than anything else, summed up Billie's true style – where the masculine style emphasized her innate femininity. Those who knew her admired the understatement, and for suiting the subtle look as well as she did. 'In private life she is the most feminine of creatures' described her sister in the 30s.

Billie's daughter Carole remembers her as 'a fairly graceful type of person and aware of herself in the way that actresses often are.' Carole talked about her having a presence – the sense you get, when you've been used to making appearances from a young age. Billie's ideal look was a pared-down subtle femininity. I'm told she would have happily been perceived as Twiggy was in the late 60s, wearing one of those Tommy Nutter suits cut by Edward Sexton. She might have appropriated a version of this look in her private life, but this definitely wasn't the look she brought off on stage even though she wore her double-breasted suit with great style. Her build made that type of femininity difficult, and the overall Billie Houston package presented something too convincingly masculine where her stage character was concerned.

Renée and Billie were different characters and this made their exchanges unpredictable. Renée was the freer, chaotic type of artist. Billie was the voice of reason and practicality. Several stories told by Billie in mid 30s articles in the People's Journal are evidence for this. The outrageous streak she had in the 20s seems to have gone, leaving a shyer personality, subtle in her self-mockery. In these memoirs, Renée does 96% of the talking: her amusing accounts jumping chaotically in terms of subject and time. It's a surprise Billie got a chance to speak.

There's a marked different in story content if you compare Billie's stories to Renée's. What Billie finds interesting are accounts of two long car journeys, one south from Ayrshire around 1929 involving all kinds of mishaps and having to spend a night in a field. She tells another about when she was a solo driver. It's Billie's *Top Gear* analysis regarding problems with the carburetor, or her detailed telling of how she took safety precautions whilst another driver didn't, that she writes reams about. In another article she gives a detailed account of the harrowing flight she experienced in a sixteen-seater Napier airliner over the English Channel – an event recorded in the press that occurred on August 6, 1927.

The commercial air transport company Imperial Airways was hoping to start a service between Croydon and Deauville, dropping travellers on the beach outside the Casino. It enlisted celebrities including Jack Hylton, Enid Stamp Taylor, and Billie Houston to come aboard to increase publicity.

Billie arrives in Deauville 'that fearfully Ritzy French resort.'
The man next to her is Art Fowler, the ukulele wizard from *Shake Your Feet* at London Pavilion
From Vaudeville News, 22 October 1927
(By kind courtesy of University of Illinois Digital Newspaper Collection)

Somehow Imperial Airways didn't feel it worth the while to tell the guests about the perils of flying. It turned out that everyone's lives were in danger given the severe weather conditions. Only Billie and Major Brackley, the Imperial Airways inspector, maintained calm with the other guests stressed and horribly sick. I doubt Jack Hylton conducted the band outside the casino on arrival as had been the plan. Billie just falls short of putting on her aeronautical engineering hat. Her natural tendency was to display detailed knowledge and take an evidence-based approach to a story she might tell. There was no pointless musing or emotional asides where she was concerned. She was the sort who liked facts and had a passion for the British Museum. She innately thought through a situation rather like an Agatha Christie or a Graham Greene.

The British Library has an edition of Billie Houston's 273-page thriller 'Twice Round the Clock: a mystery novel' with a library stamp dated February 14, 1935. Published by Hutchinson & Co, each chapter is titled as a time segment like 'Half-Past Four to Half-Past Five.'[22] Little is said about the author in the foreword although it points out that *'few are not acquainted with the smiling, fair-haired boy.'* A man is murdered at a dinner party held in honour of his daughter at his lonely house. Telephone wires have been damaged and cars tampered with. For long hours the guests are cooped up together each aware his neighbour might be the murderer. In *Book 1* the action starts at 4 pm *the day before* and in *Book 2* the action ends at 4 pm *on the second day*. The Prologue starts on the second day at 4 am. The immediate serialization of the novel in the Daily Sketch indicates Billie's fame and public appeal in early 1935.[23]

Theatrical papers were less ready to admit Billie had a literary gift. The Era's book reviewer praises Billie's 'unlimited talent' on stage, but regrets to say 'I do not feel so charmed by Billie as a novelist.' He describes her thriller as conventional and has a less than lenient attitude to her literary efforts saying 'Miss Houston has some ability for peppy dialogue, but a murder story . . . cannot survive on peppy 'cracks' alone.' He ends on a patronizing note that must have annoyed the author. 'I look forward eagerly, however' he says 'to seeing once again Billie with Renée behind the footlights.'[24]

I enjoyed 'Twice Round the Clock' not least for the novelty of reading a detective story – something I confess I hardly ever do. The action hinges on the discovery of a special type of gas - the effect of which can be exactly timed and predicted. There's a risk that the discovery will end up in German hands. The undercurrents of patriotism and Anglo-German rivalry in 'Twice Round the Clock' anticipates films like 'The Lady Vanishes' and 'Night Train to Munich.' Provincial newspapers said they hoped the novel would be filmed, with Billie in the lead role. 'That would be 'a record for literature (are thrillers literature?)' the reviewer remarks, concluding the book is 'quick moving and exciting' and adding a 'Well done Billie 'Boy'!'[25]

Billie made her fictional male hero a '*Bill*' and uses the name of '*Brent*' as his surname. He's not a trained detective so that's an excuse for some of his actions like handling the corpse at the scene of the crime - hardly your typical police practice nowadays. A Renée-type character is absent from Billie's book. For once Billie has a platform free of all things Renée which must have been liberating. Billie channels many sides of herself into her characters. The '*Tony*' character might be a disguised Pat Aherne. The scene when the main characters are tied up contains a joke about the class system. The titled ladies are given pillows but not the maids. Music hall style jokes abound, for example: 'It's well-known that there are more screws loose in the House of Lords than in any other collection of men in the country.'[27]

I found the plot exciting but liked the dialogue most of all. It's cheeky and fast - on par with many a Houston Sisters sketch. It matches the pace of the novel. Reviewer comments such as 'the author has a gusto all of her own'[26] are apposite. The heroine is '*Kay Fane*, nineteen, Eton-cropped, too red-lipped, too saucy altogether about the face, and, making one think whenever one looked at her how much more piquantly attractive she might have been with her big crop of unruly curls which would have grown on her head if only she would let them.'[28] *Kay* is stroppy, willful but essentially very feminine. Using her eyes, *Kay* flirts with *Brent* even when bound and gagged. 'Phoo! Can the boy kiss?' is a later line. Another begins: 'Her eyes were filled with tears - One of the new detachable eyelashes - she explained, blinking hard.' Her status as daughter of a baronet doesn't wash. *Kay*'s a toff but she's more of a tough, so that's incongruous.

There are little statements about clothes acting as a camouflage and with the *Kay* character readers get snatches of the author's brand of femininity. *Kay* is assertive - often the one interrogating the fellow guests, and she dresses in extreme ways mostly to *spite* conservative-minded *Bill*. She's 'doing violence to her eyelids' and bleaching her crop just to see what he'll say about it. She will happily see him burn with a rage before she comes over fluffy and feminine to please him. Her object in life is to push boundaries but ultimately captivate her man. Still, the novel might be thought of as a continuation of the primeval Houston Sisters quarrel. There are plenty of lines like 'Can't I? Oho! We'll see. Just you wait. Just you wait, my lad!' *Kay*'s a riveting character – with the best lines in the book.

Billie's son says that if his mother continued writing throughout the time she was bed-bound in later years, she would have turned out some brilliant books.[29] Another career Billie could easily have followed was that of songwriter. She was a natural lyricist. She could sit down and invent words for a new song on the cuff. Literary identity was one thing. All the siblings had that. But who among the Gribbin kids was a better Christian soldier in the face of want and deprivation? This was Renée's calling.

Newspaper headline: 'Renée Houston gives birth to a son.'
Granny Houston: Dearie me! And to think I was nowhere near her.
Daddy Jimmie: (On the phone) What's all this I hear about ye having a son?

Identities to Play With

Renée: I adopted him in Belfast but I'm trying to kid the public he's my own.

This is a tale Renée told to her fans in 1936. The story was good for a few gags when she first went public ten years after her first adoption, safe in the knowledge that it wasn't worth anyone's effort to question her boldness. This version of the story has Mammy quietly passing out on reading the headline and Jimmie interrogating his audacious daughter. Then Renée refuses to let tiny Trevor, her baby, out of her sight, carrying him to the side of the stage while performing her next engagement. As the orchestra begins their overture she places the babe in the arms of the startled theatre manager, who is standing there in top hat and white tie. In her 1974 autobiography Renée briefly touches on the adoptions. By then she had dropped some of the screwball touches but not all. She loved to tell a good story. The *'grab 'em from the orphanage'* story of her adoptions is typical of the daredevil identity she played with. However, that's the comedienne and public person talking.

Poor Renée. The Christian act underlying the scenario she jokes about was sincere, but everyone nowadays seems to regard her motives concerning her adoptions negatively - family especially. Even in 2016 one still has to speculate as to the truth as the circumstances are cloaked in mystery.

As I immerse myself in the weekly comings and goings of the 20s variety world through the pages of The Encore, the latter's 'What The Encore Wants To Know' page is a nifty way of tracking gossip and discovering who the real 'characters' of the time were. That page ran throughout the years of the Houston Sisters' successes in London. Each week there is a jokey commentary freshly updated referring to performers, agents, audiences, topical subjects and in-jokes - often poised cryptically, so you have to guess what secret knowledge the roving reporter-in-the-know refers to. The Encore loved Renée but couldn't help but speculate about aspects of her private life outside the professional sphere. 'What The Encore Wants To Know' has a curious statement in its November 11 issue: 'Is Renée Houston's new name 'the lead-swinger'? Will she flirt with lumps of lead again? Does Eileen really think she's an angel face ... If the doctor hadn't a lot to answer for?'[30] I've no idea who Eileen is, and the comment is cryptic. Trevor Ivor Houston, born November 9, 1926, was the little boy in the crib in the basement at Elsham Road, although it takes another month for The Encore to make further comments: 'Is the Houston Museum not growing? What (do) they think of the latest specimen at home?' and 'How does Billie like being a fairy godmother?'[31]

Christmas Day had got out of hand given the distraction caused by a party for a peer requiring the Houston Sisters' presence as paid entertainment. You wonder if there was any time for a baby, given the packed diary with engagements at the Victoria Palace and the Coliseum between Christmas and New Year. However, New Year was all about Trevor, if you exclude letting a reporter come in to take a photo of Renée cradling her baby. Trevor was christened on Friday December 31, 1926, possibly at their local Catholic Church in St James's Gardens or at the Oratory. Everyone made a fuss of the baby. He was their lamb laid down in the manger. *Ivor* is a Norse word for 'Lord,' whilst *Trevor* can mean 'wise' and 'discreet'.

Billie, Renée and baby Trevor, Elsham Road, late 1926 (Artwork by Author)

'Whoever will give honour to one such little child in my name, gives honour to me'[32] is from the Gospels and explains why Renée adopted children. She was sensitive to the vulnerable. She shared the genuine hopes of all parents who adopt - to provide a home and not distinguish an adopted child from a biological child in terms of love and support. It was giving something back - changing a life using money she'd earned. Nomatter what applause greets you, it's not the same as coming to the aid of someone helpless. This was a true identity where Renée was concerned.

She was married to George when she adopted her first two children in 1926 and 1929. She obviously wanted kids and might initially have hoped it would happen with George. Sadly, it didn't prove possible. She decided to take the matter into her own hands. Trust The Encore to make a lurid suggestion about Renée and question George's paternity after only a couple of months had passed since Trevor came along! The Sisters had been less ubiquitous on the London stage in the interval. 'What The Encore Wants To Know - - How long the Houston Sisters took to celebrate Hogmanay? Who put the Hog in it?'[33] went the graceless gossip. They presumed Renée was Trevor's birth mother though.

The baby boy was adopted at three weeks, apparently in Belfast where the Sisters were appearing at the Hippodrome. The Irish News and Belfast Morning News describes the 'vociferous welcome' that greeted those *'Great Belfast Favourites'* remarking how these stars of 'no mean altitude' were better than ever and that bookings that week would be heavy.[34] In Renée's 1974 memoir she talks about an orphanage in Belfast that she went into on the spur of the moment, following a chat with her landlady. It was quite easy to do this just then. Billie, Binkie and George were out playing a few rounds of golf at the time. After Belfast, the Houston Sisters played the Palace Theatre Cork, topping the bill. They were also hostesses at a dance arranged in honour of their visit.[35] In total they were almost four weeks in Ireland.

Trevor was adopted just before the Adoption of Children Act came into force on January 1, 1927, making official registration subject to legal process in England and Wales thereafter. It was supposed to stop adoptions being carried out as financial transactions. Given the timing of Trevor's adoption, money is likely to have changed hands, as it did for many adoptions arranged privately. Northern Ireland did not bring in a similar system as England and Wales until 1931. Lizzi's name was recorded on Trevor's adoption certificate. There might be a plausible reason for this, as when the act came into force in England, Renée was still twenty-four. The 1927 law did not allow adoption 'under the age of twenty-five' so possibly Renée's mother was forced to step in as applicant. However, Lizzi was named legal guardian on the papers for a second child, Terry, in 1929, and Renée was twenty-seven by then. Legally, Renée was neither child's adoptive mother.

In the early summer of 1929, Renée adopted a little girl. She wasn't a baby, being almost four years old at the time of the adoption. She didn't like being given the name 'Terry.' Her original name was Mary Joan Teresa and Renée must have thought up the name 'Terry-Jo' from these, although the simpler 'Terry' was more frequently used. Shy as she was, you heard her insist 'my name is Mary Barry' to sympathetic listeners. Grace Mary Teresa Barry, a domestic servant had given birth to her baby on July 12 at Lambeth Hospital. The hospital itself was formed only three years earlier, from the workhouse and infirmary – the same place where Charlie Chaplin had been an inmate aged seven. When her birth was registered in August, the father of the little girl was unnamed, and Grace's home was listed as 92 Tulse Hill, then a nursing home. Kelly's 1926 Directory for Dulwich and Tulse Hill lists this as 'Springfield Nursing Home' presided over by a matron called 'Miss Betts'.

Sometime after, the little girl was placed in an orphanage, ostensibly because her mother could not keep her. In later life, Renée's daughter Terry spoke with her daughters from her second marriage about her first memories. I am indebted to Terry's daughter, Terry Kay in the USA, and her son Patrick in the UK, both of whom have helped so much with their information and thoughtful insight. The mystery deepens as a flyer was kept from a fundraising performance - the occasion 'when Renée first saw mom.'

The Houston Sisters took part in a great many concerts for children's charities in the late 20s, as I describe in Chapter 10, and one *All-Star Concert* took place on Sunday April 21, 1929 at 8pm. It was in aid of the Southwark Catholic Rescue Society's Homes for Children. The other acts included Terry's Juveniles, Joe Termini, The Twelve Tiller Girls, Georgie Wood, Balliol & Merton, and Tex McLeod. The theatre programme survives and Little Mary Barry appears in a photograph within its pages. It was placed there for the purpose of publicity: showing nine 'exemplary' children selected from homes theatrically posed like child acrobats. At first I was inclined to believe that the photo was of Terry's Juveniles.[36] Today it would be unusual for real orphans to be pictured in a theatre programme. However, this was 1929 and it was a reasonable gimmick to 'sell' the charity. Interestingly, someone has annotated the page with an arrow pointing to the youngest child with the word 'Terry' printed to the side. This 'cute' photo, her daughters strongly believe, led Mary Barry to be 'chosen' by Renée, after the Houston Sisters appeared at the concert at the Holborn Empire. Previously, I had been under the impression Terry was adopted in 1928 when I read a suggestive comment in The Encore indicating Renée had a daughter: 'Hasn't Houston Junior a better command of the English language than many twice her size,' it said. That was in May 1928.

Most people feel glad to hear of an orphaned child finding a new home and family. But if that child's mother should still be alive but couldn't afford to keep her, or was coerced into parting with her, this becomes heartbreaking given our modern sensibilities. It opens up dialogues about ethics. What hell it was then for women put into situations when they had to give up their babies! A Magdalen home existed in nearby Streatham, with the 'moral reform of penitent inmates' its aim. It's tragic that Grace Barry had to place her child in a nearby orphanage[37] and a remarkable feat if she continued as a domestic servant, getting to see her baby here on rare occasions. Keeping her servant job is unlikely. Perfectly 'fit' mothers faced social stigma and hardship if they had a child out of wedlock, and this was often the reason for adoptions. If Grace was alive she would have had a hard time giving up her daughter, and 'Mary' would doubtless have been happier to remain an 'inmate' had her mother been able to visit occasionally.

The day of adoption was traumatic for the child, carried down the steps of the orphanage by a Father Joe. She cried bitterly when placed in Renée's arms and when she met her new family it was confusing and terrifying for her. Claire Silander, the Houston Sisters' friend and their brother's fiancé, was apparently present. Claire might even have liaised with the home on Renée's behalf, being active as she was in good causes. Claire's vague memory was that the child was handed over near Waterloo or London Bridge. This sounds like the HQ of the Southwark Catholic Rescue Society, then at Westminster Bridge.

Terry was never going to forget her first family although too much identification with her first home would naturally have been discouraged. She always hoped she could someday be reunited with someone from her first family and tried to find her birth mother and birth family herself, to no avail, in 1992. Her daughter then made enquires, writing to Claire Silander. Sadly Claire provided little information when she replied. Renée too, had never been clear at all about how she adopted Terry except for the 'flights of fancy' she would unhelpfully drop into conversation about Terry's father being Jewish. You can't fully rule this out. The theatrical world was a place where Christians and Jews mixed. Many theatricals who 'made it' lived in Tulse Hill and Brixton in the 1920s. Might a connection have existed between the Houstons and the home in which Grace worked as a servant?

Terry didn't start looking for her birth family until some years after Renée died. She and Renée last met in 1975, after a thirty-year separation, at which time Renée gave her pages from her precious cuttings scrapbook - perhaps a gesture of reconciliation and perhaps to ensure the programme for the *All-Star Concert* was in her possession. During all the years Terry was in the USA her letters to Renée had been very infrequent. She seemed to ignore Renée's enquiries as to whether Terry's kids knew about their 'grandmother in England.' Despite the 1975 meeting, Renée never replied to a letter Terry's daughter sent her later, seeking genealogy information on her natural grandmother. I have traced a couple of Grace Barrys who might have been Terry's mother - living in later times, at addresses in North London, but I can't make any worthwhile conclusion.

There are a few comments made by Renée regarding Trevor and Terry having the same mother that complicate matters. Given the far apart locations of the adoptions, this might best be ignored. In the 1936 'memoir' of her life up to that date, Renée makes a reference to Trevor's natural parents. She says Trevor's father had been killed in an accident three months before his birth and that his mother was tasked with earning her own living. Renée asked her friend if she could have him. Her 'delight knew no bounds when she agreed,' and Renée went ahead with the first adoption. Her decision was to pretend the baby was her very own. This story might be romanticism on her part but it's worth a mention what with the dearth of information. The story about Renée agreeing to take a friend's baby is one Elana Aherne also heard so it's probable in the case of Trevor.

If she acquired Trevor in Belfast it begs the question what friend in that city agreed to such a proposal? Could it have been one from the party of theatricals on the bill with the Houston Sisters - from the *'Company of Star Artistes'* at Belfast Hippodrome?[38] Later on, in a newspaper report from 1938, Renée changes tack, referring to 'Trevor Ivor and Terry Jo, whom I adopted when their mother, *my* best friend, died,'[39] bringing Terry into the story here. Her first mention of Terry's adoption was in a Radio Pictorial interview in October 1936. If Trevor and Terry were siblings and were the offspring of Renée's friend, the friend must have died or fallen into greater misery to be faced with abandoning her older child.

If that friend was Grace, Terry's mum, she was already a mother of a one year-old daughter when she gave up Trevor. She might have lived in Ireland or had some theatrical connection. She might have asked Renée's help knowing she couldn't support a new baby on the way, having a toddler already. They could have set it up so her baby arrived in Belfast, allowing Renée to adopt him from there. She might have worked as a domestic servant in London, struggling to keep in contact with her daughter. After this she might have died or lived a separate life. This is all conjecture. That Renée's best friend could be far removed from her on the social scale - working in service, is unlikely. I don't go out of my way to travel on these flights of fancy but the legend of Miss Houston sends me on them.

What about the other wonderful question: Was Renée Houston the birth mother of one or both of her 'adopted' children? AND, while we're there, were there other children she had given birth to who were never 'legitimized? 'No, no, no' – as Maggie Thatcher would say. Well 99% of me agrees with Maggie. This was an era of hiding things under the carpet, aided by inexact public records. For divas of film and theatre, speculation about mystery offspring is often their lot. It's ironic that attractiveness makes you more culpable. Would we make the same enquiry of a less attractive person? Renée's youth, showbiz glamour and financial independence produced a suspicion that she did as she pleased and never got into trouble, because rich people can buy themselves out of anything.

She was sporting a crinoline in November 1926 in a photo taken at a ball at the London Royal Opera House two weeks before she went to Belfast and there was that curious comment in The Encore about her flirting 'with lumps of lead' before she left. Trevor has some facial similarities to Renée' in photographs. The 1% of me admits that Trevor might have been her own baby and Belfast was somewhere to which she 'just went back to collect' to quote a line in Tom Gallacher's play. In *Renée Houston Rehearses Her Life - A Musical Play in Two Acts*, which Gallacher wrote in 1974, two of the characters gossip about Renée's adopted children. The playwright got most of his information from 'Don't Fence Me In' - the actress's book. It set him guessing on this subject, as it did other people including myself. Adoption paperwork does exist which throws water on this. In Terry's case, a birth mother is named but I was not told who Trevor's birth parents were.

The story of her collecting her own child from Belfast is a good story and furthers Miss Houston's mystique. Nothing though, could be gained by concealing a truth that she was Trevor's birth mother. Other famous women at the time like Dorothy L Sayers and Rebecca West had children outside marriage and adopted them to make them legitimate. In Dorothy L Sayers case she never admitted she was her child's mother but Rebecca West always admitted it. In Renée's case, she was married to George Balharrie in February 1925 so there was never a concern about 'legitimacy'. She always had a ring round her finger. This undermines the plot line about her adopting offspring from a time she was unmarried. There was never a need to spare her daughter's shame that drove Lizzi to name herself the children's legal guardian. The truth is Renée maintained she adopted Trevor and Terry all her life. She didn't lie to these two children, or conceal the existence of any other child.

I wondered about the possibility of Lizzi being party to the act of faith that brought these children into the family or even the initiator. Lizzi grew close to the little boy. She chose to leave Trevor the majority of her possessions when she died in 1943 – according to Renée's bankruptcy court records from 1948. Aged fifty-one when Trevor arrived, Lizzi was either appalled or glad to be a grandmother. She assumed a central role in the rearing of Trevor and later his sister Terry but this might only have been because she had no choice. The financial rewards Lizzi and Jimmie had stacked up over a decade and a half of putting on their own music hall act were meagre. They owed their security to their daughter. They had to fall in line. Members of Renée's family say, quite openly, that these children were dumped on Lizzi, who had to face the practicalities of her daughter's impetuous action.

In fact Lizzi was not entirely alone in terms of childrearing as nurses and various helpers were hired. George keenly played a role in the early lives of Trevor and his sister and was always nearby. It's impossible to tell how responsibility was shared. In accounts penned by Renée, placid George is forever excluded, except for her mention of his fear about a comeuppance back at the Houston home when she adopted Trevor. Two decades after George died she would allude to the fact that theirs wasn't a 'real' marriage. He was officially her husband though, so his paternity was assumed for both Trevor and Terry during the first seven years. Officially or unofficially they took his name 'Balharrie.' Pat Aherne married Renée at the end of 1932, and the adopted kids lived with them for a while at *'Well End Lodge'* - a remote farmhouse near Elstree with animals adding to the menage. After George died in 1939 Renée's adopted kids used the name 'Houston' and not 'Aherne'. Still, Pat did commit to family life, and Terry was said to be close to him, staying with him for a while when he moved to the States. Trevor used the name 'Balharrie' in the 50s when he married and later on.

I don't know why Renée didn't 'legally' adopt Trevor and Terry. If she put her name on the adoption papers it would have underlined her serious commitment. Mysteriously, she didn't do this. Her mother had legal responsibility although in practice it didn't make much difference to family life. It's possible that Renée didn't put her name on the papers to maintain 'privacy' for the kids' sake. These were not public adoptions – not for the first ten years. It's common now for famous people to allow their infants to be featured in press articles. Renée, by contrast, was very private about her children to the point of being mysterious. She never conceded to a press story until the kids were much older. Adoptions by famous people weren't subject then to the kind of public scrutiny we have today. If she had been open about adopting children at the beginning she would only have received praise. Renée didn't want a pat on the back for this and played down this part of her history.

Again, this leads me back to my argument that she was motivated by her Catholic faith in her decision to adopt – something strong in her identity. A lot of thought, planning and soul-searching might well have existed, on her part, and on George's. One should be cautious of the cynic who interprets her decision as a mere ego trip. Renée had a self-making principle, thinking money could change lives. Nowadays, property, cars and plastic surgery are priorities when people have serious money to spend. It was the priority of Renée Houston, however, at an early point of her career to improve the lot of someone needy. Many women in the theatre and in the film world adopt kids today despite hectic schedules. They do so usually when they are better established and often are quite public about it.

Renée was a provider *and* mother. In fact, many people were dependent on Renée – not just kids. She understood her role was for life and strove to provide a better home than the orphanage, although that's easier said than done. She wasn't an everyday mother. This was an identity she played with. Renée was in no position to look after children on a day-to-day basis. She had to be an absent mother with her constant workload. More of her time was spent entertaining us! I expect this is why family members talk about the 'act of largesse on Renée's part' when they refer to her adoptions. There was an impractical side to it - felt by all her children.

31 Northwick Circle, 1929:
Jimmie,
Granny Houston,
unidentified man,
Billie holding Scottie dog,
Trevor,
Marion Silander,
Claire Silander

(Photo: by kind permission of the Aherne Family)

Almost all their young lives, the two older children were surrounded by grown ups and older relatives. From 1933-36 their busy parents decided Trevor and Terry would be better off staying on with their grandparents and the rest of the clan at Northwick Circle. It was a home they knew and it saved uprooting them – even though they would move to Sudbury with the older relatives after a couple of years. In these houses Granny Houston resided - the voice of sense and always generous with attention. This was the matriarchal environment Renée had herself known and trusted. Pat and Renée needed to be close to the film studios. There was inadequate space in the house they chose to base themselves: at 41 Glendale Avenue in Edgware, thirteen miles to the northeast. The younger childrens' nanny and cook were based here. This arrangement led to the family separating into two groups. On a positive note, it didn't force George to suffer a change in status quo. For the two older kids, at eight and seven years of age, it must have felt sad to be excluded from Mum and Dad and the two youngest kids. Trevor never showed any sign of resenting Tony and Alan for the privilege. Renée and Pat re-united all four kids at their home in Stanmore later on. Alan told me the business of the adoptions was something the adults kept secret for a great many years[40] and he wasn't sure if Trevor was told he was adopted. Regarding this point, I don't think Renée would have let it be known to the press before telling Trevor. I expect she told him when he was nine or ten.[41]

What impact did the adoptions have and were they successful? One aspect of the Adoption of Children Act was that it ushered in a 'secrecy' connected with adoptions, so that the natural parent should know nothing about where the child was to be placed. In Trevor's case, being adopted into his new family so young, he had every chance of transitioning smoothly. He was a happy, smiling, very good-looking little boy, blessed with the tall gene that his brothers envied. Until he was in his thirties he blundered his way through life and in some ways was a bit of a *loose cannon*. The relationship between Trevor and his mother was a forgiving one all the same, and from the looks of it, survived the ups and downs. They remained fairly close. Terry, who had always known she hadn't been born into the family, was less happy. One of Renée's nephews in England feels his aunt didn't provide a loving home for these two children and a lot of people were shocked by the set up. The son and daughter from Terry's marriages in the USA have few stories to tell about their mother's life in England but the general impression of Renée from these years is that of a bossy, sometimes churlish adoptive mother – an area I shall explore in Chapter 17.

She had mood swings but I discount stories about her being physically abusive. Balancing home and career was going to be hard. The job she did and the lifestyle that came with it put pressure on her. The attention she gave was divided but Renée loved all her children and saw her wider family as a 'net' for sharing duties. When actions that come from a desire to do good backfire, we find ourselves saying 'we can but try'. Aware of Renée Houston's faults, I see her as somebody who did the wrong things for the right reasons - something I'm quite expert at myself so I have sympathy. Despite her faults she was a woman of faith. With her two eldest kids, roles were later reversed and mother became child, and got abandoned. And which self is the identity we should have been true to?

Chapter 9   The Artiste at his Work

Oh those Houston Sisters! Their joyous and unaffected act has more than a sparkle of genius. Last night the Palace audience clapped and stamped and shouted its approval. They were prepared to love the roguish Scots maiden with her tousled curls and her childish legs and ridiculously short frock, and they did . . . It was wholesome, utterly irresistible fun – we could see them every week and then want more![1]

A book by Rafael Sabatini was found among Renée's possessions. Her books tended to be romantic novels set in different times and places. In this one she would have made sense of strange rivalries within the Estates-General at the beginning of the French Revolution with a strange hero who changes sides like he changes socks. He confounds his enemies with eloquent oratory and swordsmanship. Actor he isn't, but his pose in a *Commedia dell' Arte* troupe as *Scaramouche* reveals how good he is at performing and writing - steering the troupe to dizzy heights. She would have grasped something in its opening line: *'he was born with a gift of laughter and a sense that the world was mad.'* I think of her full of the joys of *Scaramouche* ready to Fandango down the aisle to confound Billie, Binkie or anyone else on the train. Those train calls were a hoot for the three girls in the early days. Of course, they would deviously bag a compartment all to themselves. 'Have you got diphtheria?' said Renée loudly if a person dared enter the one they had occupied. 'My sister has diphtheria. It's terribly sad.' Worse blinders would be resorted to if that one didn't work.

The amount of transport required of the 20s music hall artiste in order to reach a wide audience is disturbing in its magnitude. Travel can be stressful, although Trainline tell you otherwise. Everyone in the profession toured. If a journey could be done in a few hours such as Brighton or Portsmouth from London, you took the car. If detailed provincial engagements were to be met then someone was needed to sort out the train calls, cars, and taxis. Jim Houston or George Balharrie did this for the Houston Sisters. The Midlands, North of England, and Scotland represented neat links in a chain in a typical theatrical tour. Stars shot up and down the country like mercury in a thermometer. The effort of playing theatres maddeningly far apart geographically marked out the dedication of the performer.

The reason why you couldn't escape a hefty amount of travelling in Renée and Billie's day was because variety was the nation's most popular entertainment and there was no television. Radio transmitters were new and limited. Travel got you out to your audience. You could do the same act for five consecutive weeks in different towns, as people wouldn't have heard it. Do it on the radio once, and it couldn't be done again. Touring could be intense in the 20s and 30s but how much you could do in a given time was limited by the speed of travel. Today, tours are more extensive. *Paul Merton and his Impro' Chums* had an impressive set of tour dates. I caught the show at Glasgow's King's Theatre. In the early days of the *'Comic Strip'* Jennifer

Saunders and Dawn French took in thirty-one theatres as they travelled Britain.

A copy of The Era from July 16, 1924 has the title 'Smoothing the Path of Theatrical Travel: How the L.N.E.R Helps *The Profession.*' With planning due for that autumn's provincial tour, the article tries to convince readers that the London and North East Railway could be relied upon as Britain's most enterprising and progressive railway group. The author addresses the theatrical profession's worry that ease and rapidity of transit is in jeopardy, given the amalgamation of the five principal railway companies of England and Scotland. Surprisingly, theatrical traffic had been coupled with that of the fish trade a generation or so before. The article cheerfully asserts that the ancient reproach of 'Fish and Actors' is now a distant memory. The 'amenities of present day railwaydom' by contrast, constitute a revelation to the 'old-timer' now that sumptuous railway stock, an amazing network of branch lines, express services, high quality restaurants and sleeping car services are available to him.

In fact, travel was something the 'old timers' took in their stride. They had been very close to fish, risking their lives on perilous sea voyages around the globe since Victorian times. In Vesta Tilley's day an annual tour of the provinces for six months was common. By the 20s, theatrical travel was well established with a range of luggage deals available. The modern L.N.E.R had its own theatrical traffic department at King's Cross to help with the planning of tours. The variety artiste found 'the heartiest of welcomes and more than one good friend' down King's Cross way.[2] Sad that the happy little office is now hard to find - somewhere near platform 8½ I expect. The traditional theatrical tour lives on and planning is a hectic business. Malcolm Rudland was musical director for Petula Clark's *Sound of Music.* He told me his experiences ranged from simple arrangements at seaside pier shows to transporting harps and other instruments by train - once even for a sixteen-piece orchestra. Artistes paid all their own expenses during the heyday of variety. If you weren't in the major league this was burdensome. In their young days the Houston Sisters boarded a train and sometimes weren't interested in smoothing the path of anyone's travel given their thoughtless pranks. Later, they turned cool and professional, using travel time to catch up on sleep or to produce material.

Joyce Critchley started in variety at a very young age as a dancer. While she was never with the Tiller Girls, she later joined the Mary Devere Dancers and the Annette Short girls. There were loads of touring companies by the 40s and they always went by train. Joyce recalls that members of one troupe had their own carriage - a label on the window naming their company, and performers generally didn't mix outside of this. Joyce never saw the Houston Sisters perform but knew of them. On one occasion she came into contact with them during a train call. She was in a compartment with eight girls and they were all singing and having a good time. The Houston party were next door in their own compartment trying to get some sleep but the girls never knew this, engaged as they were, in a right old sing song. All of a sudden a fearsome Renée Houston burst through the door of their compartment. They noticed she was carrying a huge bag of sweets. She threw it at them and said 'Have these and shut your bloody mouths!' I asked Joyce if the train travel involved was very tiring but Joyce said it wasn't. She thinks most performers enjoyed it. For others it could be an uncomfortable experience. Young Bruce Forsyth slept on the overhead luggage racks.

If you went to your local theatre on a night in the 20s and 30s there were usually seven or more acts playing. Advance warning about headline acts might be determined a fortnight earlier if you glanced at the tour listings in the theatrical press. Like planetary trajectories performers travelled to theatres of the land, returning to the same one six months after a full cycle. Week after week something new satisfied the most fastidious in the audience. Let's consider a night at London's Wood Green Empire – on the Stoll circuit following a 1912 takeover: an event that worried local Non-Conformist clergy (concerned with theatre-goers' moral health) enough to encourage a boycott. In 1918 Wood Green gained a reputation as *unlucky* for magicians when spectacle turned to tragedy. Chung Ling Soo's trick *Condemned to Death by the Boxers* backfired, and American William Elsworth Robinson (not really Chinese beneath his makeup) was killed before the audience's eyes. On a good day he deflected oncoming bullets with a china plate. In those pre-health and safety days, anything could happen and did. Some sources say his wife, who was his assistant on stage, killed him, after discovering he was having an affair!

Could an evening's entertainment be possessed of more human energy? Glancing at what your entry ticket bought you at Wood Green on March 21, 1928, you might see where I'm coming from. Appearing on this date is Bransby Williams - waxing about mystery plays in his wonderful speaking voice. Here are the Houston Sisters with a new gag, singing '*Are You Happy?*' Harry Claff rolls out his comedy novelty *The White Knight*, Rich and Galvin provide more laughs, and Victor Moreton sings humorous songs. The Flying Flacoris fly from the trapeze, Cornalla and Eddie do a humpsti-bumpsti act, and finally the Skating Nelsons close the bill showing they can do anything on roller skates. The old Wood Green Empire, now a Halifax, dreams silently about its past like many former theatres - a neutralized sleeping beauty.

Chung Ling Soo
(Author's Sketch)

Bransby Williams
(Author's Collection)

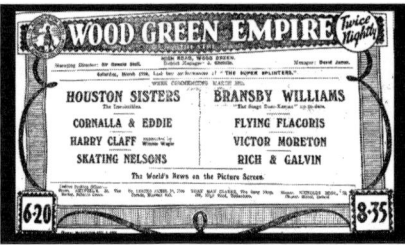

Advert for the Wood Green Empire
(Courtesy of Hornsey Historical Society)

The Artiste at his Work

Great variety acts are on the streets of London today. There's the human beat box and harmonium player who manages both in synch. There's the wiry spectacled unicyclist who takes his trousers off to the blaring music of Prokofiev. Both these acts grace Leicester Square and I half wonder if there's not some force that draws them here: a ruthless roofless Alhambra spirit. There's the drummer on the pavement outside a famous department store at Oxford Circus with metal-ware, plastic-ware, upturned saucepans, pots and frying pans sprawled out around him. Crowds gather on the street and people watch transfixed from the tops of buses. There's the young lady of Covent Garden whose singing of ballads comforts you as you pass by on your way home. Where's the Oswald Stoll of today to build a palace worthy of classical Rome, to book all this talent and usher them into a marvellous career leaving the streets to just be streets? We could do a lot worse with entertainment. Could academies foster a *talentocracy* based on the currency of pleasure, teaching British youngsters the skills possessed by performers in variety's golden age such as wire walking and rope tricks? New careers and businesses might be founded as performers specialize. Tablets and smartphones cast aside, people would come flocking ... and they might build attractive new theatres at the same time as all the new housing....

An essay summarizing the year 1926 in the variety world warns against shortsightedness on the part of bookers causing stereotyped programmes. It reminds us that a large public still exists for the ordinary music hall. Audiences wanted a good entertainment with value for money, and in some cases, acts were becoming stale.[3] The Houston Sisters had their bundle of gags carried over from Saltcoats but now they were variety '*A-listers*' they were a continual focus for the theatrical press. The weekly 'Across the Halls' column in The Performer was one means to judge an artiste's standing. Comedy acts were praised if they brought out new material but not if things got repetitive. The Houstons were ticked off in June and July 1926 soon after their Royal Performance. On June 30 we read of the Sisters 'perfect procession of tab calls - But why not vary the story of the *Three Bears* occasionally?' A week later it's 'The Houston Sisters can claim to be the Alhambra's favourites, though they still plough through that *Three Bears* story!'[4] This theatrical paper – the very 'organ of the VAF' was kind but critical with its all-seeing eye. Barely anything negative was written in The Performer about the Houstons over the next eight years. This is partly because they changed material enough for the paper to declare in 1930 that they 'surely hold the record for the number of new acts they have introduced in the last few years'[5] and partly because superstardom guaranteed respectful write-ups.

Selling the Houstons' star factor is hard because it's about theatre, and film footage isn't there. The mainstay of Renée and Billie's professional life was variety. Fame existed in the here and now: fleeting, and then gone to dust. The more traditional stars were often hostile to the prospect of being filmed. The risk of over-familiarity was too great if people saw the act at cinemas. It meant material was used up fast with no facility to recycle a joke. Variety sketches sometimes turn up on film but these are relatively rare. While individual variety stars crossed over into television, acts themselves didn't. We relish the memories of those who witnessed performances, recalling the skill and star factor of vintage performers. In the new century the number of witnesses diminishes. Thank heavens for individuals and societies that share and keep alive this cultural memory.

People might recall Renée made films but the vast work she did on the variety stage is unknown. What's left to examine? Descriptions of the Sisters' act in the theatrical, national and provincial press have to be the main source and reading as many reports as possible forms my picture. It's a bit like restoring one vase from ancient Greece from the fragments of more than one version of the same vase and it's very fruitful. Fifteen of the Houston Sisters sketches can be assembled. Thank heavens too, for the press that recorded their turns. The level of coverage the Houstons got when they appeared in the major halls proves they gave their biggest rivals a run for their money.

Their turn came and Renée and Billie might be introduced together on stage, or stride in from opposite wings. *Bill* might surprise the audience emerging from the auditorium. Renée's voice had a high-pitched plaintive sound whereas *Bill*'s was gruff. What the Sisters sounded like is significant. From early on, people liked their accents. *More Dam Things* was the final touring revue the Houston Sisters appeared in, between December 1934 and April 1935. A Scots journalist witnessed it and wrote of their style, noting 'an analysis might suggest it consists of a constant recurring of some of the idioms of speech and expression of their native city.'[6] When they came home the Glasgow style was 'upped': the 'oo's' and 'r's' of vowels and consonants allowed free reign. It's sad to read the younger generation of Scots in the 21st Century might lose their rolling 'r' due to natural evolution of language, if experts are to be believed.[7]

Staleness comes when 'attitude' is at a deficit. A street performer today might be churning out poor stuff but have mesmeric presence. Once you do something people like, why not milk it for a period? When you think of the amount of times Will Fyffe did his *Ninety-four today* and *The Engineer*, or the times Robb Wilton did *The Magistrate* you realize that if the formula was good, people want to see it again and again. GS Melvin, a Scots comedian a generation older than the Houston Sisters who had appeared on stage with their parents, was famous for his dames, girl-guide leader burlesque, and his 'I'm Happy When I'm Hiking' song. Melvin writes in 1926 that 'audiences do not want clever stuff. They want the obvious.' While he dislikes being multi-sided and believes his type of artist isn't any different to actors of the legitimate stage, in his 'Is Versatility a Handicap?' article in The Era, he concludes that 'more success comes to the actor who merely plays one type of character.' Versatility, he says, is going to restrict your success.[8] It puts me in mind of acclaimed actors who play themselves whatever the role. Renée falls into this category and yet came into her own in the revue format with its potpourri of characters. That she could stay 'in harness' for four decades has much to do with versatility.

She and Billie joined GS Melvin for a couple of weeks back at the London Palladium in late October 1926 for Maurice Cowan's revue *Life*. The sketches have names like *It's Ripping to Dance*, *You Know What Authors Are*, and *Seeing is Believing*. The titles are evocative of the gay 1920s. Clarice Mayne, dancers Hooker and Seaward and Sam Wooding and his band featured. It was thoroughly versatile stuff.

It was most common for the Houston Sisters to develop a sketch organically over a period of seven months, sometimes longer, until it finally went into the ether. Some, to be honest, had a ten-year vintage, like their *Spanish item*. Of course an old idea might look radically different to its original down the line. Billie and Renée 'lived' the sketch, investing it with something amusing to them. They often drew on films and 'celebrity' lifestyles for jokes. For a week at the Coliseum in 1928 alongside acts like Nervo and Knox, and Arthur Sinclair and Maire O'Neill in a playlet, they exhibited *Rehearsing a Drama*. In this, Renée is 'obstreperous as usual,' insisting she knows best how to best portray a vamp. Billie is both hero and villain and directs her. At Hackney Empire three months later the 'stolidity of Billie' and 'the mercurial manner of Renée' in the same sketch, was enough for The Stage to comment on the 'finish of their style.'

Oh, to have witnessed *Society Reporter* - a gag with Shirley Houston as a reporter from something like The Tatler, conducting an interview with the Sisters backstage: Renée and Billie pulling the reporter's leg something rotten. When the Sisters took *Society Reporter* to Holborn Empire on December 28, 1931, Renée was *Mistress of Ceremonies* throughout – introducing Elsie Bower and Billy Rutherford, Clapham and Dwyer and praising Lily Morris, who sang about the 'Commercial Traveller.' It was the Holborn Empire's first *'Crazy Week'* and the flow of impromptus was impressive. A similar chatterbox offering by the Houston Sisters was *Private Life*. In this sketch, from late September 1932, they get out of bed at 5 am but the early start doesn't prevent them being late for the theatre. Renée added thumbnail impressions of well-known stars, a short step dance, and the sisters closed the act singing. *Private Life* travelled to Edinburgh in October but was back at London's Victoria Palace days later.

Granny Houston provided inspiration for the 30's routine *Grandmother's Hundredth Birthday* – a visual sketch involving all three Houston sisters, played to adoring audiences everywhere from Shepherd's Bush to Blackpool. Shirley's Holborn debut was inside a picture frame - as a portrait painting rather like the *Gainsborough Girl*, but one capturing Granny in her vibrant youth. Keeping a straight face can't have been easy for Shirley, with her real Granny in the audience. It was an organic sketch - a 'bright little act' the Sisters broadened per iteration. The Sisters wore the 'picturesque' costumes of Victorian times with Renée in a particularly huge crinoline. The Performer is full of praise when the gag reached the Coliseum, describing not only how 'Renée's beauty adapts itself to any period' but that 'the amount of fun she can get out of a crinoline must be seen to be believed.'[9] It's left to the imagination what jokes concerned the *Duchess*'s past and what flights of fancy were achieved with the skirt, but the turn warranted a replay at the Coliseum a month later when the Sisters joined Nellie Wallace, Phyllis Neilson-Terry and Bransby Williams in his *Chelsea Pensioner* guise.

Grandmother's Hundredth Birthday
(Artwork by Author)

Holborn Empire programme (1930s)

Bud Flanagan

Sophie Tucker

Young Ted Ray

Cartoonist Van Dock
(Artwork by Author)

(Photos: Author's Collection)

A versatile new Houston Sisters gag with a hint of topicality was born in March 1928 at London's Wood Green Empire, perhaps inspired by the song 'Council Houses' Victor Moreton was singing just then. *Locality* reflected the new homes councils were building using government subsidies. When the Sisters took it to the Victoria Palace a few days later, *Bill* - proud occupant of a 'wee but and ben', gets annoyed at Renée's 'palpable lack of respect' for his new abode. The Stage commented on the re-use of old material[10] but Renée gave her *Glesca keelie* a new prominence. At London's Alhambra, with a quarrel outside the front door of *Bill*'s superior res, *Bill*'s 'new found snobbery' was 'a decided hit.'[11] So began a two weeker at the Alhambra, initially in the company of Yvette Rugel - *miniature prima donna*, Talbot O Farrell, Johnny Marvin- *crooning on guitar and saw*, the acrobatic Jovers, and *Auntie - A Gate a Bike and a Gamp*.

They added a few innovations to *Locality* the second week and we learnt that *Bill*'s father's promotion to the position of factory foreman enabled the relocation. Renée calls round but *Bill*'s still declaring 'he may no longer play with her because she's 'common'. They quarrel but make it up with a song and dance. This time the *Irresistibles* were item 6 on the bill following Chris Charlton - *and his deceptions of 1928*. Naughton and Gold item 9, and *Last of the Red Hot Mammas*, Sophie Tucker - item 11. Could this *little house* on the Alhambra be the one that had a notorious trick dealt upon it by the *Crazy Gang* – as mentioned in Renée's autobiography? She and Billie went inside the *wee but and ben* for a costume change only to be grabbed by those crazy hooligans before they could finish changing. Proud *Bill*'s little house got pushed down on that occasion. People took note. *Locality* is among the Sisters' routines reported most frequently in the theatrical press. Strangely enough, a couple of years later a comedy revue was staged at the Palace Theatre, Newcastle upon Tyne called *Council Houses* so memories of this might possibly have inspired it.

Less common were the sketches that saw an airing once only, or a few times. These didn't get a sure hit reaction. In *'funny little difference'* in 1926, *Bill* tries to lose Renée but his tactics are foiled and Renée's idiocies dominate conversation. Another time *Bill* offers her a coin to buy a glass of milk hoping she'll go but she chides him for throwing money away and notes his resemblance to a bedraggled cat. With the word 'cat' placed, a quick tribunal concerns the life changing experience next door's cat has suffered. Embarrassing references to *Bill*'s vanity emerge in *Ill-Treating A Cat*. Focus transfers to what the time is, and the little ditty 'Why?' is sung before they vanish. There's *Annie Laurie's Wedding* with *Bill* attempting to sing the famous number with interruptions from common little Renée – intent on syncopating it and reducing the ballad to its cynical elements - causing them to fight out the matter in song. Perhaps the dialect didn't register with Holborn's audience and this is why this routine is rare.

In 1932 *Artiste's Studio* featured the assistance of Bud Flanagan and Chesney Allen – often on the bill with Renée and Billie at this time. Bud's father had opened a fish and chip shop in London's East End after fleeing from a Russian pogrom. His son got a job as a callboy at the old Cambridge Music Hall and that was his first step on the tricky showbiz ladder. Here, he emerges as a stooge to lift the temperamental *Mexican artist's model* played by Renée on to a pedestal, with her jumping off and going off the deep end about it. This act with Bud and Ches finished with a rumba number.

Image from a music score and publicity for Sunny Swanee (Author's Collection)

You can't ignore the musical side of the Sisters' performance and the training that came from having Lizzi and Jimmie as parents. For dozens of acts, a song is often the single thing we remember centuries on. Not all acts sang but many did, and some sang and did other things. The Houston Sisters were in the latter category. At the beginning, end, or middle of the turn, they belted out happy fizzy numbers like Harry Warren & Bud Green's 'I Love My Baby, My Baby Loves Me' already popularized by Elsie Carlisle and Josephine

Baker. You might get a foot-tapping, sentimental sing-a-long like 'Sunny Swanee,'[12] with Renée and Billie singing 'I still remember - late September - Nineteen Twenty Three', wistfully looking back to those 'ne'er forgotten - fields of cotton - Sunny Swanee way.' Their version adds verses about going home sweet home with toothbrush and comb. With numbers like Elmer Schoebel's 'Blue Grass', and 1932's 'Bedtime story,'[13] they put their signature on classics. The Houstons always featured a song and they did this twice nightly or more for at least a decade with no microphone.

The act's music had to be top line to guarantee success. Renée and Billie had offers to sing music by well-known and amateur composers. Layton and Johnstone were offered hundreds of copies of songs a week and sometimes did their own songs. OK, the Houstons weren't divas of song but you might say they carried the banner for later comediennes who sang. In songs like 'Oh! Rosalita' *Bill* crooned and Cuban Renée was *his* gal. Attempting 'a tango mixing graceful dance movements with some strong he-man stuff... the girls finished big' at Camberwell Palace on September 14, 1931. At the Palladium two months later the same song is called the 'funniest part of their turn' with Renée – a high blonde 'at her best in a costume with a distinct hiatus in it.' It's easy to overlook the role their musical director played. George could be counted on for all those early appearances, ready to take his place in the pit to conduct the signature tune that heralded the Sisters' entrance or set other comedy routines to music.

Columnist MWD in The Observer reflected on the slow grave music of the Scottish accent. The Sisters' fondness for American tunes however, made him sigh, fearing an extinction of Highland ballads with the Charleston emerging victorious. Surely the pugnacity of the Scots would count against such change? And yet the Houstons insisted on jazz versions of cockney ballads! A writer in The Era adopts a similar concerned tone about changing times and the 'modern' youngsters the Houston Sisters typified who have a 'disregard' for reels and pibrochs. Yet, the 'predilection of this pair for syncopation' had to be witnessed. The press frequently mentioned the girls' syncopated singing. People got over the shock of the new. London audiences accepted the rough-edged Scots kids in these routines. Would a dance on the stage to such rhythms by English sisters have been too close to home?

The sheer amount of songs they covered proves they were a highly musical act - even with 99% of their vast output vanished into the ether. We can't associate songs with them but listening to the same tracks performed by others who made recordings, for example, Jack Hylton and his Orchestra is a joy, and you reach into music of this era. When the cheeky vocals complement the vibrant saxophones your grey day brightens up.

The Houston Sisters put hours into rehearsing music but recorded little that remains for posterity. Recordings possibly exist on obscure labels. It's a lack of foresight both on the Sisters' own part and their manager's that they did not make a good sound recording deal early on. Renée's Columbia recording contract in mid 1935 came too late. During her career, Gracie

The Artiste at his Work

Fields recorded in excess of one hundred records and George Formby double this amount so when you compare what possibilities existed with the likes of Decca, His Master's Voice, Rex, Regal Zonophone and Columbia, it's shameful the sisters failed to record more in the decade they were in the limelight. The writer and historian John Fisher writes of Gracie as being a songstress who did comedy as well.[14] George Formby was seldom seen without us hearing him sing. Even if the Houston Sisters were foremost a live comedy act, a song was always expected from them too. Perhaps their tendency to patter and chatter instead of singing whole ballads made them less of a gramophone commodity. Their recording career could have been better managed. The same could be said for their film career. Still, some of the music they included in their act sounds catchy even in the 21st Century. One I admire is 'It's OK Katy with me' (by Ed G. Nelson and Harry Pease). It's as R&B as it comes:

> If u want loving, some LOVE, LOVE, loving and want that loving just like a NOTHIN
> *It's OK Katy with me!*
> If u want kisses, some KISS, KISS, kisses, the kind of kisses that u've been MISSIN
> *It's OK Jimmy with me!*
> Do u wanna go out? Do u wanna go out? Do u wanna go see a show?
> I'd rather stay home, I'd rather stay home, with the lights turned way down low.[15]

There's Fred Rose & Walter Hirsch's unforgettable 'Deed I Do' - a smash hit in 1927, sung by the Houston Sisters at the London Alhambra that August during a rare departure from the nursery, with *Bill* in immaculate male evening clothes and Renée charming in a party frock. It was recorded soon after by Benny Goodman's band, then - in the swing era by Peggy Lee and later still by modern artists including Diana Krull and the Paper Moon Trio.

There's the strummingly addictive 'Shinanaka Da,'[16] all about a Turk who, all through 'Tuesday, Wednesday, Thursday' *'played a guitar, and smoked a cigar'*, and *'laughed a ha ha ha ha ha ha'*. Trust me, this one-step - a frolic in the dance halls of 1929 - is so psychedelic it must be forty years ahead of its time featuring alternating skiffle-sounding riffs and glockenspiels. While not the natural choice of song to accompany *Bill* troubadouring on guitar whilst dressed in an Eton suit, the guitar sent Renée into frenzied dance - disrobing progressively. You got the unexpected with the Houston Sisters in the roaring 20s, and don't think for one minute her mother was pleased about it.

The lead up to that mild striptease concerns a forthcoming house party *Bill* is invited to. He's no intention of taking his common little sister. Renée, of course, is coming, finding ingenious uses for the contents of her fancy dress box. This was first seen at the Palladium in February 1929 considered in need of 'tightening up' by The Performer, before they took it to the Coliseum in early March in the unaccustomed position of closing spot, due to doubling at Hackney Empire (evidence of their turn-working on the same night at different theatres). At the very same time when the Alhambra and big Stoll theatres in London were seeing Burns and Allen on their London tour, the

Houstons were praised for beating singing rival 'uncle' Henry Hearty to the post of 'Pride of Denmark Street'[17] in their speed in adopting 'Shinanaka Da'.

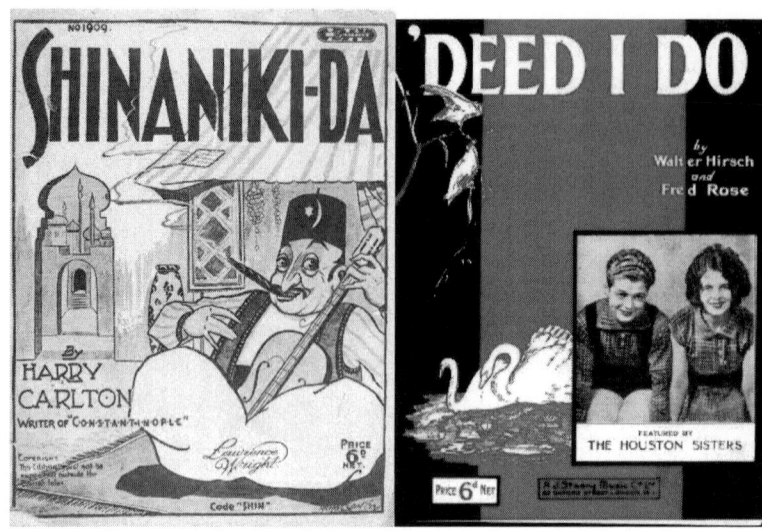

Sheet music for Sinanaka Da and Deed I do (Author's Collection)

They took it to the South London Palace at the time Ida Barr was singing a political song on the flapper vote - a ballad that registered big given the Equal Franchise Act of 1928, finally giving women the same voting rights as men. GH Elliott was also there singing 'Up with the lark in the morning,' and 'Me and the man in the Moon.'

A 'storm of applause' followed Renée and Billie when they took Harry Carlton's number to the Metropolitan on April 24, 1929. Later still - alongside Marie Burke and violinist De Groot in June at the Alhambra, the *Irresistibles* gave the same number a priceless rendering with portions of costume shed lavishly among the audience to the sound of rapturous applause.[18] Returning to Stoll's Coliseum a month later, on the bill with *Countess Phelmore - Masked Singer*, 'Shinanaka Da' was Renée's 'souvenir stunt' - still strumming here a year later in May 1930, when the Houstons were alongside Naunton Wayne, and balancers Frank and Eugenie.

A strong visual contrast was already apparent with the *Irresistibles* but they were happy to go one step further if something could make them funnier. In the late 20s Ivor Vintor was *England's Smallest Comedian* and naturally his routines were youthful studies. When the Sisters were at Holborn Empire on February 13, 1928 they introduced Ivor into one of their quarrels and this got a big laugh. At the time Ivor's description of the trials of wearing an Eton suit sent titters into the audience[19] and I expect that planted the seed that grew into a new image of *Bill* done up in Eton togs - first seen in their act at the Palladium, as reported in the Daily Mail, February 18, 1929. The Sisters acquired a visual image first, working out a routine after.

The Artiste at his Work

Left: Ivor Vintor
from sheet music
(Author's Collection)

Right: Billie and Renée
(By kind permission of
the Aherne Family)

Below: Cutting for
The Houston Sisters
tour dates for the late 20s
(From Renée's scrapbook.
By kind permission of the
family of Terry Long)

In May 1929 the illusion of *Bill* 'strutting in his Etons,' bragging about his school while Renée 'pulls his newly trousered leg' was done with such spontaneity you could lose yourself believing it was genuine. Conrad's Pigeons, Billy Merson and the Houston Sisters' good friend Stanley Holloway were there that same night at the Coliseum – the latter doing songs and telling tales. Off went the Houstons to Blackpool Palace on July 22 where the Etons were exchanged for a sportswear, with *Bill* 'very grown up in his white flannels and his striped blazer and boasting shamelessly about his new school.'[20] This was Julian Wylie's *Show Of Shows* with Max Miller, and Mona Vivian and Billy Danvers - singing a duet called *'Lancashire Love'*. By August at the London Alhambra, the routine had developed into *Home From School On Holidays* with Bill trying desperately hard to make Renée serious during their holidays. It's your standard Houston Sisters fayre but it was a funny enough idea for The Stage to comment how 'four boards and a genial little quarrel are apparently all that they require to set the house agog.'[21] That line up also featured Alfred Latell - *animal impersonator*, Noni - the clown beloved of Coliseum audiences, comedy girl Gladdy Sewell, and Alexander Oumansky's ballet. For some in the audience, the Eton suit gained rationale as real-life chappies were descending on parents that summer.

As the lifespan of the sister act began to draw to a close, they began touring in *More Dam Things* managed by impresario Tom Arnold, who later became well known for his spectacular ice shows. The name is a pun on Sonnie Hale's *One Dam Thing After Another* from 1927 that starred Jessie Matthews. The 1935 show was fast moving, in two parts with an intermission. Each part consisted of *1st Dam Thing, 2nd Dam Thing, 3rd Dam Thing* and so on – numbering eight in the first half and ten in the second.[22] Renée is given first writing credits with young Ronald Jeans and Douglas Furber secondary credits. Jeans went on to become a comedy playwright and Furber would soon be known for his lyrics for *'The Lambeth Walk'*. Mark

151

Chesney was musical director and Claude Boulby, business manager. The girls could exercise influence on the overall design. The revue started in the provinces and finished in London and Brighton. It wasn't in the same league as the *Crazy* Shows pulling them in at the time, such as *Life Begins At Oxford Circus* at the Palladium. The Houston Sisters' salary was still top bracket - about £100 a week – equivalent to about £3,500 now.

Week commencing Monday, December 31st, 1934
TOM ARNOLD
Presents
THE HOUSTON SISTERS
in
"MORE DAM THINGS"
A New Revue
Book by Renee Houston,
Ronald Jeans, Douglas Furber

Notice for More Dam Things (Artists Impression)

Left: Tom Arnold (J. Lewis family Collection)

Right: Max Miller (Author's Collection)

More Dam Things featured eleven artistes in the company and two or three guest acts. As well as the three Houston girls there was racy Jack Daly - *Irish Personality Star*, singing comediennes Sara Preece and Gloria Day, character artiste Lance Lister, dancers Fox and Sally Evans and tumbler Percy Val. In the first part we were taken for a *Riding Lesson* with the Houston Sisters, a *Groom* - Lance Lister, *Miss Fairgrit* played by Shirley and a model horse. There was a *Cuban Scene* with dances to dazzle by the Radiolympia Girls and Shirley who hoped to avoid comparison with her *Irresistible* sisters using the stage name 'Shirley Brent'. In *Dowager Fairy Queen* Renée sang 'Nobody loves a Fairy when she's Forty.' The second part featured a dancing lesson *Dam Thing* followed by the playlet *Perfect Harmony* in which Renée and Daly were young couple *Fifi* and *Nickie* whose newly wed exuberance of affection quickly breaks down. In *The Customer is Always Right*, Renée played different roles within *Whitefridges* - a large London store. She was a shop girl reprimanded and made to appease complaining customers and a French-accented coiffeuse. Finally, came her '*Garbo*' - 'strikingly true to the original' - an exotic and ultra-sophisticated customer in long flowing robes paying a call to the store. Billie did well in the same scene 'capital as a man about town' strutting about in the latest cut in men's eveningwear.

Rich visual contrasts appear and risks were taken. A publicity photo surviving from January 1935 shows the small and impish *Bill* and Renée, he in jodphurs and she a' la Shirley Temple, standing in front of a life-size model horse with a young man dressed in a callboy uniform. John Duncan was the young man and a note says that he was an orphan boy who had got the sack before being adopted by the Houstons as their stage manager. He was *Mr Whitefridge* in the earlier scene. One of Renée's stories, told to her son, reveals *Riding Lesson* was one of naughtiest ever Houston Sisters sketches. With Lance Lister on the horse, singing a grandiose song, an open sack of manure would emerge by the rear of the horse care of Johnny Duncan. With the audience in fits, stoical *Bill* bore the lesson's disruption with a pained look. This 'vivacious series of episodes and crosstalk incidents' was a swansong for Billie and Renée whose appearances together were coming to an end. *More Dam Things* stopped at Nottingham, Birmingham, Stratford, Glasgow, Sunderland, Sheffield, Edinburgh, Hull, Holborn and Brighton. The revue was flexible alternating the lineup to include Larry Adler on mouth organ, the Four Franks, and the Marconis – *Argentine Accordionists*. Reaching Holborn, *More Dam Things* was described as a cheerful, bright and extremely clever entertainment full of real surprises, and the 'glorious dancing displays were something to rave about. Here was an opportunity to take a show round the country, adding several unexpected sketches. The Houston material was typical but their act had reached its highest state of perfection and they took greater liberties.

Looking at reactions to the Houston Sisters', one word that keeps recurring is 'freshness'. Reports on their act in December 1925, say it was 'refreshing in its individuality and abundantly humorous so far as material and method are concerned'[23] and an 'unusual atmosphere of freshness' is remarked on eight months later proving 'conclusively that we have good acts of our own as any which are imported.'[24] We're told in 1930 after a Chiswick Empire visit 'their turn is always distinct and different from all others'[25] and how, in March 1932, Renée's 'quips and gags are always delightfully fresh whilst her humour is most infectious.'[26] The act's 'delightful spontaneity' then rolls forth into 1933. Even in February 1952 lines about these mid-Thirties music hall idols, finally back together again, inform us 'they have lost little of that freshness and vitality, that artistry, that made them household names in more than one country.'[27] They had sustained the act fifteen years, and spent the last nine of these at the very top. People close to the variety world tell me that to sustain an act over a long period of time is an achievement of the highest magnitude. I see it now, although when I was young, variety had been made to leave opprobriously by the back door. Kids in the 80s assumed variety stood for all that was embarrassing, second-rate and amateur. Who would admit to watching *The Good Old Days* televised from the stage at the City Varieties Theatre, Leeds? Having experienced few live performances, I was no judge having, like my contemporaries, been brought up on a poor diet of television.

For centuries a force has existed that knocks away what's gone before, even things that were perfectly good. Those thirsty for change vie with those experiencing neurosis in a state of flux. In the 20s technology tinkered with entertainment, lustful to replace flesh and blood with something new and scientific. Wireless radio and talking pictures were the two 'techno' enemies – potentially destructive to variety's existence. Were audiences going to stay home and listen to variety on the radio? Were performers to brave it in half-empty halls? Was the space where you earned your keep going to throw you over, reserving its room for the cinema only, now that a combination of exciting action and sound was available? It's a tough environment for a variety entertainer at the best of times, and much worse when the juggernaut of change threatens to toss you on to the junk heap.

After the First World War enough money still existed to run theatres, stage gaudy revues, and pay stars shockingly high salaries. Advances in technology pointed to economy and a cheaper way of listening or watching variety entertainment. Radio and film was better surely? The money at stake shifted into new hands, as well as the same old hands. What happened in the 20s laid the foundation stone in the *Palace of Cheapness*. There's a parallel debate now about 'online' and 'cost-reduction' versus everything else. The worldwide web is the sinister overlord intent on devaluing worthwhile experience. Too much 'process' accompanies each new technology so the fun becomes the process, not the content. We ask will newspapers die and moan about the state of education. We debate whether TV licenses are necessary and moan about quality. We feed techno-tots whatnots, and screen-agers non-stop internet, talking all the while about Attention Deficit Disorder. Great white walls offer cognitive behaviour therapy, taking away the costly human. Things hang on, like my mother's transistor radio in the bathroom. Variety has hung on as always, throughout the modern age. TV has had a very long innings, and will soon rival that which variety theatre had before.

From 1910 to 1930 films and variety co-existed in Britain either separately in picture houses and variety theatres or alongside each other in cine-variety houses. Picture houses always had pianists or orchestras constituting the live 'turn' to enhance the moving image. EM Sansom, in his essay 'The Variety Year,' writes at the end of 1926 how *Kine-Variety* had grown in the previous twelve months. He disdains the era's equivalent of the advert break: 'Where is the manager who will have the courage to rid his programmes of the advertising films which break up the best of entertainments to book intelligently a full quota of turns . . . as in the old days.'[28] Opinions about cine-variety were divided and you either thought films and variety combined well or you didn't. English audiences liked the combination less than their American counterparts, preferring films only according to a report in The Performer.[29] Americans still have a greater toleration for ad breaks eighty years on. In the very early days Renée and Billie leapt at opportunities to play at obscure cine-variety theatres, not exactly loving the experience and receiving modest pay. In 1927 picture-theatre managements were criticized for not understanding variety in their craze for cheapness, and paying ridiculous low sums when they combined variety with films. Unsurprisingly, Germany was said to have the right balance, better standards, and led the field: the 150 cine-variety houses in Berlin alone serving as proof.[30] Whatever the case, these houses survived into the late 30s in the UK. Their movies, interludes, live turns and star appearances might even be accompanied by orchestrals simulated by organs from John Compton's Organ Company, or Wurlitzers. This was the case at Kingston's Regal Cinema and the Egyptian-themed Luxor Theatre that graced

Twickenham's Cross Deep (between 1929 and 1944 after which it became an Odeon cinema). Renée appeared at both these cine-variety venues.

Silent film posed no threat before 1929, being a different species to the variety stage. You only have to go back to the early 20s when Minerva Films: a collaboration of Leslie Howard, AA Milne, Nigel Playfair, Aubrey Smith and Adrian Brunel aimed to raise the standards of British cinema focusing on film comedies. They found the West End music hall to be so strong that nobody had use for a film equivalent. Then British Lion made the first complete sound film, 'The Clue of the New Pin' at Beaconsfield. The advent of irresistible sound made possible by sound-on-film processes like Fox 'Movietone' revolutionized US cinema and impacted Britain all the more.

In May 1929 whilst Stoll had his London's Coliseum and Alhambra 'wired' with the Western Electric systems, The Performer moaned about 'the reverse of good showmanship' and that conceiving a type of entertainment which 'curtails the flesh and blood turns,' permitting instead a 'shadowy mechanical representation allied to a gramophonic sound reproduction is something the writer ... does not believe patrons of theatres would like after the novelty of the 'Talkie' has worn off.'[34] For a short time film was a 'turn' in its own right with the Alhambra featuring 'British Movietone News - *Events of the day shown in a wonderful way*' regularly advertised on its playbill.

In a speech he gave in November 1929, Stoll admitted that 'the public are eager for the Talkies' and The Performer announced that 'with profound regret we learned that the Alhambra London is to become a cinematograph theatre on December 23 - having been leased to British International Pictures (B.I.P) under the chairmanship of John Maxwell. They put up so much money to have a theatre in the West End to present their products that it didn't matter that the house had a bright variety history and had always shown handsome profits as such. B.I.P are paying £1000 a week for the theatre.' London's Empire and Tivoli theatres were also rebuilt as cinemas while the Pavilion and the Hippodrome went over to revue. By late February 1930 a thousand cinemas were equipped with sound reproducing apparatus[35] some struggling with non-standardized equipment. Many of the variety theatres were on the road to cinema conversion.

In the late 20s Fleet Street journalists as well as those who spoke for the VAF took a negative stance, publishing articles headed by the scare-mongering question 'Is Variety Dead?' There was a falling away in enterprise, some argued, adding that variety needed a younger formula to survive. The Daily Mail, in an article 'Plight of the Music Hall' talked about the death of talent but placed the Houston Sisters among those who represented true talent still to be found.[31] Views were expressed about the long-term effects on our culture. In analyzing change and examining results we looked across the Atlantic. Perhaps Britain got off lighter than America, where the effect of radio and Talkies on traditional vaudeville was more crushing. Stoll features among the portraits in 'Hannen Swaffer's Who's Who', when the elegant theatre critic penned that 'Every Monday he sits the Coliseum programme through, even the turns he has seen a hundred times. Variety is dying under his eyes. Not even his great discoveries, Gladdy Sewell and the Houston Sisters can save it.'[32] Bransby Williams, meanwhile, reassured people, pointing out that 'there's always this cry in the papers that something or other is dead. They say variety is dead, then next minute they are asking all the variety artists on a Sunday to appear at matinees for charity.'[33]

Since they were little girls visiting Jimmie and Lizzi, Renée and Billie absorbed the beautiful painted stage scenery and backdrops, the whiff of greasepaint, and the electric thrills exchanged between performer, orchestra and audience member in his red plush seat. The halls represented a spectrum of humanity – a place, as Renée puts it 'where you discovered and re-discovered the special camaraderie of the variety theatre – that odd mixture of comics, dancers, jugglers, singers and dramatic actors ... a world of friendship, an exclusive world inhabited by special people.'[36] It was an old life she and so many others in variety were familiar with. How powerless they were in the face of this upheaval! The place where the Houstons had first conquered a London audience, the London Music Hall, closed as a theatre in 1934. For some stage artistes the Talkies, as they muscled in, added to the state of *in terrorem* but variety took the knocks and battled on, fragmented but not beaten. Variety would evolve and survive. Renée and Billie were among those who looked ahead and went where opportunities were: adapting and compromising.

Radio, the medium that fast became part of our lives, transmitted from BBC studios and via outside broadcasts from 1923. These were often from big London theatres wired for sound plus state-of-the-art cine-variety venues like the Regal. Medium wave transmission was possible from several big cities in the UK. A transmitter towered above Selfridges, Oxford Street, and there was one at Daventry in Northampton for long wave transmission. Two million radio licenses were issued in 1926[37] and the 'cat's whisker' or crystal set was tuned to the correct frequency. Sketches and songs had been heard on the BBC since 1922. WH Berry was an early voice and after John Henry's debut in 1923, he was in a domestic sitcom with his wife Blossom from 1925. The same year saw *Radio Radiance*[38] broadcasting the fun of the concert party. Peter Eckersley was the BBC's first engineer and something of the spirit of variety existed in his love of spoof reporting. This was combined with his technical know-how. Eckersley's spirit, however, didn't refresh the palette of the BBC's first General Manager, Scottish Presbyterian John Reith. The BBC offered light classical music from the beginning. Dance music was broadcast from the Savoy hotel, conveniently located near BBC HQ at Savoy Hill. It allowed keen individuals to practice steps at home although singing was definitely subservient to music. Noisy jazz was held in disdain and crooning abhorrent. In 1929 the BBC banned singing for a while.[39]

As the 20s progressed the BBC broadcast documentaries of the 'improving' type, folk songs, and a half-hour variety show in the evenings.

The latter was sacrilege! From early on, theatres reacted with a ban on variety artistes performing on radio without express permission from managers. This forced the BBC to find its own stars like Mabel Constanduros, who excelled in monologues and created the *Buggins* family. Mabel later gained a career in the halls through radio work. Her popularity carried her to the Coliseum where she topped the bill in 1929. The main beef of theatre managers was that they felt broadcasting injured the value the artiste had to the music halls. They had a point. The BBC had very quickly assembled a massive roster of artistes, writers and bandleaders.

It still had to prize the well-known artistes away from the theatre managers and agents. Shrewd negotiation by the BBC was required. The radio debut of the Houston Sisters occurred when they were one of the three acts selected from the 1926 Royal Command Performance lineup for broadcast. The other two were Billy Bennett and Bransby Williams. After this, the Sisters made two appearances in March and April 1927 on the new 'National Programme' in the *Variety* slot which went out at about 21.45. On New Year's Eve, 1929 they were heard in *Vaudeville*. The early dates prove the Houstons were among the earliest female broadcasters on the BBC. Stoll, who allowed the sisters to go on the air, cut a deal with the BBC as his 1927 article 'Music Hall and Wireless - What Managements Should Do' indicates. For him, £1500 was a reasonable recompense for losses sustained due to the BBC contracting variety artistes. Some performers, however, were playing with fire. Bransby Williams chanced to lose his contract with Charles Gulliver MD of Holborn Empire, by broadcasting his *Padre* sketch on the BBC.[40]

Whilst theatre managers hoped to safeguard their position, many stage performers considered radio opportunities to be as attractive as those in theatres, cine-variety circuits, and films. The Houstons saw radio's potential. Of course, some held wireless in contempt but it was managers of the big theatre circuits who took the fundamentalist 'variety view.' But weren't they restricting the freedoms of artistes? In 1928 came a new waft of negotiations when VAF took a kindlier view saying it was ok to broadcast artistes from the stage fortnightly, suggesting that different material for broadcasts be selected to that used on stage.[41] In March 1929 the BBC broadcast sketches by Malcolm Keen, Olga Lindo and Houston Sisters in *Just a broadcast*.

Stoll, against the ban, agreed that same year that publicity generated from wireless was a valuable asset: 'I have never opposed broadcasting on the grounds that it was injurious to the artistes or the theatres. My opposition has always been based on the fact of a monopoly of broadcasting being held by the BBC.' Stoll's idea was that theatres should be able to set up their own stations and do their own broadcasting.[42] Nevertheless, the ban dragged on with negotiated deals per artiste. While the Houston Sisters made few broadcasts in 1931, Max Miller and GS Melvin made their microphone debut from the Palladium and it was remarked that in Max's case, his gusto worked well on the air and that the 'artiste who *excels in attack* is the one to whom even radio audiences will warm the quicker.'[43]

The VAF were also keen to highlight that pros attempting a radio career didn't have it easy when BBC officials were hardly 'scouting' in search of new talent. Artistes enjoying phenomenal reactions were not given opportunities to go on the air whilst the BBC favoured certain lucky artistes, it claimed. A 'snobbery complex' existed in 'the sacred portals of the BBC,' damned the article's author. The lucky ones obtaining handsome fees were always 'well-educated.' The 'BBC needs to broaden its outlook'[44] it raged. Two years later the same point is made, as well as the point that the BBC, having a monopolistic position, could well afford to pay more for talent.

Children of variety entertainers I've spoken to tell me the BBC did not pay well. There was a geographical disadvantage in the early years, given that the BBC was London-based. Unless your engagements were in London, it meant taking a week out to rehearse. Special writing was needed and that came at a premium. Commercial radio offered healthy competition from the early 1930s. Performers flocked to these stations. Before then, it was only in the USA (where broadcasting was always commercial) that acts got paid fabulous sums by sponsors.

The BBC paid for the Houston Sisters, happy with their *University of Life* education, and the girls were on air a few times in 1933 whilst hard negotiation continued between the BBC and the new entertainment kings. Big changes in variety occurred in late 1932 when the upper echelons of Moss Empires changed. Charles Gulliver was ousted, and Mark Ostrer, CM Woolf, RH Gillespie and George Black became Moss's new directors. These top dogs had an interest not just in theatre but the production and exhibition of films. Gulliver was also ousted as MD at Holborn Empire and in 1933 Woolf and Mark Ostrer became its joint MDs with George Black directing WC1's theatrical powerhouse. Black's role was to look after the variety side. The broadcasting ban was renewed in January due to VAF pressure, illustrating how much resistance to the Radio Age there still was. Black, seemingly on the side of the pros, argued it harmed theatres when personality artistes went on the air. He suggested a *special permission clause* on contracts. Didn't his theatre suffer a financial loss amounting to £10,000 per night in cancelled seats when Gracie Fields went on the radio? Black argued that the only benefit to artistes could be in gramophone record sales pointing out that since the advent of radio 'in America there is not a single Vaudeville theatre left.'[45] However, it was proving a battle lost for the entertainment kings. Radio won the war.

Renée and Billie accepted the changing world, with a readiness to live in the here and now. Their aspirations were really no different to their 21st century equivalents. In February 1925, Renée said their ambition was 'to go on to the films'[46] and in August 1926 in an interview in The Era, we hear from Billie that 'Four different film companies have been making enquiries about us and, perhaps sooner than we expect, we shall be fixed up.' Renée pipes up with: 'we have both determined to be cinema stars,' adding 'people will laugh at us for saying this, just as the good people of Scotland laughed at us when we told them that we intended to come to London to take London by storm.' Billie hints of their numerous offers to go to America until Renée interjects, 'Yes, '*but*,' as you say.... what Billie means is that I am terrified of the sea. My last experience . . . just about finished me. A sister-ship to ours lost a propeller, and we had to go to her assistance. My word - didn't the ship roll!'[47] While conceding that films were their 'next great hope,' Renée didn't see that without an international tour, relying on films to spread their fame was as doomed as the lost propeller. The Houstons talked about films as soon as they made it big but they were taking too generous a helping of bread and butter from theatres in London and the provinces to bother too much with film companies. If they offered paltry sums what was the point?

With their energy and talent, it was a miscalculation to turn down the American offers. Fear of travelling by sea was an excuse. Renée would travel 5943 nautical miles when she and Donald Stewart visited South Africa in 1938. It's interesting to muse what chances might have become available had Renée's fear of travelling not kept the Sisters firmly on our shores, and what American opportunities might have led to. The Houston Sisters were not going to make much impact in silent films that failed to convey their essence, which was their patter. Talkies were different. If they had managed to play some limited vaudeville dates in America in 1926, they might have benefitted, as their friend Sir Harry Lauder did, from a prepared audience in America and a film distribution deal that cashed in on that audience. He reportedly made £10,000 from his film 'Huntingtower' - the George Pearson film in which he played an ageing Glasgow grocer. In Lauder's case his film had a soundtrack. A trip to America was easily worth the interruption and hardly would have dented the fantastic run of success the Houston Sisters were having in London at the time. Vesta Tilley did six American tours and got a contract from Hammerstein's agent for £1000 a week, although Marie Lloyd failed in the States.

I think America would have appreciated the Scottish Houstons who captured the mood of the moment wherever they went. Going there would have helped them in the long-term. After Jessie Matthews played to audiences in New York and Toronto in the mid 20s, the British musicals she made directed by Victor Saville appealed all the more, making her an international star – rare among British performers at the time. That graceful and lithe creature was the undisputed female version of Fred Astaire so her fame went without saying. If the Houston Sisters had kick-started a following across the Atlantic, in the same way they had nurtured a fan base up and down the UK, they might not be as forgotten now. An epitaph to the Houston Sisters might include the sentence 'refused to take America by storm.'

They did realize their determination to be cinema stars in March 1927, joining a film being made at Gainsborough Studios in Islington. It wasn't much but it was a start, and they were the darlings of director Adrian Brunel and his supervising editor Ivor Montagu. Both were intrigued by these new finds. The son of Lord Swaythling, one of the richest men in England, Montagu became a communist and started the London Film Society in 1927. The society drew its inspiration from foreign directors and included among its members enthusiasts like Walter Mycroft, Harrow-educated Adrian Brunel, and many members of the intelligentsia like Shaw, Wells, Huxley and Augustus John.

In a corner of a film studio. **ADRIAN BRUNEL** chatting with the **HOUSTON SISTERS.**

The first full length film in which the Sisters dominate one short scene: 'Blighty' (1927) directed by Adrian Brunel (By kind permission of The British Library)

The Houstons' *office* scene had to be rehearsed many times, with the director crying out 'Retake!' This was always at the same moment - when the head of the firm walks in, takes a bottle of champagne out of the safe and uncorks it. Eventually this got a moan from one of the Sisters - 'Oh, why do we always stop just here'[48] came the cry. The scenes featuring lead actors: Lillian Hall-Davis (who had starred in 'Boadicea'), Godfrey Winn, and Ellaline Terriss (huge star of musical comedy in the Edwardian era now making her film debut) were far more sedate with on set mood music utilized to create a sense of melancholy in the finished result. When production started in December 1926, the film was to be called 'Apres la Guerre' but that was abandoned when Michael Balcon hit on the catchy title 'Blighty.' When the film had its preview at the Coliseum, George Bernard Shaw was among the many notables who came to watch.[49]

While many variety theatres converted to cinemas in Britain in the 30s, the Houston Sisters didn't fear. Variety's top comics had, since Victorian times, been in demand to provide escape from depression and drudgery. Variety fuelled cinema and every American studio had room for personality stars, comedians and song and dance men and women. 20th Century Fox gave us wonderful musicals - many with Shirley Temple. There were tough films about gangsters rolled out by Warner Bros. We got Fred Astaire and Ginger Rogers in dance films as well as horror films from RKO, plus low budget horrors from Universal. We fantasized about the American dream when we watched a romantic comedy from Columbia Studios, whilst Paramount permitted us either to lose ourselves in sophisticated stories set in Europe or to laugh with the Marx Brothers, Bob Hope, Bing Crosby and Mae West. In Britain, many artistes from variety, particularly comedians crossed into films, and the venture met with huge success. These included Leslie Fuller, Gracie Fields, George Formby and Will Hay. Jack Buchanan, a lad from Helensburgh, had appeared at Glasgow's Panopticon. He made Hollywood films after appearing on Broadway and was a star on both sides of the Atlantic.

At the beginning there weren't enough films so there was a breathing space for variety theatre. It's possible the old halls and picture houses might have co-existed longer with talented performers to keep both going if film companies hadn't lured the fan base to the cinemas *Pied Piper* style. While the breadth of entertainment was greater, theatre-based variety never promoted its stars in the same way that film studios did. It didn't have the fantasy escapism of the movies. Olympian ideals were nowhere more exemplified than by Metro Goldwyn Mayer: famous for high quality productions. Fantasy was the zeitgeist: ideal looking people all the rage, with the Nazis, many of whom were cinema junkies, believing they could plan an ideal race in Central Europe. It was a moment when unreal aspirations dominated, whilst achievements on a human scale and the all too human side of life, made light of by comedians on a theatre stage, started to run close second. The intimate connection between stage and audience began to wither in the 30s. Thankfully our British disregard for pomposity and artificiality stopped us getting carried away.

The period in which the Houston Sisters enjoyed their greatest fame teemed with technological innovation. It was the age in which mass use of the telephone began, when the turbine engine was invented and an era that saw achievements in the field of powered flight. As I flick through the pages of a newspaper while looking at the write-ups for variety acts in the London theatres, I see a column nearby talking of the latest advances in physics. In April 1927 the Houston Sisters skit: *'Cohen's Accident on The Omnibus'* is the most convoluted theatrical creation ever there was. The wheeze has Renée crazily rushing up to the centre line having witnessed an accident involving a chap called Cohen. She taxes *Bill*'s patience until he's led off on a false scent by her chatter about a 'Scotsman's bag'. 'Was he in the right?' asks Billie. 'No,' says Renée, 'but Cohen's in the bag.' No amount of definition gets us anywhere and finally we hear that all this is just about Cohen getting thrown off the bus for not paying tuppence. Their senseless mirth brings the house down and Billy Bennett has a job following them. At exactly the same time as the roaring laughter at London's Alhambra, tiny particles ejected from radium with the fastest energy of motion of any particle known to science, were set spinning when Sir Edward Rutherford performed beautiful experiments to illustrate the alpha particle phenomena at his well-attended lecture at the Royal Institution.

Chapter 10   London and Everywhere by Storm

In September 1926 The Sphere, an illustrated journal with a whiff of jeunesse dorée emanating from its high quality pages, dedicated space to the Houston Sisters: the clever pair of Scottish performers 'who recently took London by Storm,'[1] and their photo spread included two 'new and exclusive studies by Vandyk.' She's fluttery and prettier than ever, clutching her doll whilst looking away, defeated by *Bill*'s latest slight. A little girl persona could be maintained for a surprisingly long time as Mary Pickford had proved so divinely and Shettleston's scrawny waif knew the secret. She had her own way of sending up prettiness, not that it stopped her wearing little bows in her hair to the very end of her life.

Three months after The Sphere, a high quality book of thirty-six soft-focus portraits of society beauties and actresses shimmering in subdued light paid tribute to that same wallflower. Hugh Cecil was the photographer who conceived 'The Book of Beauty.'[2] He first photographed the Prince of Wales in 1925 and, like Vandyk, supplied The Tatler and The Sketch with copious portraits. Later, he took the official photographs for the postage stamps of Edward VIII. Renée visited his studio at 8 Grafton Street.

Each plate has a poetic title and is accompanied by a poem on the left hand page. Beneath Renée's portrait photo the caption reads '*Incomparable*' and *"There be None of Beauty's Daughters"* by Lord Byron[3] is the accompanying poem – about the spiritual presence of water and the magical power of music. Renée's sweet Scottish voice must have been likened to *'the charmed ocean's pausing'* and her elfin beauty worthy of the godlike persona enchanting of all the children of Beauty. What Renée thought about Hugh Cecil's book is unknown but the lyrical dedication she received is prescient of words Cecil Beaton used to describe Audrey Hepburn in his 1950s books.[4] Renée is the least expected 'beauty' in the book. She's in the company of Lady Diana Cooper, Viscountess Curzon, Lady Lettice Lygon, Lady Bridget Parsons, La Marquise de Casa Maury and actresses Natacha Rambova, Isobel Jeans, Juliette Compton, and Edna Best. Her inclusion could be read as a seal of approval from people in high places.

People in the performing arts need champions. For a new artiste storming London connections must be built from scratch. On February 27, 1927, the Sisters were in the cabaret lineup at the *Gallery First Nighters' Club dinner* held at the Frascati Restaurant. The GFNC was formed in the 1890s after one *galleryite* booed a performance and got sent to prison and fined as a consequence. At these dinner evenings, people from London's play-going world, press and insiders rubbed shoulders and delivered witty speeches. That night in 1927 everyone made a speech offering a toast to the legitimate theatre. When Leslie Bloom, Club President, asked Renée to give a short speech, she told the guests she and Billie had never felt so illegitimate in their lives.[5] Back then, a chain of influence would connect agent with theatre insider, or journalist with titled lady wishing to attract prominent stars for her latest charity fund-raising event.

This merry-go-round allowed plenty of scope for mutual pampering and subtle string-pulls so Renée's line, 'it's not what you know but whom you know,' told frequently to her sons, isn't surprising. For the Houston Sisters the one who *'noticed'* them was James Agate - critic flamboyant at the heart of Fleet Street whose stylish observations in his *'Dramatic World'* column in the Sunday Times made everyone's ears prick up. When the girls first stormed London Agate made apostolic statements such as 'the British Music Hall has found two great artists,'[6] and 'they reached the stars at a single bound.'[7] Writing in The Encore, as early as January 1926, after seeing the Houston Sisters at the Victoria Palace, he pays them a significant tribute saying 'They are the cleverest newcomers I have seen for many a long day, and they will go far. They have a great sense of character, burlesque, and sheer fun, and every moment of their admirable and even brilliant entertainment proceeds straight from their brains.'[8] He wasn't excessive in his praise thereafter. Stars of legitimate theatre were Agate's primary concern, although he mentioned countless variety acts in his Sunday Times column, and in his nine volumes of 'Ego.' The Houstons are absent from his 'Their Hour Upon The Stage' and unlike Sophie Tucker he pays them little more attention until the mid 30s. Agate reserved most praise for Shirley Houston when she appeared in a straight role in 1935 and was less enthusiastic about the musical comedy Renée had a big success in that year. On that occasion, he sharpened his dagger about the overall quality of the show, comparing himself to the boy on the burning deck in a poem - staying 'to the piece's bitter end . . . *Casabianca-like'*. We have to wait until 1936 for Agate to say of Renée he is 'so great an admirer of this brilliant little artist.'[9]

Hannen Swaffer   George Balharrie and Renée   James Agate
(Photos: A. Richardson / Aherne Family)

His friend Hannen Swaffer, famed for his preposterous bow tie and pretty little flat overlooking Trafalgar Square, was known as 'the Pope of Fleet Street'. 'Swaff' took Sophie Tucker to his bosom. In the years after her British debut at London's Stratford Empire in April 1922, he gave her personal advice to help her, as well as praising her amazing vitality in notices. Swaff partied with his adored Tallulah Bankhead at her mews-cottage at Farm Street: his review about her the next day either cutting or full of praise. While he dubbed Gracie Fields 'the Funniest Woman in the World' claiming 'I brought her to London from her native Rochdale and she took the town by storm,'[10] he was unwilling in his books, to make similar dedications to the Houstons. Like Agate, he would have got excited if one of the sisters branched out in a legitimate drama in the 20s, as Gracie did. It's possible the Houston protective wall of family and George Barclay prevented them being championed by one particular press king but they commanded respect in the long-term.

The theatrical press was a different matter and in this narrower world they were thoroughly loved. Two years after making a hit in London, a writer in The Stage commented that when 'one realizes the inconsequential nature of their material and the great call on their personalities at each performance, it's astonishing how well they have maintained their position. Their act must be one of the hardest to perform in vaudeville, especially when they happen to encounter an unresponsive or difficult audience.'[11] After an Alhambra performance, when the Houstons had spent nine years in the limelight, Variety magazine believed the charming girls still possessed the artistry to fascinate stating that 'in song, burlesque or dance they succeed, while the humour and pantomime of Renée is an art of hers unequalled.'[12] They were 'the Alhambra's most popular act' and still 'in irresistible form.'

The terribly gay 20s theatrical world attracted all that was chic and modern into its orbit. It was a place in which *Bright Young Things* flourished. The Houston Sisters were on its outermost reaches. The imagery of music hall rubbing shoulders with the glitterati whilst *lunch is poured* adds a tinkling note to time and place for lovers of this period. Looking back, aged seventy-two, Renée tells us she knew Tallulah Bankhead and Ivor Novello very well: 'We went to parties. We met them all.' She recalled a party packed with stars including Tallulah, Bea Lillie, Novello and practically everyone else. Renée and Billie still had something of the dour Scot about them as they sat staring wide eyed, not understanding the fuss people made of them.[13] It's a joy to think of them fêted by the sublime when they were big news. One story I've heard the family tell recalls a party organized by Anton Dolin's crowd and the sexual antics of the guests were so bizarre, Renée and Billie had to run out into the garden, hiding in the bushes until it was home time. How people must have joked at their expense! This little story says more about the characters of Renée and Billie at this time, their Catholic upbringing obviously holding sway. Their regional accents and provincial airs were not only integral to their act, but ran close to the grain. It was no surprise they were fish out of water when placed in sophisticated circles.

Some members of the upper class who met the Sisters at parties and functions failed to be charmed by them. Renée and Billie promised Lizzi they wouldn't perform on Christmas Day 1926 - then on Christmas Eve, the phone rang with a request for them to entertain at a house party that a peer of the realm was holding the following evening. Stipulating a fee of 30 guineas to put the caller off, Renée felt un-Christian - reducing the fee to 20 pounds. In an instance her heightened spirits had caused her to let her mother down. She was festive and full of love for her fellow man that day having attended, a few hours earlier, the *Christmas party* that Lady Stoll had given for ex-soldiers and their relatives. She admired Stoll's down-to-earth Nottinghamshire-born wife who, like her husband, went little into society, devoting time to their charitable causes.

Left: Lady Stoll, Sir Oswald, and son (My thanks to Westminster Reference Library) Right: Coliseum view 2015

Seeing ex-soldiers' children watch in anticipation for the toy that would be selected for them from the illuminated Christmas tree tugged at the heartstrings. Billie, Will Hay, Dick Henderson, Daisy Taylor, and Leslie Sarony were among the fun providers. The Sisters had to go into society that Christmas day and, hardly au fait with such private engagements, learned to their shame what it was to feel like outsiders. Arriving at the party in their simple frocks they looked silly next to everyone else in evening dress. The host quickly got annoyed at them because they didn't have a drink. They overheard him comment 'Did you ever see such a couple of country bumpkins in all your life. Look at their clothes and they behave like a couple of half-witted kids! Won't even have a drink.' She thought of everyone she had encountered at Lady Stoll's, the day before: humble families and children who quietly waited for the single moment when someone would make them feel special. Here, around the room, everyone had been born with a silver spoon in their gobs. She looked at *Bill* whose eyes said it all. 'Not a friendly face and being ridiculed aloud,' murmured Billie, downheartedly. That bad-mannered reception gritted Renée to give the performance of her life, going in for the kill - especially where one fashion-conscious man was concerned: 'I made him look silly, criticizing his clothes - as we Scotch say in 'half fun, whole earnest.' Having earned the 20 pounds, people begged them to stay, giving Renée opportunity to quip in a voice clear as the crystal chandelier above: 'I'm afraid the two little country bumpkins are very tired.'[14]

Social changes were underfoot even if it was forty years before most of us witnessed any change. Aristocratic ladies flocked to be introduced to the two Houston Sisters, marvelling that the type of young woman whom they might have shared no more than a few humorous exchanges with as their cook or servant was suddenly achieving renown in the theatre, apparently made wealthy and even surpassing them in prestige. Courting the rich is part of the show business game, and Renée outwardly gave the impression she was charmed to rub shoulders with the upper class. Privately she was unhappy about the indifference shown by some who had possessed money for generations. She disliked anyone who spoke lightly about injustices faced by starving ex-servicemen or struggling miners. On the other hand she and Billie respected those who combined privilege with duty. She was proud of her blue-blooded namesake Lady Houston, who, after a radio broadcast in which the Prince of Wales spoke about the Miners' Distress Fund, gave £30,000. In accordance with the scheme, the government was expected to match this sum. Lady H, once the richest woman in Britain, who bought 615 parrots and taught them to shout political slogans, was a political maverick, feuding with the likes of Ramsay MacDonald.

There was a long tradition of fund-raising in the music hall. In the 1890s Marie Lloyd paid for beds for the homeless and destitute in squalid parts of London, and Vesta Tilley championed wounded soldier and children's charities after the Great War. The tradition continues today with the work of *The Variety Club* through its *'Tents'*. The Houston Sisters participated in numerous events. Back in 1926 they supported the *Wireless of Hospitals Fund*. At the London Hippodrome on February 5, 1927 along with comic Harry Green and rope artiste Tex McLeod they took part in *Three C's Charity Concert* to aid the Queen's Hospital for Children and a clothing fund for poor children. That realized £1000. An *All-Star Matinee* at Victoria Palace in May 1927 raised funds for Westminster Hospital. Seymour Hicks, Hermione Baddeley, Gwen Farrar, Van Dock, Elsa Lanchester, Clive Maskeleyne, Italia Conti and her child performers, the Co-Optimists and Norman Long performed too. A few days after, the Hippodrome did another fund-raiser for the Hospital of the Jewish Incurables.

Lady Moir organized a *June Rose Ball,* enlisting the Houstons for the cabaret at Wembley Stadium Club's dance hall, raising large sums for Westminster hospital's eye unit for kids. The Houstons were in the company of Sophie Tucker, Cicely Courtneidge and Jack Hulbert, and the beautiful actress Joan Barry - who married banker Henry Tiarks. A *Variety Matinee* for Brinsworth House took place at the Palace, Salford, in May 1928. In January 1930 there was a *Waifs and Stray's Society Charity Cabaret* at Covent Garden in aid of the Winter Distress League. When, the same month, Lady St John and Lady Titchfield organized another *All-Star Matinee* at the Theatre Royal, Haymarket, John Gielgud and Gwen Ffrangcon-Davies complete with pink bath, repeated their *balcony scene*, and the Houstons offered their services. Later on, Billie Houston gave a performance for miners at a South Yorkshire coalmine in early March 1935, and both sisters participated in a *Down and Outs Matinee* at London's Gaiety Theatre on April 8, that year. It was an astonishing show featuring Lawrence Olivier reciting Kipling's 'If', Jack Hawkins, Isabel Jeans, Evelyn Laye and Jeanne De Casalis. Charles Mayhew along with Irene and Violet Vanbrugh did mini-scenes from classic plays.

Many performances supported Brinsworth House, the Royal Variety Performance being the most famous, and individual artistes who had fallen on bad times. Renée and her stage partner Donald Stewart were among what has to be one of the best line-ups ever, when producer George Black lent the Palladium for a charity bash on August 24, 1939. They joined a company that included Max Miller, Revnell & West, The Two Leslies, Vic Oliver, Dick Henderson, Nervo and Knox, Tommy Trinder, Arthur Askey, Naughton and Gold, Flanagan and Allan, Freddie Bamberger, Norman Long, Albert Whelan, Adelaide Hall, Teddy Brown and Tex Macleod. It's surprising how many events like this took place, with theatres offered free of charge by London's 'entertainment kings'. Theatres of London are less used for this purpose in our day and age, whilst if you step outside you can barely avoid the charity muggers or 'chuggers' - often impoverished actors, forced to fundraise (far more effective to let them perform on a stage surely?).

I'm unsure if Miss Houston met Lady Houston, but many ladies of title were outdoing each other in the charity stakes, and the Rt. Hon. Ladies Plunket, Titchfield, Instone and Moir were a few of those known to the Houston Sisters. The Prince of Wales, later King Edward VIII was a great patron too. Billie definitely used to imitate him. At the beginning of her career, as the boy part of the Houston Sisters, the type of male impersonation she did was as different, say, as Shettleston is from SW1. With each successive occasion Billie came into contact with HRH, the potency of the illusion increased until *Bill* looked almost identical to the King.

How did the Houston Sisters meet the Prince? Family have told me it was definitely at one of the private appearances they were asked to give at Buckingham Palace, or at other royal palaces. Such events when performers were introduced to royalty were usually held at weekends and often on Sundays. Renée tells us that by 1936, she had appeared before the Prince – by then the King, on several occasions, and for the Duke of York - later King George VI, and Prince George – many times. Socially, royalty and people from the theatre did not mix and it was not approved of at all. Royal protocol put its foot down. Then again, it's known how the Prince eventually became fed up with the constraints he was forced to abide by. I can see the appeal of the Houston Sisters to anyone loathing the humbug aspects of English life. Here were two Glasgow girls unfazed by their surroundings: un-self-conscious, long having played oddballs in countless pantomimes. They couldn't contrast more with English society ladies, ritzy French courtesans, sexy Tiller girls, or cigarette-selling Kit Cat girls whose stockings had little trompe-l'œil cats' faces at the knees.

The Prince definitely sought theatrical friends and this isn't surprising given his involvement with many charities: his association guaranteeing the attendance of star names at benefits. Royalty has a staggering way of putting people together for good causes. He liked the movies as well as variety, backing the British National Film League's attempt to start 'film weeks' even though, at the time, there were too few films for the idea to take on. He was known for descending on studio executives, and in 1932 visited British & Dominions Studios at Elstree, watching Jack Raymond on set of 'Sorry You've Been troubled,' then Ealing's ARP studios, while Basil Dean explained a scene from 'The Sign Of Four.' He was introduced to Owen Nares and Betty Stockfield.

The Prince was also quite a *card* if legends that spring from the Aherne and Houston sources are true. Renée's husband Pat Aherne apparently used to go round to the back of Buckingham Palace and meet the future Duke of Windsor, and together they would steal off to have a drink at a little pub in Belgravia in the quiet streets stretching beyond. Nobody from the palace had a clue about it. There's an added caption to this fascinating story about the monarch who abdicated. On one occasion a Cockney man and sporting type came into the snug where the two handsome men were seated and started saying to the fair haired man: 'Oi!! Don't ya look like tha Prince,' and the Prince, putting on a most convincing Cockney accent said: 'Not me guv,' or words to that effect, proving what a good actor he was.

There's a charming story Renée told her sons in which the Prince insisted on the Houstons' presence at a 20s party he was giving. Renée and Billie were innocently sitting at a table drinking cocktails with cherries. They were teetotallers at the time, and would have opted for a glass of milk if offered. They didn't know what to do with the cherries so they thought it best to flick these under the table. When you think how a glass of whisky or gin was never far away from them in later years, it's sweet to think of a time when they were strangers to the elegant cocktail. The Sisters had been in and out of the best nightspots over a five-year period and by the end of it were familiar with the Who's Who of society. Renée's son Tony talked about going to Hyde Park with his mother, and saying hello to the little Princesses.

During the ten years before Edward VIII shocked the nation with his abdication, the Houstons got to know him well, although they never met Mrs Simpson. The Sisters would comment to their sons how there was nothing more elegant than the *Windsor knot* for wearing a tie, and harked back to similar little things that seemed to encapsulate their one time closeness to the enchanted Prince. Both sisters were extremely sympathetic to the poor man, bearing the full weight of public censure in the late 30s. They voiced sympathy long after the abdication. When Billie made her home on Paris's Isle Saint-Louis in the 60s, her son tells me she occasionally saw her old friend. Others say that's legend.

Prince Paul of Greece was another royal who graciously turned up for charitable causes for the mentally disabled, shell-shocked and neurasthenic cases. Greece was a Republic, and that's why Paul and his brother, the Crown Prince, settled in London in 1924. Paul anonymously worked as an apprentice aircraft mechanic in Coventry. It was during a fun-packed week in July 1929 that the Sisters met him - one that saw circus riders accompanied by wild animals parading through sunny Blackpool's town centre. During his stay, Prince Paul was shown a display of high diving and after ascending Blackpool's Tower he told a reporter 'it was like seeing all Paris under one roof, and for one shilling. It is wonderful.' Everything culminated in a *Gala ball* arranged by *The Stage Guild* at the Empress Ballroom graced by the presence of Prince Paul, vice-president of the Guild. A cabaret featured Max Miller, Bertini and Dorothy Langley, as well as Billie and Renée. The girls, beautifully dressed in satin were asked to join Prince Paul's table, and were photographed either side of him.[15] Boy, were they shy about meeting him! Paul was drawn to theatrical people, and one of his great loves was music. At his little flat in London's Victoria Street he displayed his talents as a pianist, so it's possible a more confident Renée and Billie visited to try out a new song, unaware that one day he'd return to Greece as its King when his brother died when, for a short period, Greece swung back to monarchy.

Sizzling late night cabaret in the 1920s is very *Sally Bowles*, and you might think the Sisters were living the high life. It was more a case of working very hard in the best places. Their brother Jim, acting as their manager, seems alone to have had the privilege of enjoying the surroundings. The Kit Cat Club, purposely built as a club, was one of the Sisters' typical late night engagements and Jim was a regular. It had a streamlined ultra-modern style and set you back a little more than its rivals with dinner at 15s 6d, Supper at 12s 6d, and Lunch at 5s. Jim's thoughts drifted to the great and the good among the audience. He once spotted the Prime Minister and members of cabinet letting their hair down, in the 'professional' section of the gallery, which looked down on the large square ballroom.

For the week starting September 19, 1926 we find the Kit Cat has a 10 pm floorshow with dancers Tamara and Fowler. American eccentric comic Chez Chase amuses the crowd eating matchboxes and matches. Space on the ballroom floor is cleared in time for the midnight spot, when Al Starita, in the small recess directly opposite the elegant stairs, leads the band. Marion Harris sings her well-known numbers like 'I'll See You In My Dreams'. Next, the Co-Optimists do a number in which they play the 'kazoo,' deafening everyone with its barbaric sound. Then, a couple of *children* have a good yawn before bustling into the ballroom in mid quarrel. Renée and Billie work the crowd causing an observer to say 'the intimacy of their act is peculiarly suitable for 'the floor.' Their Scotch pick-me-up has done the trick, and afterwards people fill the floor, with a cheeky fox trot from the band.

For first night revels, the Kit Cat offered London something that Sardi's or Dinty Moore's offered Broadway. Suddenly a constellation of theatre and film stars, as well as composers, writers and singers comes into view a few tables from you. Sophie Tucker, Ella Retford, Jack Hylton, George Grossmith, Tallulah Bankhead, Delysia, Gladys Cooper, Ethel Levey, Cissie Loftus, and Irving Berlin are captured on film in a 'Clubs and Cabaret' Pathé news item. They gather or pose as the spotlight descends on them. Ella was known for her *Sophie* impression, and Pathé captures Sophie and Ella up on the tables belting out a tune together. You could knock 'em back here! At the end of

1926, the Kit Cat club was deregistered for three months for serving liquor after hours. Marion Harris, a white singer who famously sang jazz and blues vocals would marry theatrical agent Leonard Urry in the 30s. He would represent Renée in later decades. At the time Marion was at the Kit Cat, young Leonard was over at London's Cafe de Paris - employed to dance with female patrons.

One nightspot close to their hearts was the Cosmo Club - a large venue on four floors, where Billie's twenty-first birthday party was held. Amiable friends like Stanley Holloway, Laddie Cliff and *Kisbey the Callboy* filled its trellissed piano bar for that occasion. Even Jimmie and Lizzi joined this late night gathering in the heart of Soho. Group photos survive, with Billie seated on the piano, her sister on the piano stool next to George, and Jim, Binkie and George Barclay all present. Both sisters hold a cuddly Dismal Desmond. A craze for the *Doleful Dalmatian* began after Joe Noble's cartoon used to be played at Gaumont British cinemas from late 1926. The Cosmo building still stands and has been home to O'Neill's pub for several years.

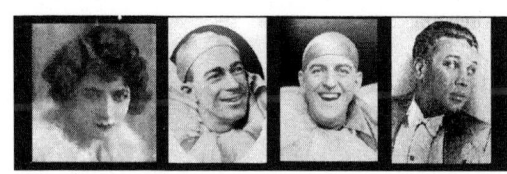

Elsie Carlisle, Laddie Cliff, Stanley Holloway, Hutch (K.Forbes Collection)

At Ciro's, Jim recalled seeing three of the four princes of the realm in that bright and glassy establishment. Famous for its African-American jazz band during the teens it was located at the Haymarket end of Orange Street. It gained a state of the art sliding roof and illuminated glass floor in the 30s, and bartender, Harry McElhone would start up Harry's Bar in Paris. A club called The Stage Door on St Martin's Lane had its topline acts appear in its dim lit cellar cabaret. The Houston Sisters joined Charles Austin, Clarice Mayne, Nervo and Knox, José Collins, conjurer Jacky Burns, George Jackley, and the beautiful actress June on this occasion on February 3, 1928. When The Stage Door opened, the staff from Windmill Street's Blue Peter jumped from that battleship-designed club to follow clubman Harry Adams here.

In late 1928, the Sisters were the popular attraction of *Playtime at the Piccadilly* – a busy West End midnight show. Jim's autobiography reveals another nightspot they were associated with - the Riviera Club, at 129 Grosvenor Road, down from Millbank. It was a peaceful haven by contrast. Crossing the elegant drawing room and stepping out onto the balcony, you gazed at the wide river and the distant little wharves on the other side. The river looked brilliant at high tide and you looked on cautiously. On summer nights supper takers felt refreshed by a luscious light breeze, and the small band, led by Percival Mackey, played subdued music. Royalty relaxed, knowing they wouldn't be gaped at, given the exclusivity of the membership and splendid isolation. The Prince had been coming to the Riviera Club for several years, often with a large group of friends, encountering former girlfriends. Jim Houston was responsible for the Riviera's floorshow, as associate producer of two cabaret productions, and his sisters would naturally have received bookings here. Some I've spoken to recall a story Renée told about herself or Billie drinking champagne poured by HRH into her slipper. The merriment of this mythical scene at the Riviera Club has worked its way into my imagination: elegant young men egging each other on run through the French windows onto the large balcony overlooking the Thames. Shrieks of laughter come from upper class ladies. The Houston Sisters sketch is disrupted, causing a look of fear on *Bill's* serious face. The *champagne in a slipper* story seems a common myth prevalent in the musical theatre of yesteryear. The film 'Evergreen' (1934) with Jessie Matthews and Betty Balfour offers a cinematic version. Some ladies of the theatre really did experience it when they'd had a success. It happened to Ruby Miller, so Evelyn Laye recalled.[16]

If the Houston's got the Moët slipper at the Riviera Club in the roaring 20s, it's become so distant, washed away entirely, into the dirty Thames. In the early hours of January 7, 1928 a disastrous Thames side flood occurred, and Jim describes the utter chaos of surging water swirling around peoples' ankles: everyone scrambling to get on chairs, and how the ladies passively waited to be rescued, perching in the meantime on the mantelpiece and grand piano. He bravely did his best to help in the hellish scene. The Riviera Club at Grosvenor Road was a casualty of one of the last major floods affecting Central London. It resulted in the death of fourteen people in nearby basements. Water levels rose to a depth of four feet in some areas and four thousand Londoners were made homeless. Even the House of Commons and underground stations near the riverside were flooded and paintings by Turner in the Tate Gallery got damaged. On the freezing morning after the flood a bedraggled and shocked Jim arrived back at 43 Elsham Road and was instantly clad in blankets by a panic-struck Lizzi. That evening Renée joined her brother to inspect the damage to the Riviera, her latent fear of biblical threats all the more reinforced. The Riviera Club survived to get converted into a home for Oswald and Diana Mosley in the late 30s. The simple single tiered classical villa has vanished, with something lacking soul in its place.

You could say the Houston Sisters woke up one day and were upper class by virtue of their stardom or from rubbing shoulders with enough important people. Renée managed to stay common enough to keep the *Glesca Keelies* ever-loyal fans, even though *Bill* was becoming 'damned aristocratic' at least in attitude. In cabaret, the Houstons were never awestruck by the rich clientele and threw out the same material as they did to patrons at the most ordinary music halls. Sometimes they found the sophistication of the regulars of Kit Cat and the Riviera 'put on', and Renée made sure to mock the debutantes and nobs on pedestals. Cabaret made for a very long day but the money was excellent. What act wouldn't take the opportunity to cash in?

Their first cabaret appearances were followed by a taxi home to Dalston to find Dulcie waiting for them with a hot supper at 3 am.

Close friendships have always existed between stars in the variety world. Vesta Tilley was a trusted friend of Dan Leno, for instance. Sometimes career rivalries would prohibit it. When the stars met the stars, they might seem a sociable bunch but some of that was definitely a front. A member of Renée and Billie's family told me Gracie Fields was considered more of a rival than a friend. Renée did defend Gracie in public and often cited Gracie as among the finest of all clowns. Pat bought a beautiful Hispano-Suiza off Monty Banks in the mid 30s. Renée liked to be driven around in it. The chances of being outshone by a rival emerging from that shiny conveyance were slim.

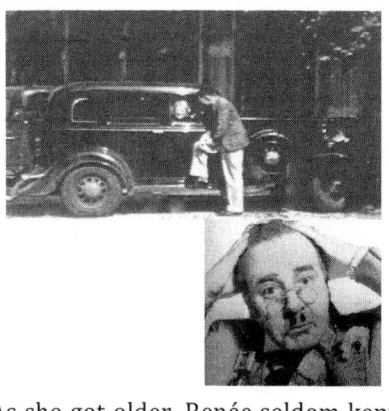

Renée in the Hispano-Suiza. The man with his foot on the footrest is George Balharrie. (Aherne Family)

Gracie Fields (Author's Collection)

Robb Wilton (Author's Collection)

As she got older, Renée seldom kept up with theatrical acquaintances. Some of it was down to rivalry – that grit common to the shoes of the entire theatrical breed. The curse of *Norma Desmond* also strikes hard for ex-Divas in their later years with crossed out names in the contacts book something plentiful. In their prime, the Houstons were quick to make friends. In the 20s, one of Renée's good friends was Jessica Merton, who with Carl Balliol had a huge success as 'England's Foremost Sensation Dancers.' Jessica was used to being flung swung around by the ankle or even streaming from the back of a fast-driven motorcycle.

On the whole family came first. Sir Harry Lauder, Will Fyffe and Robb Wilton entered the family orbit remaining special lifelong family friends. The girls didn't have time to go to many parties. Billie turned up at a bash for Nellie Wallace at Warwick Square in 1931. Only at charity balls did the Sisters hobnob with masses of the big stars and these occasions were few. The only time both sisters attended the Variety Artist Benevolent Fund annual charity ball was on November 12, 1926 at the Royal Opera House. They were like two nervous outsiders then. Singer Lillian Burgiss was perched up high in a fairy bower, theatrically lit, while the band, conducted by Lawrence Wright, played his 'While the Sahara Sleeps.' Sightseers waited outside to behold the fancy dress. Costumier Willie Clarkson was got up like the *King* in the playing card deck, Fred Barnes was a *Spanish grandee*, and the Houstons went as *Alice* and the *Mad Hatter*. Binnie Hale, Jack Buchanan and Peggy O' Neill were judges and 'best costume' was won by Dr Walford Bodie, who received a handsome gramophone as a prize. Gracie Fields and Archie Pitt, Bransby Williams, Dave O'Gorman, Marie Kendall, Layton and Johnstone, Florence Mills, Harry Tate, GS Melvin, Jack Hylton, and Sir Oswald Stoll were also guests. The Houstons were still new to London, and, for all their fearless storming the capital they were under the thumb of their parents.

They were more sociable in the next decade counting dazzling names from British cinema among their close friends. Best buddies still came from the variety world. Officially, the Houstons were in a 'super class' of high earners, although their lifestyle hardly compares to the über rich of today. Their 'legendary parties' tended to be in Southport, which became the preferred destination for annual holidays. Once, in the late 20s they invited all their friends to come north. There is a sad aspect to this story because the Sisters found nobody was willing to come to their *big party*. Most of their friends from the variety theatre were mindful where their next job was coming from. Therefore, the girls had to lure people up by offering them contracts, getting them on the bill at the Pier Pavilion. This tactic worked and their friends arrived in Southport in droves. Seaside and swimming pools epitomized the type of holiday entirely satisfying to Renée. They hired a lovely house where all their friends could stay with a week of activities laid on, such as airplane flights (for all except Renée). If we can believe one of her asides, this party emptied the coffers. Asked how the Houston Sisters' fortune had been lost, her answer would be 'Well, there was that party in Southport.' In the late summer of 1937 they were here again with radio star Ronnie Hill, actress Sally McBride and Don Stewart, enjoying the carousels and dodgems of Pleasureland. Southport is not the first destination that comes to people's minds today, when asked to name somewhere where you expect to blow all your takings in one go.

People who know something of Renée Houston are aware that she and Donald Stewart faced a harrowing examination in the courts for bankruptcy in 1948. Less familiar is the bankruptcy that Pat Aherne served as figurehead for, in 1940. He was at this time operating as manager for his wife and her stage partner Donald. Archive records for both bankruptcies shed light on financial risks associated with producing touring shows, when the burden falls on the headlining act. Expenses rack up, and provision for dependent acts is nowhere to be found. It's interesting reading, casting light on how show people try to break even. Unlike modern CEOs, they come across as far from avaricious, more like martyrs. The role the Second World War played in affecting earnings is clearly highlighted in the archival records.

When the Registrar questioned Pat in the official hearing at the High Courts of Justice, on October 30, 1940, we learn that Renée's money problems were due to accumulation of debt in the form of unpaid back tax. The Ahernes were paying it off in weekly installments at different times, to keep the debt down. As the sum increased, they were not able to catch up with it. By 1939 there was a marked difference between Renée's gross income and her net income but Pat claimed that 85% of what she earned should be expenses, telling the Registrar 'I can absolutely prove it week by week.' For every £100 she earned in 1939-1940 half of this would go on the expenses for a dress or a hotel bill. After you had taken off what it cost to support several relatives, the amount left to pay off the back tax installments was even smaller. What is astonishing is the claim for tax went back to 1932!

There was little financial planning in the early years of the Houston Sisters, when Renée and Billie were earning a fortune in the variety theatre. Gracie Fields, by contrast, had the sense to buy and develop an estate in Capri in the early 30s. Gracie did this and she also had a family clan depending on her. Luckily, Gracie's husbands were effective businessmen. None of Renée's husbands were as astute. The Houston Sisters were at their height between 1925 and 1934 – the time when variety was all-powerful, radio was still new, and variety attracted thousands of hopefuls as a career. The remuneration one could expect then was humongous, and several top of the bill acts commanded even bigger money than the Houston Sisters. In the Sisters' very early days in London their salary was a mere £30 a week, perhaps about £900 in modern money, but a family source has told me that, at the height of their popularity in the 1920s, when they combined appearances at prestigious houses like the Coliseum and the Alhambra, turn-working with other houses, and topping this with midnight cabaret appearances, they were each earning £1000 a week. That has the equivalent spending worth of £28,000.00. It's a lot, although nowadays the world's top ten footballers earn more in a single day. How we got to this situation with footballers is a mystery to me, but so is what became of the Houston Sisters' fortune. The truth of that seems lost in a Greek Dark Age.

Traditionally, pros got paid in cash at the theatre, but could at least count it out in their hand. When the Houston Sisters were handed 20 guineas for an 8-minute performance at a social function, all of that was easy to follow. Things got more complicated though. At the time top names had contracts with different organizations and this made tracking the payments more complex. From quite early on in the Sisters' career there was a lack of control over money. The view expressed by family is that George Barclay was excellent for getting work, but was far less so when it came to getting paid. In the case of Billie and Renée their finances were forever in a mess, and tax was not paid for some time. They had no idea where the money went most of the time, and it's very likely that some middleman was ripping them off. What they lacked totally was an accountant whom they could trust.

To return to Pat's examination by the Registrar at the High Courts of Justice, he explains how Renée's loyalty to her family only added to the troublesome tax situation: 'When my wife was in partnership with her sister they were known as the Houston Sisters and a lot of tax accrued there, and my wife's sister was taken very ill, she was unable to work and has not worked for the last six years, and my wife told the Income Tax people she would take over her sister's tax as well as her own, which she did, but she could not pay it, it was too big.'[17] Both Houston Sisters lived under the shadow of bankruptcy from the mid 1930s.

The heartbreaking thing is it seemed to follow Renée around for all of her career, and Donald Stewart got marked to some degree by association. In February 1956 Donald was writing home how 'Tax are asking half of everything. We have to slog all the time because we can't save anything in reserve. In June or July the solicitors and accountant have a view to cancelling our bankruptcy and tax debts and giving us a chance to start again.'[18] This didn't happen, and the awful truth is, that for all their tenacity, service and hard work as *Variety's Sweethearts,* and for all their theatrical and television work thereafter, they were still receiving threatening letters from the tax people in the mid 1960s.

Billie and Renée worked hard, and by the end of their first year in London they had done so many engagements at theatres and cabarets, it was the equivalent of three years work. By the end of 1927, they were already fed up with London and asked George Barclay to give them a rest, and afterwards send them on a tour of the provinces and Ireland. It was the first time in months they could sit back and look around a town themselves. Billie got a chance to develop her skills as an author. However, even in that first year, nothing stopped their annual holiday in Saltcoats, and they always returned from here with batteries fully charged.

Billie and Renée in Saltcoats (Aherne Family)

Billie and Renée (by Georges) c. 1911.
(Photo: Ronald Grant Archive)

James and Lizzi Houston,
1913. (Aherne family)

Above: The Houston Sisters
Photo by Herbert Vandyk, Summer 1926
(By kind permission of The British Library)

Left: Postcard of The Houston Sisters who appeared by Royal Command at the Alhambra Theatre, May 1926 (Lawrence Douglas)

Below: The Houston Sisters attend a secret political meeting. Cartoon by David Low, Evening Standard, 7 February 1929
© Solo Syndication,
British Cartoon Archive, University of Kent.

Above: Saltcoats annual holiday, 1927.

Right: Southport, 1929:
Top right: Binkie, Claire, Renée, Billie, Ronnie Rowe
Bottom: Claire, Shirley, Billie, Jack Stanford, Renée, Ronnie Rowe, Binkie. (Photos Aherne Family)

Right and below:
Cosmo Club, 1927.

Lizzi (in a dark dress) and George sit in the front row (George's hands on the shoulders of *Kisbey the Callboy*). Behind them, left to right, are Stanley Holloway, Binkie, Billie, unknown, Laddie Cliff, Renée, George Barclay and Jim Houston. (Aherne Family)

In the second photo George plays the piano and Billie and Renée each carry a *Dismal Desmond*.

Above: Saltcoats, 1926
(Aherne Family)

Above:
George Balharrie:
Renée & Billie's conductor 1924–30, Renée's husband 1925–32, and James Houston's partner in his *CineVariety Service* 1932-33

Below:
Hal and Claire Silander

Above: York Road, Battersea, February, 1935: James Houston, novelist and former West End agent helps others learn a new trade at a centre for the unemployed. (Photo: TopFoto)

Below left:
A page advert from The Performer Christmas Number 1931 with Christmas message, photos by Eric Gray and wistful self-portrait sketched by Renée.
(Courtesy of The British Library)

Below right:
Photo from November 1935 of the three Houston Sisters (Shirley, Renée and Billie) walking with dog. Photographer unknown. (By kind courtesy of The British Library)

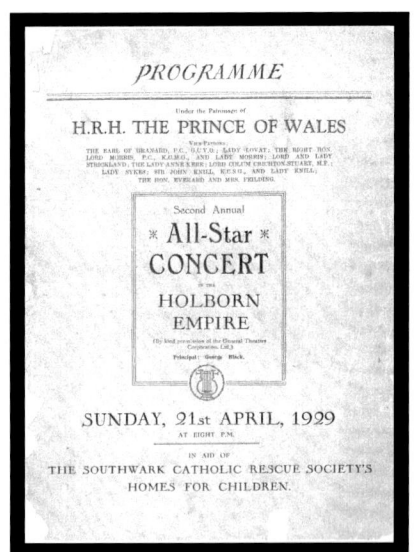

Programme for a 1929 charity concert in which the Houston Sisters performed.

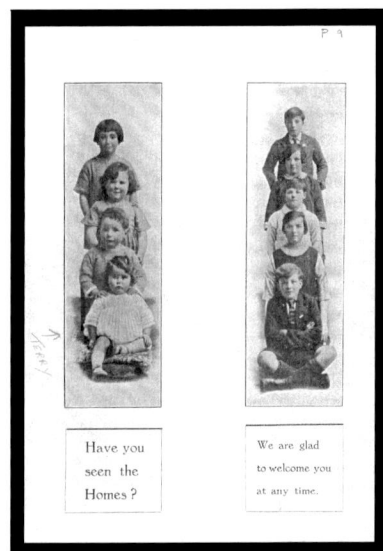

Renée adopted a little girl from a Catholic Rescue Society's home, seen in the advertising.

Above: April 28 1931: Jim Houston marries Elizabeth 'Claire' Silander at Trinity Church, Harrow on the Hill. Terry and Trevor Balharrie, a cousin - John Houston and Shirley are also seen in the photo.

Above right: Terry c. 1930-31. Terry left the UK in November 1946 and almost 30 years passed before she met Renée again. Shown is the photo that Renée gave to Terry in 1975 with the message *Fondest love to all my family, Grandma Renée.*

Below right: Northwick Circle, Kenton, January 1931 Seated are Trevor Balharrie, Renée holding Tony, Terry. James Houston stands behind them.
(Photos by kind permission of Terry Long's family)

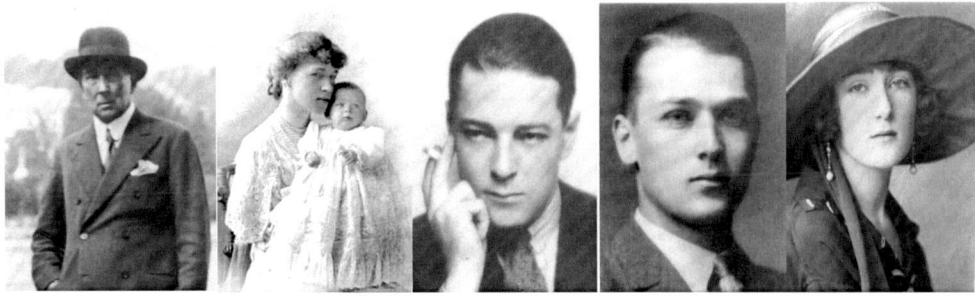

Above: The de Lacy Aherne Family: left to right: William ('Big Dad'), Lulu and baby, Patrick, Brian, Elana
(My thanks to the Aherne Family)

MISS LOUISE THOMAS.

The Ahernes: an acting dynasty: left to right: Lulu the young actress before her marriage, de Lacy heraldry, the three Aherne children at Italia Conti, Lulu (1920s), Brian Aherne at Malvern College.
(Aherne Family)

Patrick Aherne
Left: 'The *Flying Houdini*,' Centre: Teenager in Edgbaston, Right: At Tower Holme
(Aherne Family)

Left: Pat Aherne as *Richard von Rolf* with cast members. Right: Chili Bouchier as hypnotized *Ariel* with her saviour. Stills from Gainsborough's 'The City of Play' (1929) directed by Denison Clift and produced by Michael Balcon. Ian Dalrymple was film editor. It was partly made in sound with the RCA Photophone system. (By kind permission of The British Film Institute)

Above: Walter Bird portrait for The Sphere, July 20 1935 (The British Library)

Right: Cartoon by Arthur Ferrier for *Love Laughs*. "Renée Houston as 'Jenny' – A Smile-Stone in Musical Comedy History." From Play Pictorial No. 399. Vol. LXVII July 1935 page 30 (By kind courtesy of The British Library)

Laddie Cliff

Above and Right: Scenes with Laddie Cliff and Allen Kearns. Renée as Shirley Temple, Renée and Laddie. (My thanks to Michael Gaunt)

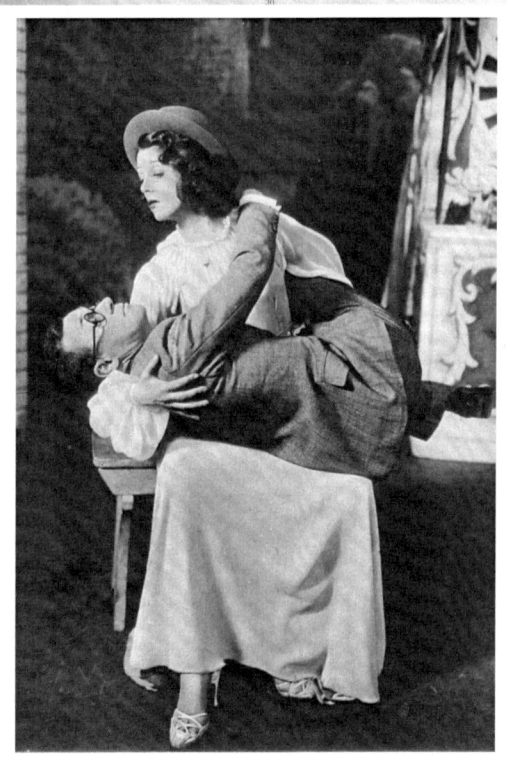

Renée as *Maggie Maclean* with Claude Hulbert as *Jimmy Oliphant* sing: 'It was 4 O' Clock in the morning':
My favourite scene from the film 'Their Night Out' (1933) directed by Harry Hughes.

(By kind permission of STUDIOCANAL FILMS Ltd)

Renée as *Titania*. Also pictured are Edward Chapman and WH Berry in the *Midsummer Night's Dream* sequence from the film 'Mister Cinders' (1934) directed by Friedrich Zelnik.

(By kind permission of STUDIOCANAL FILMS Ltd)

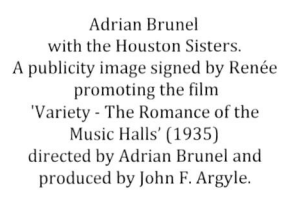

Adrian Brunel with the Houston Sisters. A publicity image signed by Renée promoting the film 'Variety - The Romance of the Music Halls' (1935) directed by Adrian Brunel and produced by John F. Argyle.

(My thanks to the family of J. Lewis)

Lost Scene from the Houstons' autobiographical film: 'Happy Days Are Here Again' (1936) directed by Norman Lee and produced by John F. Argyle.
Left to right:
Billie (*Mickie Grayson*), Viola Compton (*Ma*), Renée (*Kitty Grayson*), and Bert Cameron (*Pa*).

(By kind permission of A.Richardson)

Clockwise: Shoreham, July 1934, Terry and Shirley; Shoreham beach with Shirley, Pat, unidentified man; Group picture with Shirley, Sally McBride, Renée, Trevor, Terry, Tony and Alan (Lizzi seen at far right); Lunchtime visit by Brian Aherne to '*Abbotswood*', 1938. (Family of Terry Long)

Renée's family at their home '*Abbotswood*' in Stanmore.

Left: Brian and Patrick Aherne, Hollywood, 1946. (Aherne Family)

Above: The Wintermute Family of Wilkes-Barre, PA: left to right: Ferd. Clark Wintermute (Donald's father – a civil Engineer), Jessie Wintermute (called 'Mickey' by her English friends), and Don's siblings: Jack, Lois and Janice.
Below: Donald Stewart Wintermute, Broadway star of *George White's Scandals* (Wintermute Family)

Above: Renée at the time of the film 'Fine Feathers.' (Wintermute Family)
Next page: Renée and Don in 'Fine Feathers' (1933) directed by Leslie Hiscott. (Wintermute Family)

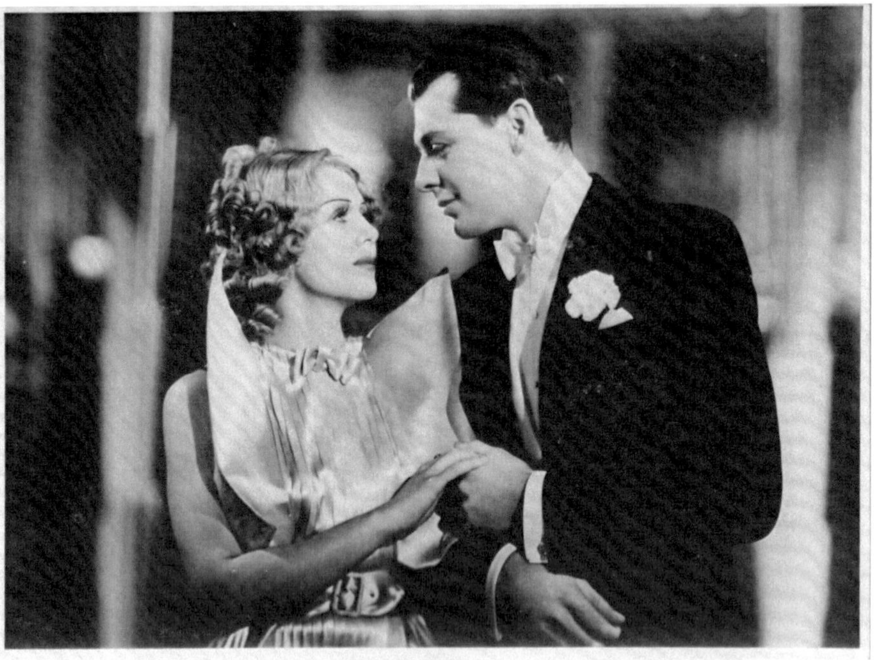

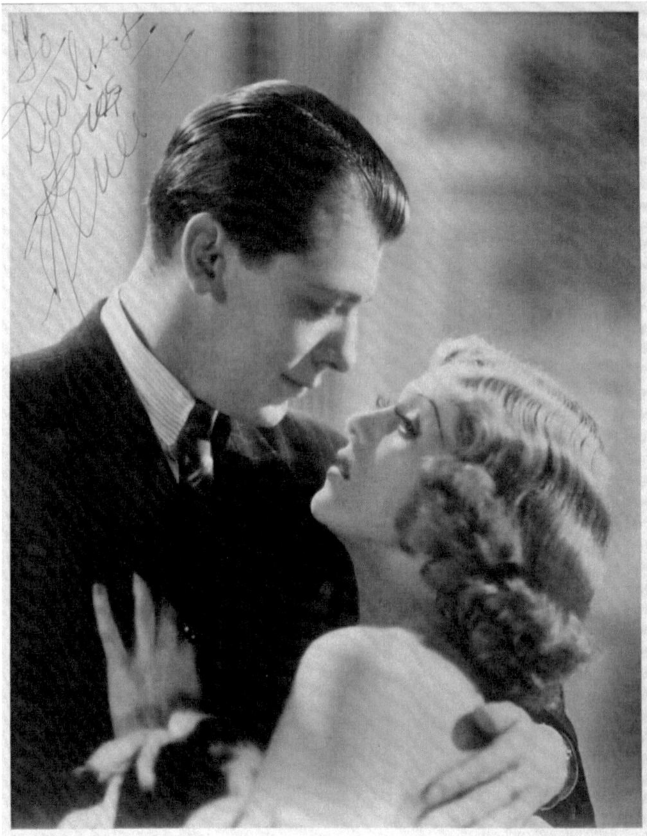

Right:
Renée Houston weds
George Balharrie
Thursday
19th February 1925.

This photo appeared in a newspaper article from February 22nd, 1925 entitled *'Romantic Wedding of Glasgow Panto Artiste.'*

(Photo: courtesy of The British Library.)

Right:
Renée Houston weds
Patrick Aherne at
Henrietta St
Registry Office
Monday
28th November, 1932.

Shirley Houston is Renée's bridesmaid.

(Photo: TopFoto)

Right:
Renée Houston weds
Donald Stewart
Wintermute,
Saturday
7th August 1948
The photo was taken in the garden
at their home in
Waldegrave Park,
Strawberry Hill.

(Photo: By kind permission of the family of Donald Stewart.)

Above:
Rehearsing a drama.

Right:
Renée with manager and husband Pat and her stage partner Donald, 1938
(Photos: Family of Terry Long, Wintermute Family)

Top row:
Southport Pleasureland, 1937, Renée and Donald pose with Shirley.

Returning to this popular vehicle the next year to pose with Mickey and her friend Annette Gebert. Summer 1938.

Middle row:
Southport Pleasureland, 1937, Donald, Shirley, Sally McBride, Ronnie Hill and Billie Houston.

Bottom row:
Scotland, 1938, Donald and Mickey during Mickey's trip to the UK.

(Photos: Wintermute Family)

Above and Below, and Next Page - *Variety's Sweethearts* in 1938 (Photos: The Wintermute Family)

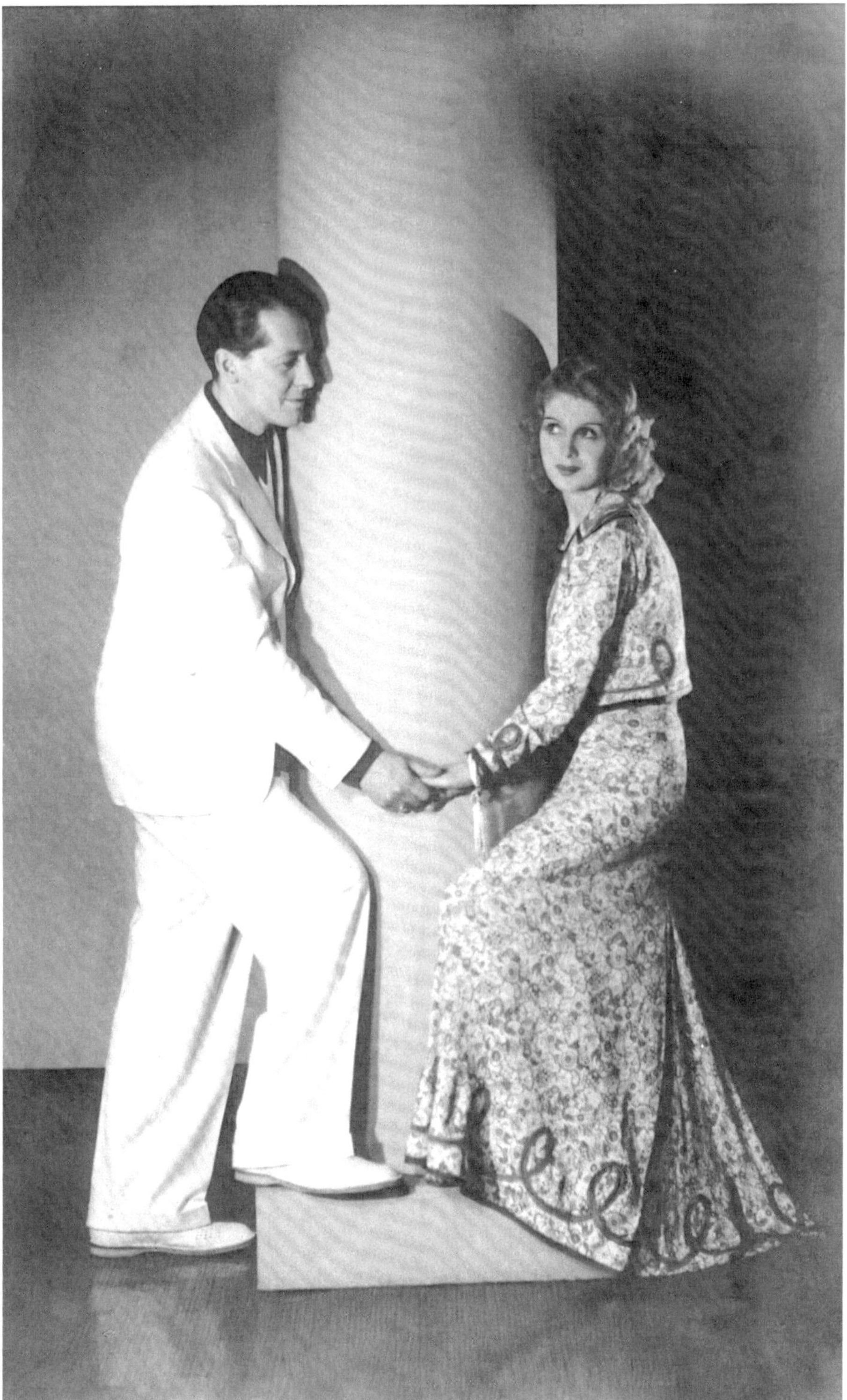

Above: Anthony Buckley portrait of Margaret Lockwood, Renée Houston, Hugh Sinclair and Lilli Palmer publicizing 'A Girl Must Live' (1939) directed by Carol Reed © estate of Kenneth Hughes / National Portrait Gallery, London

Above: Renée Houston, Phyllis Calvert and Patricia Roc pose for a film still during production of 'Two Thousand Women' (1944) directed by Frank Launder © ITV/Rex/Shutterstock, British Film Institute

Above: Renée Houston at the time of 'A Girl Must Live' (1939) directed by Carol Reed.
(By kind permission of Lawrence Douglas)

Chapter 11   The Love and Loves of the Houstons

In October 1928 Bob Wilton Smith, a RADA-trained actor, and Billie Houston announced their engagement. He was twenty-one and she, twenty-two when they perched on the steps outside the front door at Elsham Road, beaming at a Daily Mirror photographer. She loved travel, and unlike Renée, longed to go to America. Only an adventurous spirit would have flown Imperial Airlines on its trial flight between Croydon and Deauville the previous year. A photo taken at Deauville conveys her vivacity: something she had in large supply. Bobbie was an only child and a loner when not treading the boards.[1] He had been in the Sisters' orbit since his father Robb Wilton began appearing on the same bill as the Houstons. A few days before the wedding, when both sisters were interviewed, Renée, her bossiness clear to see, explained what trouble she'd had kitting her sister out as a conventional bride.

It shows the social standing of the Houston Sisters that Billie was able to marry at Brompton's Church of the Oratory, not least on Christmas Day of all days, and no expense was spared on the reception. They were married by Father Joseph Crea, and if you imagine a tray of iced Belgian biscuits you might complete the image of the three bridesmaids in turquoise blue and three in pink, following Billie with orange blossom on her mob cap and a sheaf of lilies in her hand. All the ladies wore medieval-style dresses, and Little Trevor Houston was a page. The reception was at Belgravia's Rembrandt Hotel, owned by the Vandyks - photographers the Sisters had used for stage portraits, who would later take colour portraits of Edward VIII. The Houstons worked on Boxing Day at the Alhambra, and when Billie came on she got a hearty ovation. Donning a man's old brown felt in their sketch, she was handed a bridal bouquet before they left the stage, which must have been an incongruous sight.

The newlyweds settled into a flat at Leith Mansions, Maida Vale. Bobbie appeared in *Cynara* at the Playhouse Theatre with Gladys Cooper, Gerald du Maurier, Ann Todd and Celia Johnson. He sometimes joined variety circles, and it was a big happy family during May and June 1930 when Renée and Billie collaborated with Robb Wilton, wife Florence, Ray Cardle, folk dancers Dawnya and Petrova, and the Hintoni Brothers for the *Houston-Wilton Road Show* at theatres in Croydon, Camberwell Palace, Islington and Kingston. Bobbie and Billie went to the *Water Rats Ball* at Park Lane Hotel in November but by August 1931 their marriage had broken down. So much for expensive weddings!

Differences in earnings added to the pressures of marriage. Billie's takings per week were £80 - almost £3000 nowadays, whilst Bobbie's were modest. There were separations because of his wife's work commitments and, true to his public school motto "If Right Within, Trouble Not," Bobbie didn't voice his troubles. Billie did, only too used to asserting herself among strong-minded siblings. She didn't feel at home with the legit theatre and her career objectives tended to be blatantly commercial. In their divorce court file, his wife's adultery with another actor from the legit stage is given as the reason for their split. The correspondent was Richard Cowper. Strange that Billie should go so quickly from a relationship with one actor to another, although who amongst us hasn't been overtaken by an infatuation. Unusually, the dates she had 'frequently committed adultery' with Cowper[2] occurred after the Wilton Smiths had separated. Perhaps the three of them organized a 'set up' to release the couple from marriage. Billie and Bobbie remained friends with no apparent bad feelings, and Bobbie participated in revues staged by Renée and Donald later in the decade. Desperate to be a granddad, Robb Wilton regretted their decision.

Left: Bob Wilton Smith and Billie (Family of Teresa Long)

Centre: Richard Cowper (Family of Teresa Long)

Right: Paul Eve and Billie, 1939 (National Library of Australia)

Her second husband was another only child, but Richard Cowper had been born into wealth. His family owned a large estate in Sittingbourne and other parts of Kent. A descendent of the poet William Cowper, he lived in a smart flat at 186 Albany Street, near Regents Park Barracks at the time he was cited in her divorce from Bob Wilton Smith. He used his family name Shapland Cowper on the stage, but was 'Dickie' to his friends and 'Uncle Tommy' to Renée's kids. He was six foot tall, gifted musically, witty and genial in his manner. Two years her senior and extremely cultured, he was a guiding force for Billie. At the time Billie and Renée were eating their late night corned beef sandwiches in Dalston, his musical comedy *Tell Me More*, featuring the music of Gershwin, was closing. This was at London's Winter Garden Theatre (where The New London Theatre is today). He travelled to America with the cast. Returning home, Dickie was in a handful of plays after, including *The First Mrs. Fraser* by St. John Ervine.

Billie and Dickie married before the Sheriff at the County Buildings in Glasgow on August 11, 1933, the bride in a mustard-coloured outfit, and this time with four friends to wish them well. The happy party then sped off in a saloon car back to Largs Hotel as the Houston Sisters were appearing in *Sunny Days* at the Pavilion. A few months after, Dick played two small roles. One was in *Clive of India*[3] but subsequent acting roles either didn't come or personal choice led Dick to focus on being a publicity agent. The Cowpers lived at Lauderdale Road - just a street away from her former home with Bobbie. 222 Lauderdale Mansions possessed an aquarium of tiny brightly coloured fish that impressed her young nephew, Tony, and was beautifully modern. Entirely un-domesticated, Billie hired three maids, got some idea as to the basics of housekeeping then aristocratically dismissed them. What she learned wasn't much.

Was it Dick's wealthy solicitor father, William Shapland Mandeville, not his son, who was really in love with Billie Houston? Their relationship was lasting. Billie had a knack for collecting loving father-in-laws, and Robb Wilton continued to love her like a daughter long after she had divorced Bobbie. At Shapland Senior's estate, Dickie and Billie spent a lot of time together making lily ponds when she wasn't playing golf. Interviews with Billie give an indication of her social circle: a posher one than that Renée moved in. It mirrors the *'wee but and ben'* stage routine with *Bill* having climbed some distance up, although Renée wasn't exactly 'bottom of the ladder.' Renée and Billie were hardly ever in Tatler but Billie's photo appeared in an issue once, when she attended an open-air party with aero-display in July 1936 - a fundraiser organized by Jeanne de Casalis.

Billie might as well have been in the Tatler set, where it was typical to receive invites to country house weekends, requiring gentlemen to determine whether tails or a dinner jacket were appropriate. One time Dickie thanked his lucky stars it turned out to be a ball, not an informal hop, although when he came to dress he realized their maid had mistakenly packed Billie's tails. Another time Billie was spending Christmas with 'my husband's people' as she described them. Arriving after a prolonged tour with her trunk of stage clothes as well as personal wardrobe, her suits were hung in a dressing room adjoining the room used by Shapland Senior. Dressing for dinner, the older man had a prolonged struggle getting into his togs. His wife, thinking he'd eaten too much, made a large slit in the trousers of Billie's 20-guinea suit, thinking it wouldn't show if covered by the coat.

The Cowpers were happy if you believe the snippets in newspapers over the next few years. When 'Twice Round The Clock' was due to be serialized in the Daily Sketch, Billie mentioned the 'no going back' panic that set in and the drudgery getting the book out in time. Dickie would come into the room on grey mornings saying: 'What about the book, eh?' He seemed to be the one who pushed her to see it through and in return was press-ganged into helping, having learned how to type. When the first installment appeared a photo in the Daily Sketch's photo section showed Billie in her chintz armchair: her Scottie dog Dougal in her arms and Dick perching close to her. She's regal and he's slick in his pin stripe suit. It's bizarre why an unrelated news story, running at the same time, about a marital 'scandal' concerning a Mrs Lloyd who used to pounce on her husband and wrestle him should be referred to as a 'Billie Houston affair.'[4] Did I miss an intervening story with Miss Billie losing her regal demeanour and flooring someone?

More Dam Things came to Sheffield in late February 1935. A woman in the audience died and the manager asked if her body could be put in Renée's dressing room. That week Billie, Shirley and Dickie visited a Blue John mine, with Billie and Shirley doing a turn for the miners at the pithead. A picture survives with Billie, lamp in hand, standing next to her husband who looks relaxed and smiling, with a soot-faced miner next to him. This was before an adventurous undertaking into the deepest recesses of the mine to observe how men dig for 'black diamonds' and risk their lives daily. Crawling through a gallery on hands, knees and tummy, deafened by the boom of blasting operations, and showered by particles they finally emerged into the daylight. But what greeted them was a terrible storm, forcing them to take cover in a hut until it abated. Their guide turned out to be a cave-hunter who suggested showing them some of the marvels of nature. Billie talked about how she and Shirley would happily have let Dickie go, but neither cared to remain without male protection in that deserted hut. Together they explored some of the stalactite caves but it became so dangerous they agreed Dickie go on ahead with the guide. While the sisters waited Shirley's hat got blown away and the two of them made their way out. They waited ages and ages, soaked to the skin in the car, for Dickie and the guide to return.

'Don't ever mention caves to me if you value my friendship,' Billie said, referring to that day. Her husband's disappearance with the guide might be significant. Billie was of the generation that never referred to a person's sexuality, but years later made an exception, describing Dickie as 'queer as hell'. One member of the family bluntly tells me that Dickie married Billie because he liked boys and she looked like one. Crazy as this might seem, it was not out of keeping with the times and sophisticated people might have considered theirs an ideal marriage. My sense is it was some way into their marriage when this side of him became known as they stayed together long enough. It can't have been easy for either of them.

Another man appeared on the horizon, leaving Uncle Tommy in the cavern's shade. At the end of 1937 twenty-three year-old Paul Eve left Brisbane on the *Oronsay*, a ship bound for the land of his ancestor William John Wills - the surveyor who explored the north-south route across Australia, dying at Cooper Creek. Paul, who never used the Wills-Eve surname, had once played cricket for New South Wales and won medals for swimming. Aided by his mother Ruby - one of Australia's first female columnists who wrote articles for newspapers like The Brisbane Truth, Paul began a career in journalism. Was Ruby news magnate Rupert Murdoch's godmother as one story goes? Paul began his career in Fleet Street working for several editors until the mid 40s when he became deputy Editor of *British United Press*. The United Press subsidiary edited the very American-orientated news wire for distribution to the media in the UK and Canada.

In the late 30s, Paul, who spoke with a mere trace of an Aussie accent, made use of his vast network of well-connected friends in England. Paul knew Lord Beaverbrook, and had grown up with the McGuire sisters - known as '*The Marrying McGuires*,' owing to their spectacular marriages. They entered the British aristocracy or became actresses in London and Hollywood like Mary McGuire. Patricia McGuire married Beaverbrook's son Peter Aitken in 1942 and they were lifelong friends of Paul and Billie. This opened doors. It might have been the McGuire connection that led to Billie's meeting with baby-faced Paul Eve.

In April 1938, a devoted Dickie visited Billie in hospital, giving the press daily updates regarding her recovery from a throat operation. The Daily Express on April 12 has a photo of him entering the door of University College Hospital. He promised to set her up with a dance band if she got better. Then, in early June the couple separated, causing Dickie to go downhill fast and plunging publicity-shy Billie into intrigue and scandal. Imagine two affluent apartment blocks in London's Marylebone, a doomed marriage and a dramatic suicide – *story by Edgar Wallace - directed by Alfred Hitchcock*. The Saturday papers were full of the story. On the evening of Thursday July 21, Billie called into the basement flat of her husband's boyhood friend Henry Jackson-Werndly at Hyde Park Mansions, where Dickie was in a state of desperation. 'You must do something to bring us together,' he begged his friend. Billie asked to see her husband alone to talk divorce plans. Following a quarrel in which he was heard persistently crying 'What can I do to put things right?' he jumped up and left the room. Harry Lawrence, porter at the building, encountered Cowper staggering up the steps from the flat with a bottle of what looked like cough mixture pressed in his hands and was told: 'I am dying, take this.' The thirty-four year old actor collapsed on the pavement, his face twisted in pain[5] again crying 'What can I do?' Tragically, he died minutes after the flying squad came and took him to St Mary's Hospital at Praed Street.

The Hull Daily Mail tells us that Dickie hadn't been sleeping for days on end, that the couple were unhappy and that during their interview she told him to 'get out.' Cowper's friend Jackson-Werndly provided these details. He had left the building so the couple could be alone. Billie had no idea what he was going to do. At the inquest, Coroner Ingleby Oddie asked 'Where did he get the poison?' Dr Wynne Wilson gave evidence to confirm that death was due to shock and heart failure from swallowing an irritant poison and a 'verdict of suicide while of unsound mind' was recorded[6] with Oddie concluding: 'I've no doubt the unhappy life that Cowper and his wife were leading caused him to lose control of himself and he yielded to his insane impulse to take his life and end his troubles.'[7]

Suicides were not uncommon among well-born but unhappy young men in the 30s although suffocation by gas was a more usual cause of death. The most extraordinary interpretation of these events is in a letter from Tony Aherne, writing in April 2004 about his memory of Cowper's death. Tony says his Uncle Tommy staged his own death to mirror a scene in Billie's novel 'Twice Round The Clock'. It sounds far-fetched and the stuff of comic books, but Dickie was indeed mirroring events in the novel. Tony brings Paul Eve into the story: 'Tommy found out. He made up the poison in her novel, confronted the couple (Billie and Paul) in the street and threatened to take it if his wife did not return to him. Knowing the toxin was not deadly, Billie refused. He took it and died: of a heart attack!'

Did an affair between Billie and Paul trigger the hopeless mental state that led to Dickie's death on July 21 1938? Billie was having a dreadful time of it in the first four months of 1938, recovering from her operation – not an ideal time for a love affair, surely? Apart from the old newspaper reports, what I've learned tends to be as folkloric as the brambles and thorns on Sleeping Beauty's castle. Dickie emerges as needy: his genuine struggle and tendency towards emotional blackmail prolonging the relationship until there was no choice but for them to separate.

There are a couple of other possible motives. Jackson-Werndly thought the medicine bottle was connected to a heart condition his friend had, telling the press 'I know that he had heart trouble and a few months ago he had a mild collapse.' He added that Dickie's mother had just died and that he and his father were grieving, although Dickie was normally one of the most cheerful and happiest men he knew. If Billie and Paul Eve had, in fact, begun an affair - this was a harsh punishment. She might have considered Dickie's emotional state knowing he had recently lost his mother. Three mysterious documents were left by Dickie at the concierge's desk at adjoining Oxford and Cambridge Mansions in Transept Street which indicates everything was planned, although it isn't clear what these revealed. It seems he could neither bear the shame of failure, nor the prospect of being alone, and so 'died for decency' rather like 'Boy' Fenwick in Michael Arlen's novel The Green Hat.

For Billie Houston this was the last thing she expected and she found herself in the middle of a nightmare. Renée and the rest of the family rushed to support her. Billie spent that hellish week at her mother's in Sudbury overcome with grief with a doctor in almost constant attendance. A friend told the Daily Mirror 'Billie's grief is tragic. She lies alone in one of our rooms. All we can hear are her sobs. She does not want to see anyone. She is heartbroken at the loss of her husband.'[8]

Family members tell me that Paul's mother Ruby was disapproving of her son's new relationship when he wrote to her in Australia, but only on account of a misunderstanding. She thought Paul had got himself involved with one of the Dolly Sisters. When she found out it was a Houston, everything was ok - which doesn't say much for the reputation of the Dollies. This does lead me to wonder if Paul told Ruby about his relationship prior to the episode in Marylebone. If not, the scandal of Dickie's death would surely have mattered - much more than the idea of him being tarnished by a Dolly Sister. It also didn't seem to matter to Ruby that Billie was eight years older than her son.

Paul Eve knew what it was like to emerge out of the debris of a failed first marriage. That had taken place when he was very young. He never spoke about it and his children only learned of it much later. Similarly, if anyone put the embargo on Billie's marital history, it was Paul. Their kids hardly every heard them discuss Bob Wilton Smith or Richard Cowper. Paul was a determined young man who knew what he wanted. He seems to have been a driving force, ensuring that he and Billie finally get things put right and he took her under his wing from the start. You also have to admire Billie's resilience in putting her past behind her. In September 1939 she was listed as a widowed 'Travelling actress' living at the same address - 7 Addison Court Gardens W14 - as that of Paul Eve and his mother. The couple married on November 13 that year at Hammersmith Registry Office. Shirley was Billie's bridesmaid. Ruby, who had moved to England and was an occasional voice on the radio speaking about her career in journalism, didn't attend the ceremony. The couple lived for a while in an apartment in Hays Mews.

Tall, well built, and in possession of sartorial style, Jim Houston had a commanding presence. He looks like a 'somebody,' captured in caricature by a theatrical artist. Jim first tried his luck in performer representation: a masculine world of tough guys - the kind he met through 'the Guv' in early 1926. He claims he was with the Houston Sisters at Shoreditch and that Renée dictatorially shoved a pile of letters his way saying 'Here, take these and attend to them as soon as you get home.' His ne'er do well playboy reputation was enhanced after he started going to Mother Meyrick's *Club 43* in Soho's Gerrard Street where gangsters and lords sat side by side. Before Ireland's 'queen of the nightclubs' was sent to Holloway Prison in 1929, Jim was a regular there. He might have been innocent to the majority of the accusations laid at his door in these years. He claimed that several impersonators in the West End used his name to do discreditable things. One of his old friends was found out to be a criminal.

In his autobiography Jim projects a tough frame of mind, mentioning his run-in with the Notting Dale Gang – a gang of toughs threatening the peace of 1920s West Kensington. For the weekly 'What The Encore Wants To Know' gossip sheet, Jim was one of several recurring 'targets.' He gets some of the funniest lines such as a ragging for being wily: 'Why does Jim Houston think we're in for a quick return to Variety? Is it because he is booking acts up at a very satisfactory rate?'[9] Then the paper gossips about him splashing his money about: 'does Jim Houston write his telephone numbers on a fiver?' 'Has Jim Houston come to town for good . . . For whose good? 'Where's that Hogmanay box of cigars Jimmy promised us?'[10] Finally he's fond of a fight, even fond of a knife: 'Is Jimmie Houston junior going to set up as a nose-setter?' 'Isn't Jim Houston a sharp young fellow? Doesn't the grass in his garden even come up in blades?[11] There's no doubt he had a reputation and lived up to it. Despite brushing alongside London's underworld and causing alarm among Episcopalians and Unitarians in London, Jim remained a man of energy, running with the Harriers from Regent Street Polytechnic.

Before long, he was applying for a license for his new *Cine-Variety Service* at 26 Charing Cross Road in 1932.[12] Cine-variety had definitely arrived, and Jim's idea was to move with the times - matching the right artiste to the right venue, harmonizing the best variety act with a particular feature film, and keeping a close eye on local conditions so acts met with audience tastes. Good idea wasn't it? His service provided music for venues and George Balharrie, Jim's co-director, handled this side. No longer Renée's conductor, George arranged for bands to go out with the productions, helping out of work musicians to reap the benefits of playing with a band. The boys' chief problem was 'distance', it being impossible to run the service between say, Doncaster and Plymouth, unless they already had dates to fill between those places. The cost of fares prohibited such disconnected engagements.[13] There's a lot to admire in this new venture but times were tough then for many people in business, and Jim's own proclivity towards depression counted against success. He was sick of being accused of milking others' fame. When life got him down it usually stemmed from being branded 'The brother of the Houston sisters' in the same way Shirley hated being called the 'other sister'.

Whilst Jim and Renée attended posh dinners and balls such as one in March 1929 at the Old Vaudeville Club, a degree of negligence on his part got the Houston Sisters embroiled in a court case a few weeks after that, over copyright issues connected to portraits by the photographer Sasha. Jim allowed some of the photos to be hung in frames of the Coliseum Theatre when they were only on loan.[14] Jim admitted he and Renée 'did not always see eye to eye,' but was open in saying that all her life she 'turned to him in her crises.'[15] Soon, he would stop using the 'Houston' name, forever after calling himself James Alan Rennie.

When he was thirty-two, Jim married Elizabeth McWalter Silander - gentle daughter of entrepreneur Herbert Silander who left Gothenburg and settled in Scotland marrying Marion - an Ayrshire woman. Herbert worked his way up in the lace bleaching business - one Granny Houston knew well. Betty was a Girl Guide, retaining a long connection with the movement. At sixteen, she was a student at Kilmarnock Academy. She had the looks to grace a London chorus but never wanted to even if she did strike up a friendship with Renée and Billie. This happened either at a local swimming pool or through some lark the Cummings boys planned at the time the Sisters were at the Palace, Kilmarnock. Jim waited several years for her. When their courtship officially began he would take her out to supper at Romano's in the Strand or to Henley for punting. It was probably having two Elizabeths close to him that caused him to call his wife 'Claire'. At their wedding at Trinity Church, Harrow on the Hill, little Terry and Trevor are in the pictures, with Shirley very much in bloom as Claire's bridesmaid. When they married in 1931 they were on the front page of the Daily Mirror. Such was the mystique of being associated with the Houston Sisters in those distant days.

The early years of Jim and Claire's marriage weren't easy. Enjoying the family's new wealth but barely contributing to it played on his sense of guilt. Here he was in the first three years of the 30s in the comfort of London's pristine suburbia whilst a third of his native city's workforce scraped by, given the decline in heavy industry. Until the middle part of the decade social security benefits were minimal if they existed. More and more women were going out to work and society was changing. Jim had lived the highlife, seen his sisters' success without feeling he was being true to himself. No wonder he would talk of his first 'wasted and utterly meaningless' years in London. He had gastric problems on account of his ulcers, drank too much, and suffered depression severe enough for doctors to admit him to a psychiatric hospital in South London – a harrowing experience. He had dabbled in many fields since he was a young man, enthusiastic at the onset, but his interest waned each time. Claire was the quieter partner who guided him.

His sense of duty, desire to instruct, to help others and communicate ideas increased in the years after his marriage. He helped hospital inmates then got involved in occupational centres for the unemployed. This is a side to Jim I admire. One scheme was in South London, initiated by settlement workers from Cambridge University's Gonville and Caius Colleges. With almost three million people out of work during the winter of 1934-35 these training schemes helped workers learn a new trade, providing they contributed a penny towards facilities. At the Gonville Hut on York Road, Battersea, Jim assisted in classes for cobbling, rug weaving, and building radios. Claire helped run the canteen. Jim organized the Unemployed Football Cup Competition, proudly seeing Gonville Hut FC reach the semi-finals at Wembley. He helped coordinate unemployed drama groups in the London area - once receiving a visit from actor Robert Donat. That was a gesture to Jim, whose Charing Cross agency had once helped Donat when he was unknown. The Duke of Kent and his wife visited the Hut in 1935 and the event received press coverage – one report referring to him as the 'novelist brother of the Houston Sisters' – something he hated. It suggests he was writing before February 1935. It's possible the *Down and Outs Matinee* at the Gaiety Theatre in April 1935 was connected to Jim's activities.

Happy to be *Mrs GA Balharrie* when it suited her, and forgetting about it when it didn't, Renée opened the door to romance when her love for George had turned into 'arrangement'. She had a tendency to shock her parents and anyone stuffy - ever keen to see what she could get away with. Married or not, her parents attempted to keep her on a leash and even if she wanted to hoodwink poor George, finding free time to do so was another matter with Billie, Lizzi or Jimmie following her around. She tells us a little about her early innocent boyfriends in 'Don't Fence Me In,' like the beau she let carry her vanity case. It was amusing seeing him grow ever more frustrated - forced to repress his passion. He couldn't bear it any more and one day threw her vanity case across St Martin's Lane, storming off in anger. The fun was in the chase, and I get a strong sense that pleasure came in the conquest. Catching the eye of someone she detected was interested whilst resisting her was a particular sport. It emboldened her to flirt. When she mentions her young self in memoirs you hear what a gushing flirt she was, although she gives the impression she remained innocent, and confesses she wasn't very successful at finding love. Of course she loved variety – that went without saying: one week it was an electrician, then a boy from a dancing troupe, then a conjuror, then an acrobat, then a lion tamer. She seemed to be particularly attracted to young men noteworthy for physical feats. An acrobat she was inseparable from for a while kept appearing in the back of the cab and when Daddy Jimmie opened the door on them she tried to introduce him as a distant cousin.

Jimmie and Lizzi weren't always there to open the door on her, or even chaperone her, and Renée admits that her sister Billie's disapproval regarding her romances caused many a backstage brawl. The variety environment offered tremendous opportunities to meet people. She was constrained by the moral atmosphere of the age she lived but sassy enough to exploit the loopholes that existed, allowing her a degree of freedom. She was no pushover and often called the shots. Her male colleagues in the theatre admired her vibrant personality and thought her a sensational beauty. 'Good' girl she might have been, but she wasn't average in any respect. Brian O'Gorman's father Joe would say of Renée, with a twinkle in his eye: 'She was no better than she ought to have been.'

There was Jack Stanford - *the eccentric fool* whom she liked, even though he made it obvious the feeling wasn't mutual. There was Sir Lawrence Olivier, then an unknown actor five years Renée's junior. He met the Sisters between March 1926 and November 1927 at Mrs Swan's theatrical digs in Birmingham. The Encore records Renée's presence around late May 1927 with reports 'Didn't Birmingham audiences enjoy Renée Houston's skit on the watch committee? Isn't it time the watch committee was wound up?'[16] There were several variations of Renée's 'romance' with the actor, ranging from her 'love' being unreciprocated to the couple getting engaged and almost marrying. In August 1959 reporter Bill Boorne was present when Renée began *Roar Like A Dove* at the Phoenix Theatre. She received a glorious bouquet of flowers. 'Love, ever, Larry' said the note. 'He couldn't afford flowers like that when I first knew him as a young man of nineteen when we shared digs in Birmingham,'[17] said Miss Houston intriguingly.

Dame Sybil Thorndike steered Olivier to Jackson's Birmingham Repertory Theatre in those early days and Anthony Holden in his book on Olivier tells us how ardent and passionate Olivier was then. Peggy Ashcroft gives the impression that any young woman might have become the first Mrs Olivier if she happened to be in the right place at the right time. Peggy's chance was thwarted by the noisy sound of somebody pulling the lavatory chain at Mrs Swan's, stopping the impassioned and brooding Olivier in mid-proposal.[18] Miss H might also have become the first Mrs Olivier or even been the one pulling the chain. She and Larry remained good friends even if passion led nowhere. Looking at Renée in her films at the start of the 30s, with her elfin stature, protruding upper lip, toothy grin, weak chin and fish-eyed stare, her power of attraction isn't obvious. Some wand wafted a bit of magic dust over the package. I expect her lovable and comic nature contributed to it.

The fling with a lion-tamer was more serious. She mentions him in two or three sources. This can only have been *Togare* – the lion tamer from the Balkans, dubbed the *New Valentino* in press reports. In his bandana and earrings, he was a sensation at the Krone circus, the Carmo Circus in 1928 and the Bertram W Mills Circus at Olympia. He was a great showman who entered the ring in a cape but handed this to his assistant so he was stripped to the waist. Togare was one of the finest animal trainers. He spoke to the animals with a soft voice and never carried a whip or stick into the cage. He's usually seen with a hefty lion over his strong shoulders or between two lions. *Paris* was the name of that lion - one he'd broken in as a cub, who was able to listen to him. *Paris* saved *Togare* from a tiger on one occasion. Then, in Birmingham, *Togare* heroically saved *Paris* and seven other lions by entering a cage when it caught flame. The Schwarzenegger of his day, whose stage character owed something to Douglas Fairbanks, *Togare* was a decided catch for *Miss H*. 'If you see a lion tamer who is appearing this week at Cirque de Paris, do give him my regards,' prattled Renée to the French press. 'He's a charming friend of mine . . . och he was extraordinary!'

Togare (Author's Collection)

She once described how she stepped in to help her lion-tamer when the zoo wouldn't keep one of his poor lions, giving the animal temporary digs at Elsham road. Of course Lizzi hears noises coming from the cellar and almost dies of shock, and I'd give this tale a high fabrication rating, sounding as it does like a rehash of the plot of 'No Monkey Business.' The house became a mecca for foreign artists, went Miss Houston's story: so intent was she to learn about the lives and customs of foreigners. 'Darling, have you met *Blacaman le Hypnotisant, Fascinateur de Fauves*?' she asked. Mammy braced herself at the prospect of a menagerie of crocodiles and snakes. The ever curious Encore asked 'If the lions miss R. Houston?' or 'What Renée thinks of lion-tamers?' at the end of 1928, and in 1936 she recalled how, learning that her lion-tamer had been mauled, she ran into her dressing room in tears, brandishing her fluffy lion mascot. *Togare* was indeed mauled by a lioness in the late 20s, sending him to hospital for three months, and the beast was sent to another trainer who suffered a worse fate, so sharp were its teeth.[19]

I can see Renée raving about actor Patrick de Lacy Aherne, after witnessing him do a trick turn on a cycle - something he did well. It's difficult to be scientific about when they met. 1930 at the Coliseum is normally given as the time and place, although this might have fitted the version of the story that got the biggest laugh. An interview in 1938 has her saying she first met Pat at a film star *Carnival Ball* in Birmingham. He was *guest of honour*, and she was awarding prizes. The story says they found themselves playing on the same bill in London a few weeks after, and Cupid got to work fast. Renée's story about Lawrence Olivier from her 1974 memoir mentions how a bunch of them came to see him in the JM Barrie play *Quality Street* performed in June 1927 when the Birmingham Rep was at Station Street. The de Lacy Aherne family was part of the fabric of Birmingham's famous theatre, and Pat's sister Elana was playing *Henrietta Turnbull* to Olivier's *Ensign Blades,* so what if Pat trotted along to see his sister and possibly met Renée? Or had they met even earlier? In the same memoir she tells us that in trying to impress Olivier she made sure to let him know she was on good terms with Sir Barry Jackson - big chief at Birmingham Rep. While it's unlikely she was 'in' with Jackson, if that *were* the case, chances are she knew the de Lacy Aherne family already. Olivier probably found her a braggart with her 'I'll put in a good word for you' line. Renée's crowd-pleasing story of her meeting with Pat is, however, the funniest and most atmospheric.

The Coliseum programme for the week starting February 17, 1930 doesn't name George Balharrie as the Houston's conductor although he was there, as usual, starting the Sisters' signature music. As soon as he did, the curious sound of honking backstage sent waves of laughter throughout the crowded house. This seal of approval was from Olsen's sea lions (item 3 on the bill). An *'Electric March'* by the Sixteen Foster Girls (item 5), revealed part of the circus-style set design for what was coming later: the *'Startling Horse Riding Novelty'* of Lawrowsky and Wassilowna known as the Sobolewski Troupe. The revolving stage was switched to its fastest setting for that particular spectacle. The Houston Sisters (item 6) featured *Spanish items* and their *Down on the Farm* skit. A one-act play (item 11) called *To Meet the King* - featured actress Sybil Thorndike, returning to the Coliseum after a long absence, and its small cast had rehearsed at Sybil's home because she had recently slipped and torn a muscle performing at Lewisham.[20] Her new role fortunately had her in a chair the whole time, as an invalid mother of a young airman at a seaside hotel suffering from a heart condition, and awaiting the result of an international flying race that her son hopes to win. The Schneider Cup had been an inspiration for author HCG Stevens. In the play Sybil's character begins talking with pride about her son's sporting victories, then, when her nurse leaves the room, *Ronnie*, the son, played by Patrick Aherne, walks through the verandah window. He rushes to tell his mother he has a summons to meet the king and she must accompany him. We do not know that the young airman is actually dead at this point – not until he exits, and a doctor arrives informing us the son has been tragically killed in the race. Cold shiver! The old lady doesn't hear. She is dead herself by the time the doctor finds her, her face bearing the smile that comes from seeing a vision. The haunting harp music of Norman O' Neill created a fitting atmosphere for this psychic playlet. It wasn't about the Great War although the death of a son was still very heartfelt in 1930.

Sybil Thorndike's scrapbook in the V&A details the reaction to this little spook play. Audiences genuinely loved it[21] although the sound of the voice off repeating the title: *'To Meet The King'* in the same bored stentorian tones brought to mind a railway porter proclaiming 'Next Stop Barking.' Reynolds News, mistaking Pat Aherne for his famous brother Brian, described him as a 'rather solid-looking spirit' and one report said *'Ronnie* burst in like a hungry schoolboy home from a football match.'[22] Renée, seeing a resemblance to Valentino in the young actor, made sure to get him into conversation. Whistling him over one night in the Lemon Tree pub, she teased him about *Ronnie's* line: 'Yes, Mother. I've just seen Father.' 'You didn't say it right,' said Renée. 'You forgot the rest. You should have said 'I've seen Father... coming out of the pub, pissed to the gills.'[23] They lived on this joke for the two-week run, with Pat saying the alternative line on stage – almost - to Sybil's horror. The two miscreants couldn't look at each other without falling about. The Houstons were back a second week, jointly billed as *'The Peter Pan of Variety'* – an opportunity for Renée and Pat to spend evenings after the show dining on lamb chops and petit poi at the Criterion restaurant.

Their cheeky exchange in the wings, or in the upstairs room of the pub set the tone for their love affair. Just standing next to Pat caused fireworks to go off and she wondered how when they said hello he could have this completely nonchalant air. There was no indication of how suddenly this quality could be dispelled during a stolen moment of passion. Then he went back to being a man's man: cool, mocking and uncompromising. It challenged her and she was seduced, like putty in his hands. I've heard it said of Pat time and again that he had a side to him that was magnetic, and that it was impossible to dislike him. Renée completely fell in love, and it became her purpose to egg him on. It became a scream to see Pat and Renée together, and the merriment was still there six years later when she wrote of him: 'He is truly Irish, and loves anyone who makes him laugh.' Then there were the numerological coincidences of course, when he revealed he lived at house number 43 just like her.[24]

By then, the family had left 43 Elsham Road for a *mock Tudor* Costins house at Northwick Circle[25] in Kenton where George Balharrie was heading for when he was the subject of a 'Hot Foot story.' This concerned his journey from Brighton where the Sisters were deputizing for Robb Wilton. Driver George knew the engine was amiss, as the pedal area was getting hotter and hotter. Renée, smelling something burning, woke up from a slumber to find the *Houston Chariot* on fire and George's soles smouldering. She leapt out of the car cursing. The car was left at a garage in Surrey and a few days later,

George picked it up, heading off to the Alhambra for a matinee. The car gave up a second time, and he never made it to the theatre, forcing the Alhambra's bandleader to step in to provide backchat with Renée. Although Northwick Circle was officially her home after the Houstons quit Kensington, I question if she ever lived here with George.

Within weeks of meeting Pat, it was obvious there was no going back to the kind of marital arrangement she had. If her Edinburgh-born husband had hopes something might finally develop between them, he was forlorn. She was full of grander designs, and *mock Tudor* simply didn't do it for her. The family knew about the romance. Secrecy was impossible. When not on provincial engagements she moved in with Pat at 99 Broadhurst Gardens, near Finchley Road and West End Lane. Her parents found it outrageous, with responsibility for Trevor and Terry thrust on them. Then 'the thing happened' as Renée phrases it, in 'Don't Fence Me In', apparently in the back of a hansom cab.

The Sisters were back at the Coliseum for Billie's birthday in 1930, after playing the Argyle Birkenhead and Bristol. 'We are mere jumping beans in the bigger scheme of things,' Miss Houston might have thought, sitting there watching *Charles Dudley and his Midget Gladiators* do their novelty springboard act. At this time full-page ads with large photos of The Houston Sisters advertising songs indicates their stature as stars. Renée glares face on, cupid bow lips puckered, whilst Billie, in an Eton suit, looks over her left shoulder. There was a week at the Palladium on May 12, where the songs covered were 'Every Now and Then' and 'All Hands on Deck.' The Houston Sisters shone bright not wanting to be eclipsed by the other acts. Here was Gracie Fields singing her Lancashire ditty 'A Couple of Dooks,' her folk-flavoured 'Three Green Bonnets' and six other songs. *Jerry and her Baby Grands* – an act with four American ladies each with her own piano astounded people. The fantastically suited 'Buck and Bubbles' - the first black artists to appear at New York's Radio City Music Hall were making their debut in London. Watching the Sherman Fisher Sixteen Palladium Girls do a number dressed in Highland costume got the Houston girls misty-eyed, so it was no surprise they were back at the Glasgow Empire the following month.

Then came the Palladium, then a booking at the Blackpool Palace in July. Thank heavens for Muriel George and Ernest Butcher - friends from the Coliseum - who deputized for Renée, whose sudden indisposition required they do a quick change and motor-dash from the Central Pier (after their first house) to the Palace, then a hop back to their own show again. They saved Renée's bacon. Some poor stooge on a bike otherwise would have been in a mad panic to grab a replacement act. Billie did her best to keep an eye on her sister. There was never any thought about slowing down and 'coping,' or, thinking about what was going to happen to your body. The Houstons missed being at the Coliseum for the first public demonstration of large screen television by John Logie Baird on July 28, but fun was to be had in Blackpool

The Love and Loves of the Houstons

at Renée's birthday party with guests Clapham and Dwyer and Wee Georgie Wood.

The Sisters were joining Wood again at Portsmouth in less than a month for his *Vaudeville Peter Pan* and a breath of seaside air helped. When, in September, the Daily Mail described the Houston Sisters' new act, giving the irrepressible Renée an opportunity to wear a huge crinoline it chimes with that old euphemism: 'I'll have to get the crinolines out' used by theatrical people. Audiences then got a glimpse of the third and youngest sister in the *Grandmother* sketch. Shirley's Coliseum and Holborn Empire debuts occured the week after, although her public debut in London had actually been at the Wembley Stadium Club in connection with the *June Rose Ball*, on June 1 1928, when she was only twelve. Renée might need her to step in, but wasn't there a limit to all that dressing up?

A peril of success is that something ghastly will be lurking out there to try to knock your civilization to bits. A problem for the Houston Sisters at this time was blackmail. Tittle-tattle about Renée's affair with Pat produced a series of nasty poison pen letters and blackmail attempts – finding their way to her dressing room wherever she went. Not everyone laughed at the Houston jokes, or accepted their wealth with good grace. Grinding poverty was the lot of many folk. Yet, it takes a sick mind to persist in blackmail letters and threats. Fortunately, brotherly love, until then more of a hindrance than help, suddenly came to the rescue. How long the letters had been coming is unknown, but Jim managed to sniff out a lead, listening in to a conversation one night when he and Robb Wilton were propping up the bar at the London Alhambra.

Having a James Allan Rennie for a brother proved of great benefit when all the letters were immediately passed to Scotland Yard, and the battle was won. Sadly, this was a low point for Jim. In November 1930 people read how this theatrical manager, aged thirty-one, pleaded guilty at Bow St Police court to being drunk while in charge of a motor car in Kingsway. He had to pay the maximum penalty of £50 and costs, and was disqualified from driving.[26] This would apply for five years because a previous conviction for a similar offence in 1927 was proved. A breakdown would follow, but his personal quest afterwards produced a renewal in Jim's life and career.

Back then simple tittle-tattle conspired to have the same effect as today's social media at its most poisonous – harshly judging people in the public eye. The Houston strategy was *not* to disappear on account of the tittle-tattle. People in the variety world suspected Renée and George weren't a pair despite being married. Early in 1926 The Encore innocently asked, in its commentary about the personalities of variety, how she and George celebrated their wedding anniversary, but two years later it was cheeky and unkind, asking whether George was surprised to see a stranger in his wife's room. Speaking to anyone about her condition was best avoided, given the fact there were plenty backstage people you couldn't trust. At the Coliseum, with Bransby Williams and Nellie Wallace on the bill, on October 27, 1930, Renée donned a new outfit to conceal her tummy. That lovely hall was a place she rightfully called 'home'. Sir Oswald, if he knew her secret, might well have supported her: their relationship long-standing and mutually beneficial. But he was under strain, having a lot on his plate: the days of his great *Cathedral of Variety* numbered. Stoll was fighting the issue of entertainment tax in articles and speeches, leaving pamphlets in theatre programmes. The Sisters went up to play Sheffield's Hippodrome then nine months pregnant Renée returned for a week at London's Victoria Palace on December 2, and even made an appearance at the fabulously new Luxor Cinema at Cross Deep, Twickenham the night before Patrick Anthony was born on December 18, 1930.

She and Pat had just moved into a house called *'Elmwood'*, at Elms Lane, Sudbury so Pat must have been chauffeuring Renée the length and breadth of London at this time. In love more than ever, happy for what they had, and over the moon when their little boy arrived, they were earnest in the hope that one day they would marry and make it all official.

Twenty-nine year-old Pat Aherne had appeared in at least fifteen silent films, taking his cues from ten film directors and sampling the practices and quirks of every film studio, occasionally making West End stage appearances. The uncharted ocean of early cinema suited him, given its adventurous aspects. Filmmaking was experimental in the silent era and Pat and his brother Brian began making films in 1924 - a year described as the nadir of British films when only 10% of all films shown were British.[27] Since almost every studio here was struggling to survive, the brothers were lucky to get a start. The problem of British cinema lacking a home market capable of producing profits on an expensive picture remained an issue until the 30s. Our small production companies struggled given Hollywood's flooding of the market and its hold over the renter/exhibitor chain. More money went into Hollywood pictures, which could rely on a huge market and vastly superior publicity machine. The Conservative government, sympathetic to the plight faced by British cinema in the face of American competition, brought in a new Cinematograph Films Act in 1927 limiting foreign films to 22.5% of the British market. This provided a much-needed boost. Many shrewd variety entertainers wondered what it could do for them, given that films were a lucrative way of compensating for lean periods. The VAF even held a conference about the proposed 4-500 films needed by the quota system and the opportunities for supering in these films. That was before the act came into law. The government didn't remove the Entertainment Tax, even though it should have gone after the war. It remained in place for decades, contributing to box office losses and affecting British impresarios in cinema and theatre alike. Oswald Stoll urged customers to write to their MPs to 'free the living theatre from this iniquitous tax.'[28]

Pat had made 'The Cost of Beauty' (1924) for Sam Smith and Bertie Samuelson at Isleworth Studios and 'Thou Fool' (1926) for Oswald Stoll at

Cricklewood. He'd worked for Welsh-Pearson at studios in Cricklewood and Winchmore Hill, for Archibald Nettlefold's company at Walton-on-Thames, at Whitehall Studios, Elstree, and at Gainsborough in Islington. In Britannia Films' 'Carry On!'(1927) Pat, along with actors Moore Marriot and Wally Patch, appeared in the first British film directed by a woman - Dinah Shurey - who persuaded the admiralty to lend her a few battleships to add realism in one of her militaristic movies. Cinema in the 20s is characterized by a pioneering spirit, erratic work practices, costly experiments with sound and colour, ingeniously lit sets and breakthrough cinematography achieved in 'dark' and 'light' studios. Behind the camera were geniuses supported by a motley crew drawn from different backgrounds. There was an eclectic quality to the subjects of feature films. There were comic series ('Steve Donoghue', 'Walter' and 'Bindle' being examples) and non-fiction films. All tastes were catered for.

In the later 20s, looking at the production details and casts of British fiction films in Denis Gifford's film catalogue, the pages are peppered with the names of short-lived production companies. Directors floated between these, undeterred by mergers and bankruptcies. A pool of actors including Henry Edwards, John Stuart, Ivor Novello, Betty Balfour, Mabel Poulton, Ursula Jeans, Fay Compton and Chili Bouchier make up the casts. The character actor Moore Marriot, who made his first film in 1912, was making films with Pat in 1927 and with Renée in the late 1930s. British silent films featured guest stars from Hollywood, such as Dorothy Gish, Nita Naldi and Pauline Frederick. The majority of British film actors had a stage background especially older leading men. Juvenile lead actors on the whole came through repertory theatre. John Longden is one example. He worked at Liverpool and Birmingham Reps. Connections mattered, and knowing a friend of Seymour Hicks helped him get the part of the cockney leading man in Hitchcock's Talkie 'Blackmail' (1929). He was a 'name' after this. Betty Balfour, like Renée, had been in revue, although she'd been lucky enough to meet producer CB 'Cockie' Cochran through her admirer Lady Fitzmaurice and enjoyed brilliant success on the stage in shows like *Airs and Graces* before she landed a two-year movie contract with Welsh-Pearson.

Photos of Pat Aherne from his silent films show a dark-eyed, dark haired, brooding type, not especially tall, with expressive eyes and a tough demeanour. The cinema press liked to emphasize that there was nothing Latin about him and that 'He's a Celtic as any other Irishman.'[29] In 'The Inseparables' (1929) he was impeccable in a dinner suit and white tie, and the same year, cut a sharp figure as army officer *Richard von Rolf* in 'The City of Play.' Straight as an arrow in a Prussian suit, Pat makes a handsome hero with his classic profile. He's fallen in love with *Ariel*, the hypnotized 'human thunderbolt' - Chili Bouchier. Breaking the spell, he fights *Tamburini the Great,* flooring the villain just in time for the latter to be crushed to death by a gigantic python. During the filming of the film's carnival scene, a number of film artists were injured at Gainsborough Studios when a floor collapsed and a heavy imitation elephant fell into the dry tank several feet below.[30]

Throughout Pat's early life, theatre dominated, it being the grand passion of his mother Louise de Lacy Aherne, known as Lulu, who kept her looks and trim figure long after Victorian corsets were abandoned. Lulu had great legs and catching sight of them men used to follow her down the street not aware quite how mature in years she was by then. Long before legs could be seen, she had fascinated men. An early suitor had been Austen Chamberlain who was starting his political career and was known for his speeches. Her contribution to 'Theatrical Birmingham' in the early part of the 20th Century was significant. A descendent of Sarah Siddons – an actress who took London by storm in the late 18th Century, Lulu was an actress in the 1890s. A close friend of George Bernard Shaw and one of the original *Pilgrim Players*, she appeared in *The Interlude of Youth* in 1907. Shaw wrote plays for the company and Lulu helped produce them using members of her family in the cast. Shaw used to sit on front row of the stalls, quietly reading each line and unsettling the actors who feared making mistakes. The *Pilgrim Players* became the *Birmingham Rep Company*: its first season starting in 1913. Lulu was part of a fight to save the Rep in the early days and ten years later was in its inner circle, along with John Drinkwater and Sir Barry Jackson. She acted in *Back To Methuselah* with Edith Evans and Frances Doble, with Mr Shaw making special visits for dress rehearsals. Lulu possessed an original script of *Back To Methuselah* signed by Shaw and the original cast.

Her two sons and daughter were propelled towards the theatre, acting for the Pilgrim Players. Like many with an Italia Conti training, they joined the cast of child actors for *Where the Rainbow Ends*. All three Aherne siblings were in this famous play by Clifford Mills and John Ramsey with music by Roger Quilter. It came to the Garrick Theatre, London on 26 December 1913. Their friend Noël Coward was *William the bad boy* whilst other children travelled on flying carpets, received a visitation from St George or danced as little parties of elves or will o' the wisps. *Where the Rainbow Ends* was staged at various theatres including Holborn Empire. Jack Hawkins was one of several child actors from the school who became famous.

Pat's family lived a comfortable life at 'The Plaisance' - at Monyhull Hall Road, Kings Norton. It was a town house exemplifying all the architectural merits of his father's practice. It's sad that in later years the local council built a hospital next door lessening its quiet residential pride. Summers for the de Lacy Ahernes were spent with relatives at Tower Holme - the rambling home on the beach at Pevensey surrounded by Napoleonic era Martello towers. William de Lacy's parents 'Pater' and 'Mater' were Plymouth Brethren who forbade games taking place in the house on the Sabbath. A hut outside was made available if people wanted to play cards. Tower Holme was a place sometimes criticized by Pat's younger brother Brian for its lack of event. Brian upset older relatives by his description of life here, in his autobiography 'A Proper Job' (1969).

Elana Aherne   Pat Aherne at Tower Holme
(By kind permission of the Aherne Family)

Fair-haired and blue-eyed Elana, three years Pat's junior, attained professional stage success before her brothers. In 1924 she played one of the Princes in the Tower to Sir John Martin Harvey's *Richard III* at the Prince's Theatre, Bristol then appeared in *The Only Way* in 1925. Elana toured the Far East with Martin Harvey's company in the late 20s. For her, working in the theatre wasn't about making money and you had to put up with a lot, as a letter to her Aunt Eunice (William de Lacy's sister, Priscilla Eunice Aherne) indicates. Elana writes that 'The Old Vic only offered me my bus fares to play leads in their Shakespeare plays! That sort of exploitation was the rule until Equity got going with legal contracts. The show would shut down in Edinburgh with no money, and the company left stranded without a bean to make their own way back to London - with their luggage and stage props!' At least Elana had the satisfaction of beating four hundred chorus girls in a competition to find *Marion Davis's Double.* Similar in looks to Marion Davies, Elana entered the competition on return from her Far East tour. She had a Hollywood offer as part of the deal but never went there - too afraid her wardrobe wouldn't pass muster.

Brian Aherne also inherited the fair looks from his mother's side of the family, and was tall and handsome with a commanding presence. Brian tended to come across as brainy but shy - the sort of boy to weigh over a question for a while before coming back with a considered answer. He was always top of the class yet 'pretty hot at sports too,' as Pat Aherne proudly described his brother adding with modesty how he, by contrast, was 'fond of sports and very little else.'[31] Brian might have had theatre in his blood but as a teenager, ignored Lulu's encouragement. After school at Malvern, Brian worked in a Liverpool shipping office and bent his back over a ledger for two years. The proper job made him unhappy despite its prospects and positions in Africa and India. Elana, recuperating in Middlesex Hospital following a car accident in which she broke her pelvis and wrote off her friend's Sunbeam Talbot, received a visit one day from a downcast Brian. She suggested he use her agent - Barry Jackson. An introduction to actress Peggy O' Neil – also helped get him a break in *Paddy the Next Best Thing.* Brian toured Australia with a theatrical company performing many JM Barrie plays and went on to have notable London successes such as The Stage Society's production of *The*

Unquiet Spirit, *The Silver Cord* in 1928 with Clare Eames, and *Craig's Wife* in 1929. He reached the heights appearing on Broadway with Katherine Cornell in Guthrie McLintock's production of *The Barretts of Wimpole Street*. Shockingly, he admitted he prefered films to the stage.

In films Brian made in British studios he could play ordinary young men who were also brave and likable as in 'Underground,' or perfect gentlemen, equally brave and likeable, like *Corporal Grant* in the World War One drama 'The W Plan' - a film that not only revealed his modern naturalistic acting but his wonderful voice. Brian even speaks in fool proof German in 'The W Plan' – his first Talkie. Pat believed Brian's greatest gift was accents, referring to Renée's observation that his brother's dialect in 'What Every Woman Knows' (1934) was the best Scottish accent she had heard coming from an Englishman. I'm certain she was simply 'selling' Brian in this instance. In this adaption of a JM Barrie story - one Brian had already acted on the stage, all the Scots accents are terrible, although they improve half way through.

Brian's Irish accent was another matter – one he did beautifully. He did comedy with vast subtlety and panache, whether playing an impassioned blockhead, an innocent kind fool with scholarly pretensions, or a twinkling executive who wants a little *not so innocent* fun. The parts he played during a film career lasting forty-three years demonstrate exceptional versatility and of course, he played the English gentleman to perfection. It's no surprise he made it big in Hollywood. He was chosen to portray the actor David Garrick in a film. He was fairly modest about his artistic achievements but proud of his commercial success. He retained a respect for more straight-laced traditional careers like his father's, or banking.

Brian believed the best experience was in travelling the world – a personal goal he definitely achieved given the numerous exotic trips he made – records of which are preserved in his home movies, and by the extent he developed as an aviator, satisfying his wanderlust chartering his open *Waco* and later his *Fairchild Ranger* between Los Angeles and New York. As member pilot No.6, he was one of the original AOPA members (Aircraft Owners and Pilots Association). Originally turned off the skies by his first sortie into aviation in early 1931 at the time he was on Broadway, he was persuaded by his actress friend Ruth Chatterton to persist. She had done 250 hours in her *Stinson Reliant* by then and introduced him to Bob Blair who taught many motion picture people to fly. They used to race around poles at Santa Monica Airport – later called Howard Hughes Airport.

Pat Aherne went to King Edward's Grammar School in New Street, Edgbaston[32] leaving school at seventeen and getting a job at Austin's Motor works. Birmingham folk at this time were living in fear of aerial attack, the city being a valuable enemy target with its munitions works and vital metal trade. It narrowly escaped a heavy attack in January 1916 when towns like Walsall took a hammering. Anti-aircraft guns were installed and blackout precautions enforced, despite complaints about traffic accidents in the darkness. On October 19, 1917 in far away Glasgow, *James Houston and*

Company were at Govan's Lyceum Theatre. Pat's future wife - his junior by seven months, was deputizing for her mother in *The Flittin*. In Birmingham, at 11 pm that very same evening an attack came without warning. Unable to locate the city centre in the darkness Zeppelins jettisoned the open countryside saving a final bomb for Austin's Motor works in Longbridge.[33] Early the next morning Pat cycled to work, stopping in horror at the sight of such devastation. His next job was for BSA Motorcycle Co. as a demonstrator testing motorcycles at high speeds on the worst roads. He gained a degree of fame for his showmanship in this job, especially for the demo he performed up New Street handcuffed and standing on the saddle to show everyone how 'balanced' the motorcycles were. Crowds turned out, and some years ago, Pat's nephew David met Enoch Powell who went to King Edward's and had heard about that episode in Birmingham's history. Enoch said that the legend had carried down, even though Patrick had been there four years before him. Pat soon became Birmingham's local hero known as 'The Flying Houdini' and also did hair-raising stunts at country fairs and gymkhanas.[34]

Pat tried his luck as a stuntman on an early adventure to the USA although he had to slum it washing dishes in a Chinese restaurant to pay for his return trip. Back in the UK, he was frequently to be found at Brooklands - discussing the merits of a Temple-OEC-JAP with his best friend - the champion motorcyclist Claude Temple. Claude built his own brand of motorcycle and took the trophy for the World Land Speed Record travelling at 108.41mph on a Temple-Anzani motorcycle, taking the award again in the later 1920s and in 1930. He helped his actor friend prepare for *walls of death* and crazy motorcycle stunts jumping over Brighton Pier, or sometimes off it. The bikes were retrieved later and stripped down.

Pat's entry into the film world had more to do with fearless feats than Birmingham Rep connections although family helped. He entered films just before his brother. Using the fact he'd been an able diver as a lad he landed his first part as a double for the lead in a high dive straight into a tank of cold water a considerable distance below. This infamous feat was popularized by a circus act called the *Human Thunderbolt* and repeated in many films[35] including 'The City of Play' when Pat's love interest takes the plunge. Despite his finesse where diving was concerned, that boyhood hobby had come to an end after a sadistic schoolmaster clouted him. He had nursed a ruptured eardrum ever since. What hell such death leaps were now! His painful cinema baptism took place in mid winter and he was rewarded with a chill as well as 30 shillings. Given that film work was insecure, he made an early attempt at running a garage but this went wrong, when someone made off with the capital. Pat's actress friend Violet Vanbrugh encouraged him to try the legitimate stage. I doubt he could have fooled Sir Barry Jackson about his 'considerable stage experience' but connections counted. Soon he was in 1925's *Hamlet in Modern Dress* at the Kingsway Theatre.[36] Pat apparently played five parts in the production that ran each night from August to mid

November 1925 to astonished cheers. Colin Keith-Johnston, as the contemporary *Hamlet* wore plus fours, and Cedric Hardwicke and Elana were also in the cast. Pat returned to the West End for 1927's *White Cargo: 'A Vivid Play of the Primitive, Unvarnished Life of the Tropics.'* Brian had previously been the leading young man in this Leon Gordon play, alongside Mary Clare as the reeling and writhing black temptress *Tondeleyo* whose piercing scream of fear no one ever forgot. Brian left *White Cargo* to tour Australia, and Pat joined it at the Strand Theatre in March 1927. It was the exception. His stage career tended to stay garaged most of the time.

In the silent movies, Pat played sporty juveniles who boxed or played football, 'Irish' types, spies, and continentals. He found his niche playing the kind of ordinary young man that you felt for or were moved by. He was also a very physical actor and gripped cinemagoers in rough and tumble scenes that were natural and convincing. One screen 'tough' was his role in 1926's 'Blinkeyes' - one of several films Pat made for Welsh-Pearson. The movie's slogan refers to 'the humour and pathos of an East End Dancing Girl's hatred of 'toffs.' Director George Pearson was in tune with the everyday experience and 'down-to-earth humour of working-class characters . . . acknowledging life's misfortunes' – much in the vein of variety theatre. Directing the 'Squibs' films, Pearson knew Betty Balfour's 'cockney heroine' character registered with the public – even if she herself was desperate to break away from it.

In 'Blinkeyes' Pat was a working class girl's childhood beau-turned-blackguard. He loiters around Limehouse pubs whilst the heroine - Betty Balfour - puts herself up for auction to pay off a £60 debt owed to Chinese villain *Chang*. First she's relying on Pat - *The Basher* - to save the day in the fake marriage auction. She isn't exactly loyal to him, softening her anti-toff views on meeting his rival *Kenneth* who happens to be a millionaire. Her thrown over protector has to flee the police after *Chang* gives him away. He fights *Kenneth*, underestimating the latter's prowess as a fighter. When the film had its trade review they said 'Pat Aherne is excellent as *The Basher.*' It was a departure against type because previously his looks conveyed an air of delicacy. In the General Strike of 1926 Pat was making money driving a bus and this action caused real working class toughs to set on him. He finished up in hospital with a broken jaw. Originally he'd been turned down for the part of *The Basher*. Coming out of hospital and looking mean, he got the part!

It's a strange coincidence that several of his silents have a Scottish theme or Scots characters. There was a Scots shopkeeper in 1926's 'Thou Fool', Gorbals boys saved a Russian prince from the Bolsheviks in 1927's 'Huntingtower,'[37] and in 1929's 'Auld Lang Syne,' Pat's character was *Angus McTavish*. Pat got to know Sir Harry Lauder during the shoots for 'Huntingtower' and 'Auld Lang Syne.' In the former he played the part of intrepid *Captain Heritage* - a role that required passionate love scenes with sultry Russian actress Vera Voronina – as the princess. It was a performance that singled him out as an expert at the emotional acting required for close-ups. He had the right equipment - lips that were mobile and eyes that could express heartfelt pain. Pat didn't possess the kind of beauty that some of his contemporaries in the silent movies were lauded for but he injected a lot of passion into his roles. He wrote an article for Picture Show in late 1927 entitled 'Those Thrilling Screen Kisses' about the use of shoulders and eyes, plus other techniques a film artiste must undertake to best achieve difficult close-up scenes. It was both a stamp of approval and measure of his popularity. Certainly, he was getting brilliant parts by this time.

He was also developing his abilities in the boxing ring, although it isn't clear how he got started. A good friend was British Empire Champion boxer Bombardier Billy Wells - born in Stepney - who would become the second Olympian torso seen in the opening credits of films from the Rank Organization. Billy Wells was filmed banging a gong at Worton Hall Studios, Isleworth, in 1935. Back in the 20s, Billy and Pat appeared in a film short 'The Game Chicken: Romances of the Prize-Ring' (1926) directed by Harry B. Parkinson. They continued to be sparring partners.

The McLaglens were a talented family - children of an Anglican clergyman from London's Mile End. Out of the eight brothers and one sister: Victor, Leopold, Clifford, Cyril, Kenneth, Arthur, Lewis, Frederick, and Lily, only Frederick seems not to have been involved in films. Arthur was a talented landscape gardener. Pat and Brian were friends with Victor McLaglen, the eldest brother and all his siblings. As 'Sharkey' McLaglen, Victor had boxed and wrestled in Canada and America, soldiered in the Middle East, prospected gold in India and been bodyguard to a Rajah - all prior to his movie career. Among a minority of actors without a stage background, his carefree spirit, natural charm and lack of inhibition added up to star quality.

Victor McLaglan in Dick Turpin (Author's Collection)

While he could be frightening in movies like 'The Passionate Adventure' (1924) and stood six foot five tall, in real life Victor was the most pacific person who ever crashed a fist into a jaw on the screen and this is born out by the fact that Pat's sophisticated and ladylike sister Elana once dated him.

Victor's brothers Cyril and Clifford made films at Sir Oswald Stoll's Studios at Temple road, Cricklewood in 1926, as did the Aherne brothers. When Renée and Billie Houston filmed their scene in 'Blighty', the same year saw Cyril McLaglen make five films at Gaumont's Lime Grove studio. Pat Aherne made four: one being 'The Silver Lining'[38] for British International Pictures (B.I.P). John Maxwell ran the company until 1940. While not a friend of Variety, Maxwell defended of the British film industry, wishing to remove the threats posed by big American production and distribution rivals.

Seeing Pat Aherne in the tortured role of *Thomas Hurst* in the neglected silent - 'The Silver Lining' proves beyond doubt that he had something. He might have a fondness for the guilty hangdog expression but on the whole, his acting is very intelligent and economic and you appreciate what exceptional use actors made of their faces. This 'powerful drama' of a boy who went to prison to shield another has an amazingly powerful scene when a bridegroom's bleeding hand incriminates him at the altar. Marie Ault gives a fabulous performance as the mother of a modern Cain and Abel. It's all set in the fictional village of Poppleton.

Three years on and he saw his mastery in this particular type of acting meet with little favour. Fresh new faces and personalities vied for lead roles in the Talkies and not all actors were welcomed as they crossed over from the silent films. Pat still had the looks although similar faces took over the space that once had been his territory. Ivan Lebedeff epitomized this look in the American movies. The expressive face still had currency, providing gestures were restrained, and thrilling screen kisses were as much in demand as before. In Pat's case, his voice lacked resonance, although he did adapt to sound films, and appeared in brilliant films like 'The Return of Bulldog Drummond,' with Ralph Richardson, in 1934. It was a blow to Pat that the lead roles stopped coming but he didn't mope about. Being immensely likeable he had lots of friends in the studios. Pat and Renée were friends with landlord Ernest Cox and his family at *The Plough Pub* in Elstree and the Aherne family say that Pat was one of the few actors Alfred Hitchcock genuinely liked. The two of them were often here. Hitchcock had years before hired Elana Aherne as an extra in one of his films. Of course she had to be filmed inelegantly falling down the stairs wearing a long dress[39] - typical punishment blondes could expect to suffer in Hitch films. Pat found himself in crowd scenes in early Hitchcocks, and much later on, in America, he was offered small parts in Hitch's films and TV dramas.

Brian Aherne and Cyril McLaglen starred in Anthony Asquith's 'Underground' playing bitter rivals. This B.I.P thriller about lowlife in London has quick cutting, impressive camera angles, expert lighting by Karl Fischer, and Brian chasing the murderer over the roof of Lots Road power station, grappling with him, falling into the Thames, and emerging from the river in a totally dry suit! Late that year Brian read through Rudolf Besier's new stage play *The Barretts of Wimpole Street* – thinking of Robert Browning secretly marrying Elizabeth Barrett at Marylebone Parish Church before the two poets escaped together. He looked up, not for the first time, meeting the eyes of heavily pregnant Renée Houston, who his brother Pat couldn't yet marry. She liked to stare into Brian's crystal blue eyes. That way her baby would have blue eyes, she would tell people. It was typical of the folklore Miss Houston believed in. It didn't work because Tony had brown eyes. The actress Katherine Cornell took an interest in Besier's play and Brian was soon to leave England for Broadway to play the role at New York's Empire Theatre.

Broadhurst Gardens retains something in the breeze that harks back the 30s – a pleasing olfactory sensation: one combining petrol and ladies' perfume. At the Criterion Restaurant or at his bachelor pad Pat enchanted Renée - recalling his exploits as a trick-cyclist riding 30 mph through a paper hoop whilst blindfolded. On one hand he was a free-spirited chancer, and on the other, a respectable young man from a well-to-do family from King's Norton in the West Midlands. His 'old boy' expressions amused her and she loved to copy them. What a livewire he was about the latest happenings from those madcap film studios. His film 'The City of Play', released in 1929, was partly a sound picture – and what an odd vocal assortment it had: the *man on the street* accent of Pat Aherne, the stage-trained vowels of Lawson Butt, and the *Minnie Mouse* squeak of John Stuart. Sound in cinema was in its infancy and those producing Talkies came in for a lot of flak for the inadequacies of mechanical sound reproduction, and because it was 'hard to distinguish dialogue from the grating background.[40] All British film studios were quick in finding ways to surmount these inadequacies: muffling cameras inside boxes on wheels and covering 'blimps' in heavy blankets. Pat and Renée had friends and enemies in common and much to plot together. Militant crusaders fighting for the survival of variety might say she was cavorting with the 'enemy' with the 'cinema octopus' grabbing and destroying the theatres that were hanging on as a reserve for the human actor. In reality, many acts from variety made films, like Grock - the Coliseum clown - in the film 'What For?'

'Elstree Calling' came into the cinemas in February 1930 - the earliest British sound film to feature an all-singing and dancing revue. In the USA, between 1929-30, every second film was a musical revue copied on film, and Broadway actors flocked to Hollywood like it was the new Klondike. It was no surprise that 'Elstree Calling,' with its dazzling array of homegrown artistes got the thumbs up. A reporter from The Sunday Dispatch describes it as 'an ample justification of the English voice in Talkies.' 'Shows Hollywood how to do it' went another notice, adding this latest product of Britain's cinema was 'better value for money than 'Hollywood Revue.' By now Renée was keen to learn as much inside information as possible, although she knew Adrian Brunel of course, the film's writer.

The successes American film actors were having with the new Talkies intrigued her – especially stars like Bebe Daniels, Bessie Love, and Anita Page – all catapulted to international fame. Marilyn Miller got $100,000 for a picture. Yet several things kept Renée rooted in variety and while films were an ambition, she made few inroads at the studios. Steady work with a fresh and appreciative audience at changing theatres and her strong ties to agent George Barclay contributed to keeping her grounded in variety. Sadly, the job she loved was under threat, given the cinema conversions and state of the art cinemas springing up. Stoll fought cinema's onslaught through intelligent use of gimmicks to lure audiences to the Coliseum. He displayed curiosities for inspection - like Fannie Ward - a sixty year-old who looked sixteen. The final pure variety performance at London's Coliseum was on March 21st 1931. It went over to revue with *White Horse Inn* - a Tyrolean spectacular produced by German producer Erik Charell, then it staged *Casanova* between May 1932 and January 1933 before becoming a cinema in March 1933. 'Payment Deferred' and 'King Kong' were among the first films shown there.

The London Alhambra was having a troubled time at the end of the 20s. You went there to see boxing matches on February 13, 1929, and in December that year it was agreed that the building could be rented by John Maxwell's B.I.P. as a '*Shop Window* site in the heart of the West End' to 'do for our product what the Americans do for theirs.' Maxwell expected films like Hitchcock's 'Blackmail' would have long runs there.[41]

It was a moment when British entertainment embraced American culture and music hall had its honour compromised. Cinema and variety wrestled with each other at the Alhambra for the next few years. It came back to variety at Easter 1931, with Horace Sheldon appointed conductor and George Balanchine involved in producing *Variétes en Fete*, but for a long run, the theatre only staged ballets such as *Waltzes from Vienna* and Markova's *A Kiss in Spring*, before returning to variety again on April 9th 1934. The Houston Sisters played the Alhambra a handful of times in 1934, their last engagement there being the week of October 1, 1934.

At home in your parlour on February 16, 1931, you would have listened glumly to the wireless when Stanley Baldwin addressed the nation about *The Problem of Unemployment* on the BBC's National Programme at 21.15. Perhaps you perked up a little at 21.40 when an outside broadcast recorded from the Coliseum featured the *Irresistibles* as the first act. Hearing the chirpy, child-like voice of Renée making flippant remarks to *granny* (played by Shirley) and Billie's gruff tones as she reminded her to be more respectful, you would never have guessed that Renée by then had a little girl of five, a little boy of four and a newborn.

Pat's mother Lulu was not in the least upset by the *fix* her eldest boy found himself in. Renée had the distinction of being in the theatre, and Lulu admired the Houston Sisters.

The Love and Loves of the Houstons

The Aherne brothers with their parents in Edgbaston, mid 1930s.
(The Aherne Family)

Free of censure, as people in these circles so often are, Lulu voiced no objection. Her husband, known affectionately as 'Big Dad' was always good humoured and as supportive as Lulu. Louise Thomas had married William de Lacy Aherne, a distinguished architect, in 1898. His heritage could apparently be traced to the Norman Conquest. The loving couple lived in Moseley village, Kings Norton, Worcestershire and later in Edgbaston. He built mansions for the wealthy but struggled after Lloyd George passed a law that stopped architects from being builders. He was well respected in his field. Years later Mrs Bryant of Bryant Homes paid tribute to him for giving her family its start in the business.

Pat's parents were a fun-loving couple. They loved their holidays in the south of France. Home movies frequently show them ready to shriek with laughter. One sequence filmed by Brian, outside their home in Edgbaston, shows a mischievous Pat frightening his mother by picking up a snail from the ground. I also like the moment Brian is sitting in his limousine in the street outside his Hollywood home - his arm casually out the window - only to permanently lock arms with an unsuspecting Lulu. His parents journeyed to the USA a few times, staying at his homes in Bel Air and 703 Rodeo Drive, Beverly Hills where 'Big Dad' is seen placing brightly coloured tiny terrapins on the lawn where they are free to race with each other.

Renée was aware of the difference in background between her and Pat. He had always known privilege, even if his family's security was less secure than in former times. Protestants from Cork, the Ahernes had lost their Irish estate in the 1880s, and had worked hard to sustain a position in England. But if theatre is a leveling force, where talent supersedes privilege, Renée was 'rich.' She had been born into this caste. Still, certain things such as keeping servants illustrated the difference between Renée's upbringing and Pat's. Renée was used to doing housework and domestic jobs. Servants were something to buy with money but she found it difficult to believe she had a natural right to have one. A nurse was duly engaged for Tony – her baby.

Less than a month after he was born Renée and Billie appeared at the Hackney Empire, then with Shirley, for a spot at Shepherds Bush Empire on February 9.

Left:
Brian Aherne with Lulu and 'Big Dad' on the Riviera.

Right:
Jimmie and Lizzi Houston at Northwick Circle.

(Aherne Family)

Films were something the Houston Sisters poked fun at in their routine *Gone Talkie*.[42] This has *Bill* exasperated at Renée's wisecracks and interruptions in their argument about 'what to do' and 'what not to do' to make a successful talkie debut. *Bill's* yearnings for film fame are expressed when he dresses 'in white plus fours and a mustard pullover' and his De Mille-like ideas are met with 'frivolous derision' by Renée. Somehow this finishes with the *Irresistibles* singing the hit song 'The King's Horses' by Noel Gay and Harry Graham. Coming much too soon, this was their last opportunity to appear in pure variety at Stoll's '*Cathedral*', a place close to their hearts. It was only natural dear old Bransby Williams should be there for the occasion also on the bill. Throughout the bulk of 1931, there was no change to the schedule for Renée and Billie. They had dates at Bristol, a two-weeker at the Alhambra, then Shepherd's Bush, and Blackpool in July, where Renée, on her birthday, opened the annual theatrical garden party in Stanley Park in aid of a local hospital, and gave a speech supported by Georgie Wood.

Renée must have slipped off somewhere with Pat in early August because only Billie shares the lineup with Gracie Fields and Will Fyffe at the Shakespeare Theatre, Liverpool. Then the Sisters are together again in Brighton, Camberwell, and then the Victoria Palace. Here they shared the bill with Max Wall, Blondie Hartley – Danish trapeze artiste, Hutch, Horace Sheldon, head-balancers Blum and Blum, and Flanagan and Allen – doing their '*down and outs*'. The Sisters were on cracking form and the 'ecstasy' they met was so much they 'bowed their heads.'[43] For late 1931, it was back to the Glasgow Empire, then good old Hull, then the London Palladium and then Holborn. It was tiring work.

Variety was not starving under siege even if the ramparts of the once mighty Coliseum and Alhambra now seemed vulnerable. All the same, her *Flying Houdini* arrived just at the right time for her. She always had a soft spot for Pat's salesman patter and boy did he sell films to her - telling her she could go far in the Talkies. Renée had done some film work but had little experience acting before the camera when not simply presenting a turn. Could film be the right medium for her spontaneity and personality –

especially with the audience so remote? How would her accent sound in a Talkie, and what character could she play? She needed friends to champion her. Some time in November 1931 her hair was expensively bleached, and her large curls were flattened out, creating a new silhouette suitable for a modern film starlet.

Pat's circle of friends included John Longden who he worked with on 'The Ball of Fortune' (1926). Longden married screenwriter Jean Jay in 1926, submitting scenarios to producer Maurice Elvey, who earned a reputation in the silent years for turning out twenty pictures a year. Elvey's wife - Isobel Elsom - appeared on the same bill at the Coliseum as Renée and Billie when they did *Gone Talkie*. Soon life would imitate art. Elvey gave Longden a writing job at Gaumont British, leading to the actor's breakthrough in 'Quinneys' (1927) - a film co-starring Cyril McLaglen made at Lime Grove with young David Lean as camera assistant. Longden's manly and realistic portrayal of a detective in Hitchcock's 'Blackmail' earned him a reputation for realism and versatility.

Longden was working at Blattner Studios at Elstree on a comedy called 'Smash and Grab,' at the time he signed up to be part of a company set up by Eric Vivian Earl Hakim. His friends Kenneth McLaglen and Pat Aherne joined him. Their first project was to film an original story written by Longden and Jean Jay, with Longden also directing. William Shenton, who photographed Pat in 'The Silver Lining' was to be cameraman, and Frank Parish, the assistant director. It was to be Renée Houston's first Talkie, starring Pat Aherne, Robert Holmes, Fanny Wright and Hal Waters.

Hakim, an infant prodigy violinist who grew up to become the youngest airman in the Great War in the French Air Force, entered the film industry in the 20s. His family owned a chain of cinemas including one in Cheltenham. Hakim's chief aim in forming *Cinema House Ltd* was to put on the best plays, and in their absence, the finest films. You saw un-commercial imports like 'Kameradschäft,' 'Mädchen In Uniform' and 'Das Cabinet des Dr Caligari' at Hakim's 'continental' picture houses such as Academy at 225 Oxford Street that opened in 1931. This has been described by film academics as Britain's first Art Cinema. Hakim married Nina Vanna – the Russian-born actress who fled her country during the October Revolution and worked alongside Pat in 'The Cost of Beauty' (1924). Hakim then produced 'The Outsider' (1931) and the English version of 'M- Eine Stadt sucht einen Mörder,' re-shot with Peter Lorre in the Spring of 1932. For their new project 'Come into my Parlour,' he created *GEM Productions*, and there's a sad irony to that name because twenty-five years later Hakim did time in jail for gem fraud and obtaining jewellery by false pretenses. This was Eric Hakim's second time in prison. Prior to 1934, he had been influential - credited with introducing Elisabeth Bergner and Adolph Menjou to England. He was first declared bankrupt with debts of £30,000 in 1934, and later in 1946 with debts of £51,000.[44] He went from the loftiest heights to working as a humble clerk for United Utilities in

Edgware Road, and even there he was accused of fraud.[45] In between the highs and lows he lived beyond his means as a playboy in a Mayfair flat.

The forty-six minute film 'Come into my Parlour,' classed by one reviewer as a 'whimsical comedy,' made a profit of £1,000 but today it is 'lost.' Prints might have been seized as assets after Hakim's bankruptcies. *GEM Productions* had morphed into *Kenneth McLaglen Productions Ltd* by the end of 1933 with Kenneth, whose company selected stories and submitted them to Victor in Hollywood, forced to pick up the debts. My attempt to locate the film through hopeful pleas to the film collector community has come to nothing and I have press reviews only to interpret it. The story is about a young manicurist in a hotel saloon - *Jenny MacDonald*, played by Renée, in love with barber's assistant *Gerry* - Pat Aherne - whose jealousy is roused by the attentions she receives from wealthy customer *Julius Markham* - Robert Holmes. The film took its name from the misquoted poem 'The Spider and the Fly.' When *Markham*'s attentions grow, *Gerry* follows them to a hotel room. Coming across a burglar who's just ransacked a room, they fight and when the burglar falls over the parapet, *Gerry* believes he's killed him and flees. *Jenny*'s heartbroken, not knowing why he's vanished. She finds him after he's attempted suicide while hiding in a Thames-side wharf and assures him the burglar wasn't killed. The scenarists might have taken inspiration from ATP's 'The Water Gipsies,' filmed the same year. On the whole the movie was thought unworthy of attention and did not have a trade show. In terms of exhibition, it appeared only at a few obscure picture houses. 'John Longden will need better material' went The Bioscope, adding that 'Renée Houston's break into films is not auspicious' and 'Pat Aherne mooches through his part with a series of grimaces.' Curiously, it refers to an opening bedroom scene 'in which the censor's forbearance must have been stretched to the limit,' adding 'vulgar interpretation might have been omitted.'[46]

Kinematograph Weekly, anticipating the 'mediocre quota booking' potential of 'Come into my Parlour' found it 'slow and amateurish, but not lacking in ideas,' pointing out that Renée's presence was the film's main asset. Too bad she didn't appear 'to the same advantage on the screen as on the stage,' it said, although Pat Aherne was considered 'quite good as the barber's assistant.'[47] The London street scenes were thought praiseworthy but Longden's bright ideas weren't successfully realized, and an attempt to avoid too much dialogue had backfired, giving the sense that 'the picture was only partly a Talkie.' It's mind-boggling what exactly was open to vulgar interpretations. Perhaps it was something saucy about *Mr Markham* offering his manicurist a large tip.

In the throes of their affair, filming at Blattner Studios was a convenient way for Renée and Pat to be together. People gossiped about them, and at first they didn't care. The jokey seasonal notice Renée placed in The Stage on December 31, 1931 had a sting in its tail with 'The Houston Sisters (Renée, Billie and Betty) *Wish all friends and enemies The Season's Greetings. With a Three Cheers for George Barclay.*' Their notice in The Performer for the same date has arresting Eric Gray portraits with a child-like self-portrait by Renée evoking the style of Marie Laurencin. She was twenty-nine years old and a mum but her path in life kept her suspended in childhood.

John Longden and Pat Aherne (early 1930s)
(Aherne Family Collection)

In January 1932, Renée, Pat and little Tony were lying low at *'Elmwood'* whilst headlines in the papers read *'Decree for Husband of Renée Houston - Birth certificate mentioned in Divorce Court.'* At the High Courts George was suing for divorce. It read that his suspicions about Pat began in March 1930. That month his wife had told him she was fed up with him and was going off with Pat. The newspapers described how George openly told the court that his wife and Pat lived together[48] and named Pat as the father on Tony's birth certificate. If this was ten years earlier, it might have affected the couple adversely, but they survived the exposé well apart from Renée cancelling a show at Hackney Empire in late January, collapsing just before she and her sister were due to go on. She was ready to wage war with quips at the Chiswick Empire on February 29, 1932. He might have been a 'wronged' man but George was great friends with Pat and would also have done anything for his 'Houston' as he called her. Years later Renée said he was so fond of her he almost ruined the divorce saying the wrong things when requesting a decree nisi. George became *'Uncle George'* to the kids, which must have been a little confusing for Trevor and Terry, the eldest ones.

1932 charged on, and Renée, Billie and Shirley could rely on Pat to chauffeur them to London engagements with ease and comfort. Billie would say of him that he was the best driver she knew, and she felt safer driving with Pat at the wheel than anyone else. In April 1932 notices read how at New Cross Empire locals reserved a warm welcome for the Houstons, then the three sisters were hailed in their *Hollywood* skit at Hackney, and called 'irresistibly volatile' at Liverpool's Empire for keeping 'the house in roars of laughter.' At this point the Sisters turn up in the Pathé magazine item 'Roadhouse Nights' when Renée's musical voice is heard chattering above the sound of splashes as fashionable late night swimmers plunge in the deep end. 'With it' Londoners in the 30s said they were going 'out on the Bypass' taking the car to the Ace of Spades - a pioneering summer venue serving meals late into the night in a restaurant that seated eight hundred. You could dance, and play miniature golf and even polo.

Vacating the Kingston Bypass, the Houston Sisters played the Hippodromes of Manchester and Bristol, then Swansea Empire, before heading back to London followed by Edinburgh in a bill including the vent act Coram and Gerry. Pat found a large old farmhouse for three quid a week rent, where they could raise the kids, and keep in touch with film world. Popular as ever, the Houstons had engagements at Shepherd's Bush Empire, one at the Palladium joining Paul Robeson on the bill, then a Victoria Palace engagement for Halloween, then Aberdeen's Tivoli.

The Stage, on November 24, 1932 in its 'Behind the Screens' column reported that a new film - Claude Hulbert's first feature - was going into production and that shooting would last about thirty-three days. Shortly before, Renée had been given a contract of £100 per week for a year: the whim of a studio executive. It happened over lunch in Elstree's canteen whilst she was chatting to Charles Laughton and Elsa Lanchester. This contract would later collapse.

Pat had recently had a successful screen test by MGM and prepared for a trip to Hollywood. On November 26, every newspaper carried the announcement that he and Renée were to marry, and two days later they signed the register at Henrietta St Registry Office, Covent Garden. Renée forgot to take a copy of the decree dissolving her former marriage and for a while it was 'doubtful' the ceremony could go ahead. Anxious, with little time to spare, Pat drove the registrar in his car to Somerset House where the official saw the document, allowing the ceremony to be performed.[49] Pat looks happiest in the photographs as they sign the book or pose, with the piazza behind them. He was probably relieved it was over. Renée carried a bunch of white spider chrysanthemums - symbolic of truth. Would she follow him west?

The day after the wedding, on November 29 1932, Pat sailed for Hollywood, expecting to be the male lead in a film with news magnate William Randolph Hearst's girlfriend and Elana lookalike, Marion Davies. Arriving at West Washington Boulevard, Culver City, he discovered they wanted him to play a fifty year-old man. Getting production staff to sort out this casting error Pat waited until he was assigned another part. He played golf, went to the beaches, drew his pay on Friday evenings and waited. He kept checking for news but day after day, and week after week he played more golf, did more bathing and went on drawing his money. He went mad with boredom, couldn't stand the food[50] or American manners, and felt miserable. They made 'Peg o' My Heart' with Marion Davies, directed by RZ Leonard but the part they offered Pat didn't appeal to him.

He failed to fit in with the film crowd revolving around Marion addicted to parties and drinking their own homemade gin out of a bathtub. A prudent English traveller, Pat had taken his own gin with him on the journey out, anticipating its scarcity, and didn't care for bootleg. After three and a half months in Hollywood, he came home. He was advised to return to MGM the coming May although this fell through. He had reached California slightly before his brother Brian only for his first Hollywood film role to crash.

Brian, by contrast, had a contract with Paramount for 'Song of Songs' (1933) with Marlene Dietrich that began production soon after Pat left. Brian crossed back to the UK for Gaumont's 'The Constant Nymph' directed by Basil Dean, before leaving for Hollywood permanently at the end of 1933. By then, he was an established member of the Hollywood British colony and Ronald Colman, one of Tinseltown's most famous British actors, became his most supportive friend.

Brian Aherne with Marlene Dietrich and Reuben Mamoulian about to make 'Song of Songs' (Cutting from unidentified newspaper in the Aherne Family Collection)

Chapter 12   Enduring Loves

Sir Lawrence Olivier, interviewed for *The Entertainer,* in which he played *Archie Rice*, talked admiringly about the gallantry of the music hall. He described that lone figure on a stage set against the whole audience. How we leaned forward in excitement as his sharpened consonants began to strike against the back of the pit like bullets![1] Renée was this calibre of performer, whose belligerent instinct got across to her audience. She got away with suggesting verboten topics. Just compare Britain in March 1933 with Germany, where halls were put under direct supervision. Spring-cleaning commenced throughout the Reich and in Berlin police president Von Levessow held forth.[2] Artistes that dared put over questionable material were dealt with strictly. Our Max Millers and Renée Houstons meanwhile, were free to be spontaneous and we continued to lean forward in anticipation. Thank heavens for the luxury of freedom and catharsis!

Renée had never been positive about developing a career in the legitimate theatre. All the time she was growing up, the two worlds had been too far apart. One was commercial, physical, irreverent, and by nature crowd-pleasing. The other prided itself on the immersive performances of its players and the ability to communicate ideas serious and difficult. Players from both types of theatre claimed they sought perfection. Renée didn't like the snobbery the legits had towards variety where her ties were. Now and again she got a bee in her bonnet. She liked to mention how back in Birmingham in 1926 the Houston Sisters had the No 1 dressing room whilst Olivier was at the local Rep. It wasn't easy to cross over from variety into straight roles as a degree of mutual exclusivity existed in the two cultures.

Bill Maynard, who started in variety, told me his first Shakespeare was *Taming of the Shrew* alongside John Neville at the Old Nottingham Playhouse. At the Marlow, Canterbury, he trained Neville in variety sketches at the Shakespearean actor's request, but John was unsure he could do it, and chose not to use it on stage. Bill believes that comic dialogue can be very close to Shakespeare. In *Measure For Measure* he put in touches he'd picked up from his variety training. It went down well, especially with kids in the audience. Many purely dramatic actors told him they wished they had the advantage of variety training. Most Shakespearean actors do the one thing only. In Bill's case, it was his Shakespeare work that made the Reps accept him.

Renée Houston, by contrast, didn't have the patience. The legit world, she claimed, wasn't for her, and while she made light of it, this gap in accomplishment added to her insecurities. She could have bought acceptance, continuing on from her own shot at Shakespeare in *Taming of the Shrew*. She played *Katherina* in one scene in a 30s film, now lost. It suggests that this type of acting was at least a personal goal. She also talked about portraying strong women from history. She was once keen to increase her experience but factors made her hold back. Being a victim of her own commercial success was one and satisfying public expectations another.

Responding to a question concerning the development of her career posed by a French interviewer, she is pragmatic:

Renée: But people don't want it. They expect us to be very young funny girls. As soon as we appear, they have fun. They don't want us to be serious![3]

Her musical comedy successes, long variety career, and character roles in West End plays and films happened largely as a consequence of being true to herself. From the 30s to the 60s international film directors saw the appeal of this, perhaps more so than homegrown ones. She wasn't too old to be moulded by Polanski. She never met her Fellini though. Yet Renée never became a true muse to a playwright, theatre or film director or lent herself to a pivotal new production. Frequently underused, she had to be rediscovered. Sometimes she put the blame on others, projecting an image of herself as an overlooked actress never given the breaks because producers put people into boxes.

Renée: I had played the baby for years and within weeks I had to make it by myself. Nobody thought of me for stage plays until I appeared in 'A Town Like Alice.'[4]

In fact, ideas to present her in serious dramas as well as musical comedies had frequently been floated in her younger years. The serious dramas never materialized. It surprises me that one who loved challenging people's expectations didn't persist until the goal became a reality. She might have proved herself a serious actress earlier if she hadn't joined up with Donald as a new partner, extending her variety career. Bringing in the money to support family made her think twice about taking a chance with her career.

Friends with the mighty thespians of her day: Laughton, Olivier, Redgrave, Guinness and Sybil Thorndike, 'the pals' were among those encouraging her or initiating theatrical entrées. She didn't see them as natural bedfellows. If she had joined them it would have felt like she was being untrue to herself. The variety world had been tough to survive in and sometimes coarse. There had been times when she competed with contemporary comics in sour atmospheres. The 'pals' hadn't come up the way she had. She was resistant to their 'come and join me' requests, framing herself as a variety performer and modestly making light of her acting ability. Elizabeth Seal pointed out to me how Renée's variety training placed her worlds apart in experience from other actors in the West End, and Fenella Fielding told me she sensed that Renée became insecure if theatre talk verged towards the highbrow. These two observations are very useful in understanding her.

When she left variety, she found a substitute in provincial tours and one play in particular. This was Lesley Storm's *Roar Like A Dove,* in which she played the American momma. She had done it enough times she could walk into it without rehearsal and add spontaneous extras to refresh the comedy. Nobody minded. She described it as her favourite part. For Renée, greatness lay with individual performance and the play could even be subordinate.

As she got older a powerful and substantial part in a gritty drama would have suited her had one been within reach. She could have inhabited a contemporary role, or done wonders with a Dickens adaption. Alas, *Betsey Trotwood* wasn't Scottish. She was best when she didn't have to do understatement, although she could do this incredibly well in films. Her comic calling and mastery of the revue form makes me think that had she been born later a television show comprised of sketches deriving from her own writing would have made a screamingly funny series highly conducive to modern tastes. In later years she gave professional performances to order but a measure of ambition and a measure of discipline had gone by then. Some legit actors felt she wasn't their idea of an ideal team worker or collaborator, while others talked about her sweetness and helpfulness.

She had no problem giving her audience *Renée Houston* whatever the role, and there's a type of honesty about that. In the late 60s audiences were often full of people who had come to see her exactly for that. They remembered her with affection and watched her with a smile. For the older generations she inspired real love. When I showed pictures of the young Miss Houston to Michael Gaunt, her director in 1968, he told me it was difficult to see the same woman he knew, although he recalled how flashes of her old vitality became apparent and her eyes lit up when she talked about the past, or was recognized. Those eyes, behind glasses, revealed an inner sadness when she was still. This Renée wearing glasses is one I doubt her fans would recognize.

She had survived on a blend of instinct and charisma for so long and having fun was a central part of the story of Renée Houston. In trying to understand her, her love for her sister Billie - her earliest partner, her sense of being 'at home' in the variety theatre despite its vulnerability in the changing world in the 30s, her enjoyment of the people in that world, or the camaraderie that might come via radio work, are all worth a glance: aspects of Renée's life that might be considered 'great loves.'

Next engagement – Where are we? – Untested audience - Should've 'eard the bird he got, New gags, Luggage, Theatrical digs, Fellow pros, Fears you'll end up where you started - these all came with performing in variety. Everything about the culture here was different to the legitimate stage – worlds apart – to use Liz Seal's phrase, and it was coarser, raw, untamed even. The young Renée never felt she was slogging it out. She loved the hour or two waiting to go on before the callboy knocked on the dressing room door with his *'Houston Sisters - five minutes please!'* Having a sandwich and a cup of tea, reading the paper, putting on makeup, doing a crossword, filling in a Pools coupon, talking to other turns, speaking to an agent, booker or script writer, and snoozing – these were among the mundane things a variety entertainer did during waiting times. In Renée, Billie and Shirley's case add to this list the heated up leftovers of yesterday's argument, shrieks of laughter, latest news in letters, non-stop theatre gossip from Binkie – their dresser, and ridiculous larks connected with superstition.

Enduring Loves

The latter obsession began at Our Lady and St Francis with Renée and her school-friends scaring the hell out of each other about the nun who died and haunted the convent. Later in Johnstone came that séance where she held hands under the table causing George to say afterwards what a 'cheeky little kid' she was. At the Roadhouse, Kingston Bypass, we see Renée surrounded by the audience - her tarot cards about her on the floor talking about *Bill* meeting a nice dark-haired girl. Even in her last film she's reading the cards.

Throughout the English provinces, in Scotland, Wales and Ireland, every large town had theatrical boarding houses - thriving businesses! Approved lodgings were listed in the theatrical press boasting the presence of a grand piano for musicians or suitability for large troupes. Good souls like *Mrs Cooke* of Ramsgate charged winter prices in summer months and got a little plug in The Performer while the treatment dished out to pros by other landladies was quite mean. It was imperative to book up your digs in advance. After a few years touring variety performers had favoured digs. Brian O'Gorman, who's father Joe was touring constantly at the same time as the Houstons, told me the commonest type of communication was in writing as few of these places had phones. The stooge fixed the digs weeks ahead. A late booking for a week's work might require fixing things up on arrival. That's when stage door keepers came into their own as the best people to tell you what you could find locally. Renée and Billie talked about their experiences in digs and some of their tales bordered on the supernatural. They were struck by how amazing it was that so many landladies were practicing spiritualists.

One story goes like this: In a queer old house in the Midlands, Renée's looking into a full-length mirror trying on a new hat. Herself, Billie and Lizzi are the only residents apart from the landlady and her son. She's singing to herself blithely: '. . . *so, honey, don't you cry! We'll find a silver lining, The clouds will soon roll by* . . .' She feels an awful tension, as if someone's behind her although she can see in the mirror no one's in the room. Why is there this overpowering desire to turn around? She turns her head and with a sigh of relief sees there's nobody behind. She looks through the open door - the one she had used to enter the room, and Lizzi's in the room opposite. 'You silly little fool,' she says to herself, turning back to look at the mirror, and for a second she stands petrified, too terrified to move her lips – It's too awful. With a shriek that nearly lifts off the roof she falls to the floor in a dead faint. Renée has seen a young woman standing immediately behind her fingering the material at the back of the hat. The next day it emerges that others have had a similar encounter. Lizzi – even more sensitive to the paranormal - confronts the landlady 'Who was that pale-faced young lady who passed me on the stairs as I was coming in from shopping this afternoon?' The landlady explains that a London chorus girl died in the house two years before. Séances are necessary to ask this girl why she keeps coming back.

Another goes like this: In a queer old house in Lancashire Renée and Billie are sleeping in an attic room. This landlady's a loud-mouthed sort, telling the

Sisters that a crowd is gathering that night for a *bit of a séance* in the room below them. 'There's nowt to be worried about,' she tells them. They go to bed and hear a swishing on the floor. The next day they buy a nightlight and place it in a saucer so it won't fall and cause a fire. Billie goes to bed with her boy's own story and Renée, in her frilly nightdress, writes a letter. George doesn't exist as usual in these stories. When they're sleepy Billie puts the nightlight on the mantle-piece, turns off the gaslight and they go to bed. 'Swish, swoosh' comes the noise this time from the area where the top of the walls join the ceiling. Rickety noises are heard, like the noise of a boy drawing a stick across the rails at the foot of the bed. They've seriously got the wind up. Everything's starting to fall from the shelves. The nightlight is hurled off the mantelpiece. Terrified, the two curl up in balls in the middle of the bed. The next morning they discover the carpet's been moved from the side of their bed to the middle of the floor. The candle grease from the nightlight has been tipped everywhere. What horror did all this? All the bloody landlady says is 'Jack was along last night - up to his old tricks again.' Jack was her youngest son, a wild young devil, killed at the Battle of Jutland. 'He's been wilder than ever,' the landlady tells them. 'You know what them sailors are.'

In a final story a randy fellow pro is affected by the supernatural. This married rover of a comic fancies himself a hit with the ladies and attempts to get off with a strange lady. A challenging display of sweaty passion is followed by a realization he's been trying to 'mash' with a ghost. He goes back to his deserted wife after this.

There were landladies who insisted on coming into their bedrooms to talk to them late at night. Sometimes their husbands arrived instead. It could be very embarrassing. Some digs were so ghastly that vengeance was had by nailing a kipper to the underside of a table – a method to ward off living spirits! Whether this old variety tradition was truly executed is another matter. So many halls, so many friends, so many digs, so many ghosts . . . Every minute of their off-duty time offered something to talk about. Then they were on the move again. People whose job offers a constant change of scene acquire a thrill and panache about them. Salesmen have it. So did the Houstons.

The Sisters had each other too - an enduring love. Billie fine-tuned the act, generously doing the subtle work as *straight man* whilst the spotlight illuminated her sister in her latest piece of foolery. Next to the scatterbrained Renée, *Bill* was the perfect complement. Strange that even from the time of *Tom Tom*, Billie would admit to being in the game to make money: 'Well, I don't particularly like being on the stage, but if we're going to be on it we might as well make some dough,' she would say. That pot load at the rainbow's end was forever tantalizing. Renée could be oblivious to a purse full of notes leaving the theatre at the week's end. In a story her granddaughter told me, Renée's purse was full of an insane amount of money but when travelling from London to Edgbaston, where Pat's relatives were, she managed to lose it. She was ready to shrug it off when an honest train guard retrieved the lost purse and rushed to present it to her. Genuinely grateful, she opened the purse and took out a one-pound note to pay him for his trouble. It wasn't meanness, but her sheer obliviousness to money. It only occurred to her soon after how disproportionate the reward was and she went back to give him more. When it came to big financial decisions, she was neither here nor there. It's one of the mysteries about her. She was an action-orientated leader type in so many other ways. When Billie suggested going to America in 1926, Renée's reaction would be:

Renée: Go to America? Oh, no. Never! I always refuse contracts offered to me. Nomatter how brilliant they are. I'm afraid of crossing the water.[5]

That fear of long distance travel was disingenuous. No doubt they bickered about this. Billie and Renée complemented each other as laughter-maker and feed with a healthy rivalry electrifying their act. They often frustrated each other in real life. When the Sisters quarrelled people ran for cover. Screaming fights, doors smashed open and shut, and periods of time when they wouldn't speak to each other were the order of the day. It happened with all three Sisters. The reason would always be some forgettable thing. Thankfully, they could get over it just in time for something else to be the new basis of a fight, and so went the cycle. Most acts made sure nothing relating to quarrels came to light because sneaks, backstabbers, and chiselling cheats backstage were all too ready to spread derogatory news about them, casting doubts about their ability as professionals. The Houstons however, benefitted because an ongoing quarrel was integral to their act. News of a backstage bust-up leaked but it was par for the course.

Billie's dour character gave Renée many opportunities for light mockery. Renée I see as a seasoned provoker with Billie's mind best suited to cool calculation. I had a view of Billie as quite a lamb – far less bossy than Renée. Evidence seems to point to her being a loose cannon with or without Renée. She could surprise others with the cheek she was capable of and adlib just like her sister. She could tell Max Miller jokes with an unbridled delivery that made her serious-minded son cringe on the spot. He recalls his mother's proclivity towards making embarrassing jokes at school prize-givings. Billie was also capable of devilish pranks like the one causing an unknowing Renée to walk hand in hand on stage with a chimpanzee. Judging from accounts of Renée at her most foul-mouthed, it can't have been very nice for Billie having to take on her sister in the legendary brawls. Even after the worst of these their infighting was subordinate to the act: 'We'd have a punch-up, do the show and come off the best of pals,'[6] wrote Miss Houston. It's a true pro that can instantly go into a chirpy verbal exchange following cross words or after they'd barely spoken to each other since the early morning. Renée wrote how just before their Royal Command Performance in 1926 that 'Bill said in a quiet voice, 'Best of luck!' She wrote that she couldn't believe her ears, admitting they were never the sort to exchange greetings - even at Christmas.[7] Her throwaway comment gives a sense of the natural distance they had. Then again, if any pain or hardship befell Renée or Billie, or Shirley, each felt the other's pain miserably. It was a complex relationship but the love between the Sisters stayed with them their whole lives.

Intuition lay behind the swift performance, and Renée would describe the 'uncanny understanding' that let her sister steer the comedy,' her 'accurate mental clock' providing an innate awareness of their time on stage. They never required a time-check. Discipline like this counted for a lot in variety where time was of the essence. The Houstons perfected a little turn that was very economical. Shirley Houston had the raw deal, being ten years younger than Billie. For all her talent, she was unable to match her sisters in experience – a perpetually unfair challenge.

Sneaks and backstabbers, brittle egos and jealous prima donnas exhibiting vile behaviour were to be found in their beloved variety theatre. At the Coliseum, Stoll had to deal with Grock's artistic tantrums, when the whiteface clown[8] who wore a completely bald wig a'la *Micawber* yelled 'Send for Sir Oswald Stoll,' after seeing Bransby Williams appear in his get up as *Micawber*. Grock insisted Williams had copied his makeup. He had no grasp of the Dickensian characters, still much in the public mind.[9] As she wafted on stage leading lady José Collins would say nasty and wounding things about the figures of the chorus girls behind her fan in and between her lines in the libretto. The chorus girls would say something equally nasty back, taking quite a risk in doing so.[10] It was behaviour Renée, Billie and all their colleagues loathed. A scene in the film 'A Girl Must Live' echoes this kind of on-stage bitching by the chorus.

By contrast, a kind word from a colleague boosted your confidence. Most of the time everyone felt like they were mucking in together. Many variety acts were the children of music hall acts who by their early teens had grown up with each other, and met all the acts on the circuit. It was an endlessly shifting on-the-move community. They were famously supportive of each other. I hadn't fully understood this quality until I came away from a Max Miller Appreciation Society garden party held a stone's throw away from the sumptuous Royal Pavilion in Brighton. Max's cheeky and surprisingly squeaky voice played out from the speakers. The great and the good rubbed shoulders, but the high and the mighty were nowhere to be seen. Some of the now retired entertainers had interesting stories to tell. A bevy of ladies sat singing a harmony, quietly but perfectly. The charming and effervescent Peter Waterman, an entertainer of the classic kind, performed magic literally and figuratively throughout the day. He was the first person to speak to me and demo'd a slick turn for my own personal benefit. People chatted to old friends and swapped stories. Thea McIntyre told me about GH Elliott - a family friend. With her daughter she was visiting his resting place in Rottingdean later that day. He had been one of the most popular performers in Scotland and his manner of dressing entirely in white: hat, shoes and cane to contrast to his blackface was stunning. In his routine he drifted like thistledown across the stage. Elliott's act left her in awe and Thea became a choreographer herself. I'd come across Elliott's name on a Sunderland Empire playbill so rainbow-hued it was uncanny. Fancy it dating from 1911! If I'd been Thea, appearing on the bill with some of those big names, I too would have felt less daunted because so frequently the fellow acts were folk your family had known for ages.

'Twice Nightly' variety lasting from the 20s to the 60s with a different bill every week meant you got to know the star act and the seven or so other acts during your week together. Wyn Calvin - *Clown Prince of Wales* recalled how sociable Renée was, as well as being a terrific pro. Bill Maynard, at the age of seventeen, was in the same touring show as Renée and Donald Stewart. This was the *Bryan Michie Discoveries*. In those days Bill did everything: song, dance, comedy, a cowboy act with a guitar, a George Formby type act, and one belting out Neapolitan arias. Bill's father was earning 23 shillings a week gardening in the Bishop of Leicester's garden, and Bill could earn substantially more just by playing the clubs just for a weekend. He said that the material variety performers had was always fairly rehearsed and he doesn't recall performers being over-worked. A star act brought in the crowds but new talent could be showcased at the same time. As a young man, he found something impressive and sexy about a woman, especially a beautiful one, using bad language. Bill described Renée as *upper class*. That was interesting. Still, I can see how she was among theatre's *polished brass* at the Palace Theatre, Leicester around 1945 - the time he listened to Renée's risqué language. On this occasion his fellow pros were congregating backstage. The conversation and jokes were good and a lot of steam was let off. Renée's language was outrageous. 'Unbelievable!' was how Bill put it. Why the sewer language? I asked. He said he thinks it was a kind of release. Actors are so governed by the 'appropriate behaviour' they must display before their public. They're trained to forever watch their backs. Left alone with their mates for company, there's no end of effing and blinding.

When Renée and Billie were '*Discoveries*' Bill Maynard was still a distant glint in his mother's eye. By the 30s, when they were an established act, performers were kept more on their toes owing to the pressure of managers like George Black. He was keen to draw people back to the theatres, now cinema had overtaken variety as the nation's *number 1* entertainment. In the London theatres the hugely popular duo Nervo and Knox worked alongside Renée and Billie at least nine times between 1927-28 sometimes doing their *Fall of the Apache* routine at the Coliseum. Naughton and Gold appeared twice alongside the Sisters in 1928, and Flanagan and Allen were on the bill with the Houstons at least six times between 1931-32. By 1932 a new phenomenon was assembled from those three male top liner double acts, drawing in other temporary members. This was the *Crazy Gang* - the super-act that enjoyed crowd-pulling superiority until 1940. *O-Kay For Sound* was one of the first *Crazy* shows. George Black produced three at the Palladium masterminding their success. Emphasis was on fast routines with *Gang* members darting on and off in between acts. Newspapers talked of variety's survival through Black's 'innovations' like 'Non-Stop variety,' making speed the keynote. Waits between turns were eliminated. The installation of microphones at the Palladium was another innovation. Black justified the latter saying audiences had got so used to cinema that they were accustomed to artificial voices in acoustically sound theatres. 'Black definitely gives audiences what they want'[11] – was how these reports concluded. Management was muscling in more than ever and Black blamed expensive performers for acts that were monotonous. He ticked people off for not being strikingly novel enough. It has to be accepted that Black's changes paid off, at least at the Palladium.

All this speed was dangerous and poor Shirley Houston found herself in a *Crazy* show riding a comedy cycle around the stage with that seasoned bunch of lunatics. Somebody banged into her and she lost control, flying over the handlebars, falling into the orchestra pit on top of a pianist. She sustained a bad injury to her leg and the pianist burst a blood vessel in his foot. Renée joked that 'Everywhere we go now members of the orchestra wonder if we are going to drop in on them some time.'

George Black says in his Performer article that some of the material used by his performers in *Crazy Week* came from hired funny men.[12] He needed to buy in jokes because of the rate at which they were being used. It took some pressure off the performers. Not everyone wanted to work together. You would think the *Crazy Gang* a *tour de force* with such a strong line up, but in the mid-30s, they were refusing to be booked with the Houston Sisters, fearing the competition. The business had got tougher. Whilst the Houston Sisters did their stint of *Crazy* shows, it didn't suit them and I believe they were more 'old school' in relation to their time in the limelight. When old time star Harry Champion commented about the *Crazy* shows, he would say how in his day, stars were too jealous of each other that such a thing was impossible.[13] The Houstons would have appreciated that last point.

The sheer joy of holding an appreciative audience in your palm is what justified working in variety, even for Billie, who had talked about being in it for dough. A variety manager, Will Dalton, well known in his time, told a journalist in 1933 that the 'backbone of variety are the acts that make audiences restless before they appear and sick with hysteria when they depart,'[14] and the Sisters were happy to be that backbone. They also knew that minor acts played a crucial part in creating the overall spirit of variety. There was a ranking underlying the billboard arrangement: letters decreased from the huge: reserved for the big names, to the smallest typeface. Despite this, there was little room for vanity.

On their own minor acts wouldn't normally draw a penny and frequently relied on top-liners to enable them to keep working: a symbiosis with a social conscience. Acrobats were at the bottom of the barrel in the minds of the public and fellow pros. When you think about the marvellous expertise of acrobats this is completely unfair. Often they were put on as a first or last act for the benefit of patrons who might arrive late or leave early but want to catch the higher-ranking items on the bill. Working hard and never getting money or recognition used to warrant the mock-denunciation: 'May all your children be acrobats!' It's a sad fact that some acrobats, paper-tearers, wire walkers and escapologists were underpaid. Some exceptionally talented artistes fell into no category. One lady I met at the Max Miller garden party told me her hugely successful husband would not have felt happy with the label *Speciality Act*. Having labels foisted on you is unfair.

Camaraderie among theatrically minded folk still flourishes in theatre groups but fewer towns have them nowadays. In order for the lifestyle Renée Houston loved so much to re-materialize, theatres and some kind of circuit would need to be brought back. Nowadays, it's optimistic to think that there are many places of work outside of *the profession* where it truly feels like being part of a family. Camaraderie now means the regimented lunchtime five-asides, Google Cafés, and sweeties from the office cabinet handed out to productive teams on the call centre floor. For office misfits this only results in more eagerness to retreat from work to some other place of freedom. Opportunities to work in a career like variety alongside adventurous friends from extraordinary acts sadly aren't there today. What used to be this vast informal network has diminished. Who, today, can have the same disinterest in materialism: mirroring the values of obscure theatrical bottom-liners of the past, now we're supposed to be so financially inclined? It discords too much, and the surveillance cameras would be on to you. Your creative boho nature would be likely to result in a poor performance review.

Some of the acts that were on in the 20s and 30s astound me. In early 1926 the Reinsch Brothers - Danish circus jockeys - riding around the Coliseum's revolving stage did sensational stunts.[15] Would you believe in November 1927 that Samson - *Strongest Man on Earth* could lift a piano and pianist with his teeth suspended by his foot from a rope?[16] That was nothing for Samson who lifted iron girders with his teeth all the time. He must have have been unnaturally possessed of calcium. The feel of a one-ton lorry containing twenty passengers run over him was all in a day's work and when he was bored he hammered nails through a piece of wood three inches thick using the palm of his hand. There were less dangerous acts that were visually stunning like Dr Angelo's *Living Jewellery* or the clever seaside silhouettes created by Harry Gunn and Company.

Singers like Sophie Tucker belted out 'Rose of the Volga', 'Vo-de-oh-do' or 'Some of these days.' Comics like the African-Chinese combo act Rucker and Perrin gave us *Chop Suey for one,* and the O'Gorman Brothers gave us *Missing The Train*. In one-act plays, actress divas like Nazimova could be mad, bad and Roumanian: as she was in *A Woman of the Earth*.[17] Many of these acts followed or came before the Houston Sisters. I expect that Billie in her naval uniform found herself a hit with Nazimova. Many younger actors who worked with Renée Houston in the 70s recall a whiff of mythical past glories bouncing off her. As they gathered around this Ephesian goddess, rapt in a huddle at the bar, she flabbergasted them with epics from this golden age.

She had always enjoyed getting to know the obscure underpaid acts and the mysterious continental ones. She had seen a thing or two, and liked to think of herself as non-judgmental where friends were concerned, although there were limits to who was welcome at her door. At home Renée liked unstuffy atmospheres where kids could run around and put their feet on the sofa. She might send her kids to expensive schools and have the odd servant but she never aspired to being 'posh.' She stayed true to herself. The oddballs of her profession, the creatives and those who struggled were born of her pedigree. She preferred the underdog to the top dog.

Before the Houston Sisters made a feature film together they did something even more pervasive - they became Radio stars. Big personalities on a stage, Renée and Billie only had to be heard a few times on the wireless to be recognizable by their voices alone. They were among the first generation of comics on the airwaves. The BBC variety department broadcast from the Aeolian Hall on New Bond Street, from Portland Place and St George's Hall in Langham Place. This was formerly Maskeleyne's Theatre and was used by the BBC and Radio Luxemburg. Sometimes the BBC relayed programmes direct from the Coliseum or George Barclay's Clapham Grand. By the early 30s, the BBC was outputting more than one hundred and fifty variety programmes a year.[18] Measuring an act's popularity in the public eye when so many decades have gone by isn't easy but there's evidence to prove the Houstons rated very highly.

Billie Houston
(Author's Collection)

July '36 Radio Pictorial
Cover (Author's Collection)

Shirley Houston
(Silander Family)

From the mid to late 30s they featured in Radio Pictorial - a kind of *Hello* magazine of its day with listings that fed on the mass appeal of the stars on the radio. From 1933 it made glamorous stars out of voices heard on commercial stations like Radio Luxembourg, Radio Normandie and Radio Lyons. Towards the latter part of the decade it highlighted BBC listings too. You might never go to the cinema but you could put a face to your favourite wireless stars. The magazine had unstuffy articles, jokes, photo stories, recipes, welcomed listener feedback, and offered women advice about housekeeping problems or beauty tips from Mae West, Joan Crawford, Myrna Loy and Jean Harlow. Radio Pictorial gave Radio Times a run for its money and stars got ginormous coverage. Radio Times only included BBC listings, and kept its television listings separate in a supplement. It combined radio

Enduring Loves

and TV listings at the end of 1949 when a transmitter was opened at Sutton Coldfield, taking TV to the Midlands.[19] All the stars were in Radio Pictorial: Gracie, George Formby, Ambrose, Roy Fox, Vera Lynn to name a few. Almost every star endorsed one product or another. Max Miller advertised Shredded Wheat, and Gracie Fields, everything from a garden chair to a domino.

The sheer number of artistes parodying the Houstons provides another measurement of their popularity. One of the earliest takeoffs was by Dick Henderson - the small northern comic with a supersonically fast delivery. Doris Bleach assisted him in his *Lucky Stars* show when he did his 'Houston' item. The New York vaudeville star Madge Kennedy was given curtain after curtain for a routine that included her imitations of the Houstons. She even did a good Will Fyffe! Renée and Billie needn't worry about being absent from the halls for a few weeks because there was always someone doing an impression of them in the interval. There was Anna Rogers, Marianne, and Ann Penn (who delighted Penge Empire with her Gracie Fields, Houstons, Bea Lillie, Lily Morris, and Nellie Wallace). If she didn't appeal there was a clever impression of Renée and Billie by Jenny Howard – known as 'the poor man's Gracie Fields.' She got this name because she would follow a hit by Gracie with her own cover version on the cheaper Woolworths record label. The best of them all, in my opinion, was Beryl Orde, hugely talented and popular *BBC Impressioniste*, whose career stretched into the 40s. There is a fantastic Pathé film called 'Jazz Justice' of Beryl in a mythical police court where the defendants include Gracie Fields, Zazu Pitts, Renée (in a black curly wig), and Billie (in a short blonde wig), all impersonated splendidly by Beryl, as they answer the judge's questions.

Beryl Orde   Gracie Fields
(Photos: Author's Collection, By kind permission of K.Forbes)

While it all seems to have been done in jest and good humour, a large *'Special Request'* advertisement in The Performer placed by Miss H, in late 1931 icily wishes 'all mimics to refrain from any kind of imitation . . . as the ladies have greatly suffered from it during the past years.'[20] She had been a topliner long enough to feel she had the right to make this demand. Renée has to be admired for expressing her feelings about competition in the variety business where many wouldn't dare, and this shows how confident she was at this early date. There would be many future situations when she proved herself to be a vociferous on a certain issue. She and Gracie were the two who spoke out against the issue of impressionists basing far too much of their act on the lampooning other artistes. The argument was a sore point and they articulated it well. We take it for granted nowadays how the Internet proliferates things in record speed, but back in the 20s and 30s, radio was the demon medium - unleashing copyists onto the airwaves.

Many comic turns were extremely sensitive about having their better gags or delivery looted and hoped that something might be done to keep tabs on the situation. Five years earlier Little Tich had talked about the hard work comedians have to do, getting material up to scratch and fighting to get the bookings. He mentions in an article that certain 'creators of style' suffered from the spread of copyists, telling us how in the old days authors would work exclusively for one comic. Now this is rare and it's toughgoing to keep a large repertoire you can call your own. Tich rounds off his intelligent discourse observing that being put through the mill sorts the men from the boys.[21] It was common then for managers to encourage their acts to copy other artists. There was a saying in Renée's day that 'a gag created on Monday will be copied by two or three others by Wednesday.' This was a time royalties began to be required as radio stations were utilizing gramophone records made by artistes instead of employing live artistes to entertain the public. Britain, like the USA, needed to find a solution.[22]

In 1931 among the famous individuals Renée was burlesquing in her stage act was *Greta Garbo*. She captured the Swede's voice particularly well and her new parody was thought diverting.[23] Impressionistes in turn saw fit to burlesque *Renée's Greta Garbo* and it was the extent they did this that got right up Miss Houston's sensitive nose. Again she saw fit to complain about it. Yet, when you count up how many times Renée did her *Garbo parody* you might wonder if Miss Garbo's best material wasn't being snatched. Wasn't the Swede due a royalty? I'm sure she would gladly have taken one.

Radio rage was present in the Houston household in October 1935. Renée thought a bit of background radio might be nice as her dinner guests assembled round the table at her home in Glendale Avenue, Edgware. Suddenly, as she listened to a BBC broadcast featuring Janet Joye, the Birmingham impressioniste who was freely using the *Houston-Garbo parody*, her lips became as fixedly oblique as her gaily-painted Cubist teapot. She declared she'd not stand for this and her poor guests heard nothing else but Renée's rage the rest of the evening. In a front-page story in the Daily Express, entitled *'BBC Apologize to Renée Houston,'* we learn that the apology quickly came from the BBC with Renée sounding sportsmanlike about Miss Joye. When the Daily Mail ran the story Renée emphasized the ruthlessness shown by impressionists lifting material without a care. She mentions how Gracie Fields suffered on account of this, not just Billie and herself. She harked back to the old days when the profession was marked with more courtesy. Permission used to be requested. Another press report gets closer to what seem to be Renée's actual words: 'Audiences who have not seen or heard us get prejudiced in advance by bad and sometimes malicious versions of our acts by performers who cannot be bothered to think out their own material.'[24] This report reveals that Gracie had threatened action some years previously against any future impersonators. Reading this it sounds like no comedy artiste was safe. Radio was but a saloon in a Wild West 'free for all' with Renée the latest sheriff.

Tracing gags can get a bit pedantic. The Houston Sisters influenced many a fledgling comic. They themselves were cognizant of fellow acts in that long lead-up to storming the capital, and afterwards. It's worth mentioning how in June 1929 the Houstons shared the bill with Burns and Allen[25] at Manchester Hippodrome. Renée was sure to pick up a few tokens.

The O'Gorman Brothers: Dave and Joe (By kind permission of Brian O'Gorman)

The fabulously funny O'Gorman Brothers: Dave and Joe, contemporaries of the Sisters, anticipated Eric and Ernie. The O'Gormans led the field with the physical element they added to their act and were famed for 'non-follow on' routines. Brian O'Gorman, watches Eric and Ernie on TV and shouts out 'Dave and Joe!' thinking of his 1939 Holborn Empire programme headlined by his dad's act with Jack Hylton's band and fourteen year-old Ernie present. It's easy to forget how lasting the influence was of some of the personalities from the interwar period. The scrapheap of comedy offers fabulous recycling opportunities for everyone from The Goons, to Peter Cook and probably everyone else. Who doesn't observe and learn from the wings, have a crack at something someone else did, and hope to go one better?

Renée's criticism of radio copyists underlines her respect for her fellow stage entertainers. She wasn't against the radio as some individuals from the variety world were. As regards her standing in the eyes of pros, I can see evidence from reading articles in *Radio Pictorial*, that Renée had a huge amount of friends in the profession in the 30s. The singer Phyllis Robins was a darling friend who gave Renée lots of encouragement when she blossomed out at the Hippodrome as a solo artiste. The tuneful Carlyle Cousins were also good friends. They lived in a 400 year-old Tudor cottage just outside Elstree and Renée often got Pat Aherne to drop her off there.

Clockwise:
Burns and Allen
(Author's Collection)

Ben Lyon
(from Renée's scrapbook. By kind permission of the family of Terry Long)

Phyllis Robins
(Author's Collection)

The Carlyle Cousins
(By kind permission S. Taylor)

She and Pat and Donald treasured their friendship with Ben Lyon and Bebe Daniels. The Hollywood couple came regularly to England after 1933, settling here in 1939 to become established radio stars. They were fond of Renée, and always managed to stay in the same hotel as her when they played the same provincial theatre.

During the years of the Houston Sisters the girls were perfect troopers deputizing for other colleagues like Harry Tate,[26] Little Tich,[27] Tex Macleod,[28] and Robb Wilton,[29] and this gained them respect. Renée looked to her variety colleagues for reassurance at the times she felt let down by television producers or stranded among highbrow theatricals unsympathetic to her. After Renée persuaded Donald Stewart to join her in a new act, he shared her love of the 'on the road' lifestyle, even though that bumpy ride became hell in later years. He liked it best when they had friends on the bill and the crowd shared sociable suppers, and drinks parties at digs and hotels.

A performer who, in her later years, had her most sustained success on BBC radio in *Petticoat Line*, Renée first hit the airwaves in Savoy Hill Studios in the 20s. She blossomed in the 30s, revealing herself to be an experienced hand at the mike - one of the least nervous stars facing a microphone. This is astonishing given her nervous disposition. While some radio performers lived in fear of forgetting their lines, Renée could always extemporize and offer something alternative that was often more hilarious than what she was originally supposed to say.

At least until the early 40s, BBC producers liked her intelligent artistry. She said herself 'they have a way of treating you at the BBC that makes you feel so important!'[30] Producer Howard Thomas wrote how Renée wouldn't and couldn't work from a script, and yet the BBC put complete trust in her: those BBC boys turning the mike over to her with one hand trembling on the control knob. This trust was later forfeited it seems. In the 50s Renée was more tightly managed in case she made an unacceptable faux pas. She had to supply scripts then and a lot of stuff was submitted, binned, and improved.

Before the war, when whole families gathered in front of radios Renée was thought the least person likely to offend anyone. The BBC chased her for work then. She was not, however, given any long running show - something that remained the case until the 60s.

Enduring Loves

Herbert Harris was asking in 1938 why the BBC wasn't turning 'one of the microphone's biggest assets' into a television star. Why, he asks, didn't they say to her: 'Renée, we're going to make you the Jessie Matthews of television'?[31] Perhaps they feared her. She'd been too eloquent in her complaints about imitators. That future *Petticoat* was no 'yes woman.' She might have a go at them on the air.

| Bryan Michie | Nina Devitt | Bert Ambrose | Ronnie Hill |

Just like in the theatre, she could invent a sudden piece of crosstalk to share with the leader of the orchestra, like Charlie Shadwell. She always got laughs from the boys of the BBC Variety Orchestra and those at Portland Place. The electric relationship she had with them might be a reason why the BBC didn't trust her. Being the *irresistible* she was, she couldn't resist taking her shocking schoolgirl pranks into the studio. A final thing I must drag up from the Radio Pictorial is an interview with Verity Clare when Renée tells her about one time she got specially dressed up for the mike:

> Renée: I always have a new gown for every broadcast.
> Verity: What, every broadcast?' Even when you have no audience?
> Renée: Certainly. Every broadcast.
> You see. I always have the same boys to play for me.
> (waving at the orchestra boys). They see me every time and it's up to me to keep them interested. I feel that if the boys are interested, then my broadcast's alright. I have never done two broadcasts in the same gown. I wore a negligee last time.
> Verity: A negligee?
> Renée: A negligee! And what a negligee! I was stuck for an act and couldn't think what to do. Suddenly my little goddaughter said to me. 'Auntie, why don't you do an act in your dressing room?' It seemed a good idea so I used it.[32]

225

Chapter 13   Film Star of the 1930s

Critics declared Claude Hulbert to be 'on the topmost rung of the Talkie ladder' as the upper class fool in charge of a company who combines guileless innocence, moral rectitude and idiocy in a single character. Renée's fish-faced and toothy-grinned *Maggie Maclean* - prim and proper in sensible tweeds - has naturalness and a lack of vanity. This quarrelsome little clown takes you aback. Each one of those three adjectives is important in understanding the limitations of Renée's film career.

Claude Hulbert and Renée Houston in a scene from 'Their Night Out'
(Publicity cutting, by kind permission of J. Lewis family)

Very quickly in 'Their Night Out,' Renée makes something delightful of *Maggie*, the Aberdeen manufacturing client that *Jimmy Oliphant* needs to entertain, but where should they go? She has 'an awful fancy to see a nightclub' - surprised these really exist and desirous to satisfy her bluestocking curiosity. Soon she and Jimmy are dancing to the music of a blackface band in frock coats and striped Golliwog trousers. Glaring indignantly at the low-backed frocks women wear, *Maggie* orders a reproving glass of milk once back at their table. Binnie Barnes, who had just played *Katherine Howard* in Korda's 'Private Life of Henry VIII' appears as *Lola* – chanteuse and con artiste, who sashays across the floor in Pola Negri headdress and backless gown, its bias-cut fabric erotically stretched over her hips. Singing lyrics by Peter Mendoza: *'I'll put a board in my window. I've got love to be let or sold,'* she moves close to men, eyeing stuffed wallets whilst wives or girlfriends cringe in disgust. Innocent *Jimmy* tells *Maggie* 'See her. She's good' and *Maggie* replies 'Doesn't look good to me!' The frighteningly statuesque Lola sleazes: *'The best central heating you could request. You're fond of fittings and hmm, fixtures.'* Hovering and vamping obscenely, she steals Jimmy's wallet with sleight of hand. *'I can give new love for old.'*

The Duke and Duchess of York were watching this very scene thoroughly intrigued. They had been ushered into the studio at Elstree after only one hour's notice of their visit. Renée, Claude, Binnie, and director Harry Hughes didn't have time to be nervous. After the take, the principals were seated drinking their milk before being presented and the Duchess asked if they found it hot and tiring under all those lights.

In the next scene *Lola* and the nightclub owner want to frame somebody to cover their own misdoings, but the club is raided. The police bundle onto the cabaret stage and *Maggie*, thinking they're the next turn, claps enthusiastically. Lights go out in the mayhem, people escape and *Jimmy* tries to get *Maggie* to safety but it's *Lola* hanging on to him by the time he's outside. *Maggie* has grasped *Lola*'s motives watching the vamp race off in a cab with *Jimmy* to a gambling club. *Maggie* follows and has a quarrel with a taxi driver checking his meter then bargaining the cost to the nearest penny. Inside the club *Lola* has vanished with *Jimmy* drunkenly slumped over the bar. 'Oh! So this is where you've landed!' *Maggie* exclaims, entering the sordid premises.

Renée had a funny face then: tiny with childish eyes close together. Her flair for musical comedy goes without saying. While it's the era of the Talkies, I was struck by her presence. Sound or no sound, she's a female Chaplin – perhaps the nearest thing to one I've ever seen. At the bar *Maggie* gives *Jimmy* a homily periodically taking gulps from a line of champagne glasses. *Maggie's* starchy puritanism is temporarily in abeyance and the pathos of her forlorn life comes to light through inebriation.

Maggie: I suppose you call yourself a gentleman. A gentleman indeed! It's me that's the offended party. It isn't the action of a gentleman to take an innocent girl all the way from Aberdeen, and bring her here to this den of iniquity.

Maggie: (Taking a gulp) I suppose you think because I am alone in the world that I am unprotected. Get rid of that now. I've got friends in Aberdeen who would protect me at a moment's notice. One in particular is a *captain in the boy scouts*, and if he thought there was a person like you alive, he would buy an excursion ticket and come down and tell you something – yes, you can take it from me.

With this reference to *Bill*, wide-eyed *Jimmy* answers to every charge while not listened to. The champagne causes *Maggie* to hiccup at the end of each sentence:

Maggie: A girl brought up as decently as I have - I'm surprised at you! (hich) You're a naughty boy (hich) running away, leaving me like that in the middle of *Londin*.[1]

Jimmy listens with a hangdog expression and finally they get up to leave, giving the other an elegant bow redolent of the music hall. *Maggie* knocks the stool behind her and an entire row of stools collapses like dominoes. She looks behind with a nonchalant air, they bow again, and this time *Jimmy*'s action results in the stools behind him collapsing. Calmly they put the stools back and *Maggie*'s coat is caught on the stools. Another collapse. They return to have another drink after replacing the stools, toast, shake hands firmly and bow. *Maggie* knocks down the stools again, looking back at them with a shrug. This the best scene, producing as many laughs today as it did eighty years ago. Renée and Claude extract every ounce of fun.

Someone places *Lola*'s headdress on his head as he and *Maggie* emerge outside in the doorway. They sing 'It was 4 O' Clock in the morning, when we said good night last night' - the big number[2] - in one of British Cinema's finest musical comedy moments. The departing guests add the repeating chorus 'And then we had another' with genuine bonhomie, and one guest sings a verse with a husky contralto that Renée imitates. How tiny Renée is in the gaggle of people! Her size destined her to play a certain type until the camera learnt to disguise this in later years.

Binnie Barnes, by contrast, towers dangerously over *Jimmy* and *Maggie*. Unbelievably, *Maggie* throws aside her easily scandalized nature at the end of the picture, her underfed, badly outfitted figure sashaying *Lola*-style among the tables. She would need to be Jodie Foster in 'Bugsy Malone', with a cast of children to seem physically proportionate, and it isn't surprising the scene was called an 'anti-climax' with Film Pictorial decrying: 'Why that was inserted, only the B.I.P officials can say? It is utterly illogical.'[3] To The Picturegoer the finale was 'incomprehensible,' robbing *Maggie* of sympathy, yet admitting 'here is a find for the British film industry . . . if she is carefully groomed and given the right parts. If Hollywood gets half a chance they'll take her, so it's up to our own companies to make the most of her talent.'[4] Renée would have been glad of the positive comments but by the 70s, the film was a half-memory only. She found the plot tiresome and never worked with Harry Hughes or his editor again. Yet 'Their Night Out' has much in its favour. Claude's chinless young man is a Woosterian dream and there are memorable characters like *Simpson* the butler - Gus McNaughton, who thinks he's the world's best detective. Some of the sets document the home beautiful circa 1932, down to the Clarice Cliff tea service and the outfits of supporting actress Judy Kelly are also a designer's dream.

When the film was released in March 1933, B.I.P was celebrated for comedy films and company manager John Maxwell was glad to have Renée on board, their paths already having crossed. Glasgow was where he built up his cinema chain that became the ABC circuit.[5] Other big shots at B.I.P included studio manager Joseph Grossman and film critic turned producer Walter Mycroft. B.I.P's rivals in 1933 were Gaumont-British[6] and Twickenham Studios, presided over by Julius Hagen. The latter was admired for his deals with Hollywood big players. Generally, the view then was there were not enough British films but the push to increase output resulted in a gamut of comedies. Commentator PL Mannock warned that these were being overdone and we were getting careless in terms of material, adding an early warning about the 'lack of control over scheduling and finance.'[7] 'The Private Life of Henry VIII', however, enjoyed massive international success - boosting the industry, at least for a while.

Renée braved the choppy Irish sea that freezing December, to join Billie and Shirley in pantomime at the Opera House, Great Victoria Street, Belfast, remaining there until January 25, 1933. She had proved she could be glorious in front of a camera and was back at Elstree with Claude and Gus McNaughton for 'Radio Parade' (1933). Archie De Bear directed. He was one of the original *Co-optimists* - an act that began in 1921 (along with Davy

Burnaby, Laddie Cliff and Stanley Holloway). 'Radio Parade' has a theme of 'radio' running through each scene with a concept of 'seeing' what you are 'hearing'. Based on a pretend broadcast, there's patter from the announcer, music, comic intervals, harp music, more comedy, syncopated singing, witty impersonations of inanimate items like train noises, comedy again, comic instrumentalists, more from the announcer and so on. There's band music before six pips, and finally a goodbye from the thoroughly English announcer Christopher Stone. Listening in to the wireless from different places, suggests homesickness - explored through the use of shots of New York City, Chicago, a log cabin in the Limberlost, and London's Broadcasting House seen just before the installation of Eric Gill's statue of *Ariel* with the controversial penis that prompted calls for reduction, so myth has it. Photography was by James Wilson who introduced unusual close-ups such as the feet of the Houston Sisters, before panning up to reveal them, as well as nifty fade-outs after each act.

Claude Hulbert and Gus McNaughton have an air of institutionalized idiocy, emerging through doors, passing down corridors and reappearing in strange places. They take notes and spy on stars, perhaps to copy material. You can be sure they've incorrectly taken down the mention by Renée of *Presbyterianism*. In the hilarious *gangster's club* scene they dodge machine gunfire as they patter and take a bow. The Sisters' performance is polished. The Sydney Morning Herald mentions 'the power of the Houston Sisters' and how the producers created a show that's 'naked and unashamed, instead of timidly dressing it up as a musical farce,' making the point that 'an audience in Sydney could not see and hear so brilliant an array of notable variety performers except through the medium of the talking film.'[8]

Renée waited anxiously for the next letter with US postage stamps from her husband. Agent George Barclay had bookings for all three Houstons, and on February 13 it was the Palladium alongside Max Miller in plus fours, Lucan and McShane in their *Matchseller*, and GS Melvin as a Victorian lady cyclist. People complimented Renée's new hair - a brilliant shade of Titian. She did some radio alongside *crazy soliloquist* Leonard Henry. Suddenly Pat returned home and a child was conceived.

The Californian interlude had not been what he hoped but he cashed in, his window on Hollywood appreciated by The Picturegoer: 'The player is the thing,' he said. 'Hollywood itself is amazing . . . There is not a real house in the place . . . . You're always waiting for a director to spring out from a street corner and yell 'Strike that set!'[9] Pat, Renée and the children moved into a farmhouse, with trees for camouflage, dark ponds separating it from the lonely road and wide wide views of the countryside of South Mimms. They needed to live in proximity to the studios at this boom time.[10]

Well End Lodge, Near Elstree, 2015 (Photo: Miranda Brooke)

'*Well End Lodge*' is where Mr and Mrs Aherne kept a farm – or tried to. They couldn't bear to kill the chickens and ducks, and when the calves were sold at market Pat was assailed by grief returning to buy them back at an increased price. A neighbour promised to keep them. Cyril McLaglen, making several talkies at Elstree and at Ealing, turned up one day at the farmhouse and stayed far too long. Unfortunately for him, he had the bedroom above the lounge: the one where they heard funny noises day and night. Filming 'Their Night Out' with Pat away in California, Renée could never remain here by herself. It didn't surprise her that Cyril wasn't quite the tough-guy he played on screen. When Renée and Pat took a walk outside one day and looked up at the top windows they saw a strange yellow miasma gushing out from the window of Cyril's room. The miasma wasn't itself supernatural but was Cyril's sudden fear expressing itself in urinal extremities. He lived with the fearful ghosts a month more then fell out big time with Miss H. Usually one who hated goodbyes, Renée was unsentimental in showing him the door. His visits to the pigsty with a local lass resulted in her ending up 'in the pudding club,' so the story goes, and Cyril made out Pat was responsible. Renée located some proof to the contrary. Cyril later went to Hollywood, ironically falling out, many years later, with Pat's second wife.

There were the long stretches of 1933 when Renée was away from Pat when the Houston Sisters toured Edinburgh, Hull and Belfast, and June through to August when they were engaged at Barrfields Pavilion in Largs – the harbour town in Ayr close to their hearts. With old friends like Harry Kemp, Pete Davis and new ones like Donald Peers, Alec Finlay and Rita Andre, the Sisters larked around in pedallos in the water. The motto for Kemp's *Sunny Days* was 'No Fun Like Work' and you sense the wag he was in his foreword to the programme, referring to the week they were entertained by officers and men of HMS Valiant. He quotes the crew's misprinted invitation 'The party will be *gin* at 11.15.'[11] There are several formal photographs of the company, some colour, at the Scottish Screen Archive showing a back row of musicians with the Houstons in front – Billie's hair brightly peroxided and Renée in a flounced dress. A postcard shows Billie in white tie and dinner jacket and Renée on the piano showing signs of her pregnancy. The BBC broadcast *Sunny Days* on July 12.

John Alan Burns, 4th Baron Inverclyde, was grandson of one of the founders of Cunard. This former Eton schoolboy endowed the National Sports Training Centre at Largs and had been married to the actress *June* between 1929 and 1933 although they had parted. Renée had known June her before she married. Alan Inverclyde became friends with Renée and Billie. His family seat, Castle Wemyss, was on Scotland's foggy coast where the Clyde flows into the Firth. The Sisters, frequent travellers between Wemyss Bay and Bute, knew the castle was where Mary Queen of Scots supposedly met Lord Darnley. The Queen was a subject Renée was passionate about. She had also heard tales of hauntings by the castle's *Green Lady*. Alan answered questions historical and supernatural and Renée and Billie were often visitors. He would have his sleeves rolled up at the gas stove in the castle's kitchen, frying a ham and egg supper for six people, because the servants had gone to bed. 'It makes you form a more human picture of the nobility,' observed Renée.

The Sisters participated in a revue written by John Watt and Harry Pepper staged at *Radiolympia* - the exhibition organized by the Radio Manufacturers' Association and held every August at Olympia, near to the Sisters' old home at Elsham Road. The artistes were in a specially constructed theatre - its stage lighting transferred from Drury Lane. The Houstons, Nelson Keys, Anona Winn, Lupino Lane, Cyril Smith, Norman Long, Harry Pepper, Horace Kenney, Flotsam and Jetsam, Dorothy Ward, Clapham and Dwyer, Julian Rose and the BBC Dance Orchestra, directed by Henry Hall[12] complemented the big names. It was Lupino Lane's first time live on air. Next, the Houstons played the Shakespeare Theatre, Liverpool and Cardiff New Theatre on September 25 - with Nina Devitt's *Eight Stepping Sisters* on the bill. Renée's pregnancy was a less maniacal affair than when she had been carrying Tony. The lead up to Christmas 1933 saw the brief return of Brian Aherne and happy get-togethers.

They left *'Well End'* and its resident spooks for a modern and spacious bungalow-like home at 41 Glendale Avenue in the parish of Edgware - a short drive from the studios. The road crosses a gentle little stream, Edgwarebury Brook, marking ancient field boundaries and 'Glendale' - like the 'jewel city' overlooking the San Gabriel Mountains in Los Angeles was a sign of the Aherne family's future Californian connections. Here Alan Brian was born on December 11, named firstly after his godfather Alan Inverclyde - whose quiet charm impressed Renée, and secondly after Uncle Brian. Lucy Brown and Gertrude Minnie Hunt were their first home helps. Space was an issue, so Trevor and Terry stayed with Lizzi at Northwick Circle – several miles away. Sometimes they visited, as one family colour home movie reveals, with the older children in the garden fishing in a tributary of the stream and little Tony Aherne emerging from the rushes like one of the *Water Babies*. Renée is barely seen, lying down on a bed inside patio doors, but you see Tony with lovely eyes and long lashes in the foreground smelling a flower. The camera passes to an impeccably dressed Pat Aherne, then to George Balharrie. Film Star Weekly – another *Hello* of its day, featured a photo of a Pat and Renée standing among the daffodils outside their home.

Photo of Pat and Renée outside 41 Glendale Avenue Film Star Weekly, 1935
(By kind permission of The British Library)

London in the early part of 1934 saw a lot of the Houston Sisters. There was cine-variety at Brixton Astoria and dates at the Hackney and Chiswick Empires – at the latter alongside Elsie and Doris Waters. On January 25 1934 they were at the re-vamped 'Trocabaret' on Coventry Street. Radio wave transmitters were powerful, and the chatterings of 'Les Houston Sisters des irrésistibles' were received in France in February. The Sisters made a rare appearance at London Pavilion on March 25[13] for a charity event organized by the Variety Artistes Ladies' Guild to help orphan children, and the deserving poor of the variety profession. Renée then left for Elstree to shoot scenes for 'Mister Cinders,' commanding second billing in a part 'specially written in to suit her own inimitable comedy talent.'[14] The part was small but memorable.

The song 'Spread a Little Happiness' scored by Vivian Ellis was tried out in a forgotten show *The Flower Princess*, reworked in February 1929 in *Mister Cinders* at the Adelphi Theatre starring Bobbie Howes and Binnie Hale, and in a production at Berlin's Kunstler Theatre. The libretto was by Clifford Grey and Greatrex (Rex) Newman – the latter, a genius highly in demand. Ellis described Rex as an albino whose permanent address was a railway compartment en route to seaside towns where his *Fol-de-Rols* were playing. 'Spread a Little Happiness' was a magic salve as the pain of the Depression set in, and, by 1934, executives at B.I.P believed a film version was due. German Jewish director Friedrich Zelnik was chosen - the first European to post-synchronize a movie. He had left Germany, Hitler having taken power the year before. The effervescent leads were Clifford Mollison as *Jim* - the male 'Cinderella' and Illinois-born Zelma O'Neil as *Jill*, a hybrid Prince Charming and Fairy Godmother in reverse. *Jill* is an heiress recently resident

Film Star of the 1930s

along with her millionaire father *Henry Kemp* and her cousin *Minerva* at a nearby stately home. *Jim* is the 'poor relation' living with kind but meek *Sir George Lancaster* and his awful wife, *Lady Agatha*, who treats the young man like a menial, and plots to promote *Lumley* and *Guy* - sons from a previous marriage. When he can, *Jim* attends the local amateur dramatic society and one day saves *Henry* from drowning letting *Guy* take the credit. The *Lancasters* are invited to the millionaire's costume ball, and just before this, in order to evade a police officer she almost knocked down on the road, *Jill* disguises herself as new servant girl, *'Sarah'*, at the *Lancaster*'s home. She unexpectedly falls in love with *Jim*. Observing injustice, she influences events, and sings Ellis's song to *Sir George*.

The opening number 'Where's Jim' is catchy, each verse switching to a new member of the cast expecting *Jim* at everyone's beck and call. That's how we first encounter Renée. With the most perfect curly hair imaginable, barely any makeup, and as natural in her manner as a character in a film from 1964, she is the 'over-informed' village post-mistress, *Miss Phipps*, who crosses with the leader of their local dramatic club, played by Edward Chapman. He irks her, questioning whether the *Queen of the fairies* in their *Midsummer Night's Dream* should be Scottish. She crosses with *Merks* - the village policeman played by WH Berry. The Western Brothers - Kenneth and George are the 'ugly sisters' in reverse. With monocles, puns about Oxford bags, and trademark arrogance, they are in top form. They send up class in 'Mister Cinders', and wrote two songs for it. The Western Brothers show how pompous and awful people with servants can be. In one of the last scenes where Jim smashes up the breakfast table and shuts up his cousins, it's pure redemption. Well-harmonized, with the odd ordinary vowel slipping out, George and Kenneth exemplify the 'stuff' of variety: an act of original design, perfected through years of working together. The result never fails and seldom is an audience disappointed.

Clifford Mollison's handsome brother Henry is the villain. The crime hinges on the distraction caused by the amateur dramatics club, who perform the worst ever Shakespeare while the gleeful upper-crust guests look on. Renée reappears as *'Titania, Queen of the Fairies,'* clad diaphanously as in the John Simmons painting: fragile but Scotch and very prickly. She enriches the scene, making it the funniest with her effrontery to the policeman. Things get worse after her fickle revenge on *'Hermia,'* - starchy colleague from drama group, on whose head she places the ass's head so firmly that nobody can get it off. The cockney policeman tries to help, but Renée can't work without a quarrel, lampooning each suggestion he makes with 'I 'aven't got an 'atchet....I 'aven't got an 'ammer neither!' After the ball, it's a hat, not a glass slipper, found belonging to the mysterious hero. *Jim* captures the thief, leaving him bound and gagged outside the police station. In the last scene true identities are revealed and the fairy tale ends. The cinema press remarked on the 'great comedy cast' as well as Otto Kanturek's cinematography. The trade show was at Prince Edward Theatre on October 15 and, on release, Kinematograph Weekly confirmed 'Mister Cinders' 'did for film exactly what the original stage show did in the West End.'

As if they had been stacking up during Miss Houston's short interlude at Elstree, there were more variety engagements than ever after filming concluded. The Sisters played the Paramount, Newcastle on May 17 1934, then both Chelsea Palace and the Metropolitan on June 4 both alongside Tod Slaughter in his *Heard in Camera* sketch. At the Met, an observer wrote how the 'Houston Sisters consolidate old friendships and win new admirers.' Sophie Tucker, with Ted Shapiro at the piano, was everywhere and delighted punters at Holborn Empire in May 1934, and shared the top of the bill with George Robey at the Palladium on June 7. The 'Last of the Red Hot Mammas' also toplined Golders Green Hippodrome for the week commencing June 18 with the Houstons coming second, with Billy Merson, Gillie Potter, Frank Boston & Betty, *Omar The Whirlwind* and the Accordion Kings lower down the bill. Stalking off to Hastings's White Rock Pavilion on June 23, the Sisters appeared with *Petulengro and his Nineteen Lady Hussars* then had July dates at the London Alhambra, doubling at the Trocadero. They topped the bill again at the Chelsea Palace on July 12. They saw their *Restaurant* sketch rated 'one long laugh' at Shepherd's Bush Empire, and received cheers at Bradford on July 26, before crossing the Channel for a continental trip.

Henry Giovanna from the Moriss Agency heard that the sisters were holidaying on the Riviera and suggested they play Geneva: 'Why not play there and get paid for your holiday? You speak French well enough,' he apparently said. While some of Renée's relatives today cast doubts on her fluency, she mentioned this skill often enough, sang French songs, and used it to communicate with a Czech lion tamer. Her training from the convent was good, and her linguistic ability went without saying. Could the Houstons do their act in French given its distinct British nuances? In Deauville after a perilous crossing in 1927 Billie knew little more than 'Jamais' – a word she and Leslie Henson answered every question with, finding they still seemed to get everything they wanted. Billie mastered the lingo later on in her life. Renée had cuttings from French papers about the 'Charming Scottish Fantasists', and an interviewer for Comœdia in 1929 writes how Renée was 'happy to speak our language, albeit in a picturesque way.'[15] Many acts went to Paris in the 20s and 30s and were perfectly acceptable in English, but Renée wanted to go one step further.

They stopped for a day or two's high jinks in Paris then played two weeks at le Kursaal - Casino Municipal, starting July 30, 1934. Working through the weekends was a downside. On Quai du Mont-Blanc with elegant sweeping Pont du Mont-Blanc to its far right, le Kursaal was at the heart of the city, looking on to the Rade de Genève and its Jet d'Eau. Cherished for many years, the 1885 building was demolished in 1969 despite strong protest, and up rose Hotel Noga-Hilton - latest in 1978 chic, soon to be Saudi-owned. Memories of le Kursaal are wiped but rare photos show that this casino was huge: monumental staircase, terrace, dance halls, cafés spilling out onto the pavements, with a theatre and gaming rooms all under a zinc mansard roof. Renée and Billie saw the Quai du Mont-Blanc in its low-rise heyday but they weren't impressed. They said the hotels wouldn't even send their postcards.

Left: Le Kursaal Casino and Music Hall, Geneva (Author's Collection)
Right: Lords Shrewsbury and Inverclyde (Author's Collection)

At least the party could enjoy a route from Geneva through the mountain passes, admiring the beauty of the Alps Maritimes, to Juan-les-Pins in the Antibes, where the Sisters were booked to play two destinations. Wild parties had taken place here - attended by Cole Porter and Scott and Zelda Fitzgerald when Frank-Jay Gould - railroad millionaire and original for *Gatsby*, launched Juan, taking ownership of French Riviera landmarks, such as Hotel Le Provençal. The Houstons were too late for the parties, and besides didn't hang on to dough long enough to be classed idle rich. Their first booking was Juan's Casino. The audience here not only included Russians, Germans and Chinese, but Renée also wondered if the *Glasgow Fair* was being held there that week, given the masses of Italians present. The Italians failed to get their jokes, causing the Sisters to lapse into untranslatable Scots: 'Did you ever see such a *glaikit* bunch in all your life?' Noël Coward and his witty friends were seated in the audience. Noël burst out laughing so loudly he spilled soup down his shirtfront. The Sisters saw a lot of Noël for the rest of that week. [16]His yacht was anchored at Juan and the three had fun desecrating a few Riviera customs that week.

After the Casino, the Sisters played The Hollywood Café, near Plage Hollywood, and went down well with the wealthy patrons. It might have been the 'jazz age' with illustrious stars like Josephine Baker, Tino Rossi, Yves Montand, and les Frères Jacques playing Juan at this time but that age of glamour deserved a trounce. Despite a respect for the language, faced with all things Continental, Renée and Billie are like holidaymakers from a 'Carry On' film. When Billie first visited France in 1927 she pointed out how the British are always being told how rotten their hotels are, 'but how would you like to walk into the cloakroom of a hotel and have to buy your own soap? And pay a shilling for it, at that!' Renée also found the continental hotels and shops over-priced. She remarked how one night in Juan, a food bill for three people was over £35 and the hotel cost over £100. When the hotel bill arrived they barely had money to pay it. For her, the trip seemed to be all about giving the hotel authorities her hard-earned pay. It was hardly a holiday. Pat, who was with them, was annoyed they had to work so much.

Back in London on August 25, they recouped their losses as 'unexpected visitors to the Alhambra,' deputizing for absent Julian Rose.

Northwick Circle, leafy, well connected for the Bakerloo line, with a tennis club inside the circle, gained house numbers in 1934 and *'Carntyne'* became number 31. The enclave seems to have been stubbornly Scotch. *'Carntyne'* itself at one time had eleven residents, representing Ayrshire, Lanarkshire and Midlothian. Next door was a McDonald in a house called 'Drumadoon', and on the Houstons' other side lived a Murray. In 1931, Claire's eighteen year old kid brother Harold - or 'Hal', along with Claire's widowed mother Marion - known to all as 'Auntie May' came to live with them. May's husband, a businessman from Newmilns, had been a good friend to Renée. Once mistress of a grand home, money was now in scarce supply but she would reinvent herself as a businesswoman in Northwest London, investing in a café at 170A High Road, Wembley. Scandinavian cookies would restore her fortune. How Jim coped with his mother-in-law resident for a few years was another matter. Jim turned *'Carntyne'* into a dog-lover's paradise when he started breeding pedigree dogs. Hamish felt outshone, and the neighbours stoically tolerated the noise and bounding energy from oriental-looking Chow-Chows racing around the garden or the pack of Great Danes that pulled Shirley along as she grabbed the leads.

In 1934, Shirley turned eighteen, Terry was nine, and Trevor was eight. Kind and affable to all members of the house, George Balharrie said little about the howling, although I expect he hated it, valuing space for concentration as many musicians do. Nor did he say anything about his tiredness and night sweats, although he could hardly disguise his weight-loss or those awful occasions he coughed up blood. George was stranded when Jim, his erstwhile business partner and ex-brother-in-law left London in late 1935. Lizzi and Jimmie cared for George, who was like another son. On August 29, aged 31, George was admitted to Brompton Hospital - then a large "E" shaped red brick building, with an outpatients department, ten wards, a compressed air room, and a Turkish bath for respiratory sufferers in the basement. He was diagnosed with chronic pulmonary tuberculosis, as the inpatient register records. Admitting he had TB was brave. It was unfairly considered 'a poor person's disease' although it affected rich and poor.

The Houston Sisters went on with the show, playing the Glasgow Pavilion on September 1, the Alexandra Theatre Stoke Newington, then London's Alhambra on September 24 when Will Hay did his *On the Way to Cambridge* skit, then Brixton's Empress. At Leicester Square's Moorish palace for a week starting October 1 they fascinated audiences – their last appearance here because this old landmark was saying farewell to everyone. They were on the National Programme's 'Variety' broadcast on October 6, with Layton and Johnston and Billy Merson, then a week at Folkestone's Pleasure Gardens billed as 'England's Greatest Burlesque Artists.' Golders Green Hippodrome saw the Houstons along with Billy Cotton's Band, the Western Brothers, Wilson Keppel and Betty, and Talbot O'Farrell in its lineup on October 29.

By this time George had been at Brompton Hospital's Frimley unit a month, a confined location where sanatoria patients were prescribed two pints of Guinness daily and nutritious food but didn't allow physical activity except when beds were wheeled on to the verandas. He remained here until February 2 1935 at which time he was 'much improved' moving later that year with Lizzi, Jimmie, Granny Houston, May, Hal, Shirley and the kids to a new home - Gloucester House Harrow road, near Sudbury Town station. Jimmie enjoyed having Sudbury golf course on his doorstep and typical of showmen of a certain age he was in the Variety Golf Society, attending its meetings. Renée's youngest boys visited the house at Harrow, and Trevor impressed them with daredevil stunts, once jumping off the roof with a rope tied round him. Lizzi had to make a quick dash to get him out of a pickle. After everyone left Northwick Circle, Jim, Claire and the dogs left for South London, then for a few years, rented an old cottage called *'Green Briars'* at Cranbrook near Benenden in Kent. Here he got to grips with writing, with Claire acting as his stenographer. They had a daughter, Elizabeth Pamela but tragically she died in infancy.

George would have liked the score of Renée's next film that featured Finck's 'Decameron Nights Suite No 1-3' even if the film was 'artless nonsense' - just 'a succession of robust gags that are clean and enjoyable.'[17] Fred Newmeyer who had made pictures with Hal Roach and Harold Lloyd in America directed 'Lost In The Legion' but Leslie Fuller – famed for his none too clever and cowardly English hero, guaranteed success at the box office. Kids and Victorian great granddads alike laughed their socks off at Leslie in the early 30s. He had been in Fred Karno's troupe and had entertained troops during the First World War. He formed his own concert party in Margate. Although demand for Leslie Fuller comedies waned his films are forerunners of the 'Carry Ons' - each film seeing a crazy gang of comedians placed in unlikely settings. Benny Hill and Bernard Bresslaw are his comic progeny.

Bill and *Alf*[18] are cooks on a ship carrying French troops to Algiers. Being careless in the culinary department, *Bill* falls foul of bullying *Sergeant Mulligan* – played by Alf Goddard. In a rough sailor's dive in Algiers we meet the local chorus line stranded with no choice but to shake a leg to keep body and soul. We get an impromptu *Swan Lake* from *Bill* and a comedy Charleston from *Sally Hog*. Gracie Fields' sister Betty, who had been in two films with Leslie, played *Sally*. A local *Sheik* lusts after the British girls, and Renée's *Mary McFee* tells him in the thorniest terms 'They've been looking for a long time for you in Loch Ness'. No amount of upbraiding can prevent the *Sheik*'s retainers from abducting the two dancers for the harem and *Bill* and *Alf* get into a fight trying to save them. Renée modernizes her appearance in this film, updating the Clara Bow package, to a sleek blonde and she appears more petite and pouting than before although her brittle one-liners roll off the tongue with familiar ease.

Left and Centre: Publicity cuttings from 'Lost In the Legion' (J. Lewis family)
Right: Betty Fields (Author's Collection)

The 'strip poker' game when *Bill* and *Alf* leave their guards naked in the cells is funny and soon they're lost in the desert - 'Looks like Southend when the tide's out' they say. In record time they've been forcibly enlisted into a Legion troop. Santos Casani is *Tani*, the *dago* who knocks *Sergeant Mulligan* cold to everyone's delight. Casani - an ex-pilot in the Great War, danced the Charleston on the roof of a London taxi making its way down Kingsway with Josie Lennard back in March 1927 - one of the era's notable publicity stunts preserved on Pathé News. In the 30s he was a familiar voice on the radio and ran a school of dancing at 90 Regent Street to teach you the fundamental steps of any dance in three lessons.

This film doesn't win any points for political correctness but is an honest record of English humour. Our impatience listening to splutteringly fast incomprehensible French is one example. Because *Bill* and *Alf* smugly laugh at the flattened *Mulligan* they get put in the cells, only to burrow out of course. The funniest scene is when the *Colonel* falls into a tunnel the escaping prisoners have dug. A sudden Arab attack enables *Bill* and *Alf's* escape. They pinch the 'veils and whatnots' from the 'Queen of Sheba' and 'Lady Godiva' – local ladies having a wash in an oasis. Disguised and fully veiled in nikabs they enter the harem to rescue *Mary* and *Sally* but when the *Sheik* requires his dancing girls to strip they're doomed. Suddenly the Legion arrives. A fight leaves the *Sheik* in an *Alibaba* vase and *Bill* opens the gates. Following an Arab defeat this action wins their freedom from the Legion.

The 'rubber-faced comedian' had made ten comedy films between 1930 and when Pat Aherne worked with him in 'Pride of the Force' (1933). Pat's in a few scenes in 'Lost In The Legion' although he doesn't do much apart from look good in a uniform. This Foreign Legion burlesque made in autumn, 1934 is noteworthy for being the only occasion you can see Mr and Mrs Aherne in the same film though not together. When Leslie had been in 'Pride of the Force,' he met his wife to be, Nan Bates, on the set, and Nan became friends with Renée, asking her to be a godmother to their twins a month after shooting 'Lost In The Legion' ended - at a ceremony at St Alban's, Teddington. Nan asked Gracie to be godmother too, so with Monty Banks another one of Leslie's co-stars, it was like one big family. All were reunited a year and a half later at a garden party at Nan's home when we see Gracie, Renée, the little girls and others from the film world. On December 6, 1934, she and Billie returned to the Kingston Empire, where long before, as an urchin full of dreams and energy, she had learned some magic tricks.

Mid week entertainment listings in The Evening Standard tell us what the average man or woman could expect to see in the capital on December 12, 1934. At Stoll's ornate Picture Theatre, occupying a whole block of Kingsway, you could see *'the One and Only Greta Garbo'* in 'Queen Christina', and Madge Evans and Robert Young in 'Paris Interlude'. At the London Hippodrome Bobby Howes and Binnie Hale were paired up again for *Yes, Madam!* The Palladium had the new *Crazy Show* with its three sets of comedy duos, and there was *Revuedeville* at the Windmill Theatre. George Formby was at Holborn Empire with Anona Winn, with a note that *Where the Rainbow Ends* was back for Saturday's matinee. At the St James Theatre, Gladys Cooper and Raymond Massey were in *The Shining Hour*. The Holborn Empire was now the only theatre in Central London giving traditional music hall programmes, with the trend towards *Crazy Show* formats, and you had to go to the suburbs if you wanted more. Just twenty years earlier central London had had sixty Empires and Palaces of Variety.[19] Having performed in a large percentage of London theatres for fifteen busy years, the *Irresistible* Houston Sisters, in the face of these striking changes, chose to appear in their own revue starting January. They also started taking films seriously and began considering individual performances if West End opportunities arose. Before then, they shared a bill with Gracie at Holborn for a week starting December 17, 1934. The Radio Three, The Melvilles, *Keith Clark with his cigarettes*, and Calient the wire walker. Accompanied by Harry Parr-Davies at the piano, Gracie belted out 'Sing As You Go' then brought tears to people's eyes with 'Ave Maria.' *Bill* also was close to tears, trying desperately to teach Renée how a film starlet should act, with Renée's raising the roof as she took off a certain Swede with a famous slouch.

She must have taken some of *Bill's* advice where starlet appearances are concerned, because on January 21, 1935 Renée looked striking and beautiful dressed in a gold sheath gown and magnificent black velvet coat with a hood lined with gold. John Chetwynd-Talbot, a hands-on farmer on his estates, had a respect for clever people in the arts. At nineteen he met the fashionable Nadine Crofton - known for her operatic singing. She was soon to be his wife. Up until then he had been one of England's most eligible bachelors, due to inherit the titles 'Earl of Shrewsbury and Waterford' and 'Earl of Talbot.' At the age of twenty-one, Chetwynd-Talbot threw a coming of age party at Ingestre Hall Staffordshire, his 17th-century Jacobean mansion, with master staircase and staring portraits of previous owners. He invited Renée to his party to provide entertainment for his guests. Miss Houston of the *Irresistibles* worked her magic and this is the party described in 'Don't Fence Me In' when, after her performance, *several chapters from Debrett's* come up to her room to hear, in privacy, the stories she hinted at. She had been joking offering to divulge the 'blue' versions and hadn't expected them to take her seriously. The debutantes couldn't resist her or those stories. I expect the fee was princely enough to cover the overtime required by these highborn ladies with their sans-gêne tendencies. You have to forgive their naïveté. I hope they weren't corrupted! Lady Joan, Chetwynd-Talbot's sister, would have been among them. John and Joan and their friend Francis Howard Bickerton, the Antarctic Pioneer appear to have known John F. Argyle, whose company Argyle Talking Pictures was behind Renée's next two pictures. Bickerton and Lady Joan married couple of years later. A little schmoozing of people of influence probably had something to do with Miss H's presence at Ingestre Hall. One newspaper at the end of 1935 called John Argyle 'England's youngest producer.'[20] Talented as he was, at twenty-four this skinny, narrow-faced young man had barely started shaving. His black hat and circular black-rimmed spectacles gave him a quirky air. In a photo seated between Billie and Renée he looks like a young whiz kid.

Renée's blonde glamour continued throughout January then, hanging up her black velvet and gold, she reverted to the insolent half of the *Irresistibles*, darkening her hair, and donning a transparent frock. Both sisters were to do their stage act before a camera for 'Variety - The Romance of the Music Halls' (1935). Argyle Talking Pictures claimed 'no expense is spared' for this *'Pageant of Variety'*[21] and the publicity afforded much hype. Names of its top-liners were deliciously kept secret in January then revealed in the run up to release. 'Variety' had thirty performers including Sam Barton- trick cyclist, the Houston Sisters, Nellie Wallace, Billy Cotton and his band, Bertha Willmott, Denis O'Neil- popular radio tenor, George Carney - popular 'swell' of the halls, Bobby 'Uke' Henshaw, Olsen's sealions, Anita Low, Van Dock, the beautiful Sherman Fisher Girls and an orchestra under the baton of Horace Sheldon. The latter was John Argyle's musical director. The cost of the acts, theatre sets and period detail must have mounted up but it was not big budget. At Cricklewood studios Oswald Mitchell assisted staging this film of variety acts - less quirky than 'Radio Parade' in terms of format, but with a storyline charting the ups and downs of running a music hall, rivalry among theatres and having to turn a profit. Members of the Livesay family: Sam, Cassie, Barrie and Jack played the vaudevillians. It was told using historical markers such as the South African war, the First World War, and the present age, mentioning theatrical innovations like high-speed variety. The passage of time was also reflected in the sixteen numbers including 'Champagne Charlie', 'Ta Ra Ra Boom De Ay', 'Man From Harlem' and 'I Don't Want To Climb A Mountain' – the latter sung by the Houston Sisters and composed by Eddie Pola and Steininger. New Yorker Pola came to London in the 20s where his song-writing career took off.

Brunel tried to capture the 'raw' experience of the performer with additional backstage realism. He made sure you not only got to see stage and auditorium but authentic glimpses behind the scenes in dressing rooms, offices, passage ways, stage door, and vestibule. He had an eye for detail – including the changing fashions in different periods for cars, cabs, omnibuses, clothes, furniture and advertisements. He was pleased with the overall product, as a letter he wrote to Michael Balcon on September 26, 1935 suggests: 'It is seldom that I can call a picture "mine", but limited though the cost was, I had a free hand in getting at the public my own way in "Variety" - an experience which was profitable when I made 'Badger's Green' and 'Blighty.'[22]

Judging from reactions in the trade press, Brunel achieved something momentous, especially when criticism about pictures being made on the cheap was rife. Broadway songwriter Al Sherman – whose songs raised the spirits in Depression-era generation was on record saying that 'British pictures are reaching a standard of perfection' in terms of production and the professionals involved.[23] Renée and Billie's new picture must have been a relief to cinema insider PL Mannock who had expressed earlier concern that 'we are not putting Britain and British people on the screen enough' at this time, although his big hope was to show off provincial subjects and the beauty of our country as well as training more of our own directors.[24] Brunel's 'Variety' contributed to the British film *production push*. It used subject matter reflecting the national culture and caught the nostalgic fervour of the time, coinciding with the Silver Jubilee celebrations of King George V and Queen Mary between 6-12 May, 1935. 'Variety' was listed as No. 5 in a Jubilee Programme of films[25] and was trade shown on March 21 at Prince Edward Theatre. Despite the praise for Brunel's work, the distribution company was Butchers Film Service - backers of low-budget quota productions and it's likely that the original deal included a clause to recoup costs by breaking the film up into shortened reissues later, considering the fact that these shorts were also handled by Butchers.[26] Once a film had been through its first exhibition run, it often reappeared in a version as a 'short' used as a supporting feature in a double bill.

The BFI's John Oliver tells me this happened to countless films through to the demise of double bill programmes in the 1970s. Variety films, because of the episodic nature of their structure were easy prey for cutting down for the purpose of reissue. This is the reason why Brunel's 'Variety' is lost in its entirety now. A few scenes like the one with the Houston Sisters miraculously survive because the short was re-used yet again, in a film called 'Down Melody Lane' (1943) – a picture incorporating footage from 'Variety' as well as other films like 'Music Hall Parade' (1939). Scenes from these films were woven together to create a story of a theatre manager reminiscing about the old days. The finished film was one of many distributed by Edwin John Fancey's[27] shoestring distribution company New Realm. Subsequent bankruptcies caused the rights of many of these second feature films either to lapse or get sold on the cheap to other companies in 'cash in hand' deals, sometimes for release in 9.5mm sound film format.

Renée and Billie's act can be enjoyed on its own although it is a shame we can't see the backstage scenes or their song. In the surviving scene, the

Houstons do their '*rehearsal*' skit - one perfected on many a stage. It features Renée's saucy repartee with conductor Horace Sheldon. I like the way it refers to well-known ladies in the public eye.

> Renée: Father Father! Where is mother?
> Billie: Your mother?
> Renée: Yes Josephine Baker.
> Billie: Why darling. Never mention that name again!
> Renée: Why Father?
> Billie: You're mother has gone for good.
> Renée: You see I'm going to get a chance
> Billie: This is your big chance.
> Renée: Claude, Claude. I have come back to you. (In Sybil Thorndike voice)
> Renée: I'm bent on telling you something.
> Billie: Aha woman!
> Renée: Oho Monkey!
> Renée: So you have returned eh? (In her Garbo voice)
> Renée: I have come back
> Billie: What is all this
> Renée: I've been so tired, so depressed ...
> Renée: Give me a penny. I want to be alone.[28]

That last line became a catchphrase. I feel sure I remember listening to older relatives jokingly repeat it when I was young, and Renée's son knew the line well, and he had never seen the extract from 'Variety'. Renée was more than an impressionist, desecrating cinema shrines where she could, with sharp sarcasm. Throughout late summer and autumn, 'Variety' competed with films like Gracie's 'Look Up and Laugh'. One paper called it 'bright merry entertainment for old and young,' adding 'you'll be sorry to miss it.' An old photo shows Adrian Brunel backstage, seated between the Sisters. He casts a look of attraction towards svelte-looking Billie in her immaculate suit while minx-like Renée in silk and white feather boa jealously restrains him.

Where was the film that would be for Renée Houston what 'Sing As You Go' was for Gracie Fields? How could she, being so closely identified as one part of the Houston Sisters, develop herself into something like the individual performer that Gracie was? Both actresses had a madcap presence. While Gracie was a trusty 'big sister' type, Renée excelled in sauce and sarcasm, not that Gracie couldn't do sarcasm. Whenever you saw Gracie on screen, she was more 'full of the joys,' her warmth more constant, whereas Renée's personality ranged from sweet to rude and bitter. Miss Houston didn't have the redeeming goodness that might make half the inhabitants of a town get on her side in a dispute with the town council, or rally around her in a street carnival to raise money for the poor. She was too unpredictable. How could she ever receive the kind of deeply felt love typical of Gracie's fans, or even rival Gracie in the cinema? She lacked someone at the top to mastermind her career: a Basil Dean or Anthony Kimmins. She didn't even have a Beryl Formby petitioning a producer on her behalf. It's admirable that she sought to mastermind her career herself and seek out parts that weren't as limited as those offered by B.I.P.

'Variety' was the first of three films Renée made in 1935. Between the first and second she was appearing on the stage in the *Love Laughs* and the second film was the independent production, 'No Monkey Business' probably made in August. Renée has third billing in the opening titles. Scenes were shot at British and Dominion's Imperial Studios - focal point for expertise in sound technology and where the first purpose-built sound studio in Europe was used for breakthrough films such as Hitchcock's 'Blackmail'.

Herman Fellner
(J. Lewis Family)

Artist's sketch: Renée and Billie
Variety (1935)(Author's artwork)

John Argyle
(Author's artwork)

Renée knew prominent figures from the German film world - Jewish exiles who had settled in England. Zelnik has been mentioned. Two had suffered broken health following Nazi persecution. Julius Haimann's Super-Film company produced some of Germany's earliest films to have single sound scenes such as 'Ich küsse Ihre Hand, Madame' (1929) and he produced 'No Monkey Business.' He moved to London in 1933 dying in 1939 in Kew – his confiscated property later being the subject of a case handled by the Claims Resolution Tribunal. Herman Fellner was a producer of musical comedy and film. One of the earliest films from the company run by Fellner and his Hungarian partner Josef Somlo was 'Der Tänzer meiner Frau' (1925) which helped Marlene Dietrich on her way to stardom. In the late 20s his company used British director Graham Cutts, as well as actors Clifford McLaglen and Ivor Novello. In 1931, with racism and nationalism increasing in Germany, they brought their money to England as well as the film rights for musical films to remake them here. A successful screen adaptation of *Die Fledermaus*, entitled 'Waltz Time' followed in 1933. Fellner had seen Renée in *Love Laughs* in 1935 at the time he was striking a deal with CM Woolf for his new company Cecil Films. The Era reported Renée was given an immense £10,000 contract by Fellner to star in three pictures following on from current engagements.[29]

Plenty of ordinary folk circa 1935 would die from shock if they were handed a £10,000 contract. Unbelievably, Miss Houston didn't know which golden egg opportunity to choose from: to take *Love Laughs* to Broadway, or take up the offer of a Richard Rodgers and Lorenz Hart show to be created specially for her, or to accept this astonishing film contract. She had truly hit the big time now both Broadway producers and prominent filmmakers were bidding for her services. Maybe it's not such a mystery why she accepted Fellner's offer - an astronomical sum – with a spending worth of £369,800.00 in the 21st Century. In Renée's memoir of 1974 she writes how the 'tragic figure of a man . . . pleaded with me to let him take over the management of all my film work.'[30] His story broke her heart so she signed up with him, although this would later prove a mistake given the status of her contract after he died. Renée doesn't name the 'tragic' man, but drops the clue that he was big in the German film business and helped Dietrich's career. It can't be anyone but Fellner. In 1936 he had produced the utterly charming 'Dishonour Bright' (1936) starring and directed by Tom Walls. Fellner had just joined Gaumont-British Pictures to make a film with Jack Buchanan but on March 22 he was found dead in his London apartment, having apparently committed suicide by hanging.

Perhaps a strand of Germanic humour might be detected in 'No Monkey Business' adding to why the film diverges from usual British comedies. The absurd plot comes from a story by Joe May - another pioneering German producer - about an anthropologist whose daughter wants to prove to her father that animals are more intelligent than men. *Jim Caroll* - Gene Gerrard is a variety showman impounded by creditors. He persuades his assistant to perform as *'Charlie the almost human ape'*. Claude Dampier is the professor's butler, *Roberts*. Renée, as *Jessie*, has the oddest role. We meet her at the beginning when she and starchy *Roberts* try to get tickets at a variety theatre box office. An African drum beats and Wally Patch and other members of the theatre's crew angrily bustle about. She's the sassy Miss H most people recognize here: chic in her hat and smart ensemble with medieval sleeves.

Next, seated in the dress circle she's selected as the prettiest woman by the frightening *'Charlie'* and presented with a bunch of flowers after the ape swings Tarzan-like up to the circle, forcing the butler out of his seat. The ape sits worryingly next to her, doffs his hat and hands her the flowers. 'Jessie put that animal down at once,' cries the butler. 'Where would you like me to put him?' she retorts, causing hearty laughter. Yet, a couple of scenes later we realize Renée's real role is maid or companion to the professor's daughter *Claire*, played by June Clyde. Renée is the most unconvincing maid the 1930s ever witnessed. For one thing *Jessie* never does any work, and is more likely to quip to her employers and order *them* around. She's someone from the lower orders but too modern and emancipated. While the professor – Hugh Wakefield - gives a boring lecture in a darkened room with his daughter asleep, Jessie, in a ridiculous maid's outfit of long dress, pinny, and frill hat, is in a rocking chair, cracking nuts under the rocker. The noises upset the professor's concentration and her laughter is nothing short of insolent when clumsy *Roberts* knocks over the slide projector. Throughout the film her character is equal to her mistress in terms of chic, wisdom, and sex appeal – a very interesting social message. At the end the two women are more like best friends. The picture quality is really good with Claude Friese-Greene's cinematography using a 'smash' fade to quickly move from Renée's scene with Gene Gerrard backstage at the theatre, to her carrying a sack of monkey nuts into the nursery for her scene with June Clyde.

The director was Marcel Varnel, whose Anglo-French education and experience staging shows on Broadway and fantasy films in Hollywood set him apart from the likes of Lupino Lane or Norman Lee – directors of typical British comedies with Leslie Fuller in the lead role. Varnel later directed Will Hay in a series of films beginning with 'Good Morning, Boys!'(1936). His reputation for encouraging improvisation among his actors to add spontaneity, and his handling of the quick gag had been demonstrated in 'No Monkey Business.' You sense the randomness of the director's personality in Val Guest's account of being challenged by Varnel to write a screenplay. This only occurred because Mr Varnel was incensed by a piece of journalism he penned.[31] The result was Guest's script for 'No Monkey Business' developed from May's story. The characters *Claire* and *Jim* display charm and fine vocals taking turns with Guest's lyrics in the club scene before stopping for *'Monkey Gland'* cocktails at the bar. Smiling June Clyde had made twenty-five films in the States before she came to England to make this movie. Musical direction was by Benjamin Frankel and the film featured music by composer Hans May who provided music for 'Two Thousand Women' ten years later. Hans May married his agent Rita Cave - a publicity girl who had had a small part in Brunel's 'Variety' before getting her own broadcasting career. She would become one of Renée's agents in the 1950s.

Jessie's admirer in the movie is *Charlie* - a man disguised in an ape costume. The ape costume is so good, I confess to being 'had' until the man beneath is revealed. That's young Richard Hearne, later famous on 60s television as *'Mr Pastry.'* Around this time Hearne was Shirley Houston's boyfriend and the two almost married. 'No Monkey Business' is dated by today's standards but offers an almost Shakespearean theme: a man trapped in a convincing disguise unable to express his true passions. After *Roberts* scraps with *Charlie* who has thieved a bit of food, *Jessie* admonishes the butler. In a touching scene later in the nursery she confides to her 'ape' hanging in his 'tree': 'Goodnight Charlie, Sweet Dreams! Aren't dreams the sweetest things in life! I'll let you into a little secret. If I can't get anything I just pretend that I can. It hurts nobody and what's more, it costs nothing.'[32] It could be Renée herself talking, and this cues to *Jessie*'s next scene in *Claire*'s dressing room. She indulges in prolonged fantasy, assuming the role of *'Lady Bubbles Bedale'* with imaginary manservant James. A fantasy phone call with Lord Eglington follows. She's speaking to herself in front of a mirror with her mistress's evening dress pinned to her - a long black and white number with a large black bow over one shoulder: 'Dupont designed it. Such a droll fellow!' She's lost in the *Lady Bedale* fantasy in the next scene in the street, having left the house in the dress and satin cloak. She talks to herself about *Lord Eggy's* invitation. *Charlie,* who's forgone the ape outfit for an immaculate evening suit follows her and makes her acquaintance in front of a playbill. It doesn't take much to get her to visit a club that's 'dirty enough to be smart,' where a false Chinaman wishes his guests will be *'very muchy welcome.'* From the dance floor *Claire* and *Jim Caroll* - romance budding - almost recognize *Jessie* and *Charlie* before the latter pair make a exit. *Jessie* remembers she must return to look after *Charlie.* She tells 'Eggy' how she's sick of 'being misunderstood' and that 'she's not that kind of girl.' He's serious about her though.

He escorts her home and for some reason, falls down the stairs. When Jim and *Claire* return, *Jessie* acts fast donning a dressing gown and locking *Eggy* in *Charlie's* room telling him 'You'll be alright - there's only an ape in there.' In a photo taken on set that has survived, Renée, standing next to Gene Gerrard, looks luminous, the camera enhancing her small features. That promise: 'I can make you a big, big star. You are perfect for the films . . . You are so beautiful and so talented'[33] that Herman Fellner made, wasn't the least bit far-fetched. A later scene in the university lecture hall is very funny, if you don't mind seeing two real apes supplied by *Reuben Castang & his Apes* dressed in children's dresses. *Charlie* - about to be undressed, makes a run for it, and *Jessie* does a Tarzan call. It's mad!

'No Monkey Business':
Renée and Gene Gerrard on the set.
(The Aherne Family)

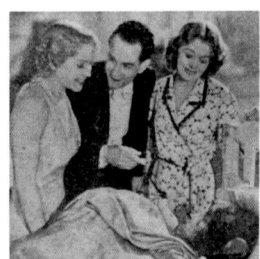

News cutting advertising 'No Monkey Business':
June Clyde, Gene Gerrard, Renée, Richard Hearne
(By kind permission of A.Richardson)

Renée got lost in the hype that went with 'No Monkey Business.' As new top gun of British and Dominions, Charles Moss Woolf saw this film as part of the British film *production push* to uplift quality and make British films more competitive in the USA.[34] He saw to it that 'No Monkey Business' received lots of hype. Independent of previous alliances with the Ostrer Brothers, Woolf inaugurated a new renting/distribution company General Film Distributors (GFD) in October 1935 with J Arthur Rank - millionaire flour magnate and philanthropist as director, and Herbert Wilcox an associate. GFD grew into the powerful Rank Organization.

The advertising that graced Kinematograph Weekly in its October 31, 1935 issue featured a pantheon of British stars – each with a giant page caricature in lavish colour. Renée Houston, Gene Gerrard and Jack Buchanan were featured. Each image had the GFD logo. Lurid adverts for 'The Supreme Comedy' signalled the film's trade showing at Prince Edward Theatre on November 12, and a subsequent review said 'this promises to be the laugh of the season and Renée Houston, Gene Gerrard and June Clyde have rarely appeared to better advantage.'[35] In practise it made little impact on general release in 1936, and Variety (US) criticized it for being so 'light a story.'[36] I'm not surprised. Something about it doesn't work. It's never been issued on video or dvd although it was shown at the BFI in 2013 in its *'Projecting The Archives'* series.

Some years ago I stumbled across a book by Dan Farson about his Isle of Dogs pub in the 60s and attempts to revive old time music hall there. I exchanged my world of London 2006 for the cockney world of Marie Lloyd, Hetty King, and Ida Barr, curious about these ladies. Trawling for information about Ida Barr I came across a note saying she was in a film called 'Happy Days Are Here Again' which had the Houston Sisters in it - an act I'd never heard of then. I just knew about Ida Barr who had gone from nowhere in London to appearing in New York Vaudeville where she featured Nat D. Ayer's hit, 'Oh, You Beautiful Doll' and scored big with 'Everybody's doing it now.' Ida went to South Africa and Australia, and toured with Houdini. In her latter years she lived in a modest flat in a tenement overlooking London's Charing Cross Road always decorated like a country cottage. She had no money unlike Hetty King, who had invested well. Ida died on December 17, 1967. When I got to see the few remaining scenes of 'Happy Days Are Here Again' I was struck by her earthy performance in feathered hat and shawl singing 'The Coster's Honeymoon.'[37] She swaggers back and forth on stage with eight pierrots behind her in a row.

> When you're getting married girls, lor lummy it's a scream,
> If you aint been through the job before.
> It aint so much the la-di-da-de business at the church,
> It's what will come on afterwards that knocks you off your perch.

Actress Sally McBride is seated second, Renée is third and Billie, fourth. At the end of the row Mark Stone is pleased with Ida. Shirley, to the left, is a bit nervous. Sally looks like she might laugh. Renée looks at the older star with a wide-eyed admiration, as if she's imbibing a new personality. You can hardly see the girls. Ida takes up most of the space. 'Ida Barr!' people in the profession used to joke – 'More like 'ida bleedin pub!'

> I'll sure be glad to get me Bryant and May's off.
> Married people needn't be shy. Good Night all, olive oil.
> My ol' man will bolt the door. I'm off to bye bye byes.

This astonishing meeting between music hall old and new – a missing link entitled 'Happy Days Revue' – *'An Argyle Production - Edited Version by FH Bickerton'* is a twenty-minute short film and all that's left of 'Happy Days Are Here Again'. The short itself has hitherto been boxed up and forgotten. Who would believe it now that the original film was 7650 feet, with an 85-minute duration?

FH Bickerton might have piloted an air-tractor sledge and discovered the first Antarctic meteorite but he was no great shakes at film editing - his new career after packing in exploring. Dating from 1938 the short is like a fragment from an Egyptian tomb. I wondered first if some calamity had struck the building where the original film material was held but the film suffered its dreadful fate because its distribution rights were sold on – something that has been the curse of many a British film. Films showing variety turns were vulnerable to this. After the film's first exhibition run a decision was made to re-issue it as a short. Renée and Billie's unique film was hacked about with in an appallingly amateur way. Extra titles were inserted.[38] Sold as 'cinematic turns,' the Sisters are denied a status as 'actresses.' Associated Producers & Distributors sold the rights to a shoestring distribution company, just as the aptly named Butchers did with 'Variety.' Perhaps the problem began when they took a chance with a producer who had barely started shaving. The film would have fared better had it been made at Gainsborough or Ealing under the auspices of someone like Basil Dean, who helped make the early films of Gracie Fields a success, capturing the grit, determination and humour of working-class society in his films. 1933's 'The Good Companions' based on JB Priestley's novel about musicians joining together to save the *Dinky Doos* - a failing concert party - seems to have partly inspired 'Happy Days Are Here Again.' Sadly, there was no Victor Saville to give the film an edge.

    The Houstons signed for Argyle's film with Norman Lee directing on July 17, 1935 – a time when Renée was appearing individually in the musical comedy *Love Laughs*. She claimed she initially turned down 'Stage Folk' – the film's original title - but they persisted, offering her a fat salary. Filming didn't in fact coincide with *Love Laughs*, as the show closed on September 14. Pat and Renée motored up to the Highlands for a deferred honeymoon, and stopping at Glasgow, Renée told the press this was more of a 'busman's holiday' as she was on the look out for 'Scottish types' as supporting players for the new Houston Sisters biopic. Sally McBride was described as one of their finds, previously billed as 'Scotland's most beautiful girl' after a recent dancing appearance. Sally, a Glaswegian from Ibrox, had, in fact, known the Houstons since at least 1934 when she had spent a summer in Shoreham with the family. Renée liked to refer to Sally as her 'cousin,' although the same phrase was applied to Binkie and several others. Sally, who had a perfect face that photographed beautifully and white blonde hair was to play *Ella*, based on Ella Pearson. Robert 'Nicky' and David Kidd – already known 'Discoveries' had met Renée via Jack Hylton who had brought these former members of the Boy's Brigade south. Nicky was a great pianist who had written his own songs aged eleven, and David had been a professional vocalist at thirteen. With Hylton's band, David - the *Boy Soprano from Glasgow* - cut discs at the studios in Chelsea's Town Hall. Billie and Renée loved David's singing of Leon, Towers and Wright's 'Bedtime story', borrowing this to close their spot in 'Radio Parade'. Renée remarked how the younger brother at fifteen could pass for twenty. She sought the most 'outstanding finds,' as she prepared for her latest creative project and comes across just then as the Madonna of her day given her single-minded 'drive'.

Viola Compton,[39] older sister of Fay Compton and Compton McKenzie, was chosen to portray Lizzi, and *'real Yorkshireman'* Mark Stone was hired as *Alf the comic*. He would appear in panto with the Sisters in *Babes in the Wood* straight after filming, and was later known for a double act he did with his wife. Bert Cameron, a handsome mature actor and bass lead singer played *Daddy Grayson*. Another comic - Harry Milton - joined the cast. He was the troubled former husband of actress Chili Bouchier. In her autobiography 'Shooting Star,' she writes how Jessie Matthews bought him a £1000 MG sports car ignoring pleas that she leave her husband alone. Chili finished with Harry and Teddy Joyce became her boyfriend. Both Hamish, and Billie's Scottie dog Dougal were canine actors and nine year-old Trevor Houston had a tiny part. This was Renée's third film that year, her second with Billie, her first with Shirley, and her ninth feature. She provided the original autobiography. In creating the script, her brother Jim, now calling himself Alan Rennie, changed the Sisters' names to *Kitty* and *Mickie Grayson*. They find fame as the *Harvey Sisters*. FH Bickerton and Daniel Birt were also credited for script and editing, if credit could be an appropriate word.

Left to right:
Billie, John Argyle, A.F Smith - journalist for The Telegraph (standing), Renée, comedian Pat Hanna, and Norman Lee.
Photograph courtesy of The Telegraph (Brisbane) December, 12 1935 (captioned: 'Working on Stage Folk') The National Library of Australia

Above
Francis Howard Bickerton, Antarctic Pioneer and John F. Argyle's film editor

A large theatre stage was specially constructed at Sound City, Shepperton. The seven-studio complex had state of the art soundproofing with everything brand-spankingly modern. Shepperton developed after Norman Loudon, a Scot from Campbeltown, bought the Littleton Park estate in 1928 on the back of an enterprise selling sports booklets or 'Flickers,' and the surrounding countryside was ideal for filming river locations and wooded islands. A thousand year-old tree stood in the grounds. Renée has several very long days to look forward to, motoring back to London with Pat and her sisters. All had evening theatre engagements. They might be back again the same night if night filming was required. Sometimes they didn't finish until 6am and stayed in bedrooms in Littleton Hall - the mansion within Sound

City. Miss H claimed bedroom number 7. Other nights she arrived at the silliest hour after doing cabaret at the Mayfair Hotel. A newspaper mentions such cabaret stints.[40] It says Renée had to fight somnolence on the part of audience when this should have been the other way round. Filming had fun moments despite the graft, and in December 1935, *'Digger'* - the New Zealand ex-soldier noted for his stage shows and films - visited the set, commenting how Norman Lee was 'a very breezy director who gets his results with patience and ease,' adding 'It's a wonder that Lee was able to get on with the picture, at all, as Renée Houston has the whole unit in fits from beginning to end.'[41]

'Happy Days Are Here Again' has elements of Brunel's 'Variety' with straight-acting scenes complementing the Sisters' musical numbers with the Kidds and sister Shirley. There are scenes not featuring the Sisters with Marie Kendall, Ida Barr, Harry Milton and George Harris - all well-known acts in the music hall and film world. The Sisters' rise to fame has an added drama of them falling out half way up the ladder of fame, each having gotten a little proud, and each sister has a romantic partner in the film. Billie Houston, who gave an interview prior to release, amusingly tells us:

> Billie: It's really a back-stage film. With songs and a bit of dancing and a lot of romantic nonsense about love affairs. Me having lovers! Doesn't that make you laugh?[42]

After seeing the trade show, Clarkson Rose reported that 'in between her romping Renée gave us one or two close-ups in a serious vein that showed what a 'mistress she is of charming expression.'[43] Remaining footage, the BFI's press book for 'Happy Days Are Here Again,' cinema press reviews, and rare old photos retrieved from dusty collections of film ephemera allow me to make a good guess as to the sequence of events as they were originally.

Firstly, the 1929 Ager and Yellen song 'Happy Days Are Here Again' accompanies the titles, and we meet the *Grayson Sisters*, daughters of a Glasgow pro. A curious song 'Don't Look In The Cellar' relates to some secret known only to the girls. Mum *Lil* gets a 'throat' and father *Jim* can't let his manager down so *Kitty* asks 'Why couldn't we deputize Dad?' They've been rehearsing in secret knowing full well their parents' act is finished. He refuses but they get their way and soon the *Graysons* have a revue of their own going. They're painting their own scenery and making their own costumes with disastrous results just as it happened in real life. There's a song called 'Hey There Circus Clown' and another 'Fall in and follow me' - the latter echoing Renée's leadership during the 1924 tour. *Alf, Maisie, Ella, Nita, Chris,* London Coster Girl *Gertie, Brainwave, Chris* and two concert Pierrots played by the Kidd Brothers join the gang. In a trellis scene Dave Kidd is in the foreground with Nicky Kidd and *Kitty* leaning on the piano. *Mickie* (Billie) in conical hat strums her little guitar. For the number 'Bench Beneath The Tree,' Renée and Nicky sing and semi-speak one verse. She gives a queenly look down at *Mickie*, then *Mickie* and Dave sing for a little while before everyone joins in, ending on Renée's high note.

Sadly, 'Topsy Turvy of 1925' is a flop and *Kitty* - little mother of the family - takes it on the chin. Stranded in a town the concert party travel to their next engagement by truck. Everyone's there: Ida Barr, George Harris (from Leslie Fuller's gang), and the rest. *Kitty* keeps people's spirits up singing 'If you 'aven't got a train then a lorry will do' with *Mickie* strumming her banjulele. We're introduced to *Bert* - dark haired with a high forehead. He's the conductor who wears a dark suit and white tie. Tony Smythe plays this weakish man who attracts *Kitty's* sympathy after he buys her pair of stockings. She sings 'Friend O'Mine' telling everyone 'One day, I'll repay that boy. I'll marry him.' *Kitty* embraces *Bert* and carts him off to the registry office causing her father to remark what a couple of mutts they are. It's outrageous how true to reality this is and that she could exploit her relationship with George in this way. Just as the Gribbins became Houstons, the *Grayson Sisters* have become the *Harvey Sisters*. Things have moved on when we meet them again in the office of provincial booker *Reg Jarvis* - Billy Watts, *Mickie* wears a small beret, blouse and white tie and *Kitty*, a fluffy white collar. *Reg* asks *Kitty* if she'll leave the profession and let him take care of her but she won't desert her family and he warns her touring will be tough, ending with the hopeful song 'Spring is Coming.' In the next scene they've turned stylish with 'Topsy Turvy Blues': Pierrots in large ruffs decorate an incredible scena – each human a different mechanism of a giant clockwork device. The *Harveys* are in centre position and *Kitty* shows a lot of leg. Shirley Houston is the shapely girl-pierrot directly below her sisters: the hands of the clock. Takings are good and the *Harveys*, still in costume, sit round a table with their parents looking a bit more pleased with themselves.

Lost scenes from 'Happy Days Are Here Again' (1936) from newspaper cuttings:
Left – With the Kidd Brothers, Right - Billie and Renée (My thanks to A.Richardson)

Reg persuades a London manager to try them out and they don little boy and girl outfits, meeting a 'George Barclay' in the wings. They close with 'Toy Drum Major.' Despite stardom, the next two scenes are downers. *Bert's* a drinker and spoils the act having had one over the eight. He and *Kitty* quarrel then part. The *Harvey Sisters*, still in their matching drum major jackets outfits then have words. *Mickie* believes she can quit the stage and become a writer turning out mystery thrillers. Depressed, *Kitty* sits on a sofa and sings 'Melancholy Baby' with only Hamish as an audience.

Time passes, and *Kitty* is a legitimate actress oozing foxy glamour with *Reg* on her arm. It's the eve of her theatre premiere. She's *Katharine* in *Taming of the Shrew*. To shoot this scene Argyle hired esteemed Shakespearean actor Ion Swinley as *Katherine's Petruchio*. Shortly before Swinley died in 1937, he was in a short extract from *As You Like It* in the first television broadcast of a Shakespeare play.

Print cuttings showing lost Scenes from 'Happy Days Are Here Again'
(By kind permission of J.Lewis Estate / A.Richardson)

Renée's shot at Shakespeare attracted much advance publicity and in stills she looks alluring in her Elizabethan pearl-embroidered outfit. Many saw the photos and believed Renée had made a full-length film of *Taming of the Shrew*, unaware it was just another scene within the cluttered 'Happy Days Are Here Again.' The scene is entirely lost. Watching *Kitty's* debut in Shakespeare, in an opera box with her admirer - a successful publisher, is *Mickie*. Soon we see the sisters, dressed up to the nines and a publisher's office is the scene of a reunion thanks to the tactful work of *Reg*. There's a version of 'Auld Lang Syne.' Crafty *Reg* has an offer they can't refuse - *'Topsy Turvy revue of 1936'* – sure of a West End run and big money. *Mickie* might have turned soft-eyed and sloppy in the direction of her publisher but the *Harveys* decide to go after the big money. Being kind-hearted souls with a wee dram of Scotch modesty they send a telegram to the old concert party back home, asking they join them. The former Pierrots hit the West End and the whole thing is a phenomenal success. The performance of 'The Coster's Honeymoon' by *Gertie*, played by Ida Barr, is one turn followed by the Sisters' *'Dope'* turn – a transition left intact in the 'Happy Days Revue' re-issue - odd given Bickerton's over-zealous editing.

Lobby Card Photo from Ebay (Author's Collection)

Film Star of the 1930s

The Houston Sisters in their famous act entitled, "So This is Hollywood," from the picture HAPPY DAYS ARE HERE AGAIN (A.P.D.) reviewed in this issue

The 'Dope' scene, before *Bill* leaves to muck around with the *real* people in Hollywood
(By kind permission of The British Library)

Kitty mimics a cockney in the style of Ida Barr: 'Isn't it *noice* eh?' Yet suddenly they drop being *Kitty* and *Mickie* and are Renée and Billie. What became of continuity I don't know but the *'Dope'* turn is amusingly risqué. Renée wears a short white skirt and bonnet and *Bill* is the bee's knees in *his* suit. The sketch concerns the eating of something cocaine-like from a box that might just as well have come from Woolworths.

Renée: If ma granny knew what I was mixing with. Let's try it.
Billie: Don't be so idiotic darling. I'll show you exactly what you do with dope, you take it in your hand ...
Renée: I'll do everything but I'm not doping.
Billie: If you're going to take the stuff, take a good dose of it.
Renée: Getcha!
Renée: Here's a teaspoon over here. I'll get it. Come on *Bill*, I'm going to watch the effect on you. Not so hot is it!
Renée: As they say in Scotland it's a bit *wersh*, meaning it's very sour - ho ho ho!
Billie: Shut up a minute – Do you feel any different?
Renée: Look at this – Epsom salts! (The 'dope' turns out to be Epsom Salts)
Renée: Don't blame me. I didn't rush you for it
Renée: What'll I do while you're in Hollywood making pictures?
Billie: Get in with the right people. Listen darling, you run around and make yourself popular.

Holding the box, she jokes with 'Jimmy' - Syd Seymour - who's conducting his *Mad Hatters Band*:

Renée: Jimmy's having a laugh! Hello Jimmy (crosses to bandleader)
Billie: Leave Jimmy alone! Never mind Jimmy!
Renée: Oh Jimmy. Why did you finish with the saxophone? Why's didn't you finish with the harp?

Reneé is told she needs to hobnob in English society whilst *Bill* will pursue the all-important contacts in Hollywood. Reneé has other plans:

Renée: You mean to muck around with the *real* people! (strokes *Bill*'s head)
Renée: You leave it to me my dear, and I won't leave it to your talent to get you where it takes.[44]

A seamless transition enabling a costume change allows her to make good her vow in *'This is Hollywood'* - a sketch showing the meeting between Greta Garbo and *Bill* in Hollywood. Renée looks incredible in a figure-hugging dress - a dead-ringer for one of Adrian's Hollywood creations, entering stridently, with an imperious sideways face eyes upwards, lips all pursed and overdone, and massive eyelashes.

Renée: (as GG) No autograph today. I never see anybody.
Renée: What are you doing in my house?
Billie: In *your* house?
Renée: Yes. In my house.
Billie: I'm afraid it's my fault you're seeing me. I rented it.
Renée: Rented it? Rented it? Oh, I don't understand you English. You rented it. Oh I see you mean you have borrowed it. Well, I want it back. Get that and get out quick.
Renée: Since you are here I would like to tell you me about this England of yours.
Billie: Well, I don't exactly know what to tell you, I'm sure.
Renée: Have you any beautiful women - Marvellous women?
Billie: Marvellous! Many of them. Thousands of them.
Renée: And have you no famous . . . no, interesting people?
Billie: Yes, very many.
Renée: I suppose it is a very small place... Capital of Wigan, isn't it?
Renée: Tell me ... When you were in England, did you ever hear of a man called Hannen Swaffer?
Billie: Yes... Hannen Swaffer. Well, that's the funniest thing. He's my uncle!
Renée: Your uncle, yeah!
Renée: When next you see your uncle, I would like you to give him a message from me. This is my message...(BANG! Shoots gun)
Renée: I think I go home.[45]

Her burlesque of the sphinx from 'Grand Hotel' is perfection. She leans forward a moment, then flops supine on the long leather couch, her movements acrobatic. With a look of surprise she swings around then leans back to look sulky, elbow on knee. She strokes her arms in anxiety, writhes, rubbing the knee of her slinky dress. At the cue of 'Hannen Swaffer,' she squirms her body with electricity, but ends up with her body deadly straight. She waves her head, strokes the chair, leans back and shakes her hair. One wonders if Swaff, who sometimes got banned from first nights, liked the pun. He had extreme views on cinema stars and was famously 'sick to death of Greta Garbo's eyes.'[46] No wonder Miss H's slinky alter ego wants to take a shot at him.

'So this is Hollywood': Renée as Garbo with Billie in 'Happy Days Are Here Again' (Artwork by author)

It is a shame that the straight-acting scenes and those with a love interest haven't survived. What's left in the obscure 'Happy Days Revue' is a small mercy though. Following the Garbo scene is a song number with fourteen chorus girls. We hear George Harris sing 'I'm Small But I'm Full Of Vitality'. Marie Kendall sings 'Just Like The Ivy'. *Alf* returns wearing a loud checked comedian suit for the 'Put me amongst the girls' number. Syd Seymour adds a touch of live showmanship and a scantily clad solo dancer takes the stage. For the finale, each of the ten Austrian Dancers in long white skirts with black spots has a partner in evening dress, making a line in front of a small on-stage orchestra. The *Harvey Sisters* with feminine hairstyles also wear white gowns, joining the curtain call either side of Alf. It's a spectacular vaudeville ending. Fifteen songs are featured in all, some provided by Lawrence Wright and some by Eddie Pola, with other music composed and arranged by Guy Jones.

Problems dogged the film. Monthly Film Bulletin commented that 'although the cutting is neat, there are still several loose ends and lapses in continuity which cry for editorial ruthlessness. The cameras are often irritatingly immobile.'[47] The film was still much anticipated. Near to its general release in March 1936, the trade press believed the faults would be offset by the cleverness and versatility of the Sisters 'who seldom leave the screen,' even if the camera didn't serve them well enough. It concluded it would draw family and provincial audiences. One notice raves that Renée 'has the audience with her' from the word 'go' and that 'Billie too registers effectively, although of course on quieter lines.'[48]

John Argyle relied on personal appearance and use of contacts to ensure the film reached its audiences. Following the Birmingham trade show, he gave a cocktail party at the city's Midland Hotel attended by the Houstons, Georgie Wood, Sandy Powell and cinema trade officials. By August, it was reported that 'Happy Days Are Here Again' had been booked to over a thousand cinemas throughout country and that Billie Houston, John Argyle, Mark Stone and Ida Barr were to make a guest appearance at the Rosum, Walsall on August 24. There was no high profile launch in a London cinema. This largely independent film didn't help the Sisters' careers much. A family saga from the pen of a Houston couldn't match the studio-written screenplay that was catapulting other variety stars to prominence. The film's distributor also lacked the influence of GFD. Argyle didn't worry. He had just signed a new three-picture deal with B.I.P. Never again would cinema exploit the Houston Sisters' act. Renée chose not to remember this film when she spoke of her career in the 60s and 70s. I think they must have felt screwed over.

All three Houston Sisters, as well as Sally and the Kidd Brothers, went to Columbia Studios on November 20, 1935 to make a record to publicize 'Happy Days Are Here Again.' Side 1 featured 'Topsy Turvy Blues', 'Rhythm' and 'Bench Beneath the Tree' and side 2 had 'Hey There Circus Clown', 'If you haven't got a Train', and a repeat of 'Topsy Turvy Blues'.[49] The Gramophone was negative about their efforts, especially for excluding patter from this disc, concluding 'they don't succeed.' The Houstons were so typecast that expecting creative doors to open was unrealistic. Gracie Fields avoided typecasting. If only the sisters could have learned from her. Only a few months earlier, Renée, draped in furs, looks pleased in a photo captioned 'Renée Houston signing a Columbia gramophone contract – a hallmark of success.' She might have looked the part but didn't flourish at Columbia. Nevertheless, she tried to make up for it by being a radio star.

Commercial broadcasts might pay well but BBC work paid much less than stage, films or recording, Renée seems to prove yet again she was less astute in money matters than *Our Gracie*. She was glad to appear in the *Gala Variety Performance* at Broadcasting House on October 26 alongside Yvonne Arnaud, Douglas Byng, Jean Sablon, Ronald Frankau and Nat Gonella and his *Georgians*. The film world had limited scope. Things she wanted to develop and build upon were difficult to get off the ground despite having friends in high places. 'Happy Days Are Here Again' was the nearest she got to being a film's creative force. Writer and journalist Herbert Harris asked why she didn't try her luck at straight dramatic acting. She shrugged and said:

Renée:　There's one character I'd like to play, but I don't suppose I shall- It's Mary Queen of Scots. I've read everything there is to read about tragic Mary.'[50]

It wasn't simply about acting the part of the Scottish queen, whose character she knew inside out. She wanted to produce the play herself. She saw herself as more than an actress. She got an offer to go to New York in early June 1937, her second one: from Lee Schubert for a forthcoming Broadway musical Bea Lillie had turned down. Schubert was arriving on June 8 with a contract and script and everything was set for a voyage aboard the Queen Mary. It's not known why or how the project fell through. She initially accepted the offer. She was happy building up her act here with Donald, although he could have come with her. Who knows what her destiny might have been if she had conquered Broadway?

Even though she was an absent mother, who saw her kids about once a week she had a homebody attitude. She didn't like to be far apart from her parents and the tribe for prolonged periods. She would get future offers for America but always there was a reason she couldn't go. More interesting to her was her Mary Stuart project. She told a reporter about the play she had written about Mary, pointing out how English history books took a prejudiced view and admitted that what Scots were taught in school didn't chime with what was taught in England. Speaking French with a Scots accent would be a cinch for her. Renée was attracted to the fact that Mary Stuart was a wit and a practical joker and her play made use of the laugh factor.

Renée: I am putting Bothwell in his place, as the mere nitwit of convenience which he was. Mary had only one real lover: Rizzio.[51]

Sadly no film or theatre production came about, as in the case of other plays she'd written that she wanted to make films of. There was that film scenario penned in 1935 about a Scottish fishing girl with an urge to go on the stage and 'Nights That Pass in a Ship' - a farcical comedy about a little stowaway on a liner that had a part written in it for Robb Wilton. She certainly had vision, high hopes, and had the instinct of a producer.

The overcomplicated plot of 'Fine Feathers' - a film for British Lion released in 1937, concerns an attempt to deceive the people of a Ruritanian kingdom that their *Crown Prince's* hated mistress - cabaret artiste *Madame Barescon* – is not living with him, so as to make that country less unstable – making way for a dodgy American financial syndicate to invest in it. The mistress loves *Jim Warren* - the syndicate's executive, played by Donald Stewart. With Leslie S. Hiscott directing the film, there's a possibility the creative team had a comic inversion of an Agatha Christie story in mind for 'Fine Feathers.' Hiscott directed the first film to be made of an Agatha Christie work - The Coming of Mr Quin, and is famous for his treatment of her plots in early British films. Why the plot could not have been simpler is a mystery as screenwriter Michael Barringer had written the story primarily with Renée in mind.[52] While Barringer dictates the action, the whole purpose of the film is the romance between *Teenie McPherson* and *Jim*. Playing a shopgirl stranded after her fellow picnic makers get drunk and leave on their charabanc without her, Renée is the key to the plot. She turns up at a Surrey mansion where *Jim* and *Felix* the butler persuade her to impersonate *Madame Barescon* and go off to Paris to 'be' her on the stage. *Teenie* is a great part for Renée and she fills it splendidly despite the story's flaws. She speaks French very effectively in the nightclub scene - the one where she gets scattered in rose petals.

'Fine Feathers' is a romantic comedy – fairly new territory for Miss Houston even though she was Pat's love interest in 'Come Into My Parlour.' Girl-next-door *Teenie* sees dishy *Jim Warren*. He's alright in her eyes, although the butler and the gang of seedy toughs certainly aren't. In just a few scenes Renée launches into her exuberant stuff with her 'You can't catch me' routine, mimetically running from the manipulative *butler. Jim* and *Teenie* hold either end of her dress - comically shrunk after the rainstorm - bouncing up to each other as they hope to stretch it back to size. There's sexiness in their movements and patter. At the beginning of this scene, for an almost unnoticeable split second Donald looks like he's going to crack up laughing. Later we have a dash of Garbo as *Teenie* channels *Madame Barescon* in order to carry off her feigned identity. Of course she forgets herself with smatterings of broad Scots dropped in - her 'Tha suits me!' - as un-Continental as you can get. Then, there's the clever scene where the shoulder fastenings of her gown somewhat do the talking – each side taking turns to become undone. That's the scene when *Teenie* is won over to the idea of helping *Jim*, trying on *Madame Barescon*'s gown and finding Jim's arms around her as he offers gentlemanly assistance. A 'scintillating comedy with music', is how the film's pressbook markets the film, referring to the 'two famous broadcast artistes' whose new partnership was 'gaining nationwide popularity.' The chemistry is evident from their very first scene as *Jim* opens the door and *Teenie* re-enters the mansion, to the last scene in the Paris nightclub when the police are out for them. It's the most unlikely getaway in film history, as they slip out kitted out as a couple of storybook *Bonnie Scots* in tartan kilts and tam o' shanters.

Resentment boils up when *Teenie* observes the real *Barescon* making a play for her adored Jim. To make him jealous she flirts with obese Ruritanian official turned nightclub king *Hugo* - played by Francis L. Sullivan and has a vase-shattering showdown with her aristocratic rival. Robb Wilton's in great form as *Teenie*'s uncle. He's incapable of being her protector, and it's her protection of him that makes her feistier as she takes on *La Barescon*. In a gentler scene, Renée and Donald make on screen magic with Donald presciently natural as 'feed' taking over where Billie left off.

Jim: Gosh, I'm not even a good crook.
Teenie: You certainly are not. You're a washout!
Oh you crook, how I have you! (Shirley Temple voice)
Jim: Shut up will you.
Teenie: Don't you shout at me!
Jim: You're a swell kid.
Teenie: Everybody wishing I was someone else, and me wishing I was...

Film Star of the 1930s

At the end is Renée and Donald's melodic and touching duet 'I'll Step Out Of The Picture.' The performance is as slick a combination as Fred and Ginger or any other divine couple you might name. They were visually stunning together. The cinema creates illusions and people believe them. Early on, tongues were wagging and the publicity photos from the film, oozing with sex appeal, made the illusion even stronger. But it was an illusion at least for three years. A film with a hated mistress of a royal heir is a coincidence given the unfolding events of 1936. Even when the film was re-issued as a 9.5mm 'Pathéscope Presents' feature for the home market, some years later, sensitivity was still running high and Graeme Newnham believes this is why the 'Pathéscope' print of 'Fine Feathers' has a disclaimer placed at the very beginning before the titles: *'The story of this film and all names, characters and places mentioned therein are purely imaginary.'*

'Fine Feathers,' of course, was sold off as a short, and that is why there's a 'Pathéscope' print. In the 50s and 60s these could be issued to the home cinema enthusiast: a perfect length to fit into one cassette of 9.5mm film. Often only these shorter re-issues survive. This is the case with 'Fine Feathers' and several British Lion films from this period. I wish someone would restore the sound quality of Renée and Donald's lovely duet, or even improve the quality of the entire film, of which several original scenes are lost. It's a saving grace it survived as a 9.5mm collector's item. If we weren't missing parts of the action, it would be easier to understand the filmmakers' true intentions, and perhaps the plot would seem less convoluted.

Renée isn't well served by costume designers in her early films with the exceptions of 'A Girl Must Live' and 'Old Bill and Son.' In 'Fine Feathers' the fabrics don't always work in front of a camera. You have to see through that, and see through her eyelashes – so long and heavy they'd shame a drag queen. In the duet scene she wears a high fashion silvery outfit – its upper part with winged sides high above the shoulders. It achieves a shimmering effect under the lights and diverts attention from her narrow shoulders. Having said that, the medieval black velvet gown, fringed with 213 ermine tails we see her in as she tries on *Madame*'s clothes is shoulder-less. This is also on the film's poster. 'Wouldn't you love 213 ermine tails on your frock? I get an awful kick out of them,' Renée innocently told a reporter.[53] She poses with an arresting gaze over one shoulder reminding me of Jean Harlow in her ostrich trimmed negligee on publicity images for 1933's 'Dinner At Eight.' The Harlow film was accompanied by a slogan 'fine feathers make fine fans' – the source for this new British Lion picture. Renée might not have had Harlow's blatant sex appeal but shared the *Blonde Bombshell*'s vocal talent and breath control. Her crosstalk with her leading man has the same warmth and humour of Harlow. Renée had been 'talking the movies' almost as soon as the Talkies appeared, being the natural mimic she was. Her bombshell was by imitation, yet her American movie starlet - an alter ego frequently seen, guaranteed laughs. In 'Fine Feathers' she looks her best in a floor length dress in pleated chiffon with huge sleeves and flounces - a design she adapted for stage dresses. She's wearing it in a photo taken on the day of filming when executives at Beaconsfield gave Renée a surprise birthday party on the set.

Renée's birthday party at Beaconsfield Studios during the production of 'Fine Feathers'.
Left to Right: Herbert Smith, Sally McBride, Arthur Alcot, Donald Stewart, Leslie Hiscott (director), Pat Aherne, Francis L Sullivan, Jack Hobbs and Marcelle Rogers.
(By kind permission of the Aherne family)

Lost scene from 'Fine Feathers'.
From Renée's scrapbook
(By kind permission of the family of Terry Long)

Renée's son remembers Sally being a regular visitor at their home in Stanmore, and there was talk of a short romance between Sally and Donald Stewart Wintermute - also a member of the household. Did Sally marry an American and leave the film world, as Alan believes? She was appearing with Matt Martell in Tommy Morgan's summer show at Rothesay and at the Empress, Glasgow in *Summer Breezes* with Doris Droy in 1944. She was in the city in 1953 when Renée stayed with her in Parnie Street.

Donald: If I come back with a nickel, I will find that I've gained a wealth of knowledge to compensate me.[54]

That's a line penned by wide-eyed Donald Stewart when he first came across at the end of January 1935, landing at Monte Carlo - his base for seeing the sights of Europe. He missed his American coffee but had a reverence for all things European and all his life appreciated his surroundings. The numerous letters written to relatives in Pennsylvania prove how informed he was about Europe's culture and politics. He hopped across the channel and easily found work in London, first in the mammoth cabarets Charles B. Cochran presented at Park Lane's Grosvenor House. These shows were the kind every musical star took part in at one time or another. A swift audition got him into André Charlot's revue *Char-A-Bang* at the Strand's Vaudeville Theatre in April 1935 with Elsie Randolph, Richard Murdoch and John Tilley in its large cast.[55] Charlot was great at discovering young talent and was Donald's foremost supporter. The young American from Wilkes-Barre went from strength to strength after this. On June 20 Donald and Elsie Carlisle were vocalists with bandleader Ambrose when a gramophone record 'Fare Thee Well, Annabelle' was made. Then, in early August, he was listed alongside Elsie Carlisle and Ronnie Hill as a 'well-approved singer' with Ambrose's band at the Palladium.

Film Star of the 1930s

Donald Stewart, 1935 - A new star in British films
(Wintermute Family)

He did his first movie - 'First A Girl' – a Gaumont-British production. Starring Jessie Matthews and Sonnie Hale - a remake of UFA's 'Viktor und Viktoria'. Looking thin and boyish, Donald jumps on the nightclub floor to sing solo vocals for "I can do everything, but nothing with you" with a line of girls in stripy outfits doing Busby Berkeley-inspired feats - legs like piano keys disappearing in mirror images. The catchy 30s number has the line 'I can wiggle my ears' and was such a hit Donald cut it on gramophone. After that, he was back again in another huge Charlot show at the Vaudeville, with Richard Murdoch, Arthur Riscoe and June Tripp. *The Town Talks* was a big hit in late April 1936 with a score by Vivian Ellis. On Columbia's label Donald recorded 'The Trees in Bloomsbury Square' and 'You Have That Extra Something.'

Postcard Donald sent Mrs Wintermute advertising The Town Talks (Photos of June and Arthur Riscoe)
(By kind permission of the Wintermute family)

Wilkes-Barre, a city surrounded by the Wyoming Valley, is named after two MPs in England who supported Colonial independence. Here, Donald's father, a civil engineer from Pikes Creek helped develop, among many other properties, the city's first bank. Don's mother Jessie, known as 'Mickey' by close friends, was originally from Brooklyn and enjoyed a luxurious home with maids and money for her children's education. Mickey was bereaved in

1931. Photos I have seen from the Stewart family indicate the level of comfort the family enjoyed. Many years later poor Mickey was swindled out of the bulk of her husband's money by a conman in Wilkes-Barre, causing the family's once high standard of living to take a dive. There was a sense of embarrassment about this.

Donald, the eldest of four, was privately schooled in voice and dance, attending Coughlin High School. In pages of 'The Breidlin'- the high school newspaper, he was regularly mentioned as a member of its junior and senior 'Glee Clubs'. He's always in a central position in photos. A line-up in a 1928 Breidlin photo has a caption 'Who is that patriotic fellow in the red, white and blue blazer?' 'Oh – that's our head cheer leader Don Wintermute.' Donald graduated soon after his youngest sibling Janice was born. A letter from a friend from Donald's early days – a time when he used to summer at Lake Nuangola includes crumbling clippings from local papers, talking about Donald being seen with many lovely ladies at local dances 'dancing as smooth as silk . . . not showing favour to any particular one of the young ladies present.' He was quite the ladies' man.

He graduated from the American Academy of Dramatic Arts in New York City, and immediately appeared in 1928 as a singer and dancer in *George White's Scandals*. White, a talented impresario, who was very handsome and a gambler on a grand scale, produced these revues using the Ziegfeld formula and was almost as lavish until he suffered huge losses in the Wall Street Crash. Sadly, he suffered worse scandals later on after committing a driving offence. Donald joined at the time White's ladies were still decked out in gorgeous jewel costumes by Erté. This Broadway vehicle gave countless big names a start: WC Fields, the Three Stooges, Ethel Merman, Ann Miller, Bert Lahr, Rudy Vallée, Louise Brooks and Eleanor Powell are some of them. Donald was engaged to the latter - the graceful and athletic tap dancer who became an MGM film star on account of her machine-gun footwork. Donald broke off his engagement to Miss Powell. The story his kid sister heard was that 'He didn't want to marry her bossy, meddling Mother' who was a backstage problem.

Donald was a singer in *Ballyhoo of 1932* - another Broadway musical comedy, and before he came to the UK, had one serious relationship behind him – one he could hardly sustain not having the means to settle down and support people at the very beginning of his career. Thankfully he emerged from his Broadway years with few scars, on good terms with everyone, and with his head firmly screwed on his shoulders. Those shoulders had rubbed against the great and the good and he considered Hollywood but first sought an opportunity to stand out from his contemporaries. He had been chasing this dream ever since he was a small boy on a soapbox in the yard at his family's sprawling homestead in Wilkes-Barre. By the time he was leaving the New York Met, he was, nevertheless, romantically involved again with Lily Pons - a talented lady of distinction. The French-American opera singer known for her coloratura soprano repertoire was principal soprano at the

New York Met and years later featured on a US postage stamp in 1997. Donald chose vaudeville instead of opera, a discipline people had told him he was good enough to master. One of Don's friends on Broadway was the young Bob Hope. Hope needed people in the wings to act as prompts for his jokes and Don stepped in as a reliable prompt many a time.

During the time Don first worked in the UK, the theatrical press occasionally talked of the *evasion of income tax* by foreigners here for limited but highly remunerative engagements. In theory, all visitants paid tax although there was a difficulty chasing the foreigners, and some got off without paying.[56] Don and Renée first worked together around May 1936 and his earnings would have been closely scrutinized given the fact he had to repeatedly negotiate his visa and status over a fourteen year period. He put up with all this, content to make England his residence whilst remaining an American national throughout. He lived as part of Renée's entourage for more than ten years before marrying his Queen of Scots.

Chapter 14   Star of Musical Comedy

Going solo on the variety stage didn't suit Renée or Billie as each functioned best with a partner but there were now openings in other types of theatre. By the time *More Dam Things* had closed and Renée's rehearsals for *Love Laughs* were in progress, stories about the 'break up' of The Houston Sisters were circulating: the Portsmouth Evening News one newspaper following this closely. Renée put them right on the question of a fall-out in April 1935: 'There is no question of any disagreement between us,' she said. 'It's simply that we have both had opportunities to break new ground. We shall still be together from time to time for film and radio purposes.'[1]

Billie was the first to achieve something independently with her book 'Twice Round The Clock,' written before 1934 ended. It was serialized every weekday in the Daily Sketch[2] then hit the bookshops.[3] Renée followed close on her heels in the writing stakes. Their last stage show had incorporated reams of material she had authored. At the end of the year *More Dam Things* was voted one of the 'Plays of the Year' for 1935.[4] If this wasn't proof of writing talent what was? The revue's success motivated Renée who, aged thirty-two, thought of herself as a producer. On good terms with the entertainment kings in both variety and film worlds, she wondered what she could achieve. She was bursting with ideas. I believe she could have moved into production if women had been able to then. She didn't have the luck of Barbra Streisand and Madonna to be alive in later eras. A press article describes how Renée had written a film scenario by herself, saying how she was going to play the part of a Scottish fishing girl with an urge to go on the stage. Her script included a part for Pat Aherne (not Billie). In the article she declared that if the men at the top wouldn't take up the film she was going to form a film company to make it.[5] Only someone as outspoken as Renée could say such a thing. She felt she was a genius striving for recognition.

Could her writing ambitions have been driven by Billie's literary success? John Betjeman, writing in The Evening Standard, suspected that Renée's Scottish fisher girl film was a counterblast to Billie Houston's book, icily saying that Renée was desperate to prove that there were other writers in her family.[6] Betjeman was probably the first person to make such an incisive and not so flattering observation concerning Miss H. There was no harm in a little competition with Billie and everyone else for that matter. Soon after Billie's novel was complete, Renée was putting together an autobiographical memoir intended to be the basis of a screenplay. The writing might have been initiated by her relationship with producer John Argyle when production for 'Variety' began. It seems this project was in the pipeline immediately after their meeting, and the story was ready in July when the deal for the film 'Happy Days Are Here Again' was sealed. Jim Houston was also involved in making a script, so Billie's two closest siblings were hot on her heels when it came to scribbling.

A business-savvy reporter questioned the reports about the parting of the Sisters saying: 'As for permanently breaking up their act, perish the thought!' and went on to explain how Renée was destined to stardom in her light comedy roles - something that would send up the market value of occasional reappearances with Billie in their popular vaudeville act.[7] This was certainly true. Achieving things independently didn't mean never again harnessing the power of the old act. Besides, they would be back together in pantomime at the end of that year and other joint appearances were to be expected, especially in films. The Sisters were keeping all options open, letting their fans know what to expect. They made a handful of appearances together until the later months of 1936.

There were three main reasons why the double act was not sustained. One reason was the breaks Renée was getting in musical comedy and films. Another was Billie's health and another was the prospect of Donald Stewart as a stage partner and opportunities for a fresh act. Both sisters had individual ambitions driving the separation. Renée had more scope to diversify and survive outside of variety. There were more romantic lead parts in musical comedies than writers willing to specially create parts for the Houston Sisters. Many theatrical contracts were offered when Renée was in *Love Laughs,* including ones from Jack Waller in England, and Lee Schubert and Lew Leslie in America.[8] Billie's determination to carry on with Shirley or other partners indicates that she was not ready to stop the variety act. She would have stayed in the act with Renée and expressed interest about rekindling the act in the late 30s and 40s. Health finally put the kibosh on this option.

Billie wanted a less hectic schedule. She might try to do more writing and was open to individual parts in films and theatre herself. The talk about her health wasn't made public in 1935-36 and that was Billie's decision. She went along with the plan that each of them try to find success individually, and accepted the compromise. She would have appreciated the breathing space to and the time it enabled them to devote to their personal lives. It's possible Billie did quite well out of Renée's stage successes and a Variety Magazine report tells us that whilst on *Love Laughs*, Renée was paying her sister 50% of her salary from the Hippodrome show.[9] If Renée had a mind to offset Billie's loss of earnings, it shows her respect for Billie. She also apparently carried Billie's share of back tax dating back to the early 30s.

According to Tony Aherne, the Sisters folded because Renée got a lucrative contract with British Lion films. The film deal was announced in the press in February 1936,[10] although in Renée's own account British Lion bought her existing contract (negotiated six months earlier with Herman Fellner). The film contract was the overriding reason but Renée did not 'fold' the Houston Sisters immediately. During those six months she made a film with Billie and appeared with her in pantomime. She spoke about 'giving the act a rest' at the same time the contract with British Lion was mentioned in the press. Her screenwriting for 'Happy Days Are Here Again' was complete, and her autobiographical memoir conveniently repackaged in series form in The People's Journal entitled 'Step-By-Step To Stardom'. In the first instalment, Renée and Billie give views as to the Houston Sisters' future:

Renée: Billie and I are still the best of pals. She couldn't quarrel with anyone. So don't you believe what you may have seen or heard. Isn't that right, Billie?
Billie: Perfectly correct, my dear.

They knew people were used to seeing them. They were a brand, recognizable by children in a 'comic book' sense. In advertising their pictures alone conveyed their strong personalities. An advert in the early 30s for Jay's Furniture is a good example with a little extract of comic crosstalk between the sisters supplied in the ad, illustrating their commonsense. They suited ordinary things about the home and also cigarettes, which both sisters advertised individually. Sometimes there was a working class flavour to these ads which, in conjunction with their image, seems to anticipate cartoon characters from 'The Dandy' or 'The Beano': comic journals that would appear a few years following the closing down of the Houstons' act. Occasionally they advertised creams and perfume. They weren't always defying the sacrosanct, but a time of economic gloom what the Sisters had to say as they cast their *common* eye on a face cream made interesting reading.

Renée liked to stress that 'Billie and I are still fond of each other as we ever were. Blood is thicker than water, and we are much too sane and sensible to end a partnership which has been so happy and successful.' She points out how each had to forego the home-life held dear to them, especially given the travelling that the act required. Many years later Renée said that she put up with criticism levelled against her for causing the separation. Critics saw her as acquiring airs and graces and longing for the polish and veneer a career in films and stage could offer. She writes that she could not defend herself well as Billie did not want the world to know she was seriously ill. She let those mutterings continue. Nothing in the press explained the true situation with Billie.

Billie had extremely expressive eyes. With those eyes she could communicate a look of innocent surprise, misbehavior, or draw you into jokes that were light-hearted or slightly perverse. She widened her eyes to express mock disgust, loaded criticism, or horror. They were watchable for their playfulness and humour. Her eyes caused her problems but not until the late 30s when she was diagnosed with exophthalmia. In the first few months of 1935 it was actually another health problem she had to deal with. All in all, she did not say goodbye to her theatrical career without a fight and that battle would last for a few more years.

It was the very last week of *More Dam Things*, according to Renée, that Billie first said she might 'pack it in' on account of her health. An old man in the audience dropped dead in the aisle that week in Brighton and it frightened the life out of both of them. Only twenty-nine Billie had, by then, been going on for years - night after night bravely putting up with her injury.

Billie later told her children that this damage had occurred when she had fallen on stage, hence her continual treatment for the spine. The worst part of it all was that Billie was a victim of private doctors who did well out of her. She was not the only 'star' who got exploited like this. The medical treatments she received for the original spinal injury were far from ideal and one treatment resulted in a new problem.

Although nobody is clear when her original fall happened, it could have been long before, when *See You Later* was at the Empire, South Shields - in September 1922, at least if Renée's 1936 memoir is reliable. After Billie landed on top of one of the musicians, losing the grip of the line dancers, she was rendered unconscious for half and hour. Renée doesn't attach significance to this accident. She says Billie's injury didn't turn out to be quite as serious as feared, adding all the same that that the crown of her sister's head was like a switchback, that one of her fingers was dislocated, and that Lizzi could barely see Billie for bandages - arms, legs, head! Was this the injury that had a long-term impact? If it was, Billie lived with it for thirteen years and never appeared incapacitated on account of it.

The only records I have of her coming out of performances before 1935 are in February 1929 when an influenza attack caused her to collapse on stage at the Brixton Empress and in November 1929 when, 'due to the indisposition of Billie' the Houstons could not fulfil an engagement at the Argyle Birkenhead. Whatever the origin of the injury, the subsequent operations she had to 'right' it, using medical treatments of the day, definitely caused complications and continual pain. What a cruel irony that a procedure to correct a problem results in worse discomfort! Billie no doubt gagged about 'backing it in' at the end of *More Dam Things*.

In October 1935, Billie appeared in a legitimate drama *Down in the Forest*, as *Andrew MacWilliam* – 'a laddie of naïve irrepressible determination to rise in the world'. This was a Scottish play by GF Malloch – a writer hailed as the next JM Barrie. This light comedy was tried out in Birmingham and Edinburgh, and was due to move to the Palace Theatre of Varieties, Cambridge Circus the following spring. A house gathering brings together a theology student, a Labour leader, a self-made colliery owner, a determined spinster anxious to wed, a canny bachelor and an ornithologist. Kathleen Boutall was *Miss Spencer* who captures the bachelor lord. Patrick Curwen and Edward Sinclair also had prominent roles. With the *nightingale* hardly native to the Scottish woodlands, mischievous *Andrew* has his eyes set on the *bawbees* if he can start a craze that attracts bird lovers. Hiding in a tree tootling on a bird whistle, he fakes the birdsong. *Andrew* is central to the plot: his actions determining the motivations of the other characters. His nightingale imitations start to beguile men and maids into plighting their troth in the moonlit wood. He even gets called '*MacPuck.*'[11] He owns up to everything after saving the professor's face – and obtains largesse for his education. An additional sub-plot about miners' wages doesn't work.

While dated, this was the type of saga about eccentric characters that would have flowered into a classic British film of the Powell and Pressburger kind, given the chance. What's amazing is that Billie is playing her first straight role in the theatre still doing a male impersonation, but not of a vaudeville kind. She was cast as a real boy in a drama! Taking male characters in Shakespeare and having them played by women is a well-trodden path. Billie's forgotten 30s play was quite historic in terms of sexual role reversal on the mainstream legit stage.

Real life intervened as it was wont to. Injury was added to insult when poor *MacPuck* slipped from the 'tree' *he* had to climb in the woodland scene, and sprained *his* ankle badly on the last night in Edinburgh.[12] As usual Billie dealt with her injuries. By late 1935, Billie's sacrifice of limbs for art was something she had down a fine art. She was also trusting heavily in her doctors, hiding her troubles, and performing with gusty exuberance perhaps in a moulded jacket. Perhaps Renée was right about her being accident-prone. *Jack* and *Jill* had gone down that hill. *Jill* fetched her pail of water while poor *Jack* went tumbling. I shall return to Billie in Chapter 16.

The thing I find most extraordinary about 1935's hit musical comedy *Love Laughs* is that Renée carries a show on her shoulders that runs ninety-six performances at the London Hippodrome and all the time she's just being Renée - not rigorously keeping to the traditions of musical comedy as a performer like Jessie Matthews might. She was merging the form with looser more rebellious aspects of her music hall presence. She took a risk and it worked a dream. She makes no mention of director Campbell Gullan - the accomplished stage actor and fellow Glaswegian, twenty years older than her. This is strange as he was a key supporter of the Houston Sisters in theatrical circles. When Laddie Cliff came to see Renée at the end of *More Dam Things* at Brighton, he knew he would be on to a winner bringing her to the West End. He was producing the show along with Clifford Whitley, who he met in the flying corps in World War One and went on to appear with in the *Co-optimists*. *Love Laughs* was the latest in a string of similar-titled musical comedies - many of which had Stanley Lupino as lead. It succeeded *Sporting Love, Love Lies,* and *So This Is Love.* They ditched the title *'Here's To Love!'* taking inspiration from a proverb from Shakespeare's *Venus and Adonis* – about love picking through locks like a locksmith and finding a way.

The first scene of *Love Laughs* starts in a film studio, familiar territory to Renée. At Coronet Studios, *Welstree*, they're making *'Jewel Princess'* – and the costume changes of the 'film' chorus range from veiled harem beauty to gipsy, then Tyrolean, followed by cowgirl – haphazard enough to symbolize madcap studio life. The boss, *Cyrus Manders*, played by actor James Carew (who had made films with Brian and Pat) isn't impressed with *Gus* - publicity man and *Tony*, his storywriter. Laddie Cliff and Allan Kearns played these two heroes. *Manders*[13] gives them a month to make good or be fired. *Eve* -

Barbara Newbury - is the starlet in love with *Tony*, who flirts with *Lord Tollington*, borrowing the *Tollington diamonds* for her scene in the film in the hope of attracting *Tony*'s attention. The substitution of false diamonds for real results in *Gus* and *Tony* getting sent to prison. *Eve* and *Jenny McGregor* – the studio's continuity girl - played by Renée - bring about their escape.

Laddie's new show was full of unusual touches. Each scene had an unpredictable charm. His own character *Gus* was less of a publicity manager and more of a secret service agent. In *Dartmoor Prison*, the convicts are horticulturalists tending a garden singing a 'Pastoral of Spring' and reading books by Beverley Nichols. The kind of prison they've been clapped into is one in which chorus ladies are introduced as a refining influence. Farcical scenes characterize the second act as they evade arrest pretending to be scarecrows and trick-cycling ice-cream vendors along a country road (with *Tony* dressed as a woman). They get caught but are freed again when *Jenny* vamps the sergeant, and the heroes steal away disguised in police uniforms. The last scene is a costume ball at *Tudor Hall* – a country club reminiscent of Ingestre Hall, with everybody supposed to be a celebrity in the film world – another amusing touch for film fans. The jewels turn up, a chauffeur is accused, and *Gus* and *Tony* are cleared. Given this haphazard scenario, I trust Renée's account about Laddie Cliff telling her to simply *make up* her part. What she improvised worked well and I expect her old friend was very pleased. Laddie was said to be a modest man who often let other people take credit. It isn't a surprise that critics of *Love Laughs* wondered why he and Allan Kearns 'sacrifice themselves on Miss Houston's altar.'[14] Characters that Laddie himself brought to the stage were imbued with a touch of pathos similar to those of Chaplin and Buster Keaton. I read that in his spare time he liked solitude and preferred country trips alone in his car.

At Glendale Avenue, meanwhile, the Houston nursery seemed alive and well with Renée - the *child* at the centre of proceedings. *Dismal Desmond the Doleful Dalmatian* still ruled, and the rooms were laden up with toys. Fans who congregated outside the Hippodrome for *Love Laughs* continued to present her with them. 'I'm an awful baby about stuffed animals, 'Miss Houston told a reporter. 'I've got a stuffed lion at home - one of those great big ones. Baby plays with it on the floor and he's a wee bit frightened of it ... it's as big as he is ... do you know what that cute kid did? He got his brother to take one of the eyes out so he can creep up on the blind side of the lion without it seeing him![15]

But the real babies in this menagerie were getting a wee bit confused. Greta, their nurse tried hard but the manic energy *Love Laughs* created had a negative side. The *Jetsam Jottings* column in The Stage tells us that 'Tony, her youngest child was so afraid that his mother would become insufferable after her success that he ran out into the Watford by-pass, and was missing for a long and anxious period. He was found in time for Renée to go to the Hippodrome and repeat her triumph, which, for La Houston means 'bringing the house *doon*.'[16] Renée herself amuses us in her 1974 memoir, with her account of the story. In her account their nurse rushes in saying 'Master Tony has disappeared.' Then Tony is found standing in a field three miles away with a daisy in his hand. The papers apparently report this saying *'Renée Houston's baby lost, found and spanked'*.

Poor Tony Aherne! He was only five years old then, and he can't have been getting the attention he craved. Those cuddly toys were no comfort and seemed like dumb intrusions. If modern child psychologists were around, they would insist on reading more into those *Jetsam Jottings* in The Stage. Why was he afraid of her becoming insufferable? Why was he afraid *for* her? It sounds like the little boy was bearing a kind of worry or guilt on her behalf, and goodness knows why. He was awfully attached to his mum. When she felt panic, so did he. Or was this a sign of compulsive behaviour, a need to run away to some envisioned place – a deep and tragic flaw that at times, even when he was old and retired, made him stand apart acutely? In his late sixties, Tony would write of 'his huge sulkings around the age of ten: depression, detachment, self-absorption, depressed, isolated, masochistic, bullying.'[17] He would write poetically, how he 'met the young Tony who fell from a star, a fall very far, and Renée Houston was the name of the star.'[18]

London was experiencing a heat-wave in the first couple of weeks of July 1935, and a theatre critic in The Bystander asked if somnolence that sultry evening might have caused him to 'miss a vital link to make the scenes logically clear,' admitting that when James Carew came on he suddenly realized 'there must be a plot after all.'[19] Almost all the critics for *Love Laughs* refer to the daft, uneven plot. There was so much 'oddity and inconsequence' that one writer considered these the 'twin keynotes of this show.' The Manchester Guardian writes how what plot there was had a certain amount to do with locksmiths, and jokes that if ladies didn't carry the family diamonds to film studios and leave them with the 'kind of constable who has been representing law and order in the English theatre since Dogberry's days, musical comedy might have to cease for lack of matter.'[20] Syd Walker, as the *Sergeant* in question, was on top form. The great convict ballet scene of *Love Laughs* with the Sergeant, *Gus* and *Tony* was entirely organized by Laddie - his clever feet and eccentric steps guaranteeing its success, while Frederick Lord choreographed the other dances.

Renée:
Cutting from her scrapbook
(Family of Terry Long)

The London Hippodrome
(Miranda Brooke)

The Telegraph points out that there was a plot 'bits of which kept cropping up, and not mattering . . . But Miss Houston was the show.' It goes on to explain that triumph came as soon as she did her number 'I'm Mad About Music' with Laddie. From then on she could 'do what she liked with the audience.'[21] This was the fifth number - the first one Renée sings. A photo records this amusing comic prelude with Laddie like a baby on Renée's lap. Both of them brought an abundance of physical comedy to *Love Laughs*. It was fairly typical in several of her plays or films for this type of slapstick scene. The scene involving the chairs in 'Their Night Out' is another one. The antics of 'I'm Mad About Music' impressed a critic who points out that when Renée 'needs to wind herself round Mr Laddie Cliff . . . she moves hardly at all and yet puts across the recognition of a quicksilver personality.' The same critic draws attention to the ease in which she could play sexy, referring to her 'pungent comment on ancient and Hollywood crudities in the technique of using body line tactics for allurement.' He mentions her mobile mouth and lightening vitality that has come from trained artistry and also her common touch – the sort shared by Marie Lloyd and Gracie Fields. She astounded London romping though her part, and so the realm of musical comedy heralded its latest radiant personality. I love the image of the cast drawn by the incredibly talented Arthur Ferrier – with Renée caricatured as *Jenny* prominent at the centre of the image, in front of a large star. Underneath it reads '*A Smile-Stone in Musical Comedy History'*.

However, not all press reports were positive about the show. Even the music by Noel Gay was thought 'not remarkable' whilst tuneful. James Agate had hardly an inch of praise for this story of convicts successfully laughing at locksmiths. He ransacked his brains for something favourable to say, concluding it is at least 'free from the mawkishness of Galsworthy's *Escape.*' Since he arrived in time for scene 3 only, and missed 'Mad about Music,' his slamming of the show is a bit unfair. Of the material in *Love Laughs,* he's aghast at the thought that such things 'deliriously succeed,' and goes on to analyze, perhaps with accuracy, how Miss Houston 'does not so much act in musical comedy as prey upon it and upon its devotees, since there is not one single aspect of this kind of entertainment which she does not scarify and hold up to ridicule.' He wonders why she is content to 'welter in inanity', when if any other musical comedy actress had been present 'they must have died of shame!'[22] His words convey a *hidden* thumbs up. It's not obvious.

Did she 'save' the show, as Agate concedes at the end of his review? Perhaps Renée saw its limitations, and this is why she didn't carry on with the tour of *Love Laughs,* prompting an ad in The Stage: '*Wanted – A Star Comedienne*' to take her part.[23] She was the show. Business was very good and one pleased person was RH Gillespie – financial controller of the London Hippodrome, known as 'the Man who accounts for taste.' He and his two sons were devoted to number crunching. At the pre-London opening in Oxford, the student audience shouted 'We want the Houston girl!' The crowds loved Renée's craziness, and the shades of her Houston Sisters self. Pressmen commented on her mercurial wit, telling readers that this was an actress to listen to – and it didn't matter how insignificant the prattle might seem.[24] The show featured her intimacy with the conductor - all too familiar – and a bunch of critics echo WA Darlington in his feeling that the show stopped when she left the stage and began again when she came back. In the number 'Love Laughs at Locksmiths,' with Billy Mayerl holding the conductor's baton, Renée, in lofty lady-like accent, breaks off mid song - objecting to Mayerl's frivolous accompaniment then slipping into her native Scots. Mayerl plays the accompaniment with such pathos that Renée rushes off in floods of tears. Returning on stage she's *'Greta Garbo* for no particular reason. She just is.'[25] In fact some critics thought Renée continued her *Garbo* 'turn' a good deal too long before the curtain came down.

Renée cut a 78 rpm disc based on the fame of her big show. 'Love Laughs At Locksmiths' was recorded on November 3, 1935 on Columbia's 'DX' label. Sadly, 'I'm Mad About Music' - the musical high spot of the show was not recorded, but the other side of Columbia DX716 features a very funny monologue entirely of Renée's creation. It's called 'The Eternal Triangle' - a wonderful testimony of her ability to speak in the tongue of all classes and tribes, flashing from one idiom of nonsense into another with ease and wit. Among her Eternal Triangle characters is '*Maltina*' and the concept might be understood more if I tell you it's a send-up of the men, women and children in bubble dialogue exchanges in the Horlicks cartoons that used to be found on the pages of magazines in the 1930s. I can't help but hear Renée singing in my head when I take my cup to bed with me.

After *Love Laughs,* the next miracle on the stage that Renée was about to perform beyond her forthcoming Christmas panto was uncertain. She writes in 'Don't Fence Me In' that a producer wanted to take *Love Laughs* to Broadway but she did not think they were offering her enough money and turned down the offer. There were reports of how CB Cochran had commissioned Scottish playwright James Bridie to write a new musical play especially for her. Lyrics and music were to be by Richard Rodgers and Lorenz Hart - the team responsible for such successes as *One Dam Thing After Anothe*r, and 'Evergreen'. Cochran was to produce, after the termination of Renée's pantomime engagement.

Bridie plays - mostly lively morality plays sometimes offer scope for big performances from Scots characters. *A Sleeping Clergyman* (1935) about three generations of a Scottish clan is one. Tyrone Guthrie, eminent director and sometime actor was responsible for Bridie's theatrical debut in 1930. Like AJ Cronin, Bridie had studied medicine at Glasgow University, which explains plays like *The Anatomist* (1930). Theological themes were prominent in plays like *Tobias and the Angel* (1930) and *Susannah and the Elders* (1937). He might have had Renée in mind for the latter, which made *Susannah* an incorrigible flirt worse than the sorely provoked *elders*. However, when performed at the Duke of York's in October and November 1937, he chose Joan White for the lead. Renée was also keen on a *Mary Queen of Scots* play and she might have asked Bridie to adapt her own story.

There was enough confidence that Bridie's vehicle for Miss Houston was in the pipeline that an advert for it was placed on January 1 1936 with a date

- April 13 and venue: Opera House, Manchester, even though no play was actually named. Renée proudly mentions the contract herself as late as May 1936, saying that her new three-picture film contract did not debar her from her involvement in the play. Sadly, the *Houston-Bridie* collaboration fell through: 'Ah did meet James Bridie tae talk aboot that. Nice wee man. But it didnae come taw anything' - goes a line in the play – a play about Renée, written in the 1970s, by Scots playwright Tom Gallacher.

Shirley's theatrical career started to light up when she appeared in *To Be Continued* - a Tom Arnold revue at the Alhambra, Glasgow between June 23 - July 5, 1935. The stars were Jack Daly, the Radiolympia Girls, Jock McDermott and his band, and Shaw and Weston. She was fully independent of her two sisters. Renée made sure to let people know that some credit for this was down to her, writing in her 1936 memoirs about how she helped her sister over the phone, supplying her with material. As a consequence of this, they ran up a phone conversation costing 25s, and impressed the telephone girls apparently.[26]

Shirley's next role was in a 'straight' play. Having directed *Love Laughs*, Campbell Gullan took *Closing at Sunrise* – *a* play by RJ Carruthers, to the Royalty Theatre in Dean Street, Soho, opening on September 23, 1935. Directed by Dennis Val Norton, the action of *Closing at Sunrise* takes place at 'Ted's' – an all-night coffee-stall in a West End cul-de-sac, with Cockney comic Mark Daly's racy humour and rhyming slang making his stallholder chat colourful. Norman Shelley is an inebriated sea captain rolling in and livening things up, while a gang of forgers skulk about ready to take advantage of a new victim. Betty Marsden is *Pamela*. Later a familiar face in British television, this was Betty's West End debut.

Nineteen year-old Shirley, with a flawless Cockney accent is *Doris* - cabaret singer and wife of a seedy musician whose happy-go-lucky spirit ends in disillusion before she's shot by Anthony Ireland's villain. Shirley proved her 'professional blood was thicker than water,' as a critic pointed out. Still, it was a venerable stage that would never again witness the patter of thespians after 1938 – a distinction Shirley could take pride in. In the 20s the Royalty had seen the first West End productions of Noël Coward's *The Vortex*, O' Casey's *Juno and the Paycock* and Ibsen's *Pillars of Society*. Before this a succession of theatre dames had run the theatre, and both Sarah Bernhardt and fourteen year old Ellen Terry had made appearances here.

Sunrise stayed at the Royalty until November 9 then went to the Duke of York's until December 14 playing ninety-six performances in all. Critics praised Shirley's strong scene when she betrays the villain, admitting her character had little to do until the last act. The story was thought a little melodramatic. James Agate writes how 'Nine-tenths of the play is about the humours of a coffee-stall,' then praises Shirley whose 'first appearance in the West End, is about three times better than most West End actresses in their last appearance. I look forward to seeing Mesdames Billie, Renée and Shirley in Tcheckov's *Three Sisters*. Theatre-managers have had odder notions, and will have them again.'[27] The compliment ends with a slight sting in the tail but it's kinder that his comment about Renée weltering in 'inanity'. I'm sure Renée would have appreciated being taken seriously by Agate as his line about her could have been kinder.

Three Generations of the Houston Family: Lizzi, Shirley, Granny Houston and Billie photographed on the stage at the Royalty Theatre (or in the cafeteria) on the opening night of *Closing at Sunrise*
(By kind permission of the Aherne Family)

Some journalists of the theatrical press suggested Renée should aim higher than musical comedy: 'Miss Houston's duty to herself is clear, she must go on the legitimate stage to give her abilities a fuller opportunity.'[28] It might sound like a career route, but the instances of music hall artistes forsaking their own acts for the legitimate stage at this time were rare. Less than a year later, another critic argued that if Renée could 'suppress her own sense of humour, and refrain from guying her lines, she could act a complete role in one of the grander or more fashionable manners with perfect success.'[29] Could she ever stop guying?

Next came a booking made eighteen months previously care of Emile Littler - the younger Littler brother. Having struck gold with *Aladdin* the previous year, as well as marrying his principal boy, Emile anticipated big rewards with *Babes in the Wood* – his second investment. He was talking a risk casting the Houston Sisters and Douglas Byng – one of the most famous *drag* performers of his day. Some thought the latter a little too 'sophisticated' for a children's show. It was a resounding success and Emile had a long and hugely successful career as a Pantomime king ahead, managing his business from his HQ at Pantomime House in nearby Oozells Street.

Littler paid well. The Houston Sisters' salary was in the top bracket - £100 a week if not more – in the region of £3,600.00 now. They decamped to Birmingham to appear at the Prince of Wales Theatre in Broad Street. Commencing Christmas Eve, 1935, Renée liked to describe *Babes in the Wood* as a bonus featuring the Houston Sisters now the act was taking a break from the variety stage. In the opening scene we're in the village of *Happy Go Lucky* outside the *Horse and Hiccup* inn where we meet *Sir Diddlum Dumpling, Sheriff of Nottingham* -played by Mark Stone and *Simple Simon* - a doleful Horace Kenney. *Wilhelmina Whackster* - Douglas Byng's latest grotesque, is the Dame engaged to keep the *Babes* in order in their nursery. She makes her boisterous entrance on a bicycle very much in the *Auntie* tradition. Thankfully, *Fairy Sunbeam* is on the side of the *Babes* who are wards of the *Sheriff*. Harry Condor directed the orchestra and journeys were to be made

Down Lover's Lane, and into *Butterfly Land* for a mesmerizing display of colour care of the girls from *Eugene's flying ballet* flying over the heads of the audience - some somersaulting in mid flight.

In part II, at *Sir Dumpling's Castle* we meet *Maid Marion*, played by Betty Huntley Wright, who sings 'Red Sails in the Sunset' on a darkened stage with a chorus waving headlamps. We travel to the depths of *Sherwood Forest* where striking theatrical effects are achieved using a large silken sheet, and we make the acquaintance of a horse, a dog, and a rabbit, before *Pie Face* and *Kind Heart* – a Good Robber and a Bad Robber grab our attention. That's Con Kenna, without his flying suit, and JH Graham. There's the outlawing of *Robin Hood* – that's Neta Underwood's dashing principal boy. He has declared his love for *Maid Marion*. Then comes the abduction of the *Babes,* and a sojourn by *Wilhelmina's Cottage* before visiting the mighty *Palace of Robin, Earl of Huntingdon*. Everyone appears in the happy finale.[30]

Billy Mayerl   Ralph Reader   Sir Emile Littler
(Author's Collection)

For the Houston Sisters, it was like coming back to where they had started. It was a great highlight of their career, and Billie would say many times after, how this was the type of show she and Renée loved the most. They could appear as children but invert this and tell adult jokes. Of course, if it were a matinee day, when all the kids were there, they kept the jokes mild. Douglas Byng recalled that the children still laughed at the jokes for the grown ups and curiously refers to there being more than one occasion when they had to dislodge Renée from the curtain, rescuing her from mid air at the finale while the orchestra was playing.[31] The mind boggles as to what she was playing at. The Sisters always got a fantastic reaction when the 'all star brighter pantomime' played twice daily at 2 pm and 7 pm.

Renée's start to 1936 saw a continuation of the twelve shows a week for *Babes* in Birmingham. So popular was this pantomime that excerpts appeared on the wireless on January 17. Performer and writer Clarkson Rose paid tribute to Billie a great 'feed', and remarked how Renée 'adlibs to her heart's content,' having 'one over the eight' in a drinking scene with Billie' – which was going a bit too far.[32] Rose refers to a scene when Billie slips her hand down *Wilhelmina Whackster*'s stocking to produce a hidden bottle of alcohol which the two *Babes* proceed to get drunk on. Was it right to go against pantomime tradition? Too much comic improvisation raised eyebrows and puritanical observers thought the Sisters had got drunk for real. 'We definitely weren't drunk', Renée assured Mavis Nicholson in an interview years later.[33] One youngster watching the pantomime was Ian

Messiter, who would recall forty four years later that *Babes* was the occasion he first came under Renée's spell. Shirley Houston was in *Babes* at the same time - in Frutin's production at the Edinburgh Empire, with Tommy Morgan and Peter Sinclair. Was the *Horse and Hiccup* an Anglo-Scots brewery?

Miss Houston's next port of call, on February 2, was Columbia Recording Studios, where with Pat Aherne and Henry Hall's Band she made a Gramophone record of her sketch 'True to me' - this version benefitting from special quips reserved for her real-life husband. There's a hilarious denouement – identifiably *James Houston and Company* territory: the sort Renée had grown up with. That special inheritance explains her natural expertise stepping between dialogue and song with her husband, as feed. Other musical sketches survive in print and on gramophone record. In 'I Do (A Song Under Difficulties)'[34] - the song on the other side of 'True to me' Renée demonstrates what a beautiful voice she has but suddenly stops for a patter session with *Nicky* and explains she's just bought the song and paid a bloke a fiver for it. *Nicky* isn't impressed and says it sounds cheap.

Nicky: Couldn't you sing something with a little class in it?
Renée: What would you like?
Nicky: What about an aria by Schubert?
Renée: That's what you get for marrying a Varsity man.
 What were you? Oxford or Selfridge?[35]

A little later Henry Hall's band get on her side against Nicky –sounding like a Greek chorus. '*He knows nothing*' repeat the band several times in unison.

Renée: Now listen you boys, what's the point of butting in when a husband and wife are having a barney!
 You might do something to help me - you being so fond of collaborating.[36]

Tunefully, she sings a line, and a SFX is provided by *Nicky*. He's delightfully deadpan whilst he produces the latest ruinous noise to accompany her.

Renée: (Sings) Every morn I hear the birdies singing, I do. [Birdie song]
Renée: Say what's the meaning of this?
Nicky: I'm trying to help you.
Renée: Giving me the bird right in the middle instead of at the end?
Renée: And the village church bells they start ringing, for you. [hooting car horn]
Renée: Say what's the idea?
Nicky: Church bells.
Renée: (Sings) My idea of a family is one or two or three or four or more.
 Don't you think you better to stop me boys - haven't I had enough?
 Oh, Please believe me when I say I love you. Yes honey I do.[37]

She was at London's Park Lane Hotel - guest of honour at a Lady Ratling's dinner on February 16, then Pat whizzed her and the kids to Birmingham. Just two days later, a friend called the theatre with news that entry to their Glendale Avenue home had been broken, and the place was ransacked. Robbers had forced the garage door allowing access to the study via a connecting door. All you could see were dressing table drawers scattered all over the floor and wardrobes torn open. The thieves had made off with the best items in Renée and Pat's wardrobe, not hesitating to add to their haul the silver spoons Renée had sentimentally collected for each of her children – a horrible inversion of the *Robbers* and *Babes* story if ever there was. Renée felt the violation with recurring thoughts as to what kind of person could do such a thing - something other victims of burglary will appreciate. For the first time in her career she couldn't summon up the old Houston resilience to go on, and needed a week off from *Babes*. The headline 'Renée Houston Has a Breakdown' drew people's attention in the Daily Mirror the following day.

Then, just a week later the hands of Fate swung, and depression subsided when, on February 26, 1936 she signed with British Lion, the film company owned by the Smith Brothers who took over management of her earlier contract with Fellner. This was good news: a three-picture deal that Renée calls a 'three year film contract'. This big money deal guaranteed her 'fifteen weeks filming each year at a truly exciting salary' subject to an annual increase. Telling this to her fans in newsprint and calculating how much she would make by 1938 based on 'annual increase only,' Renée comes across as horribly arrogant. She concludes she shall be forced to save because she won't be able to spend all the money coming to her.

For the time being, Renée, with hair a new shade of yellow gold, was back doing turns at the Brixton Empress for the week commencing March 23 1936. *'Nicky'* - not her husband on this occasion - but Nicky Kidd, assisted the 'Star of the Moment' and her other assistant was *'Tony.'* If this wasn't the other Kidd brother, I expect her five year-old son was brought on stage for a short while. It's strange that the Kidd brothers didn't bill themselves. She did her relentless *Something Spanish* routine, and was glad to be back with friends. They included Jack Doyle - *Film Star Boxer with the Golden Voice* with his wife Judith Allen. There was Neilson & Hagen - Two Old Salts, *The Three Romps - Crazy Acro-Lassies*, Bert Weston -'idioto inebriate' and Rex Roper and Maisie – *The World's Only Juvenile Lariat and Stock Whip Experts.* Variety always meant colourful company. A Fleet Street theatre correspondent laughed at the way the 'comedy bombshell' told him a while back she was 'through with the variety stage,' having no home life, telling readers 'it is our gain that Renée cannot quite bring herself to say farewell.' She was on the air on the National Programme's *Variety* on Saturday 28 March with Tessie O' Shea and Flotsam and Jetsam. She had just survived some unpleasant business in Edinburgh I'll describe in the next chapter.

Summer 1936 was a high water mark for all three Houston Sisters in their separate capacities. At Chiswick Empire, in September 1936, despite physically towering over Billie, Shirley was receiving praise in the new Houston Sisters act. It was different in style to the one with Renée but The Era said they came out 'with flying colours.'[38] Billie and Renée individually got on to the front cover of *Radio Pictorial* showing their popularity as radio stars at this time.

Renée by then, was *Kirstie Cameron* in the provincial tryout of Jack Waller's new musical comedy *Certainly Sir* at the Royal, Birmingham. Book and Lyrics were by RP Weston and Bert Lee. This was the third in a trilogy of shows. The first two were *Yes Madam* and *Please, Teacher* - successes for Bobby Howe. Sally McBride was one of *Certainly Sir's* twenty-four dancers, but she had to pull out to have an appendicitis operation. A picture shows everyone on stage in fancy dress, with women in medieval gowns and hennins, a pirate, a Valkyrie, a court jester, and a matador. Whilst a headline states that London musical shows were now bringing in £20,000 a week, after this one moved to the London Hippodrome on September 17, it only ran to twenty performances. The most interesting thing about *Certainly Sir* was the fact that Ralph Reader choreographed it. He pioneered the *Gang Show* - the phenomenon encouraging Boy Scouts to stage their own variety shows – a trend continuing to this day. He also led community singing at FA Cup Finals. He choreographed a delightful *Dresden china* ballet and burlesque-ballet of *Nelson and Britannia* for *Certainly Sir.* A smattering of Tchaikowsky, Smetana, Offenback, and Chopin accompanied these scenes.

The idiotic plot goes something like this: *Peter Pomeroy* - Carl Bernard is so in love with madcap *Kirstie* - socialite daughter of a Scottish Elder, that he falls into a cataleptic fit on seeing her. *Kirstie* has a 'corpse' on her hands at the fancy dress ball at the *Lanchester Hotel. Sebastian Withers* - Mackenzie Ward is also in love with her and helps her push the corpse on wheels to *Sebastian*'s house, lay it out on the billiard table and instruct *Hepplewhite*, his butler, to get rid of it.

As *Kirstie Cameron*
Certainly Sir
London Hippodrome
Summer 1936
(Aherne Family)

England's *Prime Minister of Mirth* - George Robey, played the butler – in reality part of a gang of crooks. He seeks to blackmail his master. *Sebastian*, fearing a police enquiry, takes *Kirstie* and her friends for a holiday on his yacht. Through the agency of *Lavinia Skindle*, the butler's past become known to *Kirstie*, enabling her to turn the tables on him. There were a few good numbers like 'I'm Forty' – the chirpiest number in the show, which Robey sang with a chorus of parlour maids and 'I'm not surprised, I'm amazed' - a song that gave him a new catchphrase. Mackenzie Ward and Renée had good number in 'We're a pair' and everyone sang 'Dip with the Ship'. In the final scene the corpse (that had looked like a floppy Guy Fawkes wheeled across the stage) suddenly turns up alive and throws another fit.

Something about the 'three comic' experiment didn't work with Robey, Houston and Mackenzie Ward who were seemingly disconnected. Miss H seemed subdued. Robey couldn't get intimate with the audience. His typical 'Don't encourage me' Robeyisms were absent until just before the interval. The principals jarred when together. Critics thought they were called on to make bricks without straw and complained that there was hardly a funny line in it. James Agate suggested that 'that ferociously witty mastiff, Mr Douglas Furber,' who brought magic to *More Dam Things* a year or so earlier, be at once 'unchained, and let loose upon the book.'[39] The Hippodrome audience was unforgiving. Robey came to a line in the script: 'This is the worst moment of my life' and he knew what was coming when the gods shouted 'It is!' On the first night, at the fall of the curtain, boos were heard from a section of the audience.

A little sophisticated advertising wouldn't go amiss to make up for this loss of face. 'I know something about Perfumes,' ventured Miss Renée Houston about compact perfume *Aziadé*, 'and *this* is good.' She's more convincing in her chic telling *Swan Down* products how she and Billie were 'fastidious with regard to our stage makeup only using the best of everything.'[40] Billie, meanwhile, was polishing off with *Kraska* nail varnish, telling Radio Pictorial readers she preferred 'the quieter mellow shade of rust' in the country.

When it came to film make-up, Renée had an aversion to one side of her face being touched. She told reporter Dorothy Drake that make-up men thought she was crazy allowing only one side of her face to be made up. Perhaps she knew what did and didn't work under lights better than anyone. Dorothy felt she had a weird complex about her looks, feeling this was 'all wrong as she is undeniably pretty.' The Houston Sisters certainly suited the camera lens, being small featured facially.

Early photos show Renée's big expressive eyes, look of mischief and dark auburn hair. Her face was pure theatrical clay, alternating from very pretty to odd-looking. She told interviewer Herbert Harris that, as a little girl, her parents made many jokes about her, especially the gap between her front teeth that was characterful. Renée suffered awful toothaches on and off for a long time when she was young. Information about tooth decay wasn't so prevalent if you grew up in the early 20th century. In the 30s the answer was more often to have teeth pulled out than maintain original teeth. It happened to Renée and countless others, and she had to lose one or two front teeth in the late 1930s. She had new dentures around 1939, and the gap-toothed look was gone forever. Alan remembered seeing an advert which went over the entire side of a London bus with his mother's smiling face '*Did you Maclean your teeth?* That gave Renée a transformed new look and ushered in her new glamour. She wore this new look very well, and was probably relieved to shed her little fool image of the 30s.

She used to tell people she studied ballet when she was very young. This was true and she loved to go en pointe. Many people who met Renée said she had the tiniest pair of feet they had ever seen. At the time of Herbert Harris's interview, a man came to the door of her Stanmore home, trying to sell her silk stockings. He measured her feet out of curiosity because he too, had never seen feet so small. She also had the young gene. Photos from the early days of the Houston Sisters show an uncannily youthful Renée Houston. Her childish pose could indeed make you mistake her for a ten year old – well sometimes, anyway. Billie too, had a baby face. 'You've got to make an effort with your looks' Renée told interviewer Gwen Robyns in 1949, removing all her war paint to let the young journalist comment on her face *au naturel*. What was beneath the makeup were 'two genuine dimples, and very few telltale lines,'[41] which the journalist found amazing considering the hardworking life she had had. At thirty she looked about fifteen. She looked sleeker, even younger, as the years went on. She was lucky in this respect.

So many people who have spoken about Renée, either in interviews or in press reports, say how little interest she had in the beauty she once was or the success she once had. People commented that she had no discernible vanity. It would have been something of a joke to her, to be known for her looks only. Apart from 1926's 'Book of Beauty' - something she didn't instigate, you seldom saw Renée exclusively using her looks as a currency. In the early 30s Miss Houston's version of the *'Clara Bow'* look was eclipsed by a movie star look of sleek yellow gold hair falling in soft waves to her shoulders. With her bright blue eyes, she had a passing resemblance to the German-British actress Lilian Harvey. Is that why Renée and Billie are the *Harvey Sisters* in 'Happy Days Are Here Again'? There's a photo of Pat Aherne visiting Renée on the set of this film. Renée looks like *Tinkerbell*, perched cross-legged on top of a wicker basket, whilst Pat rests a knee on the basket leaning over her while she gazes at him lovingly, and touches his arm. Renée is in the white dress she wears in her *'Dope'* scene minus the black ribbon trimmings. Her hair is ringletted and she wears a lot of make-up. To refer to Herbert Harris's 1938 interview, he tells us that one day in her dressing room at the theatre she received a phone call from a famous sculptor who asked her to sit for him. He told Renée he was opening an exhibition *'The Most Beautiful Women in London'* and wanted to do a bust of her. Of course, she gave an excuse. She couldn't believe he could be being serious.

With her over-the-top eyelashes and overdone makeup, if she did glamour it was mostly for laughs. In the late 30s when teamed with Donald Stewart on the stage, she began to look and act extremely glamorous. Still, she summoned up a parody of glamour and not far below the surface was the scrawny self-deluded girl from the backcourt. While modest about her looks until the end of her career, she was not afraid of keeping step with youth by studying every pretty girl she met. She had good models in Lilli Palmer, Audrey Hepburn and Sophia Loren, all of whom she worked closely alongside. She would later cringe at the way she was photographed for television. Wanting to look her best in 1971's 'Carry On At Your Convenience' she waived her aversion to one side of her face being touched, nominating young actress Jacki Piper to take responsibility for applying a piece of sellotape to either jawline to provide a little 'lift.' Jackie told me she adored Renée and felt privileged, remembering Renée as someone blessed with good looks even before this treatment. By the mid 70s Renée had no vanity.

> Mavis Nicholson: You were very pretty!
> Renée: Look at me now – pretty awful![42]

Her stage clothes needed to express her exhibitionist side. For stage or studio young Renée favoured brilliant colours like jade green, blue, and cyclamen mauve. At twenty-seven, a French reporter described her as 'skinny-looking in a flounced green dress' with 'white complexion and red hair.' At thirty-four, although the red hair and flounces were gone, she was still bold about clothes. Her son Alan told me his mother was friendly at one time with the famous fashion designer Schiaparelli. He recalls seeing the designer among a party of his mother's friends who regularly came to see her at the theatre. Renée would sometimes say to him that *Schiap* named her perfume *'Shocking'* after her. It's not a recorded fact in *Schiap* histories. It's one of the little Houston legends that might or might not be true. I believe it because Renée embodied the designer's vision. 'I was the first woman in London to wear a purple lipstick and in fact started the fashion in Paris in 1935'[43] is a similar legend I don't altogether rule out.

'I always wear freak clothes,' she told reporter Verity Clare. 'I don't like plain things ... No personality. I like unusual, rather exotic models; they suit my type.' She goes on to say how she designed all her dresses, taking a rough sketch to costume designer Lou Brooks who made all her important gowns and knew just what suited her. Once well known for his theatrical designs, Brooks is sadly forgotten now. Alan recalls that one dress by Brooks cost 200 guineas and his father was none too happy with the expense. Even if she was on the radio, a great outfit was all-important. 'My rule for the studio is look as smart as you can. It always makes you feel good to be well dressed and that feeling's bound to come over the air to your listeners'[44] was her line.

Those 'freak' clothes were really the stuff of dressing rooms as she dressed down at home. Some of her early 30s outfits in her personal wardrobe look unflattering. Later in the decade she had a wardrobe full of chic black clothes. A reporter caught up with Renée when she was travelling by train with Donald Stewart to a Film Ball at Derby after an appearance in Nottingham, finding her 'as charming in person as she was on air.' She also remarked how 'unspoiled' Miss Houston was: 'Her dress was exceedingly simple and smart. She wore a slim black satin skirt, and a little tight jacket blouse with tiny puffed sleeves made of a sprigged thick white satin.'[45] Even if she dressed down, her son Alan remembers people coming out of shops to look at her if he walked down a street in London with her.

Chapter 15   Kidnapped

A large picture of Renée's smiling face advertised *Kensitas Costlier Tobaccos* with written testimony that the wrappings of this brand were so 'moisture-controlled' your packet would still be in 'perfect smoking condition' left in a bowl of water for ten minutes - watertight words from one who seldom smoked. She seldom drank too, for that matter. Not then. Cigarettes had yet to gain a bad press in April 1936 although Professor Ernest Kennaway, director of the Institute of Imperial Cancer Research, had just proposed a potential link between smoking and lung cancer. When Digby d'Avigdor organized a charity luncheon at the same Institute, HRH the Duke of York and Archbishop Lang, brother of actor Matheson Lang, were VIPs. Renée's star presence was called for and the future King George VI signed Renée's lunch card '*To Renée from Albert*'. Such a shame this memento got thrown away years later, along with so many of Renée's possessions. She had recently spoken to HRH on November 14, 1935 after a cabaret at Claridges. 'Believe me folks,' she told fans soon after, 'he's a very nice fella! And I'm not the only Scotswoman who seems to think that our royal princes are a bit of all right. Two out of four have taken their wives from North of the Tweed - and one of them has still to vote.'[1] She was ever the royalist.

Pat and Renée
(Renée's scrapbook: Family of Terry Long)

Cigarette advert

Empire Palace Theatre, Edinburgh
(My thanks to Bob Bain)

Sid Field
(J.Lewis Family)

The London Casino[2] was complete after a renovation and doors were open, whetting the taste for a more exciting West End. But for Miss Houston it was Edinburgh's palatial Empire Palace Theatre[3] she was heading, and high time *Leicester Square Looks Round* as producer George Black might have it, given that this was the name of his new revue. The revue had been touring almost a year in the English provinces and a sketch entitled '*1945: a vision of the future*' predicted women working and men remaining at home with comic Sid Field host at a male gossip party. Sid took it to Glasgow and Renée and the Kidd Brothers joined in Edinburgh. Here the stage was immense - big enough to hold ice shows. The Festival Theatre nowadays seats 3000 and still draws a gasp when darkness slowly turns to light and mirrors reflect a gilt circus of riders, nymphs, Nubians and cherubs. In 1936 William Henshall was the Empire's proprietor and James Rutherford Hill - known as Jimmy Hill - was its manager. All the way to 1962, Jimmy would stand in the foyer welcoming patrons.

Renée had a curious dream the night previous to April 28 1936 - which happened to be Billie's thirtieth birthday. 'I dreamt', she would tell a reporter, 'I was being chased over cliffs by men, one of whom had a knife. I wakened with a scream.'[4] Tuesday April 28 was also an uncomfortable day for my grandmother in Dennistoun in the East End of Glasgow. It was the day before my father came into the world and strange things passed through her mind too – crafted images of beauty just like that publicity photo of Valentino in 'Monsieur Beaucaire' she kept for some reason til the day she died. Among the unfolding events making headlines in the big wide world were the finance scandal shaking Austria, *Il Duce's* decision to crown Italy's king as Emperor of Abyssinia, and the imminent visit of *'Golden Gloves'* - an American boxing troupe - soon to disembark at Plymouth. Students at Edinburgh University were also about to throw down their textbooks and let off steam for their annual *Rag Week*.

Renée and the Kidds were breaking in the new show and appeared in *Leicester Square Looks Round's* running order twice, their turns separated by an hour. She had played the Empire with Billie in *More Dam Things* a year previously and expected a lukewarm reception with the Scots so used to the interplay between the Houston Sisters. Some 'mouth' was bound to ask where Billie was, She buoyed herself, thinking of her film contracts, but audience reactions mattered more than weighing things up in business terms. Superstitions connected to George and Billie lingered at the back of her mind. Putting worries to one side that evening, she joked about how soon she would wreck her gown on stage. It wasn't worth stepping into that Lou Brooks dress - not until the callboy shouted 'on in five'.

How murderous intervals are! In those airless dressing rooms you're a Jack-in-the-Box before you're 'on'. Nicky Kidd was with her, polite and complimentary, no matter how many times he'd heard the jokes or seen her repeat the same pose. Just at that moment the Huns invaded Paris. All of a sudden dozens of boisterous young men filled the Empire. A central core of rugby-players and rowdy chums forced their way into the theatre's stage door from the normally silent side passage leading there. Two of them managed to tie up stage doorkeeper John Ferrier in his office while others guarded the vestibule, making sure one side of the exit door was tied with rope preventing anyone bolting the door from the inside. The star of the show was the barbarians' target. Vulnerable indeed was this modern Saint Geneviève. Lots of heavy footsteps and voices followed, and an intimidating male voice outside the room thundering 'Come on we want you!' There was an ugly declaration of 'Right now boys' and Renée, in suspended belief, asked Nicky to see if this was a fight outside the door. It was, as Sid Field learned - receiving a thump in the face, as he tried to intervene. Nicky opened the door only for a gangly testosterone-filled twenty-three year-old stranger to push his way in. Nicky protested and was forcibly held back, dreading what was going to happen to Renée. He really believed she was in danger with more thugs pushing their way into the dressing room. Showing immense bravery, Renée told them she wasn't going anywhere. She tried tough words, remonstrating, shouting, and struggled to resist, kicking and slapping the aggressor now manhandling her. It really was a performer's worst nightmare - especially for the jittery Miss H. Very quickly she was being lifted off her seat and carried outside. Two young men told Jimmy Hill they would not return her until he paid £23 towards their charity.[5] The humiliation wasn't so dissimilar to that teachers would experience dragged out of University campuses by Cultural Revolutionaries in China in the late 60s.

What on earth was happening? Her dignity at stake, she began sobbing and crying out "Daddy, Daddy," hysterical with fear and unaware of the volume of her voice. She was bundled out of the theatre into a car sideways through the window and Mrs Lowe of Lothian Street witnessed all from a ground floor window. She caught Renée's eye. 'Don't let them take me. Don't let them take me!' came the plaintive cry. Rushing to the actress, Mrs Lowe clung to her but was thrown aside leaving the actress in a state of fear and dread. The raiders and their plunder only got a short distance to West College Street, when, unexpectedly, the driver turned on his companions: 'I thought this was a gag - I'm not going to drive you to the house you mentioned.' To this, he received a smack, and was told to drive on.

Renée, maximizing the opportunity this interruption created, courageously grabbed the steering wheel so the car stopped with a jolt at the kerb. Her attackers must have decided to give up because she was able to free herself. She rushed back to the theatre in her bra and knickers. The sight was so outrageous that one of her pursuers actually came running after her and threw a blanket over her for modesty's sake. Reaching the Empire, she collapsed. Henshall ensured a strict police watch on the artiste's dressing room and of the street to the rear of the theatre fearing a repeat kidnapping. Officers patrolled Potter Row in the vicinity of the stage door entrance.

I've stitched together as much detail as I can about events as they unfolded before a trial eventually took place. On Wednesday April 29 Chief Constable Morren took statements at the theatre while a doctor, James Deuchars, examined Renée. The results of an X-ray revealed a day or so later that one of her ribs was broken.

The incident was all over the papers with speculation about prosecutions of the young men responsible. At first the *Rag Week* kidnappers looked like they'd get off with a rap over the knuckles when a letter signed by William Henshall, James R. Hill and Miss Houston was sent to Sir Thomas Holland - University Principal asking that the culprits be dealt with leniently:

> 'We, the undersigned, would like to take this opportunity of communicating our thoughts . . . we feel that, as a great number of students participated, we would not like to see the victimization of certain individuals. . . . the incident is over, and we are sure that the students concerned in this outrage must be extremely repentant. We are thinking of the future of these youths.'[6]

This show of forgiveness is extraordinary. However, Henshell had instructed his solicitor to issue a writ of damages against the University's Student Representative Council (SRC) for 'losses' suffered by the theatre. Recouping costs was on his mind, especially since the second half of the show did not go ahead on the Tuesday. They received an instant apology from Holland who stated that Miss Houston's 'generosity would not relieve the university authorities from dealing with the students who carried out a raid of such a stupid nature.' JM Mathieson, speaking for the SRC, made it known that the students' action had no official connection with *Charities Week*, deprecating their conduct. He hoped no victimization of individuals would follow.

Pat Aherne, rushing to his wife's side, answered press question growlingly, telling them he considered this one of the 'most astounding cases of hooliganism'[7] he had ever encountered, describing how his wife was black and blue all over. A second VIP apology came from the City Council's Lord Provost Gumley who telephoned Pat. Casting doubt on those who believed a fall out had occurred between the Houston Sisters, Billie immediately jumped on a plane to Edinburgh. On arrival, she had barely taken off her coat when the press asked her opinion. She was horrified. She found her sister in a terrible state and later on gave her no holds barred opinion:

Billie: That experience in Edinburgh might have killed her. I was shocked. So was everybody. Shameful business. Sons of gentlemen they were. They were fined 5 pounds apparently and Renée Houston is still suffering from nerves and hysteria.[8]

On April 30 the story broke in Canada, Australia, France and apparently Russia and China. Le Journal wrote about '*Le Beau Courage De Renée Houston -la comédienne kidnappée*' who had been admitted to hospital following an ordeal. Various members of the British press, as well as members of the SRC were received at the hotel by a solemn Miss Houston: 'I am sorry I look like this,' her fragile voice began, 'but I can hardly lift my head. I've sprained my ankle and look at my arms!' She listed her injuries: ribs – in plaster of Paris, claw marks on her legs, a strike to her mouth. To be bundled into a car was awful for someone who suffered from claustrophobia. Pat Aherne, at her bedside, added how a doctor needed to administer a sedative. Renée's statements fluctuated from the vengeful: 'If my husband knew the true facts he would set fire to the university' - to the conciliatory: 'I don't want to punish a lot of schoolboys,' and she carefully stressed "I had good reason to be afraid and in a panic at what happened to me.' Yet, in order that good causes should not suffer because of the action of a few irresponsible individuals, she said she was happy to appear at the students' charity ball at the Eldorado, Leith. By the end of that day however, Henshell flatly forbade any member of his company attending, saying they'd risk breaking their contract if they did. John McGovern, parliamentary member for Renée's hometown, Shettleston, made public his plans to address the House of

Commons with a formal question the following Tuesday. What stance should be taken under the law regarding the actions of fundraisers who molest innocent people in achieving their charitable aims?

Life went on for a few days with Renée appearing at the theatre each night amidst applause, saying to her audience 'I am not in my best form but I hope you will forgive me. The wee bit of me that is left will sing.' Wisecracks included asking if there were any respectable students still left. An incredible seventy students confessed to the kidnapping. On Friday May 1 the University's Principal had narrowed down the list of culprits to fifteen students. Now that Henshell had brought a prosecution case, the police - led by Superintendent Peebles, organized an ID parade so that John Ferrier, Henshall, and Reneé could identify ringleaders from a line of twenty students. Pat accompanied his wife, who wore a chic tartan coat and a hat with a black feather. After it was over with, Renée acted the minx, telling reporters how she'd met more handsome policemen than ever before.

That afternoon those students who had confessed talked to the press. They highlighted the negative effect it had had on *Charities Week*: 'Miss Houston took it seriously,' they suggested. 'We did not bargain for that. Hence our failure, and all this.'[9] The students pointed out that the theatre was much patronized by undergraduates who were known to the management and that the idea had been to kidnap Renée, hold her to ransom briefly, but to return her in time for her next call. They admitted it was a mistake not making the actress or anyone at the theatre party to the idea. In the heat of the moment they didn't see how genuine her protest was.[10]

The following Monday Renée and the Kidd Brothers went on at Chelsea Palace[11] alongside Bruce Bairnsfather and Donald Peers. She also had a week's work at Café de Paris: her salary reportedly $500 a night for the one-number nightly appearance. 'My nerves are still shot to bits,' she told a Fleet Street reporter on May 4. Back in Edinburgh the SRC reps were striking back after their meeting on May 5, when a motion was carried to seek legal advice, believing press reports about the whole episode were exaggerated. A charge as to the *'illegal purpose of securing custody of Miss Houston, and forcibly detaining her until payment of £25 paid'* had been made against three students: John Roderick Mackay Johnston, Kenneth Brauer, and Walter Edward Scott - each pleading 'Not guilty' at Edinburgh Sheriff Court. Sheriff Jameson postponed the case for six weeks in order to avoid interference with the students' professional examinations and a trial was fixed for July 16. In the meantime a bail of £5 each was allowed. Scott, an art student at Edinburgh University, had his charge dropped a few days before the trial.

On Tuesday May 5, in the House of Commons, John McGovern asked the Lord Advocate, TM Cooper if his attention had been drawn to the 'violent assault on Renée Houston at an Edinburgh theatre, where she was dragged from her dressing-room, forced into a waiting motor car by Edinburgh students, that she suffers from injuries to her body and was left in a hysterical condition of collapse; He asked whether he will take steps to ensure that the law will be set in motion against the persons responsible for this outrage?' The Lord Advocate answered the question:

> Yes, Sir. I have already taken action with regard to this regrettable occurrence, two persons having been apprehended and brought before the Sheriff on Saturday, and a third on Monday. The number of persons who may be implicated directly or indirectly is considerable, and, pending completion of the police investigations now in progress, I am not in a position to decide what further action may be necessary. [12]

McGovern thanked him, suggesting that police authorities might be instructed to see that persons are not embarrassed, molested, insulted or assaulted when they aren't inclined to 'contribute to funds in the way that has been done in the public streets of our cities?' A further question was asked by sixty year-old MP Alfred Denville:

> May I ask the right hon. Gentleman whether it is considered satisfactory that, in a case of this sort, the accused should be offered a £5 bail, and whether he is also aware that in any other country but this, kidnappers would be taken to the nearest lamp-post and strung up?[12]

I can hear the titters from the backbenches and it's no surprise that Denville himself was an actor and impresario who ran a repertory company and founded Denville Hall – an actor's retirement home in London's Northwood. He was also a leading member of the General Franco-friendly *Friends of National Spain*. MP for Newcastle-upon-Tyne Central, he lost his seat in 1945.

Renée's experience in Edinburgh prompted friends in variety to rally around her more than ever and she, Judith Allen and Jessica Merton were initiated as Lady Ratlings on Sunday May 2, 1936. Annie Jones was *Queen Ratling* at this time the ceremony was held at the Comedy Restaurant. The Stage on May 7 had a small cartoon[13] of an old man reading a newspaper: '*What's a Rough-Hoose mean?*' asks a little kid looking over his shoulder. '*Och, treating Miss Houston rough ye ken.*' The entire stage profession seethed with resentment at the victimization of one of their own by privileged medical students who the columnist said 'should be medically studied for the benefit and enlightenment of us lesser mortals.' They were third year medical students too. The 'bowing and scraping' in Edinburgh, and the 'poundsworth of bail' dished out to them was considered pretty poor. However, he had praise for the hard work of the police on May 21, adding 'It is good to know there is still one law for the poor and the rich alike.'[13]

A week later Renée's cheek was shown to be undiminished. She 'travelled' into the auditorium at Hackney Empire, making references to students, Scotland and damaged ribs. The events would be subject to a greater level of analysis at the Sheriff's court. The way the Defence vindicated the accused is fascinating, and the same could be said for the unexpected way in which public opinion in Edinburgh turned against the variety star. On Thursday July 16 Miss Houston stepped out of a taxi wearing a light fur coat. She removed her large hat, using it as a shield to cover her face from photographers as she dashed into the courtroom with her husband in tow. A picture in Paris Soir shows one accused student walking down the street with his lawyer covering his face with a newspaper. All appeared before Sheriff Jameson. Charges were defined as 'assault' on Miss H and John Ferrier - stage doorkeeper, as well as the charge of 'forcible detention' of Nicky Kidd.

Neil MacLean KC and JR Philip defended John Roderick Mackay Johnston, who admitted he was the ringleader and the one shouting 'Come on we want you' outside the dressing room. James Gilchrist KC and RH Sherwood-Calver defended Kenneth Brauer - a South African in the university's rugby team. He was the one who carried Renée out into the street. Peter McNeal was another medical student who had set up the early meetings to arrange the kidnapping. David Watson, a veterinary student, said he thought Renée was acting when she was shouting "Daddy, Daddy" in her hysterical fashion. These two students were not aware Renée had actually escaped the car and had returned. Another medical student, Hugh Stanton Purvis, told the court about a hand wave they used as a signal to let those outside know Miss Houston was off the stage. Dr Deuchars gave testimony of the bruises on the arms and legs of the actress, her lacerated upper lip, and the shock she had suffered. Jimmy Hill and the stage door keeper were witnesses, the latter confirming they had had no previous warning of the students' plans, and that it was only after the mob arrived, demanding their £25 ransom, that these young men mentioned to him what a marvellous advertisement this would be for the theatre.

MacLean KC diminished the prosecution's case finding any way to question trust in the actress's version of events. He asked her if the bruise on her leg was not the bruise she had referred to during her show on the previous Monday. She had apparently said in her turn 'Look what I've done with the handle of the door.' She denied this had any connection. The exact manner in which the actress was handled was scrutinized. MacLean claimed Brauer carried the actress out of the dressing room in a reasonable fashion, handling her in a way to make her safer. MacLean indicated the students were justified in ignoring her hysterical reaction, thinking she was just acting a role. He made a case that Renée's claustrophobia made her exaggerate and say things were far worse than they were. His strongest card was questioning her 'unawareness' that it was *Rag Week*, arguing that George Formby, Arthur Lacey and Valerie Tudor were artists famously kidnapped in the past by students in Liverpool. He told the court his client had told Renée this was the case, and had asked her to come quietly.

On questioning witness Mrs Lowe, MacLean asked 'Was she scantily dressed?' receiving a 'Yes Sir, she was,' and the lady stated how, when she told the boys to leave Renée alone, they replied 'Get out of the road and mind your own business.' Renée was in the box nearly an hour. Cross-examined by MacLean, she was reported as causing considerable amusement by answering questions in the pawky Scots accent characteristic of her variety performances. Outspoken as ever, she twice complained of the attitude adopted by members of the court.

James Adair acted as prosecution, stressing to the court that his client did not know her kidnappers were students, let alone that it was *Rag Week*. She spoke to the court herself. She thought the students were a gang of toughs. They seemed to spring from everywhere. It was like a rugby scrum. She denied that her claustrophobia made her imagine this, declaring she had 'the greatest memory in the world.' She had never heard of it happening to her fellow artists. She adding that being the good sport she was she would have put on her dressing gown and gone with them 'if they had told me what they were doing.'[14] She admitted there was no smell of drink about the men, but said they used filthy language. She told the court she felt in great fear of serious assault. Checking her words she admitted she told one young man: 'If you kick me again I will hit you on the *something* mouth.' MacLean picked up on this and pursued a line that her own filthy language met the filthy language of her intruders, forcing Adair to ask her what was that *something*? Miss Houston had to tell him and the court. Gasps of horror!

At the end of the trial, the Sheriff Court dismissed the assault charges relating to the stage doorkeeper and the detention of Nicky Kidd. Mackay Johnston was fined £5, and Brauer £3. The mediocre fines were paid in court. A crowd outside, mostly women, had waited half an hour to see her but it wasn't to sing her praises. When Renée left the courtroom in the luncheon interval she was booed and hissed whilst the students were cheered. She was suddenly unpopular in Edinburgh. Policemen had to make way for the actress. She had to return there in 1938 as a subpoenaed witness and the case dragged on, due to the fact that the students were medical students. Again she got booed and hissed. She says she let the case go, which might indicate that at some point she had pressed charges despite her public statement of 'I forgive the boys.'

Local people were unhappy about the bad press *Charities Week* received but soon it became yesterday's news. Brauer graduated in 1938. Mackay Johnston graduated in 1940 becoming a Lieutenant in the Royal Army Medical Corps the following year.[15] Today little reference to the incident survives in the minutes of University Court and Senate or in the files of the University Secretary. Renée writes how, in 1942, when she invited a group of Scottish soldiers to visit her home, one was Walter Scott who confessed his shame to her. He turned out to be the driver who had refused to continue driving believing they'd gone too far and had received a thump for ruining things. Renée handed him a gold-enamelled cigarette case in gratitude. Tragically, it was returned to her a few months later by his regiment.

Perhaps as a means of preparing their duets for Renée's latest film 'Fine Feathers' she was at the Paramount Astoria, Tottenham Court Road, on May 18, partnered for the first time by her leading man in that picture, Donald Stewart. Bryan Michie - blonde Apollo of BBC radio - strove to get her for

Half An Hour With - the popular show he compèred. Bryan and John Watt had met Renée when she played a prominent role at the *Belfast Radio Exhibition* in October 1934. Later she did a floorshow at the Mayfair Hotel in which Bryan was a compère. She duly appeared alongside Ronnie Hill, and the BBC Variety Orchestra conducted by Charles Shadwell. Bristol born crooner Ronnie Hill, who composed music, had partnered Billie on stage as early as January 1936, and he might have introduced the Sisters to Donald Stewart, his fellow singer in Ambrose's band. Billie meanwhile, had her own show at Chatham and she made her first radio broadcast as an individual artist with an accompanist on violin and accordion. The Radio Times listing refers to her as 'you know- the 'Boy' one.' Billie was back on the air as guest comedienne in *Ladies Please* - an all-woman radio revue (apart from Ted Ray, who must have enjoyed being the male 'victim'). On July 7, 1936 at Shepherd's Bush Empire, Renée and Billie staged a *Reunion* saying how happy it was to be together again, receiving a fantastic response in return. Renée gagged and Billie sang a song. The two younger Houston Sisters were appearing in a new act, appearing on the bill with Billy Danvers and Jimmy James.

Renée was not the only family member to face a courtroom drama that year, with journalists hovering in the street to get a scoop. One night James Houston senior was in the bar at the Chiswick Empire chatting to a fan of his daughters. He took her and her friend to the dressing room to introduce them to Billie and Shirley. Later that evening he met one of these women at a local pub. They shared a train ride back to Wembley. A few days later Violet Evans brought a case against Jimmie, claiming he pushed her against a fence and kissed her during their walk from the station. She pushed him away and ran home. Waiting for Wealdstone Magistrates Court to pass a verdict, Lizzi and her three daughters waited four hours in a car parked outside. In the courtroom the sixty-one year-old apologized to Mrs Evans's husband, admitting he had had too much to drink that night. His lawyer JF Eastwood, an MP, made much of Jimmie's weak physical condition. Daddy Jimmie was quite possibly already suffering the effects of cancer. The case illustrates Jimmie's dependence on alcohol. Eastwood made the point that even a seven year-old child could resist any assault by his client. He suggested Mrs Evans had requested money from Mr Houston, and questioned why if she felt she had really suffered an offence, did she return to the theatre a few days later to pick up the signed photos she was promised? Jimmie was acquitted. Looking frail and ill he collapsed in his wife's arms and was kissed by his daughters.

Coverage of the kidnapping saga made Miss Houston more famous and talked about. People turned up to see her at her shows or switched on the radio to hear her broadcasts out of curiosity. Before 1936 a photo of one or other of the Sisters occasionally turned up in the national papers. A report might mention her saying goodbye to her husband on a station platform, or run a few lines about her latest film. Popular as the Sisters were, they weren't as newsworthy as titled debutantes, Hollywood stars or legit stage actors. Being featured on a humble cigarette card in a series like 1936's *'Radio Stars 2nd Series'* endorsed your celebrity status back then. If you were in politics, journalism or entertainment Pathé might also feature you in a cinema short – in a series like 'At Home With' or 'The Stars As They Are.' Ramsay MacDonald, TP O'Connor, Gracie Fields, Nellie Wallace, Tom Walls, and Tod Slaughter are a few of the 'names' who got this treatment.

Renée had been negotiating with several producers for her next West End show. For a while the theatrical press claimed she would appear alongside Stanley Holloway in *Du Barry* – a new operetta at the Lyceum, then came news she was paired with George Robey in a musical comedy Jack Waller was producing at London Hippodrome that Autumn. The filming of 'Fine Feathers' at Beaconsfield was now complete and she wanted to forget the claustrophobic nightmare of Edinburgh, and instead concentrate on her family, soon to be gathered together in a lovely new home in Stanmore, Middlesex. It would be a reunion with her two eldest, who had been staying with her parents the last couple of years. In the meantime, they were all having a summer holiday.

'Do pop in and see us when you're down Shoreham way,' she said, and filmmakers from the 'Empire Review' popped in and made the cinema short 'Renée Houston at home' in August 1936 coinciding with the holiday. Here we see the Houston family and friends enjoying candid moments sitting outside a beach bungalow. Renée and Pat had rented bungalows in Shoreham-by-Sea the last few summers. A gossip columnist had spoken about the 'nice little gift' Pat gave Renée for her birthday. Renée, busy filming, had to wait a few months to see what the 'little' gift was. It was a yacht and she christened it 'Mrs Pat.' The article tells how the words *'Mrs Patrick Aherne'* were not only engraved on her wedding ring but that all the china, glass and cutlery in the yacht had 'Mrs Pat' embossed on them with a shamrock.[16] Pat was proud both of his Irish heritage and his sea legs. He would get the most use out of this 'little gift'.

Pat Aherne the skipper, The 'Mrs Pat' (By kind permission of the Aherne Family)

Shoreham's 'Bungalow Town' was a theatrical colony famous long before Renée and Pat came to enjoy this shingle spit of West Sussex that had also inspired film pioneers with its crystal clear daylight and deserted solitude. American William Dickson visited in 1898 with the first viable 35mm movie camera (one he invented at the Edison research laboratory) and shot scenes of a typical English seaside, blazing a trail for others like scenic artist FL Lyndhurst who founded *Sunny South Film Company* and made a film on

Shoreham Beach in 1912. When the film colony grew staff lived on site in chalet homes – some with fronts and backs created from redundant train carriages sold off by the Lancing Railway Carriage Works. Marie Loftus - famous music hall singer, discovered Shoreham in 1905 building the first of her sea front bungalows. 'Pavlova', her final home here with its many bedrooms, was a showplace. Many famous theatre people followed: Florrie Forde, Marie Kendall, Ernie Mayne, Hetty King, the Melville family who owned the Lyceum Theatre, the Lupino family, and Gladys Cooper: choosing names for bungalows that were exotic or panto-inspired like 'Puss in Boots' or 'Sleeping Beauty'. Sports people like Sir Malcolm Campbell, Bombardier Billy Wells and jockeys from the Sussex Fortnight were also attracted here.[17]

A carefree nature and unique spirit had characterized it in its early years, and Shoreham was still an enchanted place where adults could forget their troubles. They were cut off from the road by the River Adur and the harbour to the north, with sea all the way south to Étretat. Fifty miles from the *Smoke* fresh clean air ruled. The older kids played games in and around the town's Victorian 'Fort' with Trevor carrying one of the wooden shields he'd painted with a blue cross. He led a gang of children carrying lamps at night. Alan Aherne recalls that they spent most of their holidays here – always very happy ones. Family and friends stayed two weeks at a time and the kids went out fishing in 'Mrs Pat'. Pat loved it so much here he suggested they should buy a small cottage and live in this part of the country permanently.

Shoreham, 1936: Clockwise: Pat Aherne, 'Pirate attack',
Terry and Tony with sheepdog, the Kidd brothers with Alan and Shirley (Aherne Family)

All four of Renée's kids are seen in the 'Renée Houston at home' film, looking a little awkward at times, apart from two year-old Alan on his mother's lap. They all look absorbed in the story Renée is reading them. I recognize George Balharrie sitting outside the house wearing a tie. Shirley, with a fag in her mouth, is seen when Renée mops the deck of their yacht. When Pat pops up out of the hold, he gets the worst of the mophead. Shirley had never been without a cigarette from the days she was as slim as a cigarette herself to when her figure was a fuller one in the 80s. That's young Trevor piloting 'Mrs Pat' and laughing at their antics. Tony Aherne is the little boy in the corner of the shot while his mum is seen showing off her size-one feet. Other people present, not in this film, were the Kidd Brothers and the children's nurse. I watched the *egg whisk* scene when Renée looks at the camera, winks and eats a strawberry, and wondered if she had ever touched an egg whisk, but Alan told me Renée was an excellent cook. She was ever inventive and one dish she excelled in, that everyone liked (apart from him), was grapes with fish, or Sole Véronique to give it its posh name.

Kidnapped

Top: Pat Aherne, skipper of the *Mrs Pat*; Below: Kathleen, Greta Alan; Renée with Alan, Tony and Trevor
(Photos: Aherne family)

I've never seen Pat look so relaxed as he does in a home movie taken of him as skipper as he and Claude Temple take the boat out to sea. Another time, accompanied by the three boys, he piloted 'Mrs Pat' along the coast of Shoreham-by-Sea to a town with a harbour wall of ancient stone. There were steps leading to a pub at the top of that wall that seemed to tower overhead like a castle. The boat would do brave service in the historic evacuation of Dunkirk in May-June 1940. The story goes that artist John Alexander Powell - a close friend of Pat's - took the boat out to help the evacuees, escaping shortly before it was shot out of the water by the Nazis. Either the entire boat was lost or the wreck of 'Mrs Pat' was broken up for parts. Even Pat's fishing tackle was requisitioned. When he made a return visit to England in the 60s the thing he most wanted to do was to see Shoreham again. Of course it had changed so much it was truly heartbreaking for him. Shortly after Dunkirk the army gave twenty-four hours notice then destroyed almost all the bungalows as they fortified the coast. 'Bungalow Town' suddenly ended - a casualty of war. Ugly concrete lookout posts were assembled at the sea front and change continued when other parts were cleared to make way for Shoreham Lido, itself demolished at a later date. Modern residential developments of Shoreham's quays sadly fail to captivate.

Alan's father shot many films with his Cine Kodak and made his own film of the family's holiday. The Aherne family kindly let me see the film. Pat is in front of the camera in a memorable scene. All four of Renée's kids are whispering and cooking up a plot. Above a stone rampart, stripped to the waist with a bandana around his head, Pat brandishes a bottle of rum. Realizing these diminutive 'Pirates of the Caribbean' are about to attack, he springs up to challenge them. Trevor, Terry, and Tony look intimidating with their false beards. Alan looks unaware it's a spoof. Pat is rowing away for his life at one point but soon the happy tribe is seen together, waving from a small boat. The red brick ramparts – parts of the old Shoreham Redoubt, are seen in the background of the picturesque home movie shot in colour.

In September 1936 Pat and Renée, and the four kids were living at '*Abbotswood,*' Uxbridge Road, Stanmore, surrounded by green open spaces and quiet tree-lined roads.[18] There was space for everyone plus a couple of guest bedrooms. Significantly, they were living somewhere brand new at a time when the majority of people lived in cramped properties, many in Victorian slums. '*Abbotswood*' boasted modern fireplaces, a layout that was enviably stylish, and fashionable decoration. It was rented for an annual sum of £170.00 - a reasonable £6,500.00 in today's money.

One room had that status symbol of 1938 - an HMV television in a polished wooden cabinet. Designed to vertically enclose a long cathode tube and reflect an image on the mirror lid, nobody remembered it ever working. There was a lawn and large courtyard out front and an extensive back garden with a tennis court and play areas. All this land gave a feeling of true luxury. Trevor and Terry had their own rooms and Tony and Alan shared. The two older kids dominated the adults' attention and Alan tells me he and Tony felt overshadowed to a degree. They all got on well, nevertheless.

Kathleen Murphy and her sister Greta (or Gretchen) were two Irish girls who had first lived with the Ahernes at Glendale Avenue. Greta, the boys' nurse, was employed initially then Kathleen came over from Ireland to be family cook. All the kids went on holiday to Ireland with the Murphy girls at different times. Kathleen's family came from Port Rush in Northern Ireland and Trevor and Terry went there on holiday in about 1938 – visiting her folks. Another time the two younger boys were taken to see the Giant's Causeway and also to County Cork, where they visited Blarney Castle. Kathleen, being quite a big girl, had to step down from the donkey cart.

The Hollywood-style glider at '*Abbotswood*' Renée, Kathleen and Donald, 1937.

On the reverse of the photo Don describes the sitters as 'Lily the Loser,' 'Katie the Conqueror' and 'Don Juan' (Family of Donald Stewart)

Left:
Kathleen at Terry's Wedding, 1944

Right:
Renée and Kathleen at '*Brighthampton*' in 1964
(Family of Terry Long)

Renée always enjoyed a good gossip with her servants and Pat used to tick her off believing she should be more distant. Terry's daughter believes that

Greta was like a mother to the children. The story might have been different with Tony. Seeing his old nurse when a member of the family showed him an old home movie, he apparently became very upset, saying how he didn't want to be reminded of *horrible Greta*. Kathleen, with her heavy brogue, was loud, jolly, and full of jokes. Seated between Renée and Donald in a photo on a 'glider' in the garden, Kathleen's lovable presence is obvious.

Some years later it emerged that Greta and Kathleen, each of whom had a steady boyfriend, had also been cooking the accounts and charging their boyfriends' coal to Renée. She ended up dismissing them for this reason - a difficult thing to do knowing how attached her children were to them, Alan most of all. The Murphys had been a big part of the family, and Kathleen would remain close to Terry. Kathleen was at Terry's Wedding in 1944, and after getting US residence visited her in Cincinnati in later decades, reminiscing about the old days at the Aherne home. Kathleen met up again with Renée in 1964 and a happy-looking photo indicates that they had put the past behind them. As late as the 1990s Kathleen's husband, Bob Gonzaga[19] was in regular touch by letter with Tony and Alan.

Other adults helped look after the two youngest boys now and again. Claude Temple's wife was called *Charles*. Claude and *Charles* were a constant presence in Pat's circle. They came to pick up Alan and Tony for lunch several times to help the boys' parents. Uncle George would visit. It's interesting that there should be a point in time when all three of Renée's husbands past, present and future, should be under one roof at *'Abbotswood'*. George Balharrie and his girlfriend would give young Alan a bath. There might be a visit from uncle Brian. He was very good at fixing things - the only adult with time to repair Alan's pedal car. Pat might have been the qualified engineer, but at home he was apt to suggest getting somebody in to do things rather than be a handyman himself. Alan tells me how as a child, he bonded with Brian over the pedal car, and arriving at Brian's home in California years later they continued where they had left off, on the later occasion repairing a piece of Brian's furniture.

Tony, Trevor, Alan and Terry Terry at 'Abbotswood' Kids loving their new home
(By kind permission of the family of Terry Long and the Aherne Family)

The childrens' friends were sometimes invited to tea. The kids were forbidden, however, from playing with the village children for fear that they might pick up a London dialect they would not be able to lose later on. Their parents were sincere about this. It's funny to think of it now, but it reflects the typical attitudes of the time. Speaking well signified getting a nice high-paying job. Renée and Pat were not alone in having this rule for their children and as film actors, they valued manner, dress and accent all the more. Tony spoke very well indeed but faced other pressures. When some of his peers discovered he was born illegitimate they cruelly teased him. Even though his parents married as soon as they were able to, Tony had a real hang-up about this.

At White Gate School on Elms Road, a short walk away, Alan remembers doing very well in handwriting and that the reward for this involved trotting up to the classroom upstairs to have some stars put into his exercise book. Terry was in that classroom wearing her green school dress and waved at him. Trevor, Terry, Tony and Alan all went White Gate School.[20] After White Gate, the boys went to Alquin House, a local prep school in Old Church Lane.[21] Because the war had just started school activities included crocheting individual squares with a hook and some yarn before passing these to the teacher who crocheted them together. These became blankets – handed over for army use when finished.

Outside of insisting that the kids develop posh accents, the boys' parents were not disciplinarians. Renée was likely to laugh when her children were naughty, encouraging them to be practical jokers. She might scare them into submission by her moods or tongue lashes but she didn't smack them. The only time Alan's Dad smacked him was when he was found kicking the glass-panelled doors that separated a very big room into two rooms. In the room beyond the glass panels were the stack of quality silverware and Sunday best dinner services given to his parents as presents. These items were interesting to examine, such as the box full of special cutlery all for the purpose of eating fish. Alan and Tony used to love to polish silverware like this, putting the special knives in order of their crests. They used to beg for this job. Once, Alan had friends over, and when one little boy accidentally smashed an expensive china plate displayed on a cabinet, he was beside himself with fear when they had to tell Renée. 'O don't worry,' she said, 'I've thousands of these!' They got a reaction they least expected when she suddenly picked up a couple of the other plates and smashed them herself, The adults were just laughed whilst the children stood there, gob-smacked.

There were adults dropping by at Stanmore whom the kids later found out to be notable people in the variety world, or 'stars' from the studios. Alan remembers George Barclay coming round to the house standing with his back to the fire, lifting himself up on his toes. He remembers Barclay being quite a tall man although a photo seems to indicate that Barclay was quite stocky. The Kidd Brothers were often visitors. A picture I received from Donald Stewart's niece, dating from about 1938, shows Pat, Renée and Donald, all looking very smart, raising their silver cups in a toast while Renée holds a small cocktail shaker in her hand. Pat rests his cigarette hand on a cabinet and his cine-Kodak can be seen beside him. Alan identified the '*Abbotswood*' curtains to the right of the threesome in the photo, which were a lush shade of green. Donald moved into the house at the same time Renée and Pat did, being part of the Tom Arnold revue Renée was in then. By 1938 he had been her stage partner two years and throughout this time, occupied an unusual position as houseguest. Pat was still following his own career in films, although the period between 1935 and 1939 was a lean time for him in terms of roles. He was acting as Renée's manager and Donald was, therefore, indispensable from a business point of view. The handsome American, capitalizing Renée's time, was quietly resented by her son Tony.

As partners, Renée and Donald naturally spent long periods travelling and working and a good double act thrives on closeness. Regularly, Donald left for Belgium or elsewhere on the continent for a few days, re-entering to fall in with the visa regulations. American citizens could not stay in the country for lengthy periods. Donald, who in transatlantic passenger lists gave *'Abbotswood'* as his address, had genuine respect for both Renée and Pat. He was glad to be Renée's partner in the professional sense, and it was England and Europe he was slowly falling in love with. Renée was not his lover then.

Donald's youngest sister Janice kept letters her brother sent to his mother over a thirty-year period. Donald's mother Jessie, known as Mickey to everyone, went to England for a long holiday in 1938. 'It's just been swell,' went a letter from Donald. Mickey opened 'the last chapter of the High Seas Series' on the seventh day of her return voyage back east. That holiday she got to know the entire Houston tribe, her son's surrogate family. Donald never let any piece of news go by without his mother knowing first, writing her amusing letters every month.

Mickey's warmth and charm attracted people to her, and the 1938 holiday was the beginning of a long-lasting friendship between Renée and Mickey. Donald tells us about that visit: 'Meeting you at Southampton, the train to London, taxi to Stanmore, the dumb taxi driver messing around with the trunk. Our night at the Trocadero - Up to Southport - On up to Gourock to visit Shirley - Our trip to the Highlands, and back to Gourock - The long run to London and then down to Paignton - Up to Bristol and back to London - Then you away to Holland and Paris - Back again and up to Birmingham - Back to London for our last day.'[22] Renée also had a bunch of letters she sent on board for Mickey to open at designated times on her sea voyage. She made sure to tell her how valuable a 'property' Don was from their point of view: 'Well Mickey darling. Sorry I wasn't there to see you off, but spiritually I was there just the same. I must say I loved knowing you, and only wish my health had been a bit better while you were here. Now don't be feeling too bad about leaving Donald. He'll be well cared for, and furthermore I am going to do all in my power to make him achieve your ambition - Hollywood. I agree with you thoroughly he should be there.'[23]

I don't believe Renée was being sincere because Don was far too valuable as her stage partner in England. She answered her letters to Mickey as 'Your sincere friend' or 'Your Dizzy Friend Renée' and her letters were frothy and fun. She and Don took turns with who was going to write 'Mickey Mouse' or 'Mickey Houston' on the envelope or pen a cheeky line to make Donald's mother blush in these entertaining letters. Even though she was happily married to Pat at the time, Renée's subtle dominance over the young Donald was beginning to come through. She sounds like Donald's wife as well as Pat's, even in September 1938. She sincerely respected Mickey even though it is a little cruel to read the snippets in her letters that hint she and Donald might get over to Broadway if her play turned out to be a success. How ideal it would be for son and mother to be reunited! She tantalized poor Mickey with these suggestions for years, and they never happened.

For all his love of England Donald came complete with American ideas about style where home interiors were concerned. He would sometimes be found giving a makeover to some dark wooden furniture - the 'white' look then being in vogue. Dull wooden items would appear in one part of the house completely transformed. Donald didn't discriminate regarding his raw material and famously gave the 'white' look to several antique tables and cupboards. Alan recalls the grown ups saying how Vera Lynn had stated that she was much against covering up wood with thick white paint and how this was something she would never do. Vera was a regular visitor at Stanmore. At this early point of her career she was becoming a popular radio star. She and Donald were fellow singers and Vera knew Renée at the BBC and at British Lion where she sang in variety shorts with the Joe Loss band. She also recorded under the Crown Label at Crystallite's premises nearby.

Often, a bunch of adults from the film studios got in late at night and there would be a drinks party with lots of laughing and joking downstairs. 'Mum always had her entourage,' Alan recalled. Renée and Pat would hold forth over a well-dressed and sophisticated crowd of guests. Alan and Tony sometimes would be asked to come down with their nurse Greta and walk around and say goodnight to everyone. Alan remembers Merle Oberon being a frequent evening visitor - one of the kinder and more sensitive individuals among the entourage. Alan, five or six at the time, never forgot the time she came to Stanmore with toys under her arm. She gave him a wind-up baby and Tony a toy drum. 'I really liked Auntie Merle,' Alan added. 'She was the only one who insisted on meeting me when I first went to Hollywood.'

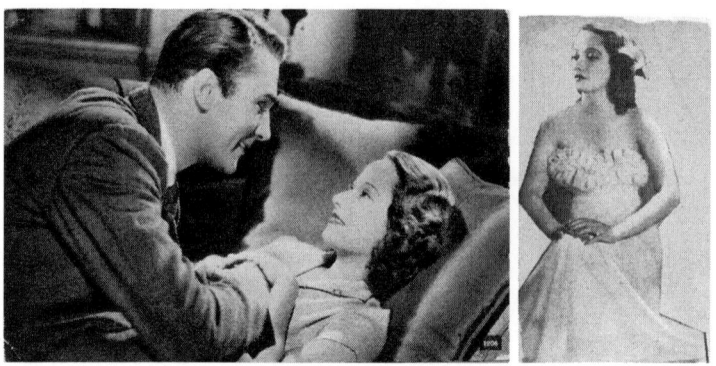

Left: Postcard of Brian and Merle in Beloved Enemy (Author's Collection)
Right: Merle from Renée's scrapbook (By kind permission of the family of Terry Long)

A story the Ahernes tell is that Merle was engaged to Brian Aherne for a short time in the latter part of the 1930s. If this is true, I wonder if she could have been on the rebound. Merle was a great big star in Hollywood after 'The Private Life of Henry VIII', and she split her time between making films in the UK and the US. She and David Niven lived together in Hollywood, with Merle putting in good words with directors on her lover's behalf.

She and David Niven had been madly in love, but things had cooled down by the time she made 'Beloved Enemy' (1936) - a love story inspired by fact, set during the time of the Anglo-Irish Treaty. Brian's *Dennis Riordan* is a kind of Michael Collins character. His love interest is English, not Irish, which departs from the true story. Merle plays an English diplomat's daughter and David is a witty young captain in the English army. Sam Goldwyn decided the film should have two alternative endings, one in which the hero dies a martyr (for UK provincial audiences) and one when he survives (for the London audience). The film builds up a sense of tragedy but has a message of hope. The love scenes between Brian and Merle have a genuine tenderness that brings tears to your eyes. I love this film. Sadly it is not easy to obtain.

Back in 1930 she had a tiny part in 'The W Plan,' seated in a café. She was a young hopeful then and Madeleine Caroll was the star. Slightly before, she had worked at London's Café de Paris welcoming customers at their tables. Dressed to perfection she turned heads as she was swept onto the dance floor. Every man who had her on his arm was envied. Subsequent roles came with films like The Battle (1934) proving her truly mesmerizing presence on the screen: combining exoticism, perfect features and a voice that stopped you in your tracks. Merle was also a fashion icon – and possessed the 'best collection of fur coats either side of the Atlantic.' The fascination she had was legendary. She was once engaged to Joe Schenck with a huge diamond ring but they broke it off amicably. Her passions for Leslie Howard and Niven didn't escape Hollywood gossip and this only increased her mystique. Earlier affairs with English aristocrats and celebrities like Hutch were less well known. Brian was just as susceptible, presenting the irresistible Merle with a distinctive and massively expensive engagement ring. She was back in London in 1937 to film Korda's 'I, Claudius' (1937) cast as *Messalina* with Laughton in the lead and a difficult Joseph von Sternberg directing. This was the time she was visiting Renée and Pat, and holding parties at her fashionable home overlooking Regents Park.

Brian Aherne suddenly broke off the engagement and Merle was unhappy about it. A 'good citizen' had leaked a rather embarrassing story about her to Brian's parents. When Merle was an ingénue actress working at the Café de Paris, Pat Aherne had had a short fling with her. Their tryst had taken place at the Green Room - a club closely connected with the theatrical world that for some years occupied the first floor of 46 Leicester Square. It was all water under the bridge for Pat and Merle, and Renée didn't let it affect her friendship with the actress, but the Aherne brothers were apparently ordered by their parents to stay out of Merle's orbit. Hints were dropped to Merle to return the expensive ring to Brian that she duly ignored. She got everyone's sympathy following a serious car accident on March 17 1937. It was an awful thing to happen to an actress, and it resulted in 'I, Claudius' being abandoned. In hospital she was treated for cuts on the right side of her face, behind the ear and on the neck[24] and afterwards she recuperated at the home of her friend, Lady Morveth Benson.

Who should come to visit her at the Middlesex Hospital but Renée Houston: a goodly caller full of charm, who spotted the expensive diamond ring on Merle's fragile finger. 'Darling,' said the garrulous Scot concluding her visit, 'what a gorgeous ring, may I try it on?' Merle conceded, and with the ring off, all her friend could say was 'It really *is* beautiful. Bye-bye darling' before upping with the ring which found its way back to Brian. Her motive for interfering indicates a loyalty to the de Lacy Ahernes. In later decades pride in the family's Irish ancestry only seemed to bring mockery on Renée's part. Imagining Pat a descendent from Irish king Brian Boru was good for a verbal drubbing. Whether Lulu really believed this is another matter.

Merle Oberon didn't bear any grudge towards Renée or her family over the issue of the ring, remaining a family friend and taking Alan to a jamboree where they watched tanks do manoeuvres whilst cannons were set off, and listened to a brass band. She married Sándor Korda fairly soon after and became Lady Korda when her husband was knighted in 1942. She bore Brian no grudge and they shared billing again in the war film 'First Comes Courage' (1943) directed by Dorothy Arzner.

Of Vivien Leigh, Alan said 'Vivien was sometimes a guest at Stanmore but my parents stopped inviting her because she had an unfortunate habit of being very foul-mouthed.' His parents admired her all the same. Alan doesn't remember Olivier visiting. The limited London-based audience of *televiewers* could see Renée on October 19, 1938,[25] when she was a guest during the premiere of Vivien's film 'St Martin's Lane' which co-starred Charles Laughton. Direct from the Carlton Theatre, Haymarket, a number of celebrities were introduced by Elsa Lanchester to the programme's commentator, John Snagge. As well as Renée, they spoke to Vivien, Rex Harrison, Tyrone Guthrie, Robert Newton, Moore Marriott, June Clyde, Alfred Hitchcock, Eddie Pola, Frank Lloyd, Arthur Christiansan, Graham Moffat, Erich Pommer, Charles Laughton, and Penelope Dudley Ward.

Olivia de Havilland (From Renée's scrapbook. By kind permission of the family of Terry Long)
Brian and Joan's Wedding, Lulu and Big Dad's visit to Hollywood, 1939 (Aherne Family)

Renée became Joan Fontaine's sister-in-law after Brian ceremoniously called on Joan's mother asking for her daughter's hand. Joan accepted and they were married at Saratoga on August 26, 1939 within a month of meeting. An article in Life from May 4, 1942 says that Brian was originally the beau of Olivia de Havilland before he was 'seized' by Joan. Both sisters were training as aviators receiving guidance from Mr Aherne. Brian and Joan enjoyed a very 'English' lifestyle taking tea at 4pm and dressing for dinner.

Renée loved to tell people about her Hollywood contacts. Writing to Donald's mother Mickey she says 'I will be seeing Brian on Sunday or Monday so I'll pin him in a chair and make him send off his picture to Lois. I'll write to Olivia de Havilland regarding the one for Jack. I'm sure it will be fine.'[26] She was quite good at obtaining photos for Donald's siblings. Sadly, Brian and Joan divorced after five years. On the whole the contact Renée had with Brian's Hollywood pals was slight. A stack of novels Joan Fontaine used to read, as well as some of Renée's were mixed up together finding their way into the possession of the Aherne boys, suggesting a possible book exchange. Joan was more of a friend to Elana. The two struck up a close and regular correspondence by letter that had a special significance with them being pregnant at exactly the same time. I've heard that Joan lost the baby she was carrying and this very sad event is something that contributed to the breakdown in her marriage. In other stories Joan seems to have had an expert line in delivering unkind quips to Brian at the time they split up. Yet, in photos and home movies Brian and Joan laugh and joke together and seem a very loving couple. Renée used to hear snatches of gossip as the years went by, long after her marriage to Pat had ended. Around 1966, Joan Fontaine and Vivien Leigh swapped homes when they were working on films: Joan in Britain and Vivien in America. One of the antique snuffboxes from Vivien's collection went missing at the time Joan was at Vivien's. Most probably a servant pocketed it, as it's unlikely Joan took it. Nevertheless, Vivien, who wasn't well at the time, created a complete fuss about it. The snuffbox was never found.

Always stylishly dressed, and full of vivacity, Binkie Nairn was a mainstay of Renée's entourage. Having known the girls since their Shettleston days, devoting her energies to Renée and Billie as their dresser, she was perhaps the greatest friend the Sisters ever had. Ronnie Rowe, an inventor, who was Bob Wilton Smith's cousin, married Binkie in the late 20s, and a decade later they lived nearby in Stanmore. Their first son was born in July 1930 and Alan and Binkie's boys played many a game of cricket on the lawn outside *'Abbotswood.'* Once, by accident, someone slung back and struck poor Ronnie with the bat. The boys often forgot they were under strict orders to keep quiet when they were playing in the garden in the mornings. There was hell to pay if the adults' nerves were fraught the morning after the previous night's drinks party. It happened often that there were guests staying over and sleeping in late. The young cricketers would get a yelling at.

There might be a reporter running a story about family life at the Houston home as well as the odd visit from a radio presenter from the BBC or the commercial stations. A fake tea party was set up in the living room one time for a photo story. Brought up in a theatrical home you were used to displaying 'perfect scenes of family life' expressly for the benefit of others and, after the reporters left, experiencing the 'less perfect' reality. A big day ahead in the theatre put pressure on Renée. She took her rest time very seriously. Alan recalls that when he was very small sleeping in the same bed as his mum, the puffy eiderdown was a thing to dread. He had a habit of getting restless and couldn't stop moving around and she would get angry if he moved. She needed lots of rest to be on form for all those masterstrokes on the variety stage and in pictures. The bedrooms at *'Abbotswood'* had modern gas fires - asbestos-type ones you lit with a match and watched the inner white bit become red-hot. While Renée always gave her public a laugh and a joke, home was a place to vent her stresses but the venting wasn't so bad then. Stanmore is where the Aherne boys say the family was at its happiest. If ever they referred to 'our house' it was *'Abbotswood'* they meant.

From the point of view of Renée's kids, 'stardom' was a pain, and normal family life longed for. The standard theatre and filmgoer in the 30s and 40s was, by contrast, fascinated by these god like personalities, and comforted by the illusions seen on stage and screen. The ultimate bore for Alan and Tony was to be forced to wait a lifetime in a taxi, or in their father's car, whilst Renée and Donald passed slowly down a line-up of fans at the stage door as they made an exit from the theatre. The boys stuck out those relentless autograph signings. Tony would later say that being forced to be part of his parents' lifestyle screwed up his education. He resented them for this, particularly all those occasions when they got pulled out of their beds to parade like cute little things in front of the Elstree brigade, as well as the late night taxi rides. This, he said, would cause him to spend most of the next day asleep in class. Ultimately it caused his exam results to take a dive.

Renée, Pat and Tony in 1935 (Aherne Family)

Some of their backstage recollections are, nevertheless, fun to hear, such as a story about one time when Renée was on the bill with Georgie Wood. In the dressing room Alan innocently asked his mum 'Who's is this tiny dressing gown?' thinking it belonged to someone in a fairy tale, and not noticing Wood in the corner beside the mirror. The best places his mum worked were those by the seaside as that meant a little holiday was thrown in and everyone would be in a jovial mood. Brighton, Portsmouth, Morecambe Bay, and White Sands at Bournmouth were places Alan recalls going to several times. Morecambe was his favourite. For him, the most pleasurable times were when it was just his mum and dad and no hangers-on. In digs they all played endless games of *Houston Rummy*. His mother had made up the rules hence the name but they were happy to stick to the new rules. Eating their piping hot fish n' chips they used to remark that if the paper covering the chips was the News of the World, then the print wouldn't come off, but it came off from all the other papers.

Pat, Renée, Lulu, Tony and Alan arrive in Edgbaston to meet 'Big Dad' 1936 (Aherne Family)

Both Renée and Alan liked fish n' chips. Their kitchen was no different to anyone's then, with brands like OXO, Bovril, Kellogg's, Heinz, Crosse & Blackwell making the shelves entertaining in their brightly-coloured packets. Alan liked the '*monkey gland*' steaks his mother used to make, the pun lost on him for over sixty years, until I explained. He remembers his mother collecting cocktail glasses. These would all be shimmering on a glass trolley, then one day Alan was wheeling himself around on a kid's wheelie, smashed into the trolley and broke the whole lot of them.

When Pat and Renée lived at Stanmore, Billie Houston was living ten miles away in West London in Lauderdale Road, Maida Vale. After marrying Paul Eve she moved to 7 Addison Court Gardens, part of today's Addison Gardens, only down the road from her old house in the streets behind Olympia. An independent creature since the age of ten, Billie was better at escaping the Houstons. Renée's boys came to visit her at her modern town flat. People remarked how she loved children and even seemed happiest in their company. When Tony was little he never called her 'Auntie' but always '*Bill*' and was furious with Renée for appearing in *Love Laughs* without his darling *Bill*. Her flat wasn't somewhere to crash your toys into the walls. A curious plant was growing from a seed in a saucer that transfixed Alan and Tony, and they asked Billie questions about it. The seed looked like it had a mouth. Auntie Billie was Alan's favourite aunt. She also told the best stories. They would be up in her bedroom listening to tales she just invented there and then such as the '*Talking Tree*'. Her voice was grave, holding you in suspense. Then came an unexpected characterization.

Chapter 16 Who's Your Love?

> *'I defy you to name anyone who can get lines across better than Renée Houston. She's as good as Mae West and fifty times as attractive.'*[1]

In the film this Sunday Pictorial reporter is referring to, Renée's character doesn't get her man unlike Mae West. Neither did the real Renée Houston hold her man as the 30s drew to a close. Mae West would say she could trap a man but could never find a long-term use for him. Renée, by contrast, wasn't planning on going it alone.

She had fascinated a few film magnates but she wasn't the sort to just do as she was told. When you're the one heading a show that's always on the road and responsible for many people, you have to have your say. Glad as she was her film career had taken off she had much more power as regards her stage work. She regarded it as her bread and butter, never neglected it, and sought now to win over audiences with her new stage partner – a handsome American, even if the landscape of entertainment was beginning to change. Moss Empires had turned many of London's variety theatres into cinemas by then but nationwide sixty regular halls, sixty super-cabarets, sixty touring revues, hundreds of concert parties, troupes, and social clubs, as well as nine BBC studios characterized the variety world overall.[2] Alfred Denville, the theatrical producer MP who spoke up in the Commons about her treatment in Edinburgh had earlier tried to find out why General Theatre Corporation and Moss Empires were closing so many of the old houses they controlled. The variety combines defended their position telling him it was impossible to run theatres[3] fifty-two weeks in the year with the burden of entertainments duty coupled with the fact they didn't have a Sunday opening privilege like cinemas. Still, enough variety theatres continued living and breathing regardless of radio and cinema.

The King delivered his sad words over the radio on December 11, 1936 and left the country the next day, marrying Mrs Simpson in France soon after. Something longed for in those waiting years had been denied and it was like a crushing blow to many ordinary people. They felt sympathy for the King, yet for him to go after just eleven months fed the fires of cynicism. Images of fair-haired pleasant-faced young men casually posing in double-breasted suits would lose the currency they once had. If Billie's stage identity didn't abdicate, what was to follow wasn't certain. That autumn, she and Shirley appeared with their *Romance Of Song* sketch at several theatres including the Edinburgh Royal. On Radio's *Light Fare* Billie's singing came to the fore with the Horatio Nicholls and Edward Lockton number 'You are my song divine.' Renée and Billie attended the ceremony for the opening of Alexandra Palace although they were not in the lineup of performers.

Donald joined a supportive family when he teamed up with Renée in the touring revue *Merrily We Go* that started its run at Holborn on November 23, 1936. There was tap dancing by Hal Menken, Shirley's *Cuban Capers* dance, *society dancing by* Fox and Evans, and the Sherman Fisher Girls choreographed by Sally McBride. Added to this were the Edmondo Khayyam Troupe – *springboard acrobats*, Freddy Dosh – the BBC mimic and creator of strange noises, and Bobbie Wilton Smith. Jack Stanford provided his *Dancing Fool* and Will Fyffe lent his stellar status. The sketches included *Wife Vs Secretary* with Shirley as the secretary, *On the Hike* with Renée as over-enthusiastic *Gertie*, *Within Reason*, and *Hollywood Episode*. The seventeen short scenes were divided by an interval in which Syd Kaplan's orchestra played Nicholl's 'On with the Show.' Short excerpts of 'Fine Feathers' featured in the second half to sell Renée and Donald's showbiz glamour.

The Times found it too long, considering the Houston brand of mischief had lost spontaneity although conceding she still possessed her usual zest for embarrassing fellow-artistes and orchestra members. They took the show to Finsbury Park Empire – a No. 2 theatre on the Moss Circuit, and did a long stint at Birmingham Hippodrome in December, using different guest acts like Max Miller, GS Melvin and Teddy Brown. In January 1937 Renée and Donald were at Holborn again sharing a bill with Vic Oliver, and after this, they took a break from *Merrily We Go* although the tour was picked up again in a road show format between March and July.

Renée signed for Kurt Robitschek's *All for Laughter* at the Victoria Palace, in which she and Donald were seen twice, first in a quarrelling sketch, then in a singing act - the earliest workings of a formula that would characterize their act for many years to come. Other acts in this show were Con Colleano - famous for death-defying somersaults in the wire-walking line and unequalled in the terra-firma, pianist Lee Sims, Cravon - *clever cartoonist*, and Gillie Potter – *off the wall monologist*.

In February 1937 Billie provided cheery, irresponsible Houston-style humour at the Met, Edgware Road. Tommy Handley was also on the bill doing his *Disorderly Room* skit on army life. Billie was working with Ronnie Hill, still doing her male impersonation but descending to flirtation with the drummer amongst others. Ronnie was blue-eyed, light haired and pleasant-faced - not unlike Billie - and either side of the mike, dressed alike in evening clothes, the effect was visually stimulating. He played piano and Billie sang. Somehow, they never clicked. Years later, Billie maintained a resentment towards him, never mentioning him except for an occasional reference to him as 'the great mistake'. In March she was appearing with Nina Devitt at Blackpool Tower and advertising *De Reszke Minors* cigarettes, handsomely dressed in her sailor's outfit. She and Nina were performing twice nightly at the Empress, Brixton on April 19 when Billy Costello - voice of *Popeye the Sailor* in Max Fiescher's Popeye cartoons - made a personal appearance. A few days later they were at the Met covering popular songs like 'When My Dream Boat Comes Home.'

Billie worked solidly throughout 1937 in spite of the troubles she faced with her spine. She two-timed Ronnie and Nina, both of whom achieved fame on the radio with Ronnie the star of the popular *Air do Wells*. Billie made her television debut soon after, in *Starlight* – a TV show that dates from the day after broadcasting began at Alexandra Palace. All the big variety stars featured on it. While the Radio Times's listing says she appeared on Monday January 4, 1937 the *programme-as-broadcast* records - the best source of actual television transmissions and truest timings, say Billie's *Starlight* occurred on May 25. On this occasion she sang 'I Need You,' with 'Yoo-Hoo in Your Eyes' rendered by Nina. The original Radio Times blurb refers to the broadcast having a biographical context - unusual for such an early TV programme. Soon after, it was announced Billie was breaking off with Nina, who was touring Australia. Joining up with Ronnie, they took *Say It With Melody* to Edinburgh, Reading, Newcastle, Hull, Portsmouth and Bath in the latter part of 1937. They performed on radio's *Merry Go Round* and *Variety*.

Renée sometimes brought little Tony Aherne into the theatre. Variety stars got £5 a week or more for product endorsements inserted into stage turns. Tony participated in one in which his mother would say, in stretched out fashion: *'Oh Mars is mar r r r r rvelous'* echoed sweetly by Tony. There was a lot to be gained by advertising. Having a bottle of something in a star photo in Radio Pictorial or elsewhere with its label clearly viewable was an easy '£5 a week job'. Commercial radio was best of all. Renée's first BBC radio broadcast with Donald Stewart was on *Music Hall* produced by John Sharman, transmitted January 16, 1937 at 20.00. If a competition existed between Donald and Tony as to who would be first to make a broadcast with Renée, Tony looks a winner as his pre-recorded patter with his mother might have been made a few days before, going out on the air on Radio Luxembourg on January 17. The Era wrote that 'Miss Houston's six year-old son Tony is coming along nicely as a comedian.'[4] Renée, in Tyrolean chic, looks fashionable and serious. Tony also looks quite confident in front of the mike. The occasion was the first of a group of Radio Luxembourg broadcasts - each fifteen minutes long, in the *McDougall's Concert* slot between 15.30 and 15.45. Producer Howard Thomas gave it the Kordaesque name 'The Private Life of Renée Houston' and seven programmes went out on Sundays and Wednesdays sponsored by the leading brand.

Thomas loved his visits to the Houston's home in Stanmore, arriving first to stir up publicity for the coming Radio Luxembourg series, concocting an interview with 'breezy boisterous' Renée. She said that she was not only delighted to take the microphone into the nursery for the kids' birthday party but that she would guarantee authenticity: 'People will probably think it's the *Marx Brothers* or the *Crazy Gang*,' she told Thomas 'but that's how things are at our place.' She told him they were not going to put on their *best behaviour* voices just because a microphone was 'dumped'[5] in the corner of the room. The article name-dropped lavishly, boasting that members of Renée and Pat's entourage like Billie, Merle Oberon, Betty Fields, June Clyde and Florence Oldham - *singing pianist* would turn up in forthcoming programmes. One very important voice was *Martha* - Renée's 'Yorkshire cook' – in reality Alan and Tony's Irish nurse, Greta. Renée would call her *Mrs*

Who's Your Love?

McDougall and every compliment she paid her cook, *Martha* was to plug *McDougall's Self-Raising flour*. Together they gave the coffers a good dusting.

Left and Below: Renée broadcasting on the air with Tony, Alan and Greta. (Family of Terry Long)

Left: Playbill for Billie (Courtesy Bob Bain)

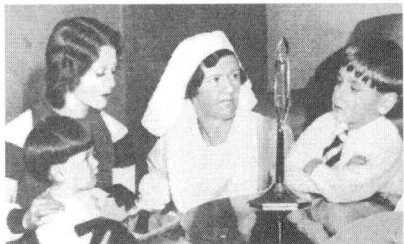

Below: Billie and Ronnie Hill (Family of Terry Long)

Tony featured in Luxembourg programmes sponsored by other manufacturers. He knew just the right moment to utter a profitable one liner like *'Oh Mummy, can we have Horlicks!'* and with the breeziest confidence. Renée turned up in more adverts and slots but ultimately rattled the nerves of Thomas's technicians who apparently feared she might swear on air.[6] Still, her laugh factor was as good in 1937 as it was in 1967.

When the massive Regal Cinema opened in 1932 in Kingston upon Thames, its £10,000 Wurlitzer Hope-Jones organ, which could produce the sounds of every instrument in a symphony orchestra, was the only instrument of its kind in the world. It's famous sound would be heard on BBC radio for many years. On March 2, Houston and Stewart appeared here in *Radio Round-up*. Senator Murphy - *monologist*, and the Hillbillies were acts bringing an American flavour to the Regal, and Renée and Donald's success in leading everyone in community singing caused the song 'Home on the Range' to became the Regal's anthem.[7] At Holborn Empire on April 25, they appeared with *Vic and La Marr* – dancers often likened to PT instructors, and Lucan and MacShane. Renée and Don did their *disintegrating conjugal bliss* sketch and upped the 'romantic' dimension on this well-mined resource whereas *True to me*, recorded with Pat only a year earlier, had been surreal. Morton Downey on the same bill, sang the classic 'Pennies from Heaven.'

Renée's first television broadcast with Donald was *Cabaret* - live from Alexandra Palace on Friday April 2 1937 earning them £35 - about £1,300 now. George Barclay arranged their first BBC contracts. They did a routine from *Merrily We Go* accompanied by Nicky Kidd. The BBC Photo Library has two photos of them glittering in evening dress and looking very snug together. Soon after, Renée went to Paris to add more glitter at a *gala performance* to mark the opening of the Paris Exhibition. This was held

307

between May 25 and November 25 at Palais de Chaillot with other events at Musée de l'Homme and Palais de Tokyo, the latter venue having been created specially for the Exhibition. Apparently Miss Houston had been 'preparing pawkiness in French' which says something about her dedication.

Maurice Chevalier Photo (previously owned by Renée) and lobby card   (Author's Collection)
Donald's photo of a playbill for Houston and Stewart,1938, Donald Stewart (Wintermute Family)

There is scant information about the engagement. An interview with Robin Russell reveals she was in the line-up with Maurice Chevalier at the Casino de Paris - perhaps a guest spot in Henri Varna's revue *Paris en Joie* that had been hyping the exhibition since February. Chevalier partnered by Nita Raya topped this revue. It also featured the *Helena Stars* - all English girls, and Clara Novello, mother of Ivor, leading a choir wearing Welsh National costume. It is possible Renée did something Scottish-themed. A photograph of the young smiling French icon, from the estate of Renée Houston, signed with a dedication 'To Renée – a fine artist, from Maurice,' dates from this time.

Donald serenaded Renée, or tried to, with 'If You Were the Only Girl in the World' and they sang 'It isn't the Clothes' composed by Nicky Kidd for *Starlight* on live television at Ally Pally on June 8, with Nicky on piano. People liked it and they were back on the same show on June 29. On June 15 in Stratford, and on August 26 in Reading, they appeared alongside Billie and Ronnie, but not in same turn. High and low they toured: Blackpool, Boscombe, Ilford, Dublin, Kingston, Norwich and London. At Holborn on November 1, with Will Fyffe, George Robey, Roy Fox and his band, Lucan and McShane and Tex Mcleod, Renée was possessed of all the same 'gay self-assurance' as well as 'impudence' in her new partnership.[8] At Trocabaret, two weeks later, when the O'Gorman Brothers were also on the bill, she failed to impress, and The Billboard found her 'coarse at periods, and 'only mildly funny.'[9] Individuals were hampering her film career just then – enough to cramp anyone's style.

She was in the thick of it with the Smith Brothers of British Lion, who had failed to find her a decent project since 'Fine Feathers'. She and Donald shot scenes for the picture 'Melody and Romance' in the early summer but these would be cut out - their parts given to Jane Carr and Garry Marsh. The only trace of Glasgow in this now obscure film comes from among the voices of children in the street scenes. Twenty-six years would pass before Renée shared a film scene with Charlie Hawtrey. The actor later famous for Carry On films is un-credited in 'Melody and Romance.' Alastair Sim was going to play an eccentric 'professor' – father to the sisters (played by Renée and Margaret Lockwood), but Sim's part was also cancelled. Maurice Elvey directed Renée's eleventh film *that never was*. It was about a talented young conductor and showman from Wapping played by Hughie Green - who creates a big act with his gang after he fails to get a contract from the BBC.

Opportunity knocks for the heavily American-accented *Hughie* when the grown up sister of the young lady he likes overcomes initial prejudice about him coming from Wapping, persuading a manager to set him up with a big radio performance. The most surprising scene has Hughie, presiding over auditions, masquerading with a *Charles Laughton* voice so weird it bowls you over. In a huge inferno, he saves his sweetheart's life as the film cashes in on recent newsreel footage of Crystal Palace dramatically destroyed by fire. On the whole, it was a lousy picture and before Renée and Don were booted out the atmosphere couldn't have been more acrimonious. Imagining them in their original parts, their screwball personalities would have carried it but the Smiths chose a version leaving the humour to the kids. They try hard but can't carry the film.

When they made 'Fine Feathers' at Beaconsfield, all was harmonious as the impromptu birthday party held for Renée, and Pat's backstage home movie of everyone fooling around indicates. Sam W. Smith formed British Lion in 1927, initially to film the works of Edgar Wallace - the company's chairman. When Wallace left for Hollywood to script 'King Kong' (1933), Sam's brother Herbert, thirteen years his junior and previously at Paramount, came to supervise production in England. Sir Seymour Hicks, Margaret Lockwood, Stanley Lupino, and Sandy Powell were signed at the same time as Renée. Sam Smith loved variety and used artistes like Florence Desmond, Jessie Matthews, Sophie Tucker, and Stanley Holloway in his pictures. There was talk of making unparalleled musical films such as an Ambrose picture.

1935, however, saw the company turn into a major producer-renter organization, calling itself *British-Lion-Republic*, when the Smiths cut a deal cut with Ray Johnston, in New York and rejoiced in handling Republic's huge output - although they were supposed to boost British production too. By the end of the year the 'greatest programme of pictures ever attempted by an independent company' began with sixty productions including four 'epics' in colour, and eight outdoor action movies. A priority vehicle was a story by President Roosevelt! American directors were engaged and Paul Robeson, Ben Lyon, Gene Autry, Irene Dunn, Ann Rutherford, Marie Dressler and Polly Moran were touted as leads.[10] With the Smiths tracking the American market, this might explain why no British themed story suitable for Renée emerged. Her falling out with the Smiths was irrevocable. She signed a new contract with Gainsborough on July 6, 1937 and her first picture was expected to be with the *Crazy Gang*. Some press reports claimed the contract was for one year with options, whilst others called it long-term.

With the company intent on accelerating growth Herbert Smith had taken a mercenary attitude to high-paid stars under contract. In her 1974 memoir Renée says Lion wanted to get rid of her because she was expensive. Her original contract, bought by the Smiths from Herman Fellner, which she tells us was supposed to guarantee two more films, was re-negotiated with disagreement on both sides. When Renée's case was heard before the King's Bench Division in the Trinity term eight months after the 'Melody and Romance' fiasco, the contract mentioned was only to engage her as star artist for fifty-two consecutive weeks for £3,750.[11] It does not mention the three-picture deal. Renée claims Lion found fault with her personal life in order to break the contract and went on to use scandal-mongering tactics to manipulate her. Something of this is born out in newspaper evidence of Lion counterclaiming, declaring they were entitled to terminate the contract owing to 'her conduct in their studios'. What they meant by 'conduct' was the 'affair' she and Donald allegedly were having – blatant enough, they attested, to disturb the peace of Beaconsfield.

The evidence British Lion had against Miss Houston, obtained via 'dirty tactics,' isn't clear. If Donald and Renée were having an affair it can't have been the first that ever happened on a studio lot, even though I doubt the affair had begun. Renée explains that the Smiths used skullduggery to oust her, trying to turn youngsters like Hughie Green and Maggie Lockwood against her and getting people to sign an affidavit saying she was uncooperative. She refers to the Smiths' line in blackmail knowing she was married with four children and threatening to leak a story in the press to ruin her career. Her husband was apparently forced to pay them off. It's true they could smear her and affect the success of her act if she were guilty or not. She tells us her South Africa trip, made soon after, was because they needed to keep the issues from public gaze.[12]

However, Renée brought the case for unfair contract termination to court six months later deciding to risk the 'dirt' the Smiths had on her, in the interests of justice. No pleading or other document from the King's Bench Division survives to judge what the real disagreement was, or the 'dishonour' at the studios. Nor do affidavits for this time period survive. It's possible Renée dropped the case to avoid scandal, and the Smiths were 'quids in' breaking the contract as well as receiving a nice hand-out from Pat.

1937 ended at Wood Green Empire on December 13 with their friend Hutch, and at Sunderland Empire with Robb Wilton. Renée was now to be separated from her family for three months and sank into depression. You can tell this from her eyes in the photographs taken, like the sad picture in The Daily Sketch of her looking at her sister from the train window carrying a *Toy Soldier* doll. Her account of leaving England and the goodbye to Billie is shot through with pain in her memoir of 1974, although she cheerfully talks of the opportunity to be with Donald and how precious that was.

She writes as if she and Donald were together, but I don't think this is accurate. 'Don't Fence Me In' should be interpreted from the perspective of a grieving widow and as a paean to Donald. If they were an item, it would have been difficult given the constant presence of the all seeing and all knowing Ma Cox, landlady from Pat's local pub, ready to tell on them. In South Africa she and Don look restrained together in photos, although one has them holding hands. If they loved each other they kept it platonic - even if her head was in a spin. Donald holds Renée protectively in his arms in those BBC studio photos, making it look as if they were lovers but it's theatre - the skill of illusion every actor profits from. It's likely Pat would have come to Africa too, if he didn't have to hold down his day job and manage the kids. Donald was the partner with whom greatest success could be achieved and together they looked gorgeous. The affair came later, in the war when the partners were dependent on each other for strength, sanity and survival.

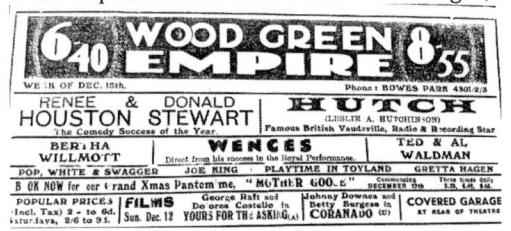

Wood Green Empire advert
(Courtesy of Hornsey Historical Society)

Two images of Renée with Alan just before leaving for South Africa
(scrapbook: Family of Terry Long)

On January 20, 1938, she looked sadly at Alan, perched on top of a travelling trunk at Stanmore the day before her trip. Her children's feelings mattered. This forced absence was to help protect them. Her heart was breaking at the sacrifice. But go she would. At Waterloo, with faithful chaperone Shirley, both lean out of the window of a non-smoking carriage, wrapped in furs with huge floral bouquets. Renée gives Pat a big kiss. Was it public relations intended to show her marriage was as strong as ever? His weaknesses she forgave and he was reliable, doing his bit to keep the troupe going. Flagrant tittle-tattle about her leaving on a three-month trip with a handsome partner to whom she wasn't married didn't exist in the press, and a married woman's honour went unquestioned back then. Readers had more respect for people in the public eye, unlike the 21st century when celebrities are 'fair game' for scandal stories. Even if there had been gossips trying to smear her, Renée had all along made her own choices, caring little for *Mrs Grundy* and her social conventions.

A London correspondent for a Cape Town newspaper met her at an impromptu luncheon party before she left England. Impressed by her engagingly friendly manner. His interview was published in the Cape Argus prior to her arrival. Renée told him how terrified she was about the journey out. She was writing a play in which most of the action takes place on board ship and needed to get the right atmosphere. 'I've just spent a fortune on frocks, and I've got French models and all kinds of lovely things,' she added, mentioning her *Mary Queen of Scots* costume for the ship's ball, and joking about the courtier outfit Donald dreaded parading in given the balloon trousers and slashed doublet, to say nothing of the hose. Her excitement turned to sadness when she spoke of the gramophone records she had made of Pat's and the children's' voices. 'I'm going to play them every day to prevent myself from getting too homesick.'[13] And so they left the country with accusations of adultery and scandal simmering at Beaconsfield. There were other entertainers bound for South Africa, and at Southampton they were joined by the Hungarian Gipsy Boy's Band.

They boarded the *Balmoral Castle*, a tired old liner, commissioned in 1910 and scrapped in 1939. The passage to South Africa was about three weeks, travelling at a service speed of nineteen knots. Shirley found the sea voyage relaxing and Renée fared very well given the trepidations she always expressed about long-distance travel. She was only sick for twenty-four hours and wrote later of the fun she had entertaining groups of children on the deck of the ship by telling them stories.

Making contact with a new overseas audience makes sense if you're predominantly a stage act but Renée and Donald's engagements took up little of their three-month trip. In the '*Bio-Vaudeville*' or cine-variety held between March 15th and 24th at the Alhambra, Riebeeck Street, they were in the second half. Audiences saw an Edgar Wallace feature or one with Gracie Fields beforehand. One reviewer thought their best skit was *September in the Rain* in which she sang in the Mayfair manner, Garbo manner and with intonations of Bow Bells and Glasgow.[14] Other songs they did were 'I'll see you Again', 'If You Were the Only Girl' and 'Rose-Marie'. The Cape Times, whilst admiring their talent, said the audience wasn't satisfied by their exchanges or their badinage with conductor Cecil White. Renée's 'gay, meaningless patter is too meaningless,' it said. London or the provinces might encore as they know Renée and love her, whereas 'Cape Town expects jokes'. Microphones were criticized because they were unnecessary. Renée, it thought, was 'too finished an artist to need such a distortion.'[15] They appeared at the Empire, Commissioner Street, Johannesburg before returning to Cape Town. Both theatres were run by African Consolidated Theatres Ltd - its local monopoly of the film and theatre industry in sway in the two decades after 1927.

Tourism in Johannesburg and audience   (By kind permission of the Wintermute Family)

The tourist aspect was appreciated by Shirley, Mrs Cox, Donald and Renée, socializing with distinguished travellers, with Mr Stein from 'Pleasure' magazine who organized events, and with the wives of men in the *Bio-*

Vaudeville show like Lulu – wife of comedy golfer Eddie Smith, and Tish Lee of Broadway's Stone and Lee - seen between two spears in photos taken near Jo'burg, when the North and South Zulus at Rose Deep did a tribal dance. Many shots were taken here with the party looking on under parasols. I like Donald's scribbles on the backs of photos like 'Just a native study' or how one tribal dancer has 'had offers to go all over the world but management won't allow it.' Home movies feature the games played with groups of children and some of the official dinners. They were friends with Major Reeds and socialized at 'The Killarney Club' – its veranda stepping down to a garden. Don, Renée, Shirley and Marjorie Reeds larked about in the pool. In other photos *'La Toots' Renée*, Shirley and Don are dazzled by the sun outside their Deco apartment.

Renée, Shirley and Ma CoxRenée and DonRenée at Jo'burg
(By kind permission of the Wintermute Family)

Touring the country provided sightseeing and adventure opportunities. Shirley and Don climbed Table Mountain, which was not without drama in the days before the cable car, and on the whole the trip was greatly enjoyed by all. Everyone in Renée's party was shocked by Apartheid. By April 7 Renée and Donald were gone but the Gipsy Boys Band - *The Sensation of Europe* were still playing at the Alhambra.

Renée's world record for how many huge dolls or massive bouquets you can carry when press photographers descend on you at train stations remained unbroken when she arrived back at Waterloo. Wearing a hat with a huge white feather, she carries a basket, large doll and a cuddly toy whilst Donald carries a huge model yacht – all intended as presents. Terry was too old for dolls but Billie wasn't. However, the big doll went to Donald's kid sister Janice via her mum Mickey: 'Just you dare go home and say we didn't love you! Have you been looking after my Popsy? Tell Janice she must take special care of her, because she's very temperamental. She's a very unusual young lady. She was originally born in America - sailed out to Africa then sailed back to England and now here she is returning to her hometown - that accounts for her highly strung condition.'[16] Renée could have been describing herself.

The arrivals from South Africa look relaxed in the photos, but Renée was smoking continually. This was quite a change considering she barely smoked before. Pat was quite disgusted and blamed Donald for getting her hooked on smoking, and drink. Like a typical husband of the time, he didn't approve of his wife drinking. It didn't matter that he spent a good while in the pub. In fairness to him he had a *6 O' Clock rule* restricting when he began, and unlike his wife in the years to come, stuck by it. Stepping ashore from the liner *Winchester Castle* on April 11 Pat took away their spirited merriment, giving them the news that Billie had undergone a serious throat operation at University College London Hospital ten days before.

Billie had a thyroid condition. Iodine deficiency is nowadays given as a cause. She had a swelling of the neck due to an enlargement of the thyroid gland. Being on the stage she had no choice but to try to reduce this. Her eyes suffered because of the condition although not as much as later. She lived with it. The year before she had fainted five times at a performance in Carlisle in *Say It With Melody,* having to rest in a darkened hotel room. The papers called it severe sunstroke owing to the open car journey she made travelling up north. There's a Houston legend some members of the family tell that Billie had the same ground-breaking experimental procedure to treat goitre as the Duke of Windsor, and that she and the ex-King were the first in the country to have it. It's unclear if the Duke really had this, even though he has a faint protrusion of the eyeballs in some photos. The eyeball bulges from the orbit, rather like the eyes of a Greek statue, and photophobia, discomfort and double vision result from the condition. Sadly the operation on the gland didn't eliminate the condition. It only expressed itself all the more in exophthalmia. The newspapers didn't bother with the science and reported that the operation, necessitating eighteen stitches, was to stop her losing her voice. It's true that she'd over-extended it all those years as that unmistakable stage baritone beloved by music-hall fans. It had taken its toll on her. Business-minded as ever, Houston HQ didn't admit that. Asked by The Daily Mirror if the strain of the deep roar she used in her stage technique had contributed to the trouble, Jimmie Houston denied it: 'Her yell is as good as ever,' he said.[17]

At this stage, Billie coped with health issues and expected she'd be on the mend. She wasn't ready to quit show business, even if her health had been a factor in the Houston Sisters' separation. The spinal injury was not fatal. She 'branched out,' of course, in *Down in the Forests* - that legitimate sojourn in the woodlands, showing she never gave up, but the goitre added to everything. Billie would be better remembered if she had been immortalized in the feature film she was then contracted for. In April 1936 she was under contract to Dave Bader, an American filmmaker based in Europe, and the film was 'Annie's Lorry' – a romantic comedy everyone believed was a sure hit. Bader and David Evans had written the screenplay, and were ready to start it in mid July 1937. Billie was to play a girl who inherits a lorry, dresses as a boy, drives it by day, and by night appears as herself. Her lorry-driving competitor is the hero of the tale and doesn't realize her duality until the end of the picture. Variety Magazine mentioned the project as early as April 1936 but a year on, troubled by exophthalmia, Billie pulled out. The project, so close to realization, got shelved.

Bader dabbled in animation and was a great friend of producer George Pal - famous for his groundbreaking shorts featuring 'puppetoons': models composed of interchangeable wooden parts filmed frame-by-frame doing hilarious things to a fabulous musical soundtrack. Bader worked for Pal in the 40s and 50s. Some say that Pal, who made 3D cartoon advertising films for Philips Radio in Holland in the late 30s, made Walt Disney look like a hack. Not only does 'Annie's Lorry' sound memorable but who's to say Billie couldn't later on have turned up in a musical film alongside 'puppetoons' – a magical thought. Her collaboration with Ronnie had ceased in January 1938 – the time her sister's ship vanished into the horizon en route to the southern hemisphere.

Still up for panto, Billie started 1938-1939's season as *Dandini* in William Henshall's touring production of *Cinderella*. She was at Liverpool's Pavilion and her glandular operation made her susceptible to throat infections. Struck down, she came out temporarily and Renee Reel - comic pianist and singer, stood in for her. The production was beset by ill luck with Sid Field as *Buttons* also getting influenza. Billie, like the pro she was, tried to return, struggling on for a week at the Pavilion Theatre, York. Then, all her doctors advised her to go into a nursing home. Sustaining a show was hard. One-offs were easier and she would turn up to open fêtes and give prizes at theatrical gatherings in the 40s and 50s. Variety magazine wrote how Renée and Donald work nicely but 'it is not the old Houston Sisters' brilliancy ... Billie was far and away the best 'straight man' in the country.' Renée had 'unconsciously become sophisticated,'[18] losing something of the personality that made her outstanding.

Wracked with guilt for having escaped to warmer climes whilst her sister suffered, Renée rushed to the hospital to find Billie unable to speak, with weights on the back of her head to keep her chin down so incisions could heal better. Dick Cowper had put a message out on April 12 that the operation was a success but during the next fortnight, reports indicated otherwise. Renée was frequently by her sister's bedside until Billie was released from hospital on April 25. A great photo shows Billie looking triumphant carried out of hospital on a bed, surrounded by Shirley and a bevy of nurses. It captures the joy and mischievous happiness ever present in her eyes – that rare quality Billie had to disarm everyone and make people instantly like her. Sadly, she would have an ordeal of an emotional nature in little less than three months time.

Other people suffered maladies and before the year was out. James Alan Rennie's ulcers forced him into hospital and out of boredom, he wrote his third novel 'Footstool of the Moon'- a science fantasy about treasure-seekers in a lost world, encountering a Brontosaurus and an apelike people. Claire corrected and typed his manuscripts, taking the swear words out. Renée and Billie used to poo-poo Jim's published efforts, and Renée's boys childishly imitated the mockery until they got to know Jim in their teens and admire him. Jim's first novel drew on his experiences travelling in Canada and was highly praised by The Sunday Times. He was widely read and at one point was propelled into the bestseller list above Dennis Wheatley.

Donald endured an appendicitis operation in June 1938 and once recovered, he and Renée met theatrical engagements in Bristol and Coventry and he joined her at her beloved Coliseum on September 11, 1938 in a lineup including Nat Mills and Bobbie. As 1938 turned into 1939, strange things were afoot with people being asked to think about their safety and health. There was talk of what to do in situations like an air raid or gas attack. *Thirty somethings* across the land gained interesting part time vocations or were recruited as air raid wardens. Some considered joining the Home Guard.

Poole Street in Islington, with its dirty factories and cobbles, was a far cry from Cape Town's white beaches and breathtaking sunsets. Gainsborough Studios had seen many improvements since Renée and Billie filmed their scene in 'Blighty' over ten years earlier. Ted Black was now head of production. He had a sharp nose for business, having helped run his father's circuit of music halls in the North East, and shared his brother George's belief that entertainment was best when it reflected British characters in realistic settings: on evenings out, and on holiday. He didn't care for escapist plots yet he dared to allow sexual frankness on the screen. 'Bank Holiday', directed by Carol Reed, featured a couple not yet married planning a shared weekend, the hopes of an ordinary girl trying to win a beauty contest, and fights breaking out amongst cockneys sleeping on 'Bexborough' beach.

Emery Bonett's 1936 magazine serialization about chorus line girls competing for a distinguished man, provided the basis for a saucy screenplay developed by Frank Launder, Austen Melford and Michael Pertwee. Not many British films had dealt with the titillating subject of gold-diggers so this broke ground and had the whiff of candid sexuality that Ted Black approved of. A writer in the Sunday Graphic amusingly describes Gainsborough's new picture as 'Not for prudes. It's all about chorus girl and the things they say to each other made me blush such a rosy red I looked like a ripe tomato in spectacles. My, it's a grand cast and joyous entertainment. But it's rather vulgar, dears, so mind which aunt you take to see it!'[19] Emery Bonett had been a showgirl herself so there was added realism in 'A Girl Must Live'. Renée plays vulgarian *Gloria Lind*, with Lilli Palmer as crafty schemer *Clytie Devine*. Renée's entrance in the film is clever. 'What can you say when a man gets talking poetry,' says *Gloria* as she explains to *Clytie* why a man compared her to a beautiful wicked snake.

You see a cynicism in her face, perfectly suiting her character. The Houston trademark had once been naïve confidence, and in the old days, she had played the fool. It's a wonder seeing the development from her *Maggie* role in 'Their Night Out' in 1933 to *Gloria* in 'A Girl Must Live'. Carol Reed's direction steers the Houston character to a hard-boiled corner that she occupied for the rest of her acting career. The power politics of studio heads had made her quite brittle, but as far as her star appeal in movies was concerned, she was at her peak.

To show up the behaviour of *Gloria* and *Clytie*, a perfect lady was cast, revealing that hearts of gold might still be found among the bomb-proof mink exteriors. This was Margaret Lockwood, as good girl *Leslie James*, who received news from Ted Black on the third day of shooting that she would go to Hollywood to make a couple of films. Reed, a former dialogue director at Ealing Studios, had made his first film, 'Midshipman Easy,' with her, and 'A Girl Must Live' was the fourth of seven collaborations between these two quiet but talented personalities. One unusual piece of cinema acting training valued by Carol Reed, was to go to the Old Bailey and watch the expressionless face of a guilty person accepting a severe sentence. He had been an actor himself. Aged eighteen, Reed had overcome parental opposition to make his debut in *Heraclius* at the Holborn Empire.

British people across different walks of life are celebrated in the film displayed in theatrical digs, dressing rooms, and elsewhere - all thrust into fast dialogues. I had to watch the film a few times to catch all the jokes. On the set, Reed asked his actors to 'up the tempo' although he never raised his voice with them. Kathleen Harrison is sheer gold as *Penelope*, the charlady, the only honest voice in the digs who removes every bit of mystique and insincerity from the residents' high line in conversation. *Clytie* and *Gloria* couldn't tell the truth to their dying fathers if they knew who they were, she tells naïve *Leslie,* who's been dosed on their white lies.

Moore Marriott, Renée, Lili Palmer, Mary Clare, Margaret Lockwood
(Specially-posed photo for UK publicity article - by kind permission of L.Pearson)

Moore Marriott's sanitary engineer asks *Gloria* on a date. 'You won't make a convenience out of me, *Mr Hythe*,' she tells him. Mary Clare's overblown nag of a landlady is memorable and Naunton Wayne, fresh from his success in Hitchcock's 'The Lady Vanishes' is understated as Hugo - elegant conman and pickpocket who plans to extort money by getting rich men into compromising situations with chorus girls, in time for him to 'accidentally' walk in and witness it. 'Sorry old bean, thought it was the bathroom' is the line he's supposed to use as he walks in as a witness. But *Hugo* gets soused and ruins it all of course, going into at least two wrong destinations, including the bathroom, slurring his 'line' each time. The final thumping he gets from Renée puts me in mind of the hiding delivered to her on-screen son in 'Carry on At Your Convenience' thirty-five years later.

Hugh Sinclair, as the *Earl of Pangborough,* needed lots of practice playing snooker for the billiards room shot. A Londoner by birth, he was educated at Charterhouse, joined Liverpool Rep and appeared in Shaw's *Major Barbara*. He spent eight years on the American Stage getting his big chance in *Charlot's Revue* understudying Jack Buchanan. He starred in 'Escape me Never' and later in two early screen adaptions of the Charteris stories bringing 'The Saint' to the screen. Sinclair has one of the most attractive male voices I have ever heard. As for the Scotch voice, it's terribly tuneful too. Tokyo the dog, abducted by *Gloria* because he compliments her monkey fur cape, is worn under her arm. He howls in unison with *Gloria*'s top notes during the scene where she does her audition song. There are top marks for casting here and it proves animals can work on film.

George Robey, fourth billed as *Horace Blount* – financier of a new show and victim of the girls' manipulation, was seventy, and the long hours at the studio by day and appearing in the halls at night was overwhelming. He married his manager Blanche Littler[20] the day before filming finished on December 1. On its release Cyril Connolly said he endured twenty-five minutes only in order to see Robey, finding 'A Girl Must Live' a 'slow fire draw,'[21] which doesn't say much about his powers of perception. Unlike *Certainly Sir*, Robey and Miss Houston were on to a winner as their crosstalk illustrates. 'Weren't you in Cannes last Christmas with Lady Bartleby?' *Gloria* asks *Mr Blount*. 'No, I was in bed with sciatica,' comes the answer.

Renée is so gutsy and watching her, I feel the audience share the knife-edge of her curses and the energy of her deeds and misdeeds. From the hallway *Gloria* is seen blasting down the stairs like a hurricane, seizing *Tokyo* - her landlady's pooch and last minute fashion accessory, deaf to protests that last time she snatched him she left him on the tube. 'Nice girl that,' sighs *Penelope*, as *Gloria* disappears into the street. At the audition there's a suggestion that *Gloria* and brash American impresario *Joe Gould* - Dave Burns – have met before. She once sang *Sea Breezes* for him in Southend, she tells him, even if all he remembers was the sound of wind blowing over the mud flats.

Lilli Palmer was once part of a sister act herself – the *Soeurs Viennoises*, when she and her sister Irene danced in the nightclubs of Darmstadt and Paris. She is 'feed' in the backchat scenes with Renée, delivering her own one-liners acidulously. Not really Viennese, she was German, from Posen, but made sure to tell people she was Austrian. Her Jewish parentage put her in danger and she ended up an emigré in England's film community, renewing her work permit every three months. She didn't have permanent status until she married Rex Harrison in 1943. In 'Don't Fence Me In' Renée tells us how the fight scene with Lilli - clad only in their scanties, was spoilt each time by their giggling and the only way Reed could up the ferocity between his

Hungarian Rhapsody and his *Aberdeen Angus* was to promote a real punch-up. He resorted to telling tales, playing on their insecurities, telling Lilli Renée hated Jews, and telling Renée Lilli hated her because she coveted the role of *Gloria*. Soon enough Renée found that when they came to shoot a take for this scene Lilli had her in a 'ju-jitsu grip', heaving her 'over her shoulder with a tremendous crash.'[22] Boy, did she injure herself, almost breaking her leg as she landed!

This was early during filming so it's some wonder she manages to shine through the film regardless of a painful injury. Her son told me the studio put the message out she had 'housemaid's knee'. Either they were unsympathetic slave drivers or Renée didn't want her injury known. Her later scenes were aided with crutches. When the other girls dance the 'I'm Savage' number, *Gloria* is absent from the frame, reappearing between cuts at the side of the door before *Clytie* makes a late entry and finds herself in trouble with Joe. Barely sympathetic about her injury, Carol Reed was very happy with one of the best catfights on film, confessing his manipulative tactics afterwards.

The Times wrote that 'the Queensbury rules go to the board, and their fights . . . would make an all-in wrestler hang his head in shame at the thought that he once imagined he was tough,'[23] whilst The Empire News, Manchester recorded that the two 'tear lumps of each others' hair out and generally misbehave in a manner that even the folks on Lambeth Walk might frown on.'[24] Sixty-three year-old James Agate liked it, finding the manipulative methods of *Gloria* and *Clytie* resonant of Balzac's 'Splendeurs et Miseres des Courtisanes,' pointing out that 'the scene in the bedroom, where every available missile is dispatched with unerring aim, has not been bettered, and perhaps not equalled, since the first custard pie was thrown.'[25] Renée and Lilli were proud of the scene that has pantomime touches such as *Gloria* and *Clytie*'s sword-fight after they grab a couple of fireplace pokers, with *Gloria* pulling the rug from under *Clytie*'s feet. It beats the fight between Dietrich and Una Merkel in 'Destry Rides Again' and Renée and Lilli are beautiful at their most physically agile.

Set design in the film is impressive and art director Vetchinsky or 'Vetch,' based his *'Blue Roof Nightclub'* on the geometrical theorums of ancient Greece. It was one of the largest sets ever built at Gainsborough. Vetch was an authority on Tudor period furniture, managing the construction for the dining room at *Pangborough Hall*. It's strange that expenses didn't stretch to providing real food for the actors to eat in the buffet scene. The caviar was a concoction made from thick motor grease and ball bearings.[26] Jack Cox's photography illuminated the leading ladies in the *'Blue Roof Nightclub'* scene. He utilized a 'Crook-Varo Zoom' camera lens, quickly moving from wide long shot to intimate close-up – thirty yards from the front of the auditorium to the handsome face of Sinclair's *Earl*. 'A Girl Must Live' was the first time this lens was used in a major shot on a large set in a UK production and it intensifies the chorus girls' romantic thrill all the more.

Film Pictorial's roving reporter 'The Nomad' went to Poole Street, meeting the stars coming on set, or descending to the floor via a gigantic lift. 'Austrian born' Lilli tells him that the onyx stone ring on her finger was given to her by her father - one of the first gold diggers in South America, Carol Reed says he's taking a well-earned holiday in Switzerland at the close of production, whilst Naunton Wayne and George Robey say no more than 'pleased to meet you and all that'. Renée has most time for The Nomad, calling him up to her small dressing room, decorated with pink table lamps and doll-mascots, where her talk is animated whilst modest: 'Aye, Lad, it's a good part. Have you heard me do my number? I expect I'll be pretty awful. But those dancing girls and the support they give me is something not to be missed. Tis a good number, too. Manning Sherwin and Eddie Pola wrote it. It's called "Who's Your Love."' Renée gave him a preview before going down to film the take.

The music, conducted by Louis Levy and Charles Williams is catchy, fast-paced and stylish. The Nomad added that 'With her happy, carefree voice, Renée held the entire production staff spellbound,'[27] not to mention himself. This was surely the break 'this grand artiste' so well deserved.

Renée poses for a UK magazine story in an outfit from 'A Girl Must Live'
(Press cutting - by kind permission of L.Pearson)

There's a frank attitude to sex in the film, and class and social mobility are handled with the lightest touch. As *Joe Gould*'s girls travel by coach for a weekend at the *Earl's* mansion, *Clytie* dishes a polite putdown of *Leslie's* dress sense, whilst *Gloria* reads a book on etiquette. Later, unaware that the Earl could prefer *Leslie*'s subtle charms, *Gloria's* aside to *Clytie* is 'Just hear it! If I wasn't the perfect lady I am I'd slosh her in the chops.' The film might show the snobbery of the time but defends the gold-digger. Margaret Lockwood's character has run away from a finishing school she can't afford, taking the name '*Leslie James*' as she tries her luck on the stage. When the real *Leslie James's* mother hears *Pangborough*'s aunt say 'I know what these stage women are,' she deflects the comment with a Kate Carneyish 'I would. I was one myself.'

The film isn't a British repackaging of RKO's 'Stage Door' of 1937 in which Constance Collier provided old thespian pretentions in a West 58th Street boarding house. This doesn't rival the quirky Bloomsbury boarding house in 'A Girl Must Live'. Comparing the two movies illustrates national differences. The British chorus girls are bitchier than 'Stage Door's implausible sorority sisters one of whom is an insipid character starving before she cops it - jumping from the stairs - all because she can't get a break. The 'Stage Door' girl fight is a mere slap on the cheek. Thankfully, Gainsborough didn't rehash the awful *Terry Randall* character played by Katherine Hepburn in the RKO picture. George Robey's cringe-worthy sugar daddy is better than Lucille Ball's civilized Timberwolves from Seattle. The American chorus of 'Stage Door' has black sequins, top hats and trousers as they dance to perfection while their British counterparts are in black sequins, wizard hats and are very under-clad with a lot of leg shown. Speaking alternate lines to the audience in the conga line, they have the saucy suggestiveness of a real Vivian Van Damm Windmill show. Renée and Lilli did, however, draw on Ginger Rogers for inspiration, copying her hairstyle.

At the very end of the film we're back at the seedy and aptly named *Blue Roof* and the Crook-Varo Zoom Camera Lens travels thirty yards and this time focuses on the wizened old *Duke of Grandonald* in evening jacket, kilt and sporran, smiling with toothless lechery. That's Moore Marriott 'the English Lon Chaney' again, with another of his many faces. He's well up in Burkes Peerage – something that gives the girls hope. *Clytie* and *Gloria*, back at square one now *Leslie* has hooked the *Earl of Pangborough*, reunite in gold-digging single-mindedness. *Gloria*, with a big wink, questions if it might be possible to fix him with a monkey gland. The ninety-three year-old might just 'lay doon an' dee'. You have to hand it to 'A Girl Must Live' for being so unswerving in its message of amoral ambition. Incidentally, the monkey gland joke is one Renée comes back to quite a lot in later years.

On the whole the combined effort of all who made this film wasn't ignored, receiving considerable praise after its first showing to the press on July 28 at the New Gallery Cinema at 121-125 Regent Street – occupied by Burberrys in 2016. A bunch of hospital nurses were invited and laughed themselves limp. Of Renée's performance, Archie De Bear thought she stole the movie 'for real humour and intelligence and force of personality, I have rarely seen equaled.' Anthony Gibbs in the Sunday Chronicle and Referee praised Renée's shrewdness, calling her a 'diabolically ingenious little minx.' She impressed PL Mannock in The Daily Herald, and US Variety found her 'splendid' concluding 'it's one of her best performances on the screen.'

The film was on full release in the UK on September 23 1939, less than three weeks after Britain entered World War Two – bad timing for an actress on the crest of wave, never before so well placed to trade on her boisterous spirit and wide sense of comedy. Joyce Jeffreys in the Sunday Pictorial stressed how the picture 'certainly equals any of Hollywood's best comedy efforts,'[28] and Moore Raymond in the Sunday Dispatch said it had more jokes 'about you-know-what than half a dozen Hollywood laugh-getters.'

Left: Cutting advertising A Girl Must Live from Renée's scrapbook (Aherne Family)
Right: Eddie Pola, who created songs Renée sang in several of her early films (Family of J. Lewis)

It's sad that a film that went one better than Hollywood didn't make more noise. In the United States, the film wasn't on general release until 23 March 1942, when distributed by Universal Pictures. It deserved bigger success. If you count the re-release in the UK in 1948 and a TV deal in the USA in 1953[29] that's a fair amount of mileage, but one day 'A Girl Must Live' may receive some of the appreciation afforded to other British classics.

Donald left Southampton for New York on October 5 when Renée started at Gainsborough and just ten days later she cabled him to return as the two of them were commanded to appear before their Majesties the King and Queen in 1938's Performance at the Coliseum on November 9. George VI, Queen Elizabeth and the Duchess of Kent took their seats in a royal box hung with red white and blue carnations and everyone stood for the National Anthem. George Black was compère and the first set of acts included the twenty-four Tiller Girls, Vic and Joe Crastonian, Leslie Holmes and Leslie Sarony, and then Murray and Mooney. Evelyn Laye was on next singing 'Love Makes The World Go Round' followed by the Stuart Morgan dancers. Renée and Donald were up next. Unable to wear their latest stage outfits - kilts made up in *Royal Stewart* tartan, they were their sophisticated selves. She disguised her leg brace under a long flowing gown in delphinium blue. They sang Noel Gay's setting of "Between You, Me and the Gatepost.' The badminton act of Ken Davidson and High Forgie followed, then Jack Payne, The Three Aberdonians, Les Allen, Will Hatton and Ethel Manners. Elsie and Doris Waters were also there filling the house with laughter with their Cockney charm.

This Performance was a celebration of London's musical theatre as it was just then, featuring a large dose of music and lyrics by Noel Gay and Douglas Furber. Artistes from the cast of *These Foolish Things* were present and Richard Hearne and Rosalind Atkinson did their *Lancer's burlesque* sketch from *Running Riot* - a show at the Gaiety with Leslie Henson and Fred Emney. Lupino Lane featured highlights from *Me and My Girl* - the hit at the Victoria Palace that ran to 1,646 performances in all. Under Lane's direction, the stage filled for a finale with a hundred luminaries of the variety world singing and dancing 'The Lambeth Walk': a melody inspired by the 'jaunty coster walk' that Alec Hurley used to do. The Royals were visibly delighted identifying so many well-known faces like Will Fyffe, Florrie Forde, Tommy Handley, Violet Loraine, Gus McNaughton, Ruby Miller, Ethel Levy, Dorothy

Ward, Kate Carney, Clapham and Dwyer, Ella Retford, Harry Tate, Suzette Tarri, Vesta Victoria, Kate Carney, Anona Winn, Talbot O' Farrell, the O'Gorman brothers, Harry Champion, GS Melvin, and Bransby Williams – all having a few seconds in the spotlight as this cavalcade of cavalcades passed around the stage.

Murray and Mooney, Elsie and Doris Waters, and Clapham and Dwyer   (Author's Collection)

Renée and Donald played the Coliseum soon after, in *Hill Billy Round Up*, with Florence Desmond, Jack Daly and Buster Shaver with his Tiny Stars. The use of 'midget' variety stars and the language to describe them didn't cause the consternation it would now. They doubled that week at The Grand, Clapham and tripled on television in *Cabaret* on January 26 1939, alongside Julie Andrews' stepfather Ted – described as a banjoist.[30]

Two days earlier, George Balharrie died in the arms of Pat Aherne at Brompton Hospital. He had been readmitted on March 28 1938, and was ordered to go to Frimley Sanatorium again between July and October. Renée writes that she did cry for wee George in 'Don't Fence Me In,' admitting that it was Pat who insisted they go down to Frimley to see him each weekend. Family members recall that if there was one subject she never willingly talked about, it was George. On the rare occasions she did, she never credited him with anything. Her answer was to carry on – to feed the children that George never sired. It was typical for her to escape to an alternative *Island of Despair* – one where *Robinson Crusoe* made his home. She did so at the Alexandra Theatre, Birmingham. Their short stay on the island was to deputize for George Robey but it was just enough time for Donald to make his pantomime debut and get a taste of things to come. It was directed by Derek Salberg, whose famous family continued to run the 'Alex' until 1977 and back then, the main entrance was on John Bright Street.

They were at Kingston Empire on February 7, with Noni and Elizabeth Welch, in a Coliseum lineup on February 21 with the Australian Air Aces, then Bristol's Hippodrome, and then the Embassy Peterborough with Will Hay. Finally, with Shirley and Robb Wilton, they did their first stint on *Caprice Parisien* - the non-stop Revue at the Prince Of Wales Theatre on April 3, replacing Tex Mcleod.

Donald's sister Lois, nine years his junior, and about to graduate from Waylister College Connecticut, got a letter from him. Donald often brought Lois up to speed with general news from England. Lois was the sibling he felt closest to. The letters would be read over the table to Donald's mother and the other siblings. Reading his long letter they learned the daily schedule in the Prince of Wales was from 2 pm to 11.30 pm: 'We make 14 appearances per day and it is killing us'. Donald goes on to say how they had one more week of it and 'it will be a gala day in our lives to get out of the place!' Killer schedules impact the performer, hastening the need to unwind, and taking a glass and a bottle of wine to the seclusion of a hotel room. The problem is finding you've drunk the whole bottle in next to no time. It's a pattern many have experienced whilst adapting to the pressures of performing. It becomes habitual, and you don't get hangovers so you think everything is all right.

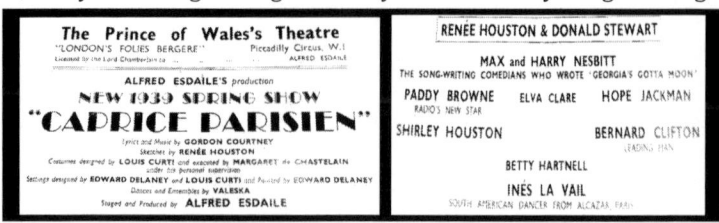

Left and right: From the Caprice Parisien Programme (Author's Collection)

In that letter of May 1, 1939 Donald spoke candidly - 'as I see it from this side of the fence.' Donald's niece has kindly allowed me to quote from this interesting letter: 'I am still and always will be, a patriotic American,' he told Lois beginning his letter enigmatically, 'but when you love something or someone, you must be able to see the faults as well as virtues possessed by that something or someone.'

He was eager for Lois and her classmates to have a broader understanding of world affairs and what he saw coming. Donald was of the opinion that America was no longer isolated - it's biggest danger being 'our stubborn insistence on living in what is now a fools paradise' and maintaining an isolationist stance. He felt the rise of the Axis Powers was no longer just a European issue but one 'the future of the entire world depended on,' adding 'for two years I've seen this coming. Over two years ago I said that the greatest guarantee for peace would be an iron bound alliance between America and Great Britain. This would automatically ally three great nations, America, Great Britain and France, and would possess almost half the fighting strength of the world. Add to that Poland, Roumania, Russia, Turkey and the South Americas, and who could defy it?'

He believed America could have impacted the outcome of the Munich meeting of 1937. If only Chamberlain had been 'armed with the knowledge that he had the strongest of allied forces in the world to back him up. Do we [America] realize that Germany is twice as powerful now as she was six months ago, and every time she is allowed to walk into a country unmolested, she becomes stronger? If a maniac makes it clear that it will eventually be forced on you, isn't it better to knock him out when he's comparatively weak, than to wait until he's put on weight and gained enough strength to possibly give you a beating?' Donald concludes that 'reason plays no part in the life of any of the Axis Powers. Their ideas, desires, and in fact, their whole life is backed only by fighting for power.' This fascinating letter, striking in its honesty, ran to several pages.

Who's Your Love?

He and Renée took part in London Hippodrome's *Summer Show* alongside good friends Stanley Holloway, Vera Lynn, Reginald Foort, Mantovani, Henry Hall and Charlie Kunz. It was a nicer experience than *Caprice Parisien*. Donald loved the country he'd made his home. Strolling through the streets, he stopped for a second, absorbing the capital just as it was then. It had a distinct character - a paved with gold quality but one manifesting a dignity and reserve – with none of the flaunted wealth essential to the spirit of New York. An American could appreciate the difference. I doubt he'd have approved of London taking on New York's mantle in years to come, and appreciated that simple things with bags of character are easy to lose.

At Glasgow Empire on June 19, they were equally billed as *Variety's Sweethearts* then the New Royal Norwich, controlled by Prince Littler, engaged them for a week on July 3. Shirley sang songs assisted at the piano by her partner Charlie. When the same players were booked at Hull's Tivoli Theatre on the week starting July 11, The Hull Daily Mail detailed a publicity event for the stars' arrival. Although planned locally, it was likely Gainsborough pictures were keen to publicize 'A Girl Must Live', soon to be released. Sending its stars on evangelical style tours to promote pictures was quite common then. Renée and Donald look happy shopping in Hull with Renée calling the locals 'Darling' at every opportunity. At Comet Radio, Donald admires a gleaming eight station, push button controlled radio set. The offer of the day was 'a radio in every room' with service thrown in, and the price decreasing to a tanner a week after the third year. Renée poses next to it in the monkey fur from her latest movie. At the Waverley Hotel a man offers her 'lucky' honeysuckle out of his buttonhole and another supplies a pin to attach this to her outfit. Renée insists on borrowing a penny to pay for the pin – it being unlucky to take one as a gift. Donald explains 'We're a bit superstitious on the stage.' Cheesy Gags are plenty at Northwood Motors with a 'singer driving a Singer' and a photo shows Donald at the wheel of a vintage Singer roadster. On Hessle Road, Renée models the latest Doll hats, before they visit a cups and medals store on King Edward Street. A huge silver cup, originating from Glasgow, necessitates her quip 'Can't be silver!' They get catalogues for inexpensive Christmas presents from Hull's largest 'Christmas Club' and Donald asks where Father Christmas has his rooms. At Needler's chocolate factory Renée asks the girls on the production line: 'What do you say when your young man brings you a box of chocolates?'[31]

Just before the war variety appearances in Brighton and Devon gave an opportunity for Renée and her family to enjoy a short seaside holiday before she appeared in a charity event at the Palladium. In late September the *Sweethearts* were at Columbia recording 'Goodbye To Summer' (by S.Botterill and H.Philips) with an orchestra conducted by Ronnie Munro. Then they did their first rally for the RAF's barrage balloon detachment, occupying the grounds of a school near Stanmore. Alan Aherne tells me that air balloons were manufactured here. Others appearing for the RAF put up at

'Abbotswood' were the Carlyle Cousins, the McGuire Sisters and Ted Andrews. Children were being evacuated now, and there was a sense of restless waiting during the *Phoney War*. Reminiscing the Great War, and singing old songs and recording them on a gramophone record was one way of making sense of things. At London's HMV studios on October 9, accompanied by Jack Hylton's band, six hundred soldiers and military wives sang songs like 'It's a Long, Long Trail'. A photo in the Daily Mirror shows Renée's fourteen year-old daughter 'Terry Jo Houston' among the singers, with a corporal on either side. Looking at least ten years older, she resembles a young Ava Gardner, dressed sophisticatedly, making me wonder if the fur she wears, with its matching hat, might be borrowed from her mother, if she was indeed still living with her mother at the time.

The following week *Variety's Sweethearts* played the Glasgow Empire with Vic Oliver, Scott and Whaley, Silvestri – juggler and football manipulator, and dancer Renée Dymott. At New Cross Empire on November 2, they featured songs 'Never Break a Promise' and 'I Shall Always Remember' - the latter described as a semi-pathetic, semi-burlesque rendering that brought a tear to people's eyes. They topped the bill in *Brighter Blighty* at the Theatre Royal, Edinburgh on November 14 alongside Bert Denver and May Moxon's Girls.

After 'A Girl Must Live' Renée and Don were booked to do the tour for *Black And Blue - George Black's intimate rag*. It had had a pre-London run at Brighton Hippodrome from February 1939, after which it was launched at the London Hippodrome. Scenes featured music by Harry Jacobson and Ronnie Hill under the direction of John Weaver and script credits went to a team made up of Diana Morgan, Robert MacDermot and Peter Dion Titheradge. Renée, Donald, Cyril Fletcher, Shirley Brent, Maurice, Ruby, Joyce, Bonar and George Colleano, Betty Broughton, Dick Evans and Anthony Neville filled the parts of Frances Day, Vic Oliver and Max Wall in the successful West End run.

By the time the tour began, under the management of Tom Arnold, Renée got a nasty shock. Reading the script the jokes sounded all too familiar. She recalled a time at the end of 1937 she had come to see George Black about lining up a show for her and Donald, and he suggested she leave some material with him. Black gave her material to a friend of his.

Flyer for Black and Blue, George Black, Renée at time of 'Old Bill' (Author's Collection)

Renée, in her 1974 memoir claims she had no foreknowledge of her material being used in *Black And Blue* and that credit should have been hers.

Members of her family back this claim. She had only given it to Black to have a look at it in 1937, although you wonder why she hadn't asked for it back. Looking at the Brighton programme, it looks like a Houston revue with the usual *Wife, Lover, Husband* scene, a Film Magnate's Office scene, a *Newlyweds Bedroom* scene with maids from three different periods: *Regency, Victorian* and *Today*, two scenes contrasting *Opera of Yesterday* with *Opera of Today*, an *American skit* and finally an *Art Gallery skit*. There are nineteen scenes in all – some of these merely a song.

'George Black's intimate rag' had added several standalone scenes like *Bob Bromley and his Personality Puppets*. Vic Oliver's scenes had been unique such as *The Beaumont Skittish News*. Abbot and Costello and Eddie Pola wrote material for some of his scenes in the West End version. There are however, enough patent similarities to *More Dam Things* and *Merrily We Go* to indicate it was lifted from Renée's jotting book. Renée claims she made no noise about this issue upon first reading the script. She says she later let Tom Arnold and Peter Dion Titheradge – both of whom had no part in George Black's action - politely know she had authored the bulk of it. It isn't quite true that she was polite about it. She found Black deceitful and the idea of being un-credited was too much. It says something about Black that he didn't see it in the same serious light and expected her to simply get on with it, after purloining her work. By the time she had come to Black's office that time, she had the right to call herself a 'master' of the revue form, and when you think of the West End production's long season, you can understand how cheated she must have felt. Renée had been in the business too long and wouldn't let an injustice go for the sake of appearances. Nor was she cowed by the might of producers as many are: beaten into a belief they're lesser mortals than these top guns.

She confronted Black and ripped him to pieces in public looking glorious in the moment, believing she was right, and coping with the consequences after. It's courageous considering Black's almighty power in the business. He apparently said 'She'll never work for me again,' and she never did, after the tour ended. Every name under the sun poured from her motor mouth. Both barrels were smoking when she took down the variety magnate, as had been the case with those cowboys, the Smith Brothers. Thankfully for Renée, George Black died in 1945. The extent to which Ted Black was brought into the feud is not known. Renée's position at Gainsborough was uncompromised when she made 'Two Thousand Women,' although it explains why she had to wait a few years for a part like this. Maurice Ostrer slowly levered Ted out of the company in the years after 1943.

Despite the explosion, *Black And Blue* was a resounding success and luckily Donald negotiated a good deal with Tom Arnold so he and Renée took home a more than generous 10% of the receipts – if this detail in her memoirs is true. Destinations for *Black And Blue's* tour included Wolverhampton, Birmingham, Nottingham and Finsbury Park Empire, and people found it had everything it ought to have. In a late scene *Park Parade*, dancers were invited from the audience. *Variety's Sweethearts* were thought to be a 'joy for audiences' and Shirley, having a fling with Bonar Colleano at the time, was seen to 'prove her worth' with 'a sense of character in her comedy.'[32]

Another reason Renée breathed fire was she was about to lose her father at exactly the same time. She was destabilized. The true anchor in her life, and one authority able to silence her was beginning to sail away. During the last few years of his life he dealt with the effects of an appalling and unpleasant form of cancer. Renée was in a highly emotional state when he died on November 27, 1939. She returned to work, having said farewell and Donald met her on the steps of the Hippodrome lit overhead by a huge melting sun, making her remember Daddy Jimmie's comments when, as a child, these sunsets had alarmed her. 'My Old Papa was right,' she said 'There's a party going on in heaven.'[33] Lizzi never recovered. For the forty-one years since the day they were wed at St Paul's Catholic Chapel, Shettleston, she had been in Jimmie's company each day. In September 1938 Jimmie, Lizzi and Granny had left Sudbury, migrating northwards to live near Renée. Jimmie still made people laugh and gave them all a song on the piano when his little grandsons had visited them at 37 The Grove, Edgware - a suburban home let for £95 a year. Alan remembers his grandparents' Chinese lacquer piano, and Daddy Jimmie tinkling away. Alan was climbing over him, slapping him on the head with childish excitement.

By September 29, 1939, Jimmie, Lizzi and Granny were at *'Abbotswood.'* Officialdom invaded people's homes that *National Registration Day* when each person in a household was recorded on a form and given a schedule number to help Neville Chamberlain's government prepare for rationing based on the prediction that food would become scarcer. *'Abbotswood'* had eleven residents according to the 1939 Register with Jimmie listed as 'Incapacitated.' In December, Pat took care of the funeral arrangements for James Brown Gribbin and 1940 began with Renée and Donald's appearances in Birmingham and a *'Tea With The Stars'* charity event at the city's West End Dance Hall. Dates at Finsbury Park, Leeds and Chelsea Palace followed.

There's a photograph showing Renée and Pat riding a tandem bicycle to Denham studios due to petrol rationing on March 7, 1940. Renée was shooting scenes in a film bringing Captain Bruce Bairnsfather's cartoon character to life. A new cartoon had revived and updated the old one with *'Young Bill'*, son of the original. At the end of 1939 the War Office allowed a unit to shoot location scenes in France including scenes of British troops behind the lines. Tests were made for the lead actors in January. The idea for 'Old Bill And Son' came about through negotiations between Herman Fellner's old partner, Josef Somlo, Harold Boxall and CM Woolf. Alexander Korda was producer and Pat's friend Ian Dalrymple directed, collaborating with Bairnsfather on the story. The early scenes introduce the English family central to the plot before action moves to France where old ties bind England

Who's Your Love?

and France in spite of cultural differences. Doughty and placid-natured *Old Bill*, played by Morland Graham, is reunited with his old Gallic buddy from the Great War when he joins *Young Bill* at the front, serving as an auxiliary. He's the butt of several people's jokes. John Mills, released for five weeks from service after special permission was received, played the cheeky son who competes with a friend for the attentions of a French waitress played by Françoise Darcey. There are good performances from Mary Clare, René Ray, Gus McNaughton and Ronald Shiner. CM Woolf wanted Renée for the movie on January 31 but his attitude about how 'Old Bill And Son' was shaping up was unenthusiastic.[34]

Most of Korda's input began in mid May. His mysterious transatlantic trips kept him away from production before then. He was critical both of the film's ending and the concert scene in which Renée appears. Korda obtained Woolf's approval to spend £6000 on added scenes and retakes, whilst a grudging Dalrymple saw a lot of his work left on the cutting room floor. What got cut and what got extended isn't known. The finished film has humour, realism and romance although it plods along for long stretches.

Over half way through Renée steps out of a car – the epitome of glamour. Casting an eye over her new environment, her *Stella Malloy* remarks what a dump she's found herself in. She's a singer determined to entertain the troops, although Roland Culver's *Colonel* is inclined to send her straight back, uninformed about her visit. In a saucy scene prescient of Carry On films she gets round the *Colonel*. Later, she is introduced by a reluctant *Old Bill* at a concert hall rigged up as the *Blitzkrieg Palace,* with an *Entente Cordiale* banner. Vincent Korda's art direction features Bairnsfather cartoons on the stage backdrop. She might be *Stella* by name but it could only be Renée Houston commanding the floor and simply being herself. Her performance is fresh and instantaneous and for her version of 'Roamin' in the Gloamin' – she borrows a tartan hat from a Scottie. When Donald, as *Canuck* the proverbial Canadian, assists her on piano, they sing 'The Smile I left behind Me' by Vivian Ellis - rallying the audience. Even disapproving *Old Bill* sings along and you can't help but feel uplifted.

Making the audience wait before a beautiful actress is 'revealed' can enhance a film but Renée should have been introduced earlier in 'Old Bill And Son'. It feels as if one film has ended and another has begun and that *Stella* might have landed from another planet on arriving in France. She's funny in her scenes with *Old Bill* who views her as you would a Martian, and is forced to make arrangements for her concert. Generally, her scenes don't gel with the rest of the film, and this suggests a scenario based on compromise between producers who couldn't resolve their conflicts.

I think Renée and Donald do a cracking job in the concert scene. Renée's son told me that after she shot this scene and saw the rushes, she returned to the hotel and sobbed with joy that it had come out really well. With all her experience to date, she was still apprehensive about her screen image. The film succeeds when she is there, and Dalrymple, a year younger than she, directs her well. He was Victor Saville's assistant in the making of musical films with Jessie Matthews and would later work on documentaries at the Crown Film Unit. He might have been for Renée what Saville was for Jessie, if the musical elements of the film had flourished more. I like these scenes most. Taken as a whole, I agree with CM Woolf who called 'Old Bill And Son' an 'unfinished picture.'[35]

At the concert, the intimacy and small scale nature of military entertainments is realistic and the sincerity of troops buoying up their hopes makes anyone watching sympathetic to those fighting abroad. While Renée dominates proceedings, the presence of René Ray and Françoise Darcey on stage symbolizes Anglo-French friendship. For a second you see a touching moment with John Mills's character pleased with *Stella,* as if he is congratulating her after her act. Renée described Mills as 'one of the loveliest blokes' she knew, mentioning he stayed with her family during filming, a few months before he married Mary Hayley Bell, although Mills' daughter Juliet couldn't recall her father mentioning Miss Houston.

'Old Bill And Son' was made in the early days of the war when nobody could predict the outcome. Charles Drazin, Korda's biographer, points out that no one could be blamed for this.[36] Filming had progressed when the Belgians surrendered on May 27. France capitulated and an armistice at Compiègne on June 22 meant the French army was disbanded and two thirds of France was occupied. The production team kept changing the ending of the film to keep it in line with events, but by the time of its release on March 10, 1941 there was little relevant about the film. It still received appreciative comments in newspapers such as 'Laughter All the Way in a Front Line,'[37] or 'Producers Josef Somlo and Harold Boxall have done a nice job.'

There's a mention relating to Pat's 1940 bankruptcy, in papers in the National Archives, that Renée suffered a breakdown in May 1940. It's brought up in connection to a period when they faced a loss of income and Pat refers to his wife being in a very bad air raid just after May. She 'had a nervous *break* and could not take the dates.' The air raid could have happened anywhere, and was only a taste of further dreadful things to come. The breakdown was not her first, and I believe something troubled her or came to a head here – perhaps the root cause to her drink dependency. Nervousness was a peculiar phenomenon in Renée's case. Many who met her believed she had a naturally nervous disposition. If ever she went out motoring she insisted Pat go at a steady pace and was particularly bothered by speed. If she saw anyone lean against the car door she got hot and bothered, expecting they would fall out while the car was in motion. She lost it one time when she had a driving lesson. Pat had given up persuading her to consider going up in a plane. Gone were the days of him attempting to 'sell the joys of flying' or suggest they sell their boat and buy a plane. Renée's answer would be 'I'll go high enough to shake hands with a midget.' For someone so sensitive about planes, trains and automobiles in fast motion she was living at about the worst moment she could.

There's a manic aspect to Renée too. Back in 1929, a French reporter who interviewed the Houstons noted what he termed an *Irish* characteristic: that she was 'garrulous, visibly in need of activity . . . her thoughts succeeding each other in an uneven but natural way.' Throughout the 30s a word bandied around in relation to Renée - as frequently as the word 'fresh' was applied to the Houston Sisters was 'mercurial.' Her ability to change mood was only admired and of course it was never pitied. Some people thought she had hidden depths, even if they couldn't conclude who the *real Miss Houston* was, given all her alter egos.

The writer Herbert Harris, great-grandson of poet Robert Southey interviewed Renée in 1938, and makes an interesting point that on the occasion Renée first went into a nursing home [the time she was in *Babes In the Wood* and her home was burgled], she couldn't stop being high-spirited, despite having had a breakdown. The nurses used to think she was kidding them when she was actually very sick[38] and this puts me in mind of those Edinburgh students who thought she was having a joke at them, when she was really experiencing a trauma.

Her son Tony, who looked back at his childhood with a dry-humoured sense of resentment, saw it as the source of his own episodic depression as his diaries reveal, although which period of his past was to blame is difficult to tell. His mother is far too absent in his diaries, and I suspect that by the time he was in his early teens, her way of coping with her problems meant she put up barriers. Finally a shutdown happened in their relationship accompanied by a kind of amnesia on his part. He wrote: 'I was denied access to what my mother's real personality was – feeling or thinking: she seemed all fantasy: acting: a mask.'[39] He was a recovering alcoholic when he penned this line, pondering the slogan from the AA's 'Big Book': 'the dark past is the greatest possession you have. The dark past is the key not the lock.' He was trying to come up with a self-inventory that might help him. Many unlocked doors might have revealed what was to blame for Tony's 'lost youth.' One, I expect, revealed that his mother could never just be 'mum' and nothing else.

When Anne Donaldson interviewed Miss Houston in 1965, she noted Renée's 'constant restless activity that seems something more than the natural tension of an actress just about to go on stage.'[40] This 'manic dispositional type' had a chattering mind that worked overtime, finding a niche in entertaining others. Perhaps she had no way of controlling it. Even before Miss Houston was a victim of the worst kind of wartime bombing this nervous and manic streak was showing signs.

The timing of the breakdown she had in 1940 is curious. They had just moved from Stanmore to the small village of Alveston, located to the east of Stratford-upon-Avon where they hoped to be out of harm's way. I say 'moved' but this isn't true, as a writ had been issued to both Ahernes. They were surviving on ready cash from a bill of sale on the furniture from *'Abbotswood.'* This might be the real reason why they left London. The marriage had started its rocky period. Stress about money and forever losing it the next minute was yet another factor adding to Renée's troubles.

Renée and Don appeared at the Glasgow Empire between April 29 and May 6 1940, then on May 23 returned to Finsbury Park. The theatre stood close to the tube station, set back from Blackstock Road, where Vaudeville Court is today. In *Design for Glamour* Billy Russell brought 'fresh material to his amusing dissertation on behalf of the working classes', pianist Freddie Bamberger supplied his usual *sophisticated nonsense,* whilst Cawalini's dogs, and the Sherman Fisher Girls also featured.

An old family friend of Pat's found them their safe haven in the Midlands in April, and the next month after the boys finished term at Alquin House, everyone settled here. There was a popular belief that the Fuhrer, admiring the Bard so much, would never bomb Stratford. Everyone crammed into *'The Old Vicarage'* – and this gradually got worse when successive evacuees came to stay for lengthy periods. The house was 650 years old, with beams, thick walls and huge old fireplaces containing the little steps a boy sweep in olden times used to climb.

Rationing was introduced at the beginning of 1940 making everyone mindful about nutrition and food for the next fourteen years. Granny Houston made sure that when the milkman came she got the right measure, dipping a jug carefully into the vat. The Ahernes were luckier living in the country where things could be obtained fairly easily without coupons. When Renée and Donald came home at weekends, Donald had a system going where he went off on a bicycle with two shopping bags hung over the handlebars. These weekend visits to the village allowed the family to eat like kings after a wangling of the best black market items going. Charming the leaves off the trees in this way says much about Donald's character and wonderful talent. Unfortunately, when the two *Sweethearts* went away again on Monday, Alan and Tony quickly got hungry again.

In this quiet corner of England, moonlight shadows were cast on the graveyard next door adding a supernatural quality to life. So many of the ancient gravestones bore the name *'Higgins'* for some reason. Agnes, the family's cook and daily 'treasure' was highly superstitious, hearing footsteps along the corridors. Alan was inside the little church with his mum and Tony one day when they heard a horrible sound. Renée panicked and went running out like a madwoman, followed by Tony and Alan. They found out it was Pat making the noise on purpose though the rafters and let's just say she was particularly unappreciative of his acting on this occasion!

Used to towns and cities, the slower pace of life in a South Warwickshire village was appreciated by Renée and her children. They could not escape the war, and Alan recalls an oil bomb one night flooding the pastureland with oil – terrible for the cows that were covered in it. Alan saw his first shrapnel on the ground and a lot of it there was. A local woman, Mrs Rider, lent Trevor a donkey she no longer had use for. Trevor put the donkey to a new use, chasing the small boys. Tony and Alan had no choice but to run into the graveyard and stand on the tiers of the gravestones to escape the animal. A little cart came with the donkey and you could also ride it bareback too, except for the times if would extend its paws out in front - a sign it was ready to roll over. The vicar's wife used to call out to the kids when Renée and Donald were on the radio, but used to hearing the boring patter at home, they weren't interested in the least.

After the first couple of months of the Blitz few people in blackened, smoking London could continue their normal occupations. Auntie May's Wembley-based café was now a food store. One item it stocked was banana powder - used in drinks and a substance held in absolute reverence by the hungry children. She arrived in Alveston with Hal Silander. Unlike his older brother, Hal was exempt from service owing to a hernia condition that required him to wear a support belt. He became a government food inspector in the early war years then worked at Stork Margarine in Stratford.

The family took a second cottage *'Ferryview'* in the village to accommodate everyone now *'The Old Vicarage'* was bursting at the seams. The new house had small windows in the lounge and when Alan had his seventh birthday here they couldn't buy toys so he had a cardboard castle and a set of tiddlywinks Auntie Billie gave him. They played with these on the table and the tiddlywinks doubled as soldiers. Pat found an ingenious way of making homemade lead soldiers out of a mould, and painted these for his son. Agnes, their cook, left when Tony fired a small gun at her Pomeranian and it became Auntie May's job to watch over Tony and Alan. Renée travelled a lot so May was a great help. Donald built an extension to the second cottage – a log cabin that went down to the Avon. Their local pub, 'The Exchange,' run by Frank Needle, provided a hub and they were ensconced here as the Battle of Britain was raging, and Alan recalls the 'wurrr' sound made by the sirens followed by a thud – although nothing happened. They listened carefully for a 'screaming bomb' and Shirley put people at ease informing them that 'if you can hear the screaming bomb that means that you're safe.' Having finished with Bonar Colleano, she had recently acquired the veneer of authority that comes with being the fiancé of the son of the Mayor of Stratford, so she knew what she was talking about.

The summer months of June and July were a time of paranoia in Britain. This followed the defeat at Dunkirk in late May and early June, although the brave actions of those involved made it appear a victory. Belgium's surrender followed. A *Low* cartoon in the Evening Standard "Very well – alone" gave the message Britain was better without aliens. The new Prime Minister, Churchill made his "collar the lot" speech on June 11, 1940 and a ransacking of German and Italian cafés and businesses in cities followed. People began to witness the horror of light bombings and fear set in about parachute landings by *Gerrys* as well as conspiracies in the midst.

Harold Nicolson, Minister of Information, sensed the negative atmosphere and felt too much had been said about Fifth Columnists. He appealed to 15,000 people at a free open-air show known as the *Rout the Rumour Rally* on July 21 1940 in Hendon Park. He stated how the government had no wish to restrict human converse or damp neighbourly gossip. He also wanted people to know that the freedom of the press was something that could still be cherished.[41] At this 'cheerio crusade' the minister was joined by popular stars whose unpaid services were requested by the war effort. A dark-haired Renée, separated from her 'alien' partner, had the crowd in her hand and Will Fyffe provided a further Scots take on the wartime atmosphere. Jack Warner quipped about Italians winning the boat race then Sergeant Will Hay spoke about the grounding that comes from our British sense of humour – pointing out that most of the well-known Nazis weren't even aware what a funny-looking bunch of caricatures they were. Flotsam and Jetsam, Jack Hawkins, Lucan and McShane, Phyllis Robins and the Band of HM Grenadier Guards conducted by Major George Miller were also in the line-up. An ecstatic crowd enjoyed the gags and took part in patriotic community singing. The rally was broadcast on the BBC Forces Programme that day.

Entertained in Aldwych Tube, Bomb Damage, 1940   (Author's Collection)

By August 1940, 175,000 Londoners were arriving every night seeking shelter in the Underground and heavy raids on September 7-8 forced many to make what was a sanctuary a home, forcing a reluctant government to supply bunk beds and toilets on the platforms. By the time the London Blitz was over, a quarter of a million Londoners had lost their homes. Those still in homes gathered around their radios while JB Priestley's short propaganda 'talks' about British spirit brought comfort and helped them carry on. Renée and Don braved the dangers of London throughout August and September. At Finsbury Park on September 5 compère Harold Berens introduced them in the *'Dorchester Follies'* line-up with Buddy Logan, massive Charles Jones in drag, and Renée's old pal Frank Boston. The small, folded paper programmes for Moss Empires theatres cost 2d and carried illustrated ads for TCP - *'simply indispensible'* to those on war service and chosen first aid antiseptic in factories. *Variety's Sweethearts*, departing by train, got out in time to escape 'Black Saturday' on September 7.

'Keep Calm! Don't Worry!! The Raiders May Not Be Coming Here' says the programme for Renée's next stage show. A copy kept by the family has been annotated either by Terry, Renée, or Pat with small suggestions and observations. In Stratford, the Shakespeare Festival, directed by Iden Payne, had returned from touring the Garrison theatres and finished a season that had seen 80,000 theatregoers made to carry gas masks with them as they took their seats. Sir Archie Flower was chairman, and Henry Tossell, its General Manager, was tasked with running a small Rep company that could provide entertainment for the growing homeless evacuees living uncomfortably in other peoples' homes.

Adding to these numbers, huge amounts of servicemen including many Canadians were stationed at Stratford. The local papers announced that, to meet requests for entertaining the Forces, Renée Houston would head a company at the Memorial Theatre on September 20-21, with Pat Aherne as compère, Donald, the Three Gales, Sylvia Atkinson's *debutantes* (freshly graduated from a school of dance in Stratford-on-Avon) with piano provided by Vera Gregory. There's a cheeky pencil scrawl on the programme slandering violinist Dea Gombrich as 'The most awful girl in Alveston.' Shirley choreographed dance routines that included 'Exit To Music' – a number from 'Happy Days Are Here Again.' Fifteen year-old Terry Houston was a prominent supporting player, often accompanied by another young dancer called *Manya* - possibly dancer Manya Zarina. Terry's parts include *Ivy* in *Outdoor Sports* and *The Storm* in *Rain Ballet*. In *Cameo 3* Terry was a *Bright Young Thing* with Pat playing a Bolshevist and Renée an Adventuress. Terry played the *daughter* in *Go To It*, and a *tourist* in *Nautch Dance*.

Shakespeare Memorial Theatre 1930s from postcard (Author's Collection)

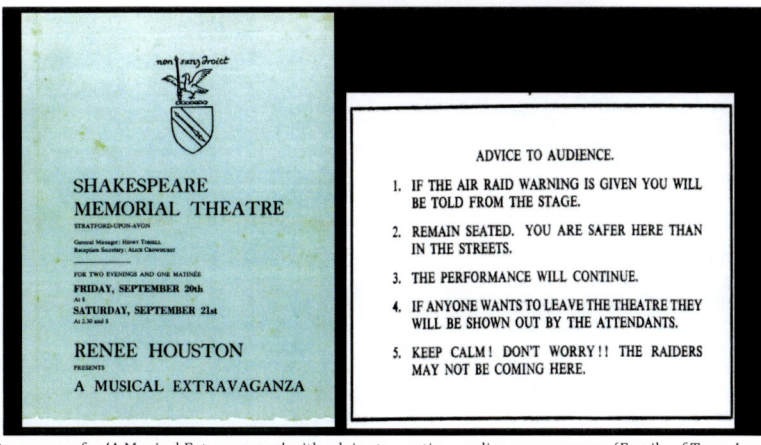

Programme for 'A Musical Extravaganza' with advice to wartime audience on reverse. (Family of Terry Long)

Donald's friend Jay Laurier, known at the Memorial Theatre for his gallery of Shakespearean achievements happily returned to his vaudeville roots. That April Laurier had played Falstaff in Merry Wives of Windsor at the Memorial Theatre. The *Musical Extravaganza* was just an experiment, Tossell stressed, continuing only if receipts showed it was 'what the public wants.'[42]

Ticket prices ranged from 6s, 5s, 3s 6d and 2s 6d, with a balcony at 1s 3d. Renée claims it was she who persuaded Tossell to put on the show. It was quite a challenge to get a theatrical company together at this time with petrol rationing, and also because the National Service Act meant actors could be called up in mid-season. The Houstons had the advantage of coming as a unit and being locals. They were also content to take a cut in pay so the benefit of having them at the Memorial was very clear to Tossell.

The Houston presence caused few ripples on the Avon. They weren't going to disturb these ancient surroundings, and instead fitted in with respectable local circles, counting the local vicar and his wife among their friends, and the family of the local vicar at nearby Loxley. For Pat, country life came easily, and in his free time he enjoyed hunting, fishing and shooting. The vicar's attractive daughter shared these interests, and became a great friend.

Columnists in the local newspapers talked about the desirability of planting cabbages, the scarcity of eggs, and the generosity of local people contributing to the *Heart of England Spitfire Fund*. One industrious man planted peas and sold them dried to raise a considerable sum for the cause whilst another spent a year saving up £3 in nickel threepenny pieces. Other local opinions expressed included ones like 'buying packet suet makes women lazy.' Stratfordians also debated whether or not the annual *Mop Fair* should go ahead. Cases were reported of local people being fined 10s for blackout offenses when they left a covered window open by accident or for lighting a bonfire. On September 11, the local papers ran the story 'Renée Houston Fined At Stratford.' She was fined £1 for the offense of 'harbouring an alien' by not announcing Donald's presence to the local police. Annoyed at the summons, she dismissed the law, making suet of the detective who fussed about it: 'You cannot summons me. Wait until I get in court! I'll tell them what I think of it,' she braved, although she ended up humbly making a plea of ignorance. The papers reported her pawky dialogue:

> Magistrate: We accept your plea of ignorance and shall let you off with a fine of £1.
> Renée: That is very nice of you. Thank you very much
> Renée: Have you a pound Donald? (Calling to him at the back of the court)[43]

Actor Ben Lyon encouraged Donald to join the US forces as he had been aching to serve as a pilot, having taken flying lessons during his early days on Broadway. However, after writing to the US Embassy for advice, Joseph Kennedy told him he would best serve his adopted country through entertainment, and serving as an American character in patriotic British films. After the first performance of *Musical Extravaganza,* Renée jibed about her 'very friendly alien' to the audience. Bookings far exceeded expectations, the newspapers reported, although the cheaper seats were most in demand, and there was a shortage of these. A *Second Musical Extravaganza* was held between 3-5 October. The local paper declared that she was 'certainly not rusticating' in rural Warwickshire, and that her 'reappearance was most welcome in these grey war days.' Len Clifford and Freda Fayre joined the revue, and there were new sketches like *Delicious and Daft* and *Moonlight Mimosa* whilst Pat's funny stories were much appreciated by the lads in khaki and 'suavely filled the interludes.'[44] A *Third Musical Extravaganza* was staged between 9-12 October, featuring Donald in the vent sketch that Billie used to do, with the same doll of course, as well as *Hollandaise Sauce* attractively served by Renée - strangely suggestive of revues of the future. There was *Memory Lane* – a war episode in song and tableaux. The whole company enacted a further picturesque scena *Sleepy Lagoon*.

Despite the geniality onstage, a new set of management fall outs were coming with Renée taking on the Memorial Theatre's board of directors who now planned to close the show, prompting an emphatic 'You can't do that!' Like a prototype for one of the characters in JB Priestley's screenplay 'Let The People Sing', she was earnest in her rant about keeping the *Musical Extravaganza* going. When these brave servicemen couldn't afford the price of a seat in the theatre and were instead turned away in droves she lost patience with Sir Archie Flower and the stuffy board over its inability to make concessions. They weren't 'a money-making concern' they told her, condescendingly. She considered them guilty of elitist double standards when they had the effrontery to imply she 'desecrated the portals' using the word 'bloody' in her act. Didn't Shakespeare freely use words like 'bastard' and 'whore' in the plays? Then she was in trouble because the revue had a sketch about a drunk. Wasn't Falstaff known for his drinking? Fancy this coming from Sir Archie - chairman of one of the biggest breweries! Talk about the kettle and the bloody pot!

The children were quick to adapt to their new life. The boys transferred to King Edward VI School in Church Street, Stratford-upon-Avon, founded in 1553, where William Shakespeare was taught Latin, Rhetoric and perhaps Greek. Tony was a day pupil from September 17- the school term starting a little late because of the harvest. Growing up posh kids did not endear Alan and his brothers to Stratford's local ruffians. Kitted out in herringbone jackets, caps with a Maltese cross, stiff collars and occasional straw boaters, they occasionally faced a stoning by the more bloodthirsty creatures to be found in the Forest of Arden. Trevor was hit in the face in one attack. At fifteen, Trevor's classmate and best friend was Tony Davis whose *Ryvita* dynasty family had been evacuated to nearby Tredington. A schoolmaster called him 'Dabber' because three kids in the class shared a *'Davis'* form of surname. Trevor and all his mates used it and when Renée heard it, she convinced Tony to keep it. 'It's what we call a marquee name,' she told him, and Dabber agrees she was right. He learned from her when he became part of the Houston circle. He and Trevor used to do a minor comedy act in their young days, and Renée saw them and tried to help them with their careers. Dabber cites Renée as the one who started him in the business. He was a comedian before he took to managing artistes. Alan was caned a few times at King Edwards. He never did any homework. His mother was never around to intercede or take a close interest in his school-life. All the same, Alan said that his mother was always able to put a situation right – and could come up with solutions.

Variety on the radio
Left to right: John Watt, Renée and Don, John Sharman
outside St George's Hall.

(Images by kind permission of the family of J. Lewis)

It was so cold during that winter of 1939-40 that through the kitchen window you could see the outline of the leaves on the trees imprinted in the ice. On the kitchen wall were traditional bedpans with tops and long handles you filled with embers from the fire, rubbing them over the bed to warm it up for a while. They used to collect newspapers for use as tapers, because of the lack of matches. Outside, the little surrounding lanes like Mill Lane were pitch black. Walking into the village from *'The Old Vicarage'* Alan remembers triangle-shaped boards lined with chemically treated paper on the route. These were an official safety measure to identify the presence of gas, changing colour if gas was detected. Everywhere was advice about preparation for some coming disaster. In late November 1940, as part of a scheme for securing photographs of public buildings, the bust of William Shakespeare above the tomb in Holy Trinity parish church was photographed in case enemy action might result in damage and reconstruction.

Pat was adjudicated bankrupt on August 10 1940, because of unpaid bills including one quarter's rental of *'Abbotswood'*, £8, 12s, 4d owed to the Gas Light and Coke Company, and £18 still owing for his father in law's funeral costs, although he had put £10 cash down for this. You wonder again why Pat, as Renée's manager was as bad at managing money as she was, where their income went, and if pride might have been the main reason why he didn't use her income to cover such trivial costs. Funding their children's education was costly and there were servants to pay, although not many.

Pat had to explain to the Official Receiver that his earnings as a film actor had fallen to £250 a year compared to 1926-34 when the sum had reached £3000 a year. Since 1934, with the changing styles, the 'tough guy' or 'hero' roles he had played were less in demand. His liabilities were £2214 of which £1600 was due for income tax, and he had no assets. He argued he had been assessed on the earnings of his wife, having included her income in making his returns for Income Tax purposes. Nevertheless, it was clear that inadequate provision was made for payment of tax. His conduct was thought good and he got a bankrupt's discharge on December 30. The contrast in the careers of the Aherne brothers could not have been greater with Pat in the invisible role of Renée and Don's manager, and Brian, in big budget films like 'My Son, My Son!' (1940) and 'Smilin' Through' (1941). Brian was nominated for an Oscar for his portrayal of *Emperor Maximilian* in 'Juarez' (1939) with Bette Davis and Paul Muni, but he didn't forget his homeland. From Hollywood he was a generous benefactor of the British Red Cross, presenting them with £30,000 and four ambulances[45] - a gesture that couldn't have been more needed at that crucial time.

The war changed everyone's life and soon after his work at Stratford's Memorial Theatre came to an end, Pat was drafted into an engineering role at Branson's tank factory in Birmingham to develop gas tanks for aircraft. His task was to make the tanks stronger and safer through the application of a rubber substance as a coating. If the gas leaked, this material swelled up and was more likely to contain the gas safely. The technology was later used to make Hawker Hurricanes. When Pat originally enlisted in the army he was told he couldn't fight being deaf in one ear, and was pulled into this particular war work because of his earlier apprenticeships with Austin and BSA, coupled with his understanding of car engines and motorcycles. The downside to this war work was Pat was stuck out in Coventry, one of the most dangerous places to be throughout World War Two - on one occasion suffering the heaviest bombing the country ever experienced. He was separated from everyone in Alveston, working long hours for weeks on end at the Coventry tank works. When Pat was able to visit the family, he would always appear on a motorcycle. Later on, he was stationed there permanently and ages passed with his sons never seeing him.

Sometimes a frost descended where relations between Renée and the Aherne clan were concerned. Lulu needed money back she had loaned to Renée several years before. Elana went round to hassle her for some of it. They knew they wouldn't get it back otherwise. Stopping outside the dressing room with the payment received, Elana overheard Renée telling other artistes in her show how she had to 'pay the Aherne family to keep them,' adding disingenuously: 'They're living off me.'

Considering the amount of time Renée's job in variety took her away from her husband, it's a surprise their relationship remained strong for a decade. Like many couples across the land, Pat and Renée's marriage suffered from estrangement and damage caused by war. It was a crazy time with what used to be 'normal' turned upside down. Affairs and snatched moments of tenderness offered a way of coping with the stresses and loneliness. The marriage was under more strain because of that certain lady from Shakespeare's country with whom Pat had shared an interest in sports and country pursuits. She kept up with him whilst he was stationed in Coventry, offering him companionship he was glad of, and she remained in the background all the while until Pat left for America later in the decade.

Renée's sons used to refer to her as 'The Loxley Lily'. It was impossible to close their ears and eyes to their mother's vendetta against this scarlet woman. The fact that their mother could be hot with jealousy and rage against 'The Loxley Lily' reveals the hurt she felt and the value she still placed on her marriage. It indicates an affair with Donald was not yet established or was denied. Of course a showdown between Miss Houston and her nemesis was inevitable, with embarrassed onlookers not knowing which way to look. The most dramatic incident occurred later on when Renée and 'The Loxley Lily' had words that started in the house, continued out into the garden, until finally Renée pushed her into the river.

Shirley's romance with the mayor's son came to a tragic end when he crashed his motorcycle into a wall and died. People were beginning to value those closest to them and it was wrong to wait forever in order to marry, with the state of uncertainty. Returning from a tour with Renée and Donald during which she had been billed as *'The Queen of Rhythm'* at the Hippodrome Dudley, Shirley was ready to settle with Hal – who was her sister-in-law Claire's youngest brother. Everybody liked Hal. He was relaxed, laid back, unflappable and cheerful. His nephews recall Hal's positive nature and that he was reassuring and tolerant of others.

Left: Shirley and Hal's wedding (Auntie May and Lizzi on either side) (Courtesy Silander family)
Right: Terry as Shirley's bridesmaid (By kind permission of the family of Terry Long)

Lizzi sent out 'requesting the pleasure' invitations on gold paper for those invited to the wedding of Elizabeth Mary Shirley to Mr Harold Silander at the

New Church, Alveston, Stratford-on-Avon, on Tuesday December 24, 1940 at 2 pm. There was a gathering afterwards of the Houston clan at *'The Old Vicarage.'* The Silanders had a double-connection to the Houstons, via Jim and Shirley's spouses. Shortly before her marriage, Shirley was baptized a Protestant.

Terry seemed all grown up, even though she was only fifteen. The training she had received at Grove Park School, Kingsbury - located in beautiful surroundings that disappeared with the ugly redevelopment of Brent and Wembley in the 1960s - hadn't placed too much emphasis on academic achievement. The theatrical limelight she was thrust into at Stratford was grittier than she expected and the experience only left her determined not to take this up as a career. She didn't want to live up to the standards as exhibited by Renée.

In the Midlands, she had a first taste of independence as a Land Girl billeted in a countryside hostel with other girls, learning a little about operating machinery, managing livestock and agricultural calendars. The work wasn't easy, and some Land Girls were badly treated by farmers. At sixteen, she was going to dances and even contemplating marriage to her airman boyfriend 'Had' - a Canadian. She had already dated an English airman called Tom. In the latter part of 1941, when the kids came down to Brighton with Renée and Donald, someone joined their entourage who read tealeaves and was 'kind' enough to inform Terry that death was coming to her Canadian. Just a short while later 'Had' was shot down in action and Terry was traumatized. It didn't help when her brothers found it a good joke to tease their poor sister for a while after saying she had 'the evil eye.' Terry experienced her first wartime tragedy early on. Soon she would be part of a fresh Houston saga that could rank alongside some of the better episodes of *Dynasty* over two score years later.

Chapter 17   Tough Glamour

On with the motley, and the paint and the powder,
The people pay thee, and want their laugh you know.

The performer must laugh it off when landing in a heap. Certainly that was the case for Renée and Shirley after they hurled themselves into the ladies' loos to escape a glass roof falling on them on November 14, 1940 - the night Coventry was bombed. The company was twelve miles south at the Regent, Leamington Spa when this incident happened. Following the *Musical Extravaganza* they had taken the same show on tour, renaming it *Careless Talk*. Faced with severe difficulties affecting wartime transport they left to play the Empire, Edinburgh on December 3, and Renée's new offering was a rendition of 'Alice Blue Gown' with verses sung in turn, in the style of an American girl, a Mayfair debutante, and finally as a Glasgow singer with a raucous style. Shirley and Alec Finlay sang, and contortionist Eva May Wong suspended herself artfully. Before going on to Aberdeen, Renée, Donald and Shirley played Glasgow, embraced by loyal fans whose city had endured a heavy bombing that November. A very young Nicholas Parsons - then dreaming of a career in radio and variety - witnessed the Glasgow Empire performance. He was an engineering apprentice at Clydebank, somewhere that would suffer devastation in March 1941. Nicholas told me he enjoyed Renée's spontaneous and improvised performance and the special quality she had that brought the house down. Glasgow has a special place in his heart, being the place he was discovered, on radio's *Carroll Levis Carries On*.

By the time *Variety's Sweethearts* were back at Glasgow Empire with the O'Gorman Brothers and Walter Niblo on April 28, 1941, they had experienced a horrific brush with death - something they couldn't laugh off. The dangers variety performers faced whilst travelling across the country in the worst periods of bombing in the Second World War has received comparatively little attention. In March 1941 Renée and Donald were due to appear in Sheffield - an important target given its steel production. It was the time of the Hull Blitz that killed hundreds and left that city the most severely damaged in Britain. The train Renée and Donald were on hit a Luftwaffe landmine - an enormous steel canister containing about 2000 lb of explosive - dropped by a large parachute. Derailed, they were lucky to survive with injuries and had to be cut out of a tangled mesh of steel wreckage. Donald was badly injured in the face and the worry played on Renée's nerves long after. Railways were targets but on April 17, 1941, Al Bowlly, credited with inventing the modern singing style, made his return journey from High Wycombe to London - only to be killed that night at home by a parachute mine. Nowhere was safe but such is the way with pros that within a month Renée and Donald were off on the road again.

They coped in two ways. One was a regular steadying drink to take away these memories, and the other was in the physical comfort they could offer each other. England was on fire, and they were phenomenal in their passion: secret, loving and tender. It felt like madness - an element of a fantasy world they shared, but one making desperate times bearable. Around the country others were barely coping and the bombings in Birmingham made a nervous wreck of cinema manager Violet Godfrey Carr - floored by an unexploded bomb that fell right on top of her. Finding her in a pile of rubble, the warden said 'Never mind dear. At least your watch is still ticking.' Violet told him she wasn't wearing a watch - it was the bomb next to her.[1]

It wouldn't be the last time the *Sweethearts* had to pick themselves up and dust themselves off. They played the Empires in Edinburgh and Glasgow on May 4-6 in *May We Introduce,* collaborating with Leonard Urry in a stage show combining changing topliners and his *'Famous BBC Discoveries.'* Leonard, based in Jermyn Street, had taken over from George Barclay as the *Sweethearts*' agent in June 1938 and brokered their early radio and television deals with the BBC. Barclay concentrated his attentions on the Clapham Grand - the music hall he owned until his death in January 1944. Here, the Guv continued to give unknown variety turns a chance. Renée and Donald escaped the raid on London on the night of May 10, 1941 when the 'Bomber's moon' aided enemy destruction. They recorded shows for the BBC Forces Programme from safe studios at Bristol then Bangor, chatting to CF Meehan about their rise to success in *Partnerships*, and appeared on *The Happidrome*[2] alongside Charles Penrose, Tessie O'Shea and Tommy Handley. In the next few months *May We Introduce* visited Kingston Empire, Peterborough's Embassy, Wood Green, Basingstoke's Grand, and Finsbury Park, often with tall, elegant Shirley as the compère for the *Discoveries*. In February 1942 the whole Houston camp decamped to Buckinghamshire within easy reach of Denham and Pinewood studios and not far from Beaconsfield – although that was home to instructive documentary films.

Bourne End is a little paradise. The ripples on the Thames are less steeped in tradition than those on the Avon. I found the crystal clear river breathtaking, bathed in afternoon sunlight and enhanced by the colours of autumn. With time fast-forwarded to the present, Alan and I tried to locate where he lived in the last years of the war when the harsh discordant noise from aircraft and chilling sound of evening raids made it far from peaceful. When Alan and I first communicated on Skype, me in London, he in California, he talked about looking out of his front door and seeing the sky covered in what looked like pieces of a chandelier. He remembered the sight of Allied aircraft during the Thousand Bomber Raid in the summer of 1942 and years later in America met one of the actual gunners who left those long trails in the sky. I met Alan several times in London, when he was visiting his brother, and grew very attached to him. His manners were old school Hollywood, his dress impeccable and the California climate, health regimes and twice weekly tennis games have kept him trim and ageless. On more than one occasion, people who we got talking to in pubs found it hard to believe that he could possibly be in his eighties.

We retraced a path from memory, blessed also by the kindness of strangers. This was serendipity or a result of Alan's unmistakable charm. Today, several peaceful riverside homes line the stretch of the Thames and look over to the empty meadows of Cockmarsh. Beyond the houses, a quiet lane called Riversdale has no public access to the river. From Bourne End station you turn right towards a crossroads – the dead centre of the village in 1942 with its grocer store and old pubs, before heading in the direction of the riverside. A ramble to Ferry Lane is where you cross the river, where the King's Swan Upper, who lived to a ripe old age, once dwelt. The bridge takes you to Cookham with its historic houses and village green.

Billie and her husband Paul Eve first made Bourne End their home at *'St Andrews'* in Abney Court Drive, within easy reach of the station. Then the rest of the Houston clan moved to Bourne End, slightly to the south of Billie and Paul. *'Shibden'* – a pleasant red brick home on Riversdale, was plain in construction with a red brick loggia bringing light from the River Thames, which flowed to the edge of their back garden. A beautiful copper beech tree stood in the grounds. In summer the river was at the bottom of the garden and in winter the garden was at the bottom of the river. The water levels created a half-moon street of land and an island where the rockery was. Tony, aged twelve and Alan, aged nine, used the punt to navigate to the island in this wonderful playground. Mr Turk had his boatyard across the Thames in the Cockmarsh, and punts were frequently used to cross the river in Alan's day. No one has punts today, and nobody can even remember *'Shibden'*. It's been demolished with a newer house in its place.

Left: *'Shibden'* – riverside home Bourne End (1950s) Right: Cook, Marion, Tony, Terry, Alan
(By kind permission of the Aherne Family)

In 1942, whether you were in Warwickshire or Buckinghamshire you were equally vulnerable to raids. You could act out your own ones on a Teddington Studios set. Renée and Donald were in reach of BBC producers and contacts in the film world and Teddington, home to Warner Brothers-First National was one of the few still operating at this time. Warners first cast tough-guy American actor Brian Donlevy to play *Sky Kelly* in the film 'Flying Fortress' but Donlevy was unable to come over and a member of the production team spotted Donald whilst he and Renée were in a *May We*

Introduce show. He was even better suited for this starring role alongside Richard Greene - *'the Brylcreem boy'* as people called him. Renée used to say that Richard and his wife Patricia Medina were the most beautiful couple in show business. Greene had been in America and requested he be released from a contract to return home where he could join the 27th Lancers. His unit gave him permission to play *Jim Spence*.

The action of the film concerns the highs and lows of two American aviators. Originally friends, they're estranged, then individually come to England initially enlisting in the RAF. They bury the hatchet and join ATFERO - the Atlantic Ferry Organization – the strategy Lord Beaverbrook agreed with the Canadian Pacific Railway to transport aircraft east from Newfoundland. It's a morale-boosting, *special relationship* tale, especially in the scene when the Anglo-American crew charts a Boeing B-17 Flying Fortress over Berlin and devastate factories. The scene when *Spence* climbs out of his plane in mid-air to close a hole blasted in its side was based on a real-live incident that happened eight months earlier. A Royal New Zealand Air Force pilot had managed to climb onto the wing of his plane to smother a burning engine, earning the Victoria Cross for his heroism.

'Flying Fortress' heralded the friendship between the *Sweethearts* and AH Salomon or 'Doc' as he was known. Doc had been studio manager since the Warner Brothers UK subsidiary began, and a stuntman in early American films, doubling for stars and once wrestling with *Rin-Tin-Tin* - the dog star. Doc was a keen gambler and tidy sums of money were won and lost during parties Renée and Don attended at his home. They began friendships with Bradford-born director Walter Forde - an ex-comic who had acted in silents at Walton Studios and future *Dr Who* actor William Hartnell who had been making films for ten years. As for Donald, British critics got a 'Big Surprise' with the considerable acting ability showed by the man known as Renée's stage partner. In America, one of the reviewers mistook Donald for a Brit and criticized his 'phony American accent' upsetting Don's mother Mickey. At the time of 'Flying Fortress', and for a period after, the *Sweethearts* were often to be found at Teddington.

In March production began on 'The Peterville Diamond' with the same director. With his fast delivery Oliver Wakefield suits the part of the *Baron* – a gentleman jewel thief who, despite a lack of chivalry, seduces the diamond ring off the neglected wife of an industrialist. The story was an adaption of Laszlo Fodor's play *'Jewel Robbery'* with a more moral leaning. The production has a richness that makes it appear to date from later decades, particularly the scene when the *Baron's* partner - Bill Hartnell - is chased in and out of the hotel lift. Anne Crawford, at twenty-two, had just received a long-term contract from Warners and shows her gift for comedy as ignored wife *Teri Mortimer*. Nattering with Renée on set, Anne lapsed into a broad dialect. Educated in Edinburgh (though born in Palestine), she once wrote a school play aged nine. The atmosphere was joyous with Walter Forde playing the piano on set between set-ups.

Donald is excellent in 'The Peterville Diamond' right from the first scene as *Charles Mortimer* - a man obsessed by number crunching. It was an ideal film for Renée and Donald, not as a 'domestic couple' but nevertheless able to send each other up. The scene where she tries to get a car started is funny but she isn't well used in the film. Her son informs me 'The Peterville Diamond' earned her 700 guineas a week all the same - an incredible £20K now. There's an escapist element to the film with action set in exotic South America. Too bad a more British subject couldn't be found for Renée to suit her character, as George Formby pictures were found to suit him. Then again, with her blonde, modern, American look, Renée – as meddling *Lady Margaret,* had moved away from your typical indigenous character. Her stage partnership with Donald willed this change. In 'The Peterville Diamond,' it's as if the British characters have been transplanted into an American film. Walter Forde films at the time were like this, and the faster paced style of dialogue suited actors like Arthur Askey. Renée might have followed in the same footsteps, but nobody came up with a variation on a Lucille Ball-vehicle. Lucille's 40s films like 'Du Barry Was a Lady' (1943) or 'A Girl, a Guy, and a Gob' (1941) could easily have been the basis of a Houston picture.

In the first few months of 1942, the Theatres War Service Council, connected to ENSA had four variety 'companies' to entertain the forces. It also had three 'parties' for the entertainment of munitions workers. In The Performer and The Stage stars coming into the scheme were announced. A *May We Introduce* company headed by Renée and Donald was listed. Other companies formed around Elsie and Doris Waters, Stanelli, Randolph Sutton, and Canadian impresario Carroll Levis. Sometimes it was a bureaucratic nightmare to ensure the availability of performers. ENSA, who advised the Ministry of Labour, had a committee to deal with applications for deferments of called-up artistes. It was still difficult taking a show on tour. Petrol rations were cut and an order, issued by the Ministry of War's transport section limiting luggage amounts, was a concern for pros. An Advertising Lighting Restriction Order – invoking worries about uneconomical use of lights made things worse. Despite all this Renée, Donald and their company got a new revue up and running. When billed it's full title was *'Donald Stewart Presents - 'Let Loose: A Crazy Musical Melange'* written and produced by Renée Houston. Sometimes it was called *'Let Loose: 'A Plot - A Story - A thriller - A Comedy'*. It was taken to Swansea on September 21, 1942, to Dundee on November 2, then Aberdeen on November 9 and Inverness on November 16. In the Scottish shows they were beginning to cater for numbers of American servicemen in the audience.

The Scottish Theatre Archive has a programme from the Inverness show describing the fifteen scenes including the oddly named *Child and the Contortionist*, and a big scene called *Hawaiian Memories*. The revue had the usual Hollywood send-up with *Linda Moore - leading lady*' played by Girwan Dundas and *'Fifi Laye - leading nowhere*' played by Renée. In that scene Renée's son Trevor Houston played *The Backer*. In *Contrasts in Romance* Donald and *BBC Discovery* Hazel Bray were transported to the *Capulets*' orchard performing *A: Balcony Scene in Romeo and Juliet*. Straight after came *B: Somewhere in the East End*: the sense of tragedy destroyed with Miss Houston's modern *Juliet*, and Neil McKay's modern *Romeo*. In the same scene Glyn Evans - *'Wizard of the Accordion'* played a butcher's boy, George Harper a baker's boy, and Les Roy a grocer's boy. Renée was in another scene called *Gypsy Frolics* - playing a ballet-dancing *Wood Nymph*. *'Let Loose'* featured a lot of swing music and a *Parade of the Allies* finale. Other artistes featured were Peggy Ashby, Rosamund Bourdice, Tony (Dabber) Davis, Felicity Fairfax, Thea Hayden, Lois Heath, Frances de Lacy, Betty Leigh, Jack Phillips, and Leslie Travers - *Edinburgh's own songstress*. The conductors were HH Charlesworth and Stanley Passenger.[3]

Let Loose was how the young and vivacious Hazel Bray came into the lives of the Houstons. She made an instant hit with sixteen year-old Trevor. Her breathtaking soprano voice melted people's hearts. Eric Winstone's band, highly in demand for concerts for the forces, used Hazel on vocals at Leicester's Savoy Theatre in January 1939 and she remained associated with this band throughout the war. A Leicester girl, Hazel joined *'Let Loose'* although she was away from them in December 1942 - booked to appear in *Cinderella* at the Bristol Empire alongside Randolph Sutton. Hazel, Trevor, Shirley and several others were official members of Renée's *National Service Entertainment Unit* throughout 1943. Like Dabber, Hazel would become a full-time fixture in the Houston entourage, travelling with them and living with the family in Buckinghamshire for the next year. Alan said she was a friend to Renée's daughter Terry. At Bourne End, in the relatively free and easy atmosphere, the love affair between Trevor and Hazel blossomed. In fact the pantry, the only room at *'Shibden'* with a lockable door, was their most frequent rendezvous. It became known as 'the room for making love.' They were both very ready for a deep and passionate affair, and Hazel more so - despite her angelic image. Both came in for no end of teasing by the younger boys for their passions in the pantry.

Thea McIntyre, performing all over the British Isles and the north of Scotland in ENSA shows, said her act - the Hislop Sisters, were paid £10 each, starting in the *C company*. Nevertheless, they loved raising the morale of those serving in the armed forces with their singing, dancing and comedy routines. In early 1943 Renée and Don were guest artistes at an ENSA concert for war-workers from a factory-canteen accompanied by Oscar Rabin's Band. It was broadcast as *Break For Music* on the BBC on February 1. The way ENSA worked was that Renée and Don had to commit to certain weeks of the year. They also worked outside of ENSA and, like Irissa Cooper, were among the 20% of British acts employed by United Service Overseas

(USO) - the organization that continues to this day entertaining US troops all over the world. In wartime Britain the USO and ENSA originally were supposed to act in collaboration regarding camp shows, but this didn't work in practice.[4] Wartime USO shows were highly profitable for artistes.

There was a recycling of *May We Introduce* at the Leeds Empire on April 8, with Jimmy James, and at Bradford and Edinburgh with Clapham and Dwyer. On May 17 they were back in London at Finsbury Park Empire with Clapham and Dwyer again, Randolph Sutton and Ronald Frankau with Monte Crick at piano. This was the time Alan Aherne witnessed descending into the London Underground during a bombing. His mother started entertaining everyone sheltering in the tube. His Mum and Don were plastered at the time but the audience truly loved it. The boys were boarders at St Paul's - Field Marshal Montgomery's old school – no longer at Baron's Court but evacuated to Easthampstead Park near Crowthorne in Berkshire. Alan hated it, especially being put to bed at 6 pm, while older boys could stay up later. When they came home to *'Shibden'* at the weekends it went back to being fun.

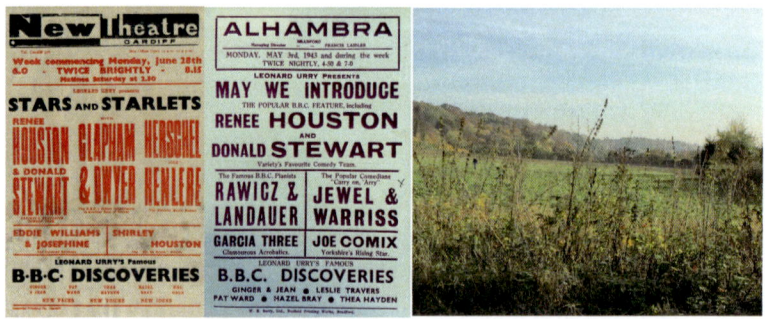

Playbills for 1943 touring shows and View, Bourne End, 2015 (Author's Collection)

At *'St Andrews'*, Billie produced a little girl, Carole Michele in 1941 and a little boy, Anton, in 1942. Paul's mother Ruby lived with them and ventured into the village or did the riverside walk often with both babies in the pram. Billie remained in bed for prolonged periods then. She was recovering from further operations. Alan didn't know Uncle Paul very well at this time. Without fail Paul left early every morning, taking the train from Bourne End to Fleet Street where he worked. The younger kids barely saw him. Enough adults were congregating in their parents' homes in Bourne End though - taken for granted by the kids. Only later did they realize some of these figures held important positions. For a year, journalist Walter Cronkite and his wife Betsy lived next door to Billie and her husband. He was Anton's godfather, and in years to come would be well known in America for presenting *CBS Evening News*.

In 1998 the Dewsbury Arts players put on a play by Mike Craig about the life story of Robb Wilton directed by David Wood with Martin Clarke as *Wilton* and Chris Saville as his son *Bobbie*.[5] It covered Robb Wilton's variety debut with his *Mr Muddlecombe in the Court of Not-So-Common* turn. This was the JP who delivers judgment on the kind of cases that never find their way into law reports. Renée used to credit Wilton as being the best of all the

English comedians. Bobbie lived in the shadow of his famous father, hiding emotions in an atmosphere of merriment and showbiz dedication. In 1936 Bob junior had toured with Houston and Stewart in *Merrily We Go* but he normally played legit roles. He was in the stage version of *The Amazing Mr Clitterhouse* at the Prince's Theatre Manchester in 1937- later made into a film with Edward G. Robinson, in *The Distant Hand* at the Q Theatre in May 1939, in *Desire Under The Elms* at the Royal, Newcastle, and in *Golden Boy* at the Alhambra, Glasgow in March 1942. Bob trained as a gunner in the Royal Artillery for a short while but was discharged that September owing to neurasthenia. He felt lonely. He hadn't settled since his marriage to Billie ended. *Men in Shadow* at London's Vaudeville theatre was his latest play. Written by Mary Hayley Bell, wife of John Mills, it was described as 'one of the toughest and *most violent in action* written by a woman.' There was only one woman in the cast - Thora Hird – in her West End debut. Bernard Miles directed it and the actors included John Mills, also recently invalided from the Army.[6]

Left: Bob Wilton Smith on right, with parents

Centre: Men in Shadow lobby card

Right: Teddy Brown

(Photos: Author's Collection)

Bobbie was a funny chap by day but one of those men in shadow by night. Early one evening, glad to have some film work lined up at Denham studios, he took his landlady and her sailor son out to celebrate but stayed out, and didn't return. Someone found him unconscious with a fractured pelvis early on Thursday August 5, 1943 in the basement area of a mansion block in Marylebone. They rushed him to Paddington Hospital where he died two days later. A wallet of notes was missing, but the verdict was accidental death. Poor Bobbie was too generous and also wore his heart on his sleeve, but why tell them all your secrets - all the old things, as the old song said? And to a lady he'd only met that night – one he shouldn't have. In her room he knew it was a mistake and decided to leave. One door led nowhere. The window, he thought, was a short jump to the basement – the proverbial quick exit. But a leap from the second floor was too great. The dreaded war made everything pitch black, and he'd had one too many to judge. It was a tragedy for all who knew him. Robb Wilton used to come regularly to see Billie and there was lots of hugging. Her kids remember meeting him in East Sheen and he would say, tearfully, 'These could have been my grandchildren'.

Renée, meanwhile, amused everyone in an alternative tale set on different levels of a building. The '*I'll fetch mummy joke*' was based on the visit of the air raid warden, and the chain of communication from Terry to Granny Houston - resulting in the warden thinking he'd come to a madhouse. Granny, ninety-three but looking sixty, was wise as ever, using her cutting tongue when it suited. She always addressed Renée using her old name 'Rina'. Whilst 'Old Granny' was invincible, 'Granny Lizzi' drifted into a world of her own, obsessing about the chickens in a little coop next to the house and watching river fowl journey along the river as if she too was wishing to return to a private place. Alan liked Lizzi's cooking but any food was good then as wartime was making everything scarce. Lizzi was becoming even less in touch with her surroundings than her 'incapacitated' mother, and Auntie May stepped in, working wonders in the kitchen, growing tomatoes beside the garage, and taking advantage of under-the-counter deals via the local pub.

Years later Renée told Maureen Cleave how her mother used to feed a swan at the bottom of their garden and how an officious lady next door continually complained about it being a waste of bread. Patience was not something Miss Houston was known for and soon they had a big barney about the matter. 'You listen to me,' Renée said, entirely out of sympathy with this busybody's official talk. 'If you say one word to my gentle mother, I'll feed YOU to the bloody swan.'[7] Alan once saw Lizzi uncoil her hair. She never cut it. It stretched to the floor and at the ends the colour was chestnut. Lizzi had to go into a nursing home at Maidenhead and it was here she died on December 7, 1943 aged sixty-eight. She was buried in the churchyard at Woodburn Green.

Renée and Donald were doing more charity concerts than ever. At the end of May they went up to the Odeon, Motherwell to participate in an *All Star Variety Show* in aid of the Red Cross POWF and NFS Charity Funds. This time '*Donald Stewart's BBC Discoveries*' was on the playbill. One regular discovery had the name Joe Comix. On Sunday 20 June, in the august surroundings of the Albert Hall, *Variety's Sweethearts* appeared in a *Grand Celebrity Concert In Aid of The London Fire Service Benevolent Fund* compèred by Gerry Wilmot, with Dennis Noble, Richard Tauber, the Western Brothers, and Anne Shelton. The concert was broadcast on the radio and a script has survived, illustrating the typical male and female patter that made their double-act so popular – this time with jokes thrown in about rationing and the girth of rotund xylophone star Teddy Brown – 'It's taken me years to get round that guy.' Renée and Don make their entrance with the song 'When You and I were Seventeen':

Donald: You must have been lovely when you were 17.
Renée: Yes I was, but the bustles didn't suit me.
Donald: I bet you've seen a few wars.
Renée: I started most of them.
Donald: Why don't you grow old gracefully?
Renée: You've given me a complex.
 How would you like to see your own mother doing this for a living?
Donald: My mother wouldn't wear a gown like that for a kick-off.
Renée: Oh, neither would I.
 I've got the sauciest pair of shorts you've ever seen.

Tough Glamour

Donald: What is that gown made of? Is it supposed to be sequins?
Renée: Yes, supposed to be made from the scales of 5 thousand herrings. Stuck 'em all on myself.
Donald: Sounds fishy to me - and stop wriggling.
Renée: I've done that to make them shine - I can see them on that man's nose over there. They don't leave much room to sit down in these utility gowns, do they?
Renée: There was a time when people used to throw eggs and tomatoes at me?
Donald: Yes, and she didn't have enough sense to catch them.[8]

Alan's mother made him represent the family at mass – a Sunday morning walk to Cookham and back. His mother never went. Having what seemed like *two husbands*, she trod an unconventional path, exploiting the 'theatrical lifestyle' stereotype for what it was worth. She didn't flout convention. Children's feelings counted, and I expect she felt guilt. If it weren't for the kids, there would have been no holding back. If those mornings were reserved for *Variety's Sweethearts* she felt she was getting even, with Pat finding comfort in the arms of 'the Loxley Lily.' Donald was in love with Renée and ready to come up with a solution to her floundering marriage, but she couldn't make up her mind not sure how things would pan out. *'Shibden'* was still a Catholic stronghold, at least until Auntie May, in her downstairs room that overlooked the garden, confessed one day to a shocked Alan, that she was a Protestant.

October saw the *Sweethearts* back at the 'Alex' in Birmingham for *Merchant Navy Week* – an annual event that began in 1940 when the Mayor of Walsall appealed for a 'comforts service' to raise funds. The loss to merchant shipping caused by U-boats was horrendous, and by the end of the War over 30,000 merchant seamen had lost their lives - a bigger loss than any of the armed forces.[9] When Renée and Donald, Gillie Potter and Arthur Askey offered their services they raised £1,800.00 for the fund.[10]

In Bourne End that March, Donald faced debt and tax problems with liabilities amounting to £1,225 of which £860 was income tax. He suffered a loss on a show he was getting together after putting up a considerable amount of money from his own funds in order to pay salaries and upfront costs. He managed to sail through a crippling financial period to make a success of things. The show would entertain troops from the United States Army Air Forces (USA AF) gathering nearby. Donald paid his creditors in full and was discharged from bankruptcy a year later.

The Red Lion Pub, Bourne End   Iron bridge, Bourne End (Miranda Brooke)

351

When he assembled the troupe they rehearsed in a big room in a hut next door to The Red Lion Pub in Hedsor Road. The social life for both the troupe and Renée's family revolved around this pub and the *Sweethearts* counted the landlord and his family among their friends. Just a few years back the Red Lion and the hut were demolished. New houses stand on the site that once saw rehearsals for Donald and Renée's shows for the USO – the entertainment initiative that President Roosevelt had started in 1941.

Wherever US military personnel were stationed, USO camp shows were staged with free coffee, doughnuts, and all kinds of other supportive services offered. GIs began to arrive in early 1942 with the number of Americans in England ever increasing. The USA AF would eventually fly from sixty-seven airfields in the UK and their presence was undeniable in Buckinghamshire with an HQ in underground bunkers beneath Daws Hill in High Wycombe, and a local girls' school requisitioned to house staff. Eisenhower sent Texan Brigadier Eaker to England at the end of the year to assume command from February 23, 1942, and *Ike* himself would be stationed here from June that year presiding over the Allied Expeditionary Force in preparation for *Operation Overlord* from his Bushey Park HQ and private home in Kingston. RAF Bomber Command was at Walters Ash, four miles north of High Wycombe headed by Air Chief Marshall Arthur Harris. Here, Halifax and Lancaster bombers, and specialist Pathfinders, like the de Havilland Mosquito, rapidly came into service. Good relations existed between Eaker and Harris and disagreements regarding which type of raid was best were ironed out. Eaker's private residence was *'The Mill House'* on Riversdale, a few doors down from Renée's home. It hadn't been sub-divided then. Eaker participated in the first Flying Fortress bomber strikes in August 1942 – a couple of months after Donald had shown the same heroics on film.

Left to right:
General Doolittle,
General Eaker, Mrs Eaker,
AGM Harris outside
'The Mill House'
in Bourne End
By kind permission of
Alan Haynes

When Eaker was reassigned to head the Mediterranean Allied Air Forces, Eisenhower appointed Californian Jimmy Doolittle as Commander, so he became the Houston clan's neighbour in early 1944. A Schneider Cup winner, Doolittle was an aircraft pioneer who helped develop and test the technology to take off, fly and land an airplane using instruments alone. It's incredible to

Tough Glamour

think of the Houstons in Bourne End knowing the man whom the fate of Europe depended on. There were continuous rounds of entertainment with visits by film stars like Clark Gable or bandleaders like Glenn Miller[11] performing 'In the Mood,' and private parties at *'The Mill House.'* One of its rooms was transformed into a cinema with glittering stars of the screen often there in person. The son of Doolittle's chauffeur Stan Haynes, remembers his father driving out to a Norwich air base to pick up Jimmy Stewart. As neighbours, Renée, Donald, Shirley, Billie, Paul, Jim and even Granny Houston were at times drawn into the rounds of morale boosting initiated by the USA AF. One of the great things about knowing Doolittle, as Shirley told her sons, was the joy of being asked to dinner at the General's – with US Forces food exempt from rationing. Still, when such perks weren't available, Auntie May kept the clan nourished, and looked after the chickens. Granny Houston was ninety-four in 1942 when a bunch of celebrities, including Hutch came her birthday party. She kept people in good cheer. 'I'm ready to go but He won't send for me,' she would say.

Bob Hope 'America's No.1 soldier in greasepaint' came to Britain for the USO on one of his four major tours. He phoned and spoke to Renée. He was after Donald whom he knew from Broadway. Bob got hold of Donald and saw him once but all he said apparently was 'Where 'r the women?' and once informed, Bob was off, and they never saw him after. Across the Thames on Cockmarsh, Doolittle's son would land and row over to visit his father. Once, after a mock dogfight, Doolittle feared his son might have been shot down. Alan took Doolittle in a punt over the river. Despite the military presence, dangers persisted and an enemy bomb exploded a short distance away from their house, leaving a crack in the window of the toilet to commemorate the occasion. The landlord of The Red Lion, Mr Swan, had another house in the village. When this house was hit, their eldest boy who had sustained an injury in the bombing came to live at *'Shibden'*. Alan and I walked up the bank of the river from Cookham back to Bourne End alongside the meadows where dogs ran riot, loving their freedom and even jumping into the river. Stopping near the iron railway bridge that returns you to Bourne End, we pictured an aircraft flying under that bridge – for a training exercise.

'Two Thousand Women' is one of the most patriotic films I've seen. It's set in an internment camp for women in France during the Nazi occupation and focuses on friendship between women internees as well as clashes. It offers a romantic storyline and an exciting plot hinged around the escape of British airmen hiding in the camp, only achieved through the valiant efforts of the women. The film has no dependency on the outcome of actual events. The dynamics between the characters are everything. It has a stellar cast and caters for a female audience. Renée's scenes in the picture started off my interest in her. I knew nothing about her variety career or career in musical comedy when I first saw it. I liked her *Maud Wright* character: common, wisecracking, cigarette puffing and brave - someone who fought her own corner and that of others too.

Frank Launder had just made the highly acclaimed factory drama 'Millions Like Us' and had earlier written scripts for the *Crazy Gang* and Will Hay. He's the unseen star of 'Two Thousand Women,' directing it so the script gels in the polished way it does. Michael Pertwee added snappy dialogue. Both had been writers on 'A Girl Must Live.' When the writers created *Maud* - the tough Scots character, they must have had Renée in mind. The route from *Gloria* to *Maud* is a logical one. Renée knew casting director Weston Drury and men at the top: Maurice, Harry and Isidore Ostrer - entertainment kings who had started in the East End as Ukrainian refugees before they founded a merchant bank. They had the controlling interest in Gaumont-British Picture Corporation including the film unit at Poole Street.

Actress Thora Hird describes how she was acting in a play at the Club Theatre, Notting Hill Gate when they asked her to play *Mrs Burtshaw*. She said it was typical then for studios to offer actors film parts after spotting you on stage one evening.[12] Thora mentions that the film was made at Lime Grove - an easy bus ride for her at the time. Renée's contract with Gainsborough Pictures, signed in Bourne End and witnessed by Donald Stewart, offered her a weekly salary of £300 - roughly £8,616.00 today, and the contract says that filming commenced on September 15, 1943.

'Mandeville' - the fictional camp in which the inmates have to obey Nazi authority might not reflect the vast majority of camps in France in which Jews, Gypsies and other undesirables had a dreadful time, but it's not inaccurate in depicting what some women from Great Britain, its Empire and America experienced. For appearance, *'Mandeville'* takes the *top end* in prison camps as a model. This was Vittel in the Vosges department of eastern France - the best camp in Europe, set in beautiful grounds. If you were lucky enough to be interned here it was like living in a hotel. Only its barbed wire fence and Nazi flags let you know you were in prison. The water, spa and fine Art Deco hotel make it a luxury spa destination today. Ex-inmate Molly Hall wrote about how the 3000 women of Vittel were well treated by the Nazis and better fed than in 'free' France. Each woman was allowed to receive one Red Cross food parcel each week.[13] A still from the film shows Renée, Phyllis Calvert and Pat Roc looking at the contents of Red Cross food parcels with a stack of these behind them, although if this had been a scene it was cut. Ironically, during the two months of filming the actresses were starving hungry due to rationing. In 1947, when 'Two Thousand Women' was due for release in Hungary, it was banned when the Democratic Women's Association didn't like the portrayal of camps as 'pleasant hotels' and SS men as representatives of human kindness and politeness.[14] As a depiction of German characters through 1943 eyes it wasn't so bad – at least not yet.

A harrowing picture of life in internment camps would have been counter to the upbeat *British* spirit the film captures, and would have killed the comedy. However, effort was made to make the vulnerability of being a prisoner evident as well as giving *'Mandeville'* authenticity. When the two older ladies are taken away to a tougher camp because of their disobedience this is very apparent. Nicky Nicholson, a camp survivor, was technical adviser to the production team. She had been a *Percy Athos Follies* dancer - arrested in France in 1940. She hadn't been at Vittel. She wasn't that lucky. Her experiences as an internee had been harrowing before she escaped. She had also faced a nightmare journey across the Pyrenees before reaching England in 1943. Miss Nicholson gave a personal talk about her internment prior to the film's screening at the Gaumont Cinema, Haymarket on September 17 1944, as a press release at the BFI faithfully records.

'Two Thousand Women' takes an independent view of the winning of the war given that the characters are British women, two English airmen and one Canadian. The internees are all Commonwealth subjects with a few French sympathizers thrown in. There isn't an American in sight even though Vittel had hundreds of women holding American passports. Perhaps this exclusion might be a reason why the film was very slow to get a US release. Having said that, Carol Reed's 'The Lady Vanishes' made four years before, lacked American characters and was a great commercial success in America. Seeing Britain's Empire take on the Nazis by themselves at the time of the UK release might have been counter to the American propaganda machine. At the time it was made there was some reluctance in Britain about the handing over bomber force to the Americans. Britain wasn't totally dependent on allied help. Theatrically, the lack of American characters is a bonus as Britain's lonely and parlous position is even more keenly felt. You feel that ultimate victory is in the hands of brave souls unseen at the sidelines – personified by the women of *'Mandeville.'* The film is a morale-boost to every woman who assists men around her to bring about victory.

The collaboration of women from different backgrounds, within a prison, reformatory, or internment camp is a winning theme. In a non-war context, American pre-code films like 'Paid' (1930), 'Hold Your Man' (1933) and 'Ladies They Talk About' (1933) paved the way. 'Two Thousand Women' is one of the first films to update the formula to a war melodrama, although there's a short scene in Launder and Gilliat's 'Night Train to Munich' (1940) when Margaret Lockwood is in a horrible concentration camp. 'Two Thousand Women' is a template for future *Second World War* women's dramas, especially those with the internment set in distant parts of the world. All the ingredients are here. Who's to say it didn't inspire 'Three Came Home' (1950) – the Claudette Colbert picture, in which Renée's colleague from variety - Florence Desmond is an inmate in a camp in South East Asia! The internment of women by the Japanese was ably depicted in 'A Town Like Alice' (1956), *Tenko* - the 1981 TV drama that ran to three series, and 'Paradise Road' (1997). When 'Two Thousand Women' was released to British audiences on November 6, 1944, people were actually subject to the horrific dangers of the war.

There was something for everyone in the characters, with upper-class *Miss Manningford* played by Flora Robson, no nonsense northerner - *Mrs Burtshaw*, and snooty middle class pretender *Mrs Hope Latimer* - Hilda Campbell-Russell. Jean Kent gave slutty *Bridie Johnson* great style and nonchalance. Clever actress Betty Jardine was *Teresa King* - 'group sector leader' whose secret later comes out. Betty and Jean tear each other's hair out in a very alarming scene.[15] The brawl over an old tin can in the grounds between *Hon. Mrs Primrose Ogilvy of Sutton Banfield, Leicestershire* and *Mrs Woodbury, widow of a wholesale butcher* was something cinematically new: the expression of a baser instinct opposed to the social distinctions and deference everyone had known in the 30s. The running commentary of the fight given by Renée is a favourite scene of mine. She sums it up with her comment 'Life in the raw – that's Mandeville.'

A still exists (either a scene cut from the rushes, or staged publicity) that shows a helmeted guard separating Renée and Thora after what looks like a 'punch-up'. One wonders if Launder tested out his actresses for the best scrap. He stated later he should have 'concentrated less on the comedy and more on the drama,'[16] but I'm glad he didn't because the comic dialogue is what makes the film in my opinion. Maurice Ostrer's inclination towards escapism and heightened emotion in order to distract war-weary audiences is spot on. Where casting was concerned, Phyllis Calvert had more of an incisive grasp on what would work than Frank Launder, brilliant as he was. Phyllis steals the picture as *Freda Thompson,* and I don't think she could have played Pat Roc's character - originally destined for her by Launder. She was astute enough to point this out to him.

In Renée's 1974 memoir she says that all the actresses got on well and Thora Hird talked of the film in positive terms, referring to the wonderful cast. Renée's family tells me that Phyllis Calvert was a guest on a few occasions at 'Shibden' and friends with his mother. Years later, Phyllis, in her interview with Professor Brian McFarlane told him that it was a great film to work on, largely harmonious, 'except that Renée Houston and Flora Robson did not get on at all. She didn't elaborate on the Robson-Houston tension and sadly no one remembers hearing what was the source of the anecdote. Alan suggests that it was probably because Flora had top billing. Flora's only comment about the film is that she thought her *Miss Manningford* a dull part.

Many Gainsborough actors were happy to work for Maurice Ostrer and Ted Black. They weren't remote figures and you could always come and speak to them. They allowed directors and even actors some degree of freedom in doing their job. Renée was allowed to get away with a great deal during the production of 'Two Thousand Women.' The most extraordinary thing is that she brought her own weight to bear on direction and held sway over Frank Launder - something he didn't appear to resent as they were on good terms for a long time after. She pushed her luck on several occasions but vanity wasn't her motivation. Usually inclined to steal scenes and dominate a shot, Renée was suddenly happy to ensure the camera captured someone else. Where we first glimpse Renée, she's on a balcony calling down to Phyllis Calvert, and next to her a pretty girl emerges by her side. This was Hazel Bray, Trevor's fiancé, playing *Lucy Wilson*. Renée thought of Hazel as her future daughter-in-law, and this is why Hazel is prominent in many of the scenes whilst totally unmentioned in the film's credits. Hazel was not supposed to be prominent but Renée directed her or, should I say, pushed her to the front. Such practice is pure Renée Houston at her disobedient best.

Left to right: Phyllis Calvert, Flora Robson, Betty Jardine, Hazel Bray, Christiane De Maurin, Muriel Aked: Scene from the film 'Two Thousand Women' (1944) directed by Frank Launder
(Photo: By kind permission of ITV/Rex/Shutterstock)

Didn't others mind? I expect Flora Robson wasn't too pleased. Alan believes nobody wanted to cross his mother. Renée just went ahead 'directing' Hazel like this on the take. She was, after all 'being' true to her bossy character *Maud Wright*. Hazel is very good in the film with a few good lines. Her fresh and cheeky personality comes through splendidly. Towards the end of the film when the women put on a concert for the Germans whilst covertly managing the intricacies of the airmen's getaway, *Lucy*, wearing a virginal dress, goes on stage to sing her version of 'Home Sweet Home'. The scene is very memorable. She sings the song movingly and the emotion is crucial to the message of hope implicit in the film.

Hazel frequently lived with them at Bourne End and Renée felt assured her protégé would marry Trevor. She was like another daughter, so close and affectionate was her nature. During the filming Renée had intervened on her behalf to an extent few other actresses would dare. Hazel loved Renée for it, buying her future 'mother-in-law' a big crystal bowl to show gratitude. Renée, at forty-one, was more concerned about the next generation than ever before. She was genetically programmed to nurture a younger performer, providing breaks, kind criticism, and sacrifice – just as Lizzi had given her. With Hazel she needn't sigh with despair, as she was wont to do with Terry. The latter had been deaf to her advice, resisting her manipulations, had long been uncommunicative, and was now gone! Hazel was the daughter who didn't disappoint. Renée was having a parenting crisis. A need burned inside her for reassurance. All she could see now was a painful reminder of shortcomings, bad habits, and neglect on her part during the last seven years. She couldn't be brutally honest about it and could barely believe it. All she wanted was to hold her little child again.

> *Sing, and be merry, playing thy part, Laugh, Punchinello, for the love that is ended. Laugh, for the sorrow that is eating thy heart.*

A domestic drama unfolded in the months preceding November 1943, and members of the family have different accounts. Terry revealed only fragments of her early life to her four daughters. That differs to the story of bystanders like Alan, and doesn't follow occasional reports in the papers in terms of chronology. Terry maintained she ran away from home at fourteen - around July 1939. This doesn't seem right. Her photo appears that September in The Daily Mirror, at the recording held at HMV studios in London, although this might have been after a failed runaway attempt.

A year or so later, she was living at '*Shibden*', according to Alan. There's an account from Billie's daughter, who was tiny at the time. Carole told me a story about being outdoors with her mum. She was aware the war was on, and heard grown-ups talk about Eisenhower. It seemed strange that all these servicemen should be everywhere. Seeing Terry riding her bicycle up the road when they were heading into town made her ask questions about her.

Billie:	Would you like to be like Terry?
Carole:	Yes.
Billie:	Why? What's Terry got that you'd really like?
Carole:	I'd like breasts and a bicycle.

The sixteen or seventeen year old Terry Houston in this scene sounds a little more confident than the vulnerable character searching always for emotional sustenance, that family members have instilled in my mind. Some tell me she was meek, not defiant – the type who often suffered under tyranny: domestic or otherwise. At several points of her life, she attracted those who tried to abuse her in some way. Yet cycling in the town she doesn't seem put off being the focus of all eyes. GIs lining the streets then were notorious for wolf whistles and calls of *'baby, will you stop for me.'*

Terry's version of this Houston saga is different. At fourteen, as a runaway, she worked for a milliner sweeping the floors in return for a room over the shop. Terry's daughter in America believes the shop-owner was kind to her mother, and living here might explain Terry's love for hats. It's possible that when Carole saw Terry, she had left home, and was already living her own life unconcerned about people observing her. However, England was not an easy place to be a runaway during the bleak years of 1940, 1941, and 1942, given rationing of food and the scarcity of flats. Living with no support from your family would have been tough, although there were hostels that looked after women supporting the war effort – as depicted in the factory girl film 'Millions Like Us.'

It's more likely that Terry ran away from *'Shibden'* in the summer of 1943 at seventeen. After this, she spent almost one and a half years living locally but independently of Renée and Don as an unmarried woman. She did not meet her husband to be until about a year after escaping, during which she worked in a munitions factory in Slough. After marrying at the age of nineteen in November 1944, she spent almost two further years based in the UK with barely any contact with *Variety's Sweethearts*. The big question is why run away? Why was she unhappy? What had gone wrong and what was so terrible about having Renée as a mother?

Summoning up the image of the four year-old crying her eyes out, carried down the steps of an orphanage by a Catholic priest, is the best place to start, in attempting to answer these questions. She had been a cute kid selected from a home for orphans. Terry's daughter tells me she doesn't believe her mother felt truly loved by Renée.

Terry referred to the adoption in her own words as a 'publicity stunt' when she wrote a letter to the Nevada-based International Soundex Reunion Registry in January 1992 trying to obtain any information about her birth mother. Asking Terry's daughter if her mother didn't feel blessed, when alternatives might have been staying in the home or being placed with less caring adoptive parents, she told me:

> 'I think if she was really forced to consider what could have been the alternative, she may have conceded that she was indeed fortunate. Older children, as those pictured in the program, are less likely to be adopted with each passing year ... Mom was indeed blessed, but I think she dwelt on the sad moments more.'

Fourteen years had followed that charitable act. Outwardly privileged, young Terry lived in comfortable houses with the showbiz side of family life affording a rarified quality. But many experiences Terry had in these years were counter to her own will. Unlike scenes from Renée's early life, Terry's *'Carntyne'* – the name given to the house in Kenton, did not represent an idyll. Having joined the family, Terry spent the first three years living in proximity to Jimmie and Lizzi and other members of Renée's family. After that, there was a period of at least six months when she, Trevor and Tony lived with Renée and Pat Aherne in Barnet, North London near the film studios. Consequently, Terry and Trevor returned to Kenton for two extra years. She was back with Jimmie and several members of the clan, while Renée, Pat, Tony and Alan lived separately in Glendale Avenue near Elstree thirteen miles away. The two adopted children also lived exclusively with their grandparents on Harrow Road, Sudbury for a further year, before all the kids were reunited in 1936 at *'Abbotswood.'* The tensions of her early years marked her view of family life forever, expressing itself in sorrow. Looking back, the positives were obscured. There is a darker aspect to Terry's resentments. I use her daughter's words here:

I asked Mom a question once about her adoptive grandparents. She remembered them well. When I asked her specifically about her grandfather, she dismissed him with a look of disgust, referring to him as a "dirty old man". I didn't press further, but there may have been a very valid reason that Mom ran away from home at the age of fourteen.

While she spoke fondly of Lizzi, the memory of Jimmie was enough to make Terry 'cut off the conversation.' It's unclear how 'dirty' the old man was, what had happened and how frequent it happened. He had always been known for his prickly temper and verbal threats. However, other information from this time suggests a weak Jimmie Houston beset by ill health and he might have done nothing wrong. In September 1939 the kids lived with Jimmie again shortly before he died of cancer. It's possible that something troubling had happened years earlier and that this lay behind Terry's eventual departure from home. It's plausible that, aged ten or eleven, she tried to tell grown ups about the actions of someone trusted by all and wasn't believed. This would have made her bitter. Molestation in families is often not believed and Terry would have been forced to keep her own counsel if this were the case. I am speculating about possible causes as to why Terry buried her past.

On the few occasions Terry spoke to her son about her early life, or about Renée, she did so in a resentful manner, and the memory that seemed to resonate more than any other was that her adoptive mother sent her out to do 'family laundry' for relatives. Terry's son says his mother said she was a 'nanny' or 'servant' in the family. Her children take a balanced view, a little mystified by the 'laundry' story, admitting that it's more likely Renée did love Terry. You can see where Terry was coming from if you consider the time she spent living away from the heart of the family. Why did Renée take credit for adopting her but not adopt her officially? Being sequestered off with grandparents, Terry and Trevor might have questioned if they were an afterthought, wondering some days if Renée wanted them.

I'll never know the truth as to the 'domestic exploitation' but I expect the Houstons would naturally at times have found a role for Terry doing laundry. There are a lot of soulless tasks to do behind the scenes to keep a family show on the road. It could have been she was expected to pick up the jobs Binkie used to do - jobs never given to boys. Annoyingly, that's how things went and how they still do. On the other hand, I see little evidence of Terry being treated in a different way to her siblings. She was never excluded from family holidays. She was a big part of the fun in Shoreham.

Many photos were taken of Renée and all four kids 'poshing up' at the time a magazine did an exclusive on the family. They all look happy, none more so than Terry, whose fondness of Alan is apparent. Alan was the one she loved most and they kept in touch in America. Far more frequent than the 'magazine exclusives' were the times when the kids were presented to adults from the film studios late in the evenings when the entourage descended on the house. They were expected to act charming whilst the difference between their mum's public face and private face was patently obvious. What hell it is, putting up with adults who are 'always right' when they clearly aren't! Renée ruled over them and yet she wasn't accessible, surrounded as she was by other adults. Like Terry, Tony viewed his parents' raison d'être, in crushing terms. He felt betrayed. Tony's introspection was life-long, as if a wound had been inflicted in childhood:

> Accept the things I cannot change. I cannot change my dreadful past.[17]

At least Terry had the support of Kathleen Murphy, before and after the unassailable Irishwoman's time employed in the Aherne household. Kathleen told Terry's daughter that Renée would scream at Terry and send her upstairs to look for something and call her 'stupid' when she couldn't find whatever it was she was sent for – obviously hurtful to the girl and horrible for those looking on. Having your ears boxed by a totally neurotic parent is not unusual - something many children are forced to put up with from time to time. Too frequent, and it becomes understandable why a child wants 'out.' A take on the Houston's household offering a further alternative to Alan's positive memories comes via Terry's daughters.

> Babette told me she had rented the video, "Mommy Dearest" while mom was staying overnight years ago. She said mom refused to watch, saying it reminded her too much of her childhood and left the room.

Similarities to the Joan Crawford home abound, and some family members quote lines from Tony, about life with Renée Houston making the atmosphere chez Crawford look positively tranquil by comparison. However, I'm very aware of the danger of magnifying a few bad memories and seeing Renée as Britain's Joan Crawford. Renée's temperamental threats never resulted in violence as far as I know. Her manic fear about her personal safety and that of others doesn't indicate a violent parent. Alan says she never hit him. She could be very fierce in her manner. Renée and her siblings had been brought up in an atmosphere where a *skelping* was common. The toughness she projected was the expression of an ingrained habit.

The give and take that comes with loving parenting might have been absent. Renée had a drink problem from 1941 onwards – a habit that can lean towards irrational and selfish behaviour as well as ugly tongue-lashing. She was, of course, picked out of the wreckage after her train was bombed that year and she kept her pact with the variety *devil* - going on unfailingly with a brave face whilst a jittery wreck inside. Home life saw the fall out, particularly Terry's final months as part of the family. Negative perceptions became fixed. The child is frequently the needy one who 'takes' more in the 'give and take' relationship. Terry got to the stage she could 'take' no more.

Stalwart in her front line role and locked into it because of her earning potential, Renée became 'out of touch' with the rank and file. Terry's departure brought it home to her. After the terrible shock I feel she immediately wanted to make amends. The situation shouldn't have ended in a separation. The Houston saga later becomes one of a desperate parent who wants to make up but has lost the trust of children. Terry's daughter believes that reconciliation would have happened earlier but a combination of lingering resentments, circumstances and above all distance prevented this. Sorrow did eat the comedienne's heart, like the *Commedia del Arte* jester, but she couldn't change. The attention she had received from her own parents growing up was divided. As a working mother she never faced the fact that she couldn't cover all fronts. Her idea was her wider family mucked in.

Terry and Renée had a different outlook about what counted for satisfaction and success. Terry lacked the self-making principle that characterized Renée and her emotional neediness did her no favours in her mother's eyes. Like many girls of her generation Terry was brainwashed by the pressure to be a good wife. Renée was an odd one out in this respect. This type of ambition had passed her by as a young woman. She hadn't found it necessary to 'catch' a man, nor was she seduced by the materialistic promises a man's status and power might offer. Pat swung it with his Hispano-Suiza but it was nothing compared to her achievements. The glories of her career were everything. A good 'catch' was all very well but it wasn't half as impressive as catching an audience and holding their attention. When Renée makes a rare mention of Terry in her 1974 book, you sense she enjoyed working in tandem with her daughter at the time of the *Musical Extravaganza*. Had Terry been content to adapt to Renée's 'environment' on a permanent footing, their relationship might have stood more of a chance. Terry didn't see things from her point of view.

Even when she was in her thirties, Renée seemed less 'grown up' than her kids. There is an intriguing moment from a 1975 episode of *Petticoat Line*. The subject the panellists are discussing is adoption, particularly whether or not adoptive parents should tell their adopted kids about their birth parents. When I listened to it, I half wondered if Anona Winn and Ian Messiter were trying to get Renée to open up on this subject. On the panel show, Renée is talking to the author Janet Hitchman, who was an orphan in real life:

Janet: Most people with sense tell them from the start. It's a fact that if you are born to someone, it's different to the fact that you have been chosen. The child doesn't choose them. The adopted child should be allowed to find out who his or her parents are. I was a complete orphan. I was obsessed with knowing who my parents were. I didn't want to meet them. I just had natural curiosity. The truth should be told.

Renée: Well, darling heart. It's a matter of opinion. As you know from my memoirs I divulged for the first time that I adopted two children. They were very precious to me and still are. I didn't want them to know, because I wanted them to be part of a very happy family. Then a school-teacher told my daughter one day, and my daughter was very distressed about it but she wasn't half as distressed as I was. I was affected because I was a possessive mother. I cried so hard that she and my son never allowed it to be mentioned in the house again.[18]

Listening to Renée's comment you feel that she loved her adopted kids, but the last bit about her son and daughter being the ones to put the embargo on the subject is curious. Renée was the one crying and feeling the pain of the situation. This is a role reversal between child and parent surely?

People were at cross-purposes in the family home: Renée, with her 'opera glass view' of the world failed to get behind something initiated by her daughter - away from the stage for instance. Either she hadn't the time to do this or was too used to being the focus herself. Terry, in turn, didn't invite her into a closer relationship. They didn't confront the reason as to why they didn't gel. Renée was proud of her 'open-minded' theatrical family whilst Tony was suffering from not having his mother present long enough to make him secure. Is it less than magical and more of a curse that theatre should dominate family life? Of her three sons, Trevor had a talent for dancing and a degree of confidence, but he didn't take it seriously. Only Tony was potentially capable of following her into the profession. It could have happened if he wasn't so shy.

With production of 'Two Thousand Women' in full sway, Renée was too immersed to track her children's movements. Terry concocted an escape from the enemy-controlled house around this time, rather like the three British airmen in the film, although in her case it was with the knowledge of the least suspected among those two thousand women. She arranged a place to stay. Unseen, she transported her belongings by bicycle to her new residence, telling nobody in the family. It's never been clear where this initial residence was but I doubt it was very far. She did not want to be separated from friends. She might have used her original name 'Mary Barry' as she sometimes did later on in America. Once she was sure of her independence, she needn't fear being seen by family. Alan tells me Terry planned it carefully, having already enquired about her rights from a solicitor who could provide assurance that her mother had no legal right to force her to return home, once she was eighteen. That she went to such lengths is significant. Clearly she felt there was no future at home. It's sad that she had decided that home life had little value. It's worth pointing out that she left when Pat and Renée's relationship had broken down. Terry's courage in taking events into her own hands has all the marks of a person with a self-making principle – even if it took an extreme action to prove it! She didn't have a lot of money and had to rely on herself. Her life began when she left.

The filming of 'Two Thousand Women' was coming to an end. Hazel Bray, the un-credited starlet had the looks, and boy did she have talent too! But Hazel made the great mistake in not coming clean about her knowledge concerning Terry's escape. All Renée's efforts to help her future daughter-in-law's career and make her son happy would backfire when this betrayal came to light. Terry had flown the nest in mysterious circumstances with a distraught and neurotic Renée left behind. At the beginning no one knew where Terry was. Eventually, Renée learned of her whereabouts but by then could do nothing to get her back. Hazel struggled with her guilt, having been knowledgeable but sworn to secrecy about the details of the getaway. One day, Renée discovered that Hazel had known her daughter's plans from the start, even assisting as a co-conspirator. Hazel knew she was about to get it. Entering the room sheepishly, the young actress with a voice like an angel witnessed a hideous rage that required venting – a volcano smoking in the most violent way. Reaching for the large crystal bowl Hazel had given her, Renée hurled it across the room directly at her, missing the terrified starlet by a few inches. It smashed into two thousand pieces.

At home and possibly on the film set at Lime Grove in November 1943, Renée turned against her treacherous protégé, ordering Trevor to split up with the young actress who had played a role in Terry's escape. She lost no time telling all and sundry about the injustice she had suffered. Hazel's name is missing from the credits of 'Two Thousand Women' and Renée's anger might well have been the trigger. Cantankerous outbursts came Hazel's way. Renée had a major falling out with Trevor who held on to his hopes of marrying Hazel. When Trev was drafted into the army in 1944, Hazel pursued her career, instigating new jealousies and finally their relationship dwindled. Trevor's bitterness against his mother lasted though. Miraculously, Renée and Hazel patched it up some years later. Hazel went back to appearing with Eric Winstone's band, and soon after was recording tracks that resonate with the mood of the time: anything could happen today, gone is all that's past and only tomorrow exists. 'It Could Happen To You,' featuring the Winstone orchestra with Alan Kane and Hazel on vocals, expresses the vulnerability of young love, so careless in those stolen moments - wondering 'how your arms would be'.

Renée lost her own mother in December 1943 and dealt with the loss - her daughter absent, unsympathetic. I'm surprised Terry didn't come to pay her respects. She would have heard about Lizzi's passing given that the event was mentioned in several newspapers. Quite possibly Terry attended the funeral although it's unlikely she helped her mother cope with her grief.

Renée was never a popular figure as far as St Paul's school was concerned. The teachers were not happy when, at weekends, she sent taxis to take Tony and Alan direct from Easthampstead, to Bourne End and back again. Using petrol for 'unnecessary reasons' in a time of rationing and shortages brought Renée in for severe criticism. When she wrote to the headmaster to say she was taking them out of school to send them to Scotland she received a typed letter back telling her she was a selfish mother who had no regard for her sons' interests. She didn't mince words in her reply, telling the school that she would 'rather be the mother of three healthy nitwits than of three dead intellectuals.'[19] Taking the boys out of school was apparently a bone of contention between Renée, by now having regular 'fainting fits,'[20] and Pat - backed by his parents - who wanted the boys to remain. For safety, Lulu and William lived at *'The Dower House,'* Stratford upon Avon. Their last Birmingham home was *'Norbrooke'*. Renée's son Tony said his evacuation to the Highlands had more to do with his mother not wishing to pay huge school fees than the falling bombs.

Tony and Alan had just enough time to say goodbye to their friends including Mr and Mrs Swan's children, and to see their father, who put up the money for everything relating to the boys' expenses. After packing up necessary belongings, the *troupes* left for the Highlands of Scotland with their mum and Donald leading the march. The younger boys remained here for the last months of the war. En route, they stopped at several places so Renée and Don could play variety theatres. The *Two Leslies* were frequently in tow. There was time for a radio performance from Glasgow that went out on May 24 1944. *Scottish Half hour* turned out to be a little shambolic, causing *Variety's Sweethearts* to complain through Urry to the BBC about Renée's name being pronounced as 'Reenie' during the performance. Also a record was embarrassingly played twice over.

They stayed for a while with Sir Harry Lauder at his grand home in Strathaven, south of Glasgow, where Uncle Harry took ten year-old Alan fishing on the Avon Water. Jim had served as a flying officer in the RAF until 1943 but his old problem with ulcers came back to trouble him and he was invalided out of the Forces in 1943 with a RAF pension. Jim and Claire returned to Scotland when they left Kent. They settled in the Highlands, south of Inverness with Cromdale their nearest town. Today the area comes under the Cairngorms National Park. At Milltown they raised animals and attuning himself to the quietude, Jim devoted his time to his writing. The landscape and its legends inspired his research into Scottish history and folklore - subjects for several later books. Tony Aherne was a bookworm, and although his interest in wide-open spaces and outdoor pursuits was limited, he liked staying with his uncle and aunt. He had a special affinity with Claire and loved her most among all the relatives. His stay was the beginning of many subsequent visits. He got to know the people of Milltown and could escape his anxieties. No longer would he echo his mother's bad mouthing of Jim. Alan attended the village school with his brother and came into his own in the surroundings of the River Spey. Jim, who had changed to a Protestant denomination, attended a little church with Claire in Cromdale. Sometimes the boys came to mass with them and noticed that Jim had developed very anti-Catholic views.

With the boys safe in the Highlands, Renée and Donald focused on USO camp shows travelling to different parts of Scotland with a company of artistes. Dabber Davis provided stage management. At one point it seemed the entire personnel of the Navy and RAF were based in Scotland as they prepared for the invasion of Europe. There was a huge American presence in Scotland especially in Glasgow. In that city, Dabber booked the entourage into the Adelphi Hotel at the corner of Union Street and Argyle Street. They did a big show at The Gaiety Theatre in Ayr, with servicemen filling every seat. Dabber recalls that with so many people from the profession drafted into the forces at this time, both male and female, it was a tough task assembling a company that included the full complement of girl dancers and singers. Achieving that was a coup, given that everyone in the business was putting on a revue up and down the country. It was common practice to keep the girls out of the Forces by officially registering them in a show. The beautiful girls they had went down a storm with the massive crowds of servicemen. The Houston and Stewart shows for the USO enjoyed a great reception. The troops were crammed like crazy into Nissen huts put up in rain-lashed locations all over Scotland. Occasionally the choice of performer went right over the heads of the average GI - particularly operatic singers.

The Two Leslies

The Adelphi Hotel, Glasgow
(Author's Collection)

Army Nissen hut

The boys in the services loved Donald – a fellow American from Wilkes-Barre who had been on Broadway. They had seen him in his films. All the Americans thought Renée was hysterically funny. Dabber recalls that afterwards many officers would come up to Renée, telling her she should be in the States. Of course she would never pursue this. When would she ever get on a plane? There's evidence to suggest she did cross water for the USO, to appear at encampments in Iceland of all places! A newspaper cutting at the time of Donald's death implies this.[21]

Archie Andrews - the high-pitched unpredictable little dummy was one variety star helping win the war in his conversations with ventriloquist Peter Brough. *Navy Mixture,* for the BBC General Forces, featured the pair early in their radio career. By the next decade his *Educating Archie* series had given many new British stars a spot as Archie's friends and tutors. Renée and Donald were also in *Navy Mixture,* and at the end of June were at Bath Pavilion appearing with Ronald Chesney - *Britain's greatest harmonica player* and Betty Driver - famous in later decades for Coronation Street. Just two days after D-Day a 'Salute To ENSA' article in The Stage tells us that Renée and Donald were among the artists who were extremely popular with the RAF.[22] They worked hard, appealing to both GIs and British forces.

A sinister new type of bomb was hitting London, as determined on the destruction of variety stars as on reducing everything else to smoke. The flying bomb or V1 was the world's first cruise missile: each one dropped by unmanned gyro, and capable of blast damage over a wide area. People called them Doodlebugs because of the strange eerie noise their engines made. Very quickly they were causing devastation to East London and a single one hit the Guards Chapel near Buckingham Palace on June 18, killing 121 people in one go. Pat had come to London from Birmingham for a visit and was

Tough Glamour

staying at a gentleman's club. Coming home at night a V1 exploded, throwing him into the street where he sustained a serious injury to his arm and back.

At *'Shibden'* Auntie May was on the phone to her eldest son who was in the services. In a coded fashion, he tried to explain something. Renée took the phone and worked out that it was something about a landing in Normandy but no stairs were mentioned. Paul Eve was one of the first journalists in the Reichstag reporting from Berlin that final year of the war. Billie's family left Bourne End in August 1945 and went to live in East Sheen whilst Renée and her family stayed on a few years. At this point of the war men in the armed forces were in the midst of the fight. At home, heavy raids were anticipated. You kept calm, praying for victory. Who chose to stay near London if they could help it?

Donald had just completed a film with Vera Lynn. Walter Forde directed 'One Exciting Night', with extra dialogue by Emery Bonnett. It was produced by Columbia's British Division, which had output seven George Formby classics. Donald played *Michael Thorne* - a government official, formerly a theatrical producer. As in 'A Girl Must Live,' you hear a spectrum of English accents. Vera Lynn appears as a United Nations Welfare Services volunteer, dismissed by Irene Handl's superior officer for being too popular with the boys. She's also a singer, trying to make a start in the business.

Left: Vera Lynn Sheet Music for Kennedy and Boulanger's 'My Prayer' from One Exciting Night' (1944)

Right: Private photo taken on the set by Donald's friend, sent to his family.

(By kind permission of Wintermute Family)

She bursts into song throughout the film, and eventually gets noticed by all the right people except by the irascible character Donald plays. She does him several good deeds, finally saving him from death at the hands of a gang seeking to steal a valuable painting belonging to him. The film has many complete surprises, like Donald playing an additional part as an English crook who 'dons' a rubber mask to impersonate him, and Vera Lynn intrepidly climbing out of a window. The numbers Vera sings, like 'My Prayer,' are superbly performed. The film was released as 'You Can't Do Without Love' six months later in America. Subsequent US reviews meanly called it 'evidently British Made' and criticized the 'unintelligible' dialogue.[23]

On July 5 a V1 struck Teddington Studios destroying two stages, the administration block and other buildings. It caused the deaths of three employees, including Doc Salomon. Donald, who had come to meet Doc that very evening narrowly escaped with his life. Doc had not only been Donald and Renée's self-appointed *trainer* as regards how to perfectly stunt a car crash should they have use for it, but was also their main supporter in the film studios. Doc's sudden death stumped Donald's film career when things had been going so well for him. This was the reason for the empty gap between 1944 and 1951 when he and Renée made no films. The studios had to be rebuilt. They weren't up and running until the end of the decade. Renée shed tears having been so close to losing Donald in the bombing.

Being human we can't tell when a harbinger of trouble comes our way, and even exploding bombs can't shake us to our senses. It was the day before this bombing that Terry, vulnerable in her independent life as a munitions worker in Slough, met a good-looking GI and was smitten with him. Lieutenant George Joshua Hill was serving as a transportation officer with the Ninth Air Force during the war – stationed at different times in England, France, Belgium and Germany. Hill came from Plainview, Oklahoma. His mother was from a German family from Nippert Lake. His home was then a Texas airbase. Free of the Houston household, fate brought these lovebirds together. Having said that, Terry had always been given the freedom to have boyfriends. Renée was surprisingly lax about her children having relationships in their teens. Trevor was only seventeen and his mother was already thinking about his future marriage. Terry's Canadian boyfriend in Stratford was also accepted. Renée Houston, of course, got married one day at a registry office, and came home expecting her parents to accept the idea. The impulsive mother met her match with an impulsive daughter.

Back in 1925, there had been no GIs waiting to cart their brides off to faraway places. According to a newspaper Terry and George married in November 1944, although the marriage was registered in Eton the following year. Kathleen Murphy and Terry's friend Joan Averil are in the wedding photos. George was stationed in Germany, at first taking periods of leave to be with his wife in England. Soon, Terry made the trip to the war torn continent herself, staying in Ansbach, Munich and other cities for parts of 1945 and 1946. This seems to have been a happy and sociable period of her life. She even attended the Nuremburg Trials - an experience she found very interesting.[24] Their plans to seek a new life in Texas would soon become a reality. Terry would be the first Houston to emigrate full of hope and in search of opportunity. I don't see Renée denying Terry her chance of happiness, even if it meant she would leave England. Lt. George Hill was definitely returning to Texas. Renée would adapt if the only alternative to that was goodbye forever. She didn't want that. There seems to have been a reconciliation between Renée and Terry in 1945 because Terry was writing to her about George writing on the back of a photo: 'Doesn't George look cute, Mom?'

Left: Joan Averill, Terry and George in Germany

Right: Lt and Mrs George J Hill in Texas

(Family of Terry Long)

The *Sweethearts* journeyed to Scotland again. Here they played Aberdeen where the newspapers described Renée as 'more svelte and glamorous than ever'[25] and Inverness, where John Worth was a great friend. There were more USO camp shows and in late August they did a *Music Hall*. Letters had been exchanged between the BBC Variety Booking Manager and the Ministry of Labour and the National Service's International Labour Branch (based at Alexandra House, Kingsway) to obtain permission to use Donald in the broadcast. He was officially an alien. It went on air on September 2 and *Music Hall* was one they would return to at least five times up to 1947, earning 50 guineas each time.

On September 4 they were back at the Ilford Hippodrome - Matcham's Edwardian theatre located on Ilford Lane and High Street. They went to Portsmouth's Coliseum, and then Golders Green on December 3 where, in the patter with Donald, the audience learned how Renée was longing to play a principal boy. This is exactly what she did – going into HG Brandon's production of *Robinson Crusoe* at Croydon Hippodrome presented by Lew and Leslie Grade.

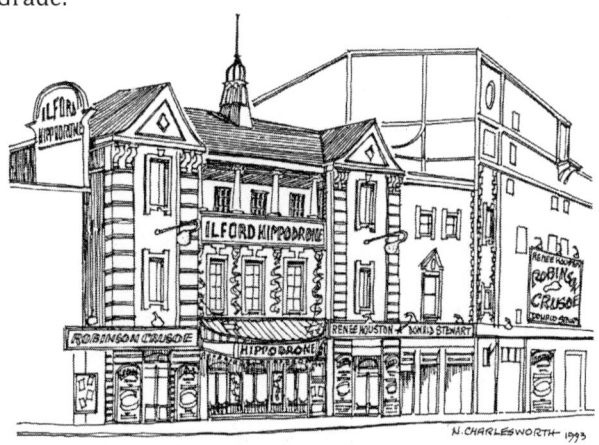

THE ILFORD HIPPODROME: Pantomime, 1945
Robinson Crusoe at Ilford © N.Charlesworth. By kind permission of Nick Charlesworth

It ran from December 27 1945 to January 6, 1945. The Stage wrote how Miss Houston played *Crusoe* in 'traditional style,' introducing enough of herself to keep fans satisfied. Donald was considered an excellent *Will Atkins*, especially sinister when lit by the atmospheric green lamp. There was Dawn Drummond as *Fairy Marina* and Dick Montague as *Mrs Crusoe.* David Litell played the *Cannibal King*. Notices were full of praise for the Hazel Ellis Girls, the Franceska Juveniles and Kirby's flying ballet.

The plan was for the company to take the pantomime to Ilford for January 12, but before they left Croydon, Renée fell foul of Miss Eleanor Frances Elliot, who ran the Franceska Juveniles Dancing Troupe. She was the sort for whom no amount of green lighting could do justice. Renée would have dropped a house on that witch any day. On Saturday January 6 after the curtain there was an issue with one of the 'juveniles' who was complaining of an earache. The star intervened, standing up to Miss Elliot in front of the cast telling her she was unkind to the child. She made it clear the dancing mistress ought to earn her own living instead of making it out of children.

Little did Miss Houston know she had met her match and this trivial issue triggered a scene in some ways more frightful than that backstage at Edinburgh's Empire in April '36. The younger Miss Elliot and the older Miss Houston had a slanging match and brutal scrap ending with Miss Elliot falling over. It provided grounds of an assault charge that came to court two years later and this woman was a very unlucky acquaintance to have for several years to come. It has to be said that, according to Miss Elliot, Renée was violent and stank of booze. Sourness and backstage hostility followed them to East London the next week and when they got there everyone was blown up by a V2 rocket. The show had just begun when a thirteen tonne ballistic missile landed on a row of cottages behind the Hippodrome, killing fifteen and injuring many. It caused a shock wave striking the rear of the theatre. There was no siren to give people advance warning on that evening of Friday January 12. Travelling at 3,000 miles an hour you had no chance of seeing or hearing the rocket before it struck.

Ilford Hippodrome post bombing
(© RCL Vision, Courtesy of Redbridge Museum and Heritage Service)

Afterwards, the noise of the sonic boom from the upper atmosphere was heard all over London. Miraculously, with the exception of one poor soul, everyone in the theatre survived, although many had to be pulled out of the rubble.

I remember the 1995 celebrations in London to mark fifty years since VE day. I was watching an aerial display on Blackfriars Bridge. Vivyan Ellacott, the stage director and theatre historian, who had started his own theatrical career long ago in pantomime, was former manager at Ilford's Kenneth More Theatre. He created a show on that same anniversary, based on the bombing of the Ilford Hippodrome that used to stand on the same spot as the Kenneth More, before it was bulldozed in 1957.[26] Vivyan told me that in designing the 1995 show they sought eyewitness accounts of the bombing. They dramatized a letter sent to him by one of the actual chorus girls from Hazel Ellis's troupe. This was Patricia Penfold, on stage on the night of the bombing. Patricia's letter reveals that she and her friend went to stay with Renée Houston in Bourne End after the bombing. Alan also mentioned his memory of the two girls from the show staying with them. Their relatives stayed too! Alan also encountered another member of *Robinson Crusoe's* cast in California some years later.

Trust Renée to offer help to colleagues affected by the crisis. Even before this there are occasions I have found where she sticks her neck out for others, particularly young people experiencing problems or a form of injustice. One can speculate she was calling time on her own proclivity towards maternal neglect – determined to right these shortcomings. Terry, occupied with her new husband and hopes of happiness was staggeringly aloof in spite of this near fatal event, which can't have been unknown to her. At the time she wasn't even far away from her mother.

I asked Vivyan Ellacott, if he might have press cuttings, finding little more than a note in the Daily Mirror from April 27, 1945 mentioning the bomb hitting the Hippodrome, saying that the cast of *Robinson Crusoe* played on despite it all. He said that newspapers were prohibited from giving precise locations of bomb attacks for security reasons, and that detailed contemporary information is often scarce. He told me that the dressing room area was blown up as well as part of the back wall at the rear of the stage. Some of the flying-grid system and the fly-floor area was destroyed and fell on to the stage area. The auditorium initially did not suffer any damage, and the entire audience could be evacuated in a state of great shock, although two days later the auditorium ceiling collapsed into the empty stalls. What actually happened as regards the players onstage (based on eyewitness accounts) was the Stage Manager rushed on, urging people not to panic and to make an orderly evacuation. Next, the orchestra started playing 'exit music' while the theatre was cleared. The musicians did so despite being sprayed by the fire sprinklers in the pit - activated by the blast.

The account based on that of witnesses is less dramatic than Renée's own account that has her blown completely off the stage, coming to her senses cradled in the arms of a man in the audience - 'a nice wee man I met some years later in Bournemouth.' Vivyan, tells me that several men in the audience actually clambered on the stage to help the injured lying in the debris, and that Renée was not thrown into the pit by the blast. Renée talks about Donald being thrown into the wreckage - his head gashed open in five places, and he certainly did have to have metal taken out of his head owing to one of the war injuries: land mine, buzz bomb, or rocket. He had to go to hospital for several years after the war for treatment on his head.

Renée's memory of singing *'The Fleet's In'* – whilst 'the bloody roof came in' is accurate, being one of the overtures used in productions of *Robinson Crusoe*. She and Donald also sang it in *Merrily We Go* back in the 30s. I have to hand it to Renée for her skill in recording momentous events in nutshells as she does in 'Don't Fence Me In' and other sources. Her memoirs exhibit a brilliance that leaves Gustave Flaubert in the shade. I can never forget her account of the wall outside the Hippodrome bearing only a fragment of poster with the words *'Ren and Don'* remaining.

It was a hideous experience to live through and they were lucky to survive it. In spite of Renée's attempts to dissuade them from coming, Shirley and Hal came to see the show that night and Shirley was expecting her first son at the time and had a very narrow escape. Shirley had asked to remain in the dressing room. Renée tells us that she had a premonition something ominous would happen. Interestingly enough, seventy years on, Shirley's son devotes much of his time helping members of the armed forces, who have experienced the terror of bomb blasts.

Chapter 18   Variety's Sweethearts

At the end of January 1945 *Variety's Sweethearts:* two performers dedicated to comedy and song at a time of shock and freezing cold, drove through blizzards to entertain workers at a staff canteen for *Worker's Playtime.*[1] Leonard Urry's home had been razed to the ground by a V1 in early 1944 so Lew and Leslie Grade[2] had been handling their contracts since the previous August. They played a final week of *Robinson Crusoe* on February 12 at the Coliseum Portsmouth and their resolve to return to work so soon after the Ilford trauma is striking. After this, they were the headline British act in *Atlantic Spotlight* - a transatlantic offering boasting a master of ceremonies each side of the pond. Recorded at Leicester Square's Empire and Monseigneur News Theatre, it went on air on 31 March 1945. Brighton was surviving the war in its plucky way and the *Sweethearts* were a week here from April 16, 1945, joining a Tom Arnold show, *The Merrier We Shall Be,* at the Hippodrome. Then, alongside the BBC Revue Orchestra and an audience of servicemen, they were back at the London Casino (renamed the Queensberry All Services Club) to record *Variety Band Box.*[3] They made many return visits to this show. Its cast included Jewish comic Issy Bonn, Morton Fraser, Richard Hart and twenty-three year-old Hattie Jacques. They recorded the similar *Strike A Home Note* from Scotland, having taken the night train. It went out on May 3, and they made an appearance at Glasgow's Pavilion before visiting the Highlands, laden with gifts for the evacuees.

Granny Houston had never once doubted victory. Her only regret was that they hadn't let her take a swipe at that crank, Hitler. Some cried on the morning of May 8 and others went crazy with joy. Some longed for reunions and others feared them. Churchill said 'there was never in our history a day like this'. Who hadn't had a close escape and hadn't shivered with fear at what might easily have transpired? Soon everyone's job was to rebuild a world. Popular variety entertainers sailed on the wave of cheer, washing up on the shores of Blackpool to people revues like *Taylor Made,* and *Hip Hip Hooray* in late June (with George Formby, Tessie O'Shea, and Suzette Tarri). For the latter, The Stage tells us Renée and Donald's act was 'not too well placed in the programme.' The *Sweethearts* complemented the London Hippodrome's summer show. Max & Harry Nesbitt, Jimmy Clitheroe, Donald Peers, Nat Mills & Bobbie, Peter Cavanagh, and Henry Hall were other stars here. A show with Georgie Wood and Dolly Harmer followed in Bristol on August 6. After this was a full month spent in Scotland.

They played the Glasgow Empire at the time of VJ Day and were dining at their hotel afterwards with Alan and Tony present. Late as it was, celebrations for the end to hostilities in the Far East were in full flow in the streets outside. The porter came to get Renée and, looking worried, told her that four representatives from one of Glasgow's gangs wanted to speak to her. 'Where's Renée Houston,' they asked forthrightly. Donald protested. He didn't want them to take her – not over his dead body. 'She'll be alright Don,' promised one of the men when they came out to talk to them. He took the liberty of unclipping Renée's diamond and ruby brooch, handing it to Donald in a symbolic gesture. 'Keep tha' til we bring her back,' he said cheerfully. This time Renée, normally so nervous, gave this impromptu role all her energy. 'They're my city men,' she acknowledged, letting herself be taken through the streets by of a couple of unlikely escorts who, by virtue of their questionable CV would certainly protect her from harm. Hoisted up onto the shoulders of these gangsters she fronted the procession - a figurehead of national pride. If it was frightening she was also humbled by it, thinking about that other Renée Houston – the little holiday entertainer in Rothesay. Where had she gone? A jubilant crowd of loyal Scots awaited her in George Square where she was placed on a platform like a victorious Olympian athlete. She caught the mood of delirium and the night saw a good few reels before she was returned safely to Donald as promised.

Earlier that year their tenancy ended on *'Shibden'* and there was no suitable place to rent nearby. Alan tells me that Pat Aherne sold his car and other possessions and gave the cash to Renée and Don as a down payment towards a new house, purchased in April 1945. It cost £5,750 - approximately £149,000 today, and evidence suggests Donald supplied the lion's share of the funds, cashing in the bulk of an insurance policy. Records in the National Archives indicate that the house was purchased in his name. It was a huge red brick Victorian Gothic mansion in the eastern part of Bourne End. High up in the hills, and near to the point where Hawks Hill and Harvest Hill coincide, it commands far-reaching views downhill. *'Green Trees'* is subdivided now but when it was Don and Ren's home they certainly could say they were living elegantly in this rambling old mansion that might have come in handy for exterior shots had Launder and Gilliat made their St Trinian's movie nine years earlier. The bedrooms numbered nine although I wouldn't be surprised if this didn't include the many servants' bedrooms, or if extra rooms existed that Alan and Tony had never found. Renée would later refer to the house as 'unlucky,' referring to a jinxed broken sundial in the garden. Strangely, Gracie Fields had called one of her homes *'Green Trees'* back in the 30s and that wasn't lucky for her either.

'Green Trees', 2015 (Miranda Brooke)   *'Green Trees'*, 1945 rear view (Aherne Family)

The journey from London to Bourne End isn't long. It was my first visit, with Alan Aherne as my guide. Providence seemed to be on our side. People we met kindly offered to drive us up to *'Green Trees.'* At the fork of the road the tennis courts of one-time neighbours all those years ago had impressed Alan. As we passed by Hedsor Hill Alan muttered the words 'Hedsor' turning!' showing he's inherited his mother's sense for a good sound bite. You notice the huge camellia the front garden, and another under Granny Houston's former bedroom window. You could cut yourself on the leaves of the Pampas grass. Their old house was named after Mr Green - an enthusiastic plant collector who assembled this arboretum that boasted magnolias, fatsia, vines, and even a giant redwood, that once stood opposite the front door. This wasn't the only portend of Alan's future. He remembered that at the top of the house was a door to an empty closet hung with a strange colour image of an angler holding a blue marlin. It originated from California. From Bourne End Station Alan used to catch the Marlow Donkey to his latest grammar school - Sir William Borlase.

Alan and Tony's rooms were on the uppermost level overlooking the garden and somehow, via a system of ledges, the boys could access the roof to patrol the sky for sightings of aircraft and even get sand and a stretcher up there. To simulate a bomber at the moment of Messerschmitt attack they assembled a balsa wood aeroplane, lit it, launched it, and watched it crash land on the roof. They failed to burn the house down on that occasion. Beneath the tower as you went through the front door, was a spiral leaded staircase, never noisy, being made of a dead metal. On the far right hand side of the house of the house, a gate led to a cherry orchard with an air-raid shelter. The boys regularly sneaked in through the gate, stole cherries a plenty and hung out in the shelter.

Near here, one hallway led to a boiler room, one to the coal store, and yet another to a cellar where fruit and veg were carefully stored. Near the boiler room buckets of water and sand were stacked up - in case of a fire caused by bombs. Rooms on this side of the house mostly constituted the servants' domain. The greenhouses were forever a source of controversy. When winter came the coal was used to maintain their temperature - something the children thought terribly unjust. Donald was pretty good at growing asparagus and sweetcorn, and not many people were enjoying fresh sweetcorn then. Then there was the head gardener, the under-gardener and the assistant gardener too. Was it necessary to have all these leeches, especially with Donald around? This set the tone of the angry debate held by the boys in their hideout. Those superfluous gardeners hated the boys in return. There were girls from the village constantly employed to clean and cook, and there was a nurse for Granny Houston. Renée and Don were living beyond their means at *'Green Trees'*. You couldn't describe Don as wasteful though. He was busy, always putting his skills at DIY and carpentry to good use. When Christmas came around, he made young David Aherne, the boys' cousin, a marionette theatre out of wood. It looked fabulous, only you couldn't take the top off to put the marionettes in. David had spent the first three years of his life in South Africa and this had been a troubled homecoming for his mother. David and Elana arrived at *'Green Trees'* with the turkey Brian Aherne had sent over, thinking it proper to share it with Pat's boys. When the tin was opened the contents were rotting. It was a vile sight with head and legs intact. Brian had, of course, insured his parcel, but the grown ups were too polite to write to him about it.

Granny Houston, a *bleacher* by profession made her perfect bed. Below her room was the library with its white marble fireplace and doors with push/pull door handles with gears in them. Granny was still a big presence, especially when the mansion was full of stars visiting for a few days, like Hutch, Sidney Greenstreet and Phyllis Calvert to name a few. Granny read all the film papers and was a mine of info about the film world. When Tony or Alan talked about some starlet Granny would say 'Not a patch on your mother or Auntie Billie for looks.' Sidney was a very good friend. When one dancer came here, a West Indian girl, the villagers said she was the first black face they had ever seen. A well-known comedian who relied on a joke-book was a regular. Some periods saw a full house here, with Shirley and Hal moving in, and the clans all gathered. Then, when the adults disappeared on tour the boys were alone for several nights. Of course, they got scared remembering the chilling climax of one of the supernatural stories Mum or Shirley had told them. Catholic families can't help but generate a store of tales guaranteed to play on your mind some lonely night. Real murders local to Bourne End were a further source of hauntings. One ghost was a poor soul whose corpse apparently rolled down from the top of the hilltop. Local news could be exciting and controversial. The husband of a woman lower down the hill turned out to be a German spy working for the British. This information created a buzz and the boys duly impressed their friends with it.

Not all memories were happy. The 'friendly invasion' by American GIs came to an end with demobilization and for Renée and Terry the end of the war saw separation after only a brief reunion. Terry was leaving for America by boat in December 1946. She travelled alone, became sea sick, and was so ill on arrival she was taken by ambulance to hospital. Soon after, she was transferred to Randolph Field, San Antonio - an army airbase typical for being remote and sparsely populated. No glass bowl was thrown when her daughter came to *'Green Trees'* to say goodbye. Later, someone sent news that the young couple lived in a trailer in their camp with folk around them roasting a slaughtered sheep over an open fire. Donald would criticize Terry's choice of husband, calling him a hillbilly.

In England, coal might have been in limited supply but the power struggle between fifteen year-old Tony Aherne and Donald fumed noxiously all the same. The problem came to a head one night when Renée and Donald came in late at night, worse for wear, failing to notice the strategically-aligned pieces of Tony's expensive Staunton Crystal chessboard. Left in the path of the clumsy *Sweethearts*, it took a complete smashing. It was a silly accident but Tony made a huge deal about it, and the next day Donald had had enough and smacked Tony. He felt very guilty. He was trying to exert authority but he wasn't the boy's father or even married to Renée. Donald often said that he and Renée had no real life together. Alan told me that one time, when things were very bad for him, with money worries mounting up and other things, Donald contemplated suicide, and tried to carry it out, but saw sense not to. Reports of Donald being even slightly depressed are unexpected and seem uncharacteristic. Yet performers are special people who experience pressures ordinary folk may not share and surprise us for better or worse.

Pat Aherne, known for keeping his cool, wasn't much of a presence at Bourne End. He still arrived on motorcycle whether from Birmingham - a hundred miles away, or somewhere less distant. While the family was at 'Shibden' he got free of the tank factory to take up flimsy non-speaking roles in a couple of films at Welwyn Studios for Associated British – formerly B.I.P. Even if he could not survive on these earnings film acting was what he knew best and he kept his hand in. It was rare for a horror film to come out of Ealing Studios and Pat accepted the tiny part in 'Dead of Night' (1945) in the *Ventriloquist's Dummy* segment. He was after all, still married to the sometime vent's dummy - prettier than *Archie Andrews*, although operated by Donald Stewart.

He initially tried to return to his old line as a car salesman but the market was depressed. The return to *Civvy Street* for many men was an austere experience and there was no money to buy flash cars for the vast majority. And still Pat was used to having gentlemen for friends and being waited on by charladies. Pat was capable of courtesy: helping his sister Elana out of a pickle regarding her marriage separation. He checked her into safe accommodation, left the country, leaving her with unpaid bills. He and Renée had had much in common in terms of financial haphazardness and amnesia regarding bills. His son Tony, later writing of his own inability to budget, recognized this in himself: 'Get aware Pat – This is crazy. This is *Mr Pat Aherne* and *Renée Houston* behaviour!'[4] California could offer a better quality of life and Pat came to the decision there was no other choice than to try to get work there, potentially utilizing Brian's contacts. This new attempt, fourteen years on, was out of economic necessity. He had been struggling since his bankruptcy. Both his parents had died in the last years of the war. Looking at the debris that used to be Birmingham and London, he must have questioned what remained for him in Britain.

Whilst Pat and Renée had enjoyed a decade of happy married life, by 1942 far too much had happened, and their separation had thrust Donald into the position of husband and protector. Alan feels that were it not for the war, his mother and father would have stayed together. With Donald, Renée had got through the worst of the war. They had survived as a close team.

And still Pat believed that Renée might come to California if what the Aherne family tell me can possibly be true. They say he planned to establish himself out there first, then to come back for Renée and the kids, getting her permanently away from Donald. Pat apparently hung on this this idea until 1947, wanting to keep his family together if a chance of reunion remained. It's an explanation I find astonishing and my line of thinking is more inclined to the idea that he left because of work, and because he had lost his wife. Why would he generously contribute to *'Green Trees'* if he assumed that they might relocate to California before too long? Pat's lawful admission for permanent residence in the USA began on May 9, 1947 while he stayed with Ronald Colman and his wife Benita Hulme at San Ysidro, Montecito.

Brian had made Pat believe that if he went to America, he would introduce him to his agent in order to get him the right parts. One story says Pat arrived in southern California at the airport to be met by Brian. They walked to his car where a woman was seated whom Pat had never met before. They drove to Brian's desert hideaway located thirty miles beyond Palm Springs, between the Coachella Valley and Thermal. Brian first observed what would become *'Thunderbird Ranch'* one day whilst flying up ahead in his jet. For a while this would be the largest table grape ranch in America. It would offer him a second career - something to fall back on. It had an added benefit, being one of those remote places Hollywood stars like to escape to. He purchased the farmhouse from a couple of schoolteachers and also installed a landing strip here - ideal to fly to and from Palm Springs.

Pat had no idea how the woman in the car was connected to his brother since Brian didn't introduce her. Throughout the drive, Pat talked incessantly about the wretched state England was in and the countless things the 'Bloody Germans' had done. On arrival, they got out and Brian said to him – 'I wish you wouldn't talk like that. I don't think you should say these things. My wife's German and she spoke German in her house when she was young.' Pat had no idea Brian had remarried and that the lady in the car was anything but American. Pat received little in the way of a Hollywood break on account of a single faux pas, even if it was a car journey's worth to be more accurate.

Thank heavens Renée wasn't present, as she would have had more to say and her language would have been even more to the point. Brian's new bride, formerly Eleanor de Liagre Labraut was upset about it, and Brian was doing right by her at the time. Perhaps he could have put his neck out a bit more for his brother. The brothers' relationship fluctuated over the next two decades and occasionally got icy. In the 70s, in a letter to her aunt Eunice, Elana writes how Pat 'would have taken his own brother to court a few years ago. Yet they're fond of each other - only 18 months apart . . . They're as different as chalk and cheese. I love 'em both with all my heart.'

After saying he was sorry, Pat accepted a job as manager of Brian's ranch at Thermal. Pat might have been a jack-of-all-trades but this was mainly with machinery, and while he had tried a bit of farming at *'Well End'* – in the early days with Renée, he had no experience of viticulture and even less with the Spanish language. He was a fish out of water on the semi circular-shaped curve of land, where rattlesnakes slithered, and vines needed nurturing throughout the long season before green, red and black grapes became plentiful. Eleanor didn't want Brian to be away too often at the ranch. She also didn't want Brian to fly. This was why Pat was needed there, and it wasn't easy work for him. Later on in the life of the ranch, one story claims Eleanor won the property off Brian in a game of poker and disposed of it soon after.

The most atmospheric among the many properties Brian owned was 1038 Palisades Beach Road - a Santa Monica Ocean Front beach house that had originally been owned by Nick Schenck. It's what you would call *classic Hollywood*. Cary Grant and Barbara Hutton had it before Brian. Cary Grant would always sell on his ex-properties to friends and had a great line in sales talk, convincing them of the property's investment potential. Brian had already acquired a Beverly Hills home from the Grant portfolio. Over tennis with Cary and David Niven there would be much discussion about who had the best feather in his cap property-wise. At the time Brian first acquired the beach house, Cary Grant was caught on film hamming it up for the camera with Katherine Hepburn in some of Brian's home movies. He and Katherine Hepburn were making 'Sylvia Scarlett.' Another frequent houseguest was Greta Garbo, or *'GG'* as she liked to be called by friends when she wasn't being *'Mrs Brown.'* Garbo was Eleanor's closest friend and Eleanor later helped her find her flat in New York. Being very wealthy in her own right Eleanor owned expensive New York real estate and she and Brian had a home at 324 East 51 Street.

When Garbo was a guest at the beach house she wasn't so admired by Brian who found her poolside habits at odds with his sense of decorum. As Brian told TV producer Bill Frye, 'It can be goddamned embarrassing. When I go down to the pool in the morning to have breakfast, she's already out there sunning herself, stark naked. I never know which way to look.' Garbo preferred Brian's unstuffy and easy-going brother, who was less embarrassed by her Swedish ways and shared her adventurous instincts. Alan told me about his father's friendship with Garbo during the time Pat was able to escape *'Thunderbird Ranch'* for months at a time. While officially 'hiding' at the beach house, Garbo would accompany Pat on walks along the crumbling bluffs of Santa Monica Bay. She was fairly sad at the time, getting advice on diet and 'positivity' from dietician Gayelord Hauser. Both were vulnerable, and it's a testimony to the universal appeal of Pat that she found in him a kindred spirit. He didn't have a decent job at the time or know what he was going to do long-term. He genuinely liked her and they would buy a loaf of bread and cheese and go and sit on the beach. They went on several fascinating trips together including boat trips and a journey into the desert. Together they hatched a plan thinking they could raise pigs fattened by dates. They reared a pig that had a breed of baby pigs. It was terribly distressing for the child-like Garbo when *mother pig* eat one of the *baby pigs*.

What I find extraordinary is that for the last sixteen years, Pat had been used to seeing his wife do a sharp take-off of Miss Garbo. As Garbo burlesques went, Renée was probably Britain's greatest and most famous exponent. It was too great a thing to hide now he was in the real Garbo's company and had a friendship going. I believe she would have loved hearing all about it, and would have asked him to go through the highlights from Renée's classic turns with Billie. I'm certain of it. Who's to know Garbo wasn't a Houston Sisters fan and wasn't pressing Pat for information about the *Irresistibles*? They were famous enough. She would have been clued up about Pat and his Houston connections from speaking to Eleanor.

Over a forty-year period the Ocean Front beach house whispered its secret memories whenever members of the Aherne family spent time there. Some of Brian's home movies show just how dazzling a place it was. Not many people could lay claim to weekend parties in which the likes of Ronald Colman, Errol Flynn, David Niven and Merle Oberon gathered about looking relaxed and happy. Cary Grant was still wandering back to the beach house thirty years after he sold it to Brian. Nearest neighbours Ben and Bebe Lyon seldom vacationed here, having made England their main residence. They were better friends with Renée in England.

In Hollywood, Pat was in touch with old friends Cyril McLaglen and Alfred Hitchcock, the latter having settled there in 1939. Pat got a small part in Hitchcock's 'Paradine Case' (1947). While Brian's 'help' didn't guarantee success for Pat in terms of his film and TV career, Joan Fontaine was a fan. She walked into the Brown Derby one day when Pat was sitting there with Vincent Price. Seeing her ex-brother-in-law, she told Vinny: 'If I'd seen him first, I would have married him.' One time Terry arrived, especially to see Pat. Her life in Texas wasn't yet coloured by regret. A photo was taken with Pat, Cyril McLaglen and Terry standing next to a prestigious car – a Jaguar. Pat quit the job with Brian in order to assist a wealthy Russian - *'The Countess Binoskha,'* in plans she was undertaking to build a new home. I doubt he had any more knowledge about building houses than running ranches, but people believed in him. By the time Pat was a free man, a few years later, *The Countess* had grown fond of him.

Back in the old world the last months of 1945 were busy ones for Renée and Don, travelling to entertain the traumatized people of Coventry on September 31, then a *Worker's Playtime* at a factory canteen near Leeds where their expenses at the Metropole Hotel were covered by the BBC. Then their patter was relayed direct from Hairmyres Hospital, East Kilbride, for *Heather Mixture*. Since 1940, war casualties from Britain, France, Poland, Canada, New Zealand and Australia had been sent to this government-designated emergency medical service. There was a week at Aberdeen's Tivoli Theatre on December 5, 1945, before returning to Bourne End only to find the atmosphere still one of checkmate. The Scottish Programme Executive dangled a contract in front of Renée and Don for six radio shows but when this changed to four shows, Donald told them it wasn't worth their while with the travel. Not only were they overworked, Renée was in pain and her abdomen was swollen. She tried to ignore it, suffering excruciating pain for a spot at the Queensberry on Boxing Day for *Henry Hall's Guest Night*, going into a nursing home where she had an appendix operation on January 2. She was back and better than ever on April 22, 1946, for a one-week show at Brighton Hippodrome with top billing given to George Robey and fellow acts the O'Gorman Brothers and Ted Ray. As a ten year old, Joe O'Gorman's son Brian met Renée, who quizzed him if he knew who she was. She found it a hoot when he hesitantly addressed her as *Mrs Houston* and after that she talked to him about her schooldays. In his book 'Laughter in the Roar,' Brian mentions Ross Mansions – the theatrical digs near the theatre. Favoured by all the big variety stars, Renée knew it well. The indelible memory of meeting Renée, whose personality 'filled the building,' came to be a short chapter in Brian's excellent book.[5]

BBC producer Bill Gates, known for *Worker's Playtime* in the war years, left a memo in the BBC Written archives describing how it was broadcast three times weekly from factories throughout England, Scotland, Wales and Northern Ireland, and started when the department was in North Wales with isolated factories nearby: a time when there was little entertainment for workers. The lunchtime shows proved an enormous success. For reasons of security they didn't mention where the factories were. In the immediate post war years Renée and Don's contracts occasionally name the location and South Lambeth Goods Depot, Crittalls Manufacturing Co Braintree Essex, West Auckland clothing Co Bishop Auckland, Edison Swan Electrical Ponders End, and EK Cole & Co Southend are some. On June 6 Renée and Don featured in another *Worker's Playtime*, available to listen to on You Tube but the location isn't noted in its contract. The screams and cackles from the audience don't sound like those of workers - more like children and parents at a holiday camp. There was less restraint then. How canteen behaviour has changed! Could it be Homerton with that reference to Well Street:

> Donald: What's your favourite aria?
> Renée: I think I like Well Street best

In this performance Donald plays a reporter interviewing a Renée who is evasive, vain and disingenuously upper class. Asked to reveal her age she quizzes him about who he interviewed recently and when it turns out it was Shirley Temple, she says 'Bung me down as the same age.' The BBC engineers would have assembled a small wooden stage in the canteen with microphones overhead hung from the roof. The audience surrounds the *Sweethearts*. 'That's my public down there with his finger in his mouth,' says Renée in a modest departure – cued by a plant in the audience – her son. The humour is salty, and after Donald sings a perfect rendering of 'Just you wait and see' with great operatic flair,' Renée tells of her long path to success and how she was once 'under Jack Warner for a time - but he couldn't seem to get the best out of me' silencing the titters afterwards. It's saucier than I expected for a lunchtime transmission in 1946. Renée's attention turns to folk in the audience - 'She's laughing – that one in the green pinny before us' and I recognize shades of Charlie Kemble. The green pinny is recalled at a later point. Rothesay territory was forever green even if time had marched on. The high-pitched cacklers fall apart when her 'upper class' drops off and she lapses into song with 'I'll buy that dream' accompanied by a rollicking piano. Grander things seem less significant compared to 'a cute one like you in the nursery' – cue next verse, with clever asides for each idea:

Renée: A honeymoon in Cairo – Who wants a honeymoon in Cairo?
I'd rather have a weekend in Soufend with you and the kids eh! Noice!
And we'll settle down in Dallas - with a little plastic... A *plastic palace*?
I'd rather have a pre-fabricated anytime - wouldn't you?

They end singing 'I wish you were the shadow that I walk with in the park' so typical of Houston and Stewart with her racing in lines in different voices. At forty-four she still sounds like a seven year old. The audience sounds very happy and I'm told, flocked around them afterwards for autographs. Renée and Don's popularity as guests on *Playtime* is born out by the amount of contracts that exist in the files at BBC Written Archives. The earliest is August 1941 when Marjory Lipscomb, the Light Entertainment booking assistant engaged the *Sweethearts*. In the early 50s, when they were less in demand, Renée and Don frequently asked BBC executives about their chances of getting back on. Amazing that *Worker's Playtime* ran until 1964!

Terry aged 20 in 1945

The home Terry and George Hill would soon find themselves in was both pre-fab and little, but it was no plastic palace. When Terry settled in San Antonio Texas at the end of that year, she had gone from a comfortable, cossetted lifestyle in England to tough physical reality. She had exchanged the beautiful countryside of Bourne End - her last home - for somewhere with barely enough room to breathe. Right at the start she and George were head over heels in love so none of the bad things mattered.

Because she came from England, her arrival made news in Texas and several newspaper clippings mention her and one carries a photo of the newlyweds next to their Christmas tree. They were the talk of the town without any mention of Renée Houston, or Pat or even Brian Aherne. Sadly, America was a great shock to her, particularly Texas, with women wearing jeans and smoking cigarettes. These were not things she was accustomed to.

Her English ways hardly made her fit in with the other young wives in airbase communities. Their culture was completely different.

Love mattered more. Family and children would always dominate her life. Babies became her occupation and soon there was a high bunk bed for infants in the corner of the one-room trailer. Life for Terry became even less of an American dream. Raising young kids in a small place left her at her wits end. Then came the stresses caused by her husband's alcholism and the trouble he got into after foolishly making passes at other women. Worst of all was the sexual discrimination she put up with from one of George's sons from a previous marriage - a congregational minister! Eventually there was no choice but for Terry to divorce, and with her three sons she moved to Fort Worth. There was no question of running back to England. She had made her life and stuck to it. She also couldn't afford to travel back for holidays. Terry went to Pittsburgh, Ohio – miles away, escaping the UFO objects that caused automobiles to shut down on the highways of Levelland, Texas. Her second husband provided her with a far nicer house, more babies and more stepchildren. Later still, she moved to Cincinnati.

At Lewisham's Hippodrome on June 13, in a show that included Stainless Stephen and Ann Shelton, the *Sweethearts* were out of season, with a pantomime skit with Renée burlesquing *Cinderella* and *Aladdin* and Donald refusing to have anything to do with the nuttiness. Then it was Wolverhampton Hippodrome on July 1, then Leicester's Palace Theatre, where young Bill Maynard was one of the *Bryan Michie Discoveries*, then Manchester alongside *Troise and his Mandolines*. From September that year Renée and Don stayed a couple of months in Scotland doing the Glasgow Empire on September 3, a *Workers Playtime* on September 13 and a *Scottish Music Hall St Andrew's Day* broadcast transmitted on November 30, 1946. Back in London they could afford to cancel a television appearance on the BBC's *Close-Up*.

Most things closed up between January and March, with snow falling every day somewhere in the UK. Shirley and Hal had left '*Green Trees*' to live in a flat in Oxford Road, Reading and the earliest memories Shirley's son has are the terrible floods they encountered there with buses making bow-waves through the streets. For a year or so Hal had acted as stage manager for productions featuring Houston and Stewart but he had to watch his health, having had a hernia. He had almost died from peritonitis during an appendectomy operation. He was a deputy manager at the Gaumont Cinema, and after two years became manager at the Odeon, Henley on Thames – a job he did for about six years and a position of importance. He had the right contacts and knew Earl St John - second in command to JA Rank. The family would move to a beautiful Georgian home at 26 Queens Road in 1949, where Shirley had two more kids. She continued her career but was a far less absent mum than Renée had been.

One benefit of being frequently away from home is that you're less likely to be held in contempt given your rare presence. *Variety's Sweethearts* had servants and a 'country house lifestyle' but you wonder if Renée got any benefit being on tour so much. They were over-reaching themselves paying the running costs of *'Green Trees.'* Slowly it bankrupted them. They appeared at Portsmouth's Coliseum on March 10, 1947 with the Australian Air Aces, and at the Camberwell Palace on March 16 – recorded as *Variety Bandbox*. After some Scottish dates they returned to Bourne End to say goodbye to Pat.

Granny Houston aged 94

There was news that Terry had had a son so she was now a grandmother. Soon after Pat left the family lost Granny Houston. She died on May 10 1947- just two weeks short of her 97th birthday, and a week or so after was buried in the churchyard at Woodburn Green. Losing someone thought to be invincible was an emotional blow to Renée who would later write that the old girl only decided to die because she was bored. The war had put pay to the last vestige of social life Granny had enjoyed. Before she got too old she had travelled back to Scotland on her own, letting people escort her to the station only. She was fiercely independent. In the mid 30s she went to Johnstone then spent a fortnight's holiday stopping at Largs, Dunoon, and Rothesay. She spent most of that holiday with womens' guilds in Glasgow and the west of Scotland. When she returned to London she beamed at everyone, threw down her stick and said 'Man, I feel champion.'

In late July 1947, the courtrooms witnessed the Houston eloquence - always heightened when a sense of justice was considered at stake. Renée and Don went to the High Courts over the assault charge brought against Renée by Miss Elliot, dating from early 1945. The verdict on Miss Houston confirmed her bitter temper and she was fined £45 damages and costs, although Mr Justice Cassels had no doubt she was provoked. He concluded the younger woman exaggerated when she claimed Renée pushed and kicked her down six flights of stairs. 'I only counted two'[6] said Miss Houston, referring to Miss Elliot's 'flights of imagination,' although she didn't seem to deny she gave her one big kick out of the stage door into the street.

Renée met her aggressor with plenty of violence in return. Two flights are enough! It's not something to be proud of. Perhaps in the 40s an era of self-righteousness was creeping in along with the changing comedy scene. Miss Elliot kept a close watch on Renée's act, especially on the radio, in case an opportunity for litigation might arise. It did after a *Music Hall*, relayed from Leeds City Varieties on December 13, prompting a letter from Miss Elliot's solicitors to the BBC. It resulted in exchanges between Renée and Mr Roche of the legal department. Renée admitted she and Donald had used the names 'Elliot' and 'Frances' on stage for the last two years. Roche took a disciplinary attitude, forbidding her from using the name, threatening the BBC would make her indemnify them for any claim brought by Miss Elliot. When Renée tried to give Roche her own view of the case with Miss Elliot, he said the Corporation was not interested in her private affairs.

When BBC producer Michael Mills invited Renée and Don to a rehearsal at Macklin Street off Drury Lane, he made the artists participating in television's *Variety Express* check that their music publishers weren't banned. Could this be because Michael Bentine was one of the acts? Bentine, then appearing in revues for Val Parnell was becoming known for his off-the-wall humour. Another year would pass before the word 'Goon' was associated with his act but comic styles were changing. More traditional was the *Sweethearts'* radio broadcast - *Saturday Night at the Palace.* They played Walthamstow Palace on October 13 with the country eagerly anticipating Princess Elizabeth's wedding.

At the end of November they did radio broadcasts from Glasgow's Lyric Theatre and Kelburne Cinema Paisley. On the latter date Renée recorded a chat with Charlie Kemble reminiscing their early concert party days. Renée's BBC correspondence was sent care of Billie at *'Denmoor'* - a Georgian mansion in Fife Road bordering Sheen Common and Richmond Park.

Paul Eve had managed to get the house because of bomb damage. It had a balcony, huge Adam fireplaces and thirty-seven bedrooms, with servants' quarters like in *Upstairs Downstairs* - not that Paul Eve's family had servants. They had a series of European refugees stay with them between 1946 and 1951, including a German girl. Being young and Australian Paul thought he could do up the house. Donald helped him a lot being a great carpenter. All the youngsters would venture into the park with Paul and Don to get wood for the fires, and a whole tree trunk would fit comfortably in the fireplaces. Renée and Don were in and out of *'Denmoor'* in early 1948. Lots of friends were around and the local pubs in East Sheen dispensed a lot of spirits while the Houston Sisters had the locals in fits. Billie was up and about for long periods at this time, enjoying regular games of golf in Richmond Park. It was one of the Wills-Eve family's happiest homes.

Billie Houston (Author's Collection)

Betty White's agency represented *Variety's Sweethearts* for a short time, and wrote on their behalf to Mike Meehan at the BBC about their idea for a radio series featuring sketches and providing a platform for using 'Discoveries,' with Donald moving things along as compère. The lukewarm reply said similar suggestions had already been considered. They journeyed in Scotland at the end of January and early February recording their eight-minute act in Glasgow on *Variety Party* produced by Robin Russell. It was another show they came back to. Down south they appeared at Collins Music Hall in Islington while Harry Wright and Albert Connolly's agency made entreaties to the BBC. Letters asking the BBC for work start around this time and continue over a ten-year period, revealing the new theatrical landscape and the struggle countless performers have had in securing a reliable salary for at least a limited period. It says a lot about Renée and Don's urgent need to replenish the coffers.

Trevor Houston came out of the army in May 1948, finding little sign of his family at the old home in Bourne End - just creditors enquiring about unpaid bills. Trevor caught up with everyone at East Sheen. He based himself in the Twickenham area, creating an enterprising business around old torpedo boats rescued from the war. This glorified tugging job could apparently pay when the weather was good, or so he said. He also had a hand in a few enterprising businesses that were not strictly kosher. He found a home at 58 Waldegrave Park, Strawberry Hill - a large Victorian villa built in the Queen Anne style with red brick and attractive tracery, and this became Renée and Don's London base. *Variety's Sweethearts* were at Birmingham's Hippodrome on Hurst Street when a notice for unpaid bills was served on them on May 21. This wasn't the first time such a thing had happened, and the lack of concern Renée displayed as regards these bits of paper was marvellously aristocratic. Then, she and Don played New Cross Empire on May 31, supported by Stanelli – the Royal Academy violinist turned comic. The next day she was granted a decree nisi with costs. Marriage to Pat came to an end - the reason stated being 'desertion ... since 1941.'

In the leafy roads around Strawberry Hill, Alan took any kind of job – distinctly un-showbiz ones such as scrubbing steps. One day he found himself photographed doing this and it was put in the newspapers. Donald got him another job - delivering beer to people in the neighbourhood. With two heavy bags – one on each handlebar - he would do the rounds downhill and uphill. It brought in 20 shillings a time. The downside was there would be notable people in the area inviting him to their homes in the hope they might be able to boast Renée Houston as a dinner guest. He got his first 'proper' job working in High Holborn as an apprentice at a publishing company that made official greeting cards. He took a bus to Richmond, another to Hammersmith – then tubed it to Holborn. He had the job of collecting his teams' ration coupons and getting sandwich orders from the Red Lion pub. He took his own sandwiches to the British Museum and sat next to a statue of Nefertiti – one with dyed fingernails - careful to appear respectful lest the statue's curse might be true. He and his mum were yellow and blue peas in a pod. Money illustrated this more than anything. Keeping down a job required him to mind every cost, whether it were season tickets, lunch, or the shoes he was wearing. Renée, by contrast, had no handle on money - a fact exemplified at Bourne End where their outgoings had been sizeable and unrealistic. What a shame that empire had crumbled.

The *Nefertiti* found in the friezes of Strawberry Hill was a domineering queen. She needed to be needed, and needed to rule the limelight. Her sign was the sun - source of infinite energy. Thank heavens for her *Akhaeton* - a man she cared deeply about, and one prepared to let her shine, happy to let himself be showered by her gold. He loved her dearly too. It's possible love had happened at first sight, but they had remained chaste when it first burned. She was ready to be his queen now. Maybe she was *Nefertari* or 'charming woman.' She certainly was that. Donald was dependable - helping her through her lows, putting her first, working for her, supporting her and quarrelling divinely. He gave her his love for almost thirty years, and his life was not a long one. Renée, eight years older, wrote to Mickey before they married in order that she might obtain her blessing. The lady from Wilkes-Barre had sensed the close bond between Renée and her son on her first visit in 1938, and gave her blessing, pointing out how half-witted both were delaying marriage so long. Mickey, a tiny, youthful sixty-five year-old came again to visit them in May of 1950 following a visit by her daughter Lois.

Mickey knew Donald could have conquered Hollywood in the late 30s if he had tried and that had been her dream. The war and Renée Houston had come during the preceding eleven years, lessening her son's chances of independent fame in America. She loved her son dearly and accepted his choice sacrificing those old hopes. She seems an extremely unselfish woman who was always in touch, and a guiding light who made the distance between them negligible.

She was a surrogate mother for Don's wife too. Mickey began a voyage back east after the 1950 visit, with a letter from Donald: 'You were upset because you were thinking of the eleven years since you last saw me, and it worried you, for fear another long time would elapse. If I can't get work in the States I'll come the cheap way on a merchant ship even if it's only a week.'[7] Such letters are poignant because it was something they spoke of so many times but Donald was never able to make that journey home. It seems astonishing but it didn't happen. Renée writes a postscript to the letter to 'Dearest Mickey Mother' telling her how she 'kicked up one hell of a stink today' when someone tried to use the baking pan Mickey had left them. 'After you left, we both went to the cinema together and silently wept. The poor dog goes to your door and whimpers.' For the next sixteen years Donald and Mickey and Renée were in touch every month if not more.

The *Sweethearts* were on the Bernard Delfont circuit appearing at Chatham Hippodrome, and for the week beginning August 2 they played Finsbury Park Empire at a time when the Andrews Sisters were appearing at the London Palladium.[8]

The Andrews Sisters (Author's Collection)

On the morning of Saturday August 7 Renée and Donald were married - each stepping out of a big Rolls Royce at the registry office in Caxton Street as crowds whistled and waved. The groom wore a morning suit and the bride - a beige *New Look* dress with a veil of bird's nest netting over her swept up hair and 40s wedges on her feet to create height. When the doors of Caxton Hall opened a little later, Renée looked small and lissome carried in her husband's arms, dangling the small bouquet of white and yellow roses, with her mother's wedding ring on her finger. She beamed with happiness as reporters from the News of the World got their photo.

Neither Tony nor Alan attended the big party held after the wedding. Donald would say he'd been denied the proper family life he'd wanted for so long. There was no need for secrets any more. That night the couple got a standing ovation when they went on at Finsbury Park Empire and their dressing room was ankle-deep in confetti, very fitting, as in so many ways, the variety world was their true home. They caught a train to Scotland for their honeymoon although couldn't help appearing once at the Glasgow Empire. They stayed at Dalblair Hotel in Ayr, a beautiful and stately guesthouse not far from the beach, run by the well-connected Jessie Burns - a good friend of Renée's whom she used to call 'the Scottish Elsa Maxwell' owing to her talent for looking after people. Sadly the Dalblair has gone.

Above: Hotel Dalblair, Ayr in 1948
(Author's Collection)

Right: Cartoon showing
Renée and Don, Max Miller, June Richmond.
The Casino, 1948.
(By kind permission
of the family of J. Lewis)

They came back refreshed and ready to make a declaration of bankruptcy on Wednesday August 18. The following Monday at the Casino on Old Compton Street[9] Renée and Don were back not only to play up the 'sexy angles,' as one notice reads, but to introduce a note of novelty in their dramatic classic skit. The sound of American jazz orchestras, often with talented pianists and excellent female jazz vocalists characterize the zeitgeist. June Richmond, the 18-stone singer sang 'Don't Fence Me In' and other bluesy swing-numbers at the Casino. Max Miller topped the bill with blue jokes and duets with blind pianist Alfred Thripp, declaring to the audience that 'No dollars are going out of here tonight.'[10]

Donald looked subdued, and I can understand why, as he had had a notice served on him at the theatre, just before he went on. It referred to the £300 borrowed from a Lionel Clarke of Reading that he and Renée hadn't repaid and it prompted a court summons. The tax authorities were waiting to pounce. The period of high living at *'Green Trees'* ended when Don sold the property in January 1948, apparently having a surplus of only £52 left after its sale. Where had the money gone? The combined earnings of *Variety's Sweethearts* had been high in the later years of the war. Why had they got themselves into this state? The answer is a combination of things: no accountant, incapacity to organize money, believing you're immune to consequences, borrowing extravagantly, supporting a number of people, dismissing the warning signs, and letting things go. You could try justifying it on account of your high expenses, on being constantly distracted by work, or even that it was your generosity to others that left you high and dry.

The messiest part of their 1948 money crisis was the tax side of things. Traditionally, the tax authorities had a special 'variety artistes section.' Their reputation of keeping track of everything - down to the smallest one night concert - was well known. While variety artistes were considered self-employed, they couldn't work unless somebody offered then a contract and there were gaps between periods. Usually paid in cash, their earnings were sometimes 'shares' – calculated as a percentage of takings at the box office – causing more variation. For tax purposes you got assessed over a three-year period and on the highest year's earnings - as if you earned the top figure every year of the three. Renée and Don were stung for non-payment for 1942 to 1943 - a time when their earnings had been especially high.

At the start of the war only one in five of the working population paid income tax, and a small proportion within this group paid supertax or surtax: the top rate. Renée and Donald were liable for the latter - a truly confiscatory system. In the UK today there's no equivalent as supertax was replaced with the higher rate of income tax in 1973 and Margaret Thatcher reduced personal rates significantly in the 80s. In America too, the top bracket income tax rate was over 90% in the late 40s and today is less than half that amount. Each *Sweetheart* has a court record surviving from this time, and the unpaid income tax shows that Renée owed £2579 (about £67,000 today) and that Donald owed £2859 11s 11d (about £74,000 today). Reading their case notes I thought of all they had done for the war effort, often being in the line of danger, only for the ungrateful victors to wring out of them everything they could, moneywise. Renée used to say to people 'we worked hard during the war, and as soon as the war was over they chucked us aside and brought in foreigners.' This is true. Val Parnell was seeing to it that profitable American acts enjoyed a greater share in terms of British entertainment.

She and Donald appeared at the High Court of Justice on September 3 then their case was transferred to Brentford's Court House. Bankruptcy is a 'gruelling experience' to live through after you have fallen into the trap, as the actress Sherrie Hewson describes, when she faced the same misfortune half a century later.[11] She writes about how the appointed bankruptcy administrator insists you hand over things at a certain time on a certain day, and how you dare not tell people about your predicament, unless you're happy to see a 'change come over them instantaneously.' As well as these tax demands twelve people were chasing Renée for debts and there were four people chasing Donald. To pay off the biggest of his debts, Don was using insurance policies, sending over a good deal of money from America at a very poor rate of exchange.

Between October and December 1948 *Variety's Sweethearts* had to return all possessions to the receivers. It's harrowing, reading about their stuff - all sold off fast - their pathetic 'goods sold and delivered.' There was a Wilton corridor rug and an Indian runner - making £95 cash. There was one cheque payable for £300 that Renée had banked at National Provincial Bank, Edgware Road branch. Yardages of plastic in white, pink and red, as well as 91.5 yards of fancy plastic, and eighty-four yards of muslin are listed - coming to a surprising £67 16s 2d. Renée's unopened bottles of 'Passionment' and 'Indiscreet' - two perfumes by Lucien Lelong, fetched £8, whilst bottles of 'L'Origan', 'Emeraude' and 'No.5' came to £15 5s 8d in a job lot with her makeup. It puts me in mind of the verses in 'I'll buy that dream' - one of the little songs you hear on the *Worker's Playtime* broadcast preserved on You Tube. There was joy in Renée's mind – a world of hope - nomatter what things might pollute the air:

Renée: There's one thing I do love – perfume. I love the perfume of the trees in the country on a summer's day just after the rain. I like the perfume of a little baby's hair - it's something you can't buy in a bottle.

Those bottles of French perfume were about the only things left to sell. The bulk of the furniture and silver had been sold to a man in Bourne End at the end of 1947, and more stuff including jewellery was sold to Biggs of Maidenhead.

On Friday December 10 at the Court House, Renée and Don faced a humiliating public examination with official receiver John Melville Clarke and Registrar Lloyd Williams. Whose name should be mentioned first in the interrogations? Only Eleanor Elliot - who was apparently owed £97 although her apparent proofs of debt increased the sum even more. 'As far as this particular woman is concerned I do not feel that I owe her anything,' said Renée to her questioner. She was asked why few possessions could be exchanged for cash, and why she did not negotiate better prices. She admitted she 'was too humiliated to consult anybody,' and that the book she kept with all the figures in it regarding the items sold got lost in the removal to her sisters' place. When Renée mentioned she hoped to pay back Donald I sense how wretched it had been when life at *'Green Trees'* fell apart. Donald had put up the money for the house. In the case notes for the hearing you see only too clearly how much Renée loved this man, who bore the crisis with such grace. Other relationships would suffer under the strain.

As regards the debt to Mr Clarke, she said they had been trying to pay it as soon as money came in, emphasizing the irregular nature of her work - 'Our business is a funny one' she said, describing how you might have nothing one week then the next a theatre and a broadcast and something else. Researching the *Irresistibles* and *Variety's Sweethearts* I wondered if all the train fayres built up over decades contributed to their bankruptcy. When the newspapers ran the story, Donald and Renée said half their earnings went in expenses, and joint 'living expenses' were £4000 a year (about £100,000 now). They keep to the same story in the case notes. The cost of a gown for Renée was given as about £36 (now £800) and she got through a good few of these being one to regularly trample them: 'A gown does not last with me anytime.' There are costs for hiring suits for Donald, a small fee for Dabber Davis - their latest manager, and taxi costs that amounted annually to £3000 (today's money). Details of hotel and other professional expenses aren't given.

It was salary fluctuations making salary disproportionate to outstanding tax that caused the most trouble. Renée tried to explain to her questioner that the salary they now received was a third of what they got during the war.[12] Only a fifth of earnings was left over each year, with personal expenses making up the bulk. This seemed to confirm it was their 'extravagant' lifestyle that caused their insolvency. Still, the calculation was based on the untypically fluid work they had in the war years. By 1948 Donald was accurate when he told his questioner: 'We live quite a simple life.' Both he and Renée carried themselves well in their answers under examination. Donald suggested a scheme offering the tax authorities 20% of net profits earned by himself and his wife going forward which was appreciated although not taken up.

Renée inclines at times towards the disingenuous. She tells the official receiver Trevor was supporting them and that her household contribution only covered the cost of milk, that she was expecting £80 from Pat Aherne but had received nothing. She put the knife in, telling them that Pat had paid hardly anything for years. She talks of how she had her mother dying of cancer for five years, and 'tried to save her' and of 'several operations' she had had after the bombings. She gets into a conversation with her questioner about the help they give others: 'we meet a lot of people who are up against it' but is told 'You must not be generous with other people's money'. Renée answers 'Yes, *Robbing Peter to pay Paul*; I realize that.'[13] She tells him she was responsible for eighteen people, in order to 'save their dignity.'

Renée clarifies that Donald is not morally responsible like her, but was kind enough to help her. To the newspapers I'm sure it was with sincerity when she told them 'I run my home, look after my four children and do my own cooking as well as my theatrical work. I have sold furniture and jewellery to keep the home going.'

Many entertainers got in trouble over tax and bankruptcy. Bill Maynard remembers being totally broke in 1961 when the Inland Revenue took everything and that he paid off all he owed and lived with relatives after moving his family's belongings down on the bus. 'It's considered very infradig to go bankrupt,' Bill told me, 'You just have to start again.' Ken Dodd went through tax examinations in the late 1980s. Jimmy Jewel, the Sheffield comedian - for years part of *Jewel and Warriss* - ignored or forgot about demands from the tax man and eventually got called in: 'Well Mr Jewel - what with delays - no forms submitted - no allowances and the interest - you owe us £30,000!' He needed a double brandy to recover. Hughie Green talked about being 'strained through the sieve of a financial court, being probed and prodded, like a prize zoo specimen.'[14] When Scots comedian Dave Willis retired in 1951 he bought the Bute Arms Hotel, Rothesay, but sadly went bankrupt. He had to return to summer seasons at Perth and Whitley Bay and admitted to people 'I havenae got a sausage.' BBC producer John Ellison, known for his scoops in getting Hollywood stars and Hitler's personal attendant on his pioneering TV chat show *In Town Tonight,* was affected by bankruptcy, and his sophistication belied the fact that he had to live in a caravan. Like Dave Willis, Donald and Renée took the punishments - a couple of performers who gave all and never took a long holiday from their hard working schedule. There's unfairness about the 1948 bankruptcy and its repercussions. Their joint salary, even during lucrative times, seems miniscule compared to the super rich in the 21st Century, although comparing money then and now is a very inexact science. It would take *Variety's Sweethearts* eight years to get back on track.

Together they got through it. To reporters outside the courtroom at Brentford, Renée was optimistic: 'while there is life there is hope, and I am one of those people who always expect to get enough work to pay.' To the papers, she added 'We don't want sympathy. We are quite happy as we are.'[15] Then, came a remarkable occurrence, involving none other than Sir Winston Churchill – former Prime Minister and one of Renée's confessed fans. The story is from the Aherne family and while I've not found evidence to confirm it in the Churchill archives or in Hansard, I've every belief in its likelihood. It concerns telegrams that haven't survived.

The ex-PM stuck up for Miss Houston at this low point, instilling a little of his trademark defiance into that beleaguered variety star. In conference with a group of pressmen, parliamentarians or party colleagues, Renée's name was brought up in conversation. Some old pussyfoot was outraged as to why anyone could rack up such a big tax bill and pointed out to everyone how shameless it was, especially since it wasn't the first time she had gone bankrupt. Churchill's exact comment isn't known but the story goes that she heard that Churchill had either defended her or excused her. She promptly sent him a telegram saying: 'Darling, I've always wanted to kiss you!' To this, Churchill replied with the words: 'Darling, I have always wanted to kiss you too.' Sending telegrams was something she did frequently, and this flamboyant means of communicating was something she'd been well known for since the 30s. Herbert Harris listed it among her hobbies and said she shared this habit with Ziegfeld, the famous American showman.

But what had she done with the fortune? This was the question everyone wanted to know including young Evening Standard journalist Maureen Cleave, who visited Renée for an interview in 1974.

> Renée: Fortune, Pet? Three or four fortunes more like. Was there ever a variety artist who died rich? No Flower, we didn't keep any money. Everybody helped everybody else. That's what we're here for.[16]

In autumn '48 the *Sweethearts* carried on at the Empress, Brixton on October 7 alongside Peter Cavanagh, Peter Brough and *Archie Andrews*, then the Dewsbury Empire. A radio show called *Fanfare,* recorded at Manchester's Apollo Ballroom came next. When Renée and Don returned to Brentford, they dovetailed in appearances at Chiswick Empire in Don Ross's *Thanks For The Memory* and unbelievably, we read in The Stage how 'the flippant spontaneity of Renée Houston is wonted joy and merriment.'[17] They also deputized for Nellie Wallace at the Liverpool Empire showing what troopers they were. They appeared at Edinburgh's Empire on December 12, alongside *Buster Shaver and his Wonder Lilliputians* and went on to Glasgow for the festive season. Lavish hotels were off-limits now but there were cousins, aunts and uncles on the Gribbin or Houston side, always in the know as to when she would be back in her native city. Their door was always open.

At this time a hundred programmes per week were coming out of the wireless, produced by the BBC's Variety Department. These included twenty scripted peak-hour comedies. In a Radio Times article, variety chief Michael Standing told listeners how training in stage and screen work was a positive disadvantage, suggesting that masters of radio art were artistes specializing in radio to the exclusion of other work. He gives the late Tommy Handley as a prime example.[18] If you could work well without an audience, like Gillie Potter, you tended to be a success on the Radio.

All the same, Dabber Davis liaised with the BBC sending Houston and Stewart scripts to Dicky Afton. The *Sweethearts* were in Glasgow rehearsing episodes of *Heather Mixture.* Designed for the export market, Howard Lockhart - BBC Scotland producer, was insistent that Renée sing a Scots song like 'My Ain Wee Hoose' each time. She was asked to make references to an

'Aunt Maggie' in Australia and an 'Auntie Jeannie' in America. Donald was urged to tell his family when it would be transmitted in New York.

It was around this time, whilst visiting her hometown, that Renée became the latest 'victim' of two star-struck lassies from Townhead. Mary Devine and Jean Smith, aged fourteen and thirteen, had a wee enterprise - checking if a star was present in a hotel by phoning up, then wheedling an appointment with the star posing as reporters - or if that failed, waiting for the star to enter the hotel lobby. *'No Star's safe from the Townhead Terrors'* went a headline and the girls recounted with pride how they'd snared Sophie Tucker (she wis awful grumphy), Chico Marx (he wis awful sad), George Formby, and Eleanor Powell.[19] I can imagine Renée admiring their chutzpah and I doubt she would have been *grumphy*, unless they caught her on one of her bad days.

Finally the BBC let *Variety's Sweethearts* do a TV broadcast with wow factor. Ronald Waldman, the young and charming Head of Light Entertainment thought they deserved a break. A letter from Renée to Waldman about their availability seemed to initiate their appearance on *Rooftop Rendezvous* for which Dicky Afton was producer. After they okay'd the material for *Rooftop Rendezvous*[20] the BBC wisely didn't go with the initial script despite Renée describing it as 'my best effort.'

It had been a skit in Regency costume: an over-the-top burlesque on 'legit' drama. In a little room with a candelabra on a table, a femme fatale called *Amber* hears footsteps and is ever hopeful that her lover *Bruce* will come through the door, although it turns out each time to be her cuckolded husband *Charles*. The scene opened with the Campbell Connelly song 'Red Head'. There are few pearls in the original script:

Don: A rude wakening for you my beauty! Not quite the visitor you expected! Eh! (*very Legit*) But having come straight from my club where I picked up some juicy bits of scandal.
Ren: What did juicy?
Ren: (*oblivious to this outburst - is eating grapes*) Have a grape Charles dear, do. You paid for them.
Don: And how I've paid for them! You who have crushed my very soul offering me a crushed grape!
Ren: Sorry Charles, shall I remove the pips?
Don: You with your Jean Simmons stare (*reaction*) - and your Mae West tactics!
Ren: And you with your Regency Buck Ryan get up. Leave me Charles. You bore me.
Don: Leave you? I'll be glad to. You - who have destroyed me – and my pocket – and my father's pocket - and my grandfather's pocket ...
Ren: Now Now! Same pocket handed down.[21]

The original script concerns nothing more than singing a song. The BBC favoured the more familiar husband and wife dynamics: the bickering that harked back to the Houston Sisters - hence the new script. 'Galway Bay'[22] provides opening music with 'Anything I Dream is Possible' sung at the

Variety's Sweethearts

tuneful end. In between is a sublime set of interruptions as Donald attempts to sing a ballad. It's gloriously idiotic and has more than one reference to their bankruptcy.

Ren: Pardon me old boy.
Don: You'll pardon me for a change - this is my broadcast. (*pushes her aside*)
Ren: Then you're in the wrong building. This happens to be Television.
Don: Now look, you be a good little girl and run along. (*puts his arm around her*)
Ren: Don't start fussing me in public. Try and remember that on stage we're only partners. Cheek of him! You'd think he'd all the money in the world.
Don: I'm going to sing. (*angry*)
Ren: Funny so am I.
Don: There have been many complaints because I'm not singing enough.
Ren: Some people don't know when they're lucky.
Don: Kindly leave the Stage.
Ren: No Dear. You carry on but I want to be in the picture (*cue for Galway Bay*)
Don: (*tries to sing a few bars from same with interjections from Renée*)
Ren: Oh boy! Here it comes again - Image of Donald Peers isn't he?
Ren: You've got the lyrics all wrong.
Don: Stop interrupting!
Ren: Go on! Sing it again and I'll prove it to you.
Don: If you ever go across the sea to Ireland (*begins again*)
Ren: Will you bring a pair of fur-lined boots to me? (*sings*)
Don: That's sacrilege. This is a lovely song.
Ren: Yes but someone might take me seriously.
Don: If you ever ... etc (*again*)
Ren: Skip Galway and bring Dublin back to me. Bring the clothes, the food, the drinks and all the lunches, and I know I've got two poached eggs for me tea.
Don: You're a glutton! Besides you can't get all that in Galway.
Ren: Then tell them in the song?
Don: You have no romance in your tones.
Ren: I'd rather have a steak in my stomach.
Don: Just swallow the words and watch the song go down in Galway Bay.
Ren: I'd rather swallow the bacon and eggs in Dublin.
Don: You know you ought to se a Psychiatrist.
Ren: I do very often.
Don: How is he treating you?
Ren: Marvellously - took me to the pictures last night and dinner the night before.
Don: If you ever ... !! (*waving his arms*)
Ren: He's gonna scream now.
Don: If you ever ... etc (*again*)
Ren: Take my advice and go from Holyhead cause if it's rough enough and you should go from Fleetwood - you'll lie there wishing you were dead instead.
Don: I've suffered enough. One of these days I'm gonna loose my temper ...
Ren: You should - it's a shocking one.

Don:	And when I do ...
Ren:	I find sinister men so attractive - in a repulsive sort a way.
Don:	I'll give you ...
Ren:	Now don't be extravagant. You can't afford to give anything!
Don:	A good thrashing. I've dreamt about it for a long time and
Don:	Anything I Dream is possible ... (*into song*)[23]

Jack Jackson was bandleader for *Rooftop Rendezvous*. The rehearsals were in 'Studio A' of Alexandra Palace in front of a small studio audience as the studio was not large. I had visions of Renée and Donald being on the rooftop of the building. In reality there was nothing authentically roof-like. Instead there was a giant cyclorama depicting a skyscraper scene.[24] The show was a big success. Writing letters to the BBC had good results.

Alan was at Finsbury Park Empire the night Houston and Stewart were in *Thanks for the Memory* on February 07, 1949, and remembered meeting Ella Shields and Georgie Wood whilst standing by the curtains. Randolph Sutton, Gertie Gitana, Lily Morris, and Talbot O'Farrell were also in the show. His mum loved to introduce her sons to fellow pros.

Tessie O' Shea   Coco The Clown
(Author's Collection)

On February 27 the Sweethearts were at the Folkestone Palace with *Coco The Clown and Family*. Dick Bentley, Patricia Rossborough, and the Mills Sisters & Michael were on the same bill. This was when Coco, an international *auguste* whose real name was Nicolai Poliakoff, christened her, throwing a full three buckets of water over her. The ancient clown tradition dictates this. It was to Miss H, a marvellous compliment, and thankfully Coco's daughters took her back to the caravan and secretly helped dry her long red hair – now a straggly mess – as ancient clown tradition also required she had to be spruce for the second house. Things would look up after this christening because she was about to be rediscovered again.

Chapter 19   Milestones between Past and Future

She was like the first daffodil in spring, said Renée, recalling the unknown dancer who started showing up at rehearsals. She could also be cool and poised in the publicity stills of the corps de ballet by Anthony Beauchamp, and it's easy to see why Audrey Hepburn was impresario Cecil Landeau's treasured asset. Cecil's concept for *Sauce Tartare* suited the era: bright, international, and totally new – an era Audrey would personify. He had found her in *High Buttoned Boots* at the London Hippodrome, rushing backstage with a tantalizing offer of a part in a revue almost as soon as Audrey had made her debut. You have to admire his fast work. Buddy Bradley was choreographer and assistant producer and Andrée Howard his assistant. Responsible for décor and costumes, Honoria Plesch provided tropical jungle forests, sepia views of New York's riverside, the verdant South America of the bolero and the Spain of the castanets. The revue opened on May 18, 1949 and the opening number featured members of the ensemble as symbolic components to the 'perfect Sauce Tartare' mixed up by *the Chef* played by Peter Glover. Tall Patricia Dare personified *'Glamour'* with Terence Theobald as *'Rhythm'*, and Enid Smeedon as *'Comment'*. Delectable Diana Monks joined the show later and Renée's name for her was 'Monkey'. The perfect 'ingredients' alternated over the life of the revue as different performers came and went. Audrey was not just a dancer in the show – she was prominently featured, appearing as *'Gamma'* to Renée's *'Beta'* in *Earthward Bound - A Pre-natal Posting Station*. Onlookers were also transfixed by the Hepburn magic in scenes like *Boogie Woogie Yogi*, *Relatives* and *Oklahokum*. AE Wilson, writing in The Star, said that 'So much spirit, colour and animation has not been crammed into a revue for a long time.'

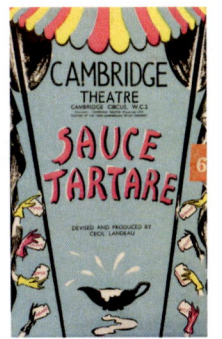

Programme for Sauce Tartare   The Cambridge Theatre, 2016 (Author's Collection)

The cast boasted at least twelve different nationalities. Muriel Smith from America's Deep South sang 'A Smile from a Stranger'- a beautiful number that Audrey danced to, while Marlana – a green-eyed Hispanic American (discovered in a Los Angeles cabaret by Cecil Landeau) did a savage jungle dance. Zoë Gail and Jan Mazurus were from South Africa, and Miquelita and her Afro-Cubanos electrified another scene. Nina Tarakanova was from

Russia, and Renée, of course, was from the bonnie banks of the Clyde. Dancer Sara Luzita, actually English, was often thought to be Spanish because of her amazing Spanish dance arranged by Elsa Brunelleschi. *Sauce Tartare* was also a welter of Spanish, Cuban and Caribbean song with lyrics by Geoffrey Parsons - already an expert at adapting continental songs into English, while Berkeley Fase, who had already set several revues at the Unity Theatre in Goldington Street, did the score. Sidney Bowman conducted.

Dabber Davis came out of the army at the same time as Trevor, having spent time in the Middle East, but before this used to knock around the Nuffield Centre, where he met Bob Monkhouse. This was just off Trafalgar Square, offering perks like a cheap cafeteria with American nosh, bar, TV room, and free theatre tickets for young servicemen. Dabber moved into production and show business, and Bob chose him as his agent when he came out of the RAF. In the meantime Dabber was supporting Renée - doing the typical 'spade work' a theatrical rep did before big agencies like the Grades came in to seal the actual deals. Dabber was responsible for getting Renée back into the West End after a long absence. She needed this opportunity with her financial troubles. The Court at Brentford, monitoring her finances like a hawk, records her engagement was £100 a week from May 18, 1949, but this was for four and a half weeks only before it went down to £35 a week. It was Cecil's return to light entertainment too, given the injuries he had sustained during war service. He was only too pleased to make Renée one of his principals, being a big fan. They joined forces, both putting their energies into this revue. Married to Madame Ciro, famous for her luxury Pearl business, Cecil was able to arrange for some of the beautiful jewels to be showcased by Audrey and other ladies in the show. The £20,000 from his backers also helped.

Sauce Tartare:

Left: Cecil Landeau
(Author's Collection)

Right:
Miquelita and the Afro-Cubanos
in the jungle scene *Babalu*
(Artwork by author)

Cecil was a strange man, Dabber remembers, the only producer he knew who, right from the word go, was convinced that an entire orchestra should be present at rehearsals. It was frankly unnecessary and would be unheard of today. It was behaviour that would prove unwise. Cecil was a true admirer of beauty. He was also able to take gambles of a kind that no West End producer since his time ever dared. Renée paints a fond picture of Cecil in her 1974 book revealing that one thing they had in common was the love of a good set-to. He comes across as passionate and 'old school' – the sort who restored peaceful relations with leading ladies with enormous bunches of flowers. He seems to have been one for primness – insisting that his leading ladies conduct themselves with ladylike decorum. Renée says she was forever trying to get one over Cecil but seldom succeeded. Only one schoolgirl prank did the trick. This was embarrassing him in front of VIPs at a reception by revealing to those present that the trimming of her hat was actually her knickers.

Comedy scenes were written by Matt Brooks and directed by Audrey Cameron. A high proportion of the sketches were inevitably 'bad,' according to Tatler reviewer Anthony Cookman. Some were incredibly funny. Taken as a whole, the critics loved *Sauce Tartare* for its 'zest and goodwill' complimenting the performers - saying that 'everyone has something worth doing,' and predicting it would play to crowded houses for months to come. It did exactly that, running to 433 performances and lasting a year. In June, Cecil was getting offers including one from Gateway Productions, to take *Sauce Tartare* to Broadway - the first American offer for a British revue for ten years, although not one that was good enough. Everyone heard about Cecil's 'no expense spared' revue, saw the publicity photos, and listened to highlights of the show on the radio. It was broadcast on the Light Programme, on August 22 and September 4.

Both Ronald Frankau and Claude Hulbert appeared in the scene *The Eyes Have It,* described as a skit on the new National Health Service. A decrepit doctor - Ronald - is dragged out of retirement by the boom in *nationalized illness*. The snag is he's unable to see beyond his own nose. In fact he's so shortsightedly incompetent that his patient - Claude - is missed, so he tests the nurse's pulse instead. Stethoscope and telephone look the same to him and are used interchangeably. 'Claude Hulbert looks at times like an anxious whitebait,' reported The Observer,'[1] as the patient sits politely while his doctor inspects the spots on the tie, not the rash on the chest. Ronald's uproariously funny performance impressed the Evening Standard. Renée had known both Claude and Ronald since the 20s. An ex-Etonian, Ronald had been a hit on the radio for his dry comments delivered in cultured tones. Zoë Gail, a dynamo of a soubrette, made up the comedy foursome and was noted for her exhilarating pep. In 1944 she had been in George Black's *Happy and Glorious* at the Palladium with Tommy Trinder and Elisabeth Welch. In *Tartare,* Zoë was the original songstress in the scene *An Englishman in Love*, and for a number called *'Lit Up.'* Her showstopper was *'A Hick in Piccadilly'* in which she appeared in top hat and tails.

Renée's *Deanna of the Dairies* - all about the transformation fame has on the unlikeliest folk, was loved by all the critics. Marlana, used to drinking three quarts of milk a day in California was finding it difficult to procure the same in England and this might have been where the 'dairy' idea came from. Many critics said the best laugh came in Renée's *The Real Thing,* in which she sits expectantly on a white satin sofa, before going on to sing of her passionate lover, who works for the MI5 and *'needs no urgin when he's done the purgin.'*[2] The MI5 sketch was worth waiting for in Act II. She appeared in a *Three Beauty Queens* skit as *Miss Brighton,* with Enid Smeedon as Miss Blackpool and Pat Dare as Miss Margate, and in a surviving photo looks slim and glamorous. She gave an update to her 'milk' sketch character in August, having transformed her into a prima donna - representing the *Amalgamated Dairies Operatic Society.* She wrote this sketch herself – an outrageous satire on advertising. She's sitting on a counter with every conceivable item on the shelves with 'AD' branding, with her dress covered in the same logo. Angus McBean photographed her for Theatre World with an *'AD'* branded milk bottle in her hand. In a Freudian skit called *The Psychiatrist,* both Renée and Nina Tarakanova play different sides of 'The Girl.' Claude is the Psychiatrist. Adele Stephens, Jean Bayless, Ray Browne, David Keller, Roy Byfield-Riches and fourteen year-old Johnny Briggs are people in the dream. The last mentioned young actor would share a stage with Renée once again before TV viewers got to know him as Weatherfield's *Mike Baldwin.* From the opening night, the reception Renée got was immense, with everyone crying for her in the curtain call[3] and for a few months she was the number one matriarchal force behind the show.

Sauce Tartare:

Left: *Three Beauty Queens* (From unidentified newspaper, Aherne Family)

Right: *Amalgamated Dairies Operatic Society* Theatre World, October 1949 (Photo: Angus McBean [MS Thr 581] © Houghton Library, Harvard University.

Jean Bayless had gone from memorizing her Shakespeare at the Co Op, Tottenham to the cast of Sauce Tartare through the efforts of her mother and Cecil's secretary. Originally from the East End, Jean got an Italia Conti scholarship and later became the first 'Maria' in The Sound of Music.[4] Jean told me that *Sauce Tartare,* and its sequel *Sauce Piquante* are among her happiest memories. The dressing rooms at the Cambridge were dingy but Jean felt they were magical. She shared with Audrey and a couple of the others and everyone got on well. Audrey and Pat Dare were particularly good friends. Of Renée Houston, Jean tells me that she 'was a second mother to us all' and recalled the 'lovely picnics on Sundays at Renée's home in Strawberry Hill - wonderful times,' and photos of the young Jean taken in the back garden record one of these visits. Jean had a special memory of Renée's 'lovely husband - so hospitable and kind,' and remembered the glass doors opening out to the garden that Donald had made beautiful. 'There were carpets laid on the grass so the company could enjoy the sunshine - drinking and eating a delicious buffet that always included trifle - all at Renée's expense.' Jean took quite a fancy to Trevor and remembers Renée sighing and saying 'He's not for you dear.' Alan led a group that included Jean to

Teddington Lock, entering the boatyard and clumsily spilling candle wax on Jean's dress as they boarded the boat he was building with his friend Lewis Roberts (a young Surrey Comet reporter). The Shah of Persia kept his motor yacht nearby, he told her. Alan had a plan to emigrate, considering Canada as a destination.

Left: Jean Bayless at Waldegrave Park (The Aherne Family)
Below: Teddington Lock and Boathouse (Author's Collection)

Unless you liked pubs England was boring. It wouldn't be if you were making a lot of money or were in love, of course. Renée and her entourage used to go to all the Teddington pubs. One was The Tide End, where they knew the owner, but the pub they frequented most was The Anglers at Ferry Lane where the landlord's family was called Goodheugh. Pubs were extensions of the home back then. Don's sister Lois was visiting at the time, enjoying a whirlwind tour of England and sampling the nightlife of London.

Renée was at another garden party - a star-studded one in Roehampton, to raise funds for the Actor's Orphanage, on the afternoon of Tuesday May 31. With Claude, Zoë and Jack Melford, she was now behind the bar, serving beer at the *Beer Garden*! The event was open to the public and featured a *West End manager's audition tent* – the most popular attraction - with Ursula Jeans, Roger Livesey, Joyce Grenfell and Stewart Granger taking names at the stage door, an *antique stall* run by John Gielgud and Angela Baddeley, an *Heiress Tea Garden* hosted by Peggy Ashroft and Sir Ralph Richardson, and a *Bar du Quartier Latin* run by Frances Day and Jack Durant. There was a *gift shop* run by Dame Sybil Thorndike and Lewis Casson, while Richard Attenborough, Sheila Sim and Linden Travers managed a *signed photographs booth*. Ronald Shiner and Jack Hobbs presided over a *shooting gallery*. At the *Fun-Fair Bar,* Vic Oliver, Jeanne de Casalis, Hermione Gingold, Douglas Byng, Clifford Molllison and Elizabeth Welch served drinks. Sir Lawrence Olivier and Vivien Leigh ran the *Race Game* - backed by the Old Vic Company. Many other prominent actors were made use of in this extraordinary event including Flora Robson, Evelyn Laye, Irene Handl and Paul Scofield.

Renée still needed to work as much as possible. She lent her image to cheap looking adverts at the time, such as *Services Sports Watches*: 'For elegance and accuracy my choice is a Services' went the ad. Thankfully she was able to earn 25 guineas at a recording at the Piccadilly Theatre - as guest victim on *Talk Yourself Out Of This.* She was given an imaginary problem that required wit and imagination to come up with a convincing alibi. A panel of three inquisitors fired difficult questions at her. She was a 'Scotland host' in *Variety Comes To Town* - when familiar voices from all the regions were gathered in the same show. Violet Carson, later to bring her fearsome 'Ena Sharples' to *Coronation Street,* was *host from the North*. Renée's comic voices were heard on the air on *Ladies' Night* accompanied by songs from Dorothy Squires and a big band care of Ivy Benson and her Girls' Orchestra.

Zoë left *Tartare* in August 1949 and Jessie Matthews, aged forty-two, took over her role. This caused a shuffle around with Renée taking over as the *'Hick in Piccadilly'* and Jessie stepping into *An Englishman in Love,* and homing into *Earthward Bound* as *'Delta.'* A new scene was created for Jessie entitled *The Seine*, with music by Guy Lafarge. Alan, something of a regular at the theatre by then, described the latter as an *adagio act*. It began with smoke blowing in and beautiful choreography using colour to set the mood. Jessie sang her number at one side of the stage whilst Audrey and Monkey, as *midinettes,* danced to the rear of the stage. It was a meeting point of generations with Jessie - premier dancing star of the 30s and much the shape and face of that decade, contrasting with Audrey, soon to be *icon* of the 50s and early 60s.

Since she was one of the original principals in *Sauce Tartare,* Renée had top billing status. Michael Thornton in his biography of Jessie Matthews, writes about the ongoing rivalry between Renée and Jessie throughout the remainder of the run of the show, describing it as 'one of the most acrimonious theatrical feuds.'[5] Not only did Renée lose no opportunity in ad-libbing impressions of Jessie complete with toothy grimaces, but transmit her slights publicly - via the tannoy! Dressing rooms and all backstage got to hear. Thornton, referring to the recollections of witnesses he doesn't name, tells us Renée got on the tannoy ostensibly to report what type of house the cast could expect that night. 'It's a comedienne's audience,' she would say, adding 'It's going to be a better audience for me, than it is for that artistic cow.' Thornton also talks about Renée spitting into the hand of her co-star and how the two ladies 'almost came to blows at the stage door.' They had to be held apart by their respective husbands. The atmosphere was apparently bad enough to make Equity send an observer to the Cambridge 'to stand in the wings to watch the behaviour.' Jean Bayless told me 'Renée and Jessie's rows must have gone way over my head,' although she told Geoff Bowden of the British Music Hall Society that Renée claimed she'd peed on Jessie's wig.[6] Jean never mentioned this to me - thinking I'd be shocked, I expect. In the same interview she said Jessie and Renée, who shared a dressing room, would push the other's stage makeup to one side.

When is a joke a joke, and what can be made of this? Dabber and several members of Renée's family tell me they were unaware of any feud between the two actresses. Renée's son tells me that Renée and Jessie had a fickle type of relationship that ebbed and flowed. If one minute they were arguing, the next minute they were very good friends so it was difficult to know if the situation was bad. In reality, they had more reasons to be in sympathy with one another. Neither had avoided upheavals during their respective journeys up the ladder. I doubt Jessie's wig really suffered such an indignity but I can imagine Renée telling people she did it, to see them look aghast.

Jessie's toothiness had a laugh-factor that was too irresistible to ignore, and the fine line between humour and spite was ripe for one who enjoyed a good set-to. Anyone could be on the receiving end of a Renée Houston prank, and the fact that it was Jessie is probably not significant. Was Renée so bothered as to be resentful of Jessie? Was she jealous? Jessie still looked trim at this time and very graceful in her dance scenes but her 'comeback' hadn't yet happened. Her mega-success of long before had plateaued[7] and she was struggling to get work. Renée's career had seen an upturn, although not to any great degree. Jessie wasn't a threat. If bitter acrimony existed, it's interesting to speculate on its source. Both actresses had been in the public eye since the 20s but Jessie was too major-league back then to consider Renée a rival. Maybe it didn't help that Jessie had met Donald before her, when she and Don were colleagues in 'First A Girl' in 1935.

Jessie Matthews in Sauce Tartare in her adagio number

Swarbrick's photo for Theatre World, October 1949
(Author's Collection)

Creakier potential vendettas exist. In the past I expect Renée hadn't been too happy with the fact that Carol Reed was romantically involved with Jessie during the time of 'A Girl Must Live.' Renée was also friendly with Evelyn Laye – whose husband, Sonnie Hale, had been shamelessly stolen by Jessie. Jessie and Sonnie married at the beginning of the 30s. Jessie enhanced her reputation further by stealing Chili Bouchier's husband in the middle of the decade. In the 30s, Jessie's film career was supreme and she was a radio star too. She turned any earlier bad press to her advantage and by the later 30s her knowledge on *matters of the heart* was considered valuable enough to make her a ubiquitous agony aunt in magazines like Radio Pictorial and Film Pictorial. This was territory Miss Houston was also competing for. By 1949 you would think enough water had passed under their dilapidated bridges. Would Renée embark on a judgmental crusade against Miss Matthews? It was probably nothing more complicated than Renée in her temperamental zone, letting her private troubles vent. True – the scenes might have been ugly and she wasn't good at making amends. I'm still dubious about the feud.

Renée's subterranean dressing room at the Cambridge had a washstand and there wasn't much space for putting on your makeup, so getting tetchy about a rival's powder puff occupying the limited space is understandable. In the airless and smoke-filled room were two light bulbs only. It was poisonous by today's standards. A bunch of people came in after the show most nights to have drinks. Alan remembers it crowded in the interval too, with someone singing an aria from *La Boheme*. Suddenly it was time for his Mum to go on. She would panic and her dresser would help, so everything would be ok. At the end of the show came invites to someone's home for more drinks – never any food! When he wasn't working, Donald waited in the dressing room. He would untie a packet containing hardwoods of different hues, take out his hacksaws and work on a piece of his latest marquetry project. Theatre people are known for filling time backstage with surprising hobbies. Absorbed in his careful artwork, Donald could forget about directors, family pressures, uncooperative colleagues and even divas. His pièce de résistance was a tabletop version of Da Vinci's *Last Supper*.

From time to time people would approach Renée with clichés like 'I want to go back to Scotland but I can't' or worse sob stories. She was the sort of person who gave them money, only to find out afterwards that the story wasn't true and it was a case of sponging. On *Sauce Tartare* there was a woman who supposedly had cancer and it turned out she was intentionally duping them. This was the real Renée, who thought with her heart - ever prone to a con. During the run, several megastars from the theatrical world came to see the show - 'pals' like Olivier, Laughton, and Sir Michael Redgrave. Coming backstage and seeing Renée they were apt to bellow 'Where has she been?' Out came the comparisons between her and great actresses of the legitimate theatre. They remembered her big film parts in 'A Girl Must Live' and 'Two Thousand Women.' Their stupefaction as to why she had been so 'wasted' in the years since was not without justification. But while Renée could act the diva backstage, she kept that in check when the pals were doing the rounds. In their company she was modest and never believed any of the talk about her being a 'great actress,' countering their great words with 'I'm just your common variety.'

Alan loved to see the girls from Italia Conti. He confessed he was a bit of a skirt chaser then, and there was a girl in *Sauce Tartare* he was desperate to ask on a date. Her salary exceeded his by so much there was no way could it work. At his sixteenth birthday party in December 1949 Audrey, 'Monkey', Enid Smeedon, and the rest of the gorgeous cast, plus crew, came to 58 Waldegrave Park for a memorable party. Dabber took a photo of the crowd including Audrey, on the balcony that looked towards the garden and underground air raid shelter – a reminder of the war they'd escaped. Sadly the photo has vanished, as has the house. On December 20 at the Cambridge Theatre, the cast acted as 'hosts' with magician N'gai, and Annette Mills with *Muffin the Mule* entertaining lucky kiddies at *Sauce Tartare's Christmas Party*. Claude Hulbert gave a funny quiz and in another scene nursery toys came to life with Audrey as an enchanting musical box ballerina. At New Year, taking advantage of the hanging mistletoe, Alan was outside the dressing rooms just

Milestones between Past and Future

at the right time to be the first person to give Audrey a kiss in 1950, or the last person to do so in 1949. The next time he saw her, she was onstage in New York in *Gigi* and he was in the audience. *Sauce Tartare* came to an end in February 1950, and Cecil Landeau opened *Sauce Piquante* on April 27 - the spin-off that substituted lead players like Renée, Claude, Ronald and Jessie for Bob Monkhouse and others. That lasted eight weeks. Audrey fell in love with a French dancer, and along with most of the cast, transferred to Ciro's for Cecil's floorshow *'Summer Nights'*.

If only summer nights weren't so brief in Britain. Package holidays were as yet uncommon, and a visit to the theatre or the movies sufficed to transport you to a place where skies were less drab, and where a few rubber palm trees positively impacted on your wellbeing. Alan needed to apply for an emigration visa and a ton of red tape awaited him. When Pat heard about his son's plans to leave for Canada, he wired telling him to come to California instead. Alan sold the boat he'd worked on in Teddington to pay fayres, and had a small inheritance from his de Lacy grandfather. If he left the decision any longer he'd be drafted for National Service. Going to America happened in a last minute way. Any plans Alan made his mother did her utmost to wreck, especially since she had to sign a paper to consent to the emigration. When she went to the office with him she made sure to let it slip that she was divorced from Alan's father. Of course a minefield of bureaucracy about his being a child of divorcees resulted. She did it on purpose.

It seemed very unlikely it would happen. Alan's leaving home was not what Renée wanted. It was a huge deal getting her to come to terms with it. Alan said with a wistful look that he and his mother didn't fully understand each other. They had never particularly argued or had any fall out apart from this episode when Renée tried to cancel his visa. It all turned rather 'pistols at dawn.' He knows she was suffering on account of him leaving the country. How foggy and rainy Britain was – six weeks of typically depressing weather! Then he packed and left in January 1950 aged just sixteen, sailing on the Queen Elizabeth. He'd sort out the emigration side of things elsewhere. That darkness and cold drove him crazy but suddenly here was a new Technicolor: the lights of New York and the candy shop. He grabbed his candy and bought tickets at the Majestic Theatre for *South Pacific* where Mary Martin and Ezio Pinza gave a cracking performance. If that wasn't heaven enough, there was California and its blue skies. There, he joined the army, and with GIs still an important presence in Europe, Alan found himself flying back to Blighty only a few months later. Stationed in Augsburg, Germany, he spent his leave catching up with everyone in London. In his absence he'd missed something extraordinary – the Houston Sisters reunited, and the heart-warming reception they received.

There was never an expectation that Billie would be able to do these shows regularly. They would do as many shows as they could manage. At home Billie had to lie stretched on a board three days in the week. She'd tell

405

pressmen she'd been in hospital seventeen times since leaving the stage, or that her favourite way of relaxing was 'to hold on to a couple of grips hanging from the ceiling.'[8] Her pawkiness was alive and well, but even in print the comedy was tinged with tragedy. By the mid century she had an impressive portfolio of illnesses and her son tells me that she was terminally ill after 1944. Problems with her throat had become more complicated and she had to rest a lot or otherwise strain herself. There were different things she was treated for - not one particular thing. She had a back op, and an abdominal op. The number of operations meant numerous recovery periods. The doctors who treated her spinal problem didn't do a good job. Despite further back operations she never regained full physical health and became dependent on a walking stick with a moulded jacket reducing pressure on her spine. Yet, if she was immobilized, it was only for a period.

At the onset, Billie regarded the 'Reunion' as a true return to the stage, even though between 1950 and 1954 only ten or so of these appearances proved possible. The first three were for charitable causes so this makes me question the explanation family members give that the motivation was entirely because the Sisters were in dire need of cash. I can understand they needed money but why didn't they maximize the news potential such a stunt offered using national newspapers and the Fleet Street contacts Billie's husband Paul had? Why didn't they plan dates for Scotland, where packed houses could be guaranteed? These strategies would have paid off. Donald did wave the idea in front of the BBC to get the Houston's new act aired on the radio. In the meantime, it suited Billie and Renée to edge their way back in quieter halls, reviving the magic so long absent.

The first performance was at the Adelphi Theatre on February 11, 1950 in front of the Lady Ratlings. Egged on by supportive friends, Renée and Billie's comeback was emotional. Donald acted as the Sisters' compère for these shows. The second one was to the Water Rats at the *15th Rat's Revel* held at the Victoria Palace on Sunday March 5. Reunions were in favour - the *Revel* being a brief alternative to *Jack Hylton Presents: Knights of Madness* starring the *Crazy Gang* - on every other night of the week at the Vic Palace.

Here, before 1600 guests including Billie's family, with the Rats and Ratlings donning full regalia, the Sisters gave a delightful turn. Encouragement from their fellow pros was plentiful. Ted Ray – as *King Rat,* opened the bill. The Gaiety Girls featured in the first act and the Windmill Girls did a Can Can in the second. Arthur English was exceptionally funny and Donald Peers closed the bill. Billie was only forty-three, but her absence and the fact that the Houston Sisters were associated with the years before the war added distance. Even with a body support beneath her boy outfit and carrying a stick, the illusion was good. They were very much their old selves.

It was something to see the iconic image of Billie Houston: her Eton crop perfect and attire brought up to date with a checked sports jacket and wide striped tie. She even produced her banjulele. Renée gagged and romped, and The Stage reported how Billie's voice had 'lost none of its depth' and how she kept up with her sister 'in remarkable fashion, considering how long it was since she last faced the footlights.' After receiving a standing ovation they said a few words, mentioning what it was like sharing *Dressing Room B* - one they had last shared sixteen years earlier. To Billie's children it was the self-congratulatory aspect of this show they remembered – more than a little embarrassing. Nobody doubted the achievement, and Billie was proud to wear a 'Rats' collar in the finale. In the photo with Donald Peers and Albert Whelan standing beside them it breaks the illusion of male impersonation a little, with *Bill* diminishing to vent's dummy proportions.

Reunion, Adelphi Theatre on February 11, 1950 (By kind permission of The Stage)

Without Renée, Billie attended the *Lady Ratlings Ball* at the Dorchester on October 18, 1950 when Ted Ray introduced the cabaret. She did a turn with Gladys Hay, and appeared in another scene wearing her eight year-old son's rugger outfit telling the Rats and Ratlings her son had at first suggested she might mention his school - St Benedicts in Ealing, only to change his mind with a 'Perhaps you had better not.'[9]

Mr and Mrs Shaw, licensees of The Waldegrave Arms - just round the corner from Renée, provided a venue on Sunday April 23, 1951 for a small variety show played to forty disabled ex-servicemen from the Star and Garter Home on Richmond Hill. Fred Ferris, the Kingston Empire's pianist provided music and Dabber was compère. The audience got to see the *Irresistibles* aided and abetted by Donald, Vera Lynn, Gladys Hay, George Doonan, Sonny and Rene Jenks, Billy Budd, and Lesley Travers. A photo in the local paper shows everyone enjoying a joke in between munching on party food. Vera is handing nibbles from a tray, and in the background you see Billie smoking a fag with her Eton crop as immaculate as ever. Renée is smiling to the right of her in the shadows. The artistes were invited to Renée's home after.

Renée and Billie next did a spot together in traditional variety on December 10, at the Hippodrome Aldershot, and on December 17 at the Walthamstow Palace. At the latter the Houstons revived the vent's dummy act and the Toy Soldier act especially for the occasion. They shared the bill with Billy Bartholomew - who played three musical instruments simultaneously, and Patricia who did a spectacular unicycle routine. It was like old times for Renée and Billie. Critics wrote how the act was 'effectively staged and encouragingly received,' and of the 'miracle comeback' now that Billie had recovered 'thro prayer.'[10] Then, in the company of acrobats - George and Esme Grande, and balancers - Bob and Rita Rema, the *'World Famous Houston Sisters Renée and Billie – Back Together'* played the Empire Theatre, Portsmouth on February 4, 1952. A paper noted that their 'unrehearsed asides and slick presentation carried them and their audience across the years between' and that they had lost none of their 'freshness and vitality . . . that made them household names in more than one country.'[11] David Aherne witnessed the age-defying Houstons. He saw his aunt Renée, and Billie and Donald at the Woolwich Empire when they followed Walthamstow.

On New Year's Day 1950 the formidable and glamorous Renée Houston pre-recorded a solo spot on *Henry Hall's Guest Night* at the Granville Theatre in Fulham where many years before she had run out into the auditorium like a madhatter to make jokes with cheery onlookers. Then came engagements at Greenock, Paisley and the Gaiety Theatre in Ayr with her poor freezing Donald in tow. In their later variety shows Renée and Donald's signature music was 'Smoke Gets In Your Eyes' or sometimes 'Alice Blue Gown.' A glissade down to the south coast saw them play Portsmouth on February 20, then back up to the Regent, Rotherham - where almost a decade earlier they came close to losing their lives. They made two appearances at the Regent, separated by a five months and on the latter occasion gave a special thank you to the musicians for the part they play in variety programmes - a kind gesture that didn't go amiss in The Stage. After a booking at Edinburgh's Empire in late July, and the New Theatre, Northampton on August 14, *Variety's Sweethearts* would tour Scotland, alongside teen pop idol Frankie Vaughan further into the month of August.

The Holy Grail for Renée and Donald was a series on the radio, and early in 1950, they began a concerted letter campaign directed at contacts in the BBC. Any regular work was welcome with television their other target. Many letters Renée and Donald sent to the BBC radio's Variety Department survive, and the most frequent recipient was Ronald Waldman. Renée had known him since he started in the business, working with her old friends like Harry Pepper. She frequently ended her letters to 'Ronnie' with 'Your aged aunt.' He was Head of Light Entertainment in 1950, ensuring airtime for the next generation of bright stars like Julie Andrews and Morecambe and Wise. After the static years of the war, listeners were keen to hear new comedians and singers. As the 50s got underway, Miss Houston's generation of comics had to step aside. Thankfully, Ronnie was sensitive to the older performers and kept the door open. Brian Willey, a sound engineer in those days at the Aeolian, who knew Ronnie well, tells me that he was very 'get-atable'. Renée also knew Lana Morris - the Rank Starlet Ronnie married in 1953.

Ronald Waldman (Author's Collection)

Another helpful friend at the BBC's Aeolian Hall was Michael Standing, and he got plaintive phone calls and letters about potential bookings from Miss H. Plaintiveness really did pay off in 1950, as they managed to do more radio work than ever before, getting good money, although they were still being put through the mill by the Official Receiver. They got a couple of *Workers' Playtimes* then a *Ladies Please,* then were asked back to Alexandra Palace for another *Rooftop Rendezvous* seen on TV screens on June 17. Renée had the luck to get a series of *Talk Yourself Out Of This*. She recorded eight episodes, impressing producer Frederick Piffard and smooth voiced presenter Harold Warrender - son of a baronet. She competed with American novelist Emily Hahn - former aide to Mountbatten, Alan Campbell-Johnson, and Kim Peacock - actor in Britain's first Talkie 'The Clue of the New Pin' (1929). A bundle of radio programmes was gold dust, and would not be offered to her for a wee while. Donald had a small part in the movie 'I'll Get You For This,' made at Teddington Studios, and because location shots were required in San Remo, Renée and Don had an autumn holiday – the first Renée ever took when she wasn't working at the same time. Don plays a US Treasury agent killed early on because he knows too much about a plot to destabilize countries using counterfeit money. George Raft, Coleen Gray, and Peter Bull were the other stars. Raft, the lovable gangster in this Riviera intrigue, became the *Sweethearts* gambler pal. In 'Don't Fence Me In' Renée mentions the luck they had in the casino. With so little security, I expect the roulette wheel was a nice way to forget the ghosts of financial past and present, bound to greet them on their return.

After a phonecall from Miss Houston, Michael Standing wrote to producers Bryan Sears, Bill Worsley and John Foreman. He felt the *Sweethearts* deserved consideration, and 'at worst a middle of the bill act,'[12] especially if they made sure to get decent material. With her heart on her sleeve, she wrote to him on November 24, telling him her telephone had been cut off and upping the urgency:

> 'During the past few months we have sold our most valuable bits and pieces, but now we've a notice to quit ... I have one week left to save my home and therefore am throwing my pride to the wind and begging you for work. So sorry to trouble you, but I feel I am losing my mind.'[13]

She tried Patrick Newman, another Variety Booking Manager with a light-hearted: 'Sorry to trouble you, but I am not doing so well on Westminster Bridge with my paintings.' He passed *Variety's Sweethearts* on to Cecil

McGivern who had returned to the BBC as controller of TV Programmes after two years with the Rank Organization where he had been a screenwriter.

McGivern got them *Season's Greetings* – a Christmas Day TV broadcast, pre-recorded at the Star and Garter, Richmond with Adelaide Hall, Peter Cavanagh and the Beverley Sisters. McGivern wrote after to tell them how pleased he was with their performance. They were actually on television twice that day, getting a spot on *Christmas Party*. BBC providence meant Renée and Don did not have to quit Waldegrave Park, and could struggle on there until October 1952. It was borrowed time and their BBC campaign continued with a new brand of paranoia in an undated letter she wrote Ronnie in the early months of 1951, all the while grateful for what he had done already, and sorry to be pestering him:

> 'Unless you are 'in' with the Gang (not powers) that be, you haven't a dog's chance. If you can use Don and I in any capacity . . . it will be a godsend. It's really frustrating Ronnie, to be praised by all and sundry and yet nothing ever happens. God knows I feel I am working better than I ever did yet nobody wants me. Since Xmas if it had not been for television and the BBC we would have starved and it looks like that any minute now. Can't even take a 'pub' because we're bankrupt.'[14]

It's true that some professions were discriminatory. Who the 'gang' was is an intriguing question. There were geniuses in the younger generation to be reckoned with. The new Crazy gang - *The Goons* – were beginning their world domination. You also had the combination of intimate revue, burlesque, Australian sophistication and satire from the happy team of *Take It From Here*. This popular show kept coming back with a funnier new edition. Jimmy Edwards looked older than his years and used to drive writers crazy scanning all scripts for grammatical errors. There was Dick Bentley from Melbourne, and Joy Nichols - a blonde from Sydney Australia. Produced by Scotsman Charles Maxwell, much of the wit came from writers Dennis Norden and Frank Muir - each over six feet tall and towering over everyone. Frank had been writing while still in the RAF. He and Jimmy Edwards both served in the *Handlebar Club*. Jimmy Edwards had come up through *Navy Mixture* and other radio shows before he appeared in TIFH items like 'Mirror of the Week' - a satirical commentary on the happenings of the day. The signature tune by the Keynotes created a buzz.

Well, you can't be outside all this – you have to mix in, Renée would say, as she listened in. The *Sweetheart's* BBC campaign resulted in fantastic returns and Renée was also on TV three times – first in *Kaleidoscope* - a charming mixed bag of features and comedy then on the *Half an Hour Variety* show on February 27. Then she and Don were Easter Bank Holiday TV material appearing with Arthur Askey, Elisabeth Welch, Norman Wisdom, Jerry Desmonde and The Keynotes again, in *All the Fun of the Fair*.

Renée had a tiny part in one scene of 'Lady Godiva Rides Again' (1951) produced by Sidney Gilliat for British Lion, with writing by Frank Launder

Milestones between Past and Future

and Val Valentine. Sam Smith died in 1945 and Alex Korda's London Films now owned the biggest share in new British Lion - its production based at Shepperton. You can't get a more 'British' film: rainy Sunday morning with bored wife - Kay Kendall looking out the window. Outside queues are waiting for the cinema to open. The usual crowd is here: Sid James running a seedy French revue, George Cole - the pushed aside boyfriend, and Alastair Sim a bankrupt producer. Launder had recently judged a beauty contest at Leas Cliff Hall providing one of this film's locations. His wife Janie is the heroine's young friend in the film. Renée plays *Beattie*, a character in *Mrs Jezzard's hostel for young ladies* when Pauline Stroud's character receives a parcel of tinned pineapples bearing her picture. 'What's he paying you for it? He's used your picture without your permission,' she nags the naïve Midlands starlet, as a cluster of girls gather around creating a frame reminiscent of a scene from 'Two Thousand Women'.

Renée was returning to pictures after a seven-year absence and accepted the tiny part with gratitude despite looking unbecoming in the scene. Her ears weren't her best feature. The Festival of Britain provided context for the 'Lady Godiva' pageant. Despite rainy Sunday mornings and fears about a rearmament because of the Korean War the Festival began in May 1951 - an attempt by London never to be black and white again, given post war recovery, super British goods, and the wonders of science. Gracie Fields opened the celebrations. Monty Banks had suffered a fatal heart attack on the Orient Express the year before. Friends flocked around Gracie – guest of honour at the Lady Ratlings Ball. Gracie however, had a good life on Capri, marrying again in 1952. Renée said she married her radio repairman. When the Rochdale Nightingale married Monty years before, that too had afforded a Houston gag.

Renée hoped to secure a spot on the BBC's *Festival Music Hall*, writing to Michael Standing on May 4 explaining her past glories. She cited her broadcasting experience that dated back to the old Savoy Hill days and the Royal Performance broadcast in 1926. She suggested that in just six minutes they could do separate turns – the first with Billie, in which she would recreate her naughty little girl character, and the second with Don. She sent some gags from a script but unfortunately it was too late for inclusion. Standing said he would be interested in using their latest sample elsewhere, as Billie had told him they had discarded the first script.

Bette Davis was Renée's favourite actress and the focus of her act's latest burlesque. Always a dab hand at channeling the gestures, even walks, of her models, she mined a veritable vein in Davis. Renée next wrote to Michael Standing from St Brelade's Bay, Jersey, where she and Don were providing an 'intimate' cabaret show for a week. A local newspaper raved about their performance and she sent a cutting to her BBC friend. She suggested that a regular guest act in the *Bebe and Ben* series might be a great idea, especially since in real life they were good friends with the Lyons. Sadly the reply was negative as *Life With The Lyons* was fully cast. He told her that the *Festival Music Hall* was being built around a fixed cast. Not the sort to be put off, Renée and Don caught the British spirit in *Hello Beautiful! A Festival of Glamour Laughter, Song and Dance* - a revue at the Empire, Portsmouth. Bernard Delfont offered them a spot in his *Do You Remember* show at the Empire, Nottingham in late August. It revived the old twice-nightly format with favourites George Robey, Hetty King, Georgie Wood, and Percy Honri. The *Sweethearts* were on it again when the show played the old Empress in Brixton's centre, and it was heard on the radio as *First House Vaudeville*, with Brian Johnston's voice announcing the acts.

Michael got her work on Ian Messiter's *One Minute Please* on the Light Programme on September 23. Roy Plomley was host and the teams were Renée, Jane Barrett and Monica Dickens versus Gilbert Harding, musical cartoonist Gerard Hoffnung and Kenneth Horne. Three air stewardesses presided over appeals. It was Ian Messiter's first attempt at a panel game of his own making and it was the first BBC show sold to an American radio network.[15] Renée and Don went up to Glasgow to pre-record *Scottish Music Hall* at the Lyric Theatre. Radio loved retrospectives, even in 1951, and Miss Houston joined Ted Ray, Leonard Henry, and Horace Kenney on *These Radio Times* to talk about the old days. Donald got in on the scribbles telling Michael about the reunion of the Houston Sisters for the first time in seventeen years, and suggesting that this would have great radio potential:

> It might be useful to suggest that I present my two kids, The Houston Sisters, at the Xmas Party Broadcast. They could do their kids act with me as their dad.[16]

Sadly he couldn't sell the Houstons, even though Michael Standing promised to keep it in mind. As in the previous year, Don and Renée recorded a *Season's Greetings* for TV, this time from Queen Elizabeth Hospital, Edgbaston. It was seen on Boxing Day. Some gaff on the *Sweethearts'* part must have upset good relations with Aeolian Hall because, apart from a *Worker's Playtime* on January 22, 1952 in Southend, and a *Mid-Day Music Hall* on February 20, 1953, the BBC offered no other radio or television contract for a two-year period. The next memo from BBC variety staff relating to Renée was not typed by a secretary, but a brief handwritten exchange on a single scrap of paper: one in red ink and the other in pencil. The difficult to read red ink is from Cecil McGivern's biro, with one part saying 'I'd better see her. One of those 6pm *drink appointments*' seems to be the sentence - or was it *drunk appointments*? Pencil lettering dated January 3, 1952 has an arrow pointing to a corner of the page saying 'Potentially great. Erratic - Both very loud and theatrical - Altho warmth - Not able to do it very - Not keen to give series - Waldman seeing them.'[17]

On the road in 1952, *Variety's Sweethearts* appeared at the Little Dolphin Theatre, Brighton, where only twenty-two people sat out in front. The reception was enough to make anyone feel like getting soused or unburdening their sorrows. They proudly 'stopped' the bill nevertheless, took five tab calls, and made a speech - 'It was wonderful,' she bravely recalled. She tried to get Ronnie interested in a comedy monologue she'd written the year before, telling him how 'it plays much funnier than it reads. I don't mind now reducing my fee a bit, . . . please let me know.'[18] Ronnie was polite in his reply but there was nothing doing at the BBC. In *Randle's Scandles of 1952* at Portsmouth's Royal Theatre on May 5, the wild and zany Frank Randle was also doing poor business and Renée and Don helped him, because that's what variety performers did. Randle strutted into their dressing room one Saturday night, saying to Donald 'I've got news for you - I can't pay you anything, but I've bought a doll for the little girl.'[19] Renée was a young fifty at the time! In May and June they did a few weeks at the unflinchingly modernist De La Warr Pavilion, Bexhill with Murray Browne, and she wrote to both Ronnie and Michael from the Hippodrome, Margate.

> Dear Ronnie. If you get sick of 'Pros' and need a couple of good amateurs in the near future, we have one or two vacant weeks. Keep your big salaries. . . PS. Do you know why we are happy? We've got nothing. Isn't it wonderful?[20]
>
> Dear Michael . . . "if anything" crops up (we) will be available next week . . . I am practically myself again, and we are very happy . . . "Dramatic Annie."[21]

All BBC sources from this period show a showbiz couple humbled and punished. It makes me sad with them being such hard workers, desperate to work their way back to a reasonable financial position. Renée had learnt from the trials of 1948:

Renée: When my bankruptcy trouble happened I never realized I could be so strong. I managed to adjust myself to the circumstances. I'm very happy to say it was the best thing that could have happened to me. It has taught me the true values in life, and I would be quite happy now with just a wee *but an' ben*, as long as I have got my man with me.[22]

Talent counted, and Ian Messiter found Renée to be among the fifteen people he thought very good in *One Minute Please*. His list included Kenneth Horne, Jimmy Edwards, Reggie Purdell, Hermione Gingold, and Yvonne Arnaud. Houston and Stewart took leave of Margate, playing Leamington's Pavilion, with Miss Houston joking about how small audiences were getting. At the White Rock Pavilion in Hastings the next week, they did a 'vintage variety show' with Randolph Sutton, before bookings in Hull, Guernsey, and Woolwich.

Her nephew David, who shared her birthday, and his mother Elana, saw the latter show - an easy bus ride from their home at Chislehurst. They loved it and David, like all nephews and nieces, got the special treatment from Auntie Renée. She had him up on the stage with 'Oh this is my nephew David.' The follow spot went on him and his own reaction took him aback because he lost his usual shyness.

Tommy Trinder (Author's Collection)

As she watched him she caught Tommy Trinder grinning in the seats behind, and with a suggestive wink to the audience proceeded with: 'Oh look, we've got Tommy Trinder!' She and Tommy caused uproar with their impromptu gagging. After the 'reunion' show, a stage-struck David went backstage with his mother to chat to the Houston Sisters. He remembered forever after that Renée drank whisky whilst Billie drank gin. He never forgot that particular detail because Renée made one of her cruel asides - that it was the gin that made Billie's eyes protrude from their orbit in the scary way they did. Her turn of phrase floored any scientific explanation. David was also left with the impression that a strand of jealousy existed between Renée and Billie although, to be fair, their crosstalk had relied on a sense of rivalry since time immemorial.

Above: Alan Aherne and Renée Houston backstage on the set of 'A Town Like Alice' (1956) directed by Jack Lee (Photo: Aherne Family Collection)

Left: *The Bells are Ringing* Coliseum, 1959. Donald as *Inspector Barnes* (C. Denier Warren, Jean St Clair, Janet Blair and Allyn McLerie also pictured)

Right: *Damn Yankees,* Coliseum, 1957. (L-R: Robert Crane, Edward Devereaux, Robin Hunter and Donald.)

Left: *Auntie Mame,* Adelphi Theatre, 1958. (Left to right are Pamela Simpson Donald, Anita Sharp Bolster, Bea Lillie, Dinsdale Landen and Jacqueline Ellis)

(Photos: Courtesy trustee of former Brevet Publishing Ltd and family of Donald Stewart)

Roar Like A Dove, Phoenix Theatre, October 1959

Left and Right:

Photographed by Anthony Buckley. Costumed for their roles as *Tom and Muriel Chadwick*

Photos: © Estate of Anthony Buckley, Wintermute Family

Left: Renée Houston with Heather Ripley
Roar Like A Dove,
Dundee Repertory Theatre,
August 1966
(Photo: British Library)

Right: Renée Houston as a staunch Marxist
(with David Battley, Jonathan Newth, and Linda Garner.
Wilfrid Hyde-White kneels in mock prayer.)
Meeting at Night, Duke of York's Theatre, January 1971
(Photo by kind permission of trustee of former
Brevet Publishing Ltd.)

Pat Aherne in California
(mid 1950s)

Alan Aherne

Anne Aherne
(Pat's second wife)

(Photos: Courtesy of The Aherne Family)

Grantown-on-Spey, Scotland, 1944
Left to right:

James Alan Rennie, Tony Aherne, Steve Silander, Shirley and Hal Silander

(By kind permission of the Silander family)

Gillingham, Kent, September, 1952

Left: Niall Lyall in front of one of his *Penny Pantry* businesses

Right: Tony and Niall

(Aherne family)

Whitehouse Hill, Chislehurst, Kent, September, 1952

Left:
Tony Aherne and his cousin David Aherne

Right: Niall, Tony and Elana Aherne taken by David Aherne

(By kind permission of the Aherne family)

Cromdale, Morayshire, Scotland, September 1952

Claire Rennie at her desk with Jim's novels and history books. Arthur Low caricatures and a cartoon of Jim dating from his days as a theatrical agent can be seen on the wall.

(Aherne family)

Cromdale, Morayshire, Scotland, Early 1960s

Claire Rennie with *Daisy Belle* the tractor and the Rennies' faithful dog.

(Aherne family)

Above: Location photo by Laurie Turner of unknown, Renée Houston, Roman Polanski and Donald Pleasance Polanski's 'Cul-de-Sac' (1966) © Filmways, British Film Institute.

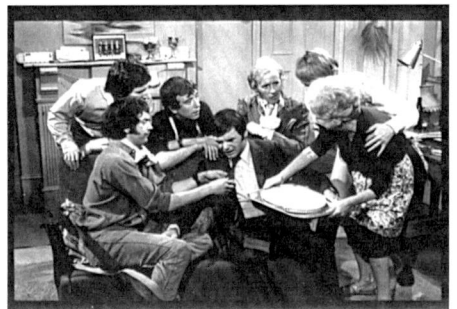

Martin Shaw, unknown, Robin Nedwell, Barry Evans, Geoffrey Davies, unknown, and Renée Houston.

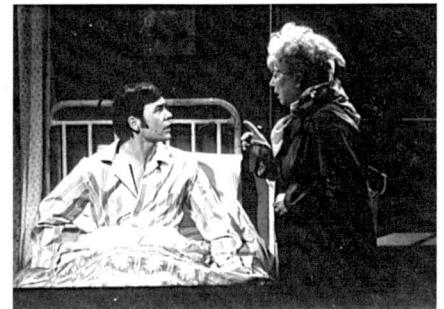

Barry Evans and Renée Houston.

(Action photos from LWT's Doctor in the House, 1969 by kind permission of Geoffrey Davies)

Renée Houston's last cinematographer and film director, Freddie Francis, seen with Peter Cushing on the set of Tyburn's 'Legend of the Werewolf'(1975).

(Photo: Author's Collection)

Right: *Little Women*, Ashcroft Theatre, Croydon, October, 1976. Renée Houston's last theatrical tour after sixty years in show business.

(Left to right: Renée, Nancy Nevinson and Patsy Blower)

(Photo: By kind permission of Patsy Blower.)

Right: *Little Women*, Wyvern Theatre, Swindon, November, 1976.

Renée Houston with actresses in Peter Clapham's touring production. (from unidentified newspaper cutting)

(By kind permission of Lawrence Douglas)

RENEE HOUSTON surrounded by her Little Women yesterday at the Wyvern Theatre, which houses the play of the same name all this week, starting last night. The girls are, back row (left to right) Janet Whiteside, Patsy Blower and Nina Thomas. Front row (left to right) Janina Faye, Miss Houston and Hazel McBride.

Kathleen, Shirley, Claire, Hal, Terry in the High Sierra Mountains, Summer 1980.

Claire and Jim either side of her brother Herbert and his wife Anne at Cooper Park, May 1964.

Anne, Louise, and Pat Aherne, 1960s.

'This is how we play golf in the USA! No use getting tired is there?' Brian and Eleanor in photograph sent to Aunt Eun, 1960.

Alan and Terry, 1990s.

David Aherne, 1970s.

Elana Aherne, late 1960s.

Niall, May 1973.

Alan and Tony, 1990s.

Brian in the Pall Mall Hotel, 1983.

The author with Alan Aherne, 2015.

Tony on a trip to California.

Left:
Donald Stewart,
Christmas Day, 1959
'Brighthampton.'

Chapter 20   Driving Me Potty

The *Sweethearts* were on the wireless on March 10, 1951, as part of John Sharman's *Music Hall* then Renée recorded a trial radio show on the evening of March 21 at the Aeolian's No. 1 studio after two three-hour rehearsal slots. For *The Houston Household* - a Max Kester production - her contract refers to her services of 'artist and collaboration on script,' stating that an extra 75% special fee would be added if records were passed for broadcast. I can't find *The Houston Household* listed in The Radio Times and she never earned the special fee. Kester had a long association with the BBC, once hosting a radio show called *Silly Songs We Used To Sing*. He also provided material for 'George in Civvy Street' (1946). He was good enough for George Formby anyway. What a pity Renée didn't benefit from his collaboration!

The BBC was on the look out for a new sitcom for the airwaves and thought a script based on Miss Houston's everyday life was worth a try. Why wasn't the experiment thought of in the 30s - the time Burns and Allen were striking it big on radio in America? Their sitcom had endless laugh-a-long jokes and themes that went viral such as the hunt for Gracie's 'lost brother.' At the time Renée was a perfect contender to be a British *Ms Allen*, given the attractive idiocies she threw up as a matter of course, but she lacked the right spouse then. A 30s foray on Radio Luxembourg was the nearest she got to a 'family series.' By 1951, although twice divorced, she now had the perfect marriage for radio comedy. BBC Light Entertainment was looking for new British writing characterized by topicality and satire, yet family sitcoms were still popular. In the UK, Bebe Daniels and Ben Lyon dominated this territory with *Life with the Lyons,* about an American family in England. It would switch to TV in 1955 after eleven series on radio. George and Gracie were ahead of the game: their show reaching the small screens in America as early as 1951. In early 50s Britain, all things American were an inspiration. When actress Molly Weir joined the cast of *Life with the Lyons* she was Ben and Bebe's Scottish cook, *Aggie MacDonald*, indicating we might not have been ready for something as classless as *The Houston Household*: a family descended from miners, servants and washerwomen.

Life with Gracie Allen quickly meant 'get me my psychiatrist' for most people and George Burns coped well with the daily idiocies and constant philosophical challenges. Their real life adopted son played their serious-minded *drama student son* in their TV show – contrasting well with his madcap mother and father. Similarly, Tony Aherne was well spoken, quick when roused, and had theatrical training. He had studied at Italia Conti in the late 40s, working at the Q - the innovative theatre at Kew Bridge founded by Jack De Leon that nursed undiscovered talent between 1924 and 1960. Returning from National Service in 1951 he still considered acting as a career. He appeared in one scene in the film 'Where's Charley?'(1952) – a film that starred Ray Bolger, Allyn McLerie and Margaretta Scott. In headshot photos taken in the first years of the 50s he wears the suits and has the slicked pompadour hair of the contemporary young man about town. He could look the part if he wanted to but beneath he lacked confidence. Long before we got *Saffy* on *Absolutely Fabulous*, Tony might have delivered droll asides to his mother's blustering on her radio sitcom that never was. Sadly, life in the real Houston household in those post-war austerity years underwent significant fracture with hopes for gentle comedy between Tony and his mother and stepfather out of the question. Renée had major son trouble at this time. Daughter trouble had come and gone, sadly for good.

Tony Aherne. Left: theatrical headshot. Centre: 1951 at Lyon's Corner House. Right: A truer likeness

Tony, whom she loved dearly, caused her anguish, and if the boot was on the other foot she made life more hellish for him that for any other child. For a start he was frustratingly quiet. Renée wrote to Mickey: 'Tony is still working as a railway clerk but he is up at the head office now. He is so eccentric Mickey - just like his grandfather, that we don't know whether he likes the job or not, but he spends his Sundays and days off here with Donald and I, and seems quite happy to sit and read, and eat and give us an occasional word when he feels like it. It just tickles Donald, we have a laugh when he goes.'[1] Eccentric was a comfortable word to use. Tony had been out of sight in Malaya but now he was back and socially awkward. His mother pricked at him. Elana Aherne hardly recognized the spotty boy sitting in a corner of Renée's dressing room silently reading. She would write how 'the army altered him and going abroad with them he was not the same homely jolly fellow he had been before he left . . . he isn't by any means the only one who altered completely after two years in the army. Have known others and some went straight into Haywards Heath mental hospital - young boys straight from good homes were shouted at and treated like dirt . . . when there's no war on one would think they could treat them better.'[2] But Tony had always had had that introspective quality. He could do droll but you didn't get bundles of fun from him, or song and dance for that matter. This paradox wasn't untypical of the Houstons. As a kid, Renée brooded on injustice. She didn't forget how it felt to stand apart but couldn't recognize the needs her son had that might bring him closer to her and to others.

Ivy Tilson was fifteen when she worked at the job centre on Denmark Street - still a world-famous rendezvous where you might catch sight of Ann Shelton, Joe Loss, Mantovani, Vera Lynn, Pat Kirkwood, Les Paul, Geraldo, Billy Cotton, or Benny Lee stepping out of a taxi. Ivy's friend suggested one night they start going to the 'Tin Pan Alley Club' located on the upper floor of a building round the corner. As well as the music crowd, you got big names too, rehearsing in the theatres. There's something likeable and down to earth about Ivy, and I can well believe many of the celebrities felt attracted to her unsophisticated charm and openness. They would say 'Hello Ivy' and she'd be drawn into their world for a little while. Danny La Rue adored her and not only got her tickets to his shows but would send a limousine to pick her up at her home: his driver presenting her with a gorgeous lily in a box. I got to meet Ivy in Holborn in 2015. She remembers meeting Renée Houston with her son Tony, possibly around the time of *Sauce Tartare* and never forgot Renée's voice, admitting that sometimes people didn't understand her strong accent. Renée got annoyed if people dared ask her to repeat things. The unwilling presence of her son was obvious and he was frequently raising his eyes to heaven, at the knife-edge of his mother's scolding. He took Ivy to one side that time and said 'She drives me potty.' On a later occasion, thrown into the mother and son drama, Ivy said to Renée, very bravely, 'You'll lose him you know, if you aren't careful.' Renée wasn't having any of this and said such a thing could never happen.

Hopes that Tony would find himself a nice wee lassie would forever be frustrated when the young fella found himself a nice older man instead. To be more accurate, he found a friend great and rare - one who seriously wanted to share his life without any crushing blows of guilt and repression. Tony's family never referred to his relationship as 'gay' and the words 'partners' or 'friends' were used. The way the law stood then acted as a compass to social mores, and being gay was incomprehensible or considered subversive and wrong in the eyes of many people. Many gay people hated themselves and nobody came out in those days. If you wanted a career and to enjoy some success, secrecy paid, so two men or two women would live together as 'friends' and there were many *Holmes and Watsons* living in houses up and down the country, desperate to be left to themselves. Before this time Tony's sense of self was fragile. As a quiet teenager he retreated into himself, never successfully making contact with anyone to help him bear the loneliness, and there was no support then. If there was an underground gay culture, he was ignorant of it, apart from a few secret experiences in the summer of 1950. Tony's 'lost youth' was something that troubled him until his final days. More than anything it was a society forcing gay people to feel like they didn't matter that was to blame. He adopted survival strategies – usually variations on a form of retreat.

To everyone in the family it was an open secret about Tony, and there were jokes made here and there but it wasn't taken seriously. Renée possessed a view about homosexuality typical of the times, believing it was a phase, however long that might be. Tony accepted the advice of a doctor to take a course of hormonal suppressants - the 'fix' offered by medicine back then. His hair, previously a little thin, gained texture admirably, but it didn't stop him being gay. There was even a girlfriend whom he felt he should have, who was quite ugly and lasted only a short while.

Renée never gave up her belief that he might be 'cured' and she was uncomfortable expressing truths or confronting them. When all your life you've put on a show come rain or come shine, you don't go in for years of analysis. She was still down to earth, the type who troops on, and was famously sarcastic. When those close to her faced tough problems she found solutions because solutions existed. In the 50s Tony's predicament didn't come with a 'solution.' She couldn't see alternatives, and her instincts told her it was wrong. Underneath, she dealt with the subject by denial, and with difficulty and pain. She mulled over the Catholic view that if chasteness were guaranteed, there was no wrong. The lifestyle Tony found as a solution didn't get a high rating in her book, and she wasn't impressed that he should be contented with this. Having courted the *Glesca keelies* so long in the past, her outlook was probably nearer to theirs. Well, she needn't worry about him being contented. He never was. He had tried to comply with moral codes observing the *irreproachable* stars of stage and screen acting as standard-bearers. He contradicted this world by his very nature but it was always going to be a struggle. He was left with a deep-rooted sense of isolation.

Would he ever consider it was frightening for her too, aware of the backlash and ignorance then? Cases of gay relationships being accepted by families did exist, but prolonged denial was common. You might think that during Renée's long theatrical career her outlook would have broadened, having known so many homosexuals. But even in the theatre, truths were known but seldom spoken. Lyricist Geoffrey Parsons shared his life and home with the singer and teacher Erich Vietheer. Douglas Byng and Lance Lister were accepted. John Gielgud would be arrested in a Chelsea public lavatory in October 1953 but his career survived unblemished. A kind of insincere exchange was ok, with colleagues in the theatre relaxed about homosexuality personally, and gay actors prepared to tailor the image they projected, to deny the truth publicly, and not upset the apple cart.

Renée's tentative enquiries about radio bookings sent to Ronnie Waldman and 'Boxie' – Miss AE Boxhall (one of Light Entertainment's booking managers) reveal that something else happened in March 1952 and for a while Renée had no time to submit scripts to the BBC. From her theatrical digs at Ross Mansions, Brighton, on March 4, she wrote to Ronnie that she'd 'had a great domestic trouble over one of my sons and it made me so ill, I couldn't concentrate on anything.'[3] A letter to Boxie on the same day echoes this: 'I am recuperating from a bad domestic shock, and work seems to be the only answer. I mean it's the only thing that keeps me to forget.'[4] The shock in question was that Trevor had been convicted for a crime and sent to serve time at the King's pleasure. This was a real disaster for the family, and difficult to cope with.

National Service didn't straighten out Trevor's tendency to take risks if a quick deal presented itself - in evidence at *'Green Trees'* when he was a nineteen year-old. That stately pile witnessed Trev spiriting away the odd piece of Houston clutter to survive austerity. It was a few bob here and there to fund bottles of spirits, but dodgy enough for those around him to suspect it a deliberate strategy. The police were not going to shop him for nicking from his own family. Schools changed too many times - an issue for all Renée's kids. Trevor had received support from Pat but they didn't forge a close relationship. In the early years he lived with older relatives and Lizzi and Jimmie who were too old to control him. His mother wasn't around to enforce rules. Pat eventually left the country and Donald moved into the stepfather role. Pat and Donald wanted the best for him although none provided a tough form of paternal discipline. Trevor was forced to follow his own path – one that was at times precarious. On one level he could be admired for being so independent. He was something of a favourite with Lizzi. When she died, she left him several possessions and pieces of her furniture, which he sold.

Alan tells me that Trevor, as the eldest boy, wasn't bossy and seldom lorded it over them. He didn't resent his two younger brothers who, in the early 30s, had lived with Mum and Dad. Tony and Alan were kept in the dark about Trevor and Terry being adopted. When Trev was nine, Renée came clean in newspapers and interviews that she had adopted children and she would have discussed it with her two eldest prior to this. It's difficult to know whether Trev coped well given the news. He was a cheerful lad outwardly. From the age of ten onwards he occasionally had tiny parts in his mother's theatrical productions - an enlightening environment for a kid to learn the business. Such freedoms and privileges could be exploited. He explored what he could get away with while he charmed and entertained. At sixteen he took part in wartime shows like *Let Loose - A Crazy Musical Melange,* at Renée and Don's invitation, and he enjoyed touring and being in the company of Dabber and Hazel. He was tall and very good-looking. Several young ladies including Jean Bayless were aware of his charms. When Donald's sister Lois, seven years older than Trevor, found herself attracted to him, he wan't so kind about her. Renée was also unhappy about Lois's attentions towards Trev and told Donald about it. That Donald was eight years her junior didn't register obviously.

Trev had a tendency to bungle things in a way that would shame a professional crook. Had things gone to plan and his little misdeeds not been found out, I expect he would have been a big success as an up and coming businessman. He had an entrepreneurial streak and an ability to take risks. His initial misdeeds were to do with his taking lead or ballast over to France by boat and exchanging it for cement blocks or vice versa. This was punishable as larceny and a newspaper report reveals he was convicted by Kent Assizes and put on two years probation while a charge for failing to report his change of residence and employment was adjourned. Later, he got himself in trouble again in an almost infantile way. To quote a letter Renée wrote Donald's mother, 'he had 'bunged' several 'dud' cheques and committed one or two clumsy burglaries, and incidentally we were amongst his victims. He was caught (ironically enough) through stealing and selling a sewing machine I had hired. Your 'clock' wedding present to us, thank God, we managed to recover that. He had also pawned and sold all the bits and pieces of family silver and glassware we never recovered. Since the house was in his name we had no option but to clear out and store our furniture. They (the police) would have claimed all that was under his roof. Billie stored some and Don and I have had to sell the bulk of it to live.'[5] Trevor's early history was no longer something to be kept quiet about, as local papers unkindly carried the headline *'Stage Star's Adopted Son Sent To Prison.'*[6] After his crime of petty theft[7] the earlier convictions counted against Trevor. The report, describing him as a fitter by trade, says he admitted the new offence plus seven other offenses. On February 27, 1952 the same court at Brentford, all too familiar with his mother's financial failings sentenced him to jail for at least six months at HM Prison The Verne on Portland. At twenty-five he was too old for the borstal.

At this emotional low point Renée, writing from Brighton, tells Mickey how she rejoices in the fact she has Donald and will survive whatever her children put her through. 'Tony has never written or phoned me since I've been down here. Alan wants to stay in America, Terry never writes, I don't even know if she's alive, and then – Trevor, and I still love them all (more's the pity) and I cannot help myself. Thank God for my Donald. He is my greatest love. He's been so patient and kind and he must be sick of the sight of my weeping face.'[8] Donald adds a note to tell his mother they found her clock 'in the second hand dealer's window – and that's how they learned about the sewing machine. He adds 'She just can't believe that after devoting so many years of her life to four children that none of them seem to care a damn. To Renée it has literally been a knock out. To have your home, family and belongings swept away in one full swoop, through no fault of your own.'[9]

When Renée had a variety engagement in Guernsey for the week starting October 6, she, Don, and Stephen (one of Shirley's boys holidaying with them) took the boat back from the island. At Weymouth Renée and Stephen, just seven, went by taxi to Portland. She left her nephew in the room outside and visited her son. Trevor was out in December 'on license' and would have had to report regularly to a parole officer in Twickenham. The family no longer resided at Waldegrave Park, and Renée and Don were then at 38 East Avenue in Hayes for a six month period when they weren't touring. 'We played this little theatre at Hayes four or five weeks ago and liked the people we were staying with at this address and we have taken the top flat (It's only one story above the ground) until we know what our plans are, Its only two pounds a week. It's a little modern house overlooking a large recreation ground, surrounded with lovely trees within easy access to London, not a long way from Stanmore. We only spend Sundays here between out journeys.'[10] Life went on in the fractured Houston household, and a letter or ten to the variety department was a worthwhile tactic: 'If we haven't been black-balled by the BBC see what you can do dear,'[11] wrote Renée to Boxie. That Christmas, she and Don paid a visit to the Reading Palace to see wee Shirley in *Jack and Jill* produced by Jack Stanley. Backstage, the older Houston sister offered advice for director and cast then cried a little. What do you do with all those memories of vinegar and brown paper? There'd been some argument concerning Billie's treatment of Renée since their last reunion show in February of that year and as Donald described the situation to his mother 'It's been a realization to both of us and where Paul has been blamed for a lot, we know now it's her bullets that he fires.'[12]

1953 was a year in which Renée and Don got nowhere with the BBC and they talked seriously of retiring to run a boarding house in Guernsey. The recent trip with Stephen gave them a taste for a peaceful environment and they looked to see what could be rented, but, as Donald told his mother, it was a case of – 'lots for sale but none to rent.' They hoped to persuade a Guernsey proprietor 'to let one . . . with an option to buy after they had cleared up their bankruptcy. Such a business would have suited them, with Donald's handyman talents. Their fame and reputation would be an instant advantage. How different things would have been!

It was also a tough year too for Mickey, dealing with the mishandling of her deceased husband's money and its aftermath. Both Donald and Renée were keen to help her, even though they were near rock bottom themselves. From Hayes they write that 'they will have saved enough money by August to send her. We can always find a *ways and means society* to send it to you. I'll go to Val Parnell for instance and get him to get one of his American acts playing the Palladium to take it back to you. It may not be much but it might come in handy. I'll never rest until we come to America and put things right for you.'[13] This is further evidence of Renée's closeness to the entertainment kings. As well as having the ear of Val Parnell, she was trusted by Lew and Leslie Grade. Ever loyal to Lew, she would propose a toast to him the time he was honoured at a *Press Club lunch* in Fleet Street in 1969 - with Nyree Dawn Porter and the Director General of the BBC among the guests. Charles Henry, formerly George Black's second in command, and later Parnell's Chief of Production at ATV was another important ally. It goes to show that her earlier showdown with Black was forgotten. She had also not done badly at the BBC in the past, even if they were ignoring her at the present time.

With *Murray the Illusionist, Maskar the Yogi Expert* and Bunty St Clare as fellow acts, the *Sweethearts* played the Theatre Royal in Exeter, and on March 30th, Renée wrote to Ronnie and Lana: 'I know you are madly in love, but that's no excuse for neglecting your aged aunt . . . I would like to do a 'television' for you soon as I have decided to 'pack up' the whole business this year. So how about a 'spot' on one of the programmes?[14] Jimmy Edwards, who had admired Miss Houston since she had graced his radio show in the late 40s[15] was signing copies of his autobiography at the Exeter branch of WH Smith, and dropped in to see his old friends at the theatre. A newspaper cutting in the BBC files mentions that at the Theatre Royal, Jimmy and Renée produced the most hilarious impromptu *'Romeo and Juliet'* sequence for the benefit of the audience. That article refers to compliments paid to Renée by her *Romeo of the handlebars*. Thrilled with this notice, Renée sent the cutting to Pat Hillyard, Head of Variety, who tried to push for them again at the BBC, hoping producer Bill Gates could get them something. Renée pressed the compliment from Edwards to Michael Standing, desirous of his help with radio or TV work in London. With Belfast and Scottish engagements coming up, she tells him about her phobia of trains, and says with a measure of honesty: 'Please try and help me Michael, otherwise I'll have to find a barmaid's job and I'd love that.'[16]

Jimmy Edwards   Joy Nichols
(Author's Collection)

It was ironic that Renée and Don were too 'expensive'[17] for the BBC - virtually homeless, penniless, and living out of suitcases as they were: touring the country with their canine 'child' Rowley in tow. Don's dog, acquired the year before, came everywhere and was always well fed. They thought seriously about leaving the UK if some opening in America appeared. The previous year Don asked his mother to enlist Lois's help with their pal Audrey - then appearing on Broadway: 'Ask Lois for the address of the theatre where *Gigi* is playing. Little Audrey Hepburn, one of the dancers from *Sauce Tartare,* is starting in it and is a sensation. Tell Lois to see her. Renée coached and encouraged her during S.T. We are going to write to her to see if she can do something about America for us. If she can I know she will. Tell Lois to say she's Renée's sister-in-law and my sister. I think they met at the Cambridge Theatre.'[18] Audrey was unable to pull strings for them, but they worked with Benny Hill for the first time, at Scarborough's Floral Hall. Thankfully that year, theatres stayed loyal to *Variety's Sweethearts*, grateful to have them, while the BBC conferred about how best to tackle the question of a reduction in her fee without getting as far as an offer.

At a number of seaside locations, the troopers kept cheery. Faded as cut-price postcards they might be, unfunny they weren't. That old gag about Donald being '100% American and half Scotch' was taken literally in Arbroath and the Montrose Burghs, with the couple described as 'Scotland's Greatest Personalities,' whilst at the Dundee Palace on May 4, on the bill with Frederick Ferrari and *La Celeste – mind reader*, their turn received rounds of applause. A photograph taken backstage shows Renée holding Don's marquetry picture of the old servants' kitchen at Warwick Castle. His skill in

Driving Me Potty

marquetry had advanced to the stage that he could enlarge pictures from postcards to three times the scale with draughtsman tracing. Don must have learnt this from his father. The image was originally going to be a tea tray but they framed it, got it valued at £45, and he had a plan to make his hobby pay.

They needed cash fast! This is illustrated by the fact that they could no longer afford hotels. A reporter from one of Dundee's newspapers went in search of them in Brown Street in Dundee, climbing up steep flights of steps in one of the tenements, trying one door after another only to be told: 'If it's Renée Houston you're after, ye'll find her in the next close.' Knocking at No. 8, there was no reply and another neighbour appeared, with a 'They're no up yet. You had better come back.' Then, a sleepy-eyed Donald popped his head around the door, and arranged for the reporter to call again later in the day.

Left: Don and Renée, May 1953 (Image courtesy of The British Library)
Right: Cutting showing Renée and Don in their Brown Street tenement digs, late April, 1953 sent inside a letter to Mrs Wintermute. (Wintermute family)

The protective people of Brown Street took the couple to their hearts. The touching story entitled '*Renée Houston – Dundee housewife for a week*' appeared with a little photo of Renée cooking at the 50s stove and Donald having tea. Used to 'three modern bathrooms in her London home' they are having fun with the wee washing area separated by a blind. The reason they're in a tenement, Renée claims, is 'I like to make a meal whenever I feel like it – and that's usually in the middle of the night. Hotels are not usually keen to cooperate, so this is the ideal answer.' She shows the reporter one of her oil paintings, gives him a lard-heavy recipe for flaky pastry, and tells how they gave lunch that week to Buddy Logan, brother of Jimmy. She's thrilled with their stair neighbours: 'When I woke up one morning I got to the window and heard a noise going on in the street. It was a crowd of kids and one little girl that I know was saying. 'Ssh, come here and I'll let you have a keek at the film star.' When Donald took Rowley for a walk, a crowd of kids came too, all of them contending to take the dog out for further walks. Two little girls upstairs sang to Donald, asking for a goodnight kiss. 'They're proud of their '*Uncle*,' Renée described, finding the way they bragged to their friends amusing. Another girl who didn't want to be outdone insisted, 'Ye're *my Uncle Donald* tae, are ye no?' as she fought for the right to dog-sit.[19]

After this came Paisley, where Donald wrote how 'they did terrific,' and Renée went for a wander around Johnstone. Then they played the Gaiety in Leith on May 19 where another reporter pursued her. She told Leith's Gazette she had 'never forgotten the Port' and was nostalgic considering that thirty years before she'd played the Leith Alhambra, and even before that the Lawrie Street Picture House. She encountered hostile comments about her *selling out* from 'one particular gentleman' who questioned why she came back. 'If I started in Leith,' she put it, 'there is no reason why I shouldn't go back to Leith.' Renée spoke with a mixture of pride and humility. 'If you behave decently on the way up, you can always shake hands with the newcomers on the way down. I don't intend coming down, because when I can't top the bill I will get out graciously.' She gave the press man the lowdown on their plans to retire to Guernsey, mentioning that on the Monday night a special friend had been in the wings – none other than Ella Hempseed - her ally from the dawn of her stage career.[20]

At Glasgow's Empress from May 26 - whilst London was fever pitch for the Coronation - reviews highlighted the redhead's 'bags of personality' and 'bad-gal pose with her impression of Bette Davis' a standout.[21] Their stay in Scotland over four months meant lots of trains and exacerbated Renée's travel phobias. In Glasgow they stayed with May Oliver, from whom Renée had learned tap dancing by imitation. Now as then, May was a sister to her. Renée never forgot these friends. She visited May Logan too - mother of the Logan family. At Dunfermline, they stayed with Lena and Cherry Grant after a show, and a week of happy chin-wagging followed. Renée made light of the fact that the earnings she and her husband were making were confiscated, making me think her old songline might be updated to: 'If you haven't got a home then a spare room will do.' They delighted the folk of the lovely Highland town of Perth on July 20, before travelling to Grantown-on-Spey to stay with Jim and Claire, before returning to Leith's Gaiety, and Edinburgh's Palladium for the week beginning August 10. A journalist would later comment on the ill-attended audiences of the Midlothian shows, all the same finding himself mesmerized by 'her ebullient wit, humanity, charm and West End chic.'[22] He writes that despite the show's meagre takings, she presented the entire cast with personal gifts on the last night's finale.

Next, Renée and Don turned their attentions west where, at the Gaiety in Ayr, nineteen year-old Andy Stewart joined the entourage. They played to Invernessians on August 17 alongside Alan MacRitchie - *Scotch tae ye'r taste* and Diane Vern - *buxom bundle of fun*. Peter Sinclair - *Radio's Cock o' the North* and Allan Young were there for the second week. It was a surprise and a half when the drummer in the show, May Harold, turned out to be the same little scamp Renée played peever with as a little girl. Knocking a shoe-polish tin along the ground was the first step in May's journey that steered her towards drums. These old Scots friends - all the Marys and Mays, were show folk truly after Renée's heart. She and Don found time to visit Rothesay, staying at The Bute Arms - Dave Willis's hotel. They laughed and talked for four days. People who remembered her as a lassie treated her as if she had never been away. Another girlhood friend, Alice Taggart - now Mrs Boyle - laid out a lovely tea for them. Renée and Don ventured south again on September 20 reaching Woolwich Empire in time for the Monday prize night - an extra award being a kiss for each winner from Renée.

Meanwhile, over at Aeolian Hall, Booking Manager and pal Patrick Newman was trying to sell her to producer Charles Maxwell, as a replacement for Joy Nichols in *Take It From Here,* referring to her new, more manageable fee of thirty guineas. Renée had, after all, apparently been an inspiration to young Joy when the latter started in show business. After a trek to Bilston's Theatre Royal in Staffordshire, Renée didn't mind what radio show she did, confiding to Newman: 'I would much prefer to be in a resident show every week (on the air I mean) than doing all this beastly travelling.'[23] Grateful to him for his efforts, Renée would soon be clear of the bankruptcy with the last official receiver released from duty. Still, she and Don didn't have a home to speak of, and when not living out of a suitcase, what remained of the *Houston-Aherne-Stewarts* stayed with Shirley at 26 Queens Road, Reading.

Tony, while working for British Rail in Waterloo, had lived partly with his new 'friend' and partly with Elana and her son David at 21 Whitehouse Hill, Chislehurst. Elana's family would later move to East Sussex. In early 1953 they were living in Henlow in Bedfordshire when a knock came at the door and Trevor Balharrie was standing in the doorway - a grown man. David, barely ten at the time had probably heard the gossip. He took a sort of instant dislike for Trevor. When his mother disappeared to make tea he observed Trevor's hand touch the handles of her bureau by the side of the wall. 'That's private!' came the voice of his angry little cousin and Trevor said 'I'm going to get some cigarettes.' He never came back. Elana was put out by it. It was the last time they ever saw Trevor. Released from his chains with his reputation a little tattered, Trev went back to his Thames-side stomping ground and found things hard as do many who have been inside. This wasn't an easy time for him and he was very alone.

He made a sincere go of it, and lived in a small bungalow on slim cigarette-shaped Trowlock Island – on the Thames at Teddington, where a little chain bridge takes residents to and from the mainland. He married his river girl - hairdresser Patricia Tidy. Trev and Tricia Balharrie lived a quiet life in their bungalow *'Ciampedie'* possibly dreaming of the Dolomites, and protected by swans and the 'salt of the earth' types on the island. Trowlock had theatrical connections and was a supportive little place. Lee and Jose Street - a double act during the 30's and 40's lived here in 1956. For a time, Trev joined the Royal Merchant Navy as a second engineer.

Houston and Stewart returned to Scotland to play Greenock on October 31, 1953 and Renée was back in touch with Cecil McGivern, writing from Sally McBride's tenement at 52 Parnie Street: 'I am still photogenic and still have loads of suitable material.' She spoke about their recent successes in Scotland and, being 're-discovered here with the new generation.' It was as if her career were starting anew – so why should she be ignored? She pointed out that all the Scottish newspapers were complaining there weren't enough Scottish stars on television.[24] I was not able to see McGivern's reply. At the Metropole, Glasgow in November 1953, Andy Stewart, in his first Glasgow appearance, joined Renée and Don before the *Sweethearts* did a brief interview with Howard Lockhart in *Personal Choice* on the Scottish Home Service. Between December 7 and Christmas Eve they were in *Happiness Ahead* at Aberdeen's Tivoli with Jimmy Wallace and Chic Murray and his wife Maidie Dickson (*The Lank & The Lady*). Renée sometimes got bored of targeting producers and chiefs at the BBC for help, and occasionally went via the stars. One who tried to help her was Frankie Howerd. He had been a radio star since the late 40s after his *Variety Bandbox* appearances. Whereas the *Houston Household* had failed, he made his television debut in 1952, in *The Howerd Crowd* and benefited from the skilful writing of Eric Sykes although he created most of his own material. From her dressing room at the Tivoli on December 7, 1953 Renée wrote to 'Dearest Frankie':

> Renée Houston calling. I loved your programme, and Margaret Rutherford was really smashing. I would love to do a spot with you . . . if you could fit it in. The scripts are so good too - I'd love it. I would be free from Jan 4th when I finish up here. Meantime darling, best of luck always.[25]

Frankie made Alastair Scott-Johnson consider the idea, but sadly Miss Houston got fobbed off. Renée and Don sat instead among a panel of worthies judging the *'Spirit of the Arts'* competition, then after Christmas were in pantomime at Kilmarnock's Exchange Theatre presented by Renée's friend and boyfriend from all those years ago, William Cummings. In *Dick Whittington and his Cat* Chic Murray played *Idle Jack* with Neville Taylor in the cast. Billy Cummings's *irresistible* redhead was feisty as ever. Chic Murray, a sensitive performer, fell foul of the redhead's wrath. In one ugly outburst that an embarrassed member of her family acknowledges to have happened, she called Chic a 'Stupid Idiot,' later shouting at him: 'How did you get on a stage?' followed by 'There's one of YOU on every street'. He gave as good back and didn't mince words. It happened during a rehearsal, and of course all at the Exchange witnessed the cringe-worthy exchange. It's extreme of Renée to do this and I've no details on the reason for her shockingly bad behaviour. She and Murray seldom worked together afterwards if they could help it.

Through the efforts of Patrick Newman, Pat Hillyard and Cecil McGivern, Renée and Don were returned to TV screens for an appearance in *Stars of the Halls* on January 9, 1954 – a nice fifty guineas fee. A new film was in production based on the spidery drawings of artist Ronald Searle. 'The Belles of St Trinian's' was a successor to 'The Happiest Days of Your Life' in which Launder and Gilliat took the theme of irredeemable corruption among teaching staff in a decaying English school even further. The school scenes in Evelyn Waugh's *Decline And Fall* possibly provided a starting place. It was a feminized version, and the storyline incorporated Frank Launder's real life love of horseracing. Launder directed, and Matthew Arnold composed the music. Little did they know this combination of instantly recognizable music, riotous little girls and fight between the forces of good and evil – with evil winning, would become the classic of British Cinema it has. It's never been bettered, and I don't think the near suicidal tendencies of those at the *Ministry of Education* and the anguish of local police could be replicated so humorously today.

Alastair Sim has a dual role as *Miss Fritton* - who runs the school with a pawned iron rod, and her devious bookmaker brother *Clarence*. Who could forget Sim's character coming into the ladies' staff room to utter the drop-dead line that he's seen far better ladies in a bar in Port Said? Renée's prickly personality and toughness make her a strange choice for art teacher *Miss Brimmer*, seen with her pulled back hairdo that also acts as a quiver for paintbrushes. Perhaps Launder thought she was so unlike your average art teacher, although that's an irony. Renée frequently painted as a hobby at home. Amongst the school's woefully unprofessional roster is Irene Handl - Cockney *Mistress of English* – an actress who was extremely well bred. Irene never spoke Cockney in real life - her *Lady Agatha* in the film 'Cardboard Cavalier' is closer to her real speech. Beryl Reid was *Miss Wilson* - monocled and golf-mad mathematics-cum-distillery mistress. Balbina Gutierrez – forerunner of *Morticia Adams* is *Mlle de St Emilion*, whose past is shudderingly sinister. *Miss Downder* - Hermione Baddeley - is the Geography teacher: expert on the Bordeaux region when awake, while young Joan Sims as *Miss Dawn* is no less profane in her teaching style.

With the *Cheltenham Gold Cup sweepstakes* the basis of the plot, the 4th Form of St Trinian's vie for advantage against the 6th Form. The 4th hope to win a packet if they shove their lolly on *Arab Boy* – the dead cert favourite, belonging to new girl *Fatima*'s father. In real life the horse was none other than Launder's real life horse *Windsor Cottage*. Their go-between is *Flash Harry*, who directs the distribution side of their distilled gin business. George Cole, protégé of Alastair Sim, landed this 'daddy of all Spivs' role and never looked back. Cole drew inspiration from Sid Field for the part: his lessons in RP from Alastair Sim never called upon. *Clarence* has an evil plan and enlists the 6th Form led by his chain-smoking daughter *Arabella* to steal *Arab Boy* so another heavily backed horse will win. Her gang captures the horse, with sultry Belinda Lee luring the stable boy. Their plan is thwarted as the watchful 4th re-steal *Arab Boy* and hide him in their dorm, aided and abetted by *Miss Fritton*. What else do you do when all the school's money (*Fatima*'s pocket money) is on a horse? How they lower *Arab Boy* to ground level using blankets as rope has always astounded me.

The abiding memory of Annabelle Heath who played *Maudie the Bookie* was the prestige of having a chauffeur collect her for shooting and bring her home again after. Her family lived at Ealing and her mother often worked at the studios with her father helping out with transport. Annabelle remembers being last in the queue of twelve girls reading for *Maudie*'s part. As each would be *Maudie* was reading the line in a similar way to the previous girl, Launder asked Annabelle to say it in a different way – a stroke of luck - as she got the part. Annabelle pulled off an organizational coup fifty-four years after the film's release, helping facilitate the St Trinian's Reunion at Oakley Court, Old Windsor – a location that had served for background shots in the film. She got in touch with the 'old girls' and anyone connected with the film, including reclusive George Cole who sent her a nice letter but couldn't come.

Polly Baber, a child dancer since the age of two, played *Celia*. Polly told me about her chauffeur-driven car that smelt lovely. The driver was a man called Tubby. Lorna Henderson played *Fatima*. It's hard to believe that the dark-haired tanned little girl was really a pale-faced white blonde. They sent Lorna off to Elizabeth Arden to have her hair dyed black and a dark makeup perfected. It took a few hours to do so Lorna's car came for her at 4 am in the morning. She lived in the East End and had to get over to Shepperton - almost the other side of the world. Still, she accepted all this without a word of complaint. The former 4th formers I spoke to were very young when they made the film and all cherish their memories from 'Belles of St Trinian's.' That magic and wonderment came from somewhere: a 'special world that surrounded theatrical people,' as Polly put it. Alastair Sim, she recalls, rested on a leaning board because he couldn't sit down in his *Miss Fritton* costume. She found Alastair and Beryl Reid a little scary. Lorna thought Alastair a true gentleman – and a lovely man.

Billie Houston's daughter Carole was in the 4th, in the scene when *Miss Fritton* shows off the school's chemistry lab to a new pupil. To the left of Alastair Sim, Carole is the chief bottler of the bootlegged gin. She recalls the jokes exchanged between Beryl and Renée, and also George Cole who was a favourite with her aunt. Carole says each child had a chaperone on set that suggests the studio must have been chaperone-heavy given the size of the 4th Form. All the younger girls by law had to have a number of hours devoted to learning each day in the schoolroom at Shepperton Studios. From what Carole told me, they used that time to study scripts at their desks, while I'm put in mind of a relaxed schoolroom with several girls sitting there dreaming of Liz Taylordom. Polly said her tutor did classes in the dressing room, teaching whichever girls were there at the same time. To the dismay of her aunt, studious Carole was impervious to the showbiz dream. Renée took it upon herself to interest a producer – a 'champion in the business' to try to change this. Once things were in motion she proudly informed her niece, not expecting the answer: 'I wouldn't touch this business with a bargepole.' Billie was a stubborn one too, Miss H would have thought, not giving up.

As seasoned professionals as Sim, Cole, Reid and Co were, I like Beryl's observation that 'there was no sense of responsibility involved in making this film at all.'[26] She recalls meals in the restaurant with large groups of children, and Ronald Searle's four year-old daughter sick at one of these - over a few of the actors. Launder must have given adults and kids a license to run riot and it was 'one jape after another,' as Beryl goes on to say, with the two warring factions of schoolgirls and adults throwing soot at one another across the barricades. In a film still, Renée emerges from the blast with a punk hairdo when the battle-weary teachers look ready to give up. Annabelle's mother is Renée's stand in when you see *Miss Brimmer* scramble up a ladder to the 4th form's dorm to be first teacher to 'safeguard' *Fatima's* pocket money. In fact Annabelle's mum would be a stand in for both Renée and Jean Anderson in 'A Town Like Alice' in 1956. Lorna Henderson's overriding memory of the *pocket money* scene was how badly Renée's breath reeked of rum. Miss Houston had refused to climb the ladder and that's why Annabelle's mother had to stand in to do that. No, Miss H didn't do ladder scenes and told them good and square, and they had to accept it.

In BBC's *Showcase* Benny Hill introduced a bill of artists making their first appearance before the camera and producer Kenneth Carter – a fan of Renée's approached her for a script so that she might guest on the show. Her appearance on Monday March 15, 1954 didn't wash with critics like Angus Hunter who wrote how the newcomers were 'tough competition for the more experienced guest artist,' whose act was 'blasé.'[27] One writer added: 'there is little she cannot do - if she tries.' Renée had a lot on her plate then, and a guest spot on a TV show was nothing special. She was best exhibiting her fun-loving talents with Don and together they were given *Thank You Ally Pally* to charm viewers with their double-act, live from Alexandra Palace on March 19. They had taken a one-roomed service flat at 14 Nevern Road near Earl's Court, as they were based in London for a while. Donald reports in a letter to his mother that Trevor and his wife were involved in the making of 'Captain Lightfoot,' an American picture directed by Douglas Sirk starring Rock Hudson and shot in Dublin. Trev's wife Pat assisted in the hairdressing with Trev providing assistance to the director. This seems a turnaround as Trev was in the merchant navy only a year earlier, but this foray into blockbuster films proved a one-off. Donald played a part in a picture called 'Tiger By The Tail' with Larry Parks and Constance Smith - quite a good part but not much money. As usual work opportunities diverted Renée from her troubles. Cecil Landeau came to the rescue.

At look around London's theatre scene in May 1954 reveals a good mix of the serious with the light-hearted. You had *The Cherry Orchard* at the Lyric Hammersmith, *After the Ball* by Noël Coward at the Globe Theatre, *Both Ends Meet* at the Apollo, and among the revues were *Going To Town* at the St

Martin's Theatre (with Hermione Baddeley, Dora Bryan and Ian Carmichael), *It's Never Too Late* at the Westminster Theatre, and *Requests the Pleasure* (with Joyce Grenfell). If you were a man about town in London's West End then, you might take your wife or mistress to Ciro's or to Churchill's (located where New Bond Street and Old Bond Street converge). There was generally a good floorshow at these exclusive clubs. At the time the script for a show in a West End theatre had to be run past the Lord Chamberlain and might be rejected even if it was just a bit more cutting edge. What couldn't be put on in the theatre could be put on in a club, so you got around the rules this way. Some floorshows were all-round great entertainment, not necessarily risqué.

Fenella Fielding was kind and generous with her memories the day I had the great pleasure in meeting her. She was at Churchill's Club doing comedy spots and songs and Cecil Landeau saw her and thought her ideal to try in *Cockles and Champagne* at the Saville Theatre. At a small party held in his Mayfair mews Fenella asked Cecil about the huge vat of immaculate roses, so large she compared it to a field of wheat. 'They're from Audrey,' said Cecil, bursting out with 'I wish she'd give me 10% of what she earns now!' By 1954 Miss Hepburn was in Hollywood making films like 'Sabrina' with Humphrey Bogart and William Holden. So Fenella joined the same revue that returned Renée to the West End again, this time with Donald Stewart as well as several dancers and actresses from *Sauce Tartare* like Pat Dare, Diana 'Monkey' Monks, Christina Lubicz, and also Nina Tarakanova who choreographed a scene. Others joined, who would find fame in television and films like Miriam Karlin – who was also quick to leave the show. John Hewer would go to Broadway with Jean Bayless and later become inseparable from his well-known *'Captain Birds-eye'* character. *Cockles* showcased talented French performer Pierre Dudan, who sang a number giving the dancers opportunity for a fascinating routine, and there was Mildred Smith whose Milan cabaret debut had been followed by the films she had made with Dan Dailey. Renée had tried to get young Andy Stewart into *Cockles* but sadly he had other commitments. Did Miss H have a role in casting I wonder? Naida Buckingham, Marie Burke's daughter Patricia, Terry Theobald, Gay Clark, handsome Bob Stevenson, Tommy Shaw (who later became a costumier), Laya Raki, and Elizabeth Seal are only a few of the names that flowed from the steady pulse of *Cockles and Champagne* throughout its resuscitations.

The unusual name of the revue was a play on dramatic contrasts - a wonderful mixture of the vulgar and the posh, expressed by the show's original cast, with Renée personifying the *'Cockles'* and Phyllis Neilson-Terry representing *'Champagne.'* Phyllis was an eminent Shakespearean actress who had appeared with Brian Aherne in *Craig's Wife* at the Fortune Theatre back in 1929. As every show needs a 'bit of a thing' between divas – this time it was between Renée and Phyllis Neilson-Terry, my sources tell me. From the sound of it, it seems to have been a fairly trifling set-to.

Along with Audrey Hepburn, Liz Seal was one of the first actresses in London to have the very short hairstyle. When she was in *Cockles*, Liz remembers Renée's sweet nature. This was her overriding memory of the actress. Liz described how Renée put herself out with costume advice, often doing alterations for some of the young actresses so they looked their best.

Cockles and Champagne:

Left: Don and Renée, opening night for *Cockles and Champagne*, Saville Theatre, May 1954 (Aherne family)

Miriam Karlin (Author's Collection)

Programme with Arthur Ferrier illustration (Author's Collection)

Renée in *Cockles* (Family of Teresa Long)

Renée Houston, Bob Stevenson, Terry Theobald and Tommy Shaw July 1954 (Photo by kind permission of trustee of former Brevet Publishing Ltd. My thanks also to Westminster Reference Library)

Fenella Fielding got the sense that Renée felt the difference in age in spite of her *'Peter Pan'* nature. She was fifty-two then, probably not the best age for most actresses, and she had to mix in with all the young dancers. She hated having to undress in front of them, and one night Fenella remembers her saying to the girls: 'You wouldn't like to see *your* old mother doing this, would you?' Nobody replied and it was one those moments where nothing filled the pause. Fenella sensed that Renée was slightly uncomfortable at the mention of highbrow theatre stuff. Someone in the cast was sounding off about some 'important' new play in the legitimate theatre, or that they were off to do an Ibsen or Shakespeare, and Renée would give off the impression such 'culture' wasn't her scene. She was known for giving members of the cast advice about achieving the greatest impact with their lines, and added to this, she selected pieces of advice about life in general for whoever was listening. There was a story running in the press in 1954 that the girls were chatting about in the dressing rooms one day. It was about modern girls choosing to take tablets as aphrodisiacs. Renée was disapproving. She wasn't against the idea of aphrodisiacs per se. She wanted to make the point that capsule popping was dangerous.

Décor was by Honoria Plesch who did *Sauce Tartare.* The finale dresses were by Victor Haffenden and the actresses wore Christian Dior jewels. Shows got off the ground because of a series of clever actions by producers like Cecil, like getting beautiful lace for frocks in three or four different shades via his Nottingham contact who had a lace factory. There would be times when a row of seedy looking men occupied the front row seats - most likely the fourteen angels whom Cecil had invited specially to rehearsals that featured the girls in their sauciest outfits. It was a way of showing them the goods. Cecil was forever doing deals with people so that a singer would join the show, sing a certain number, and in return, guarantee that necessary funds were piped into the show. It wasn't an unusual practice but it happened frequently on *Cockles.* 'The Road To Rome' - a memorable number sung by Valerie French for her London debut, originated from such a *Cecil deal.* Valerie was married to Renée's old friend - writer Michael Pertwee, and wearing rather dull clothes and a headscarf tied under her chin, began 'Road To Rome' with lines about a film actress's life in England not making an exciting impression. Suddenly as she got to the line about 'Rome' she would discard the headscarf and jacket until she was clad in sultry basque only, explaining to the audience the sensational Italian film she was in!

There were good numbers - a few by Maureen Stevens and Ronald Bullock, or by Sam Coslow such as 'Darling - They're Playing Our Song.' The *Tomorrow Mountain* scene featured the swing time music of Duke Ellington. Alas, too many numbers, too many performers, and too many scenes dogged the revue. About forty-two make up the programme, astonishing Fenella, as she counted them. One day a singer nobody had ever heard of came in and was suddenly inserted into the running order. In fact the scene was brand new! All this characterized the haphazard way *Cockles* was assembled. I learned so much about Cecil from Miss Fielding - a splendid raconteur.

One extraordinary episode involved Victor Valotti's - located across the road from the Saville. Cecil held planning meetings at this traditional café, which had a screen on the wall listing the grub available to order. The words '*Egg, Bacon and Sausage*' might be on one of the screen's many detachable wooden boards. Cecil 'borrowed' a lot of these boards one afternoon from the café and plastered the names of various scenes in *Cockles and Champagne* over each board's egg or sausage combo. He would sit there in the theatre, displaying these in front of him, endlessly playing around with the running order. What the poor café owner thought about this is anyone's guess. No-one was ever sure what items were going to be in so people tended to bring all their costumes down from their dressing-rooms to the small, quick-change room at stage level, so as to be ready for whatever. Fenella is hilarious, acting out the voice of Helen Dibley – stage manager - from all those years ago: '*Will the Witch Doctor come down to stage?*' -'*Witch Doctor to Stage,*' and her vignettes and accents are witty and delightful. Her memory and her ability to bring these scenes to life astonished me.

Cecil's design ultimately became a disconnected mish mash and members of the cast were underused. 'I haven't got anything to do!' was Phyllis Neilson-Terry's complaint, and Miriam Karlin felt the same. The six-week rehearsal period prior to the opening was long and Cecil got so absorbed he failed to consider his performers' needs. A rehearsal might go on until 2 am, posing difficulties for people getting home. Some of the girls had far to travel to. Miriam Karlin put him in his place a few times with 'I'm going home now – Goodbye!' Then Cecil might pick people up the next day saying *so and so* wasn't working in the previous night's performance when this was plainly open to question. When Naida Buckingham virtually lost her voice, imploring 'I must go home' in a pained way, Cecil was a swine, insisting 'You can go home but do my scene first.' The cast had issues with their pay packets too. Fenella tells me that Cecil was nonetheless an absolutely charming man and was fatherly towards everyone in the cast. You could tease him a lot and there was a lot of laughter backstage. You also had to hand it to him for the sheer achievement of getting people to back him to the turn of £35,000 - twice as much as he could hope to get back out of any of the theatres.

Opening night was truly horrific with a hiccup half way through. Something was done to the lights and the audience sat in the dark far too long with the curtains down, with banging and cranking reverberating behind, and the crash of something falling like a boulder from a mountaintop. People expected *Snow White*'s castle would appear, newly constructed on stage, but when the curtain went up ten minutes late only a boring front cloth greeted them - identical to the one already seen in the *Air Stewardess* scene. All in all, *Cockles* ran close to four hours that evening and the cast could hardly hear themselves for the sound of the departing audience, with seat by seat banging up, as they upped and left.

Brian Aherne and his wife were at the opening night and Eleanor must have returned to America with a good story to tell GG about the insanely long show Brian's brother's ex-wife was in – definitely a case of *schlimmer kann es nicht mehr warden.* Brian told Don he would try to produce some TV contacts for them in USA. There was still time for the *Sweethearts* to go west. Renée would now happily sail. Theatre critics left hideously early to rush off and give the show a panning. Yet, Pauline Johnson literally stopped the show in the second half. Fenella remembers her as a wonderful singer, about nine foot tall. Pauline got masses of applause for her number. She had no reviews because the critics had all gone by then.

Renée Houston, sensing the show's vulnerability, was unable to stand back and intervened. On the second night at curtain call Miriam Karlin and Phyllis Neilson-Terry were surprised as Renée stepped forward, addressing the audience of the Cambridge Theatre in slurred Glaswegian:

> I jusht want you to knaw that our grreat producher Sheshil Landoo shutting there in the bauxsh hash been faabuloush, he hash been wunnerful to ush and therre ish a grand bunch of kidsh here and the criticsh, thoshe terrible criticsh they slottered that pooorr Sheshil Landoo, sho I want you all to applaud Sheshil Landoo because you're a grand maan, Sheshil![28]

These are the words of Miriam Karlin who isn't kind about Renée and very to the point about the latter's alcoholism. Renée shouldn't be mocked for her bravery in facing the audience like this. She was incredibly loyal to her friends. Fenella recalled the occasion thinking the action was sweet but daft. If you're going to embark on a crusade of this sort, it's better to be stone cold sober. This view of Renée wasn't one held by all. When I asked Elizabeth Seal if Renée's drink habit was apparent, she said there were no signs of this.

Cecil survived the bashing he got from the press. While for Miriam, there was only so much of *Cockles and Champagne* she could take, the rest of the cast stayed true to it. In fact many individual scenes in the show received praise from the critics. One was *The World's Workers* featuring a falsely raked stage sloping towards the audience so the heads of the scene's charlady characters appeared at intervals in the gradient. Hangers suddenly descended – with a set of marvellous clothes and hats for each lady beneath. A quick change from their 'Hilda Ogden' overalls made way for the opening number: 'I'll be wearing my best bib and tucker.' Miriam was the original in *The Programmes Seller* scene coming on from the back of the stalls, dressed as a theatre attendant with a torch. She carried on with her 'umble job despite winning the pools. Fenella took over the part when Miriam left.

John Hewer was a *vicar of mirth* in one scene, P*edalling around the parish*, driving the ancestor of all vehicles in order to take Monkey to her destination. Ronnie Hill and John Hewer wrote the number in question. There was voodoo frenzy in *Drum Ritual*, with Laya Raki pursued by the jungle's answer to the Keystone cops. Fenella sang me lines from *What's it to do with me?* in a cockney accent: 'So I said to the Detective - What's It to Do with Me, Guv? – Is it my Fault if someone's in a Rut? Ard luck.'

She played the posh girl in *Queens of Sport* to Renée's huntin' woman, replacing Miriam. She remembered how experienced Donald was - supportive and ready to come in and save you on stage if something was failing. Fenella had a similar scene alternating with either Don or Renée. When she did the skit with Renée, Fenella sensed after the first week or so certain jokes weren't getting the laughs they deserved. She started doing it slightly differently on the night. Renée was able, each time, to react to the spontaneity. Afterwards an arch Renée was overheard saying to Cecil or someone else words like 'Who does she think she is, coming in here and playing around with the words!' They got on brilliantly all the same and Fenella believes that Renée appreciated anyone with the guts to challenge her on the cross-talk front. Renée was full of beans and cheeky as ever in her other scenes. In *Mrs Beatty's Home Perms* her poor clients suffered devastating effects, and in *Mrs Marchbanks* she was fruitily comic, fighting her inebriated condition whilst dealing with an over-persuasive philanderer.

Nevertheless, the Illustrated London News – so sure of itself in reflecting highbrow culture, wrote a dismissive review of *Cockles and Champagne*, and it bombed with other critics who 'longed for the days of Cochran.' After the bad start, Cecil innovated with new acts and the critics began to focus on positive angles, especially when Peter Townsend was brought in. He did a silent mime appearing on stage with a chair, bowler hat, parcel and umbrella only to get tied up in knots and double-knots as he unfolded and proceeded to wrestle with a copy of the Times. He'd been in a Cambridge revue with a partner so Cecil got them both for *Cockles* - a two for one deal.

Of course, Cecil reverted to form and was 'the world's biggest muddler,' as Donald describes, when the Saville gave Landeau two weeks notice to quit. At the last minute he transferred the show to the Piccadilly Theatre, only to find himself in the High Courts. 'Stupid Cecil had gone in there and paid for a month in advance and had not received an option to continue in writing - only verbal which he couldn't prove. He went to court, which gave us another week there, but he lost his case,' wrote Donald. The show had lost £35,000.00 in fifteen weeks and they never did capacity business.

Then came the astonishing *Cockles* strike led by Pat Burke, with the cast refusing to go on unless Cecil guaranteed their salaries that week. It was unlikely the evening's performance would go ahead but at 7.25 pm. Landeau contacted the cast who were at Equity's office in Harley Street to say he had their salaries. They jumped in taxis to Piccadilly, scrambled into costumes and went on like the professionals they were. Renée and Laya, however, waited for news at the theatre, playing no part, which says something about Renée's work ethic. Don and Renée were theatre folk of the traditional kind, sticking with the show for richer or poorer. They were getting half their salary but regarded it as preferable to travelling all over the country.

Facing eviction, even though *Cockles* was steering into its best season, along came a new venue outside the West End. This was the King's Theatre, Hammersmith. The switch came at the last moment. Cecil got an offer so the show shifted here after a two-week gap. Many of the cast had left. Brian O'Gorman came to see it here with his mother. Apart from Renée, they concluded, 'it was a very thin show.' At this point Donald describes to his mother how Shirley Houston stepped in and 'literally did all those people's work and she was damned good.' mentioning how Renée added another number. Prices were made cheaper for the suburban audience. Again Cecil muddled things. He forgot to get playbills printed. For two months, they were playing a week with no adverts and people not even knowing if the theatre was open or shut! Finally they sorted this out and there were bills all over the place. Business leaped. Then a bus strike hit hard. Cecil couldn't be blamed for that. Don told his mother how the strike 'put the final touch to this travelled and controversial show,' adding the following statement:

Donald: Renée used to tell me about him in *Sauce Tartare* and I used to accuse her of exaggerating. Now I know. Shirley used to think we were both exaggerating. Now she knows.'[29]

Binkie came to see *Cockles* along with her son Ronnie, who was tall, slim and good-natured. One day Alan, also glowing with health, called in at the theatre to see his mother when *Cockles* was still at the Saville. He hoped to see Shirley's boys but his aunt seemed unable to fix a date so he could see his cousins. People reacted strangely to Alan in his American Army uniform. Was he cast as *Pied Piper*, and would he put ideas into their heads too about going off to the States for long stretches of time?

Alan had got himself naturalized now. He had learned to drive, and had worked at the Flying Tigers, finding out that unlike England, two week's income in California could almost buy you a car. He loved the North Hollywood life but missed the British sense of humour: something that didn't travel. The actors he came into contact with in California were certainly amazing in front of the camera, but proved less witty when it was switched off. Alan couldn't forget the comedians of the variety theatre he'd encountered through his mother - hysterical on *and* off the stage, although admittedly he'd taken all that for granted in England. The loudest laughter in Hollywood came out of a can, and the image of Brian's friend George Sanders sitting morose at the bar - not chatting, just about summed up his feelings.

Pat Aherne's transition to life in the USA wasn't easy, and many years later his son Tony would ask himself why he ever went: 'Dad had friends, relatives ... Why stay there - to live and die alone ... in a land with no history ... in the dreary desert and bush - could he not recall the beauties of Middlesex and Scotland? The varieties of architecture which he claimed to enjoy. I hear his voice... 'Dear old Henley, Polesden Lacey' etc etc. There is no 'dear old

Driving Me Potty

anything' in CA.'[30] In Hollywood an actor who doesn't get the high-earning parts has to live by his wits for long stretches. Pat did sales jobs, driving miles into no man's land selling aluminum roofs, with one hand on the wheel and the other positioned out of the window. That's what being an unlucky bystander in wartime London does for you. He lived with the pain of that injury for many years to come.

After a year or two, Pat was visiting *The Countess* and one of his chums rang up Anne Kocsis - a young lady of Hungarian extraction acquainted with Pat. The story goes the friend proposed on Pat's behalf and Anne got into a car and instantly came up to the house, happy to accept. The poor *Countess* was abandoned, which is sad. Pat and Anne married in Reno in 1951 and one day Alan was given an ominous message telling him 'HQ wants to see you'. He was told 'You have a sister.' This was Louise. Years later, she followed in the family footsteps, enjoying a successful career as a Hollywood actress. Anne was a helpful stepmother to Alan. About 5,447 miles west, Mrs Wintermute, prompted by a small act of kindness on the part of the new Mrs Aherne, remarked to her mother-in-law: 'Do you want a good laugh? Pat's new wife sent me a necklace, earrings and a bracelet (not real, of course) but very beautiful. She said she'd like to meet Don and I, and I can't keep laughing. I said to Don. I wish you'd been married before, your wife might have sent me something.'[31]

Whilst living in North Hollywood Pat went back to selling English cars – on Hollywood Strip. He sold a car to Toni Mannix, and soon drifted into the circle that surrounded Toni and her husband Eddie. Eddie was a producer well known for hiding aspects of stars' private lives, and Toni was a film executive who introduced Pat to George Reeves - star of the *Adventures of Superman* TV series. Pat became great friends with George, and was able to add *Superman* to his repertoire. Pat appeared in a strange scene in an igloo in one particular episode. Even Alan did a TV commercial for a brand of fold-up boats made out of wood and canvas. The company was called 'Fol-boats.' George Reeves bought one, and the little boat turned out to be a lifesaver when George was as a real-life Superman, saving folk stranded in the water following a plane crash.

In Beverly Hills if you were friends with Ronald Colman, you were 'in.' Brian was, of course, at the centre of this circle and if Alan was lucky, he could glimpse the fabled British film colony in its prime. There were Hollywood parties thrown by Brian and Eleanor – either returning to their oceanfront home, or leaving for their chateau in Switzerland. They were generous hosts and a newspaper might publish the party's spectacular guest list, resonating with famous names too numerous to mention in full. Here were: Hitchcock, Gabor, Vincent Price, Jack Warner, Reuben Mamoulian, Adolphe Menjou, Cary Grant, Joseph Cotton, Greer Garson . . . and Charles Boyer, and even . . . Alan Aherne, second from the bottom. It was a source of amusement to Alan that the reporter rated him above George Hamilton.

Chapter 21   You Can Take It From Me

A day had been spent tending the herd and *'Daisy Belle'* - the scarlet tractor, had done her turn. Jim and Claire lit oil lamps and settled down for the night. The farm in Ballintian[1] brought in little but income from Jim's pension and books and newspaper articles sustained them. A respected member of the Society of Authors and Radiowriters Association, Jim's stories had been read aloud in successive episodes of *Children's Hour* in February and March 1949. His Houston Sisters connection might be forgotten but he dabbled in pseudonyms all the same. He was *Boone Denver* when he penned Westerns, occasionally *Morton Cleland* and at other times *Maxwell MacFee*[2] He also produced works of non-fiction like 'Romantic Strathspey', 'In the Steps of the Clansmen' and 'The Scottish People' with a painstaking level of detail and erudite study that stuns me. I could believe Jim lectured at Scots universities, as a family member told me, although I've not found evidence for this.

With their BBC accents Jim and Claire were untypical Morayshire farm dwellers. The Glasgow accent Jim possessed had softened, not that it was ever strong. His Silander nephews visited Ballintian for holidays in 1959 and 1960, gambling on the uneven bus service to take them to Claire and Jim's remote home. They were always met with a hearty welcome and the primitive Highland way of life of the Rennies was a revelation. Billie and Paul's children also made the journey up. Their sumptuous house overlooking Richmond Park might have impressed, but ironically, their debt-ridden parents couldn't afford family holidays. Carole and Anton saw remote mountain-passes few youngsters got to see. Jim, a great walker, never tired, his tall frame striding ahead as they struggled to keep up with him.

Donald still thought Renée the most glamorous woman he'd ever met. She put Dietrich in the shade every time. Given his peaceful composure, he might seem at the mercy of this divine subordinator in their private life, but this wasn't the case. They were evenly matched and his quick intellect kept her on her toes. Theirs was a successful marriage - each respectful of the other's career and they weren't inseparable, as Jimmie and Lizzi had been. Don would persuade her to take offers and he was the one who would 'dig this grandmother out of the kitchen' and get her to the theatre. In mock Scots he would call to her 'Could I have a wee drinkie?' hastening a thorny 'American' response. Don wore reading glasses now and she called him her 'Professor.' Disorganized as she was in balancing career and home life, she loved to look after *her Donald*, and adored the care and support she received in return. 'Marlene might have been a homely housewife some years ago . . . but my little girl still is,' Donald proudly told a reporter, when he wasn't jestingly teasing his 'poor wean'.

October 1954 saw a return to leafy Twickenham, this time to a first floor flat at 23 Norman Road. The smell of home-baked bread warmed your spirit and your bread roll sported nose, ears and a mouth, or your piecrust an unforgettable face. 'If you see a Santa Steak Pie – Blame Me'[3] went a newspaper headline about the domestic goddess with a sideline in plaster cast facemasks that she also vividly painted. 'Gosh! Am I good at it? Never knew I was so clever,' she'd say, whilst Don observed that her modesty was frankly embarrassing. They were sad to see their Waldegrave Park house demolished and replaced by flats. At Norman Road they could breathe fresh air again and move from one room to another but sadly they couldn't even afford to stay here long. The Wintermutes went to Dabber's wedding in June 1954 with Renée, Bob Monkhouse and Dennis Goodwin mock slandering the groom to the bride in the photos.

Left:
Dennis Goodwin, Bob Monkhouse, and Renée, at Dabber and Paddy's wedding, June 1954. (My thanks to The Stage)

Right:
Renée and her niece in Limelight, August 1954. (By kind permission of The British Library)

The hour-long *Limelight*, on August 23 at 19.55 brought Don, Renée, Billie and thirteen year-old Carole before a camera. Henry Caldwell was the producer. Renée and Carole sang a duet in the main part of the performance following an earlier scene in which the little girl played her aunt as she was when very young. In another scene the audience saw Billie strolling in to greet them. Carole remembers having to be careful not to trip over the cables running over the floor at Lime Grove. A story in the national press the next day made out that the Houston's first public reunion in years was totally unplanned and that Billie wasn't expected to show up. Of course she was too ill and would communicate with Renée live by phone call.[4] That's until she surprised all and sundry with her unexpected entrance - went the write-up. In fact Billie was present the whole time and was never anywhere near a phone. It's interesting that even then newspapers used the story of Billie's legendary illness in order to make her appearance extraordinary. In fact, Billie was perfectly well for sizeable periods by this time, even if she did relapse at intervals in which she was bed-bound.

Apéritifs at Lime Grove tasted awfully sour after an outburst, possibly arising from a remark by one of the men in suits. Renée instantly went to Ronnie Waldman. Instead of penning 'tittle tattle about your producer Mr Caldwell,' she told him, she would prefer to explain the facts to him in person, adding 'I have been very badly treated I can assure you.'[5] In her eyes, she was still the star and expected such 'scenes' to be met with sympathy. She saw Ronnie in November, telling him 'If I was starved I would not take this situation lying down.'[6] Her emotional arguments, however were running counter to the cool attitude of the Beeb. The specifics of the grievance aren't known, but the six year campaign by Renée and Don to get Ronnie 'on side' in the gambit for a TV or radio series is likely to have been set back slightly.

Donald had penned a three-page letter to Ronnie saying that earlier BBC 'justifications' as to why Renée couldn't have a series no longer applied. The excuse of her not having made a 'stir' with audiences didn't hold given the excellent feedback they got touring Scotland. Letters from fans poured in after their *Thank You Ally Pally* appearance. He hoped Ronnie might like his idea for a show in which he saw himself and his wife as joint compères. Ronnie left them with hope - 'if we should get an opportunity of using it I will be on to you like a flash,'[7] and kindly gave a publicity plug for *Cockles,* their troubled West End revue, in his *'Puzzle Corner'* in *Monday Night at Eight* – his own radio show. Renée thanked him, but a series in which they were 'resident' was what they wanted. And who wouldn't welcome the prospect of regular work as an alternative to an exhausting round of touring? With enthusiasm, she told Ronnie on June 9: 'My brother in law Brian Aherne is here on holiday and he thinks that Don and I would be ideal for the *I Love Lucy* series in this country. What do you think?'[8]

Brian and Eleanor Aherne (Author's Collection)

Brian and Eleanor Aherne had a home at 12 Warwick Avenue, managed by their housekeeper Mrs Woods. When James Stewart was in London appearing in the stage version of *Harvey*, Brian lent him his house and Stewart's family lived on nothing but peanut butter sandwiches - their food of choice! Another time, Renée and Donald were invited to dinner and it started off cheerfully. Renée always got on extremely well with Brian, and made an effort with Eleanor. She told Brian, as indeed she told everyone, the tragedy about how she couldn't see Tony because this evil man had separated her from her son. The 'evil man' was Niall Lyall. His scientific work pioneering the process for flavouring crisps and cellophane wrapped foods, developing the meatless sausage and 'sweet' hams, and heralding microwavable food, distinguished him as a prominent food technologist. Niall was a leader in an emerging field - a lateral-thinking genius whose years of painstaking committed study were not without eureka moments. Judging from the books he later published, I would describe him as a cultural polymath. By June 1954 Tony had started cutting himself off from Renée for long periods in order to live his own life and she didn't know where he was. Her performance was moving enough for Brian - one of the few who knew where Tony was living at the time. He couldn't help himself and gave away Tony's whereabouts to his mother.

Tony's life had started to change in 1952, when he lived with his aunt Elana in Chislehurst during one of the periods his mother and Don were homeless. His lack of academic qualifications mattered to him. The list of prestigious schools he'd attended looked good on paper but he suffered from a broken education. He set about getting a tutor, sat examinations and was very successful. Tony's tutor Helen got him through, and Niall was Helen's brother. A member of the Aherne family remembers the change that came over his cousin at the onset of his relationship. Tony couldn't stop talking about his new friend and when people got to meet Niall, he impressed them with his knowledge of natural sciences, electronics and computers. He was Tony's closest pal – and they complemented each other, the age difference being no issue. Tony didn't know Niall was seventeen years older than him until the day he died. Keeping Mickey abreast of the news the following year, Donald mentioned that Tony had started 'a partnership with another man,' building up a business of shops called *Penny Pantries* selling 'cooked meats, hamburgers, hotdogs and hot suppers. They have options on five places and one option on a small factory for cooking the foods . . . It is at least enterprising.'[9] Based in the Medway area, they tested the market for Niall's ideas and nutritional innovations, as well as selling old classics like pease pudding. Elana, who was Lulu's daughter down to a tee, and her son David, came to love Niall, finding him funny and brilliant. The atmosphere in their home was one of toleration.

The la-di-dah Aherne family might take pride in possessing a certain Bohemian élan but Renée Houston, child of popular theatre, had an outlook traditional in scope. Having peddled her own act so long: one that for all its apparent riotousness, was at its core 'family friendly,' she didn't rate the selling potential of Tony's 'performance.' My belief, all the same, is that if push came to shove, Renée would have been behind her son if he hadn't rejected her. She was brave enough. She admired boldness, so you would think she would admire it in Tony. The Houston Sisters had been able to go through life ignoring Mrs Grundy and doing what they liked. I believe Renée turned into such an adversary where her son was concerned because she felt edged out in the presence of a rival character closer to her own age. Tony made a lot of assumptions about his parents and dealt with problems by cutting himself off. The tragedy in all this was he assumed his father would show the same 'disapproval' as his mother and stepfather. Alan tells me this was far from true. His father would have accepted it without question. Pat had 'blotted his copybook' by leaving the country - interpreted as a rejection by his son. Tony made decisions, seeking his place in the world. Like his sister Terry, he could only do so away from his mother. He displayed a newfound confidence instead of cowering under convention.

I don't believe Renée didn't try to tolerate her son and his lover. She didn't oppose Niall just for the sake of it. There was some give and take. Tony and Niall are seen in a photo at Renée's home in Clapham in the garden seated on the wooden chairs that Don built, showing they visited Renée's home as a couple. There is even evidence that Renée and Donald shared a flat with them for a short time, possibly before or after Clapham. She wanted to be a dominating presence in Tony's life and he was escaping from her in order to breathe. He had to slip through the gap to survive.

While they worked around their issues at the beginning, the battle between mother and son never had a true resolution. Back in the 50s her heaving emotional presence was a nightmare before Tony made the break. In a letter Elana Aherne wrote to her aunt she mentions the 'scours and very unpleasant remarks' and how Renée and Donald 'were getting home after the show, tired and hungry and had a few whiskeys I believe! Then anger, threats started and unkind things were said. So, when they went away on tour, Tony and Niall just closed the flat and departed for keeps.'[10]

If there was one thing Tony was able to entirely channel his genius into, it was chess. It was an inward space to go on the attack: one in which his 'opponents' could be symbolically and repeatedly crushed, and one in which outward things so 'essential' to his mother mattered little. Tony's young cousin Anton had grown up admiring Tony's record at playing chess in national tournaments and wished he could play with the same cocky vengeance of his cousin. Pat had taught Tony the game and by the age of twelve he played like a grand master. Stationed in Malaya on National Service, he won the All Malaya Chess Championship two years running. He was national champion of the Singapore Chess Federation in 1950.[11] Tony had taught Anton at the age of three and he taught Billie too. They played incessantly. When Renée got very frustrated she put a downer on the cosy little contests presided over by twenty-one year-old Tony. She couldn't help but *drop him in it* about his not being 'normal' even using the line that he was an unacceptable companion for twelve year-old Anton. When Anton suggested a game of chess, Renée would say 'Oh no. I'm not letting you be alone with him.' Cheap snipes like this and the code of fear they represented would occasionally taint family get-togethers. Accepting her son's choice was not *good parenting* in her book. With so much happiness in her own marriage, why couldn't she live and let live? It's another of her endless mysteries that she should wreak havoc in the life of someone who should have been closest to her. Tony's sexuality never resulted in a rejection on his mother or stepfather's part. They wanted him, but on their terms.

Billie played *ladies correspondence chess*. It doesn't exist today but long before computers, in the late 40s and early 50s, you received a letter containing a little folder that unfolded into a lightweight chessboard. There were chessmen cutouts you slotted in for your next move. You recorded your moves, folded everything up and posted the letter on. In this age of online game communities, it's remarkable to think thousands of people played chess every day by post. Could Billie have been her wee nephew's ally? In her youth she'd been married to someone who had gone through something similar. Was she sympathetic? The idea challenged her, despite admiring Tony's courage. Typical of her generation, Billie seldom talked about the subject. If she ever did, she used old-fashioned words like '*Elizabethan*' to describe gay people. If she recalled Dickie, it was with a slighting tone. She was once known to go off on a tirade about the 'aggressive lesbian' who pursued her – long before this actress went on to enjoy a long career on *Coronation Street*. Billie and Renée, recalling what happened to Jim all those years ago at school, sometimes had the fear of God in them, voicing heavily laden religious opinions when it suited.

Family members tell me the sisters weren't close in this period so it's possible Billie didn't know about Niall. It wasn't in Billie and Renée's nature to be in each other's pocket. For all their early camaraderie, after their stage act ended and each had families, they weren't interested in being around each other except for family occasions or at Christmas. Renée was ever on the move so it wasn't possible for them to keep in touch as much as they might have liked. Whilst she was at Nevern Road, Tony and Niall lived off Cromwell Road - moments away. Between them were boarded up clearings of buildings lost in the war but none of this damage served to remind her war was wrong. She looked out of the window brewing up the next manoeuvre, reverting to her *Maggie* character in 'Their Night Out':

Maggie:	So this is the house of the ungodly!
Taxi Driver:	No, the *House of the Ungodly* is round the corner.
Maggie:	If anyone from Aberdeen was to see that den of iniquity! I could never sing in the choir again.[12]

Young David, staying with Renée and Don, experienced the uneasy lull in crossfire and found he had his own reason for bitterness against the distracted aunt incapable of taking his Vegetarianism seriously. At least he did not trust she did. Much as he loved her, she had this side to her that wasn't very sweet or pleasant. She was struggling with love and hate, and during the Marian Year, asked Our Lady's help and prayed for a 'cure'.

The time came for Renée to perform her *Alice Blue Gown* and there couldn't be a more appreciative audience than those turning up to see the *Rat's Revels* at the Victoria Palace on Sunday October 24. The Water Rats and Lady Ratlings designed one hell of a bash. These revels started because several of the wives of featured showmen from *Jack Hylton Presents* were Ratlings. They had the idea to put on events to raise money for charity. This '*Gang Show*' included Tommy Trinder, Mike and Bernie Winters, Harold Berens, Eddie Calvert. Ralph Reader, Hetty King and Sandy Powell.

On the afternoon of December 18, 1954 both Houston Sisters attended initial BBC rehearsals at the Aeolian, before they took to the stage at the ever-beautiful Coliseum – fifty years old. How new it had been almost thirty years before when those awestruck Glasgow youths made their debut in Stoll's hallowed 'Cathedral'- suppressing their fears about uttering the wrong word! They were back to record *On Stage Coliseum* - a special produced by Tom Ronald to be aired on both Home Service and Light Programme on Christmas Day evening. It was Renée and Billie's last professional contract as the Houston Sisters. The BBC used Fucik's 'Entry of the Gladiators' as the programme's opening music – the same music the orchestra played fifty years before when the theatre opened. Dickie Valentine sang his hit 'The Finger of Suspicion' then Randolph Sutton did 'On Mother Kelly's doorstep'. The stars of *Can-Can* - the Coliseum's current show did the next turn and later came songs from *Annie Get Your Gun*, *Kiss Me Kate*, *Call Me Madam,* and *Guys and Dolls*. Harry Locke did impersonations of street traders and foreign tourists, opera singer Victoria Elliott sang 'Jewel Song' from Gounod's *Faust* and Fay Compton did a speech from *Coriolanus*. George Gee and Yvonne Arnaud did a *husband and wife* sketch. A lone Flotsam was seen at the piano. Jetsam had died eleven years before. Ethel Revnell, now without Gracie West, did a conversation between herself and an imaginary niece. Gert and Dais discussed their gifts to Bert and Wally then Jewel and Warris took the spotlight.

Jewel and Warris   Vic Oliver   Ada Reeve
(Cuttings collection: Simon Grayson, Author's Collection)

Finally, Renée and Billie Houston appeared - Billie wearing a body support beneath her boy outfit. Bud Flanagan sang 'Hometown' and Vic Oliver did a comic turn followed by Ted Ray. Eighty year-old Ada Reeve took to the stage and lastly seventy-nine year-old Albert Whelan, in cloak, gloves and hat, emerged to the tune of 'Jolly Brothers'[13] a number from way back when! Renée and Don spent the end of the old year and beginning of the next in Wolverhampton, joining Alma Cogan at Wulfran Hall, returning to record *Twelfth Night Out* with a TV audience made up of medical staff and patients of Wolverhampton hospitals. It was seen on TV on January 6, 1955. Then, for the first week of February they were back at the Palace in Dundee alongside Jimmy Nichol, *Kardorma* and Neville Taylor in *Foolish But Fun*.

In her eighteenth film, Renée gave a memorable performance in a Republic second feature film directed by Bob Springsteen called 'Track The Man Down' in which Petula Clark and American actor Kent Taylor were leads. As a boy, Taylor ran away to join a vaudeville troupe before his parents fetched him back, sending him to engineering college. Kent Taylor's name partly served as the inspiration for *Superman*'s alter ego. Playing a journalist, he's set on covering a murder at the dog track but gets forced to report on *Pat Sherwood*, 'the biggest thing on the British stage' with a diva personality to match. She's just walked out of a West End show - a story half a million readers care about. He's unenthusiastic: 'The way I hear it she's a dragon,' he tells his boss, believing she's only good for five lines on page six. We meet the apparently incognito *Miss Sherwood* playing with her cigarette holder. She's dressed in dark clothes, black hat, and expensive-looking dark glasses. Her line - 'What makes you think that I'm in show business, and even if I were, what business could it be of yours?' - might well have been spoken by *Gloria Lind* if that chorus hoofer ever became a star of the first order. We're in the 'bar' of Victoria Coach Station where played-out *Miss Sherwood* waits to board a bus, intent on quitting London for the south coast. She backchats with the manager who begs her to return to the West End. She's merciless about the 10% he's collected from her all these years. Then a drunk, superbly realized by Arthur Lane, seizes on *Miss Sherwood* with: 'I know you,' but he can't register where he's seen her face before. He run through a list of locations where it might have been, including the Stag And Hounds in Wapping, whilst *Miss Sherwood* gives an icy reply each time.

> Drunken man: I'm sure I'll think of it soon. What about the George And Crown? Don't worry. I'll think of it.
> Pat Sherwood: I'm sure you will - before you run out of pubs.[14]

'Track The Man Down' superimposes a 50s British Cinema view of American style gangsters on top of your polite policemen, matriarchal landladies and refreshment hall white cups and saucers. The gangster aspect seems risible now but it was just the ticket back then. It's a fast-moving well-directed film although you wonder where all the American characters can have sprung. The best American accent comes from British actor, George Rose who gives an absorbing portrayal of *Rick Lambert* - tough-guy on the run, who turns out to have a bit of a heart.

Pat Sherwood comes to blows at the hand of *Rick Lambert* (Artwork by author)

Renée would work with George later, on 'Flesh And The Fiends,' but it probably says something about the speed in which these films were made that she makes a mistake in her 1974 memoir, saying it was Michael Balfour who punches her in 'Track The Man Down'. In fact it was George Rose, the Old Vic actor who went on to win *Tony awards*. In real life, he was gay but had no partner. Many years later he died in the Dominican Republic, killed by a group that included the young boy he supported. When *Pat Sherwood* is holed up in a boathouse, the sock on the jaw she receives prompted by Houston outspokenness – is crucial to the eventual rescue. The film was made at Nettlefold Studios, Walton, but they use the bridge at Teddington Lock in one shoot. Petula's *June Dennis* doesn't exchange dialogue with Renée but offers contrasting versions of chic. Petula reminds me of a Hitchcock heroine in the scene with the suitcase at Victoria Coach Station. *Pat Sherwood* was a part after Renée's heart and she played it with sincerity. Petula tells me she'd seen Renée in her variety act on the stage before and enjoyed working with her on the movie immensely. She remembers how funny Renée was but most of all remembers her glamour. The scene at the end is hilarious, when *Miss Sherwood* parodies the drunken man, who by then has thankfully sobered up. You now he won't remain so for long. She beckons him along with her - to the nearest pub, and there's an irony in that!

At the BBC, a hoo hah over material and a run in with executives followed Renée's guest spot on *The Jimmy Logan Show* produced by Eddie Fraser and aired on February 28 on the Scottish Home Service. This time Variety Booking Manager - Pat Newman, well meaning and eager to help Renée out, got her work in advance of a contract and perhaps she was deputizing given the short notice. Off she went to Glasgow, glad to help her 'wee nephew, Jimmy Logan', and it was only after the show aired that something bad hit the fan. Firstly, she saw the contract and fee - only 15 guineas, and secondly the BBC didn't like the fact she had doctored the script. There was no shame in this as far as Renée was concerned and she expected credit as the material's provider. Letters began to fly between the Scottish Programme Executive and the Aeolian. Newman moaned to his opposite number in Scotland about how Renée took it out on him remonstrating that Eddie Fraser blamed him for the mix up. 'If I thought that Eddie Fraser really did blame me,' Newman claimed, 'I'd go mildly off the deep end for maybe that's what happens when you attempt to help, as we did, by slightly cutting through red tape . . . However I take everything Miss Houston says with a pinch of salt so let's forget it all and just remember never to use her until we have a signed contract.'[15] Scotland sent him a sympathetic response claiming the star had only provided a monologue of her own and added: 'As for the Houston allegations - a tablespoon of salt I feel.'[16] She frustrated executives but Eddie remained on her side. He immediately offered her the TV show *Garrison Theatre* on March 25, live from HMS Condor at the Royal Naval Air Station at Arbroath - a 50 guinea job. It was great to appear alongside Dave Willis and this was Andy Stewart's first TV broadcast with 'Auntie' Renée. Soon after, the BBC signed Andy Stewart up for two years and the Scottish press wrote how Miss Houston seemed 'a lucky charm for the boy!'[17]

Donald continued in the West End, this time in *Desperate Hours* – a melodrama with an edge, given its bunch of psychopaths on the run, occupying the home of an ordinary American family as a hideout. Don played the chief of police - one of the good guys. A review criticized the London Hippodrome's amplifying arrangements, that made most of the actors' speech inaudible[18] but *Desperate Hours* ran between April 19 and September 10 providing a window into small town America – still an attractive place to small town Englanders. How this contrasted with real-life London was something Pat Hillyard would find out in letter from Renée on April 24: 'Donald is in 'Desperate Hours' at the Hippodrome and I go on stage in the desperate hours at Churchill's Club. It is killing me dear, and Don won't let me travel for long out of town, so I am available for anything within easy access at the moment.'[19] It was a good angle to use with the BBC, that she was nearby and ready for radio work. Sadly, Hillyard was in America at the time. A show at Churchill's meant shared dressing rooms, not going on stage until 1.30 am and getting home at 3.15 am in a state of collapse with Don leaving at 9 am for his rehearsals. She wrote to Mickey: 'Club work is horrible. Nothing but drunk men and bad women. I loathe the atmosphere. They are all call girls and I do a *'Duchess act'* on them. I speak to no one.'[20] All the same, she was grateful to Cecil Landeau who was presenting these shows. Ted Gatty and Danny La Rue were at Churchill's at this time.

Logo on branded goods from Churchill's Club (Author's Collection)

A turn up for the books arrived in mid July when Renée was asked to test for a part in 'A Town Like Alice' to be directed by Jack Lee, the brother of writer Laurie Lee, who had cut his teeth working with the Crown Film Unit. The film was to start that autumn with shooting mostly at Pinewood. Joe Janni – a refugee from Fascist Italy before becoming a producer, circled Renée a few times remarking that she must have been very pretty when she was young. 'What do you mean *must have been* - I still am!' growled la Houston. A tear-jerking impro, hitting hard about how it feels to be ignored for months by producers is what convinced them she could make people cry as well as laugh, so Renée tells us. Bill Lipscomb created a script from Nevil Shute's 1950 novel about British women taken prisoner in Malaya in 1942 omitting several scenes set in the outback, leaving writers of an Australian TV adaptation in the 80s to stay faithful to Shute's novel. Rank agreed to finance the movie.

Don, Shirley and Billie tripped north for a birthday celebration for Renée's 53rd. She was playing a hall in Manchester and the party was a surprise. The ten weeks work on 'A Town Like Alice' couldn't have come at a better time since Renée and Don were near homeless again. That July they took the ground floor maisonette of 23 Bramfield Road off Northcote Road - convenient for the shops south of Clapham Junction. This became their London base for three years. Don was in his element in the little strip of garden and made flower boxes for the lounge windows painting these pastel shades and filling them with flowers within two weeks of moving in. Renée had a little kitchen, dining room and lounge with a red settee, and there was a nice bedroom with French windows. In the evenings, she got lonely on her own but looked forward to midnight when 'her angel' returned home for the supper she'd prepared him. Upstairs, lived two ladies from Chile. One spoke perfect English whilst her sister-in-law spoke none. These ladies forwarded mail on the Wintermute's behalf. They had a home craft business making little bags and weaving scarves on a tripod thing and when Renée befriended them she sold eight of their *pouchettas* at the film studios to help them.

On August 14, Renée did a Sunday night concert at Dunoon in the Firth of Clyde. It was one of her typical summer engagements when she could take a holiday in between work and she took her fourteen year-old niece with her. Carole remembers the swimming and coach rides between shows, the presence of Dickie Valentine and Andy Stewart in the party (something enviable at the time), and how gentle Andy set her young heart a flutter. They had a wonderful week and Donald remarked in a letter home how Carole was the same age Renée had been when she went to Rothesay to work. Carole appeared in a troupe of youngsters dressed in the military uniforms of one of the women's services and she remembers being made to swear an oath to *respect* the uniform, which wasn't merely a costume.

Don surprised both of them coming up on the sleeper with Anton when a booking for Butlins in Ayr on August 21 materialized. At the holiday camp show in the middle of Renée and Don's act, Miss Houston announced 'And now you're going to love what's next – it's my dear sister's kids'. Donald wasn't happy about her doing this. Anton remembers how something took over him and he felt no fear on stage – comfortably going through his *Goons* characters with accents ranging from posh English to broad Glaswegian. The audience lapped it up so much that Donald said to him as he walked off 'I hope to God you won't do this. You'll be dead before you're 50.'

Renée was happy to show willing when radio work cropped up. Two installments of *Housewives Choice* on September 3 and September 5 paid five guineas a time and she introduced Don on the second occasion. The BBC had acquired the old Shepherd's Bush Empire in 1953 for television as a stopgap studio while it waited for White City to be ready. ITV work was also welcome and late 1955 saw Donald in an episode of *Douglas Fairbanks Jr. Presents*, filmed at Elstree for the American market. Each episode, introduced by Doug Jr and sponsored by Rheingold Extra Dry – *New York City's best selling beer*, was seen on NBC's network. Don was in a British Lion film 'Ramsbottom Rides Again' (1956), appearing as a captain of an ocean liner, with Arthur Askey, Anthea Askey and others en voyage to Canada where Frankie Vaughan, and Sid James as an excellent cowboy, await them.

Getting a spot in a provincial variety theatre was good to fall back on for Renée and Don but the traditional form of variety theatre took a battering in the years following the launch of ITV on September 22, 1955. The 'flesh and blood turns' felt even more desperate in the face of change. A combined attack by Radio and Talkies with all their sophisticated weapons was less destructive than television's bloody onslaught. In the first year of commercial television only 4.5 million TV licenses were issued to a population of 51 million[21] but the shift toward home entertainment was quickening up accompanied by technological advance. The entertainment barons - the same proprietors of old variety theatres, were quick to seize the initiative, buying up franchises for the newly created ITV network. Lew Grade's company Incorporated Television Company (ITC) looked to a future of selling TV programming to American networks. A merger of ITC and Associated Broadcasting Development Company brought about ATV, transporting Lew Grade, Val Parnell and Prince Littler into the vanguard of television variety. The old Wood Green Empire closed in January 1955 and was restructured for TV use by ATV: studios that would, in years to come, be used for Val Parnell's *Saturday Spectacular*, *The Sid James Show*, and *The Morecambe and Wise Show*. ATV also used both the New Cross Empire and the Hackney Empire. The old Granville Theatre had a short-lived life as a TV studio for Associated-Rediffusion between 1955-56, and the old Chelsea Palace - a southern outpost for Granada Television, served as a studio between 1958 and 1961. The variety artiste's holy grail was now *Sunday Night at the Palladium* hosted from London's West End. This show's first ever broadcast was compèred by Tommy Trinder, with Gracie Fields and Guy Mitchell as top-liners.

I never fail to cry each time I see the final scene of 'A Town Like Alice' when *Jean* - played by Virginia McKenna and *Joe* - played by Peter Finch are reunited in Australia. She was a secretary caught up in the nightmare and he, a young Australian soldier driving a truck for the Japanese who tried to help. You care deeply about *Jean* and the other brave women during the hopeless trek that takes them miles across Malaya barefoot, surviving brutality, starvation and death. Sixty years later the power of the film is undiminished, and in 1956 its effect was hugely significant. Renée plays *Ebbey Edwards* - nagging wife of *Arthur* and we first meet her when the women gather in the accounts office, presuming that fishing boats will transport them out of the country. 'Oh come on Arthur, don't let everyone push you around,' says *Ebbey* pushing someone with her case as she bustles in only to be ticked off by *Mrs Dudley Frost* - Marie Löhr, for sitting where she shouldn't. 'Goodbye, you old stick-in-the-mud,' says *Ebbey* to her husband when women and men are separated. As is typical in her films Renée provides a little spirited comedy, contrasting with *Jean*'s moving sincerity and also the agony born with bravery of schoolteacher *Miss Horsefall* - played by Jean Anderson.

You notice Renée's subtle Chaplinesque movements whilst dodging a bayonet-holding guard emerging from a doorway in the back of a shot. Did she insert some patter into the script? In the scene where we meet the Australian chaps one of them says to actress Maureen Swanson's flirty character: 'You're pretty quick on the uptake,' and there's a little Houston repartee with: 'She's quick on anything,' getting chuckles in the process. Every theatrical Oriental in England was recruited to be extras, even if only a few had Malayan looks. These performers were jugglers and acrobats and, if 'Don't Fence Me In' is to be believed, they all knew Miss Houston from the theatre. When squabbles ensued between the Chinese and Japanese performers she played peacemaker. Tenji Takaki, the sympathetic guard, had been a real life British POW and his other job was making lampshades.

The production of 'A Town Like Alice' didn't finish until November 1955 and they spent three days in Burnham Beeches wading barefoot in the stagnant lake full of tin cans and rubbish people had chucked in it. Virginia McKenna and the other actresses were disappointed that no foreign travel to exotic Malaya or Australia was on offer. All the villages were brilliantly constructed on the set at Pinewood! The takes of the tracking shots weren't easy to achieve, requiring much traipsing around. Members of the cast told Brian McFarlane it was so cold they were given a bottle of rum to bring their circulation back. The wonders of cinema, and glycerine sprayed their faces make the setting of sub-tropical jungle convincing. Nora Nicholson, as *Mrs Frith*, the hypochondriac who proves more physically fit than anybody, had to kneel down in a freezing white frost to say the Lord's Prayer and Marie Löhr got ill. In a later scene when the women think Peter Finch is being crucified you could apparently hear their teeth rattling - they were shaking so much with the cold.[22]

The once glamorous half of the Houston Sisters found it distressing wearing those filthy rags in the swamp. This is when *Ebbey* falls victim to exhaustion. On her hands and knees in mud drenched from the deepest part of the lake at Burnham Beeches she had the worst deal of all of them. Jean Anderson revealed this years later to Jack Lee who admired Renée all the more - 'By God, she was good in it.'[23] Virginia McKenna, incidentally, told me Renée was uncomplaining about having to do the scenes, and she recalls her being a real team player. I asked her about a drawing Renée had apparently done of her on the set that Renée mentions in 'Don't Fence Me In' but Virginia didn't recall sitting for this and had no idea the picture had been bought by Charles Laughton for £50. I later discovered that Renée did paint a picture of Ms McKenna but this was from memory after the film ended, as mentioned in The Stage.[24] Renée needed a quick buck and Laughton was happy to hang a Houston alongside his Renoir.

The critic Symson Harman praised the efforts of Renée, Marie Löhr and Jean Anderson who, under the tender hand of the director provided 'as fine a combination of thrills, laughter and tears as you could hope to find in any movie'[25] and the picture was one of the three biggest British box office hits in 1956. Composer Mátyás Seiber had created music for the CIA-funded animation of Orwell's 'Animal Farm' two years before. His score for 'A Town Like Alice' is even more beautiful and haunting. It was his last picture, as he died in 1960 in a car crash. The film was withdrawn from 1956's Cannes

Film Festival in case it offended the Japanese. Nevertheless, it got the *Belgian Prix Femina* for 1956 judged by 50 women[26] and Virginia McKenna and Peter Finch won BAFTAs. For Renée, she sensed a new dawn with dramatic roles. She wrote to her pal at the BBC 'I nearly forgot to say Ronnie, but now that Don has done so well in *'The Desperate Hours'* at the Hippodrome and I have been launched as an actress, how about the drama end of TV? After all they do have guest stars don't they?'[27] He replied encouraging her to get in touch with the then head of BBC drama, Michael Barry.

Around 1958 Renée and Don resolved to up their game and be more organized regarding future engagements, in advertising themselves to casting directors. For years, Renée had barely bothered with Spotlight, the service founded in 1927 that published handbooks of actors and actresses with photos, notes on their recent work and contact details. In the 20s you saw Brian, Pat and Elana Aherne and details of their agents in Spotlight, but Renée and Billie were never pictured, although the 1936 Spotlight has phone numbers listed at the back of the book for Renée and Shirley. Variety stars didn't consider themselves too distinct a breed to miss out on Spotlight. Many took up offers in film or legitimate theatre. I wondered if Renée and Billie considered themselves too 'big' for Spotlight sure as they were of the variety network and *insider contacts* in musical comedy, the BBC and films. Renée was now listed under '*Leading and Younger Leading Women,*' with an attractive photo by Raymond J. Hearne. Renée and Don had Rita Cave represent them from January 1956. Rita had been press and PR officer for Odeon Cinemas during the war and represented stars like Alfie Bass. Miss Houston was slow in believing Rita's 'Personal Service' advertising strapline was all it was cracked up to be: 'Bless her, dear heart, she's ok for films but doesn't understand much about TV,' she said behind Rita's back.

Donald wrote to Pat Newman and others at the BBC about his wife's success in 'A Town Like Alice' and Rita joined the 'Ronnie' campaign, reminding him that her wonderful Artiste had not appeared on the BBC for a *long long time* . . . Val Guest gave her a small speaking part in 'It's a Wonderful World' as a sex-starved neighbour who's moved into the room opposite Terrence Morgan and George Cole to their disappointment. She is un-credited which seems unfair but so is Jon Pertwee who plays a conductor. She made films with three future Dr Whos. Renée's time on screen was fleeting but she was too much of a pro for it to matter. The film was a winner.

Joe Janni offered Renée a significant part in 'The Big Money' - the £175,000 film he was producing for Rank at Pinewood with Ian Carmichael in the lead. Renée signed on March 20 for a guaranteed sum of £240.0.0 and a daily rate of £60 to play *Bobbie* – the Irish Technicolor redhead presiding over the *Red Dragon Pub*. Quick and funny and the same old Renée despite looking smaller and stouter, she pulled pints and cross-talked with punters, setting the yardstick for *Rovers Return* landladies in the subsequent decade. 'I'm afraid me young fella me lad - it's too late,' *Bobbie* tells folorn *Mr Frith* -

Ian Carmichael, who's arrived in search of young barmaid *Gloria*. Diana Dors had been lined up to play *Gloria* but she was tired of playing gold-diggers and cardboard floozies. Twenty-one year-old Devon-born Belinda Lee stepped in. She went on to play temptresses in Italian films and five years later died in a car accident in California, her driver doing more than 160 kmh.

The film, directed by John Paddy Carstairs, with cinematography by Jack Cardiff and Jack E. Cox was not actually released until 1958 having its music and titles added later. It was shelved because John Davis, managing director of Rank, gave this order on account of the film being 'not funny enough.' Certainly, a strong plot is absent from 'The Big Money' and it would have been better by far had it possessed a measure of humanity, taking its cues from Carol Reed's wonderful 'A Kid For Two Farthings.' Diana Dors was astute to keep clear of it and it was hardly going to launch Hull-born Ian Carmichael as British Cinema's bright new hope. Still, the London boozer is authentic, and individual performances by Renée, Belinda Lee, Robert Helpmann (as the bogus *Parson*), Leslie Phillips (as the *Hotel Receptionist*), and Harold Berens (as the *Bookmaker*) are a saving grace.

Renée finished her scenes and on April 1 1956, was back on to Ronnie–alternating charm and directness: 'Don't worry about Variety Salaries, just give me (or us) a break.'[28] To Michael Standing she emphasized their suitability for straight or legit work - 'all we need is work on TV and radio to help us,' she begged, suggesting *Henry Hall's Guest Night*, *The Bob Monkhouse Show*, *Workers' Playtime* and *Midday Variety* as possibilities. With an air of tragedy she described how she was trying to reach him but when she telephoned no one knew her or remembered her.

Never afraid to pick up the pen she was also writing to producers within ITV's network and it was at the BBC's rival where all was trumps up. *The Blood is Strong* - broadcast on May 3 and directed by Joan Kemp-Welch, (who did *The Ladykillers* in the 80s) was an adaption of a 1948 play by Canadian broadcaster and polymath Lister Sinclair. He also caused a storm in 1950 for his radio drama about a pregnant, unmarried woman considering an abortion. This drama with Renée playing *Mrs MacDonald*, co-starred John Laurie and young David McCallum and was about sailors and their families. As *The Blood is Strong* went out live Joan relied on hand signals to prevent over-running. Renée was very quick jettisoning a paragraph and running on the cut down dialogue.

With her first TV drama in the bag, she was asked to appear in *Thanks for the Memory* at the old Met on July 11 – a show that included GH Elliott, Hetty King, and Randolph Sutton among the artistes. Each night Don Ross introduced a *great lady of the music hall* with Marie Kendall, Ida Barr, Gertie Gitana, Clarice Mayne, and Ella Retford as choices. JV Benjamin wrote a letter to The Stage telling readers how Sutton was 'still electric in every sense of the word' and that Ida Barr 'moved him to tears.'[29] Miss H scoffed to a reporter: 'Old Timers?? - They were all at school when I started.' The article rejoices in her official debut as an old timer remarking how 'the little girl of 7 stone 4lb is now a big girl of 9 stone 6lb'. A wolf whistle from the gallery brought smiles: 'I bet he doesn't remember me. His grandfather would.'[30]

Left: *Thanks for the Memory* at the old Met, July 1956: Hetty King, Renée, Randolph Sutton and GH Elliott (The Stage)

Below: Rita Cave (Family of Terry Long)

Inverness beckoned - one show being a *Halloween Party* at the Empire Theatre on November 2, and Renée and Donald were in *Anything Can Happen* in the scene: *invite you to join the party*, then in another with Teddy Lancaster, Joe Long, Kay Mitchell, Bill Montgomery, and Leslie Robertson. A 'Tyrolean' Dave Willis joined them at their next theatre engagement, where the audience got tea and biscuits in the interval.[31] Perhaps as a training ground for their new *legit* identities Renée and Don appeared in Longwood Productions' *Rock n' Roll Murder* at the Garrick in Southport on November 28 taking this to the Empire, Nottingham in early December.

An article in the Southport Visitor tells us that writer-director Bruce Walker reveals 'the staggering secret lives of teenagers at a Rock n' Roll club,' drawing from his experience of club life in London's Soho, just as he did in his last work *Cosh Boy*. A gang member is accused of murdering *Vera* – a society woman of mature age - played by Madge White - her drunken flashes of cynical wit relieving the sombre violence of the play. Renée is *Lottie* - the tough but good-natured barmaid at the Rock n' Roll dive, and Philip Barrat – the sinister club owner *Count Guiseppe*. Donald, as the *Inspector* is praised in the article, also for his recent films.[32] While criticizing the 'infantile plot,' The Stage said Renée held it together, adding that Johnny Briggs as 'a lad hankering after something better' showed a 'natural ease of performance.'[33]

Cutting from unidentified newspaper showing Renée and Don in scene from *Rock n' Roll Murder* at the Empire, Nottingham, December 4 1956 (sent inside a letter to Mrs Wintermute) (By kind permission of the Wintermute family)

453

Their many missives to the BBC got them no more than a spot on *Midday Music Hall* – performed in cocktail dress at the Playhouse Theatre, Northumberland Avenue and broadcast on December 28. This radio appearance resulted in more criticism from serious-minded executives. A memo from CF Meehan, Assistant Head of Variety, to producer Bill Worsley, pointed out that the script 'called upon Renée Houston to act and fool about as she did in her one time double sister act. She has now, for obvious reasons, passed this type of work and should no longer attempt to be a young woman.'[34] His boss Pat Hillyard added that 'when artists give a performance that it not in our opinion up to standard because of a bad script, in fairness this should be pointed out to them.'[35] Bill Worsley covered himself, explaining how he had told Donald Stewart that his script wouldn't do as it was. 'I went carefully through it with him and suggested various spots where gags could be inserted, and he promised . . . This is a repetition of what happened last time I booked them out of sympathy and I really feel that they have now had 'their lot'.'[36]

It doesn't sound as if the BBC was going to welcome Renée and Billie's reunion any time soon. Don's letters to his mother reveal that Renée was suffering from a problem with her womb at the time, and the last few weeks had been terrible. They thought hospital was inevitable and she joked about her condition saying 'the drawing room was slipping down to the cellar.'[37] She spent Christmas resting, avoiding an operation and wrote a small play while she was ill - a farce about people in digs on tour. She and Don hoped someone might produce it or that they might get independent backing to produce it themselves. Sadly, such opportunities for actors like Renée and Don were even more limited in 1957 than in 1937. You would have thought they would have been used on the radio in the same way Ted Ray and others were. Much of the 50s saw Renée and Don begging for work at the BBC.

Their exclusion from the airwaves for the rest of 1957 was to television's advantage, but it was thanks to the efforts of Waldman and Michael Standing that the ball was set in motion. In January Rita Cave sent Joy Harrington at BBC TV Centre Wood Lane untouched stills of Renée looking 'de-glamourized' from the film 'Time Without Pity' plugging the fact that Sir Michael Redgrave was in the picture. Then on February 1, Stephen Harrison dropped Renée a note to tell her he was pleased to cast her as anxious mother *Vi Vining* in *The Day's Mischief*[38] informing her of rehearsal dates at Lime Grove. In the play a schoolgirl is suspected of being the object of her schoolteacher's lustful attentions, resulting in outbursts from his wife, the girl's disappearance and a lot of finger pointing. Renée was cast in a role that might just as well have been inspired by her reactions to Terry's disappearance ten years earlier - an uncanny coincidence. With her daughter nowhere to be found, we hear *Vi,* overwrought and talking about how, as a mother, she'd give her life's blood to be reunited with her. She wracks her brains as to why her daughter could leave, and questions if certain things in the past had addled everyone's brains and if, perhaps, the atmosphere hadn't been right for a girl to be growing up in. Lesley Storm's play had already been used for 'Personal Affair' a 1953 picture starring Glynis Johns, Gene Tierney and Leo Genn, with a moving performance from the wonderful Megs Jenkins in the role of *Vi Vining*. It's a window into a realistic British world of narrowness, innocence and town gossip - a time when there was no place to hide. You obeyed the rules, approaching your role in society with sincerity and trusting institutions. Nobody slipped through the gap completely then. The community was singular, all seeing, and all-powerful.

Was the girl seduced and murdered by her teacher? It emerges all this is nothing but fiction, but when the police drag the river – tragically the body of his neurotic wife is found. Felix Battle reported that 'glorious, neglected, red-haired, Glaswegian Renée walked away with the play'[39] as the girl's slovenly mother. Harrison sent Miss H an encouraging letter on April 1 informing her that the play had registered well in a viewer poll and contained 'some special praise for you.'[40] She was clearly making big strides in dramatic roles.

The acting aristocracy was out in force in London courting Tennessee Williams at the premiere of Peter Hall's production of *Camino Real* in April. Donald, meanwhile, appeared in an early wartime drama *O.S.S.* on ATV, then joined the musical *Damn Yankees* based on a story by Douglas Wallop – 'The Year the Yankees Lost the Pennant' –a retelling of the Faust legend set in 50s Washington DC: a time when the *New York Yankees* dominated Major League Baseball. *Joe Boyd* vows he would sell his soul for a *long ball hitter* if rivals, the *Washington Senators* could only beat the 'damn Yankees' and Donald - as *Van Buren* - manager of *the Senators* sees a turn up in his team's fortunes. Music and lyrics were by Richard Adler and Jerry Ross with choreography by Bob Fosse. It started its run at the Coliseum on March 28, 1957 and played 258 performances. Ex-Olympic skater Belita initially played *Lola* but Elizabeth Seal took over when Belita left the show. Billie Houston's son Anton remembers how Donald used to teach him baseball in exchange for cricket lessons. Donald loved his part, and was popular with his colleagues, but in an accident he slipped his disc, tearing a ligament in his back and was in great pain. He was taken to a specialist and the disc was put back in place. Renée wrote to Mickey how his nurses at Charing Cross Hospital 'are more beautiful than the chorus of his show and I keep telling them to stop vamping him.'[41] When the plaster came off, they put him in a steel belt. Determined not to disrupt the show, Donald was back in just over a week.

Renée did a TV drama for ABC – one of the original ITV franchise holders owned by Associated British Picture Corporation. The hour-long *Rappaport Always Pays* - part of the *Armchair Theatre* Series - was seen on the evening of Sunday May 12. Directed by Wilfrid Eades, the cast included Harry Green as *Harry Rappaport*, Alfie Bass as *Sam Schmaltz*, Billie Whitelaw as *Marlene Watts* and Renée as her mother *Ethel*. It was the first time she worked with Billie Whitelaw but her association with ex-laywer, ex-magician and international vaudevillian Harry Green went back to 1927.

Harry Green (J. Lewis Family Collection)

When the Houston Sisters topped the bill at the Palladium on March 21 1932, Harry did *The Cherry Tree* – a playlet about a Jew aspiring to the presidency of the USA. He had been in other plays with a Jewish message although he liked to claim he was a laughsmith, not a lecturer. English playwright EV Lucas - Harry's great admirer, was first to persuade him to act in *Welcome Stranger* at the Lyric in 1921 – a humorous take on anti-Jewish prejudice in small-town America. The papers liked *Rappaport,* enjoying Green's quickfire comments like 'It's a storm in a tea-cosy' and 'I'm talking to you like a Dutch oven,' adding how splendid it was to see players like Renée and Alfie revolving round him. Donald, busy at the Coliseum and *gazetted* about his bankruptcy adjudications in July and August, wrote to Ronnie venturing his opinion that male compères in musical shows on BBC and ITV were appearing tiresome. He suggested using Renée as a female compère as a welcome break from the stereotype. The response from Ronnie's colleague to this good idea was lukewarm.

Joseph Losey, blacklisted in his own country during the McCarthy trials, was director of 'Time Without Pity' - based on the Emlyn Williams play *Someone Waiting*. Recent campaigns for abolishing the death penalty make this a topical film given the harrowing wait of an innocent who is sentenced. The Homicide Act, restricting capital punishment in murder cases to five circumstances had just become law in the UK. Sir Michael Redgrave did well out of his deal with Harlequin Productions, getting all expenses paid, £12,000 on signing, and 20% of the distribution sale or other exploitation of the film excluding television.[42] He is *David Graham* - alcoholic author who, having neglected his son *Alec* for years, returns from Canada to find the young man condemned to hang for the murder of a young woman. The clock's ticking and *David* is desperate to prove his son's innocence and atone for being an errant father. Something connects his son's friends - the *Stanford family* to the case, particularly car manufacturer *Robert Stanford* - Leo McKern, who has had a fling with his manipulative secretary *Vickie Harker* - Lois Maxwell. Renée is *Mrs Harker* - a woman all too quick to manipulate her daughter's affair with her boss for financial gain. She spills the beans about a love affair between *Alec* and *Mrs Stanford* - Ann Todd.

Renée creates a grotesque *Mrs Harker*. Haunted, uttering drunken repetitions and looking around with squinted or rolling eyes, she urges him to have a glass with her. We feel for the painfully vulnerable *David*, knowing he could so easily come off the waggon. She slurs her words and one of the ridiculously ubiquitous alarm clocks in her room sounds off. She reveals the sound gives her pleasure: 'Just to hear it ring, and know that you don't have to go anywhere – isn't it wonderful!' She's a woman who's had a hard life now enjoying a better standard of living. Becoming aware *David* wants to extract information from her, she grouses 'I'll tell you nothing. No more to say! Not another word!' Soon she's sobbing hysterically. He leaves and she wakes from her emotional derangement. Eyes widen as she again pictures her material benefits and what opportunities might still be grasped.

She had another part to add to her inventory of sozzled ladies when, alongside Leo McKern, she was *Marthy* - one of the characters seasoned by the 'ole devil sea' in Eugene O'Neill's *Anna Christie* - a new *ITV Television Playhouse* production directed by Philip Saville. *Marthy* befriends *Anna* in the docks, prior to the damaged girl's meeting with her father. On the set, romance blossomed between Sean Connery and Diane Cilento, playing *Mat* and *Anna*. After this Renée appeared in 'The Key' - a Cinemascope blockbuster from Carl Foreman who had brought us classics like 'High Noon.' In this dramatization of de Hartog's novel 'Stella,' Trevor Howard and William Holden play two tugboat captains on convoy rescue duty during the war's darkest days. Sophia Loren is an enigmatic Swiss-Italian refugee previously engaged to a tug skipper who met a watery end. The 'key' unlocks a top floor room in an elegant building in Plymouth, where virile passion receives compassion and delicate sympathy: a key to life for some but not all.

Renée doesn't speak in the film, nor is she credited, but her chubby form smoulders for a time in the frame to the right of Holden under a sign that says '*Wines and Alcohol prohibited,*' when Holden and Howard enjoy a drinking session. Being placed under that sign is an insider joke on Renée Houston – a cruel one, to my eyes, but one she obviously couldn't care less about. Just before that scene Sophia Loren utters the words to Trevor Howard 'Don't drink too much.' Rules are lax in that *Forces Social Club* scene where Renée is a waitress, oblivious to liquor bottles crudely placed under the tables. 'The Key' is an excellent film, and who could blame people needing alcohol and sleeping pills in these dark days, especially those providing a 'Red Cross' service at sea, putting their lives at risk. Renée's friend Belita is the tired blonde who utters a line in the dance floor scene, and Renée also appears as a lady carrying too much shopping in the queue behind Sophia, when the latter – chic in her white raincoat, graces the fruit and veg market. There was much praise for director Carol Reed – reunited with his *Gloria Lind* after eighteen years, for Trevor Howard and for Sophia, and deservedly so. Writing about filming in Europe, Foreman laments Hollywood's star system that lessens the casting potential for featured parts. He contrasts this with Europe, where the Rep tradition has conditioned top actors to consider a small role if it might be a worthwhile opportunity.[43] Indeed, the British press appreciated the supporting players – like Irene Handl as the civil servant ticking off Sophia for being found when she's a missing person. There was the sour housekeeper played by Beatrix Lehman, and miniaturist performances by Oscar Homolka, Brian Forbes, James Hayter, Noel Purcell, Rupert Davies and Bernard Lee. The film opened the Brussels Film Festival. When Sophia mentioned to an English newspaper that cheesecake was her favourite dessert, fourteen of a lemon and strawberry variety piled up outside her dressing room.

In November 1957, Donald was at the Coliseum playing *Inspector Barnes* in a new style American musical *The Bells are Ringing* that ran 292 performances after a premiere at Manchester's Opera House. Lavish spectacle had moved aside in favour of intimate comic scenes – one being the premises of *'Susanswerphone'* – an enterprise letting New Yorkers pick up messages when they're out. These were, of course, the days before voicemail. Janet Blair played scatterbrained telephonist *Ella Peterson* whose messages are relayed in different voices to suit different devoted customers. Soon she and her sister become involved with certain callers, and romance is afoot between *Ella* and a playwright who's above her social station. Then the police are on to them, suspicious the answering service is a 'front' for vice. Choreography was by Jerome Robbins and Bob Fosse, with hit songs like 'The Party's Over' composed by Jules Styne. The public loved the themes of the New York party, romantic meetings in Central Park, as well as the colourfully daubed sets, the sneakers and 'Brando' studded leather jackets, supplied by Vince Man's Shop for younger members of the cast. It bucked the trend for Americana then gathering pace.

Renée came backstage to see her old friend Sir Lawrence Olivier in late October 1957, at the Palace Theatre where he was playing *Archie Rice* in Osborne's *The Entertainer*. Should she or shouldn't she take the latest part she'd been offered? This was *Big Momma* - the matriarch who pleads with her former athlete son *Brick* to give up his craving for drink. Her son is struggling with his homosexual feelings towards *Skipper* – a dead friend. *Cat on a Hot Tin Roof*, the banned Tennessee Williams tale of lies and hypocrisy, was the play in question. *Rose Tattoo* had got director Alan Simpson arrested in November 1957. Williams was, just then, very new and controversial. You could buy a paperback copy of *Cat on a Hot Tin Roof* but it had only managed to get staged because it was put on at a *club theatre* – the Watergate Theatre Club in Panton Street (now the Harold Pinter Theatre). This didn't come under the Lord Chamberlain's control. By paying 5s and filling in a club membership card you could become a patron and see the plays. The club had previously put on *View from the Bridge* and *Tea and Sympathy*.

A Daily Express article in November 1957 says Renée told Olivier her fear was public disapproval but the Knight Bachelor said to her 'Have you a shut mind? Take that part and you will open a new gateway in your career.'[44] We are told she took it reluctantly, but she was serious about acting the part, hence her visit to see her pal from the old days at Birmingham for advice. The Stage, on January 2, reported that Peter Hall's production was due to open within four weeks and spoke of the welcome Renée would receive back in the West End again, following another long absence, and how 'no artist of her generation has richer experience of the entertainment world.'[45]

Right: *Cat on a Hot Tin Roof*, New Watergate Theatre, February, 1958
(Renée Houston with Kim Stanley and Paul Massie)
(By kind permission of trustee of former Brevet Publishing Ltd / Westminster Reference Library.)

She joined an outstanding cast that included Broadway actress Kim Stanley as *Maggie the Cat*, Canadian Paul Massie as *Brick* and Leo McKern as *Big Daddy*. Renée's niece says she remembers coming to watch the actors and saw Tennessee Williams in the auditorium, although I can't find evidence of him being in London just then. I'm not sure how many rehearsals Renée participated in but around January 20 she was no longer part of the cast and had been replaced by Belfast-born Bee Duffell just in time for the opening night on January 30.

Alec Guinness had given her lunch on January 16, 1958[46] inviting Ronald Neame and Kay Walsh too. This date in his desk diary for the period is his first mention of Miss Houston. He records lunch cost £2.7.6 – not exactly the prize sum people are usually *bought for*. Guinness nevertheless had a good distribution deal that meant his new film 'The Horse's Mouth' would be widely seen in the US. If she was going to come in on this picture she had to leave the Peter Hall production as shooting for 'The Horses Mouth' was commencing on January 27 at Shepperton. Which should it be: stage role in a Tennessee Williams play, or supporting part in a Guinness film?

Taking the role in the film is a surprising diversion given Renée's new legitimate 'calling'. Had she remained in the play, Olivier's prediction might have become a reality. She left a team of great actors. Bette Davis herself thought Kim Stanley was one of the true brilliant new actresses to look out for then. A feisty role in a Williams play for a woman of increasing years was a coveted thing - not something you expect an actress to run away from. *Cat on a Hot Tin Roof* was staged in three locations at the same time – by Hall in London, on Broadway by Elia Kazan and in Paris by Peter Brook. The

November before, Liz Taylor signed to play *Maggie* in the cinema. To the Daily Mail, Renée explained she was 'a lot happier' doing the film with Alec Guinness, giving this as her reason for leaving the show. She tells how she overcame her concern about the play's content: 'It is quite true that when I first read the play I was shocked by the language and many other things.' She had left 'by mutual consent.'[47]

Reading the press reports, you see it solely as Renée's decision – a selfish decision surely? Imagine the reaction of Peter Hall and the rest of the cast to her coming out of the play a week or so before it opened! It's one of the worst things an actor can do, to cut adrift and take up a film offer at a critical time. Why leave it until then to tell readers of newspapers about her concerns about the material? Was it the Houston lack of vision to seize the day - another instance where she failed to sense long-term opportunities, grasping what was commercially sound only? Her nephew told me that he has never come across anyone quite like his aunt, more personally responsible for not having twice the success she had. The context of Williams' play is about lies and repression surrounding *Brick's* homosexual desires, with masochistic *Maggie*, binding herself hysterically to a man who does not want her. Might this have been a problem for Renée? She had experienced stress over the situation with Tony. Niall was by then a constant presence and an uncomfortable one for her. She thought if she could get Tony away from Niall he would be 'cured'. I wondered if it justified her leaving the Williams play? None of the above is a reason.

Niall and Tony visiting Renée and Don in Clapham, late 50s. (By kind permission of the Aherne Family)

There was something strange about her coming out of the show. Sadly the cast members are either gone now or are too unwell to advise me - all except one. It took a long time to discover what really happened and I was very lucky to speak to Lorna Henderson whom we remember as *Fatima*, the girl with dark makeup in 'Belles of St Trinian's.' Lorna played *Dixie* in *Cat on a Hot Tin Roof* – the grandchild of *Big Daddy* and *Big Momma* - a brat who listens in on conversations, firing a cap pistol at *the Cat* - taunting *Maggie* for being childless. Lorna has a very interesting career. Music played a part in her life ever since a grand piano made its way into her modest East End home. Her immediate family wasn't theatrical, but, as I found out (and frequently have, through the course of this research), that where there's talent, there's a theatrical connection. Lorna is related to Kay Henderson, who worked with the *Crazy Gang*, to the Henderson Twins, Dickie Henderson and his father Dick. Lorna would later grace the Palladium in several dazzling shows, singing with Harry Secombe and appearing with Max

Bygraves and Tony Newley. But, to go back to early 1958, Lorna's memory of Renée was negative.

I wondered if this was just an unlucky occasion when Renée failed to gel both with her director and fellow cast members. Directors usually got what they wanted from her with a fair amount of give and take. *Cat on a Hot Tin Roof* presents the exception to the rule – surely? Could the actress have lashed out verbally as she did because of Peter Hall's dictatorial attitude? Lorna disagreed. He wasn't nasty or rude. He knew everyone's name and was on first name terms, unlike some directors who use your stage name. He was simply a perfectionist and firm, and Lorna liked him. Peter Hall had made a rule 'No alcohol at rehearsals' and was very serious about it. Renée made some effort not to be seen but couldn't resist having the odd swig in the wings. A small flask sometimes in her bag or even tucked in her knickers did the trick and she almost always got away with it. Lorna observed the little flask at least twice. The rupture happened early on, at a read-through. Miss Houston arrived worse for wear and Hall kept on prompting her, then lost all patience. A terrible argument left an acid aftertaste and stony faces all round. She was in the side part of the stage and Hall was in the stalls and she screamed at him bitterly: 'When I want an (effing) drink I'll have an (effing) drink'. Hall told her off in a forceful voice and everyone thought that was it, especially when Renée walked off the stage.

The next thing that happened was she reappeared and hit him over the head with a beer can: not a real one. It was a humble stage prop – one of the *Miller High Lifes* left by *Brick*. There was a big thing with Equity for the rest of that day. The next day a jovial and sober Renée turned up at the theatre as if nothing had happened. Hall told her to leave. She wouldn't go so he threatened to call the police. She had no choice but to come out.

Up until the bust up Lorna says that Renée put everyone on edge being disregarding of people. She was absolutely without shame, using the bluest language whenever she let rip, making no curtailment for the fact that child actors were present. She was drunk to the level that you feared violence according to Lorna who feels very uneasy and worried about opening up an old wound, especially if anyone from Renée's family might get upset hearing this. Even that old superstition about never saying the word '*MacBeth*' on stage was something Renée turned into a joke. Storming into the dressing room, she mocked everyone present in a loud voice 'Don't say Macbeth! - Oh, I've said Macbeth on stage!! I've said Macbeth on stage! Aren't I bad!' I confessed that I might have laughed had I been present. Unfortunately, no one else backstage at the Watergate Theatre Club was laughing. I sense that Renée was breaking records venting her spleen.

Another thing Lorna mentioned was that Charles Henry – the ATV producer behind *Sunday Night At The London Palladium* had a hand in getting her into *Cat On A Hot Tin Roof* in the first place. An action like this, going over the heads of both casting and director, was sniped about. It was contentious enough for Lorna, still a young actress, to pick up on. The idea that Renée was there because of some decision by the powers that be rankled. Apparently, the majority of the cast rejoiced when Hall took Renée off the play. I tried to come to her defence. Renée can't have been the only actor caught drunk in charge? Others were worse than her - surely? 'No! No one!' said Lorna, going on to tell me she made a point of saying to her agent – 'If you ever give me an audition for a play Renée Houston is in, I won't do it.' It was that bad. Bee Duffell, by contrast, was a lovely, supportive colleague – 'a very cuddly lady unlike Renée.' When Bee took over, the atmosphere improved and the actors settled down to fulfilling what they were there for.

It wasn't Renée's finest hour. Trying to put this in context a few conclusions can be drawn. In terms of professional challenges she had accepted the part and didn't run away from it. She would have seen it through had she been able to, and she probably would have professed loyalty to Sir Peter Hall given a chance. She might even have made something great of *Big Momma*. She got chucked out. Sir Peter wasn't prepared to accept her weakness as others had. He was brave in this respect. He wasn't prepared to bow to the powers that be. Renée wouldn't compromise on who she was either. There's an irony reading the early comments in The Stage about what a 'keen observer of humanity'[48] Miss Houston was. Her humanity was out of place - the wrong person at the wrong time. I know the beer can was out of order but the *'MacBeth'* episode was not uncharacteristic of her sense of humour. It ranks among the 'pranks' she was apt to play on people. It's difficult to say if it was worse than those her colleagues on *Sauce Tartare* suffered. At the Watergate Theatre Club she was a fish out of water, sending up the serious tone of the rehearsals. Usually people turned a blind eye towards her behaviour. She was being Renée Houston. She obviously felt unwelcome at the Watergate and probably worsened in her behaviour because of this. She horrified Lorna - about fourteen then, turning the serious business of acting on its head without any respect for it. It's a shame people didn't 'get' her, or should I say, accept her 'bawdy' side because if they had, rehearsals might not have been the 'mortal' experience they were. I expect her whole attitude would be considered unprofessional now, but the flipside is we don't see diva actresses taking parts like this and making these subservient to their own mesmerizing personalities. Perhaps some of the disorderly pride that Tennessee himself admired is lost in the equation.

The evidence about her getting parts because she knew all the big boys at the top puts me in mind of the star who knows everyone in the business and whose 'maturity,' if you call it that, is an impunity from judgment whatever the wrongdoing. Lorna's account shows the unfair process of star placement viewed through the eyes of young actors. It's still common practice in 21st century theatrical productions although few admit it. For some reason it puts me in mind of a joke – one of Tony Aherne's from his 2001 diary:

>Van Gogh's girlfriend on receiving his ear:
>"You old schmoozy! You know how to get round me."

The most stunning thing is how Renée always had the press on her side. There was no scandal sheet circulating about her. She must have had the ear of big boys in Fleet Street too, because nothing ever leaked out about her or threatened her 'good name'. It shows how deferential newspapers were in Britain to veterans in show business and something about the power of reputation. This, of course, was a system that would be abused by some in extreme cases. The press story of Renée coming out of *Cat on a Hot Tin Roof* shows her in nothing more than a respectful light.

The critics dealt with Hall's production fairly negatively although it lasted 132 performances, closing on May 25. Derek Monsey in the Sunday Express said the play failed to be moving and Harold Hobson in the Sunday Times felt it lacked the pace of the Brook production in Paris.[49] Hall's version was, however, the only one that used the ending Williams wrote, unlike the Broadway production which Kazan changed, so the London production was all the more historic for this. In Oswald Stoll's day, you wouldn't see his protégés involved in a play that touched on the subject of homosexuality but times had changed. Renée had no moral issue about being in a play that pushed boundaries and could easily put aside personal worries about the content. She was flexible in terms of the playwright's artistic idea, just a bit too flexible or inflexible as regards obeying rules.

The real issue was her alcoholism, and Lorna considered that before Renée started drinking she was probably a really nice person. She wondered what could have happened to put her on that path. Her drinking caused her to be lonely and isolated. She had no friends. Some drinkers get to the point when craving makes them temperamental, argumentative and difficult, and that makes them lose friends. You also meet some people whose lack of friends is difficult to justify. They are the loveliest, funniest and most generous people on one hand but living with them isn't easy. While you appreciate them, you're pleased to see the back of them. If a true illness has developed, too many ugly moments stem from the craving, and even people tolerant of booze draw the line. Happiness can be in short supply, not just for the alcoholic. When everyone's happiness is crushed by one person's habits, it's a downer. The other conclusions that can be drawn are that Renée showed resilience in the face of being rejected. She was able to brush off the 'shame' of being taken off the play, and didn't bother to challenge the decision. I expect she felt very upset about it in private. She wasn't going to stop drinking though. She went into the Alec Guinness film mainly because it was convenient and she needed a job.

'The Horse's Mouth' directed by Ronald Neame and produced by John Bryan, was selected for the 1959 Royal Film Performance in aid of the Cinematograph Trade Benevolent Fund and Renée was among those chosen to be presented to the Queen Mother and Princess Margaret in the foyer of the Empire, Leicester Square on February 2. A long time had passed since the occasion when the former Duchess of York visited the set of 'Their Night Out' at Elstree. They had met many times since, and Renée felt a sense of admiration for this lady who had come through the war and been a strong support to her husband. Several stars were presented including Alec Guinness, Kay Walsh, Renée, and Maurice Chevalier. Lauren Bacall, Juliette Greco, Terry Thomas, Richard Todd, Frankie Vaughan, Simone Signoret, Janette Scott, Peter Sellers, and Max Bygraves were also present. Before the film, Chevalier gave everyone a song. The starry presentation featured on the radio on February 8 in the film magazine *Movie-Go-Round*.

Guinness developed the story from the Joyce Carey novel, concentrating on the character of *Gulley Jimson* at the expense of the book's social and political themes. Carey, the daughter of actress Dame Lillian Braithwaite trained as an artist before writing and acting, and I've read that the *Gulley Jimson* character was based on Augustus John. The scene where *Jimson* enjoys a drink in a little dockside pub full of beer slops and sawdust with an edgy barmaid is in the John tradition. Unlike John, *Jimson* travels into Surrealist territory with his later output. His early masterpieces like '*Sarah in the Bath*' are in the tradition of Renoir - and might be Renoirs. For the scene in 'The Horse's Mouth' at the home of art connoisseur *Hickson* - played by Ernest Thesiger, this Shepperton interior was, at the time, one of the most expensive sets constructed in a European Studio. Antique furniture costing thousands of pounds and works by Corbet, Sickert, Bonnard, Renoir, Degas, Dufy and Pissarro decorated the walls. All this cost a bomb load and required tight security.[50] Artist John Bratby, then aged thirty and a member of the *Kitchen Sink School*, did *Gulley*'s monumental paintings. Despite being seen in Technicolor, none of the paintings stand out for me – just '*Sarah in the Bath*'.

Artiste's model and Artist: *Sarah and Gulley* (Artwork by author)

Sarah's character is sidelined into a vignette and I think this role would be bigger if the film were re-made today because the history she shared with *Jimson* is more interesting than lengthier aspects such as *Jimson*'s egotistical takeover of the premises of *Sir William* and *Lady Beeder* when he discovers a virgin wall in need of painting. *Sarah* is more kindly treated than *Coker* - the vicious-tongued barmaid and chief sufferer at the hands of *Jimson* - a bigger, less interesting role that received excellent handling by Kay Walsh. Derek Hill in The Tribune describes Renée's *Sarah* as perfect, and he goes on to say 'she could have been equally good as *Coker* if she hadn't been pushed into some embarrassing knockabout.'[51] He was referring to the tussle between painter and ex-mistress - when *Sarah* is comically concussed. Tragically, Mike Morgan, the actor who played *Nosey*, contracted meningitis before filming ended and died on June 5, 1958. He was the young novice bullied by *Jimson* despite his loyalty – a further unexpanded theme.

To me, the film doesn't reach its potential and several scenes are too lengthy without good reason. I like Renée's subtle comedy but Guinness's *Jimson* is too much of a caricature. It's one of his less resonant performances and fails to elicit the sympathy the role needs. The Times is on my wavelength when it says 'only Renée Houston is allowed to offer an entirely convincing performance.'[52] Nina Hibbins in The Daily Worker talks about how Renée's 'respectable plump housewife with a smooth quiet genius for getting her own way steals every scene in which she appears.'[53] Scheming and lower middle class she might be, but she possesses that higher quality that makes her believable as a one-time artists' muse. It's a nice study and landing the role salvaged her from the fiasco of her time on the set of *Cat On A Hot Tin Roof*. The film was a success. Released through United Artists, it quickly recouped the £250,000 cost of its expenditure, earned $1 million at the box office and was the most international film Renée was ever part of.

It was a little like art imitating life for Renée to go into a role as an ex-mistress of a heavy drinker. She embodied the role of *Sarah* but equally could have tried to embody *Big Momma* – a character who wants her son to give up alcohol, who has faced rejection, and finds it hard to come to terms with realities, trying all the same to hold a family together. This would have been a more challenging role requiring that her own addiction to alcohol be a resource to contemplate as she grasped the play's message of decay. Slapstick came easier to her.

Renée might, by then, have admitted to those closest to her that she had a dependency on booze. To everyone else she kept it under wraps and, as some people might say in harsher-toned voices, she lived a lie. There she is, one time, generally being disregarding and violently screaming at someone who had the guts to confront her. Another time, she is dignified, sharing a polite joke with HRH. Such contrasts in character made her enemies recoil.

Long before, she had been a milk drinker, but it couldn't stay that way. The first person in the Renée Houston story to draw attention to her heavy drinking was her enemy Eleanor Elliot at the end of 1944. A few decades on, it was too late to confront a dependency that wartime pressures had solidified. She and Donald soldiered on. When it came to the day-to-day life of that lovely couple, you didn't see what the problem was, thinking that booze was just a necessary part of life – commonplace and non-destructive.

Chapter 22   Time and Tide

The Russians were ahead of the game with Sputnik - all the more necessity for California to up its game in aerospace. On January 31, 1958 Explorer 1 was launched into the sky by the US Army's Ballistic Missile Agency and signals sent into space could soon be bounced off this giant metal balloon floating in orbit, allowing levels of radiation to be measured. Alan Aherne was there to assist. His job in the Santa Susana Mountains was to check readings and calculations in order to maximize engine-running times for his country's first satellite. Wartime England had disrupted his education but a promising career now awaited him.

His letter arrived on the mat in that little house down Clapham way that hid a pair of glamorous film stars. There were other letters. Shirley sent a photo of her semi-detached house in Whitley Wood Road, Reading, with news that Auntie May was now in an old folks home in Wokingham. Marion died later that year at the age of eighty-one. The bells were ringing for Shirley at Reading's telephone exchange where she now worked as a *Hello girl*. At least the money was regular, although she missed the theatre. Almost never was the letter from Terry, and it was Alan who would inform her that Terry had three sons with George Hill, and following divorce and re-marriage, four daughters with John Long Jr. Renée proudly talked about being a grandmother. It sounded good, even with her family so dispersed.

Years before she would work a week on the road and tell people with pride how she caught late trains on Saturday nights from far away northern towns so she could spend a full Sunday with her kids in London. She had always been proud of the way she managed things. All along, there was never a question of coming back to an empty house. One full of the laughter of children was more to her liking. There, she would be a part-time doting mum. Everyone knew she was bringing home the bacon and the kids would nicely dovetail into those variety schedules.

Now that it was just Mr and Mrs Wintermute they tried to keep the house warm during the cold spell that lasted all the way through March of 1958. Then Trevor Balharrie came and went. His marriage sadly hadn't lasted.[1] He stayed for the winter then disappeared with all the cash in the electric meter. 'And good riddance too,' his mother carped. Not an easy business mothering these boys. She had another one to consider at the end of March, when BBC contracts arrived to engage her as *Jimmy Clitheroe's* mum requiring eight visits back and forth from Clapham to the frozen north.[2] This was the first run of *The Clitheroe Kid* after a successful radio pilot.

Renée joined a team headed by James Casey, who produced the show and wrote it along with Frank Roscoe. The son of Jimmy James, Casey was a talent spotter who discovered Les Dawson in a Manchester club and tried to help Ken Dodd whilst the BBC were slow to showcase these comics. *Jimmy Clitheroe*, the star of the show, was now well into his thirties playing the eleven-year-old, wearing his schoolboy's blazer and cap for each recording.

Peter Sinclair played *Jimmy*'s Scottish grandpa.[3] Monday evenings in 1958 brightened up when you tuned in at 8pm. The series lasted until 1972. Renée was only in series one, probably because she could not commit to all the travelling. Pat Burke – stern but less gruff - took over as *Jimmy*'s mum. In the middle of the run Renée swapped her northern town for 14th Century Nottingham for an episode of *The Adventures of Robin Hood,* seen on TV in the USA on May 25, 1958.

There was a budget of £10,000 per episode thanks to a deal negotiated between Lew Grade's ITC and American investors Sapphire Films, who worked out of Nettlefold Studios. Where Safeways used to be, the residents of Walton on Thames would likely find themselves standing next to film stars in the queue at the cash desk. The trees up by New Zealand Avenue were transformed into a corner of Sherwood Forest. No expense was spared and each half-hour episode was shot on 35mm film. *Robin* revived Richard Greene's career. Alan Wheatley was the *Sheriff* and Paul Eddington - *Will Scarlett*. In Renée's episode, a trap to catch *Little John* is foiled by the merry men. She played his *Little Mother*.

Trevor turned up for another merry visit. At least this was one son who needed her. 'Who's Sorry Now?' wailed Connie Francis on the radio and Renée would sing along with feigned emotion as she did the day's housework. She felt the pain of motherhood but didn't look back with regrets. She didn't go in for examining herself – identifying the lifestyle she had led then distinguishing cause and effect.

Offers of film work continued. The plot of 'Them Nice Americans' is a comic echo of the real life drama when Terry married a Texan sergeant, although this has Renée playing *Mrs Adams* - sympathetic to her daughter's choice to marry *Johnny*, an American GI. Her policeman husband - Basil Dignam - is totally opposed to the union. Vera Day is her daughter and Bonar Colleano - *Sergeant Joe* – the brash yank who, with *Johnny*, attempts to publicize the desirability of American sons-in-law in the village. Crazy scrapes follow, involving USA AF tank carriers and English policemen, until the yanks earn respect through their bravery. Too bad this hilarious film is currently unobtainable. I noticed *'Butcher's Film Distributors Ltd'* on the publicity and that's never a good sign. Bonar had known Renée since his family came over from the States in 1936 and joined *Black and Blue*. On August 18, shortly before the release of 'Them Nice Americans', tragedy struck and Bonar was killed in a car crash at Birkenhead driving back from Liverpool's New Shakespeare Theatre. Renée and Don's bankruptcy and debt-related issues weren't on a par with the estimated £8,000 in unpaid income tax at Bonar's death - a major upset for his wife Susan Shaw and his family. That December big names from British entertainment like James Mason, Sid James, Alfie Bass and Alma Cogan played a football match at Hayes Stadium to help raise funds for Bonar's three year-old son.

There was a part for Donald in 'The Sheriff of Fractured Jaw' in one of the funnier scenes, when Kenneth More boards a stagecoach west from St Louis, with Donald and Sid James for company. Sid is so drunk he sleeps through an Indian attack until it's averted by Kenneth More's English diplomacy. Donald, looking visibly older, tended to be cast as frustrated but well-meaning characters. He had no scenes with Robert Morley, or Jayne Mansfield, whose number in the film is very catchy. Donald wrote to his mother to tell her he and Renée would move to the new flat at *'Brighthampton'* in Oatlands Avenue, Walton-on-Thames on June 12, a lovely bright flat they had been decorating since April. It now boasted fitted carpets and a new blossom pink bathroom. Even before they moved in, he told his mother they had named the spare bedroom 'Mickey's room' in anticipation of her next visit. Renée recorded a *Does the Team Think*, for fellow Scot Charles Maxwell, at the BBC's Piccadilly studios - aired on the afternoon of June 18.

Meanwhile in Chicago, Pat Aherne was in town, invited by one of Brian's nice American doctors to attend a round of cocktail parties. He took his son along, and they met Ronald Reagan – still on the board of the Screen Actors Guild - the labour guild for Hollywood actors.[4] Reagan and Alan went into the garden to point out Explorer 1 in the night sky. At that time, the GI Bill meant Alan had the potential to get a home but trying for a Calvet loan he found nothing but red tape. Reagan, who couldn't be keener to help Brian's nephew, sent a letter on his behalf to help. It made a difference and Alan was very grateful to the future president. He regretted not keeping in touch.

On September 1, Renée picked up her dramatic stage gauntlet from the ignominious place she'd flung it, and joined the cast of *The Party* - the play that saw Charles Laughton as actor and director return to the West End after a twenty-two-year absence. The Americanisms he had acquired in that interval were thought 'out of place' by the English critics. *The Party* had opened in May that year and Elsa Lanchester had already taken credit for shaping the role Renée stepped into. Elsa had a film to do in the States. Renée was only in the play for the last three months and her role was hardly the prestigious dramatic opportunity *Big Momma* had presented – one she might have made her own if things had worked out differently. *The Party* hadn't received the best reviews either. Still, Miss Houston was keeping her foot in the dramatic door. She was close by Donald – who was in the West End too, and she was happy to help her pal Charlie Laughton.

He conveyed a man whose mental health and drinking had caused him to spend the last few months in an asylum. The latest job for former well-to-do Kilburn solicitor *Richard Brough* was earning pin money as a petty bookkeeper in a small dress shop. Joyce Redman played his loyal wife. Ann Lynn played *Henrietta* - their spoilt seventeen year-old daughter who plans a party, that is, until her father unexpectedly turns up. Ashamed of him, she telephones all the guests so they don't come. John Welsh played the *Brough*s' lodger – a man fearing loneliness. Albert Finney, dressed in a leather jacket, played *Soya Marshall*, *Henrietta*'s boyfriend, who, like her father, quails before her selfish and uncompromising demands. The young actor from Salford had yet to become 'angry' but had won the Emile Littler Prize, been at the Birmingham Rep and prior to *The Party* was in *Macbeth*. Renée's part, as always, punctuated the sense of despair. She was *Elsie Sharp* – the little store's owner - lonely and on the shelf - who adores *Richard*'s jokes and hopes he'll return to his post. When Elsa played the role, critic Ken Tynan described the role as 'a rowdy coquette who talks like the late Suzette Tarri and owns what everyone weirdly calls the nylon shop.'[1]

The playwright Jane Arden was hanging out with artists in Greenwich Village when Laughton nagged her to complete *The Party*. The play would be praised for communicating a sense of loneliness present in the suburbs[2] but criticized for a lack of credible manipulation of character. The ending, in which the self-righteous daughter realizes that failure needs pity not scorn, was panned. Better she had received a clip round the ear on account of her lack of sympathy, thought many, although Tynan identified incestuous feelings on the part of *Richard*, influencing his daughter's behaviour. Miss Houston was in lighter company when *London Lights* aired on the Light Programme on November 30, with Tommy Trinder introducing guests Roy Castle and Leslie Randall with music from George Melly.

Don looked in need of time off to relax, but when *The Bells Are Ringing* closed, he was immediately in demand at the Adelphi Theatre for *Auntie Mame*. It began its run on September 10 and lasted 301 performances. Florence Desmond later got sacked when she flew to the Bahamas to recover from a throat infection, without telling the manager. One time Don himself forgot a Matinée, going instead to the cinema. Prior to the evening performance he ran into Bea Lillie, who played the lead. Bea enquired if he'd had a nice day, and agreed that a visit to the pictures had a wise decision – what with such a low turn out at the matinée. It was only then the penny dropped and Donald almost died on the spot.

At the Coronation Hall in Denmark Road, Kingston, Renée earned 50 guineas as a contestant on *You're Turn Now* - seen on the box on February 23, 1959. *A Nest of Robins* - a new TV play with John Slater and Eleanor Summerfield in the cast had needed three weeks of rehearsals at St Andrews Church Hall W14, plus extra sessions at Lime Grove. Set ten years earlier, it was about the shame felt by the younger members of a family when a mother gets 'found out' for having been in musical comedy. Critics smashed the story by Robert Monro for these unbelievable attitudes, but perhaps the play detected the values of a society on the crest of the 60s. The hip and young could only look back and shudder when a Sonnie Hale dance number was recreated in authentic style, or look on appalled when the oldsters acted out their creaky reminiscences.

She was memorable in 'And the Same To You,' taxi-ing to Walton Studios to join a host of stars that included Miles Malleson, Arthur Mullard, Shirley Ann Field, Terry Scott and Dick Bentley. Bill Hartnell is unrestrained as *Wally* the shifty and bribing boxing promoter who ends up in an uneasy alliance with *Reverend Sydney Mullet* - Leo Franklyn, when they share a church hall as premises. From his entrance genial giant Tommy Cooper is hilarious as *Horace*, *Wally*'s assistant. The *Reverend* is dubious when his nephew (played by Brian Rix) is persuaded by *Wally* to fight after observing that the Oxford boy can box. Vera Day is unforgettable as secretary *Cynthia Tripp* - the true commonsense behind the management of *Wally*'s boxing club - when she's not asked to wear 'nationalized glasses' as a disguise of course. The scene is set for match-fixing beneath a church hall roof attacked by deathwatch beetles, with honest hero *Dickie Dreadnought* prepared to put up with just so much. John Paddy Carstairs adapted the story from a recent ITV Play - *The Chigwell Chicken* by AP Dearsley. The director was George Pollock.

The most farcical scene of all happens when upright *Archdeacon Pomphret* and his unpredictable wife *Mildred* appear and *Wally* is pretending to be the reverend. *Mildred* - played by Renée, has a funny exchange with Tommy Cooper's character then it emerges she's an enthusiast for the noble art, especially having a bet on the winner. She confides to *Cyn* that, while she might not know about boxing, horses are her hobby. Her knowledge is reasonable on the flats and over the sticks, and she's managed to buy every item of her husband's wardrobe on the proceeds. It's a wonderfully unexpected study, and *Mildred*'s revelations affect in the film's denouement. Vera Day, who worked with Renée on four separate occasions, told me she was a pleasure to work with, ready for a laugh always, and full of fun. Vera was invited to Renée's flat, and remembers looking at her cuttings book, absolutely amazed at all the things Miss Houston had done in her career.

Renée made an appearance as a guest on ATV's *Tell the Truth,* recorded at Hackney Empire and hosted by David Jacobs. The episode was seen around June 1959. Edward Thomas, who grew up in Hackney in the 50s, told me he used to go to the ATV shows at the Empire, taking up to four school friends at a time with him. When Jacobs introduced Renée Houston to the audience, Edward vividly recalls a distinctive figure sweeping on, dripping in white fur, and wearing dark glasses - which she took off just before the transmission. She had an extraordinary rapport with the studio audience, all of whom were sitting in the former dress circle. Renée looked up and said: 'Do I look my age, 85?'

On Saturday November 7, as the London fogs frightened people to death, Renée and Donald were stranded at the Phoenix Theatre on Charing Cross Road. That was the downside of living far from the West End. They slept in the dressing rooms, had a picnic supper, and the foreman made them tea. Even leaving the theatre at 8.30 am the next morning, a terrifying thick fog greeted them. A film contract for America suddenly came up. Her release from *Cat* had been dramatic but freed her to make 'The Horse's Mouth.' This time she and Donald were forced to turn the film down, or get into all kinds of problems with a contract that bound them to their stage play. The offer was for Renée to play a leading part in a new Columbia Pictures film 'The

Devil at 4 O'Clock' with Spencer Tracy and Frank Sinatra. She wouldn't get another blockbuster offer like this again. It was great she was recognized as the filmmaker's choice. Not many British actresses of Renée's generation got offers like this – not in 1959. Both *Sweethearts* were disappointed. 'It never rains but it pours,' wrote Don to his mother, and Renée explained to Mickey how dreadful it was to turn down a chance to play against Spencer Tracy 'for a fabulous salary. My friend Peter Glenville is directing the film and it's *me* he wants - it would have been for twelve weeks, and we could have visited you.' Glenville was the son of her old friends Dorothy Ward and Shaun Glenville. Renée described how she shed buckets of tears – and this left her with pleurisy.[7] Donald's mum did get to stay in 'Mickey's room' in September 1959. As always, it was sad when she departed.

It's a shame Lesley Storm's *Roar Like A Dove* couldn't have released them in order that they might go to America, especially since it was not expected to run beyond March 1960 anyway. They could have joined the forthcoming tour a bit later. The papers got hold of the story of Miss Houston's offer late that November, and the Daily Mail ran the dramatic story *'Renee Says 'no' again to Hollywood.'*

In August 1959 Donald had been cast as *Tom Chadwick, Lord Dungavel's* American father-in-law. The laird and his wife have failed to beget a male heir, producing six females instead and an inheritance dangles. *Bernard Taggart-Stuart* is *Dungavel's* second cousin from London who will inherit the estate if no heir comes. He's likely to demolish everything and put up something Swedish instead. *Dungavel's* American wife *Emma* is more interested in appearing on the social pages of Tatler instead of the The Times' birth notices. Rebelling against her incarceration in the castle, *Emma* invites Mom and Pop over from Palm Springs. *Muriel Chadwick* is a tough old American bird flapping outraged wings in the sex war between *Emma* and the laird. *Tom Chadwick* crucially arranges for *Lord and Lady Dungavel* to be alone, and suggests his son-in-law try some cave-man tactics. Ultimately we hear bagpipes at the end playing *'Bonnie Laddie - Highland Laddie'* - a traditional signal of the birth of an heir. This 'feel good' play set in *Dungavel Castle* in the Western Highlands in *1956* was performed in three acts with two intervals - covering a time span of over a year.

When Margalo Stevens - the previous *Muriel* left, Renée was asked to take over. 'Nobody fools with me,' said Renée of her new role.[8] 'This momma was born with hawk's eyes.' Her fine American accent was taken into account. Evelyn Varden and Jean Dixon had already played the part. The play had seen many cast changes since opening at the Phoenix in 1957. John McCallum, Anthony Ireland, Ann Kimbell and others had given belting performances. When Renée and Don joined, their colleagues were Patrick Barr, David Hutcheson, Faith Brook, Peter Barkworth, Ewan Roberts, June Shaw, Judy Horn, Phillipa Gill and Robin Hawdon.

As had been the case with *The Party*, the West End production was nearing its end, but this time a long provincial tour beckoned. At least Renée and Don could be together, and they had glamorous roles for a change. Renée, dressed in Worth in the publicity photograph taken by Anthony Buckley, used this as her Spotlight photo from 1960 onwards. She had abandoned her red head coiffure in favour of a radiant silver blonde. Renée and Don were ideal as the long married couple, bickering about the best way to solve the younger family members' problem. You can imagine Renée provoking Donald in the eternal quarrel:

Muriel Chadwick: Don't think it's going to be as easy as that to make it up with me! I've a lot to say before we're on speaking terms again.

Lesley Storm had the knack with plays. Success hardly changed her, even if the £20,000 received when *The Day's Mischief* was filmed, and the £40,000 from a US company for *Black Chiffon* (which Flora Robson made a success of), paid for a small Kensington home. When she wrote *Roar*, she suspected it would be a 'flop'. Then it took £450,000 at the London box office and a Broadway version earned her £90,000. Doris Day was touted as the star of a future film version. By February 29, 1960 - a few days before the end of the run at the Phoenix, the play had its 1000th performance. Lesley Storm was the first female dramatist to have achieved this record with a comedy.

Success may have been due to the charming and slightly risqué plot, as well as the splendid cast and great design. Lesley Storm took part in a radio programme about Miss Houston's life over a decade later. The first pantomime she recalled ever seeing was *Mother Goose* in Glasgow, and she told how, on a station platform at Aberdeen, she had seen a large black trunk bearing the words '*Renée and Billie Houston*' in large white letters. In her gentle Scots accent she admitted she had only been in the theatre once but wanted to be an actress: 'I thought - what a glamorous life! That did fade away. It was that trunk that started it off. I never thought that I would become a playwright and that Renée Houston would be acting in one of my plays.'[9] In the same interview, director Murray MacDonald admits it was difficult getting Renée to stick to the script as she was wont to improvise. He concedes that she was definitely fun to be with, lifting everyone's spirits with stories about her experiences.

Renée became closely associated with *Roar* – not surprising, since she was in seven separate productions of the play over two decades. She would refer to the play as '*You know what*' in her memoir. She lived in fear of what Lesley Storm might think, given that she was just being Renée Houston to her audience. 'I was really doing my own version of it,'[10] she wrote. Still, the playwright only had nice things to say when she came to see it at Guildford: 'She brought a great deal of warmth to the part, and honesty and fun.'

Robin Hawdon has become one of Britain's most prolific playwrights, and has been director of the Theatre Royal Bath, having played Hamlet, Henry V and Henry Higgins in his time. Robin told me that in his last term at RADA,

Peter Barkworth asked him to take the tiny part as the servant *Shaw* as well as becoming his understudy[11] and so Robin went straight into a West End show, remaining there six months before leaving for York to get 'proper experience in Rep.' Robin has never forgotten his first experience of London's West End: a time when the spoken word still ruled supreme, and musicals and the tourist trade had yet to dominate. He says:

> 'They were a lovely bunch of people, and Renée Houston the life and soul of the company – warm, funny, extrovert, bawdy – she always had us laughing (frequently whilst on stage), and her broad Scottish accent could always be heard backstage recounting some showbiz story or other. She was quite buxom and always alluded to her ample bosoms as 'the terrible twins' and kept admonishing them to 'stop fighting you two, and behave yourselves!''

Shortly before joining *Roar* Renée was at Shepperton to shoot scenes for her twenty-seventh film, 'The Flesh and the Fiends.' The screenplay, written by John Gilling and Leon Griffiths, was based on the Burke and Hare story of grave robbers, and set in the Edinburgh of 1828. It was one of the last films made by Triad – the enterprise owned by British producers Robert S. Baker and Monty Berman and was released in the USA as 'Mania'. It might have been disappointing at the box office but I think it's a corker of a movie.

You are still thinking about matters to do with heart and soul hours after watching it. Something disquieting comes across - how power protects some, leaving the mass of people vulnerable. There's retribution and revenge in the scenes of the capture at the warehouse and the blinding. Peter Cushing's character *Robert Knox* accepts 'subjects' from *Burke* and *Hare* without question. *Knox* takes them for his anatomy lectures and is in denial of any wrongdoing. He's assured in his belief he's right and remains impassionate when outside a mob (who believe he's complicit in the crimes) smash the windows. He's the biggest fiend of them all for all his cool intellect and determined professionalism. Finally, he admits he knew how the victims died and how vanity and ambition controlled him. There's an incredible performance by Donald Pleasance as *Hare* - always one step above everyone, and he and George Rose – as *Burke* are a gruesome pair of killers.

A raven-haired Houston is unsettling in the picture. Her 'homeliness' appears to darkest effect as seedy, jealous and awful *Helen Burke* - a historical inaccuracy. The real Mrs Burke was an innocent left behind in Ulster and it was Helen McDougal who was William Burke's mistress and complicit partner. Renée's *Helen* is so oblivious to the value of human life it's comic! *Burke* murders a young street worker and is confronted by his wife, whose concern above everything else is whether or not he's touched her. *Burke*'s face fills with honest indignation and *Hare* intervenes to protect his friend's reputation. 'William's just killed her, that's all,' he says. 'I'm glad', says *Helen*, 'that sort of thing would give the house a bad name.' When John

Braine reviewed the film for the Express, this was his favourite moment. This malevolent 'music hall' was now the fancy of 1960s screenwriters.

Helen faces an angry *Maggie O' Hara* - played by June Powell, who grapples with her but she seems to escape her due comeuppance. This was true to history as the real life Helen McDougal, once acquitted, narrowly escaped a mob out for her guts several times: once wearing men's clothes as a disguise. Some reports say she fled to Australia where she died whilst others say she was beaten to death near Doune. In this early role Billie Whitelaw is already possessed of the qualities she had that made her so unique in performance, with her self-destructive study of *Mary Patterson* - whose weakness leads to death. The 'let me take you home' scene when one of *Knox*'s apprentices tries to make *Mary* leave the brothel is powerful and moving. The scene where *Jamie* - a young Melvyn Hayes - light and lissome in his movement, gets murdered in a pigsty, is actually the most fearful and dark of all the scenes as we experience the moment a living victim is surrounded and hunted down by killers. His acting is brilliant with the black and white shadows intensifying the trauma. It was so nice to speak to Melvyn, and to rest assured that he survived such gruesomeness.

Melvyn had been in another film with Peter Cushing called 'The Curse of Frankenstein.'[12] He remembered 'Flesh and the Fiends' as a 'very dark picture.' Director John Gilling callously made him wait until the very end of the day to shoot the scene when *Jamie* is murdered, by which time the pigsty was at its dirtiest. There was no glamour on the film set at all. Melvyn added he'd been an actor since 1950 and was still waiting for the glamour! As an example of the practicality that actors adopt in earning their keep this is a good one. In one scene *Jamie* had to pass an old man in the park and slightly brush the back of his head with his hand. 'Give us a clout,' said the extra. 'It'll be worth an extra fiver.' During the brothel sequence another actor is seen with his hand on a woman's breast. He asked the director for extra money given this was 'special business.' Melvyn remembered seeing Renée first in variety and thought she filled her role with effortless skill and invisible power, proving to everyone who pigeon-holed her as a mere variety star that she was much the legitimate actress. She always came across as a true professional, he added. Robert S. Baker was impressed, because a few years later he sought her out to be in *The Saint* twice.

Miss Houston's offers of work were streaming in but her son Tony, who had remained nearby but distant, struggled to find his footing in terms of a career. His lack of ambition was something he tried to analyze later on during bouts of depression. In 1959 he decided gardening was a career he was suited to. Like Niall he shared an encyclopedic knowledge of plants and insects. Embankment Gardens with its creative planting was a place that inspired him. His partnership with Niall counted for success. They were very happy. His mother needed him but her distrust of Niall had grown. She would arrive at Tony's place of work, ready for an emotionally charged outburst, in which she let slip matters about her boy's personal life to his boss and narrow-minded onlookers. She couldn't stop her tongue. Her throwing an *Agatha Spanner* into the works led to him being sacked. This happened both at Kew Gardens where he worked as a seeds-man, and on another occasion. She might have tried shaming Niall as he had more to lose, being a respected scientist, but he was too 'evil' to confront. It was this kind of thing that led to a severance for the best part of fifteen years. Tony would return to Kew where he worked again in later years. His affinity with plants, flowers and insects was the key to his obsession with seasonal changes and outdoor temperatures.

Christmas 1959 was a happy occasion as Renée and Don loved their new home and were popular neighbours. Donald made a start in the garden. As well as his roses, he was out in January planting a hundred bulbs: tulips, daffodils and narcissi – salvaged after building work had brought chaos to the bottom of the garden. His wife took colour photos outside in the sunshine on Christmas day. I like the one of *'The oldest Teddy boy in Britain'* showing Don in drainpipe trousers and long coat. 'Boy am I a bobby dazzler,' Don wrote to his mum. Renée had got him a *Ronson electric razor* while he got her a white leather square beauty case, to carry back and forth to the theatre, even though Renée found it hard to kick her famous habit of shoving all her stuff into plastic carrier bags. The sociable folk in adjoining *'Brighthampton'* flats arranged parties on different nights – and the season turned a little hectic. They were invited to go to Lesley Storm's for a Hogmanay party but cried off due to exhaustion. Renée was worried her voice might start to go. Trevor had been in some trouble, but was coming home at the end of January. His mother was very excited about seeing him. 'I sincerely hope he's learned a bitter lesson . . . He can make something of himself if he will, and he's certainly getting a chance' was among the news sent to Mickey.

Touring for the 1960 *Roar Like A Dove* production commenced with Golders Green Hippodrome, then went to Streatham Hill's Empire, Oxford, Leeds, Manchester and Aberdeen. In between houses at His Majesty's Theatre, she recorded twelve minutes of material about her theatrical life for *Morning Call*. The tour continued to the Lyceum in Edinburgh where Donald wrote about the 'fantastically good audiences - better than London . . . They are loving Renée as an American.' They stayed at digs nearby, where Jessie Robertson, their octogenarian landlady, was sprightly as a two year-old. They travelled to Jim and Claire's the following week. He'd been in and out of hospital and his doctors had ordered him to get rid of his cattle given that the work was now too heavy for him.

The tour continued to York, Brighton, Watford, Windsor, Guernsey, then Eastbourne's Devonshire Park Theatre, then Tunbridge Wells, and Southsea on July 18. Murray McDonald sold the rights for *Roar*. It was to continue touring for up to twenty-five weeks following Don and Renée's departure. The new producer tried everything under the sun to get them to stay, offering them salary plus 5% of the takings. It was hard to turn down a joint salary of £200 per week, but they were sick of jogging all over the country. While they were away Trevor, who had put on weight and was working as a maintenance engineer for a company in Weybridge, acted as housesitter, looking after their pet budgies Jimfy (sometimes Jimferd) and Tinkle. Renée would write to her mother-in-law how 'Poor little Jimferd was so pleased to see me,' on her last visit home. 'The 'lady' bird we got for him is pretty ... she bullies him when I'm not there. Trevor treats them like babies so I am glad for poor Jimferd's sake. I wouldn't have believed one could get so fond of a tiny bird. He rushes to the cage to kiss me.'[13] Both budgies could talk, she continued: 'You should hear them!' All day long it's - *where's daddy? - my dear wee daddy* ... both yell *Dad, Dad.* They give everyone a good laugh.'

There was a finishing party for *Roar* given by the management and the men all got gold-plated Dunhill gas-lighters and Renée and Faith Brook, solid gold brooches. Renée was given her whole wardrobe from the show: gowns, shoes, hats, handbags the lot. Donald was given both the suits they tailored for him. These outfits came in handy when they attended the charity gala *'Night of 100 Stars'* at the London Palladium on July 21, with Judy Garland topping the bill that year. Renée hadn't been able to attend the 1959 one.

Donald looked into the costs of sea voyage to the States but found he just couldn't afford it. He was about to book a flight for himself when he and Renée got a statement from the company they'd set up - *Winterhouse Ltd,* finding that all they had was £230. It was the old curse of unpaid back tax - still following Renée Houston like a demon! The accountant told Don his first responsibility was to the debtors, lecturing him about getting into a position to better handle their accounts. It shows how their 'sin' of bankruptcy kept them in a perpetual stranglehold, which I find shocking. Then again, they still used money quicker than they got it.

It killed Don's planned trip home to see Mickey. They had also reached a stage when they were exhausted all the time but had to take work. They couldn't risk passing the money up. Renée was a TV contestant with Bernard Bresslaw, Bill Owen and Peter Bull on *Laugh Line,* hosted by Pete Murray and aired on July 20. Produced by Ned Sherrin, the panel was shown a funny drawing with a joke to go with it and each had to switch the characters round and invent a new joke. The winner was whoever drew the biggest laugh. In August she received a contract for an episode of *Maigret* produced by Andrew Osborn and directed by Rudolph Cartier. There would be two weeks of rehearsals at the Old Oak Club, Old Oak Common Lane, East Acton, and at Riverside Studios.

The next newspaper headlines were upsetting. Paul Eve got the Sunday papers to record a few lines to record an event he felt should make people look up and feel ashamed. The headlines went *''Teds' attack Renée Houston'* and *'Star is beaten up.'* Donald gave the lowdown to Mickey in a letter dated August 21, 1960. It happened on July 30, the Saturday after her fifty-eighth birthday. It was an early start for her, having to be in Acton at 9 am. After her rehearsal she took the London underground back to Waterloo arriving at

2.30 pm. She was always wary getting on and off escalators in high heels. Just as she was ascending to the main station to get her train home a bunch of youths started to push past. She blurted out an 'Excuse me' in her thorniest tones, and the first of these youths said 'Ah get out of it.' The next one mimicked her, and rammed his elbow in her eye, knocking her down while the other two trampled over her. One stood on her thigh. Renée was shocked by the fact that of the hundreds of people present, nobody was brave enough to intervene or even offer a hand to help her up.

> **'Teds' attack Renee Houston**
>
> WALTON variety star Renee Houston, was knocked down an escalator by Teddy Boys at Waterloo Station on Saturday night.
> She suffered a black eye and bruises.
> Her husband Mr. Donald Stewart said that Miss Houston was returning to Walton from a play rehearsal and asked the Teddy Boys not to push her. "Instead they knocked her down", he added.

Cutting from an unidentified newspaper about the incident at Waterloo sent to Donald Stewart's mother in America. (Wintermute Family)

She bumped her head when she went down and she wasn't sure how long it took her to get herself up. The fact she wasn't helped seems unlucky. Then again, free public displays of disobedience of an unentertaining kind, performed by trampling bullies and cowards were then creeping into the culture. City centres saw the trend along with vandalism: harsh forms of expression making the onlooker the victim. All flowered throughout the next twenty years whilst Renée remained a member of the old brigade – fighters sure of who they were and proud to stand up for the values of a community.

She found no railway inspector or policeman to help her on the concourse. Still dazed, she managed to get her train and finally, coming through the front door, Donald thought a car had smashed into her. One side of her face was red and there was a footprint on her thigh and the skin had been torn by the brute who trod on her. Worried on account of the fact that she was so small boned, Don took her to the doctor at once. Nothing was broken but the bump on her head had an after effect. At 7.30 that evening, she began to wander and suffered three hours delayed concussion. Most of Sunday she was in bed. Finally, in the evening, she and Don walked together around the grounds - her back swollen and head spinning. For the next two weeks her husband took her back and forth from rehearsals.

What she was rehearsing was the fifth episode in a groundbreaking series setting a standard in documentary realism. The BBC had acquired the rights to dramatize Georges Simenon's 'Maigret' stories, beating worldwide competition. Made with the world market in mind, the series was sold to America and Canada. Designer Eileen Diss recreated a pungently French atmosphere from Gauloise packets and authentic coffee cups down to the rasp of a match on a wall: one illuminating the face of Rupert Davies. He had the lead role. Davies's acting experience had been varied but *Inspector Maigret* was the most important of his career. In May 1960, Osborn and Davies travelled to Lausanne to meet Simenon at his home. Davies, who during the war, had spent five years in a POW camp in Germany after his naval fleet observer plane was shot down, fixed Simenon's wobbly desk and the writer considered him *en chair et en os*, declaring the search was over to find his detective. By 1963 *Maigret* had run through four series with fifty-two stories dramatized. The last series boasted fourteen million viewers per week.[14] Simenon wrote three extra episodes after Rupert Davies first introduced the character to television in April 1960.

The accent had to pass muster, and the BBC sent out memos closely reviewing early episodes. Shaky accents and bad pronunciation of French words were earmarked for improvement. There was an uncertainty as regards the production's 'over-insistence and over-explicitness' where sex was concerned. It was also worried that the 'lightness of voice' in the young policeman character could lead to 'a suspicion of effeminacy.'[15] The episode Renée recorded underwent retakes. This was *Liberty Bar* - named after the little bar that intuitive *Inspector Maigret* is drawn to, passing through the narrow lanes and alleys of Cannes where washing lines stretch overhead. Behind the bar *La grosse JaJa* is huge-bosomed, lovable, pathetic, piteous and guilty – a character *Maigret* befriends whilst on the trail of murdered Australian *William Brown*. Renée's black-wigged *JaJa* had a *troubled past as* mottled as a French Impressionist café habitué. In the book, *Maigret* more or less mimics the lifestyle of the dead man to understand his motivations and gets to love hanging out at Liberty bar himself in slippers: eating, drinking vermouth with *JaJa* and watching *Sylvie* - the young demi-mondaine half naked and lolling about. German actress Annette Carell played *Sylvie*. *Harry Brown*, played by Paul Eddington, arrives hoping to inherit the fortune from his dead father. *JaJa* is prominent in the Simenon story and Renée's scenes with Davies were many. Each had had a tiny part in 'The Key' a few years before. The story enfolds, taking on a resemblance to *Lolita*. When Donald saw Renée on television he could barely recognize her. Even her legs were padded causing her to waddle along: her 'fat murderess look' achieved with three pairs of thick hospital stockings. The image segued into public consciousness and she joked to interviewer Robin Russell that walking in Glasgow's Byres Road a week after *Maigret* was broadcast on December 5, a little woman came up to her wondering what had happened. Several other people were convinced that Renée was obese:

Glasgow woman: I SAW YER in the films last week.
 By heavens yu's LOST A BIT OF WEET haven't you?'
Members of the public: Tha's not her. CAN'T BE HER - she's a great big FAT woman.[16]

Fat she wasn't, but playing faded tarty women behind bars was something the BBC, ITV network, and film producers lined up as typical roles for Renée during the next five years or so. Producers often have a decided type they want to cast, looking for an easy win. She was twice in the Associated-Rediffusion hit *No Hiding Place,* produced at Wembley Studios by Ray Dicks. A series that prided itself on its lack of mock-heroics, it aimed to depict decent men good at their jobs and was actually popular with the force - the TV team often being invited along to police parties.[17] The main stars were moustachioed Raymond Francis as the *Superintendent* and Eric Lander as *Baxter.* Renée was in the episodes *'Footsteps on the Ceiling'* seen on October 28, and *'Fever'* on May 12, 1961. The series was frequently in the Top 10 - sometimes in No. 1 place – with a regular audience of 13,000,000 viewers.

George Fowler, who worked alongside Val Guest on 1954's 'The Runaway Bus,' produced 'Three on a Spree' at Walton with brilliant cinematographer Stephen Dade. It brought the 1902 novel 'Brewster's Millions' by George Barr McCutcheon up to date complete with 'lively laughs' and 'living dolls.' Jack Watling was *Michael Brewster* - an office clerk, all mixed up and shook up, and tasked with spending a million pounds in order to qualify for his £8,000,000 inheritance - in sixty days. He forms a finance company determined to make bad deals but everything turns to profit. He even becomes an impresario of a turkey of a show hoping for quick insolvency but even this doesn't work! Renée plays his landlady and the mother of his sweetheart. Carole Lesley, a talented young actress, played the latter role. She made only two further films and died far too early. Renée - the sort to inspire others to pursue their showbiz dreams – for better or worse, looks elegant in a still from the movie, with Carole looking at her admiringly.

Sir Cliff Richard in 1961, Carole Lesley (Author's Collection)

It was most likely through her Canadian director, Sidney J. Furie (whose next job was to direct Cliff Richard in a picture) that Renée got to know the popular young singer. Cliff was her travelling companion on at least two occasions when they took trains en route to concert and theatre engagements. At this point *Roar Like A Dove* continued with dates at Bradford, Margate, St Andrews, Dublin, Exeter, Bournmouth, Chester's Royal,

Norwich's Theatre Royal, then Torquay, the Rex Wilmslow, Brighton Hippodrome, Northampton, and finally the Grand Blackpool on December 14, 1960. If this wasn't like old times, then what was! Yet, despite the hotels, fish and chips, and togetherness seeing the sights from city to city, it proved a wearing year for Donald and Renée.

Trevor had turned over a new leaf, and was working as a driving instructor. Donald wrote to his mother 'He's damned good at it but it is not a good paying job. The owner of the school makes all the gravy. However, he is serving a purpose. He is taking an advance driver's test and instructor's diploma, which would put him in a position to run his own driving school. In the meantime the percentage of passes among his pupils is the highest among the instructors, including the boss. He is well liked and is building so much goodwill that new pupils are asking to be instructed by him.' It's a tribute to Don that he was happy being a surrogate dad to Renée's kids whenever they needed it. He hoped to help out thirty-four year-old Trev with the costs for a car, and took a supportive interest. 'The world today needs individuals with brains and courage to lead it,' mused Donald, casting an eye over the presidential election happening in his home country:

Donald: Sometimes you can see more looking through a window than sitting in the room. From this side of the fence there is no doubt that America has lost face and prestige in the last couple of years through some of the horrible bungling of international affairs . . . I believe that young Kennedy will probably make some mistakes compatible to youth, but I think he will bring a vitality and vigour to the administration sorely lacking for so long.'

After discussing the infiltration of Russia, tax increases and aid to Asia and Africa, Donald closes the letter: '*And now as the sun dies in the west this political sermon comes to an end as we glide smoothly out to the post office to despatch this episal to our lovely mother whom we love so dearly.*'[18]

With cooked duck and brace of pheasants served by Miss Houston, Christmas and Hogmanay in Walton-on-Thames were as sociable as ever. They watched Andy Stewart on the television, discussing him as if he was their son, identifying elements of their 'training' in terms of comedy and characterizations. One by one, neighbours began to arrive: the Tarrants, the Hutchings then the Robertshaws. The Wintermutes were first footed and everyone sang Auld Lang Syne. Trev and his girlfriend Valaria arrived at 5 minutes to 12. The party went on and on, with the guests escorting the party off for drinks at their respective homes.

Offers to appear in TV dramas kept coming. Renée played a sympathetic neighbour in a play called *Not Many Mansions*, a story about old age broadcast on January 5, 1961. Written by AD Cooper, it was directed by David Boisseau and received praise in The Times. Wilfred Brambell plays *Harry*, old and deaf as a post. His wife and her daughter look after him. The local council is rehousing the occupants of his street and his son manages to

Time and Tide

get the household rehabilitated. Joyce Carey, Margaret Flint and handsome Sam Kydd also starred.

In mid-February she did two weeks rehearsals at Kings Hall, 163 New Kings Road and a day at Studio G, Lime Grove Studios, making a 'BBC Recording For Schools' for producer Ronald Eyre. This was *Dr Knock* - a half hour dramatization of the Jules Romains play familiar to French children as a school text. Romains had written the play for actor Louis Jouvet who made a hilarious film version. In the French countryside mysterious *Dr Knock* arrives to take over *Dr Parpalaid's* unprofitable country practice and it isn't long before this 'medical revolutionary' proves he's a ruthless manipulator of human emotions. His task, he believes, is not just to cure sickness but *sell* health, persuading the local citizens that they are all very ill. There's fun at the expense of country manners and gullible gallics. Renée played *Madame Remy* and interestingly, would repeat the role again in another production for television five years later. In this one Richard Wordsworth was *Dr Knock*, Frank Finlay - *Monsieur Mousquet,* and Jean Anderson - *Madame Pons*.

Renée was engaged at Hammer Films for a miniscule role in 'Watch It, Sailor' based on the hit stage play by Philip King and Falkland Cary. She's a sedate version of *Hilda Ogden,* who exchanges gossipy gestures with Miriam Karlin, whilst a weird-looking cat under her arm looks the camera face on. While she extracts as much as she can from a raised eyebrow in her scenes with batty *Edie Hornett* - Irene Handl, she's pitifully underused. Marjorie Rhodes, Cyril Smith and Vera Day were the *Hornett family* with John Meillon as *Albert Tuffnell* - the young sailor attempting to marry into it. Dennis Price, and Liz Fraser also starred and Frankie Howerd was a funny *church organist*. It's a typical British comedy entirely based on a wedding and the events conspiring to prevent it: cars breaking down, monster of a mother-in-law and *Albert's* 'paternity issue.' Hen-pecked *Henry Hornett* tries to avoid the cross-fire and the young couple attempt to flee nagging *Ma Hornett*.

In early March filming was in progress for 'No My Darling Daughter,' based on the play *A Handful of Tansy* by Harold Brooke and Kay Bannerman. Produced by Betty Box at Rank Studios and directed by Ralph Thomas, it had Sir Michael Redgrave, Roger Livesey, Michael Craig, Rad Fulton, Renée and Joan Sims in the cast. It was Juliet Mills's debut performance in a British film although she had proved herself a comedienne on stage in *Five Finger Exercise*. She is *Tansy Carr*, the tactless and clumsy daughter of *Sir Matthew Carr*, chairman of an Investment Trust. He thinks it's high time for her to drop that 'damn cricket bat' and receive a 'finishing.' *Mr Thomas,* her father's supercilious bowler-hatted banking protégé - Michael Craig - escorts her out of school. He's really in search of life's deeper meaning though this doesn't convince. The film updates the amiable English pre-marital comedy to 1961 with *Tansy* and her American boyfriend speeding around London on a Moped as a pair of trendy but innocent young lovers. I liked the film from its opening credits onwards where you see Redgrave and Juliet silhouetted whilst singing the hip title song by Herbert Kretzmer and David Lee

You glimpse a recovering London - 'a beautiful city' says Rad Fulton's character, though bombsites aren't easy to disguise. Looking quietly chic in a light coloured coat and hat worn over her short hair, Renée's *Miss Yardley* arrives for work and walks up the steps to Carr's modernist-looking office for the first scene. She reigns as his capable personal assistant.

Hanging about her father's office *Tansy* is always dropping clangers and is free with faux pas. It's refreshing to see the environment of investment banking producing no inhibition on her part. Chatting to *Miss Yardley, Tansy* unleashes her imaginative comparisons venturing the thought of that formidable PA coming into the office one morning absolutely stark naked. Tansy gets even more entrenched - 'you never would do that because it would be so ghastly . . . ' and struggles to dig herself out of it. 'Oh, of course, you would look marvellous *Miss Yardley*.' Renée's flickering facial expressions are superb, hitting the spot, and making the scene as effective as possible. *Tansy*'s father later suggests 'when you drop a clanger like that, don't try to pick it up again, cause you'll only drop a dozen more.'

Renée is low key in her characterization. She's a woman who, when asked by her boss what she thinks about life, says 'Oh, life's all very well, but one doesn't bring it into the office, does one?' Throughout this period, she traded her arch, matron-like character as a commodity in the film market. The highly sexed woman with a ready sarcastic wit was held in check. She accepted age without vanity. *Miss Yardley's* inhibited restraint gets to *Sir Matthew,* who advises her to slip on a discarded gift of a kimono *Tansy* has grown too big for, and 'pop around to the nearest geisha house.'

Sir Michael Redgrave and Renée Houston in 'No My Darling Daughter,' (1961) directed by Ralph Thomas
(By kind permission of ITV/Rex/Shutterstock)

Time and Tide

Renée does this scene free of burlesque and is notably restrained. She gave it exactly what was required, demonstrating that she could play any mature character and be perfectly believable. She did films like this purely for the remuneration. It says a lot about where she was at this time in her career when variety – her mainstay - had slipped away. Fewer roles were within reach for one with a spirit as creative as hers. However, she was willing to adapt and, as usual, turned in a good performance.

One critic said Redgrave made the least of his 'thin character' and it was 'left to Renée Houston as his secretary to suggest that the bit parts are best.'[19] After her twelve consecutive days getting up 6 am. Donald, who had recently appeared on *The Dickie Henderson Show*, wrote to Mickey about how Renée was so well liked by her producer Betty Box and by Ralph Thomas and that she expected to do another film for this same team before long. Donald also mentions[20] she met up with Frank Launder about a new film at Shepperton, but I'm unclear what this project was.

A Hollywood film 'Parent Trap' starring Juliet Mill's sister Hayley was released to London audiences close to the time of 'No My Darling Daughter' on August 10. Juliet had little to say about the latter film or Renée, even though it was her first film and she made two more with Miss Houston. 'People don't remember,' she wrote, discouragingly, adding her observation that 'Half of America don't know who Lawrence Olivier was!' It was very nice of her to reply to me all the same and to wish me luck with my book on Renée. Facing the camera in 'No My Darling Daughter' Renée speaks with the gruffer tone that had entered her voice and looks very like her sister Billie.

The real Billie Houston by then was a British National abroad, living in a chic seven room apartment on the Isle Saint-Louis – a perk that came with Paul Eve's new Paris job. She was an avid reader, Dick Francis and Georgette Heyer were two writers whose work she lived on day by day. She and Paul had a love of gourmet food and wine, and knowledge of European cuisine became a hobby for Paul. By the early 70s Paul had produced two excellent cookbooks, including the very timely European's Cookbook – 'A Country-By-Country Guide to Common Market Cookery,' warning you to serve gin if you're entertaining Dutch people, and full of advice such as getting your poulterer to save the blood of the cockerel as a sauce thickener if you're doing a Coq au Vin. They managed to remain slim even if they didn't have to wander far for fine food. In Sheen and later in Ealing and Radlett, sons of peers sometimes came to visit, as well as a few famous faces from the entertainment world like Max Bygraves and Frankie Howerd.

There was little actual money at hand. In the days before the NHS a big drain on their resources was paying for the operations Billie needed. Paul was still paying off bills to surgeons and hospitals from years later. For fifteen years Paul was among the most highly paid executives at British United Press. He let money fall through his hands, enjoying the good things – putting off paying for these til later. Ultimately they were a family facing financial troubles. His son admits that Paul was careless when it came to money. The prize for most careless person went to his Auntie Renée.

Paul Eve always looked younger than his years. In 1956 when twenty-one year-old Mike Keats joined Paul at the BUP bureau in Fleet Street, he observed the smooth dresser with a fine head of hair. Paul looked eight years older than him - certainly not twenty. Mike, now retired in Melbourne but in touch with many former journalist colleagues, was surprised to hear someone making an enquiry about Paul Eve. He tells me 'Paul was indeed cultured and very laid back . . . never saw him in a flap when things would go awry on a story we were covering - always Mr Cool.' Jogging the memories in the 'swamp gas of his mind' Mike recalled that Paul often mentioned his wife's career on the stage although he didn't get to meet her. In the early 50s, Fleet Street churned out morning newspapers and afternoon newspapers with Associated Press cornering the market on the former. Television impacted that whole world of print, making afternoon newspapers obsolete. With the market shrinking United Press no longer thought it viable to subsidize a 'British' service to edit the news, so the London bureau was disbanded.

Billie willingly followed Paul to all of the destinations he had to go to. He once worked in South Africa and she would have gone all the way there, but thankfully she never needed to - mainly because he got chucked out on account of the critical things he wrote about the regime. It was after this that Paul became Bureau Manager of UPI's Paris office. He and Billie would be based here eight years, their son and daughter uprooted from London and educated at the Sorbonne. Paul's soft Aussie accent was occasionally heard in the UK covering De Gaulle or Cold War stories like the negotiations from 1962 to 1965 over a potential European multilateral force.

Whilst on holiday in Italy, in October 1961, Billie, Paul, Anton and Carole attended a special reception with Pope John XXIII. It was the 50th anniversary of the Vatican's Press Club. Although Paul wasn't Catholic the Wills-Eve family impressed the Cardinal who was handling the guest list, firstly because they were a whole family, and secondly because they were representative of Australia, England and Scotland. Billie was having another bout of illness but this time didn't retire. She climbed the seventy-three steps leading to the entrance to the Vatican. It was only after that Italian hospitality saw fit to make it known a lift was available. There was no way Billie was going to say no to a papal introduction. Leaving her bedroom, and donning a full-length black coat with a Spanish-style mantilla, she was introduced to *His Holiness* – something she had never dreamed possible. Popes were inaccessible – just totems on the mantelpiece at Shettleston. As they came away, Billie turned round to her son and said: 'I've just met the Pope in my pajamas.' The following year Pope John played a role in bringing America and Russia back from the edge during the Cuban Missile Crisis.

The last time people witnessed the Houston Sisters perform was in 1954 at the Coliseum. That was on British soil but they did a cracking performance at *La Brasserie de l'Isle Saint-Louis* in 1962, when Renée came over for a holiday with Don. It had been a struggle for the *Sweethearts* to afford the fayre. Thank heavens they did. A gorgeous meal was laid out, and on came aperitifs *entre chien et loup* and Champagne and Cognac. The happy Parisian atmosphere lent itself to a totally impromptu performance by the Houston Sisters. Paris gathered and gawped. Just everything returned to the Sisters: the little quarrel, the vent act, the songs, *Glescu keelies*, the cheek, the repartee. Anton tells me he's never forgotten how electrifying it was. Office workers and flocks of tourists, mostly Americans, were amazed and went crazy with their whistles. The locals were restrained, unsure who these *femmes extraordinaires* might be. Shutters opened and *du Vieux Paris* listened joyfully. Le Beatnik flocked from Left Bank and Right Bank and La Brasserie never before or since did such a killing. No dollars or francs were leaving the premises and never again was such laughter to be heard. The Sisters were never better: the speed of their speech incredible.

Renée as *Mme De Montrachet* and Laurence Hardy as *Delmonte* were thought 'delightfully theatrical'[21] in *Dinner with the Family* - a BBC TV drama broadcast on March 30, 1962 with Renée second billed. It was a play about marriage and love written by Jean Anouih and translated by Edward Owen Marsh. Set in Senlis, outside Paris, it's a world of convention: smart drawing rooms, cocktail parties and sophisticated guests. Times have changed so much and I don't think it could be put on in the 21st Century without very clunky updates. *Georges de Montrachet* - Stephen Moore holds a fake dinner party and a young penniless girl *Isabelle* - Jacqueline Ellis has to see through the illusions. Jeremy Brett, Angela Browne and Joan Hickson were also in the cast. Prior to *Isabelle's* arrival two actors arrive: *Mme de Montrachet* and *Delmonte* - only to learn they must enact the parts of George's supposed mother and father. The real *Maman* has forced him into a marriage. Marital ups and downs follow the theatrical going-ons and *George's* real parents arrive. When the contract for *Dinner with the Family* arrived, it was negotiated with Pamela Simons who inherited some of Rita Cave's clients following Rita's death on June 1, 1961. Rita had gone through two cancer operations that last year and hadn't been in her office six months, working from her nursing home until she died. Pam moved her agency several times but at the beginning was based at 3 Cork Street.

Summer 1961 saw a short run of *Roar Like A Dove* with dates that included Cromer, the Bristol Little Theatre, Brighton's Palace Pier, and Bexhill. On a lonely visit to Bexhill forty-two years later Tony Aherne listened to the lusty waves and the drag of the sea on the shingle, powerless but comforted in the midst of this force. Donald had been dealing with pain during the original touring dates for *Roar* in 1960. He told his mother his specialist had ruled out a prostrate problem, believing he had a blockage in the urinal tube and a possible kidney complaint. The X-Ray results seemed to rule out an operation but soon part of his bladder collapsed and he did require surgery. It wasn't a major operation but more painful than some. He was then diagnosed with a prostrate problem and given about thirty pills to swallow every day. He and Renée joked about him starting to rattle wherever he went. She had got used to leaning on Donald all those years, yet Donald would now tell people that 'when her shoulder is needed, believe me, I've found it broad and strong. She's lost a lot of weight worrying about me. My trouble now is how to keep her worried. Ha!' The pills worked, and he recovered bladder control.[22] He had a second operation in March 1961.

Donald and Renée refused to let this stop them living their lives. Don was soon riding his bike, making sure word got about he was ok, smoking and drinking his favourite *whisky and water*. He appeared as *General Vandenborg* on August 5 in the first tele-recorded episode of space fiction thriller *A for Andromeda,* alongside Peter Halliday, Patricia Kneale, Julie Christie and Esmond Knight. He was in five of these forty-five minute episodes and did other TV plays. They didn't pay well.

1961 continued, and so did fears regarding Don's health: 'I've been ill for sometime with prostrate gland trouble. I've ignored it because I wanted to get some money in the bank . . . Our salaries are mortgaged by the company who have been dishing out for weeks on *overdraft* . . . if I have to have an operation, I want it quick so I can get a part in Lolita at the end of November and have two episodes of a series before Xmas. I can't rest easy knowing Renée is worried about finance and bills.'[23] At the end of the year he was offered a part in the musical *Little Mary Sunshine* but this fell through when they changed his American part to a British one. It was a case of 'no job'.

People came and went. Trevor visited frequently with his girlfriend, and they were considerate of Renée when she was very worried at the times Donald had to go to hospital. The door was always open over at 'Brighthampton'. Young visitors never got any sense of their struggles - just a lot of cheer, fun and a sense of warmth. Don and Renée were forever upbeat and to the younger generation they held the distinction of being everyone's favourite uncle and aunt. Anton stayed a week with them covering the first week of tennis at Wimbledon for United Press. Shirley's youngest boy Ian came another week and was as happy as a lark playing all day with David and Carol, the kids in the flat upstairs. Sometimes Ian's brother Drew came as well, and Renée and the four kids would all be on the veranda playing Buccaneer: the noise increasing to a hysterical pitch as the game went on.

Alan arrived on September 5 for a month, having taken a *Club Charter* flight costing about half the normal fare. About a hundred British-born Hollywood citizens combined to visit friends and relatives using this budget option. They were taking life into their hands. The plane that Alan came over on would crash off Ireland turning round for its return and another *Club Charter* plane landed in New York on two of its four motors.

'Brighthampton' became a mad house with Alan's old school friends arriving now with wives and girlfriends. The chattering friends still referred to the old house at Twickenham as the *clubhouse – a place* good for a meal, where they had always been made welcome. After being without Alan so many years Renée initially almost didn't want him there for fear of getting too close and repeating the pain of parting. However, this stay turned out to be a happy one for everyone.

Renée Houston in 1961 (Author's Collection)

At New Year Donald made a call home to speak to his mother, his brother Jack, his sister Lois, his sister Janice and her husband Bob. Janice's daughter Susan remembers 'we all talked to them briefly. I think it was a three-minute phone call as trans-Atlantic calls were costly at that time. My Father recorded it and I found the tape of it.' Donald tells them that he and Renée had been to a party at the tenants at Flat 5 and had several drinks. Renée had this bad chest and they came back and were asleep when the phone rang at 1 am. In a half daze Renée grabbed the phone and the operator said a call from New Jersey and she only heard the word 'Jersey' and didn't clock until Don's sister Lois spoke. She would have spoken to everyone if she could have, but made sure Don didn't miss a second. Donald and Renée couldn't sleep for excitement after. The generosity of Mickey and the family never failed and not only had they received the fantastic present of a phone call, but a parcel arrived for them a few days later too. '*La Toots* opened it and had a great time,' and Donald, as always wrote to thank his dearest mother for her kindness.

Chapter 23   Playing Mature

Broadway called at the end of 1961 when Miss Houston was asked to play third lead in a musical. For this one and only time Richard Rodgers did lyrics as well as score now that Oscar Hammerstein II had died. It was also the first time that race and civil rights were a theme of a Broadway show. This was *No Strings,* planned for March '62. Diahann Carroll was a fashion model in Paris in love with a novelist, with Renée as European Head of Vogue - well, almost. She and Donald leapt at the chance to work in America. Alas, as Don told Mickey, the 'dream of the best Xmas present in the world for you fell to pieces.'[1] The producers changed Renée's part so an American actress could play it. There was no point in crying. A steady amount of British radio, TV and film work from this point onwards kept Renée busy. Pam Simons was good at getting her roles without too much travelling involved. She was one of the speakers in *Among My Souvenirs - The Lawrence Wright Story* on the Home Service, telling her pal Boxy, 'I did not even know there was a fee! I did it for my dear little friend Judith Chalmers, and agreed to it because I would do anything for her "for free".'[2] She also contributed to *A Star Remembers,* and in May 1962 Pam informed the BBC of Miss Houston's availability now she had finished the films 'Phantom of the Opera,' and 'Out of the Fog' and the BBC TV drama *A Matter of Conscience,* seen on May 25 at 9.25pm.

James Ormerod was responsible for *A Matter Of Conscience* –rehearsed in early February at the Drill Hall, Merton Road SW18, with pre-recording at the BBC's Gosta Green Studios in Birmingham. The latter building has since transformed into a University bioenergy facility, turning natural waste materials into heat and electricity. The theme of a natural law that causes some to lose while others gain characterizes parts of Leo Tolstoy's last novel 'Resurrection,' reflecting the author's belief in egoism. A newspaper report of a nobleman called for jury service at the trial of a prostitute for murder had prompted the book. It was this aspect of the novel that Thomas Clarke adapted. 'Resurrection' had been banned on account of its 'immorality' by two of England's largest libraries when it appeared in translation in 1901. The libraries were forced to revoke the ban because the book was so popular. The play, now considered one of Tolstoy's most compassionate works, concerns the moral dilemma confronting *Prince Dmitri Nekhlyudov,* played by Harry H. Corbett, when he realizes that *Katerina Maslova* - peasant girl turned prostitute - is the girl whose ruin he's responsible for. Shelagh Richards directed[3] and Billie Whitelaw - voted television's best actress of the year for 1960 - played *Maslova.* Renée played *Korableva* - one of the vodka-drinking and cigarette-smoking female inmates of the prison.

Billie Whitelaw, Harry H. Corbett and Patrick Cargill (Author's Collection)

Playing Mature

Patrick Cargill, a fellow actor in *A Matter Of Conscience* had written a play set in a sanitarium that became the basis for a film 'Twice Round the Daffodils' with Juliet Mills first billed as the nurse whose dedication sets her patients on the road to recovery. It's a lovely throwback to the days when the NHS funded pleasant long stay recovery environments. Even TB patients were free to smoke in the wards as a way to relax. It was the first film Renée would make for super duo Gerald Thomas and Peter Rogers although she had worked with Gerald's brother Ralph on 'No, My Darling Daughter.' She's a shadowy presence as the matron, referred to as a 'refrigerated old ice cube' by *Henry Halfpenny* - Kenneth Williams, and glimpsed only a couple of times. I wondered if Tony Aherne might somehow have found his way to being the model for *Henry* – always seen with a chessboard in front of him – or if that's pure coincidence. It's a ludicrously small role for Renée compared to her previous film. Some have told me she kept screwing up the takes and they cut down her part but I don't believe that. There weren't many substantial parts that suited her and she took miniscule ones without complaint. In the cast was Welsh actor Donald Houston who plays a loudmouth and makes the depiction of tension mounting up among a group of sequestered men quite realistic. This was a rare foray into heart-felt drama by the team behind the Carry Ons, with melancholic music by Bruce Montgomery taking you by surprise, although Kenneth Williams and Joan Sims, as tragi-comic brother and sister, provide familiar comic relief with a strong lineup that included Donald Sinden, Lance Percival, and Sheila Hancock.

Guests arrived to wish Renée's Donald well, when his fifty-second birthday was celebrated at *'Brighthampton.'* Brian and Eleanor Aherne arrived from Switzerland that day and discovering it was Don's birthday, descended with friends from California. Renée describes the party in a letter to Mickey, telling her how 'there were presents galore and everyone was beautifully dressed. My cooking was a great success and everyone brought bottles of whisky and gin so it didn't cost us much.'[4] Brian was here for location filming at Pinewood.[5] A few days later Donald joined the Ahernes' party for a slap up meal at the Savoy. Peggy Cummins, with whom Donald made the wartime movie 'Welcome Mr Washington' was at the dinner. Renée couldn't make it as she was filming. She would appear with Donald in the one-hour episode *The Runaways* – part of ATV's *Man of the World* series made at Shepperton. They were the *Van Kempsons* - two wealthy parents who meet world-renowned photographer *Mike Strait*, played by Craig Stevens, who's mixed up in the affairs of a runaway who's prone to falling in love at first sight - Erica Rogers. Leon Peers and Noel Harrison also starred. It followed Bonanza in the TV listings on 20 October 1962.

'Phantom of the Opera' is a product of the golden age of Hammer horror, created by a team led by Tony Hinds. Arguably the last great Hammer film that came out of Bray studios, it had expensive sets, an original score both for the film and the *opera* within the film, and an overall richness not

489

normally found in the genre. There was enough money to pay for Cary Grant, originally cast as the *Phantom*, although he couldn't make it. Herbert Lom donned the mask instead and didn't do a bad job. Director Terrence Fisher, assisted by Freddie Francis, brought out the human side of the villain of Gaston Leroux's 1909 novel. The scene with Renée, whose memories put *Harry* - Edward de Souza - on the scent of the mysterious *Phantom,* also provides the key to the humanity of the *Phantom* - formerly *Professor Petrie*. She's *Mrs Tucker* - theatrical landlady in the lodgings of heroine *Christine* – played by Heather Sears. Renée is subtle and believable despite her anachronistic lipstick and endows the small role with a spirit as welcome as the glass of sherry wine she brings *Harry*. In a room that might have been Granny Houston's parlour *Harry* listens to a music box and learns about the great *Professor Petrie,* forgotten by everyone except the landlady. *Mrs Tucker*'s Victoriana screen - a stray sheet from *Petrie*'s manuscript pasted in its collage surface - seems to invoke the real life actress, fond of such artwork. Edward de Souza and Heather Sears have a vulnerability and gentleness about them that engages the onlooker. The film was easy to laugh at hence comments by critics Alexander Walker ridiculing the cliché of the foolish dwarf[6] and Derek Prowse: 'Though the Sewer department is agreeably furnished with double-bed, organ and refectory table, his mask pops into humiliating pleats at each intake of breath. He should haunt no more.'[7] While the UK's distribution returns on 'Phantom' were less than expected, in the United States these were very satisfactory.

As a contemporary landlady in a halfway house for ex-cons in Eternal Films' 'Out of the Fog,'[8] James Hayter plays her screen husband. He welcomes the central character *George Mallon* - David Sumner, as a guest. *Mallon* is soon to be No.1 suspect in a police investigation into why blondes keep getting murdered on a nearby piece of ground known as 'the flats'. Renée's role is tiny again, and we hear her nag in a London accent with a soupçon of Glasgow as she tries to clean *Mallon*'s room. 'Out of the Fog' attempts to mimic *No Hiding Place*, and doesn't quite work but it's a nice picture of England in 1962 with its coffee bars, jukeboxes and shops selling modern furniture. Here the police put all their faith in one suspect without bothering about alternative killers. Just because you don't have another suspect it's no justification for hanging about doing nothing! After enlisting a pretty blonde WPC - Susan Travers, as bait for the killer, it seems the entire force is bundled into the car outside the cinema with no police watching 'the flats' when a date has been orchestrated for her to trap *Mallon*. Someone must have had a brainwave later, because they appear at the last minute in those lonely surroundings for the laughable ending. You share the final frustration and anger of *Mallon* who ultimately beats the police at their own game, aware all along they 'baited the track.' The film is worth it for the fab music alone – all credit to Ken Thorne who had provided a score for 'Three on a Spree' and would do the same on the Beatles' 'Help'.

Playing Mature

Renée was in another film for Peter Rogers – continuing the obsession with nurses. This was 'Nurse On Wheels' directed by Gerald Thomas at Pinewood studios with Juliet Mills yet again in the lead, this time as new village nurse *Joanna Jones*. Her friendly, direct approach during home visits cures the locals of their reservations. I'm convinced Juliet must have inspired many girls to choose nursing as a vocation. *Joanna*'s forthright manner in confronting *Mrs Beacon* - wife of one of her patients, adds one further string to her bow. This scene allows for a very *Houston* moment. *Mrs Beacon* is the typical canvas Renée could make much of. She projects a sense of surly denial and inability for plain-speak regarding her husband's 'tendencies,' yet at the same time is oddly desperate for him to return to his roving self. Renée was very good at these portrayals of human inconsistency.

There was a fifth and final film for Renée that year and the director of 'Tomorrow At Ten' was Lance Comfort. He's likely to have been the one who summoned Miss H to MGM's Borehamwood studios. He did the sound on 'Variety - The Romance of the Music Hall' lightyears before and had recently engaged Donald for *Douglas Fairbanks Jnr Presents* which he produced. The film, released the following summer, reveals the lack of wariness about safeguarding there was then, compared to now. Children of rich men are easy prey for kidnappers posing as chauffeurs like *Marlow* – played by Robert Shaw - who in the 70s got a comeuppance when he was chewed up by *Jaws* making him a worldwide name in the process. Here, he locks little *Jonathan* in an upper floor room of a house in Wimbledon. A house in Elstree served for the location. The wily Cockney calls on the boy's father *Anthony Chester* – Alec Clunes, asking for £50K and the freedom to fly to Rio from where he will phone through with the boy's location. Even though the police are tipped off and *Detective-Inspector Parnell* – John Gregson - arrives on the scene, *Marlow* can coolly declare 'Either you give me the money or the boy dies.' They have to seriously consider this as a clockwork device with explosives to blow half a house up has been sewn into a Golliwog left ticking away with the boy. If child death is to be averted, Marlow's on that plane. The bomb will go off at 10 am the next day.

There's privilege versus equality causing friction between *Parnell* and *Bewley* - his superior at the Yard - played by Alan Wheatley, who supports *Chester's* wish to pay up as influential people can do just that. *Parnell*'s view is that if you let someone get away Scot-free after such a crime, you're weakening policemen everywhere. *Parnell* puts his foot down, gambling on *Bewley*'s cowardice. If *Bewley* removes him from the case as superior, he'll be personally responsible. The Gregson and Wheatley dialogue echoing the eternal debate about 'rot setting in' - is the best in the film. Psychology is a cynical means to an end for *Parnell* who's tough on crime. To his colleague he urges 'Never apply to a criminal the same standards you would to yourself.' A popular actor since 'Genevieve,' Gregson is compelling, and Ken Cope is realistic as his colleague *Grey* – quick with chippy comments about the true state of affairs between ranks in the Force. *Parnell* tries to lead *Marlow* in and break him to expose the boy's location. Just as his Freudian tactics hit on something about *Marlow's* mother, that privileged idiot *Chester* floors *Marlow* leaving him in a coma. The police are thrown back on only routine checks in their attempt to find the boy in time.

It's a shame that Renée is in the worst scene in 'Tomorrow At Ten' - a scene that's vaguely necessary yet damages the credibility of the *Marlow* character nicely set up by Robert Shaw. She runs the *Golliwog Club* in Westbourne Grove along with hen-pecked husband *Freddie* - Bill Hartnell again! She's *Marlow*'s mother: 'Everyone calls me *Maisie*. I dunno why, me name's Dorothy,' she tells *Parnell,* her flawless Souf London accent superimposed over the music of *The Shadows*.

'Tomorrow At Ten' (1963)
directed by Lance Comfort:
Scene featuring
Renée Houston
and William Hartnell

(By kind permission of Euro London Films)

Trying to develop the psychological motive in this scene, writers James Kelley and Peter Miller do not go far enough. *Maisie* doesn't seem capable of vast neglect. The only thing *Parnell* and *Grey* learn is that she's a bit of a drunk who exposed her child to bars full of punters with breath stinking of spirits. *Parnell* blames *Marlow*'s parents for not even asking him why he was questioning them about their son, but he hardly has any questions for them either. The police leave the club in disgust, while Lesley Allen does a Beatnik dance and Neville Taylor plays the bongos.

The club's inspiration seems a composite of real life clubs like the 'El Rio Café,' 'Henekeys' and Soho's 'El Condor' but it's too fanciful, even if more West Indian extras are present here than there were in 'Notting Hill' (1995). The ubiquitous Golliwogs decorating the bar are as silly as the clocks in 'Time Without Pity' – a lousy design fault. All the same, the film is full of suspense with interesting lead characters. It was made before films became progressively more gratuitous in their use of children as victims. The act of locking up a small boy in a room in an empty and scary house, where night will fall, creating all kinds of shadows ably illustrates the dark side of *Marlow*. The photography is outstanding and I'm surprised poor *Jonathan* didn't die of fright. Surely most boys of his age, left in a room with nothing but a ticking cuddly toy, would have cut it open to investigate the device making the noise. He gives the toy a good beating and a drowning though.

Renée and Donald enjoyed the lights and glamour of the West End in 1962. No show oozed more glamour than *Gentlemen Prefer Blondes,* which opened at London's Princes Theatre on August 20, 1962 with Dora Bryan, its vibrant star, adding an attractive British quality to the role of *Lorelei Lee.* Michael Ashlin, Bob Cole, John Griffin, Anne Hart, John Heawood, Bessie Love, Michael Malnick, Guy Middleton, Robin Palmer, and Gerald Stern were among the cast. While reviews were lukewarm, business was consistently good and the show ran for 223 performances. A vinyl LP was released with the Jules Styne soundtrack in which Donald sings on the tracks 'Bye Bye Baby',' Homesick Blues',' Button Up With Esmond' and 'Gentlemen Prefer Blondes.' The musical originally ran two years on Broadway and when they were first going to put it on in London in 1952, Donald was considered as juvenile lead. Ten years on, they cast him as *Sugar Daddy* – a better part, even if he felt he wasn't getting the money he deserved. 'It's the story of not being in a position to fight for it. I couldn't afford to take a chance,' he said.[9]

The winter of 1962-1963 was reported to be the worst winter for eighty-seven years, and *Gentlemen Prefer Blondes* was having problems when they lost Dora Bryan for about three months owing to a miscarriage. Donald explains how 'the chorus girl understudy is completely inadequate to carry a star part. We're on 20% cuts to keep ticking over.'[10] Professional as ever with his commitments, he was looking around for something else. When the London show finished on February 16 and a seven-week tour was to follow, Renée told Mickey she didn't want Don to continue, urging him to make his salary an excuse. He did exactly that and management hummed and hawed for three weeks, auditioning twenty men to take his part before eventually agreeing to his terms. Dora Bryan also kicked up a fuss because she wanted Donald to stay, 'and believe you me she can kick up a fuss,' Renée went on to say. 'She can be very awkward when she wants to be. In fact it's my opinion the show could have run in town for another year if she had been dependable, but you never knew when she decided not to come out in the cold weather and when stuck for an excuse she told the boss she had a miscarriage. Maybe she did, but it's not the sort of thing anyone with any modesty would shout about from the rooftops. She has been doing this sort of thing for a number of years. Don had a good laugh one day when I said she was the only woman I knew who built a career on miscarriages.'[11]

Renée's asides were cruel. It's interesting she believed you should keep anything to do with babies quiet. In fact she had more in common with Dora than she cared to admit, and she should have been grateful that Miss Bryan put herself out on Don's behalf. Dora, whose parents owned a mill and a gown shop in Oldham, went into the business too early and eventually suffered the effects of a relentless work schedule on her personal life. Adored by fans, she tried to cope, making time for family when she could. Drink dependency in the Bryan household had tragic consequences. One of the kids she adopted suffered badly but Dora had, by then, sought help.

Taking credit for Don's improved salary, Renée was glad of the proposed tour that took in Blackpool, Liverpool, Newcastle, Brighton, Torquay, Bournmouth and Southsea - all seaside dates. The challenge was getting her Surrey neighbour Mrs Robertshaw to look after Jimfy and Tinkle. She admitted 'these little budgies of ours are sweet but they are a terrible tie.'

When a sequel to *Sailor Beware* and *Watch It, Sailor* was planned for the West End, Renée was cast as *Emma Hornett* and looks 100% battle-axe in costume in the programme's photo by Vaslav. The domineering mother was some leap from the miniscule neighbour part she played in her Hornett film. Cyril Smith[12] was *Henry Hornett* - a role he'd made his own. Patricia Hayes was the spinster sister hen-pecked by *Emma* and younger actors included Ian MacNaughton, John Warner, Ian Curry, and Janet Butlin. During rehearsals in London for *Rock-A-Bye Sailor* Donald told his mother that they worked Renée so hard she was almost physically broken. He talks about the chopping and changing, and how director Dennis Main Wilson and the producer were at cross-purposes. Apparently, they attempted to mould Renée into a copy of Peggy Mount – the actress who made the play famous six years earlier. Frustrated and physically low, Miss H caught the flu from another member of the cast but kept going. *Rock-A-Bye Sailor* opened at the New in Oxford, then moved to London's Phoenix Theatre on October 16. Don told Mickey how the press said she was 'copying Peggy Mount' and nobody knew Renée had been directed this way. 'Enter another of those darned sailors,' slammed Bernard Levin, telling his readers he will be dead when the final installment occurs. Levin added, however, that little was to be said for the play except that 'the great Renée Houston' is in it.[13] At first Renée didn't fight about the direction, but two weeks in, she had had enough. She stormed into the manager's office and told them straight she was going to play it her way. Despite the early frost the real Renée Houston embodied the part. This action lifted herself and the whole play off the floor. Whilst business still wasn't great, it certainly improved. It's sad that something so logical as joining her husband in the West End came at a price, and by the end of the show she felt done for, her voice almost a rasp.

Rock-A-Bye Sailor,
Phoenix Theatre,
1962.

Left: Renée as
Emma Hornett
(Aherne Collection)

Centre:
Cover of Programme.

Right:
Photo by Vaslav
(Author's Collection)

Perhaps *The Private Eye and The Public Eye* by Peter Shaffer[14] opening at the Globe Theatre afforded a better alternative to *Rock-A-Bye Sailor* for the theatregoer. That December also brought a return of the fog - the worst most continuous one since 1952. They had five days with frost and ice to go with it. Renée got stranded an entire week at Elstree, living in her dressing room.

Thankfully, she had a divan and a private bath. She only had one dress though, and washed her undies every night, drying them on the hot towel rack. When she finally got back to Walton, she was going to throw away the dress but Donald talked her out of it. Astonishing her husband with a spot of Houston absurdity, Renée made sure that the day she returned to work, Donald should observe her attired in *the same bloody dress*! On December 9 1962 Donald too, had to stay over at the Strand Theatre[15] on the worst night of the fog. Dora Bryan was able to get home by tube, so she lent her dressing room to Don. He woke up the next morning to sound of parking vans and crates being unloaded in Covent Garden.

Pressure or conflict associated with *Rock-A-Bye Sailor* might have caused the 'embarrassing situation' in early October shortly before the play opened at the Phoenix. Renée was expected at a recording for *In Town Today*.[16] There might have been a good reason for the cancellation, but a letter from Pam Simons to the BBC's Light Entertainment Booking Manager refers politely to Renée's 'indisposition at Bournemouth' as a reason why the interview never took place. Pam asked if it could be arranged for a later date in London.[17] Donald's health was starting to fail too, and the destabilizing effect on Renée manifested itself in histrionic or argumentative behaviour – something more likely to be observed from this time onwards. At home the trees at the back of their garden witnessed her truest performance in which many tears were shed.

1963 began for Renée with location shooting for 'The Rescue Squad' in Ham in Surrey and other locations. The Children's Film Foundation commissioned the film. The CFF was a non-profit-making organization formed in 1951 and run from an office at 6-10 Great Portland Street. J Arthur Rank provided support like a kindly uncle in the early days. Its mission was to make films to be screened at Saturday morning matinees in cinemas and in schools. The giveaway price of the tickets meant sweeties were more than affordable and the cinemas were filled with regular young patrons, loving every minute. That a section of the industry was devoted to children's films and not purely obsessed by profits was a reminder of gentler times. Too bad it couldn't survive. It allowed child actors to get a taste for the industry. The CFF helped the early careers of Francesca Annis, Michael Crawford, Dennis Waterman, Susan George, Keith Chegwin, Phil Collins and many others.

Produced by Hindle Edgar and directed by Colin Bell, 'The Rescue Squad' had a cast of six children with four adults. Malcolm Knight, now secretary of the Concert Artists Association, was one of the young actors along with Christopher Brett,[18] Gareth Tandy,[19] Danny Grove, Lindy Leo and Shirley Joy. Among the children's colourful adventures, Malcolm remembers a scene where he ended up in the Thames on top of a runaway fire engine. In the screenplay, based on a story by Frank Wells, the children lose a toy plane in a high ruined tower, become stranded in their efforts to retrieve it, and enlist a donkey to assist them. Michael Balfour, well known for playing film baddies, was in the movie, and Renée's character was *Mrs Manse*. Looking back to when he was thirteen years old, Malcolm recalls Renée seeing one of two young girls biting her nails and telling her that if she continued, the bits of nail would turn into a large ball in her stomach. She also told someone off for calling another a 'berk', but she was really nice to all the youngsters.

After this, Renée began her new touring production of *Roar Like A Dove* - her third so far, but this time without Donald: a few dates in the spring and a season in the summer including one at the Devonshire Park theatre. She was travelling up to Liverpool on Sunday March 10, 1963. The train was taking the young rugby team who, at Twickenham the day before, had played for Lancashire against Yorkshire in the Northern Area Championships. One member of this well-behaved lot seated playing cards was Peter Harvey who stood out with his very bright red hair. Aged twenty-two Peter was to trial later that year for the England Rugby Union Team. Cliff Richard was also on the train and the young rugby players who were Cliff's age were anxious to say hello. The Beatles were not as much in the public eye as Cliff even though they had started making records. The young men made way for Cliff as he passed along the carriageway, politely excusing himself until he reached the far end where he was sitting. Cliff was on a UK tour between February and April, after which he would travel to the USA to appear on the *Ed Sullivan Show*. He walked past the young rugby players again and was greeted with more comment. Peter tells me they hoped he'd sit down for a card game so that they might win some money from him. Yet again Cliff excused himself and continued his journey to the refreshments carriage having left a mysterious lady he was travelling with. Peter walked down to the other end of the carriage to get a look at Cliff's friend and recognized her off the television. Renée knew his game, but sensed they had something in common. She asked him whereabouts in Scotland he came from.

Peter was born in Johnstone but had lived in Lancashire since he was a young lad. In fact his grandfather was born in Grahame Street, and Peter's father was a publican, so he and Renée had a lot in common. She asked him to sit in the seat vacated by Cliff that was still warm. She knew all the Johnstone streets and places he mentioned. She told him she was born in the same house as his mother in the town's central square[20] retelling the exact location of her birthplace. She chatted to Peter about her connection to the Glasgow Empire, and when he mentioned Jimmy Logan and Chic Murray, he was impressed she knew them all. Logan was her *wee nephew* – a phrase she also reserved for Cliff. It seemed like no time when the train pulled in at Liverpool, and before she parted company with Peter she'd given him her address in Walton and invited him to call 'anytime you are passing.'

Strangely enough, the Rugby Boy's Club - in Walmer Road W11 - was used for rehearsals between May 24 and June 5 for '*Scare*'– an episode of *Z Cars*, the popular series 'about police, not crime.' Writers used casebook material supplied by former CID superintendents and people from all ranks in the force. David E. Rose was still producer when it reached its 100th episode whilst fourteen scriptwriters and thirty directors[21] worked on *Z Cars*. One of these was Rudolph Cartier, who had directed Renée in *Liberty Bar*. He was impressed enough to put her behind the bar again, although this time she's *Rosie* – a sort of *Peggy Mitchell* and *Pat Butcher* three decades too early. The action is based at *Seaport*, not far from *Newtown*, the fictional town a few miles north of Liverpool where *Z Cars* is set. Location filming was actually at Docklands. After a ship docks, two seamen have gone ashore. When a suspected outbreak of smallpox on board becomes known, *PC Lynch* - James Ellis, and *PC Graham* - Colin Welland are alerted in case disease is spread by the seamen. *Z-Victor-one* and *Z-Victor-two* keep watch but the CID turns a blind eye to the goings on at *Rosie's Naughtycal Club* where *Rosie* is the most knowledgeable person in the area.

Stratford Johns and Renée Houston in *'Scare'* – an episode of *Z Cars* in 1963 (My thanks to Immediate Media)

In her scene in the club with Stratford Johns as *Detective Chief Superintendent Barlow,* she doesn't look quite as bad as her costume notes suggest: 'caricature on tarty barmaid . . . very décolleté. . . Lots of flashy jewellery . . .'[22] Brian Blessed - *Z Cars* regular, was not in this episode. The cast for *Scare* included Tenji Takaki who Renée worked with on 'A Town Like Alice'. The *Port Superintendent* was John Longden - Pat Aherne's colleague in silent films in the 1920s and Renée's director in 'Come Into My Parlour.' Thirty years ago seemed like nothing in 1963. A note about the dressing room requirements survives at the BBC Written Archives to tell us that for the studio recording, nine actors had their own dressing room. Superstitious as ever, Renée insisted on *Room 7*. Poor old John Longden shared his. His fee was only £74 11s but Renée commanded the second highest fee at £234 3s. The episode cost £5,004 inclusive of all salaries, costumes, and 35mm film unit - about £76,560 in today's terms.

Earlier in the year she had a tiny role alongside Sid James, Charlie Hawtrey and Kenneth Connor, in the Peter Rogers film 'Carry On Cabby' directed by Gerald Thomas. As *Molly* who runs the cab driver's café, she gives cabbies a glacial look as they come in for a hot cuppa. Sid James stayed in driver mode when he starred as *Sid Stone* in his own BBC TV series *Taxi*, produced by Michael Mills – Renée's friend from BBC variety broadcasts. On June 23 she was rehearsing *Taxi's* second episode at St Augustine's Church Hall in Fulham, before pre-recording it at Television Centre. In *Barricades in Bailey Street*, written by Ted Willis and directed by Robin Nash, she played *Gig Lambert* - an elderly lady about to be turned out of her furnished room by landlady *Mrs Evans* - Rachel Thomas. Thankfully *Mrs Lambert* is a friend of

Sid's. Hearing of her plight, he intervenes in his big-hearted and impulsive way. Bill Owen and Vera Day also starred and it was broadcast on Wednesday July 17. For the next four months Renée returned to the touring production of *Roar Like A Dove* playing Wimbledon Theatre on July 15, Golders Green Hippodrome on August 5, Brighton's Theatre Royal on August 12, and the De La Warr Bexhill-on-Sea on October 9.

Vera Day, the star of three films in which Renée Houston co-starred

(Author's Collection)

Before *Roar* stopped at Bexhill, there were two weeks when Renée took up an offer from New World Pictures for *The Wonderful War* – an episode of *The Saint*. Before coming into its own on television, *The Saint* had been very popular on the air in the USA. Brian Aherne and Vincent Price had played its lead back in the late 40s. This TV episode has *Simon Templar* helping wrest power away from a rebel government in '*Sayeda*'- and tense exchanges and gripping sword-fighting add to the suspense. If only a peaceful state of affairs in a Middle Eastern country could be achieved on the back of a hoax army attack with nothing more than loudspeakers to stand in for battle sound effects! In the trench Renée, aged sixty-two, loads ammunition. She's *Mrs McAlister* - a Kuwait-based eccentric. The name suits her better than 'Mrs Parry' - originally on the contract. She's surprisingly energetic in the scene where *Karim* - Louis Raynor, *Mike Kelly* - Noel Purcell, and *Lilla* - Suzanna Leigh are the four-strong army fighting a war. At the end *Lilla* mentions 'I'll get married if I can find a husband' looking at Simon, and a chic Renée has the last line with "Funny - I was just sitting here thinking the same thing myself" coyly eyeing Noel Purcell. It's a great episode, if only to see the scene with *Simon* - pretending to be *Mr Pierpoint Sykes* and dressed in an immaculate suit and dark glasses - taking a private helicopter to meet the rebels and clinch a fake deal: 'I was diabolically arrogant and got the concessions I wanted' *Simon* says. Four months after filming, the episode was broadcast on ITV. Sir Roger Moore remembers working with Miss Houston fondly, pointing out how she got on well with producer Robert S. Baker, and this is why she returned to play *Ida Warshed* in a further *Saint* episode - *The Gentle Ladies* - a very unusual thing for an actor, especially in the same season.[23]

The second *Saint* she did was filmed at the end of 1963. Set in the village of Bosham, Renée is one of the three *Warshed* sisters: with Barbara Mullen and Avice Landone: three pillars of the community - apparently. She is more her feisty self here. I was surprised, watching the episode, to see *Simon Templar* dishing out an independent *Robin Hood* style of justice. He's extremely tough on the sisters' sinister blackmailer *Alfred Powls* - Philip O'Flynn. While the women have all along covered up the fact that they once served time for a robbery, they nonetheless grew rich on the proceeds. Yet *Simon* believes they've done their debt to society and helps cover their tracks - even dirtying the shoes of *Powl's* corpse to make him appear as if he had been a burglar in their home – although a canny police inspector doesn't fall for this. It's a striking piece of casting having both Renée and Barbara Mullen - the actress familiar as *Janet,* housekeeper at *Arden House* in *Dr Finlay's Casebook.* Was this a deliberate twist on the characters of these so-called 'gentle' ladies of TV drama? Of Renée, Sir Roger adds 'She was great fun to work with - always professional and always knew her lines, despite the short schedules – undoubtedly endearing her to the Carry On producers too, as they didn't like hanging around.'[24]

'Do You Love Me?' by Brian Poole & The Tremeloes was in the Top 5, and if you had a television on Saturday September 28 you might gather around the box to see *That Was The Week That Was,* especially since the second series began that night. After the thundering success of the first series, it was scheduled to run until April 1964. Produced by Ned Sherrin, the show had a regular team of David Frost, Millicent Martin, Ken Cope, Lance Percival, Willie Rushton, David Kernan and Roy Kinnear. They pounced on the oddities and idiocies of the 'Week That Was', leaving it shredded on the studio floor. Many guest actors turned up in sketches in *TWTWTW* including American Irwin Watson and Robert Land, a young actor from the National Theatre Company. Renée received a contract to take part in one - rehearsed in Studio 2 at BBC Television Centre, and broadcast live on October 19 at 22.30. The jokes and dialogue might have alluded to peerages being renounced in order to qualify as Prime Minister in the House of Commons. This was the case then in Westminster for Alec Douglas Home who, after a scrap for succession with Lord Hailsham and Butler, replaced Harold Macmillan. He inherited the embarrassment of the Profumo affair – the sex scandal involving the War Secretary. When the scandal's main protagonists were in court, Wilson was quick to humiliate Home and this was a source for satire. Having said that anything was game for *TWTWTW's* laughsmiths. Housing was also a much talked about issue just then.

After rehearsals in another drill hall at the end of 1963 actors gathered at BBC's Riverside Studios for a recording on January 10 1964, creating the atmosphere of *Braeside - Tannochbrae's most select residential hotel for elderly gentlefolk*. When the episode reached its audience on January 26, this lavender-water and China-tea world was different to the one that viewers of *Dr Finlay's Casebook* were used to. Normally it was *Arden House*, scented by tobacco smoke, old leather and a hint of Scotch whisky: a masculine environment created by author AJ Cronin. Renée's episode was *My Late Dear Husband,* directed by Julia Smith, and scripted by Donald Bull. One of the producers was Andrew Osborn who she knew from *Maigret*. In this Cronin story, *Mrs Clegg* - Nan Marriott-Watson is the widow of a *Major* of the Inniskillin Light Cavalry. *Lydia* - an unmarried *Braeside* resident – played by Sonia Dresdel, is fair game for *Mrs Bright* – the colonial widow who lords it over her, treating her as an unpaid companion. Renée's *Mrs Bright* dominates *Braeside* society until Ballard Berkeley's *Colonel Cayley* – 'old but still unattached,' threatens to upset the social balance. Bill Simpson was *Dr Finlay*, and Andrew Cruickshank - *Dr Cameron*. Regular *Casebook* face Barbara Mullen would be the subject of *This is Your Life* in March the next year. She shared no scenes with Renée in the episode, although the two were good friends.

1964 was a watershed year for magazine advertising, at least if I base my research on copies of the TV Times. Before then feature articles noticeably outweigh advertising space on its pages. This year saw full-page adverts for *Sunblest* bread, *Players Bachelor* and *Players Tipped,* and *Rington's Tea* was regularly *'Something to sing about'*. Half-pages spread news about *Tackle Medicated Clear Gel*, *Stergene* to care for clothes, or *New Spangles 5 Fruit Flavor*. If the *Janet Frazer Shopping Guide* didn't seduce you Arthur Askey would turn up pushing the Littlewoods version. By the end of 1964 these pages were splashing into exciting lurid colour whilst television was still a black and white world. In February people were glued to their sets to watch the fight between Henry Cooper and Brian London for the British & British Empire Heavyweight championship. If they turned over they might have seen Renée in her TV commercial for *Flash Soap Powder*. She was certainly 'Cleaning up on commercials' as The Stage would say a few months later.

'We saw the first of her *'Flash'* adverts on TV last night so they haven't wasted much time starting. It's a good advert I think. Renée is *Mrs Mac the Daily*. I think you have the original of this advert series called *'Mrs G'*. The first time Renée's commercial was broadcast, judging from Donald's letter to Mrs FC Wintermute, quoted above, was on the freezing cold evening of Sunday January 13, 1963. Sadly no trace of the commercial has emerged in the archives of Proctor and Gamble, despite months and months of asking. This was first time ever the British public were exposed to the *squeegee mop*, so Renée's niece believes. How extraordinary that Renée could add 'domestic cleaning pioneer' to her list of accolades! Interestingly, she was moving the squeegee over a checquered floor without burlesque, playing the character without comic aside. Just a few memorable facial expressions managed to convey the *before* and *after* where the floor was concerned. The advertising company hired to make the *Flash* commercial for British television needed to cast one who would typify the no-nonsense British housewife. Scottish no nonsense was chosen, and would be again, when the *soap-sudded* mantle passed to Molly Weir to sell the same product a few years later.

There was pride in being the latest *soap powder lady* at her kitchen sink in those far off days, and I doubt that the same respect would have been commanded by Chanel No 5's latest face – not back in 1963. Renée did well financially from the advert, and says in her memoir that it left her in a position where she was able to pick and choose what television, plays and films she would do. Not only was it 'lovely steady money' but 'people recognize you and stop you in the street and talk to you.'[25] The queen of commercials turned up in Farnham to dazzle star struck fans when she opened 'The Royal Deer' - the pub Hal and Shirley had just taken over in a new career move for both of them. Miss H spent no time at the sink, and was still at the bar at closing time.

In the spring Renée worked with the future *Peggy Mitchell* – Dame Barbara Windsor, and Bernard Cribbens in a scene for 'Carry On Spying.' Renée Houston is only in the film for a few seconds and *Madame* is a very minor role. Nevertheless, she's a formidable presence, announcing the two new 'oriental slaves' for Eric Pohlmann's *Fat Man* to choose from in his harem. I wonder if it brought back memories of her own experience of being flesh for the Sultan in 1934's 'Lost In The Legion.' Dame Barbara remembers the day they filmed the scene. The young actress arrived on set and was surprised to see this *big* star, and whispered to 'the governor' Gerald Thomas 'My God. Look! – Is that - - -?' She knew about Renée's fame on the variety circuit, having grown up with family nights out every Friday either to the Hackney Empire or the Finsbury Park Empire. Barbara started in the business in a charity show and was in *Love from June* with June Whitfield – when only fourteen years old. Thankfully she was too short to get placed in the chorus. She found out that they included Renée in the tiny scene because she had done a couple of things for them already.

Thomas and Rogers liked Renée, and felt a bit sorry for her. While the Carry On lot could be a hard lot, Gerald could be nice when he wanted to be, Barbara tells me. There was this respect for older actors that meant that little parts were made available to them. Things aren't so respectful nowadays, although a bit of this survives. Renée made an entrance in the film and was allowed a part that let her glam up – a sophisticated *Madame* with lacquered hair and jewels. She was someone who could make people aware of her star stature, and was known for having a bit of a temper, but she was very approachable to everyone on the set. Barbara admired her.

Don Ross, then chairman of the British Music Hall Society, Vice-President of the VABF and Water Rats member, presented *An Evening of Old Time*

Music Hall at theatres in Scotland between late March and the end of April 1964 'bringing back the glamour of *not* so long ago' and featuring talents like trumpeter Nat Gonella, Dave Willis, Peter Sinclair and Henry Vaddon. Renée joined the line up for a week at the end of April, appearing at the historic King's Theatre on Leven Street, Edinburgh. Garbed for her scenes in a sugar pink evening gown, then in a little girl outfit, a critic commented how much personality and 'lovable vulgarity' she gave out, while The Stage featured a photo of the 'unabashed veteran' wearing her tartan hat and cape.

Above: King's Theatre, Edinburgh
(Author's Collection)

Left: Renée Houston in
An Evening of Old Time Music Hall
(Photo: The Stage)

Renée was such a pro she could apply herself effortlessly whether it was radio, TV or film and still meet the obligations of a busy schedule, as her timetable over the last couple of years proved. This, however, was the kind of theatre she understood best – a familiar 'family' of performers with sustaining applause. Some of the old faces would also pop up at pubs near where she and Donald lived. George Western, of the Western brothers, still kept busy running a little tobacco kiosk at Weybridge Railway Station until 1969. His brother had died. I like to think of Renée stopping at the kiosk to share a little patter. For those waiting in the queue, impatient to buy a packet of fags, the past glories of these two humble oldsters was as forgotten as the old stone pillar on Weybridge Green[26] - the original of Seven Dials - 'the burial place of the fashions'.

And when the evergreen has withered on the bough. I still shall feel the same as I do now. That was a line Donald sang – one that warmed people's hearts during the years when time was an eternity for *Variety's Sweethearts*. During Renée's absences, even though they were short, Donald's health seemed to fail. Miss Houston tried her best to show resolve and her usual first response was to ask: what can money buy? The answer was the highest quality of nursing care for her husband - at a comfortable care home: an Edwardian house surrounded by beautiful gardens in Midhurst, Surrey. Don had contracted the dreaded TB and needed careful supervision. Renée visited as often as possible. The home, with a room for her to stay overnight, felt like a hotel with its sociable atmosphere. A lovely friend they made there was Agnes Mary, Countess of Winchilsea and Nottingham. By autumn, Donald began to gain weight and she was able to take him home. She had rearranged the flat with him in mind, and was determined to stay as positive as she could. Everything was planned with his comfort in mind. Even the staff at Walton Station could be relied on to give the popular couple a 'royal welcome' as they stepped off the train.

Renée said yes to an offer from Jimmy Logan to appear in a play in Glasgow in the coming year and soon the bells of St John's Kirk rang in the New Year, and we watched dancing in the streets of Perth on BBC TV. Producer Iain MacFadyen was a guiding force in Light Entertainment at BBC Scotland. His baptism of fire was when he picked up from producer Harry Gordon who had a heart attack just half an hour before a live broadcast. That was in the 40s when Renée and Nicky Kidd were among the artists.[27] MacFadyen was the mastermind behind *Hogmanay* – the show that saw Andy Stewart go first footing in the fair city assisted by Duncan Macrae with Chic Murray and Jimmy Logan. Jimmy Shand played accordion. The other Scottish TV channel - Channel 10 or STV - less than seven years old and owned by Lord Thomson, regularly brought traditional Scottish music and dance to its viewers in *Jigtime*. In its daytime show *The One O'Clock Gang*, Larry Marshall, Charlie Sim and Dorothy Paul entertained with parodies like *'This is Who's Life?'* or sent lollipops to children in hospitals all over Scotland. When the folk of Scotland and England switched on their KB 'Featherlight' Transistor TVs for light entertainment, the ITV network franchises never failed to deliver. It was a cheaper alternative to variety theatre and films. In England the Rank Organization and Associated British had downsized their operations. Hundreds of those familiar Odeon and ABC cinemas were closing across the land with cinema attendance falling. People talked of how the television age took away the pleasures of the past - in a similar way to fears people have about today's cyber age.

If you weren't caught up in the craze for all things *Coronation Street*, desperate to read Pat Phoenix's latest 'Tanner's Worth' column in the TV Times, or if you weren't following love stories of the day - like that of Millie Martin and husband Ronnie Carroll - then you might be a more artistic sort or one professing to be against the establishment. I doubt Renée ever went to London's Ad Lib club or if its hip young patrons knew who she was in 1964, even though she had once been thought of as undisputed *mistress of the ad lib*. Among the many stylish young men gathered here in mod suits was Roman Polanski, a young director recently dispatched from Paris to London where he stayed in Eaton Place. He had many friends including Douglas Hayward - the showbiz tailor and there was support from well-connected people like Gene Gutowski - a Polish-born producer, and Victor Lownes - known for his Playboy interests. Attitudes were changing among the cognoscenti about what was creative and how far to take realism in drama. London seemed to be the epicentre of some kind of new movement.

Abandoning old ideas and taking a chance with something hip was suddenly possible in England's capital.

Just a ten minute walk from the Ad lib was the Gargoyle Club - a living Soho fossil that had hardened as it witnessed the changes in London's social life over the decades, undergoing many *Dr Who* transformations. Synonymous with Renée Houston's London career, if a club can be so, the Gargoyle burst onto the scene in 1925, although the building is much older. Then it was a kind of Ad Lib Club in the Jazz Age albeit narrower in the society of its clientele. It was taken over in 1955 by impresario Michael Klinger and combined cabaret with an upmarket strip club on the upper floor. Klinger, originally from the East End, and his colleague Tony Tenser controlled the Cameo Poly in Regent Street - once the London Polytechnic where Britain's first kinematograph had been based in 1896. Now it was an independent cinema showing Scandinavian nude flicks. The Compton Group, run by Tenser and Klinger, provided Roman Polanski with the cash to make his films 'Repulsion' and 'Cul-de-Sac'.

The Group wanted to move from sleaze into horror, although 'Repulsion', Polanski's second film, is more than this. He teamed up with Gérard Brach, whom he'd met in Paris in the early 60s, to create a screenplay for a film about neurosis: one that would 'speak particularly to women,' incorporating 'all kinds of things new to him' as a foreigner in London for the first time such as the 'light switches and the buskers.'[28] Catherine Deneuve's character, *Carole*, was based on a young woman Polanski and Brach had known in Paris. With surreal imagery achieved through latex and tactile materials, the film parallels her disturbed mind and path to disintegration. Gil Taylor's cinematography, utilizing reflected light that bounced off the walls, aided the sense of doom. His experience in photography dated back to his time with the Pathfinders during wartime raids on Germany. He had recently worked on 'A Hard Day's Night.' Compton's gamble was a success and 'Repulsion' won the Golden Bear for Best Film at Berlin's Film Festival.

I've read that Polanski used Spotlight for casting but Renée missed inclusion in Spotlight for 1962, 63 and 64 so I think it likely that her TV commercial for Flash or one of her old films might have sold her on this occasion. As chance would have it, Miss Houston was available to play *Miss Balch*, the regular customer at 'Repulsion's beauty salon - ever confident she'll have an audience as she dispenses views on topics such as 'There's only one way to deal with men . . . That's treat them as if you don't give a damn about them.' She does this whilst the silent and passive manicurists sit on little stools by her side. The camera angles are extraordinary in the scene, either making *Carole* look small and fragile or being directed unflatteringly towards *Miss Balch's* mouth so we might fall into this orifice as she speaks her mind. Renée fitted the image Polanski had for his old lady. He started his creative process making drawings of all the characters as he imagined them, and not only was Renée symbolic of the traditional British no-nonsense character that would contrast so well with his enigmatic continental types,

Playing Mature

some kind of extremity came forth in her attitude. Whatever it was, it was unique.

She represented the old ways: a feisty spirit that is untroubled, unlike the young generation. The director distances the central characters. They occupy a world devoid of the cathartic power of laughter. Polanski presents Renée's spirit to the audience but doesn't allow her to connect. He shows one side of her spirit leaving the other side closed so she's as unknowable to his other characters as they were to her. The tiny manicurists possess no 'wartime recalcitrance' or power to burlesque and *Miss Balch* is a lone voice.

The film was completed over time and above budget and released in June 1965. 'Repulsion' is a masterpiece, even if Polanski would describe 'Cul-de-Sac' as his best film from a cinematic point of view.[29] I believe 'Repulsion' is a sum of many parts and the Houston rant is valuable even though people analyzing the film barely have time to consider this. It affords balancing humour, albeit in a vacuum. Renée's energy creeps in. It gives me a chance to escape *Carole*'s dark psychological tunnel and feel less lonely in my identification.

If radio was all you had in your home you might look ahead at what the Home Service had in store for you on Wednesday January 6, 1965. There's something called *I Remember:* with Loelia Duchess of Westminster looking back to the 20s and her marriage to a capricious wealthy man. *Round Britain Quiz*, the *Stock Market Report*, John Ogdon playing Beethoven, *Abusers and Abused* (about under pressure GPs driven out of the service) are other slots listed in the Radio Times. *Norman And Henry Bones* catered for the kiddies with Patricia Hayes voicing one of the boy detectives. Then there was *Listen With Mother*, *The Archers* and *Petticoat Line*: the first episode where 'listeners letters are answered and points of difference aired' with Renée Houston, Marjorie Proops, Jill Adams and Jane Asher, and with Anona Winn in the chair. Who knew then if this might be a programme with staying power? Renée made a TV appearance on the panel show *Late Night Line Up* on the evening of January 5 to publicize the new radio show, and Pam Simons wrote to David Dore, Assistant Light Entertainment Booking Manager, sending a signed contract from Renée for further episodes of *Petticoat Line,* telling him about her theatrical commitments, but that she would be happy to fit in as many of these appearances as she could. She managed to fit in thirteen consecutives weeks' work for the first series transmit between January and March 31.

She made a weekend trip up to Scotland to meet with Jimmy Logan and others for a forthcoming play, and did a short interview with Howard Lockhart for *Today In Scotland,* but was back in London that evening to appear in *The Marriage Brokers* - a comedy adapted from Gogol's 'Marriage,' and staged at the Mermaid Theatre throughout February 1965. For each *Petticoat Line* listing that month, the Radio Times makes mention of the play.

The first dream of actor Bernard Miles and his wife Josephine Wilson was to create a theatre of their own. It came true when they turned their back garden in St John's Wood into an Elizabethan Theatre and had Kirsten Flagstad sing *Dido* in twenty-six performances. That was in 1951. In 1959 they built The Mermaid - the first new theatre to open in the City of London since the 17th century. Located at Puddle Dock on the banks of the Thames, it breathed creative life into a bombed out and distinctly low-rise district. Miles would become Baron Miles of Blackfriars, only the second actor to be given a peerage back then but he would sadly die almost destitute in 1991.

For the Gogol play Gerald Frow produced an elaborate programme, with charming silhouettes of the cast including Renée's character *Fyokla Ivanovna* - 'gorgon matchmaker' - as one critic described her part. Richard Moore, later a star of *Emmerdale* had the part of *Pjotr* – a drunken coachman. Set in the Russia of the early 19th Century the play was about the wooing of a Russian rosebud - *Natasha Techonovna*[30] by three suitors: a painfully modest middle-aged civil servant, a de-lousing expert and a retired naval officer.

Robert Eddison as the government official stole the show according to The Spectator for a 'performance straight out of English Restoration Comedy' if you could only decide 'it is farce or comedy.'[31] The actor Robert Gillespie, who came to see *The Marriage Brokers* tells me it was directed by Julius Gellner who had just directed the most mind-numbing *Macbeth* in the universe, which Robert had the misfortune of being cast in. Whether Gellner fared better with this is hard to tell, although Herbert Kretzmer found the play 'an evening of unalloyed pleasure.' Perhaps the production needed to be redeemed in parts. Renée did just that and Plays and Players commended the actress for being 'a tower of strength' which must have pleased her.

Renée's pal Michael Balfour was in the play and John Moffat, who played *Ilya Fomitsh Kotchkaryov* – the Russian man-about-town, also got great notices. A great lover of music hall, Moffat found an instant friend in Miss H. The other actors were Bernard's daughter Sally - married to Gerald Frow, Sylvia Coleridge and Colin Ellis.

Renée (seen to the far right) in *The Marriage Brokers* (with Colin Ellis, Michael Balfour, Robert Eddison, Catherine Feller and Sylvia Coleridge.)

(By kind permission of trustee of former Brevet Publishing Ltd.)

Renée's dressing room at the Mermaid overlooked the Thames, shining light from the moody river that mild February. She would remove her blue-quilted dressing gown, step into a voluminous yellow plaid skirt, and put on a scarlet frogged tunic top. Then a big flowery hat went over her wig completing the ensemble as the weighty Russian. Pinned to the dressing room shelf were photos of her garden in Oatlands that her Donald made so beautiful and actual cut flowers filled the room creating a blaze of colour. Every night, as she rushed through the barrier for the last train from Waterloo, the same ticket collector made sure she got on ok, and always asked her how the show had gone that evening.

Beneath The Wee Red Lums opened on March 15, 1965 at the Citizens Theatre in Main Street, Gorbals. The former Royal Princess Theatre had gained a new lease of life in 1943 when James Bridie and others formed a new company. Jimmy Logan was producing the play here, along with Eddie Fraser, who had requested Renée for *Jimmy Logan's TV show* in 1955. It was soon touring many of the Scottish theatres including visits to The New Metropole theatre at St George's Cross – a landmark site Logan had bought the year before for £80,000. Buying an old theatre was a brave risk only a true prince of the theatrical world would take. For ten years he was faced with mounting costs for its upkeep and had run-ins with the local authorities. The New Metropole burned to the ground in 1974 and in 1979 Logan was forced to sell the site at a much-reduced price.

Beneath The Wee Red Lums by TM Watson was written in 1945 and set before the Second World War. It was a blend of high comedy and family sentiment, centering 'on that fertile source of gloomy mirth we so much savour - the undertaker.'[32] While thought 'flat' in terms of comedy it nevertheless had a lot of jokes taken out of Scottish life and character.[33] The production, designed by Sheila Ward, had two parts entitled *Man Proposes* and *Woman Disposes* – each with three scenes. The action opens in the living room of the two old bachelors, *Archie* and *Hector McLean* played by Alec Finlay and James Gibson, who live with their nephews. *Archie* considers these youngsters' romances: one in love with a servant, and the other with a young lady whose daddy has pots of money. He's going to pull strings in parochial and matrimonial affairs, guiding things to a happy understanding – elements that echo the Gogol play.

The living room's visitors include *Mrs Forrest* – the *McLeans'* neighbour, and her sprightly but rather lonely cook *Maggie Buchanan* - Molly Weir. Renée was *Martha McTaggart* - the nippy tongued housekeeper to the *McLeans*, presiding over her dominion as her subjects gather round the table. She reserves the sharp edge of her tongue for *Archie*. Stuart Henry and Bill Henderson played the nephews. John Grieve - a *Bridie Gold Medal* winner - was the deadpan undertaker *Gilbert Dagleish* who is cursed in love.

Reviewers concluded that Grieve stole the play. The funniest moments came when *Dagleish* conceives a passion for *Martha* whilst pursued by *Maggie*. There was praise for Miss Houston's 'unwavering attack' and critics loved her 'unique voice - dare I call it a trombone ... how it revelled in the broad Scots of her native Glasgow!'[34] Yet again Renée received praise for her rich audibility. By June *Red Lums* was described by one critic as probably having taken the stages of more church halls in Scotland by storm than any other play[35] and on Sunday May 23, a live performance from the New Metropole was televised for *Jimmy Logan Theatre Hour* on STV.[36] During its eleven-week season it played the Lyceum, Edinburgh and toured England, getting as far south as Worthing.

Ann Raitt has written a number of screenplays and novels in recent years. She was in the early Mike Leigh film 'Bleak Moments' (1971). She played *Sybil Conway*, the rich girl in *Beneath The Wee Red Lums*. Ann told me this was one of her first acting jobs after college and what stood out in her memory was standing beside Renée in the wings and how the older actress frequently coughed loud before she was ready going on. Was it a nervous thing, or maybe to clear her throat before going on stage? 'Whatever it was,' Ann recalls, 'I seem to remember it annoyed Molly Weir, who was on stage at the time with John Grieve. I remember Renée as a forceful personality, and being very in awe of her. She seemed completely in control of an audience and I was always amazed at the difference between this plump grey haired lady in the wings, and her extraordinary performance on stage.'

Scene from *Beneath The Wee Red Lums:* Left to right: Alec Finlay Renée John Grieve, Molly Weir
(My thanks to Gordon Irving)

Molly Weir was eight years younger than Renée and the two had ground in common. Molly was raised in her grandmother's house in the tenements of Springburn in Glasgow – where the streets around Huntingdon Square provided a playground in this railway suburb.[37] A star on the radio after her impersonations of Gracie and Marlene Dietrich went down a treat on the *Carroll Levis Show*, she hit the West End in 1945 in *The Happiest Days of Your Life*. Afterwards, she joined Tommy Handley in a series in which her *Tattie McIntosh* character amused millions of radio listeners. When Handley died, she switched to *Life With The Lyons*.

Petticoat Line, for Wednesday March 3 that year, required Molly to stand in for Renée - her only appearance on the show. Did Renée's fear of competition from the sprightly Molly account for that? While not enemies they weren't friends either. When Renée was passed up by Flash, letting Molly clean up on commercials in the 70s in an even bigger way, and in colour, Miss Houston saw red.

Whilst in Scotland, Renée shopped for presents for her husband and caught up with Jim and Claire. She chatted on the radio on *Home This Afternoon* that April about her long and varied career, and Howard Lockhart must have asked about her brother's autobiographical book 'Past Horizons' published in 1962 that recalled the Houston kids' childhood in Shettleston.[38] Renée recorded more material with Howard during May, and was also asked to submit scripted material to producer Shirley du Boulay on the topic of being a *host* or a *guest*, and on the particular warmth of Scottish hospitality for use in *Woman's Hour* on May 12. Renée was so often on the move. Trains had taken her everywhere throughout her life and never could she escape them. She loved to come home to Donald. Inside the bold hard Houston cocoon he always found that little girl - that 'emotional butterfly'.

She had her weekly visit to the Playhouse Theatre for *Petticoat Line:* its second series starting in October. Autumn turned out to be a fairly relaxed time. Pat Aherne had returned to England, dismayed to find that so many of the old ways he had known in his youth hadn't been preserved. Twenty years before, when he was settling into his new life, he would write home to say how rude and obnoxious he found the people of the United States to be. Returning to Britain it was the people here who were rude and obnoxious. Both 'Brothers Aherne' were on hand for reunions - happy ones - with the two siblings friends again. There had also been very little bitterness between Don and Pat over what had happened in the past, and he greeted Donald like a long-lost brother. Pat stayed with Renée and Don in Weybridge. The only person he did not see, and most wanted to, was Tony.

In June 1965 Brian Aherne was back on the London stage in *The Chinese Prime Minister*[39] and his passing drolleries were as memorable as ever. 'Poor man, having a father who couldn't spell,' sighed the Hollywood actor, having suavely seen dinner guests Roald Dahl and his wife into their taxi following a dinner party at Warwick Avenue. Brian had a fondness for absurdities, perhaps an influence that came by way of *Mrs Brown* - his wife's best friend - otherwise known as Garbo. At a literary event, someone prompted David Aherne to ask his uncle if he liked Kipling.' 'I've never kippled,' quickly came the answer from a deadpan Brian. Alan says that it was the financially savvy Brian who made sure Renée was nominated for the King George's Fund upon her widowhood, although there are no records that prove that Brian initiated this. Set up by King George V in 1911, the fund gives annuities to older British actors and actresses who have rendered such service to the profession to merit recognition, and are in a position to need assistance. From January 1967, Renée enjoyed a small degree of security for the first time in her life. Having been made a fund recipient, she continued to receive it until her death in 1980.

Chapter 24   It's Over Let It Go

> *I thoroughly resent the type of men (or women for that matter) who think that because you are in the theatre world that you'll listen to any dirty story.*[1]

Towards the end of 1965 Renée had a bit part in a film written and directed by Arnold Louis Miller, famous for his earlier comic book enterprise. It was made for distribution on the Compton-Cameo Film circuit and was a story of two girls on the 'up,' surmounting problems and finding their relationship marred by rivalry half way up the ladder of fame. If you combine 'Emmanuelle' and *Z-Cars*, with a touch of 'The Prime of Miss Jean Brodie' thrown in – you might find something akin to 'Secrets of a Windmill Girl,' which even has an echo of the plot of 'Happy Days Are Here Again' from decades earlier when the Houston Sisters were *Kitty* and *Mickie Grayson*, albeit with a different ending. Of course, a lot more flesh was on the cinema screen now. The two girls in 'Secrets' are *Linda Gray* played by April Wilding, and *Pat Lord* played by Pauline Collins. When the film opens, we see a young man and his girlfriend leave a party driving off drunkenly in a sports car. There's a crash and the police led by *Inspector Thomas* - Derek Bond, visit *Linda* to get her to identify the body. The story of the film is told in flashback.

Linda and *Pat* were opposite personalities at school: *Pat* tells lies, flaunts her body, seeks fame, and gets them fired from their safe jobs in a suburban shoe shop. A quick audition is all it takes for them to become Windmill girls, and backstage we meet *Molly* their dresser – played by Renée. For *Pat*, success quickly goes to her head and it's a downhill path via a sugar daddy and a few bad types. *Linda* conscientiously improves her singing and falls in love. The two girls part company and *Linda* goes on to cabaret fame whilst *Pat* goes from strip to stag parties, drinking heavily and dying after a wild party. The press book for the film might be designed like a girlie mag but it's a feminine storyline and *Pat's* character is complex and layered – the girlfriend we admire but fear to emulate. Pauline Collins told me that she and Renée worked together for only a few days but she recalls 'a lovely, warm person with a massive career to her name. She was one of the kindest and funniest people I've ever worked with.' This was Pauline's very first film and she tells me they had a ball making it. She was thrilled to bits to get the part and enjoyed every second of it. 'The same may not be said for the critics,' says Pauline modestly, 'but for me it was magic.' Renée looks visibly frail in photographic material I have found for 'Secrets.'

She had started turning down offers of work, fearing she might be neglecting her husband. She also feared a future that couldn't guarantee the presence of familiar people most dear. Donald had been made to wait so long before they married and had been denied a proper family life all the time she had been the 'married woman' with a professional stage partner. Could she make up for it? But Don was the one persuading her to return to work. A two-week holiday that August would do her good, he told her.

It's Over Let It Go

Holy Island - separated from the Northumbrian coast by a causeway that becomes flooded at certain times of the day, was where she reluctantly headed. You have to check the times of the tide. Cars have been washed away as far as Norway I was told, when I went there thirty-four years after Renée. A lone traveller, I was warmed by Island's friendliness. I found the drinkers of the *Crown and Anchor* – the only pub on the island, a welcoming lot.

In 1965 the island actually had four pubs and Renée drank at *The Iron Rails*: her fellow drinkers and insomniacs including Lionel Stander and Donald Pleasance. The actors and crew relaxed knowing there wasn't a single policeman to enforce licensing laws. Renée was there for Roman Polanski, to shoot another obscure film, not exactly to her taste. He made her feel special greeting her with cries that she was too pretty to do the part, calling her 'My darling,' and requesting she allow him to 'un-pretty' her. She trusted this director whom she described as 'kindness itself.' Renée's makeup had to look exactly right and Roman would apply the same dedication to styling when he did Faye Dunaway's visage in 'Chinatown.' Expensively dressed in a large straw hat and polka scarf, Renée's head and shoulders fill the image of the screen and with her mouth almost central, speaking lines of authority. While very brief, Renée's presence in 'Cul-de-Sac' is significant, because she represents authority departing, allowing chaos to reign in its stead. Renée must have been terrified speeding off on the boat when we see her leaving the island.

Richard, the gruff intruder played by Stander, rummages for something to eat and drink in the strange place he's landed: the domain of sand, seagulls and hens all the while crying and clucking. Hearing voices, he observes what is happening through a slat in a wooden fence. A young husband and wife living on the island have received a visit from an older woman and man and all walk towards the castle rampart with the young husband carrying a kite. There is a personality leap from the old woman Polanski used in the manicure scene in 'Repulsion' to this matriarch speaking lines of reservation: 'No, I'd rather get home before it gets too dark.' She calls to her son, *Christopher,* in upper class tones: 'Oh! There you are darling – do come down. We're leaving now.' *Christopher* rejoins his parents, fresh from cavorting in the dunes with the island's amoral and domineering young wife. The way Renée is photographed - looking upwards – is unusual, and we seem to be looking up at her like children. Even *Richard* seems to cower behind the slat in the wooden fence. Polanski made 'Repulsion' in order to have the opportunity to do 'Cul-de-Sac' which went even further into the bounds of experiment, and has been compared to Beckett's *Waiting for Godot*, with its contrast of wise-cracking American and Europeans epitomizing human decay.

She amused the young director who would say: 'You naughty girl Renée. You no look at your script, eh? Bad girl.' It's funny that she still adlibbed her limited dialogue. She awoke in the early mornings, sad for Françoise

Dorléac's whining little Chihuahua - smuggled into the French actress's handbag to contravene quarantine regulations. Before the day's call Miss Houston wandered about the island in contemplation, passing the old priory and saying St Patrick's Prayer to shield her within and without, and give protection to those she loved. Polanski said in an interview that 'at the end of the shoot no-one could stand each other,'[2] although I expect he got what he wanted from them in his diplomatic way. Actors like John Fraser have remarked how Polanski is one of the best directors for actors.[3] Renée had completed her scenes and left before the bad atmosphere: her experience mostly a combination of pub and prayer. When I first saw the film what struck me was the strange prescient look on her face as she looks into the sky before she leaves Holy Island. Polanski's imagery, and the music by Krzysztof Komeda are distinctly memorable.

However bright and breezy she might appear when her day began, it wasn't uncommon for her to seem distracted and unsteady as the day wore on – especially when rehearsing a new television drama. Renée received a contract to appear in Romains's *Dr Knock*. Unlike the TV play she made for schools in 1961, this was a ninety-minute episode of *Theatre 625*[4] - a high quality offering for a Sunday night audience.[5] Producer and director - Austrian-born Herbert Wise - was pressured by tight deadlines. The BBC had made it clear that production to broadcast turnaround had to be as short as possible. Seven weeks was the shortest timeframe manageable.[6] Wise didn't turn out to be quite as good a sport as Polanski. Renée reprised her *Madame Remy*, John Le Mesurier played *Dr Parpalaid* and Patrick Godfrey, Graham Armitage and Mavis Villiers peopled the rustic setting. Robert Gillespie was cast as *Monsieur Mousquet*. He started his career at the Old Vic and had directed a production of *Henry V* the previous year at the Queen's Theatre, Hornchurch. Robert gave me his account of working on *Dr Knock,* recalling Herbert as a 'coarse, *on the nose* sort of director . . . why I never watched more than one episode of *I Claudius* – couldn't stand the Romans shouting.'[7] Robert mused as to the director's choices: 'How could Herbert sack the brilliant Cyril Cusack - originally cast as the menacing physician - for being too subtle?' Cusack's removal allowed the superb caricaturist Leonard Rossiter to play *Knock.*

Renée's contract mentions seven rehearsal dates in late November, at the Cooperative Hall on Tooting Road although Robert talked of rehearsing it off the A40, where the Acton Hilton was later built. Renée's alcoholic tendencies weren't a secret at the BBC by then, and she was known to end a day of rehearsals rather worse for drink if left to her own devices. Herbert, according to Robert, had 'done his research, and taken the risk . . . determined his investment in Renée wouldn't be shot to pieces: first, by talking to her and extracting a solemn avowal that her drinking was under control.' She would happily 'join Herbert and designated staff for an alcohol free lunch every day till the show was in the can,' whilst others typically spent lunchtime at the pub. *Dr Knock's* drinkers numbered quite a few so afternoon rehearsals sometimes got fuzzy, stopping by 4.30pm. Quite early on Herbert saw Robert as a confidant, for reasons unknown to him. Despite extracting the avowal, Herbert's suspicions grew, and soon he would interrogate Robert daily. Had he too smelt her breath? Snatches of conversation regarding Miss Houston come from Robert's account:

Herbert: I've taken a chance, you know, casting Renée Houston. She's such a delicious, juicy performer, with an amazing past career. Shame she doesn't work so much now – but...

Robert: But what?

Herbert: Drink. Have you noticed anything...? Renée seems... seems to be a bit all over the place, inclined to lose her words as the day goes on.

Robert: Now you mention it, yes. She does seem to get a bit vague as the day wears on – perhaps she's tired.

Herbert: I don't understand it. Either me, or a staff member is with her every hour at rehearsal. She arrives perfectly sober in the morning in a BBC car. This woman comes in every day perfectly sober in the morning, and then I watch her getting slightly, steadily, more and more pickled and unsteady, and slurry as the day goes on, and she hasn't been near a drop of anything but tea and water![8]

Herbert, who sounds like he would sooner strain at a gnat and swallow camels than give up a crusade, became ever more prickly with Renée, and soon the inevitable accusation and row happened. Nobody ever saw Renée having a tipple. So what was he basing his evidence on? One day he had sneaked a look at something glinting in her handbag. Getting the floor assistant to take her aside as a distraction, he unsnapped her bag to find a flask tucked in there. Confronting Renée resulted in denial, tears, then a solemn *cross my heart and hope to die* promise from her. She wouldn't touch any stuff till the recording was done. After this, *Dr Knock* continued to plan. Robert felt he had learned something about drinkers and their cunning after Herbert explained:

Herbert: Know how she did it? Every time she went to the loo – we couldn't follow her in there, of course. It hadn't crossed my mind to send a girl in there with her every time she went. Renée was taking out her flask and gulping down a swift slug and getting steadily pie-eyed through my rehearsals.[9]

Cunning alcoholic she was, but she was also under enormous strain regarding matters personal, given Donald's precarious health. In her BBC contract she had agreed in advance with Herbert that she be released on two consecutive Tuesdays during rehearsals for three-hour periods, and these might easily have been visits to London clinics. That December came very happy news from California with the birth of Alan's first child. At New Year, Donald made phone calls home to Mickey and the family. Something told him he might not get another chance. And echoing the spirit of Jimmie Houston, Donald would tell his wife to carry on ... keep working ... don't stop.

Having completed Series Two of *Petticoat Line* in early January 1966, a contract arrived from ATV for *The Dear Ones* – an episode of *Knock On Any Door* produced by Peter Rogers at Elstree and directed by Cecil Petty. The stories, written by Ted Willis were based on the premise that there is story behind every door. Renée played *Marion* - a woman who moved from the Glasgow house she had lived in for forty years to *Greenlands*, an old people's home. She moved to make more room and stop being a 'burden' on her married daughter and son-in-law. In the home, encouraged by her friend *Annie* – Agnes Lauchlan, *Marion* forms an attachment to *Peter* - John Laurie. News of *Marion*'s engagement brings her elder daughter, magazine editor *Sarah* – played by Brenda Bruce, hurrying from London to gauge *Peter*'s intentions.[10] Speaking to Sarah Snow in The TV Times, Renée explained that '*Marion* is just an honest genuine little Scotswoman. They don't make any show of affection, the Scots. But they're still terribly sentimental and emotional, especially the Glasgow women.'[11] She told Sarah how warm-hearted Glasgow people are. Whilst filming *The Dear Ones* – Donald went to hospital and it was a struggle remembering lines, worrying all the while about him. Cecil Petty lost his temper at her. On the set at Elstree she met the actor Patrick Wymark, who had played the *landlord* in 'Repulsion,' and told him how they admired him in *The Power Game*, her husband's favourite TV programme. She managed a small walk on in another ITV play called *The First Thunder*, about a young idealist fighting for his fellow farm workers on Dartmoor in the late 19th century.

Donald died on a Tuesday - on March 1 - in St Peter's Hospital Chertsey. Fifty-five was such a young age to go. He had put up a brave fight against cancer, as he had with those wounds he'd received from wartime explosions. Patrick Wymark was a supportive friend to Renée, reading the lesson at Donald's memorial service held at St Andrew's Presbyterian Church in Walton-on-Thames. Donald, who had joined the church two years before, was praised for his judgments and his hate for bigotry and intolerance, in the Memoriam published in the church's newsletter that month. It says of his marriage: 'A love like theirs is a health-giving force in a society where standards are regrettably low at times.' When Donald used to say to his nephews that he was a Pennsylvanian Dutch Presbyterian, that had brought titters, but they couldn't control their tears now. In March 1966, Anton Wills-Eve was working in Paris and was told he was about to be posted far afield by his company. 'I'm not coming,' Anton told them. 'My uncle's funeral is taking place and I have to fly to London.'

Outside this immense church hall with a pitched roof was a young tree, its pure white buds rejoicing in new life. Inside, Sid James, the friend who had worked alongside Don and Renée several times, read the eulogy. Donald's funeral was very well attended with many acting celebrities. The mourners included Jews and Indians. Donald had made friends with many from

It's Over Let It Go

different walks of life. People dreaded the appearance of Mrs Wintermute. She was like a submerged nun and it didn't suit her. Everyone was used to her being brash and buoyant. Seemingly removed from the other mourners she didn't attend the gathering held after the service. Some resented her for this, saying she was jealous of the attention Donald was receiving.

In his hometown of Wilkes-Barre, the local paper, The Times Leader, refers to his being made an honorary citizen of his adopted country.[12] Only Wolverhampton's Express and Star had space to carry a photo of him – a handsome one too. A man whose energy lifted people's spirits with his sunny outlook and dazzled them with the talent he possessed, Donald never feared the future: that coming era of operating systems and programs, of trends in music and fashion that would polarize opinions, and an America in the midst of civil rights tensions. As Harold Wilson waited to go to the country in another general election that March, people anticipated the next shake up, while *Syd and Eddie* and Billy Dainty were among the bright new variety stars.

The rehearsals for another Ted Willis story - *Death of a Donkeyman* - an episode of *Dixon Of Dock Green*, required Renée's services less than ten days after Donald's funeral. *Sergeant George Dixon* - Jack Warner – authorizes that the CID interrogate the crew of a cable repair ship moored in the Pool of London overnight. The donkey man or 'greaser' responsible for the ship's engine is missing, and traces of his blood have been found in the locker. Everyone has a reason to dislike or despise the missing man, except for one. After it was on television on March 19, 1966, The Stage wrote how Renée 'played the mother of the dead man very touchingly' with Ewan Solon praised as the hard-drinking ship's captain.[13] Jack Woolgar, Paul Sarony, and Johhny Sekha were in the cast, directed by Vere Lorrimer. Paul Sarony - youngest of Leslie's three sons, who would manage international ballet tours, later moving to TV and films as an executive producer, remembers Renée as a very charming lady much held in respect by the team including Jack Warner.

Many in the profession knew that Renée was coping with her loss by keeping busy. Word about her went around and many offered her small parts in movies, just earners to assist her. She seemed in tune with a younger crowd of filmmakers with their limited budgets and giant visions. She was sympathetic to anyone taking artistic risks. For them, a seasoned professional on hand was always an asset. Renée was the sort to oblige, taking a tiny part in 'The Idol,' that starred Michael Parks as a manipulating beatnik American art student who seduces his friend's mother – Jennifer Jones - before her son takes revenge on him. While the film was praised for sponging up London's local colour, the general verdict was that the characters' motives were unexplored. The director, Daniel Petrie next asked Renée to play a *titled lady* - an un-credited role - in his next film 'The Spy with a Cold Nose,' a late 60s caper. This isn't remembered despite capturing the off-the-wall comedy of its time. It starred Lawrence Harvey as a vet running a fashionable clinic for rich pets. Lionel Jeffries is *Stanley Farquhar* – the bumbling secret agent whose idea it is to put a spying device inside *Disraeli* - the friendly bulldog given to the Russian government as a present. Daliah Lavi is the lucious Russian spy. I like the line on the poster *'The idea was implausible . . . the agents, improbable . . . the chances . . . impossible! . . . So naturally, it worked!'*

That August, Renée was asked by director Maurice Stewart to join Dundee's Rep company for her fourth *Roar Like A Dove* season, and before she began, RB Marriott, writing of her 'Golden Year' in The Stage, wrote a deferential piece about her, highlighting how her 'sense of enjoyment created a magic link between artist and audience.'[14] It was time for her to see old friends again who numbered among her audience and were keen to entertain her at the weekends. She would travel through Scotland's towns, taking in new developments, not all of which met with her approval. Of the Edinburgh Festival she said: 'I like the old place without the shenanigans.'[15]

Roar opened on August 22, and ran three weeks. Handsome Philip Dunbar played the laird, Charmian May was *Emma,* and Tony Calvin - *Tom Chadwick.*[16] Renée supplied her costume and looked ravishing in her satin, and Alan Dunsmore, reporter at the Journal, described her as a combination of gilt-striped Grecian goddess and Sophie Tucker doing a cowboy act, mentioning the 'double-fortissimo' approval that brought a stamping of feet from the audience.[17] One week from the play's opening, when a young cast member fell ill, Heather Ripley, daughter of the wardrobe mistress Nanette Ripley, stepped in to play *Janey Dungavel.* 'Youth would muscle in on the act,' Miss H would quip, declaring Heather 'a phenomenon - another Hayley Mills! If this little elfin creature had happened in London, you'd never have heard of the Beatles. She's going to steal the show.'[18] A report in one paper confirms that the 'battleship of an American mother-in-law' and the 'battleship's granddaughter' were the 'sparkling stars' of the production.[19] A joyful press photo of Renée and Heather makes the former look every inch the ideal granny, and the headline 'Heather's Double Life' tells how the little girl would go over her lines in her poster-filled room, not doing the normal things five year olds do.[20] An optician's daughter from Broughty Ferry on the outskirts of Dundee, Heather enjoyed the modest treat of a glass of coke on stage each night, before fate had it that she was indeed plunged into the international spotlight a little more than a year later, appearing as *Jemima* in 'Chitty Chitty Bang Bang' aged only seven.

Might the talent scout that spotted Heather have been one of the theatrical types following Renée, with the inevitable good word to those in high places from Miss H contributing to Heather's catapult to fame? In reality the outcome left much to be desired where both Heather and her family were concerned. She went to Ireland shunning all publicity. Although years later she looked back with pride at her success as a child actress, her life was the antithesis of fame and fortune. Heather campaigned tirelessly for

It's Over Let It Go

environmental issues, getting arrested outside the Faslane nuclear submarine base. She sought peace in Findhorn - an alternative spiritual community in northern Scotland, and lived for a while in poverty, fighting over a family inheritance.

The sixty-four year old actress was her irresistible self on the radio, peddling retorts as unpredictable as ever, in response to listeners' letters read by Anona Winn. In October 1966, a third series of *Petticoat Line* started. In December, a BBC director waved a new part in front of her, telling Renée how the play itself would rest on the sympathy viewers will have for the woman she would portray.[21] Thus 1967 began with another *'Dr Finlay's Bookcase,'* to use her argot, this time in *Over My Dead Body,* seen on March 19. *'Dr Finlay'* was by then in its ninth series. Her *Mrs Johnston* was some part to play given her circumstances: that of a wife just widowed who can't accept the death of her husband. 'No – My husbands doing fine,' she brashly tells *Dr Finlay* and all who have witnessed *Mr Johnston*'s death, including the undertaker. The *Johnstons* lived life through an alcoholic haze for years – and haven't been held in much respect by the villagers, who are now demanding that the lady be certified. Thankfully, *Janet - Arden House's* Presbyterian housekeeper saves the day, paying a visit to *Mrs Johnston*. Her mention of a plan to make a memorial for her late husband makes the thorny lady turn to her sympathetic Scottish doctors. A public health crisis caused by her husband's decomposing body is averted. Art may be inspired by life, but being made use of quite like this, makes me feel sorry for actors.

She appeared on *Desert Island Discs* as Roy Plomley's castaway and her eight pieces of music reveal something of herself. She starts off with 'The Road to the Isles' to remind her of her home. Dear old Sir Harry Lauder used to sing it and it reminded her of all the fun of Rothesay when life was beginning. She lunges into the drama of Shirley Bassey's 'I Who Have Nothing' - the version of herself she often liked to project - of a person ruled by a sense of spirit, not possessions, yet never impoverished. Her outlook might chime with hippy values then becoming so fashionable, but Renée had consistently professed these sentiments all her life. There was Gounod's 'Ave Maria' to symbolize her faith and remember Lizzi. Then 'Clair de Lune' signified the sadness and beauty in her heart. Bert Kaempfert performing 'Fluter's Holiday' created a complete contrast. Then the forsaken actress chose Jan Peerce with 'Eili, Eili' to tell us again of her unshakable faith in the power and purpose of the Lord. She chose her friend Evelyn Laye's 'Near And Yet So Far' - remembering that fantastic time in the mid 30s when she was the toast of London's musical theatre. When it came to her *Castaway's Favourite,* 'Goodbye to Summer' by Renée & Donald was her choice. It must have brought on the tears when it was broadcast on Monday February 6, 1967. I'm certain many housewives were crying at home listening in to the Island choices of a voice they'd listened to all their lives. She wouldn't have believed how much they still loved her. People in the theatrical world also reached out. On February 5, 1967 she attended the *Annual Gala Concert* of the Catholic Stage Guild and was made a fuss of. Tommy Trinder, Fred Emney, and the Beverley Sisters were among the faces here

Fay Weldon had written several ITV plays that attempted to portray female characters realistically and the general feedback she got from women was positive. In a TV Times interview she spoke of her time in New Zealand where, at parties, men talked to each other at one end of the room, whilst women huddled at the other. The latter group talked only of baking. Never had she seen such subjugated women. In 1967 Fay had a series on ATV called *Trapped*, a feminist series if one could exist. The word 'trapped' features in the synopsis for *Goodnight Mrs Dill* in which the female doctor *Dr Dove*, feels just as trapped in her cycle of affairs with married men as is *Mrs Dill* - a woman forced into a feckless marriage because of pregnancy. In the episode, Renée is cast as *Ivy* - the neighbour who propagates the myth of her own happy marriage only to reveal it was all fiction.

After the broadcast on June 3, The Stage was lukewarm about the episode, judging it to be 'a commercial for the Pill,' and felt Fay Weldon wasn't 'sentimental about the institution of marriage or the blessings of freedom' a marriage brings.[22] TV drama had changed considerably since the early 60s: a time when a vast amount of subjects were still never tackled. This was a time when even *Coronation Street* shocked its audiences with its portrayal of affairs and failed marriages. After expressing her Catholic faith unequivocally in *Desert Island Discs,* we see Renée in a drama advocating birth control. Like many Catholics, she didn't see the Pill as an evil. Still, the rapidly changing society, often at odds with traditional values, would mean that the subject matter for drama was less likely to please her. *Goodnight Mrs Dill* played its tiny part in furthering the 'permissive society.' When viewers saw fictional characters articulating opinions regarding the old values, they were better equipped to express theirs. Then came the abolition of theatre censorship with the Theatres Act of 1968. She, who once got into trouble with the watchman for saying 'bloody' on the variety stage in Nottingham, didn't rejoice in the liberal legislation. Critics of the Abortion Act of 1967 said it now looked like a 'free for all' with people exercising their freedom. No, this permissive society was not one she professed to want. Full nudity on stage didn't get her approval. Yet, her open-mindedness was curious and she was still irrepressible. Her age old support for the freedom of expression made her side with the artist and writer ready to challenge ideas.

'River Rivals' was Renée's forty-third film. The role of an eccentric old woman on a boat, apparently a pirate queen in her youth, was perfect for her, and one closer to the true spirit of Renée Houston than in any of her films of the previous eight years. She was *Mrs Fredericks* in the new Children's Film Foundation film to entertain kids that year in Saturday morning cinema. Her part was sizeable. She's like a character in a fairy tale – one who is fearsome to children at first but earns their respect and ultimately becomes 'one of them.' Perhaps Renée's unpredictable nature got her cast. She was someone not necessarily on the side of adulthood.

'River Rivals' is told from a child's point of view and the child characters have a lack of sophistication and can unashamedly express their hopes and vulnerabilities. Linda Graeme's story, developed by Harry Booth and Michael Barnes, stays faithful to a child's perspective. It's obvious in the detailed scenario this is no mouthpiece for adult values – something frequently seen nowadays in films for kids. The Holmes children: *Ricky, Penny* and *Tich* have our sympathy, more so than the privileged Craig children: *Mike, Pete* and *Molly*, but all make mistakes and cause damage. The child actors included Sally Thomsett - later a household name, Daryl Read - sadly killed in a motorbike accident, Julie Booth – who married an Italian, Cordel Leigh, Philip Meredith, and Rufus Frampton. 'River Rivals' is about a contest of ingenuity, physical agility, bravery, and honesty between two groups of kids.

It was also an action movie. The *Certificate U* film, shot in Eastman Colour, was segmented into seven parts, each one only fifteen minutes long but each with an individual cliffhanger moment. We are introduced to the children as do-it-yourself boat builders entering a local competition for best river-going vessal. The Daily Mirror loaned the sailing dinghy used by the Holmes kids. With the Thames around Chertsey and the Penton Hook Yacht Basin used for location filming by the Shepperton Studios team, the kids in 1967's Saturday morning cinema got to see the rival factions employing convoys, submarines, airlifts, and frogmen in their adventures. There were water jousts, slapstick moments involving a model plane, all of fun of a regatta (laid on care of Laleham Sailing Club) and wonderful twists. Rufus Frampton told me how great it was to get yachting lessons. He remembers Philip Meredith becoming quite accomplished in the canoe! The kids did a lot of swimming given the numerous sinkings in 'River Rivals,' but their best battles are connected to the subplot involving their rescue of *Mrs Fredericks*.

We first meet her when the children climb aboard her scary houseboat. The formidable old crosspatch puts them to work cleaning it up, but she's making the kids a hearty supper despite her gruffly given advice. Shepperton's art director Harry White converted an old river trip steamer into a Chinese Style houseboat especially for the film, naming *Mrs Fredericks*'s boat *The Golden Dragon*. Somewhere this boat may still be afloat. *Mrs Fredericks* is at loggerheads with mean-minded bigwig *Mr Craig* – played by Brian Haines - who would happily starve her into submission in a bid to get possession of her mooring. She's endlessly struggling with money and debts, and needs the children to save her by airlifting food or by thinking up business ideas for her, such as converting the houseboat into a café. She's kind and supportive in return, even acquiring power tools to help the kids repair their boat. The story has a disestablishment ring to it: of houseboaters against property and business tsars. Reading the synopsis fifty years later, I can only smile at the refreshing simplicity.

Mr Jorkins, a local boat builder played by Charles Lamb, is a nice character and there's an early drag role for Dick Emery as *Josephine Blake*. 'River Rivals' is cheeky and curious, with cracked idols revealing secret messages and a little metal box containing Chinese treasure hidden in the boat's figurehead. *The Golden Dragon* was a star in its own right. My favourite scene is when every attempt by the kids to airlift in supplies for *Mrs Fredericks* misses – damaging *Mr Craig*'s cucumber frame a little bit more each time. Finally *Tich Holmes* is a human airlift when their *see-saw catapult* backfires.

It was director Harry Booth's first CFF film. He had just done *'The Finest Hours - Churchill's Life Story.'* Fifty years after making 'River Rivals,' Rufus Frampton remembers Booth as a very serious chap who knew what he wanted and how to get it: 'he was pretty driven I suppose, and that can be kind of scary for a 13 year old - you certainly didn't cross the line with him. Having said this I have no recollection of the slightest disharmony or fall outs.' Rufus refers to the 'vaudeville/rep professionalism' of people like Booth and Renée, and how it was a 'privilege to grow up in the midst of that pedigree.' He looks back to a time when there was money available for artists and a film crew to create a work like this. The atmosphere during filming was happy. He recalls the regular sausage in buns and coffee from a canteen on wheels and how they spent much time talking together, waiting for their piece. He never forgot Renée's face: 'extraordinarily open and out there,' her genuine warmth and her persona that was one of 'loving life and here for business.' He does recall a few occasions when she got a little annoyed if takes were taking an unnecessarily long time and suspects it might have been down to the kids fooling around on the shoot.

In July Miss H accepted an offer from seasoned BBC producer Douglas Moodie to earn 150 guineas per episode plus expenses for a new domestic sitcom *Let Me Do the Talking*. It was written by David Fisher - an Australian able to get under the skin of Scots characters, given his good ear for dialect. He had written for STV's *One O' Clock Gang,* and the *McFlannels*. Each of the six episodes required a six-day rehearsal period plus recording at Studio A, Broadcasting House, Glasgow. Location filming featured Glasgow landmarks including the docks and city stores. *Let Me Do the Talking* had Renée playing *Mrs MacDougall* - mother of four - with Scots radio star Wullie Joss as husband *Hughie*, and Dorothy Paul as her wayward daughter. Renée said to Dorothy one day that she reminded her of her young self. Dorothy, full of deep admiration for her, speaks in her book about Renée's handsome looks, amazing presence, and deep and commanding voice that left the press spellbound. She was so completely down to earth, taking out her dentures in the taxi, telling Dorothy they were only props.[23] Her accent returned to pure Shettleston when you spoke to her in private.

Jimmy Logan's nephew John Short also starred in the BBC sitcom. The first episode *All in the Book* was transmitted on October 3, but the series either made little impact or couldn't continue. Renée had her travelling issues, and a lack of camaraderie in rehearsals might possibly have been a reason. If you

It's Over Let It Go

tuned in to the radio on Saturday 24 February 1968 at 13.10, she turned up on *Just a Minute,* hosted by Nicholas Parsons, with Derek Nimmo, Clement Freud and Barbara Blake as fellow panellists. *The David Jacobs Show* followed, and she was going to do a *Sounds Familiar* but Bill Worsley released her on March 27 when her projected stage tour materialized.

The play[24] had come to prominence in the late 30s. Set in the 1880s, its layer of earthy comedy is unusual for a horrifying murder play. *Ladies In Retirement* was one of the most frequently performed plays in the modern repertoire. Renée played *Leonora Fiske*, an ageing ex-musical comedy chorus girl with no relatives, who faces her final curtain on the lonely Thames marshes - victim of a murder. There are two views of Renée at the time of 1968's production of *Ladies In Retirement.*

Michael Gaunt, so generous with his memories, is fascinating to talk to, not least for his knowledge of Regency and Victorian theatre. By 1968 his theatre experience had included a season at Henley's Kenton Theatre, where he worked with Hubert Woodward and the well-connected Edinburgh-born Robin Alexandar Goodsir Smith. The latter marked him out as ready to direct a strong cast. Another Renée - Renée Stepham – legendary Haymarket-based agent - who knew which pro would work in the provinces, and which needed the work, provided the link to Miss Houston. A star name was always good for business. Michael remembers the thrill of getting invited to Miss H's home in Walton - a feat in itself they took pride in. She wasn't the most accessible star by 1968, turning down most roles offered to her. That initial meeting was more poignant than he expected. In her personal surroundings she seemed immersed in her thoughts of Donald and undeniably vulnerable.

Michael: She was still grieving when we spoke, and clearly missed him very much. She had kept, unwashed, the wine glass he last drank from with the thin piece of white ribbon still in place, that he had tied around the stem. Her eyes were full of tears when she showed us the glass.
I had inadvertently asked her if the ribbon was significant!

Michael told me that she was still a warm and friendly woman, full of good cheer during the days they worked together. He admires her for agreeing to be part of his team, and not questioning the fact that he was her youngest director to date. It was a comeback for her, and a challenge without Donald there in the background for support. He had been there to come home to after she had swished around in the Gogol play at the Mermaid. She'd done *Roar* so many times but that was easy with the *Dungavel* characters so familiar and like a make-believe family.

This role required her to play a vulnerable actress in a dark, lonely house with strange people with deadly intentions. It was new territory in a theatrical sense. Rehearsals were in the Lamb & Flag pub in Rose Street, Covent Garden, in the brightly lit first floor room. Renée worked hard but her memory was failing and lines were not easily retained and sometimes quite disappeared. The saving grace was that *Leonora Fiske* appears only in the first half of the play before being murdered. Michael tells me he does not recall her drinking during these rehearsals but he gives me a good insight into what Renée was like with ordinary members of the public:

> Michael: She was not an actress to change persona with each character. There were no transformations. She liked to be recognized as Renée Houston. I have been told, although I never witnessed it, that she would entertain those on the post-theatre train from Waterloo to Walton-on-Thames, as she returned home from the West End. She loved people.[25]

One morning Renée arrived for rehearsals an hour or so after the call, and everyone had been concerned. Coming up the stairs, she informed everyone in a breathless and dramatic manner that there had been a problem with the train and she had been required to walk along the railway track in order to get to the next station. Not a lot of work got done that day. Michael liked the whole company, having a special respect and fondness for Anne Cameron, his dark-eyed lead actress who took direction very well. She played *Ellen Creed*, the housekeeper tormented by her guilty secret. Michael Carney was *Albert Feather* - the cocky nephew who discovers the dark secret, and tries his luck at blackmail. Lynn Rainbow was pert and practical maid *Lucy Gillam* admired by *Albert*. Ann Wrigg and Jennifer Hill were the dotty sisters for whose sake their sister *Ellen* takes such a murderous action. Tilly Tremayne played sympathetic nun *Sister Theresa,* and Michael Ridgway was *Bates*.

The play opened at the Cambridge Arts Theatre on April 22, 1968 and sadly Renée badly fluffed her lines producing a fair bit of first night criticism by the Cambridge press. Her appearance had been much anticipated. Anne Cameron looked after Renée in performance, covering these lapses as best she could, steering her through a scene when a problem occurred - keeping her cool as talented actors can. Michael, who was staying with the cast at Cambridge's Station Hotel, never questioned Renée's dedication, as the *actor's nightmare* strikes one and all. A few days later the irrepressible Miss H deliciously made light of her talent in an interview with Gillian Maltby, who enquired as to the secret of her beautiful complexion:

> Renée: I'm an actress who knows every line – on my face.

After this, the play went to Nottingham's Theatre Royal where forty-six years before, young, mischievous Renée was entirely to blame for the disruption of Matheson Lang's performance in *The Wandering Jew* – all for the sake of comedy. The mature muse of tragedy appeared at Darlington's Civic Theatre, where in her dressing room she intrigued another reporter with several stories including one about John Logie Baird using her for his experiments with early television. Baird sent a picture of her from one room to another – in colour too. She mentioned how on August 9 she would be celebrating fifty-two years in the business. The Darlington reviews were excellent, calling the scenes 'silently gripping.' There was praise for the

It's Over Let It Go

entire cast, and a remark that Renée 'positively bubbled.'[26] Critic Stanley Hurwitz added how well cast she was as *Miss Fiske*, and refers to a curtain speech Renée gave at the end of the macabre drama. At least she had shaken off the early stage fright.

Tilly Tremayne[27] gave me her brutally honest picture of *Ladies In Retirement* - a production she didn't rate highly and 'a dreadful play' as she calls it. Just seventeen at the time, it seems to me that Tilly got forced by the producer to spend a lot of time in Renée's company. This version of events suggests that the *powers that be* realized early on what the cost of having a star like Renée to draw the crowds entailed. They appointed Tilly, greenhorn of the production, to look after the older actress on the train calls that took the company from city to city. The youngest and keenest actors often get lumbered with the worst jobs and unfairly so. Tilly was stooge, wardrobe mistress, understudy and star's companion. The sad thing, and Tilly stresses this point emphatically, is that nobody else wanted to have anything to do with Renée off stage. Her reputation in the company was very low. She was considered unreliable because she was drunk so frequently. On stage she liked to steal the scenes and she was not a team player. Tilly's memories are impressively vivid and she was one passenger in a train carriage who wasn't held in thrall each time the comedienne stole the show.

At sixty-five the British star had a figure that was barrel-like and sturdy. She used tons of makeup and false eyelashes and Tilly wondered if Renée's style of make-up might be a coded look identifying variety artists, rather than paying lip service to any prevailing fashion. Then again, high fashion make-up in 1968 looks rather like Dick Emery drag to me. Renée's old-time 'star personality' was out of fashion and her 'voice of commonsense' wasn't getting across to the younger generation either, just then. These youths protested against authority, spouted off about liberation and yet seemed so pampered, aloof and inexperienced. Just look at those Paris students railing against capitalism and established institutions.

Yet, her thick overdone makeup and haze of consciousness concealed inner anxieties. She wanted to connect with the younger generation even if she might refer to it as 'the ugliest generation ever, both in looks and the kind of music it makes.'[28] She was telling her *Petticoat Line* listeners that British teenagers were wonderful. How could she be relevant? She saw pictures of the younger folk demonstrating in Grosvenor Square against the war in the Far East, or burning their draft cards and bad-mouthing their President in America. Her wee nephew Anton was sent across the world to be a reporter in Saigon, finding himself alongside his godfather Walter Cronkite. She knew that this war was controversial and sympathized with the many poor souls who lacked social and political freedoms across the world. Yet, she didn't care for noisy protests or people becoming so geared up that they could cause violence of any sort. This younger generation spoke its mind but the queen of the outspoken attitude was, to them, someone switched off. They hadn't known the fiercely protective spirit, scared to death that harm might come someone's way. Courage had been the thing she admired the most but she told us to look to ourselves more than anything.

Oh those train calls! Tilly remembers Renée distinctly: you always remember your first job, especially when the memory borders on the grotesque. That memory had been packaged away and never revisited until I innocently got in touch seeking memories of Miss Houston. Tilly paints a bittersweet picture of touring life. The train call she described puts me in mind of the worst zoo in the world: two animals from either end of the species spectrum holed up in one cage. The cage containing the two actresses from *Ladies In Retirement* was one of those old-fashioned train compartments that later got abandoned. If anyone was 'fenced in' it was the seventeen year-old who knew nothing of Renée's celebrity. She had never listened to her on the radio or seen her films. Tilly found herself employed by Renée as her chief fetcher and carrier – required to do the same job, it seems, Cliff Richard was doing five years earlier.

Renée (to Tilly): Bubba. Go along to the buffet car and get me some perfume.

And she loved her perfume - it was her passion – as she used to say back in the days when she pattered on stage with Donald (and probably none but the tipplers knew what she was referring to then). 'Perfume' was her name for the half whisky bottles wrapped in foil she never liked to be without. Perhaps having a sixty-five year old giving you chores made Renée all the more annoying. And when 'Bubba' came back all her mistress could do was talk and talk. Tilly wanted only to read her book and ignore her. There were just two main themes in the older lady's conversation: drink and sex. Getting on fifty years since that summer of train calls I could hear in Tilly's voice the horror she felt as a studious, conscientious type and a shy virgin. Even though Tilly isn't a prude and can laugh at this episode now, there's a sense of resentment at being forced into a 'confidence' with the older actress.

The mature *irresistible* prattled on oblivious to the fact that the person earmarked to 'look after' her was unresponsive to her lurid line of talk. Quiet moments were there to be obliterated in this state of overdrive she found herself in. She obviously believed she was entertaining, even bridging the generational difference. Each time, alas, the younger woman failed to see the joke. The rogue side to Renée Houston's character clearly existed and came out from time to time, usually backstage to a select group of willing listeners. She wasn't incapable of acting like the show-off in a reform school playground. Nobody in the company had complained about this side of Renée. Tilly said everyone else turned a blind eye to it. Perhaps blame falls on the management for dropping Tilly in it, as Renée's helper. The rest of the cast didn't need to bat an eye as they had shoved the old dear into a single compartment to keep her out of trouble and stuck the youngest member of the cast in with her as keeper. The overriding expression Tilly uses about the content of Renée's manic conversation was 'My eyes were out on stalks.'

It's Over Let It Go

She listened to the older star lunge into aspects of her conjugal life with Donald during their variety career. How she would insist that they reach the heights of pleasure 'between the half and the quarter' - referring to the quarter of an hour before they went onstage, was one peculiarity Tilly couldn't forget. Few have such intimate traditions disclosed to them. Married rovers high up in the government sometimes get caught out in their affairs but these extra-marital proceedings seem almost commonplace to jaded modern eyes. Theatre dressing rooms have an unknown quality - more sordid and troubling when unexpected things lurk there. Think of Drury Lane and its waiting room of prospective Fanny Hills! A thin veneer shielded that piquant tradition. But who wants to hear about the sex lives of healthy Christian women – older ones - in a theatre? If you express pride in the health of your sex life what harm is there? None, if the person listening is interested and appreciative. Sadly, the talk was unwelcome. Tilly was candid about Renée – unlike most actor colleagues who either never saw this side of the star or prefer to whitewash it. 'It's dirt I can't take,' the older actress had once said in a serious moment, but soused on *perfume*, she could be wonderfully free with smut. Thoroughly corrupted by Renée's confessions on that train call, Tilly admits she had to go and ask a confidante what the other meaning of 'come' was. She was that sheltered.

This was, it has to be said, a desperately lonely woman trying to connect, to play the fool, and to entertain. Only a couple of years before, Renée had lost the only one who was hers to love. There was no other. With no 'better half' to keep her in check, here she was, re-living something in a vacuum. She was a woman who bragged she never wore knickers on train calls or bought a ticket for that matter. It's the stuff of schoolgirl pranks or a kind of Tallulah Bankhead behaviour that had long been the means to vent her devilish sense of humour. Her lifetime of *Great Railway Journeys* weren't your *Michael Portillo* kind. Hers needed enlivening. But she had forgotten the year was 68, not 28. The worst part was when a train guard, I'm presuming a rather nice attractive one, interrupted them and just like every other of Renée's utterances, her word turned out to be a truth. He politely asked to see their tickets and Renée, of course, didn't have one. With agility she offered a chorus girl's exposé to the horrified man as a settlement in kind. He fled in shock. Renée Houston, without a doubt, was one of the *loose women* of her time. The crazy lack of inhibition of variety entertainers could out-pique the ways of the free love generation. The old ways were couched in obscure language and conducted in stylish travel compartments. Why shouldn't Renée, or anyone for that matter, not think about the glamour and tantalizing promise of abandon that British Rail offered the traveller?

Not every bit of Tilly Tremayne's account of Renée is negative, thankfully. Renée was always upliftingly bubbly and was never unkind. As wardrobe mistress, it was Tilly's job to get all the costumes ready, take them to the station and put them in the skip ready for transport. *Ladies In Retirement* was a costume drama and packing a lot of heavy costumes is no easy feat to achieve. Tilly recalled one occasion when the skip got left on the platform and by 2 pm that day they faced the nightmare close to tears. She desperately began to ring theatres and hire departments in her desperate panicked state. On this occasion Renée was incredibly calm. Sitting at the bar of a hotel or wherever they were, Renée would say in her very strong Scottish accent 'They'll arrive. Don't you worry.' This reassurance helped her.

Michael was very fond of Renée and while other members might not have found her such a team player, he was very clear in stressing that Renée was easy to direct. It contradicts other accounts that say that there was nothing she hated more than being asked to do a re-take, or that she would not take criticism from any younger directors, being vile to them as a consequence. I liked Michael's account and I thought that in the care of a gentle-mannered leader, we happily address faults in our performance, welcoming guidance. It's only when people aren't nice about it that tempers tend to flare.

Where both accounts of Renée from *Ladies In Retirement* converge is the idea that she was a person who seemed alone with no friends for company. To Michael, she was lonely and vulnerable. Five years passed and he called Renée's number again, when he was part of the team at the Thorndike Theatre in Leatherhead. Each year to raise funds a theatrical garden party was held in one of the supporters' large gardens. Such events take on more magic when opened by a theatrical celebrity. On the phone, it took Renée a while to register who he was, and she began talking about the film they had made together. She realized and gracefully accepted the invite to speak at the 1973 ceremony. There was a speech written down on a piece of paper but Renée just improvised entirely and Michael recalls her dazzling performance so appreciated by all present. His small daughter Victoria presented the actress with a bouquet. Victoria had been kneeling on the grass and the lawn left some fresh green patches on her dress - something Renée made a glorious little joke about, bringing more smiles.

Billie had more or less mastered French after a few years in Paris but they settled back in the UK in August 1968, in a home located ten minutes in a car from Renée. I wondered if the sophisticated continental couple found their home in Beechcroft Manor excitingly modern? Their windows had a look of Piet Mondrian - but what a far cry from the Isle Saint-Louis apartment Cecil Beaton would have begged to visit. They were very downscaled in their 60s new build, but downhearted or lacking energy they weren't, and they loved to keep up with their sport on the television. There was a clink of glasses as Paul mixed the drinks, and filled up the ice bucket, and a cloud of cigarette smoke was a permanent fixture at Beechcroft Manor. Both their children hated smoking and Anton loathed going upstairs on buses. Did Paul and Billie remember to switch on Radio Four to listen to *Home This Afternoon* on August 27? The elf of a sister Billie had protected from school bullies with her tough fighting spirit was still chattering over the airwaves - chosen by listeners to answer questions they had sent her. Olive Cox was heard reflecting on the difference between the generations, and Billie had much of her own to say one-sidedly to the radio. The opinions of the elf, by contrast, were much in demand, although she was more of a troll doll by then. Her radio series doubled its scheduled run, requiring a weekly presence in London between October and March.

A small part arrived in a new Fay Weldon ITV drama *Hippy-Hippy-Who-Cares* - requiring Renée's presence at Teddington - Thames Television's base following the ABC and Rediffusion merger. It was broadcast on Christmas Day evening, safely after the watershed. Renée appeared on the radio again when her old friend Trafford Whitelock wanted her to talk about the early years at the Coliseum when she and Billie saw their name in lights, and when *Love Laughs* made her talk of the town. Anona Winn and Georgie Wood added comments to this first in the line of broadcasts devoted to Miss Houston's reminiscences. It's a shame they didn't ask Billie to comment. Aired on September 21, *The Time Of My Life* was also repeated on Christmas day. Early in 1969 she was back at Thames to appear in the first episode of *Life With Cooper,* a series written by Barry Cryer and Eric Merriman with Tommy Cooper lending genius to sketches whilst Renée, Peter Bathurst and Dawn Addams added to the artistic brushwork. Tommy presented a unique angle to the roles of toastmaster, political candidate, customer buying a bed, and someone joining a fox hunt. We watched this on April 8, 1969, and a later episode had Tommy don a blonde wig as *Hamlet* taking his cue from Olivier's fair-haired prince.

'I seemed to be specializing in playing fat old hags, but until now I had never played a jolly sporting lesbian lady,'[29] she said. In her memoir, Renée goes on to tell the story concerning her trip to France between April 14-18 for location shoots in a dramatization of Somerset Maugham's *The Three Fat Women of Antibes.* His 1955 short story is a satire about English women who habitually patronized the Hôtel du Cap in the late 20s. Renée writes that nobody turned up to meet her at Nice after her long train journey, and she spent the first day stranded. In her story Verity Lambert's production team is *laissez-faire* enough to forget her arrival, and of course she doesn't know the name of the hotel in Juan-les-Pins she's staying in. Misunderstandings abound, as an idiotic proprietor of a café and local French police feel they must protect her whilst accusing an innocent man of being her molester. Interpol is briefed and on the look out, while director Bill Hays scours the coast. Renée tells it much better, and the café scene is very *Clochemerle*. I doubt she was really travelling alone and her wee nephew Jimmy Logan might easily have been her chaperone, as he's among the Bridge playing characters we see in residence at the opulent hotel. Renée says that the tennis court scene was filmed in a house attached or very near to Somerset Maugham's house Villa Mauresque that had been sold by Maugham's partner two years before.

I believe her story about being violently sick in between takes for the scene when the three women stuff their diet and order indecent amounts of food. It was great working with Geordie Bill Hays. Loved by actors for being a maverick, he had made a smash the previous year directing *Close the Coalhouse Door* at the Newcastle Playhouse, and would later deliver *Rock Follies*. Known for his enthusiasm for good food and drink, several seafood platters and bowls of bouillabaisse were no doubt put away, not to say glasses of rosé. Many large whiskys were ordered too if they were going to get Renée to agree to be driven along those vertiginous passes. The outside scenes of *The Three Fat Women of Antibes* capture the light of the pointillist water and something of the ritzy hotel's glamour but you wonder how necessary it was to assemble the entire company in the Riviera. As Renée says at one point, they 'could have shot the bloody thing in Regents Park.'[30]

Playing *'Frank' Hickson* was a departure for Miss H, given the men's suits, ties, cropped hair, and monocle, but then again it doesn't contradict our image of *Petticoat Line's* brash personality either. Her gruff voice suits *Frank* - initiator of the ladies' annual slimming and health-focused holiday. It's a great role and she's in almost every scene and has the best lines, a total contrast to the sugary dames *Beatrice* and *Arrow*, played by Elspeth March and June Ellis, whom *Frank* puts through their paces, not always succeeding. *Lena* – played by Elizabeth Sellars – is an annoying slim and attractive blonde. She joins their company and bridge game, leaving *Arrow* in the shade, in the 'flirting with the waiter' stakes. There's grief all round. Renée might have been one of the *Fat Women* but felt like Wee Georgie Wood next to Elspeth and June. She'd been a wee slim *Arrow* all those years earlier when she and Billie had played Juan. Apparently, playing that masculine woman initially led the young men at the hotel to think she was a lesbian. They proved a lot less distant when she 'shook her hair out', wore a pretty bathing costume and came down to the pool. In the scene when you see the three towel-headed actresses perspiring in their wooden steaming boxes, Renée looks naturally glamorous. I like the part of the TV film when you see flashes of the *Fat Women* at a fancy dress party with Renée dressed as Britannia or a Roman centurion, defending herself against an ardent male admirer, who isn't in the least put off by *Frank* – finding her an attractive challenge.

For others, the challenge she presented was distinctly negative. Tony Aherne's feelings of anger and upset brewed inside of him. He wanted to have it out with both his parents for years but that badly needed quarrel never took place. His father - a figure of resentment for having left for the USA - couldn't make amends during his visit because Tony was nowhere to be found. Renée, less consumed by work, was quick to find an argument when sober. Tony lacked a catharsis. Added to this, his mother was still unable to accept Niall and histrionically needy all the while. Was it best to break off, cutting off that pipeline of love-hate emotions?

He 'left' his mother who was ever after desperate for snatches of news of him from relatives. Elana Aherne would write: 'Yes Renée did say very silly things before Tony. He told me so. He never wanted to see her again. I was the whipping boy in between as she was always writing and phoning with her 'How much she loved him', and it was all very worrying for me . . . I think from Tony's point of view he did the right thing . . . I did hear that he is looking fine and has put on some weight and seemed happy and ok about a year ago. Someone saw him in a pub in Richmond - a friend of Brian's.'[31] She adds how Renée 'gave him no peace,' and how 'he didn't want to hear, or have anything to do with her.' Elana would listen to her turmoil on the phone then beg Tony to see his mother. Yet, around 1970, she 'had a lawyers letter saying he had changed his name and didn't want any further communication with the Ahernes, or any of the family, from this time forth.'[32] Getting intervention from a lawyer is an echo of Terry's action so many years before.

Between 1960 and 1971, Niall went from strength to strength in his single-minded new mission – to discover the secret of eternal youth. After years of investigation and a surprisingly free exchange of scientific information between researchers in Britain, America and the Soviet Union, Niall had enough evidence to support his hypothesis – that Pollen-B was the super food most responsible for human longevity. Niall's easy to read book[33] connected to this research has several extraordinary illustrations including one of a Colombian Indian man over 160 years old - seen happily smoking a cigar. He writes about how the world's oldest men and women, in remote regions in Ecuador, Azerbaijan and India, sustain themselves on a frugal diet of which bee-collected honey scrap is a constituent. This led to isolating the key cell-nourishing ingredient. Using his contacts in the international bee-keeping world, Niall eventually turned the stuff of science fiction into a mail order business, developing a tablet form[34] of this rejuvenating food supplement, tapping into the world's pollen resources at the same time. His wish to better people's lives is very sincere. His book has testimonials of many tired individuals who perk up after taking Pollen-B. Former Miss World Eva Reuber-Staier, National athletics coach Tom McNab, sprinters Andrea Lynch and Donna Murray, strongman Geoff Capes and comedian Peter Butterworth endorse the brand. Modern science is now doubtful about bee pollen's 'ergogenic' benefits. Renée's son was in 'bloody Petersham' of all the hard to get to places. Niall and Tony shared a flat in Mayleigh House (south end of Sandpits Road) after they left Kensington in 1964. A little joke that Tony penned in his 1997 diary expresses his mother's frustration:

> Supermodel asked for the loo.
> Woman replied: 'I can show you but be warned it has no door.'
> Supermodel replied: 'Then how do I get in?'

The worst thing was that he was non-contactable. It wasn't just Renée he disappeared from but all the family. During this time, he revived his old chess league success. He was in the West London Chess Championships 1963-4 and for years the venues he played included Imperial College, Hampstead and Hammersmith Chess Club. The 90s saw him established at

Old Chiswick Town Hall. He contributed articles to British Chess Magazine over a long period – taking submissions to the office at Baker Street. Much to the despair of Niall, he also embarked on that self-destructive road, one that starts with secretly drinking - something he later regretted.

About 5,447 miles west of the tree outside Miss Houston's Walton-on-Thames home, in which angels lingered, her younger son was working on an aerospace project. One day he was on a long distance call to Auntie Billie who was very interested in what he was doing. 'We're going to the moon,' Alan said, and maybe he shouldn't have because it was a concept that caused Billie some trouble. Her survival in life had been 'thro prayer' and her religion was known to govern her opinions. After discussing the situation seriously with a priest, Billie got back to Alan and said: 'Oh no, son – you'll never go to the moon. Trying to go to the moon is like trying to get to heaven without Jesus.' Those images of the Apollo landing, and Armstrong and Aldrin walking on the lunar surface on July 20 caused all kinds of emotion. Who could help but be stunned by this landscape, even if it all looked a wee bit barren? Tears dissolved into the G&Ts round at Billie and Paul's.

Alan, now married with a three year-old daughter, was also helping out his uncle Brian as house agent and manager. The lovely Santa Monica beach house with its sheltering high walls resonated with the style and glamour of Hollywood's golden age. The glitterati of the day was lining up to rent it. Alan never met his latest tenant, the actress, Sharon Tate, face to face, but was always on the phone to her. Problems getting the right gardener for the beach house were the main subject of their conversations. Sharon needed a gardener fast. The last chap was a traditional man - objecting to the nude bathing and swimming among some in Sharon's group. Perhaps there was something about the beach house that made you want to strip off. Garbo was always doing it. The gardener refused to go there so Alan sent another gardener and Sharon was very happy: 'Oh! He's marvellous' were her words. California beach homes had several problems at the time with hippies who liked throwing things like bottles at rich homes as some kind of social protest. The protective wall was a godsend. Alan was very sad that Sharon was unable to stay at the beach house longer. Tragically, the young actress moved somewhere vulnerable and met a senseless end.

Renée got a temporary change from *Petticoat Line* when the Playhouse theatre was decked out for *Sounds Familiar* – the 'game that turns the pages of showbiz history.' Bobby Jaye and Denis Gifford finally managed to book her. Pete Murray chaired a panel that included Peter Glaze and Barry Took and the show was aired on May 25 on Radio 2. She was thrilled with her next part as a Scotch landlady whose friendly house has a bunch of handsome young male doctors for her to look after and collect their bargain £2 a week rent. *Mrs Muir* is full of warmth and gladness. You can see her making all kinds of allowances where the doctors are concerned. If Renée forgot where she was for a moment she felt happy a house being surrounded by 'sons.'

And if she was faulty with a line, director David Askey was kind enough to brush over it. It would happen for a split second but only very occasionally.

The new series *Doctor in the House* was made for LWT - the company David Frost helped form that succeeded ATV in getting the London weekend ITV franchise. The stars were Barry Evans as *Michael Upton*, Geoffrey Davies as *Dick Stuart-Clark*, Robin Nedwell as *Duncan Waring*, George Layton, Simon Cuff, and Martin Shaw - a range of typical young fellas of the day. There were just two series but I can see how *Doctor in the House* would have been popular - a kind of *Young Ones* mixing uproar, innocence and sauciness. In their writing Graeme Garden and Bill Oddie give a nice update to the familiar tale of a group of medical students and their misadventures. Based on the Richard Gordon book, it had been a play at the Vic Palace and spawned a few films. The dialogue in the 1969-70 TV series is snappy with much visual humour. The two episodes with Renée were *Peace and Quiet*, and *If in Doubt - Cut It Out* broadcast on August 2 and August 23 respectively. In the former, *Michael* wants to escape the noisy trombone upstairs and the Reggae next door. Providence takes him to No. 24 where he meets *Mrs Muir* for the first time: 'Com'on in son, in you go' she says quickly enough, giving him a tour:

Mrs Muir: And this is the wee house you know. (She points to the loo) I hope you don't mind the bath being in the kitchen. You can't expect a poor old widow like me to put on a separate bath.
Michael: I'll take it.
Mrs Muir: I was hoping you would. Do you know - there's something about your eyes that reminds me of ma poor old Hamish.
Michael: Really?
Mrs Muir: Yes. I had to have him put down last month.[35]

Was she thinking of the Scottie who followed her once on to a train and later chewed up his union jack ribbon at the Royal Performance in 1926? But he had left this world a lot longer than last month. Watching *Peace and Quiet* I thought about the advice she used to give young artists in the West End who only had a small speaking part: 'You've got to do your lines as if it's the most important thing in the world.' Barry Evans and Renée work well together. When *Michael* takes the apartment, *Mrs Muir* is jubilant and insists on inviting him down to the kitchen for a cup of tea and a nice wee slice of home-baked shortbread. Later episodes enjoy jokes at *Mrs Muir* expense - about her adding a little extra 'gin money' to the rent. All *Michael's* colleagues are moving in to *Mrs Muir's* as well – into the same apartment.

On the date of the broadcast, how strange it is to consider that there was no peace and quiet in California. One place sees a Scotch welcome and mirth, and another, senseless evil. It was the same date as the horrifying set of murders - those that marked the death knell of the 'hippy' era. Other things are sad. Barry Evans died in 1997 in rather unexplained circumstances, with an open verdict given on his death.

Geoffrey Davies, later in *Doctor Down Under* in Australia, tells me that when he found out Renée was coming into the series he looked forward to it immensely, as his parents had been big fans of Miss Houston. He describes her as a 'friendly, warm person, rather spiritual, and great fun. As I often hear from this generation of actors, Renée was always 'up for a laugh' and 'kept everyone entertained.' One of the pictures Geoffrey was kind enough to send me shows Renée presenting all the boys with a giant cake. She looks like everyone's favourite Auntie.

Jim Rennie, now seventy, steered a course through the fog but was weakening, and though the Fastnet light had turned electric, his journey ended on September 17. A man with Christ-like hands lives close by nature to fulfill himself. Likewise Jim enjoyed mountain and river in abundance. Burying him, Claire embarked on a long journey south to stay with Billie and Renée at their respective homes. Always a serious sister to the three Houston girls, she valued their cheer. The loyal wife who had corrected and typed Jim's manuscripts outlived him by another thirty-three years.

Call My Bluff on November 20 was a charming conjunction of talents and personalities with Frank Muir and Patrick Campbell each heading two teams that included Renée, the popular couple Bernard Braden and Barbara Kelly and actors Sam Kydd, Tony Britton and Joanna Jones.[36] ITV's lineup for Saturday night entertainment on November 29 included *The Saturday Crowd* with Leslie Crowther and Peter Gordeno, *Please Sir, Frost On Saturday, All Our Yesterdays*, and *The Comic* - a poignant play about a comedian.

Written by John Hales and directed by Alan Clarke as part of *Saturday Night Theatre* season, LWT employed a lot of ex-BBC talent as the source for these plays. It was a thinly disguised comment on the self-destructive side to Tony Hancock who had died the year before. Trouble piles up for *Tod* with writers, fellow performers, and wives past and present. George Cole played the lead for whom booze was the slippery slope. Renée was *Olive* - eldest of his ex-wives, a mother figure dressed in Chanel, with Isabel Dean and Hilary Dwyer playing his more recent wives. The Stage thought all three actresses brought sensitivity to their roles - their differences pushed aside by a shared concern for *Tod*, despite the fact that he tramples on them.

New Year's Day 1970 began with Renée as Pete Murray's guest on *Open House* - his morning music magazine. She hosted *Be My Guest – a* showbiz affair that Cliff Richard and others had previously hosted, returning to Radio Four's *Does the Team Think* on March 10, after a twelve year absence as a contestant. Renée was in Glasgow at Jimmy Logan's Metropole at St Georges Road, between March 9 and April 4, playing *Emma Hornett*, this time in *Sailor Beware*. In the cast were Paul Young, Jan Wilson as *Aunt Edie* and Water Carr. While critics said she wasn't 'Peggy Mount's tour de Force,' being 'too nice to be the lady monster,' they conceded that the play deserved better than the sparse audience.[37] Logan corrected this, pulling in the crowds when the Metropole produced the rock musical *Hair* in June that year.

Glasgow's Maryhill, Metropole Theatre at St George's Cross, and Trongate
(Photos: Author's Collection)

At BBC Glasgow, Renée told Howard Lockhart more memories about theatre in Scotland for the *Weekend Scot* show on March 29, then donned the *Muriel Chadwick* mantle a fifth time in a snazzy new version of *Roar* for Triumph Theatre Productions. It had thrived since its formation in the 60s with Paul Elliott, Duncan C. Weldon, Robin Carr, Jerome Minskoff and Nicholas Brent all creative forces in this company's life. Their head office moved between Woburn Place, the Aldwych and the Haymarket Theatre. In 1974 their productions were touring the world.

David Scase - Joan Littlewood's former stage manager, directed 1970's *Roar*, and Richard Todd, Robert Beatty, Derek Bond, Trisha Noble, James Beattie and Michael Percival were its cast. Starting in the south they went on to tour the Midlands and Yorkshire. People loved it. The Stage reported how *Roar* had the highest house record for 1970, having overtaken figures for *The Miracle Worker* with Pat Phoenix. Canadian Robert Beatty - a regular in popular British television shows was a great friend of Miss Houston. Beatty had played the scandal photographer in 'Flying Fortress.' The two improvised lines on each performance for the fun of it. Renée surprised the cast, arriving at Richmond Theatre in a gigantic cement mixer-cum-fork-lift, having cadged a lift that morning when the buses weren't running. Stepping off, and showing a good deal more leg than a respectable lady should, she aroused Richard Todd's consternation, but 'yours truly' was ready for work.

Chapter 25   Punishing the Shop Steward

> *Christian concern can express itself in different ways. For many it is unobtrusive assistance to people in their immediate surroundings. For a few it may be wisdom in public affairs, or an ability to inspire others.*[1]

In 1970 Pamela Weisweiller planned a luncheon to pay tribute to Catholic women and to raise funds for the Catholic Diocese of Jinja in Uganda. Catholic Women of the Year is an annual event still going strong. It fundraises for a range of charitable causes and provides a forum in which ideas are shared and discussed. Nominators propose a number of women, mostly unknown but occasionally public figures, notable for good work in parishes, hospitals and workplaces. A luncheon committee looks at the results of a secret ballot before naming the women. Whilst nowadays the number of elected women is four, for 1970's event – the one Mrs Weisweiller chaired – no fewer than eight women were chosen: worthy in the fields of health, literature, law, community work and entertainment. These were the Countess of Longford, Lady Masham, Bridget Sim, Renée Houston, Doris Leslie, Sue Ryder, Winston Huston and Elizabeth Christmas. All that was left to do was plan a venue, send out invitations and produce a beautiful menu bearing the names of the women of the year. It remains to this day an important and very pleasant *CWOY* tradition. For 1970, one hundred guests attended, as they did in 1969, when the nominations started.

For Renée Houston, who had never received an OBE, DBE or any such distinction, it was an honour. She happily attended. Her voice of commonsense on the radio, as well as speeches made as a consequence of her show, were reasons why she was nominated. The reference to Renée's *CWOY* nomination in *The Tablet* refers to the fact she had been voted the BBC's most popular woman broadcaster that year in a poll.[2] The *Petticoat* by then had a primetime slot at 6.15pm on Wednesdays with a shortened repeat on Friday lunchtimes.

Renée finished off the year guesting again on *Open House*, and playing a wedding guest alongside Ronnie Corbett and Rosemary Leach in an episode of *No, That's Me Over Here*.[3] She was a guest of honour at that year's British Music Hall Society annual dinner. It seemed that the music hall fraternity were going to be eating by candlelight, what with the electricity supply dispute. Renée finally got to be in a James Bridie play, thirty-five years after first being touted as the playwright's muse. It was at the same theatre - the Duke of York's - where she might have played his *Susannah* in the 30s. In her memoir she talks of the old-fashioned lamp outside, and the lady actresses of the past stepping out of their carriages, ushered in via the stage door.

The play was *Meeting at Night* - one Bridie wrote late in life. His friend Archibald Batty revised it. The two used the name 'Archibald James' to signify collaboration. Henry Sherwood Productions staged the play that opened on January 21, 1971 and its star was Wilfred Hyde White as amiable conman *George Triple*. He offers faith healing by post to gullible patients. The characters meet in a remote Highland pub where landlady *Mrs MacLachlan*, a devout lady Marxist does her own crowdfunding at the expense of guilty capitalists. When she isn't bossing the barman around she's holding readings from 'Das Kapital' daily at 4 pm to commemorate the hour of Trotsky's assassination. There's a romance between the conman's daughter and the lady's son and everyone conspires against the detective played by Sydney Tapfer. The Daily Mail found the play 'not solid enough to be real, not preposterous enough to be farcical, nor bad enough to be intentionally funny,'[4] and The Tablet found it a threadbare piece that 'could well have been left in decent obscurity,' admiring, all the same, the 'Glasgow accent you could cut with a knife,' of La Houston, and David Battley's barman with 'baleful visions of the future.'[5] This was an unusual role for Renée and she was modest about it in her book, believing the play a one-man vehicle for Wilfrid. Plays And Players, nevertheless, thought her devastatingly good.

Trotsky didn't quite rock, but in Renée's next film, 'Carry On At Your Convenience,' she was truer to her own ideologies in this anti-union satire, so sharp-witted that people were surprised there wasn't a mass walk-out at Pinewood Studios, and that Equity didn't discipline its members. Talbot Rothwell was scriptwriter for this Carry On classic, placing Miss Houston in a pivotal role and giving her a part you can't ever forget. Tolly Rothwell knew Renée and had been a writer for the *Crazy Gang*, Arthur Askey and Ted Ray. His hero was Max Miller. He'd also been a fellow prison camp entertainer along with Rupert Davies during the war. I like his profile of himself: 'born at an early age to mixed parentage, one father, one mother.'[6]

At *W.C. Boggs and Sons*, Ken Cope *plays Vic Spanner* - the nitwit shop steward who, under the *National Union Chinawear Industrial Employees* banner, keeps persuading reluctant workers to go out on strike, however dubious the incentive: the Rovers are playing this afternoon - kickoff's at 3 O'clock, is an example. Meanwhile, *WC Boggs* – Kenneth Williams - has his secretary *Hortense Withering* - Patsy Rowlands - sit for ages on the latest toilet to test for size and comfort while flamboyant bog designer *Mr Coote* (Charles Hawtrey) looks on proudly. Even Kenneth Williams's inkwell is a small porcelain convenience. The statutory target for 1970s popular British ridicule - the bidet - is the butt of jokes where works manager *Sid Plummer* – Sid James - is concerned. He asks if bidets are for dogs to drink out of. When told, he asks why you can't just stand on your head, under the shower. Everyone feels the same way about bidets, until *King Fowsi of Aslam* orders a thousand of them - one for each of his wives. *WC Boggs* declares he will not have his firm associated with the manufacture of so dubious an article, but on hearing it's worth £19,000.00, changes his mind, happy to manufacture in time for the feast of *Aba Nibble* – when it's his highness's custom to visit each one of his wives in turn. This sets up background for the latest strike. *Vic Spanner* has his eye on *Myrtle Plummer* - factory canteen girl – played by Jacki Piper, but boss's son *Lewis* - Richard O'Callaghan, impresses her with his flash car. Nobody's too fond of *Lewis's* time and motion study that reveals fifteen hours per week are lost through visits to the loo. It's very sad that today, even with tea breaks scarce, loo visits can put your zero hours contract at risk.

I was thrilled to speak to Kenneth Cope about his memories. He was a household name in the 60s as ghost *Marty Hopkirk* in *Randall & Hopkirk Deceased* and was frequently on *That Was The Week that Was*. Ken remembered Renée as very strong in dialogue and presence, a little fearsome even. She could come into a scene like a galleon in full sail, Ken tells me. She could also be a bit bossy, a bit eccentric, very much the 'old stage type' and very Scottish, although Ken has a tremendous fondness for Scotland. One special memory he has of Renée is that she used to mutter a line *'It's the paella fella'* as a kind of joke. She wasn't saying it about anyone or to anyone. It was a just a phrase that had got into her head and she liked to say it. It's a strange memory but he's never forgotten it. Was 'paella' a word of the moment, maybe the dish of the moment in 1971? This quirk fits my image of Miss Houston - of her finding a phrase and extracting its value just for the way it sounds. I think of it as a comic's thing even if there's a touch of loneliness about repeating a phrase for your own enjoyment.

Renée was another of the generation of great performers Ken met. He talked of the skill needed in carrying off a variety show. He had done one with David Frost as a follow on to *TWTWTW*[7] - nerve-wracking work, he tells me. He thought it touching and humbling to see actors like Richard Todd - once really big stars, accepting small cameo parts in TV series such as *Last of the Summer Wine* – a sign of the down to earth approach and practical-minded qualities these performers had when it came to work. Ken valued the courtesy and discipline prevalent in the theatre at the time he was coming up telling me a story about his time at Bristol Old Vic when the whole cast was knackered and the theatre provided mattresses for them to sleep on. He remembers the discipline that Rep gave the young actor, such as testing the set for all possible sources of error. This was why 'Carry on At Your Convenience' signifies for him a good example of pros getting a job done and hardly fluffing or forgetting a line. Filming took about four weeks although they got a bit behind. Shooting began on April 8, 1971.

In the film Renée is *Agatha*, *Vic*'s mum, and their relationship is so hateful it's a wonder that it can be so amusing. Films were pushing boundaries in terms of realism and the depiction of violence, but no other film sequence was exploring the extremes of ear boxing delivered to a son at the hands of a viper-tongued mother. It was the genius of Rothwell and Gerald Thomas that made this possible. Not only was the material realistically inspired, it was superior in scope to almost everything Renée had been given during her previous fifteen years of film work.

Agatha is a brilliant manipulator and there's a suggestion of financial struggle that divides her loyalties and underlies her verbal abuse. We feel *Vic*'s depression when friend *Bernie Hulke*, played by Bernard Bresslaw

Punishing the Shop Steward

drops him off, stopping his noisy motorbike outside *Agatha*'s boarding house. We see the parlour with its lampshades, Chiparus figurines and 20s-looking objects on the wall, and meet the mother, knife in her hand, pointing at her son. *Vic*'s insistence that he's been representing workers ground underfoot is as welcome as a fart in a spacesuit. Starting a strike again is another misdeed for *Agatha* to shame him and cut him to shreds. A little *Spanner* family history is suggested and a hint as to why *Agatha* became her dreadful self. We learn that Vic's father was the victim of a gin-ridden society. Money only matters to her now.

We hear *Mr Coote*'s call of 'Coo eee' and Agatha adopts a posh voice and a pout. She transforms herself into a woman desperate to fuss over a man – while her son looks on astounded. The opportunities for double entendres are many, with *Mr Coote* clearly loving the attention and happy to oblige her in some hinted at activity she's been 'missing' as a widow. She goes on to give *Mr Coote* a massive dish of steak and kidney pie – an immense contrast to the cold sausages *Vic* gets every day. We hear the thunderous arrival of *Bernie's* motorcycle. *Agatha* is appalled at the noise and shouts her complaint from under her 'Vacancies' sign. She's selfish in her single-mindedness, browbeating a meeker neighbour in the process.

Further compact situations involving *Agatha* and *Mr Coote*, *Mr Coote* and *Bernie*, or *Agatha* and *Vic* bring new quirks into the storyline. As always the writing gives 'Carry On At Your Convenience' its particular richness. Of course there are other memorable scenes like Hattie Jacques and Sid James and their budgie *Joey*, who picks out winners on the gee-gees. Funny as they are, I believe those at the *Spanner* house are the most extraordinary. The film sets up the expectation of something saucy about to unfold between *Mr Coote* and *Agatha* who later find themselves alone. We're not told what they're up to, until we see Agatha in her pink dress. It's a game of strip poker, and *Coote* is winning. She has to take off her dress. In an impossible but funny scene, *Vic Spanner*'s trousers have been whipped off from the motorbike as *Bernie* zooms off leaving him on the doorstep. In his combination of white underpants with red circles on them, jacket and helmet, *Vic* enters his house sheepishly, greeting that neighbour we met before as he passes. Agatha, like a gorgon, doesn't miss a chance to yell about his appearance, forgetting she's more or less déshabillé herself. Realizing, she rushes back to the poker parlour. Later on, a more subversive side to Agatha's suburban boarding house is suggested when *Mr Coote,* in his boxers, opens the door to *Bernie* - all innocent-looking and darting eyes. The toilet designer asks him if he cares to have a game.

So many things happen in 'Carry On At Your Convenience.' During the works outing to Brighton they find staff at the restaurant have gone on strike. While booze-virgin *WC Boggs* gets legless at the bar, everyone else goes on the pier to have a winkle. *Vic* loses *Myrtle* to *Lewis* in the ghost train. *Bernie* and *Popsy* – Margaret Nolan - cavort on the helter skelter. *Myrtle* gets her skirt whisked off in another scene at a club with *Lewis*. What could be more '1970s British' in character than the speeded up sequence of the *Carry On* gang jumping off the coach as they visit six pubs in turn, running into the woods to go to the loo, then bundling onto the coach after! This was what laughter was – the rule of not taking ourselves remotely seriously.

The music was composed and conducted, as always, by Eric Rogers. It adds to the jovial spirit. We learn a bit more about *Agatha*'s motivation when, appearing on her doorstep in a long white dressing gown with yellow and blue flowers, she stumbles over a drunken *Mr Coote,* who, interestingly, is holding a bottle and a *red-headed* Houston-like doll. Again, that placement is telling – a producer's evocation of Renée. It emerges that *Agatha*'s future marriage to *Mr Coote* is jeopardized by the industrial action her son is causing. *Charles* will lose his job if the factory closes down.

She's not going to see her sound financial solution imperilled. Little could be more frightening than *Agatha* railing against that little sod Victor. Her smashing of milk bottles has the curse value of an Athenian drama. This drives the showdown, when the cast of *furies* – women headed by Hattie Jacques and Renée, breach the picket line and lead their menfolk back to the lavatory pans. Ken Cope - down to earth as always - bursts my bubble concerning the filming of 'Carry On At Your Convenience,' telling me the spanking scene was 'just another scene' for him and Renée to do and that there was no problem whatsoever doing it. It's the job of an actor to manage any situation, he said, crashing my deeper academic readings, although Ken never forgot what it felt like to play it under the gaze of the gathered crowd.

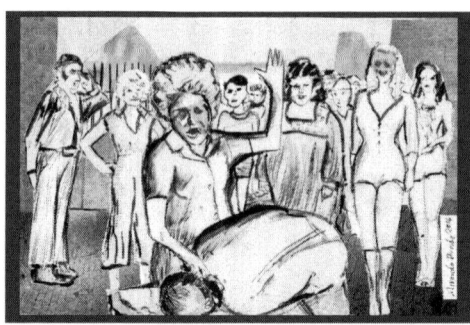

Agatha Spanner gives *Vic* a spanking (Artwork by author)

Robert Carr - Secretary of State for Employment in Edward Heath's Conservative government had been responsible for the Industrial Relations Act 1971 that had curbed the freedom to strike. Aiming to abolish closed shop agreements, he was almost killed that year when an anarchist group threw bombs at his home. When Renée Houston ignores calls for the democratic right of every worker and knocks strikers into submission - telling the strike leader to shift his arse out the way and let the good people in to do their work, she's at her most violent and reactionary.

Whereas *Pat Sherwood* had been held back with a sock on the jaw, *Agatha* goes into full swing, pulling the baseball bat out of Vic's hand and giving him sixteen slaps on the bottom before he drops onto the yard floor. It's a victory for paternalistic values. No wonder Nina Hibbin, writing in The Morning Star, states that whilst director Gerald Thomas assured her the film was not commissioned by Carr, he and Rothwell had 'done a good job for the gentleman from the ministry without any prodding.'[8] So, to use Nina's phrase, everyone goes back to being 'one big, happy, chain-pulling family.'

Renée earned £600.00 as a guaranteed sum for the film, perhaps a little more than what most Carry On actors were paid. Generally, the films were cheaply made but saw a very good return. Rather like the way Ken Cope described the training inherent in the Rep system, Margaret Nolan told me she saw the making of the Carry Ons the result of a work ethic that was raw, quick and professional. There wasn't time to do anything other than get the job done. 'They were fun to make and so easy in a way! There wasn't this manic ponsiness you get now with the huge amounts of money involved,' Margaret added. Renée's standing with Rogers and Thomas was very high, and she was all set to be in 1973's 'Carry On Girls'. However, her ill health called for Joan Hickson to be drafted in at short notice as a substitute.

Renée was turning in a good performance on *Petticoat Line* week after week delivering witty captions to the comments of guests like Jean Rook. She inspired the younger female panellists, and enjoyed the nostalgia of having Elsie and Doris Waters on the show. In her private life, the fearsome galleon in full sail was sometimes a vessel empty and rusted with chemicals, her brittleness isolating people more than ever. Donald used to take the sting out of her tail, neutralizing her verbal excesses. He used to console her after she had suffered a slight and was a layer between her and the rest of the world, softening the horrors she didn't like. As the 'feed' whose sixth sense anticipated her reactions, he had loved to see her shine. The sparks ignited in her but she was bereft. Few were coming forth with responses that lifted her with their eloquence. Her priest was an unexpected light in her loneliness.

Left: Father Bob Madden seen on the right, when on vacation (My thanks to the Madden family)

Right: Magnolia Tree at *'Brighthampton'* (Author's Collection)

Father Robert P. Madden started at St Erconwalds - her local parish church - around the same time she and Don arrived at Walton. With Donald gone she turned all the more to Father Bob, nine years her junior, who would encourage her to come to terms with her loss. His calmness, sense of humour, and listening ear were of great benefit, and he didn't criticize. They shared the quality of not being at all shy about making their views known. Plenty of these were held in common, even if he was much more left leaning in his politics. Madden hated Margaret Thatcher and the Tories, and disdained the political maneuverings of those in the church who jockeyed for positions of power. He had a great antipathy towards Capital Punishment, as he knew prisoners who were killed that he believed were innocent. Father Madden had always been a fighter and a doer. He had suffered the wartime bombings in London when he worked at St Anne's Catholic Settlement in Vauxhall and ran a youth club there.

He was now tasked with building All Saints Church in Hersham as well as founding Cardinal Newman Primary School. Renée felt inspired by her priest who, she noticed, was a heavy smoker and fond of a Scotch in the evenings. If she could assist with fund-raising at a fête to help him she would. There were wonderful ways of contributing to a cause and Madden obtained promises from other local parishioners who were celebrities like John Gregson. In such a changing world, Renée cared about good causes, guidance for youngsters, and also religious education. It wasn't a new thing. She had always been on a platform. She felt her role was to inspire others.

Renée was at the Playhouse recording an episode of Warren Mitchell's comedy *This is Living* on September 13, and doing the first of twenty-nine weekly recordings for the eighth series of *Petticoat Line* that took her up to late March 1972. That month she was invited to a lunch by the Variety Club of Great Britain at the Savoy: a Tribute to Vera Lynn and Joe Loss. She's not visible in photographs from this get-together although it surprises me that she could cry off. No reunion could have been more impressive. There was Arthur Askey, Russ Conway, Florence Desmond, Charlie Drake, Clive Dunn, Doris Hare, Dickie Henderson, David Jacobs, Sid James, Danny La Rue, Mantovani, Alfred Marks, Cliff Richard, Harry Secombe and many more present. Perhaps she left a little early before the photographs after offering a toast to those honoured by the Variety Club. Perhaps she skipped it at the last minute, knowing her vulnerability would seem all the more obvious alongside all these stars who were doing very well for themselves.

She didn't skip the opportunity to speak to young people, as a panel member in a discussion about Womens' Lib. This Radio One show was recorded on March 24, 1972 at London's County Hall and was produced by Roy Trevivian. The young of the early 70s had a world to look forward to that finally seemed easy-going. For the members of the old guard, beyond reproach in the splendid surroundings of the Savoy Hotel, the period of grafting before arriving at the threshold of success had been long. Their success hadn't depended on a single institution like TV to dominate their apprenticeship. Formality and courtesy had ruled in those bygone times when the channels that existed for plying their trade were varied. They were knocked into line in terms of manners, behaviour and dress. These *Savoyards* had gone through a lot. They might have taken risks, but in their day caution, innocence and ignorance offered some degree of protection from the evils that undoubtedly lurked below the surface.

At County Hall, the audience of teenagers in Jimmy Savile's *Speakeasy* show were innocent, even though the permissive spirit of the times indicated it was alright to be more open and publicly discuss subjects hitherto forbidden including sex. Savile commuted between London and Leeds in his scruffy motorhome, somehow managing to prearrange visits from teenage visitors at motorway service stations along the way. Someone who brought it to the attention of the aforementioned producer was told 'we will not be looking into this because they are only suspicions and because it is Jimmy Savile, it would be dangerous to do so, as we could all lose our jobs.'[9]

During July and August, Renée was part of a *summer season* at the Ashton Theatre, St Annes-on-Sea when *Ten Little Indians, My Three Angels,* and *Not Now Darling* were staged, and she was in good company alongside Richard Murdoch, Jack Hulbert, Desmond Walter Ellis, and Valentine Dyall.[10] For her seventieth birthday, Alan brought his family over, and an enjoyable party took place. Pat Aherne had not seen his seventieth birthday, dying in California in September '70, leaving a widow, his daughter and Brian, the son he had adopted on marriage. Pat had spent some time at the Movie Actor's Home at Woodland Hills where Johnny Weissmuller had also been resident (before he got on people's nerves far too much doing his *Tarzan* call). Just a couple of months before Renée's anniversary, Brian had celebrated his seventieth with old friends Marlene Dietrich and Grace Kelly who attended his party. Brian's close pal George Sanders was supposed to come but took his life ten days before. It put a damper on it.

Renée definitely arrived on time for the well-attended *Variety Artistes Ladies Guild Bazaar* at the Café Royal, in mid September – with Terry Scott, Florence Desmond, Ethel Revnell, and George Williams among the famous guests. Dressed in the fur-lined coat she wears on cover of 'Don't Fence Me In' with the addition of her Tartan trilby Renée presented prizes for the fortunate ticket holder.

Billie died on September 30, 1972 having been in hospital for a while. She wasn't old - only sixty-six but had been immobilized since the late 60s. Over-extending her voice on the stage indeed contributed to her health problems, as did her lifetime habit of chain smoking. For the last ten years she used an inhaler to breathe and believed she was in God's hands entirely. Paul's health was also very bad and he'd been surviving at home while Billie was in hospital. Anton got a message from his Dad about his Mum's condition worsening, prompting him to return with his wife from Paris, as fast as they could, to be at his mother's side. Carole's work had taken her to the Frankfurt Book Fair, and when her father called to tell her to come home she began her crossing to Dover. She didn't know her mother would go so suddenly and yet a heavy sense of vulnerability accompanied her on that journey to England. Billie had a chronic lung condition and the right side of her heart had enlarged as a consequence. She also had emphysema. Paul was devastated to be parted from the love of his life. The family struggled to cope. Renée was distant. Strong as always, she made little outward show of grief. Her iron will and ability to stand firm and carry on, only mirrored the earlier times in her life when she had lost a member of her family. You can't simply refrain from your *iron will* if that's how you're made.

So Billie's funeral didn't witness an appearance by the curly-topped little *Irresistible*. Was it fear of being left alone in the dark? Was it better to keep clear of the pain and deal with it alone? She seemed to deal with so much alone now although none could advise her otherwise. She had her weekly visit to the Playhouse Theatre to think about. *Petticoat Line* was now in its ninth series and she never missed a recording. Still, that insistence on delivering a gag, being entertainingly absurd and making life light-hearted seemed a bit of a *wash* now. References in letters I have read indicate she grieved a great deal for her sister, who was one of her true 'loves'. Different from each other they were, but they had been through a great deal together. Renée cherished those memories from distant times, not even wishing to share them. Four years later her nephew confronted her about why she had never turned up at his mother's funeral: 'Why could you not have made the effort?' he begged her admit, but Renée could only give her usual comic reply - a line that wouldn't have been out of place in the Sisters' old music hall routine: 'Oh, there was no way I could play second fiddle!'

Renée saved her precious Houston Sisters remembrances, deciding to present these in the right setting: a professional one with an interested audience. On Thursday October 12, 1972, in the midst of Billie's passing, she was joined in her home by presenter Robin Russell from BBC Scotland and a recording team to record a sixty-six minute retrospective about her life. Iain MacFadyen was the producer. The idea was devised in June 1972 with an original plan to interview Miss Houston while she was at the Ashton Theatre, St Annes-on-Sea. She told Pam Simons she was anxious not to have to travel to do it. On her contract, she crossed out the *'60'* from the *'60 years in Show business'* working title, writing a more honest *'56'* in the margin. When the programme aired in April 1973, they kept the better-sounding original name.

Renée is on top form in the Russell interview, with entertaining little asides and tales of her early days and the people she worked with. She willingly answers questions posed by her thorough questioner, who steers her back on course to get the right response about something interesting from long ago. In the interview there is no mention of Billie's recent death, even though Renée talks a lot about the Houston Sisters, reserving her liveliest stories to describe their young days. While it seems she is talking about distant times and using the past tense, Billie's 'presence' is current. Renée must have urged Russell to keep to the format not incorporating recent 'news' even though this was a perfect opportunity to celebrate Billie. Speakers Anona Winn, Lesley Storm, Ronnie Corbett and *Roar* producer Murray Macdonald feature in the talk. I believe Renée fell back on her tendency to conceal her loved ones behind a door of privacy. The thought of attracting sympathy was also anathema to her. Was she grabbing the spotlight? No, but it seems sad to compare this with Billie Houston's obituary - just a small footnote in The Stage, with little mention anywhere else.

Perhaps she was saving the best bits. That autumn she began a project for an autobiography that took over a year. This was 'Don't Fence Me In' -

published by Pan Books at the end of 1973. Brian Aherne had published his autobiography 'A Proper Job' in 1969, and she had a mind to go one better, to explain about her family, her marriages and her career. She mentions the illness that ended Billie's career. Renée credits a Peter Whittle as the one who helped and advised her. I've tried to trace him to no avail. I thought he might have taught at King Edward VI Boys, Stratford-upon-Avon but this isn't so. He might have been the Australian Peter Whittle who made films with Donald Pleasance and Harry Secombe in the early 70s. Pam Simons is another I was unable to trace in connection with my research.

I've heard different versions of how the book came about. Renée's son Alan says that if his mother had written it herself it would have been humorous but lacking in fact-base. Tony described the book as 'a pack of lies' - unfair because it isn't. Alan thinks the BBC was involved in assigning an editor whilst others mention a mysterious ghostwriter but can't remember who that person was. Some say Carole, who worked in publishing, got Renée the contract but her aunt never got round to writing it so the mysterious ghostwriter was hired. Others say the Wills-Eve family wrote it. Anton and Carole admit they were consulted, and both the Wills-Eve and Aherne families provided photos although the photos they mentioned to me weren't used. Anton told me Renée needed the money and that he spoke a few times to its author on the phone. He and Carole found the end result unsatisfactory.

Something short, fun and easy to read - the most commercial type of book - was what Renée and her professional editor decided on. The age-old formula was guaranteed to work. To me, the voice of the happy-go-lucky music hall entertainer gets over. The puns, terse observations and exaggerations make 'Don't Fence Me In' the great read it is. It captures Miss Houston's spirit. What's left out of the book was intriguing enough to lead me to write this substantially bigger book! 'Don't Fence Me In' has 80% of Renée's voice. It isn't a pack of lies because all the vague references can be supported by evidence in newspapers. Although she makes the story read better than the truth, Renée is still honest. I connect with the 'tough but kind' Catholicism that prevailed during the sisters' upbringing and identify with her motivations. I believe she felt compassion for her first husband. It's not that the book is historically inaccurate – it's just she doesn't bother with dates, being free with chronology. This was really her second autobiography but who remembered the one from almost forty years previously penned by a younger Renée? She was less of the 'old stagehand' then.

Renée ended the year with a *Sounds Familiar* recorded at the Playhouse and filmed an episode of *Special Branch* at Thames, the popular crime drama based on the activities of the Met's anti-espionage and anti-terrorist department. Her episode was about a recently engaged couple placed under heavy surveillance by detectives *Craven* and *North*.[11] She was the *Mystery Voice* in a *Twenty Questions* recorded on June 20 at the Paris Theatre. This used to be on the eastern side of Lower Regent Street just north of Charles II Street. It was here *Dad's Army* was remade for Radio 4.

She was back at Thames to participate in Dennis Norden's *Looks Familiar*, making up a team of three *'highly distinguished nostalgists'* with Ted Ray and Joe Loss. Wearing an acacia red dress, Renée looks fantastic. She can't help but laugh at Norden's bawdy introduction of Joe Loss as the 'musician with the longest baton in the dance band world, and longest run of success'. She gets an intro as that 'Permanent peg on the Petticoat Line - the most splendid Houston this side of Texas'[12] quickly jibing to Dennis 'you mean *Housto-know* the difference.' I love the following little bit of talk:

Dennis: Renée. Here's one you'll get into deep water if you don't recognize it. (Shows picture) Now, that was a singer in a band - Who was it?
Renée: That was ma wee flower Anona Winn.
Dennis: It's Anona Winn, indeed.
Ted Ray: Did she have a band?
Renée: She's had everything that one.
Dennis: Can you remember the band's name by any chance?
Renée: No dear, I didn't know she had a band, and I've known her since 1925.
Dennis: Well she had a band and it was called *Anona Winn and her Winners*.
Renée: She was a beautiful pianist and she could sing like she could when she was seventeen. This gorgeous coloratura voice - otherwise I can't stand her.[13]

In the show, Ted, Joe and Renée look embarrassed as they are shown newsreel of people doing the 'Lambeth Walk.' She tells Dennis she had her own dance for all of the old tunes not following any particular novelty dance. They have Monte Rey on as a guest[14] and at the end of the show Joe and Renée have nine points and Ted has ten, prompting Dennis's quip that he'll be receiving a life-size statue of Wilson Keppel and Betty.

Among the delights of re-watching *Look's Familiar* so many years later is seeing panellists like Bob Monkhouse in awe of special guests appearing on the show. A genuine sense of respect from the younger generation towards veterans of music hall is obvious. These older stars earned their stripes on countless stages night after night and were the benchmark against which you measured your own successes. In June Renée did a couple of dates of her *'you know what'* for Triumph - her sixth tour: this time with Richard Murdoch and his wife Peggy, and also Jack Hulbert. She started her autumn run of *Petticoat Line* then contributed to BBC1's *A Funny Thing....* a talk that featured a new personality each week, trading anecdotes about showbiz life. Renée was on it for a few weekday afternoons, beginning November 26.

On January 31, 1974 she was the guest of Mavis Nicholson, for that day's *Good Afternoon*. One of the first women to interview on daytime television, she had been spotted by Thames producer Jeremy Isaacs - a groundbreaker himself when you consider *This Week* from the previous decade. Mavis begins by drawing everyone's attention to that VOICE - familiar to radio listeners. We see Renée just 'returned from the frozen north' in an expensive sealskin jacket edged in beaver fur, matching hat, knee high brown boots – an outfit borrowed in full from Cecilia Chi Chi Zandona - her friend and neighbour in Walton. Watching a tape of the show, I notice Mavis stopping herself from bursting out laughing a few times. Renée is touching to watch.

> Mavis: I like your boots, Renée.
> Renée: So do I. I wish they fitted me.
> Look at this! (Pointing to the boots)
> There's room for two Catholics and a Protestant in each boot.[15]

Mavis asks good questions about George Balharrie and the adoptions - trying to dig deeper whilst remaining polite. Like all readers of 'Don't Fence Me In,' I expect Mavis was intrigued by the unanswered questions it raises. Renée is polished in the art of offsetting a question with funny jibes and bypasses Mavis's penetrating questions. It would be fair to say that in 1974 the majority of people from Renée's generation were satisfied in telling a fairly anodyne history. Who admitted to having had a 'complicated' life? The fashion for exposés hadn't arrived and people then didn't have access to modern records to reinforce memories. Renée relies on ready-made easy-to-recall lines taken from the roll call of 'Don't Fence Me In.' It was lovely to speak to Mavis about the 1974 interview but she didn't remember much. It was forty years back from 2015 when Mavis did *Good Afternoon* and at the time 'just another day, in our line of work.' Mavis did remember Renée's enthusiasm, and her words after the show expressing how grateful she was to be asked on. Memory is a strange thing. Many generous people I've put questions to in connection with this research are blessed with fantastic memories going back much further than 1974. In the Mavis interview, Renée begins to recount odd intriguing things such as having to give up cabaret because of over-enthusiastic fans. Her natural generosity comes across when she says 'I like to share' and 'there's always someone who needs it.' The conversation gets on to the topic of being extravagant with money.

When I saw the interview I couldn't help thinking how pleasurable 1970s shows were, even if they lack sophistication. Panellists and interviewers are visibly at ease as they light up a ciggie and feel comfortable enough to say something unheard of or daft. Miss Houston returned to Pete Murray's *Open House* for a guest appearance the very next morning - February 1, and that evening she spoke on Radio Two's *Late Night Extra,* all the time plugging her little Pan Original as much as she could.

Chapter 26 Back to the Old Caravan

Maureen Cleave from The Evening Standard arrived at *'Brighthampton'* one showery day in November 1974. The papers were full of stories about outlawing the IRA, the 'guilty' Birmingham Six, and Lord Lucan. She was welcomed indoors by Renée who wore a black lacy dress with a satin bow to one side and a big blue chiffon scarf around her head. In 1965 Renée and Maureen had shared a *Petticoat Line* panel five times and the older star remarked with pride how Maureen had got on. The interviewee had prepared a delicious tea. Dishes of apple pie arrived after a rendition from the kitchen of 'I'll be with you in apple blossom time' in basso profondo range. 'Dollop it on, Flower,' urged the motherly star, pushing the cream in Maureen's direction. Then came advice about the health benefits of cream - good for you – unlike tealeaves. Insist on a tea strainer if you've any mind! After lunch the journalist was allowed to look through books of old cuttings whilst Renée hopped to and from the kitchen, generously offering her more tea or a boiled egg. Maureen was struck by Renée's rich and bawdy voice, itself suggestive of a glorious past and an indomitable spirit. Her interview - easily the best document of Renée in this period - is a wealth of sensitive observations: 'Always on the side of the angels is Renée, though perhaps not entirely at home there,' is my favourite.[1]

Maureen got the impression that Renée's pleasure existed in doing small acts of kindness for others. Heading off into the cold evening with the task of writing up the article for her editor, the young woman glanced at the window seeing the lifeless November sky, then observed Renée reappear with her coat that she had somehow warmed on the radiator. Maureen didn't mention the glass with the white ribbon commemorating the last time *Variety's Sweethearts* drank a toast - that had lingered on Michael Gaunt's mind. Perhaps six years on, Renée was getting better.

That year Tyburn Productions was formed by thirty year-old Kevin Francis whose ambition was to be the force behind a successor to Hammer Horror films. Tastes were changing though, with a switch towards realism. Tyburn had just made 'Persecution' (1974) with Lana Turner in the lead - a late offspring made in the manner of *'Whatever Happened to Baby Jane.'* Freddie Francis, who went from stills photographer to camera operator at London Films and would later do the cinematography on David Lynch's 'Elephant Man' (1980), directed his son's productions and managed cinematography. He had recently made 'Trog' (1970) with Joan Crawford, 'Son of Dracula' (1974) with Ringo Starr, and had directed Peter Cushing many times. Cushing, described as 'the soul of Tyburn'[2] certainly lives up to this distinction in the central role he plays in 'Legend of the Werewolf.' As *Professor Paul*, he is an eccentric pathologist who acts on his hunches and takes risks, identifying that a werewolf is behind the series of mysterious murders in a French town. He utters the memorable line: 'It takes all sorts to make a world,' and complements the screenplay by Tony Hinds. This

Back to the Old Caravan

expresses the tragic point of view of the werewolf – something that clearly shows how the film departs from a *Hammer* style. Harry Robinson's music, recorded at Anvil Studios, sets up a threatening atmosphere for the 'in-the-woods' title sequence. We see Black Park in Wexham, Buckinghamshire through the red-filtered eyes of a wolf. Other scenes were shot at Pinewood.

Freddie Francis might have suggested Renée for the role of *Chou-Chou*, having worked with her in 'Phantom of the Opera'. She's the frowsy wife of the showman – memorably played by Hugh Griffith with slow-motion eyes. When a feral 'wolf boy' is caught, the troupe decide to make him the attraction of their travelling circus. *Chou-Chou*, a reluctant tattooed lady showers maternal affections on '*Etoile*' - the boy - played by Mark Weavers. David Rintoul plays the older *Etoile* who finds his naïve view of women challenged. A horse-drawn caravan bearing the signage '*Maestro Pamponi and his Famous Exhibition incredible and wonderful,*' dominates the early scenes when we meet *Pamponi* who thunders 'Wake up you lazy bitch, there's work to be done' beating the side of the van. The familiar voice of defiance cries out 'Alright, alright, you old goat!' then auburn-haired *Chou-Chou* makes her entrance, ready to give as good as she gets, although she looks undisguisably frail. Renée is only in these early scenes and that line is probably the only one with much weight. Her gestures however, are always imbued with pathos. She's often round the fire with a blanket round her shoulders – a convenient device to help restrain the struggling and injured wolf boy. 'He's going to be the making of us, whatever he is,' says *Pamponi*. Soon the show has an audience of Central Europeans gathered on little stools. There's a turn by a white terrier 'with human intelligence' that pogos across the screen on its hind legs. A painted sign tantalizes the audience about the mysterious wolf boy within a covered cage – 'Is he a wolf or human? See and judge for yourself.' *Pamponi* gives the old build up, about a certain lady of quality of the royal family of Russia - tattooed all over – one who 'will be printed on your memories for the rest of time.' Will statuesque *Princess Tamara* be as abundantly tattooed as her painted image on the Belle Epoque poster suggests? No chance, and immediately their sighs could not be more disappointed sounding.

The curtains at the rear of the caravan reveal a *Tamara* not ready, swigging from a brandy bottle. Without coming out of the doorframe, standing in her long yellow gown with yellow feathers in her hair, there's an illusion of height but little else. Her face is dazzled in the sunlight but she immediately assumes the role of proud princess, coyly revealing the suggestion of faint tattoos on her arms beneath a white gauze shawl. This Dickensian grotesque might only be gestural, but it's pure Renée Houston. Short-changing the crowds *Pamponi* blasts out 'You would not expect a lady of her breeding to expose herself further . . . so princess, I thank you.' Banging her head on the doorway after a regal kiss and wave, *Tamara* retreats into the caravan.

The voiceover of Peter Cushing explains how the young wolf boy now has human friends among this group of players, and there's another quick view of Renée looking from the caravan at little *Etoile,* who meets again the eye of Hugh Griffiths with a wink of complicity about duping the audience. Renée gives us one of those changing faces she is so good at: first a smile – a look of satisfaction, then a pucker of the lips – admiration – ending with a lower lip grimace and narrowing of the eyes - a sign of doubt. I enjoyed 'Legend of the Werewolf' and it's touching to see Renée getting laughs a last time on film. Seeing her in a travelling circus puts me in mind of her time touring with her family's troupe, with a motor lorry loaded with props and costumes during the misty years of the early 1920s. In another short sequence she watches the now grown up *Etoile* as she does a bit of fortune telling, reading the tarot cards in her hand. She declares how he will meet a pretty girl and will love her until death. 'Etoile! Are you listening to me?' she yells, before taking a swig from the brandy bottle.

A review in The Guardian has little to say for the film focusing mainly on the drawbacks of the script - 'a rather sticky wicket.'[3] Perhaps one day more respect will be paid to the film which, given the difficult time it was made, is an achievement on Kevin and Freddie's part.[4] Ron Moody's caricature as the *zoo-keeper* - glad to find someone unafraid of wild beasts - is memorable. I loved Marjorie Yates as *Madam Tellier*, a brothel-keeper dictating to her girls in a Lautrec style 'house' straight out of *Salon de la rue des Moulins*, with dialogue about spilled champagne: 'Never mind, perhaps it will clean the carpet!' In her scene with Peter Cushing, when she refuses to identify the bodies fearing business might be affected, she walks away with the scene having the sharpest lines. She didn't have any scenes with Renée and didn't get the opportunity to meet her owing to their different schedules, but confessed herself to be a great admirer. Marjorie was thirty-four with two kids at the time of 'Legend of the Werewolf.' She told me that working at Pinewood was enjoyable, remembering how awestruck she was glimpsing Robert Mitcham and other huge stars walking around the studios. There was a good atmosphere during filming and she enjoyed working with Freddie Francis, who had seen her in 'The Optimists of Nine Elms' (1973) in which she had appeared with Peter Sellers. Film buffs either love or hate 'Legend of the Werewolf,' but they would agreeon the fact that a huge amount was achieved on a limited budget. While the company had smart branding on its stationary and film materials, finance was a major issue so distribution of 'Legend of the Werewolf' happened in obscurity. A Tyburn TV series failed, and they struggled on before finding success with an unusual *Sherlock Holmes* tale 'The Masks of Death' in 1984.

Petticoat Line received a fair amount of press hype for its Autumn '74 series and was more popular than ever. The year finished with Miss Houston appearing on Radio Four's *Autograms* - similar to *Desert Island Discs*, and giving her a chance to present her choice of records. The phone rang one day in February 1975 and, a day or so after, a car pulled up bearing an exotic visitor. It was none other than Terry. A full thirty years had passed since that brief reunion at *'Green Trees'* – a period in which there had been little contact between mother and daughter. At their last meeting Terry's soft round face had been no different to that of the bright four year-old the Coliseum star had brought into the bosom of the family. Renée remembered those eyes combining passion and reserve in equal measures. The eyes were the same but the elegant lady, now Mrs Teresa Long of Cincinnati Ohio, was a grandmother herself. As was the case when Renée saw Alan, a wall of self-protection reserved for children who appear only to disappear again, asserted itself. There was a formality about the situation not least because of Terry's lady-like presence. Renée gave a fanfaronade about her current status in the theatre to interest Terry: her manner sprinkled with a dose of eccentricity to soften the situation. She seemed vulnerable compared to the times Don had been there. Here she was - a mother with a long lost child. She couldn't say no to the visit even though I'm inclined to believe that it initially crossed her mind to make excuses.

Terry's son Patrick drove her to Renée's and his memories about that day are slight. What the two women spoke about isn't known, but Renée must have been keen to hear about Terry's kids offering them mementoes. *'Fondest love to all my family, Grandma Renée,'* was how she signed photos. She gave her daughter a number of old theatre programmes including the one for the performance at the Shakespeare Memorial Theatre, and even the one for the Charity Concert at Holborn Empire – the occasion when Terry's picture had first caught her eye. Terry might have requested these in advance of the meeting. Renée also gave her whole pages from her scrapbooks – from books she had studiously maintained. Suddenly, there was an exchange with few distractions and a freedom for Terry to ask about the adoption. In the past there was never any time for pinning down Renée and having the opportunity to ask. Getting a private audience would have amounted to a luxury in the old days. Now Renée was all memories and nostalgia but she held all the cards. The information she gave Terry wasn't very detailed. Old difficult subjects were avoided. It wasn't an emotional meeting, with neither party shedding tears, and the visit was confined to a few hours. Still, Renée and Terry had definitely made their peace.

Terry's son, then in his late twenties, left his mother with Renée for the duration, only seeing Renée briefly. He recalls how afterwards his mother was totally shocked at the poor living conditions not expecting such a change in Renée's appearance or circumstances. Dinner apparently consisted of a can of tuna. This being the overriding memory of the visitors is something that troubles me. How could it be that Renée Houston lived in a hovel? *'Brighthampton'* is a very attractive place to live now and was then. When Maureen Cleave came to visit any signs of self-neglect weren't obvious. There was nothing to indicate poor living conditions even if this was a period in which Renée had isolated herself. There had at least been a semblance of genteel poverty. It's likely that Terry had been led to believe that Renée was hugely paid as you expect stars to be. In the Forties she had been, so thirty years on there was going to be a shock. Did Renée adopt a poverty-stricken pose making her economic state look worse than it was to extract sympathy? Matters become even more mysterious when Patrick tells me the old lady his Mum met that time didn't seem like the photos of Renée I showed him, and even the pictures of her Surrey home didn't strike a chord. His memory of Renée's home was that it was a very neglected council flat. He thought the location was somewhere in North London, forgetting it was in Surrey.

It was fitting that they should leaf through faded old programmes with frayed edges, because spring 1975 saw Renée offering her recollections of Sir Oswald Stoll to presenter Bill Sullivan in an episode of *The Impresarios* on Radio Two. She would declare: 'He created my greatest love, Variety, and when I say Variety, I mean Variety!' The voices of Anton Dolin, Clifford Mollison, Dennis Stoll and Georgie Wood were also featured. She was on Radio Four, interviewed by David Hawksworth for a show called *Woman's Hour Honeymoon* on May 13, and by Nick Handel for *Spring Into Summer* aired on May 26. She never tired of these radio interviews and I recall Alan saying how radio and theatre were her favourite forms of media, each being so quick and immediate. In the late summer of '75 she did an episode of Bob Monkhouse's *Celebrity Squares*, made at Elstree and produced by ATV (before they output from their Lenton Lane Studios in Nottingham). Reginald Bosanquet, Dickie Davies, Lynsey De Paul, Clement Freud, Aimi MacDonald, Alfred Marks, Arthur Mullard and Willie Rushton were fellow 'Squares'. On October 10, Renée was delighted to be on *The Andy Stewart Show* on ITV with her 'wee nephew' and little protégé. A season of *Petticoat Line* began in October - the twelfth in the series. The last time those fine points of view in response to listeners' letters were aired was on January 23, 1976. On the unlucky for some Friday 13, of February 1976, we switched on the Radio Four morning show *When Music was Magic* to hear Miss Houston looking back on the music of her Glasgow childhood, in particular her mother singing Bach's 'Ave Maria'. 'I was going to be a nun,' she told Liz Smith, adding: 'My husband always said if you were a nun, there'd be none like you.'

The Stage published a very happy-looking photo in March 1976 of a crowd of broadcasters from Grampian Television. This had the ITV franchise for the north and north east of Scotland and struggled through the recession, as did other franchises within the ITV network. Stanley Pritchard, man of theatre and broadcasting, as well as the Church, would interview a series of guests on the topic of the changing face of entertainment. His *Second Profile* series started that April. In the photograph, in front a large crowd of technicians, Stanley sits between Georgie Wood and Renée Houston. Georgie is tiny as ever and Renée has a glamorous bouffant hairdo. Georgie had known her donkeys' years, and in his *Stage Man's Diary*, wrote how they had had lunch together on the occasion she celebrated her sixtieth year in the business. 'She was a star in my book from her first appearance,' he wrote about his *Good*

Companion. The last TV show that Renée appears to have taken part in was *Hughie's Full House* on April 28, 1976, directed and produced by Ronald Fouracre and recorded at Richmond Theatre. Hughie, Bernard Bresslaw, Beryl Reid, Pat Coombs and Yvonne Marsh were companions then. How Renée roared with laughter when she watched Shirley and her son Ian as contestants on *The Generation Game*. Shirley and Bruce had known each other back in the day and were friends. Funny she and Ian were winners that evening! Does any of that gorgeous conveyor belt stuff still survive?

It was probably going to be the last time she would tour, but saying she *could* still tread the boards after sixty-years was a real talking point. Besides, she couldn't resist Peter Clapham, who came to visit her telling her she had the X factor needed to be his *Aunt March*. An ex-chiropractor turned theatre producer, he was was bringing Louisa M. Alcott's play *Little Women* back to the stage in a version he had adapted himself to celebrate the 140th anniversary of the author's birth. Clapham had appeared with the Royal Shakespeare Company at Aldwych Theatre before studying American theatre and directing 'Shadow of the Tower' (about Tudor monarchs) in New York. His CV listed films and several television shows like *The Sweeney*, his excellent contacts, and his reputation for period work.[5] *Little Women* was to run at the Ashcroft Theatre in Croydon for two weeks from October 12 then tour Nottingham, Swindon, Bournemouth, and Eastbourne. It was ideal in the lead up to the festive season with its *New England town* seen in two Christmas and New Year settings distanced by a year. Back then it cost £1.85 for the most expensive theatre ticket in these theatres and 85p for a cheap seat. Even if The Stage talked about the 'cloying' nature of the play, crowds turned out in droves, amused to see the *Petticoat Line* star in person.

Peter Clapham was no stranger to the Ashcroft, having produced and directed plays for its summer seasons. Patsy Blower, who played *Amy Marsh* remembers Peter as a very kind man. He played the small part of *Mr Marsh* himself, and toured with the company. Janina Faye was *Jo Marsh* - the character who mirrored the real Miss Alcott to some extent. Janina had started acting at the age of ten, and had already been in a popular BBC TV adaptation of *Little Women* playing *Amy*. Nina Thomas played *Beth* and Hazel McBride was *Meg*. Renée's wee young friend Lawrence Douglas, whom she had met at Jimmy Logan's New Metropole Theatre, was *Laurie*. David Davenport was *Laurie*'s grandfather, Nancy Nevinson the down to earth *Hannah*, Janet Whiteside *Mrs March* and Andrew C. Wadsworth - John. Janina tells me that when they started rehearsals it was quite obvious that Renée was now an elderly lady who needed the help, love and support of everyone involved. 'We all loved her and acknowledged her frailty and her needs,' Janina recalls. 'She wasn't difficult, just in need of that support.' For one needing to be looked after, this went a long way. Her previous theatrical tour hadn't guaranteed this.

Patsy has many fond memories of working with Miss Houston, like being entertained royally with Renée's stories about her time in films and the actors she had worked with over the years. Later, when they gathered for a drink, she supplied them with endless anecdotes. Lawrence Douglas remembered her as the life and soul of the party! Some years before, he had taken his parents backstage to introduce them to Renée. Usually reserved people, he was touched to observe how delighted they were to meet her in person. Patsy says Renée was lucky in that she had two young women: ASMs Judith Street and Polly Millar - specially instructed to look after her helping her with lines and dressing. Renée found touring an exhausting process according to Janina. The curtain went up each night at 7.45pm but there were also two Saturday performances and a Wednesday matinee. Still, her swansong was a joyful experience. For a moment did she forgot the time and place, adding a little touch she had mastered in *Hooray! We're Here*?

She still managed to do a little radio. In Croydon she recorded a short interview with Derek Brechin for *Spotlight on ... Scottish Humour* – a programme for Radio Four Scotland broadcast on November 30, 1976. She then made a short live appearance on Radio Two's *Open House*, produced by Angela Bond - aired on October 21, 1976. It was her last radio broadcast for her beloved BBC. Her theatre life was also coming to an end. Patsy Blower described the night Renée officially retired. The play had reached Eastbourne's Devonshire Park Theatre on the week beginning November 15. From the stage you could look out onto the lavish interior dating from 1884: plaster scrolls, caryatids and twinkling light. Peter Clapham guided her to centre stage, brought her forward and gave a considered little speech about her illustrious career. The audience applauded.

She naturally adapted her stage to the environment close by: street, shops, pubs, and the area outside her door – anywhere that saw neighbours coming and going. They made up her small but appreciative audience. She couldn't walk far and was a regular passenger on the Alder Valley buses. One driver: John Todman - who lived in Ottershaw, got to know her well. He said she travelled by public transport as often as she could because she just liked to chat to people. She regularly got on the bus at Castle Road near 'Brighthampton.' Todman later wrote movingly how one day she hadn't any money and asked if he would take a cheque. He gave her a ride and a non-payment of fare form, and said he'd keep it as an autograph.[6] She still didn't live in a world of money. The bus driver's testimony makes that clear.

This extraordinary old lady also seemed to live off the air for sustenance. Renée had never been a big eater as a young woman. Little had changed when Maureen Cleave visited her that time, observing that a drink and a fag were her main meal apart from a wee snack in the evening:

> Renée: I have six tables but I eat standing up.
> You know what I mean, Darling Heart, when you live by yourself.
> And when do you retire? A young man asked me.
> Ten o'clock, I told him, if you're interested.[7]

She wheeled her budgie around Walton-on-Thames. With Jimfy's cage secured onto a special perambulator they were off. Nobody could ever accuse her of neglect now. No point in one of them having to stay lonely at home if the other had to venture out. It took a long time to return so she packed the birdseed into one of the plastic bags to ward off budgie-starvation. Sometimes Jimfy even travelled long distances on trains and was a talking point when people came up to say hello. He was also a focus for a new double act with an unusual line in patter. Such joy this old dear brought to the people who rushed to greet her: those who recognized her and those who didn't. She seemed protected from danger by her irrepressible cheer and everyone she passed in town was a friend.

I was extremely lucky to speak with Ivy Keats, a Walton-on-Thames lady in her mid 90s, blessed with a crystal clear memory. While she didn't know Renée well, she had met her on many occasions just out and about in Walton. She had memories she wanted to share with me – all good ones, and that familiar Scottish voice was one she could never forget. Ivy was taking her granddaughter out in the pram when she first got into conversation with Renée, who raved about the bonny baby. Ivy's granddaughter is in her forties now, so the first encounter was probably around 1967. She asked Renée why she was sitting there on the wall, waiting by the side of the street. Renée said she was waiting for the Wellington - the pub formerly at the top of New Zealand Avenue - to open. Renée was about sixty-five then and Ivy was in her late 40s. Ivy knew that Renée had a sister and interestingly described them as 'two little blondes.'

Waiting for pubs to open was the same answer on plenty of occasions when Ivy asked her 'Are you going somewhere special?' Ivy thought that Renée was probably lonely and knew she enjoyed a tipple. She believed that, for stage folk, this came with the territory. She thought of her own parents' generation and the upbringing they had. People had tougher lives then. Booze was part of it. Ivy had many more meetings with Renée but always along the street. Renée always loved to greet her grandchildren. Ivy's impression was that Renée was kindness itself, that she made people laugh always, and told a great story. Comparing the Renée in 'A Town Like Alice' with the lady she frequently encountered in Walton, it was always a case of 'what you see is what you get.' Here was someone who never felt sorry for herself. What struck Ivy more than anything about Miss H was the feeling she 'cared about the underdog' and liked to 'help someone along,' as she put it. Renée was sensitive to anyone whom she observed to be struggling.

The evenings were loneliest for Renée. Alan told me his mother had an arrangement with a taxi driver to pick her up and take her back to the local pub in the evenings. She was often at High Pine Club – the exclusive club in Queens Road with a private bar, sprung wooden dance floor and restaurant. Outside there was a stone bridge and a wishing well. Sadly the property suffered a bad fire in 1977. Another favourite destination was the Halfway

House at 40 Hersham Road, near Station Avenue – demolished in 2003. Renée knew Julie Andrews' mum Barbara well during her years in the area, and this was Barbara's local. Having been accompanist to Ted Andrews all those years, it was no surprise that Barbara, a charismatic character, would willingly do a turn as a pub pianist. She was fantastic! Julie's aunt Joan also lived in Walton, occupying one of the flats opposite Ivy Keats in Hersham Road. Ivy knew both Joan and Barbara and witnessed the singsongs.

The Halfway House

Of course there was the Cranford Arms where Renée would catch up with her stylish Italian friend to whom she dedicated her book. Chi Chi Zandona's daughter tells me her mother and Renée were often to be found in each other's company here. It was an upmarket pub then but has changed hands now with the usual chichi pub-makeover that manages to snuff out all traces of the older type of smoky panache. Insisting she didn't need a taxi, the late nights here were more likely to result in a homecoming fall for Renée. She made new friends at the pub each time and was as generous in buying drinks as she was with her jokes and conversation. A local lady commented how she was 'lots of fun, wore little blue bows in her hair and she talked about Billie all the time.' How she loved to be the star and be centre of attention!

And at home were familiar things. There were signed photographs on the wall, the extraterrestrials on the television, Jimfy on his perch occasionally pecking at his reflection in the bird mirror, a radio voice to quarrel with. In the clutter on the floor was the newspaper with a scrawl in the white space offering a snappier critique next to Dilys Powell's film review. Aluminum foil was crushed into a racing doggie or a man with long spindly arms. Biro marks burlesqued some poor face in the TV Times. Curly fringe for my 'great friend' here, Hitler moustache there . . . Flora Robson, Florrie Desmond, Beryl, Bruce, Anona, just yoo wait and see. I'll have the last laugh. People phoned her and some were frightened away. She was always in touch with Pam Simons. There were plenty of offers she continually turned down.

There was a long period in which Trevor worked at Woolworths in Walton - a branch that closed in 2007. He kept a distance from his mum. Nevertheless, all the staff there knew her. Sometimes she came in with something to say to her boy – an amusing diversion to those who witnessed her visits. Woolworths was never without a little showbiz glamour in those days. Thankfully she had learned to keep the *Agatha Spanner* in check and brought joy whenever she appeared. Then Trevor disappeared again. He had

Back to the Old Caravan

always been terribly popular with women and the fall out after one affair with a married woman might have contributed to this disappearance. He later married again and lived happily not too far away in Addlestone.

Renée would wage an impromptu Houston quarrel with anyone plucky enough to take her on. She enjoyed a little bit of honest vulgarity as well as conversations of a serious tone. Suddenly she would impress friends with her connections to the internationally famous. She'd mention the ball Brian and Eleanor attended on June 29, 1978, following the wedding of Princess Caroline of Monaco to Philippe Junot.[8] This was the time Brian had danced with Princess Grace. Up until 1978 it was the neighbours who kept the closest eye on Renée. This was Renée Houston's retirement - a time in which she remained alert and in reasonable health.

Never her natural ally, Tony came back into the fold around March 1978. Seven or eight years had passed when nobody in the family knew where he was. Cutting oneself off can be a way of finding yourself and in that time he had put his relationship with Niall first and foremost, storing up memories of things they did together: events noteworthy, quirky, even mundane. These were times when they refused to be segregated into some corner of a 'normal' society. In late August '76 Tony and Niall set off for the Isle of Man for a new life together. This new chapter in their rich shared experience would be cut short. Tony never got over Niall's death and the years of their partnership became his past, with the *dark* past before then – that connected with Renée Houston – far less important to him.

He and Niall had loved to take winter holidays to varied countryside places, often finding themselves the only occupants of a hotel. They had delighted in bare un-swept promenades and having cafes to themselves. They didn't have the luck to be born in later generations and throughout these years public denial was expected. Tony would write how even in these faded seaside towns they were aware of their strangeness.[9] On a positive note, Niall had made a lot of money from the Pollen-B supplement business and the book published about this quest. When Niall died on Tuesday May 17, 1977, nobody could say that he and Tony hadn't made the best of things during their twenty-five years. The new men Tony met during the period leading up to the end of 1981 only sickened him and destroyed his hopes of ever settling down with anyone else. By 1997, he could speak in lighter tones, as always with his characteristically dry humour:

> I gave the best years of my wife to my country.

So Miss Houston had her son back again after his absence. She never had further cause to mention the 'evil man' and he never had any reminder of Donald Stewart to arouse his old jealousy. There was no discord during this period and mother and son shared a lonely world. In some ways his possessiveness came to the fore again. He would discourage people, including members of the family from coming over. This was not because his mother was noticeably ill or disabled but because of the shame he personally felt in her unkempt surroundings, which were apparently getting filthier as the months went by. David Aherne's son Daniel never got taken to meet Renée for this reason. Still, Tony would turn up several times a week to cook for his mum and look after her and she was satisfied with that. She managed to stay out and about, despite the agoraphobia she sometimes professed to have. If Father Madden called, asking her if she would open fêtes or appear at a meeting, she welcomed the opportunity. The two kids from next door still used to roam in and out of Renée's home whenever they wanted. When Alan last spoke to Renée he was only on the phone to her for about a minute as she put the two kids on the line and this was a time when it cost a fortune to call. Typical Renée - thinking of this.

Her death happened very suddenly and was unexpected. She had banged her head inside her home one day and had to be taken to St Peter's Hospital, Chertsey. That was on Friday February 8 and she died the next day in the early hours. The stroke that killed her was designated as alcohol induced.

Tony turned out to be a real brick and organized the funeral. Alan sent money to his brother and was regularly in touch as regards the arrangements. There was a requiem mass held for Renée at St Erconwalds at 2 pm on Monday February 18. The day seemed a lifeless one and, above the keystone with its small relief of a Saxon king, the sky was a shade of pale yellow. Below were carnations, yellow roses, chrysanthemums and a wealth of spring flowers. These tributes had started to flood in since early that morning, becoming a blaze on the forecourt and making up for the sky. That large church, designed in the late 30s with its school-like exterior, suddenly looked merry. The Houston magic was in the spring flowers, timeless as those gathered from the meadow with its distant view of the old Lightburn hospital. The largest floral tributes came from the Director General and staff of the BBC, proving that this old enduring love of hers had been a two-way thing. There was a wonderful cascade from Tyburn Films. There were more flowers and tributes from the Walton Playhouse, and from the manager and staff of Woolworths in Walton. Then cars drove into that quiet little street to the north of Walton High Street with nervous passengers, half-wondering if some twist was about to happen. Getting out, they saw the flowers and wondered *'Could she really have gone'* then passed through the sheltered wooden doors under the gently swaying statue of Our Lady carrying Jesus.

St Erconwald's Church, Walton (Miranda Brooke)

Tony led the mourners and there weren't many: Pamela Simons, Dabber Davis, Hazel Bray and her son, Carole, and David Aherne. They were accompanied by a group of neighbours and local people. It wasn't possible for family based many miles to the west to be there. They remembered her for how she was in life, for the fun and loving times. The affectionate qualities Renée had were mentioned at St Erconwalds in a spirited address. Father Madden spoke of Renée's long life in the public eye and in the public's affection. 'Anyone who has listened to the radio over the years knows that she did a tremendous amount of good,' he said. 'She was a very charitable soul.'[10] The next day, on the other side of town, Renée joined her beloved Donald at Brooklands Lane Cemetery. Today, with the passage of time, their plot is overgrown. Donald Stewart Wintermute is mentioned first and the words Wilkes-Barre, Pennsylvania. After this it says 'and his beloved wife Renée Houston, Actress.' What is written as the last sentence made me smile: 'Here Our Play Hath Ending'.

There were many obituaries in the national press. The Times said how she injected a good deal of her irrepressible nature into her radio programmes, referring particularly to her outspoken revelations. The Surrey Herald spoke to CH Carlton Smith, a local resident who had filmed with her back in the 30s. 'She had a bubbling personality and was adored and loved by everybody,' he said, and her bus driver, who still cherished the autograph she had given him in lieu of a fayre, echoed the sentiment. She was 'a tremendous person' and 'everybody loved her.'[11] On the anniversary of her death, The Stage placed a small notice from the kind fan who used to help Renée negotiate the step downs from trains at Waterloo and Charing Cross: 'For Renée Houston, who died on February 9th 1980 - In Loving Memory Your Pals Esmé & Bill.'[12]

Chapter 27   Final Thoughts

I dream of Miss Houston:

New York, don't know when, Brigitte Nielsen is in the doorway in a white trouser suit - looks a bit like Billie. She and Renée walk down the street, the latter in her trilby - fearful, chic, with a cool fire that's smoking. We hear about the aftermath of some eternal quarrel. It's the kind of movie where there's a house that people pass in and out of. Not much happens because it's already happened. We're learning about the relationships between past inmates. A boy from Edinburgh I once travelled to Iona with is in one scene. My mother's white painted chest of drawers is in another, with strange objects on top. In the basement is a shrine to Our Lady that people come from far to see.

'It wasn't my fault!' she barks, and how frightening she appears: long red hair, eyes full of anger, and a voice powerful enough to unnerve Hannibal Lecter. She scares me out of a dream. I must have done something that rankled in the psychic landscape.

She's sedate, coming out of a front door in a London street. It's summertime and the sun is shining. She's grey now, wearing a green-blue dress and we speak. She bustles out into the middle of the wide street and she hails a taxi. She doesn't have a lot of time for me.

Dame Sybil Thorndike directs a play – it's cringe-worthy but pushes the boundaries: man seduces other man either side of a grocery counter. Renée's Mrs Mop is indifferent to this type of commerce. She barely has a line – just cleans floors. Casting directors are no longer bothering with her and she's underused. She'll do her job alright: Houston face, understated, hints of disdain: the only believable character. Wake up . . .

He dreams of better things:

'Mock it, and don't ye stop' are typical words of encouragement from Jimmie - a tough coach and a disciplinarian whose business it partly is to encourage a type of cheek in his daughter. He sits back watching with an enjoyment that's slightly cruel. Remember he's travelled far on jokes and highlights elements of his own eccentricity in the unrivalled comic situations he deals in. When he's euphoric they all delight in it. Then his spirit is crushed and they all hate the times his snappy *alcoholic anger mind* awakes. There's a lot to feel dissatisfied about. Lizzi is in dire need of a rest. They long to take time off but the risk of never being hired again is real. It's all work, work and work. The Houston Company celebrates each small battle won.

Any holiday is a dream come true for kids:

Sugar and spice aren't all that nice in these tatty picture variety houses. Being too nice isn't the form. Nice with callous undertones is more effective. She has to put the bite in it. Little Mother cares for her mammy. Lack of sleep and fears about rowdy folk come second. Mammy will recover she promises. People are already remarking on the inexhaustible reserves she possesses and how she appears to be in complete command of anything she undertakes. Still, Daddy's praise isn't exactly abundant. He advises her to go with the flow. Weak thoughts will vanish. Renée flavours her cynicism. It

Final Thoughts

receives a yes vote. She has expectations to live up to at an impressionable age. She's a chip off the old block. Renée makes good her enslavement as best she can, perfecting her technique and turning exposure into something daring and unfearsome. The transcendence she achieves on stage gives an appearance of freedom. She seldom *gets the bird*. It's an environment for apprenticeship and what you can learn is unlimited. This girl's intelligence is instinctual, not based on academic training but still something to be proud of. Later on, she returns to her 'place' or at least pretends to - her confidence threatened by well-schooled actors and TV studio executives whose backgrounds have known solid privilege. This child of the theatre has never had another job. Occasionally in films she's seen 'serving' on the other side of a counter - as postmistress in 'Mister Cinders' or serving cups of tea in 'Carry On Cabby.' She's seldom doing anything if you look close and who could blame her? This is as near as she got to shop work.

Renée's heightened senses electrify the Coliseum just like they captivated the holiday folk of Rothesay. Overdosed on childhood she's putting dollies in their crib and ruling *Bill* onstage in their nursery. She and Billie do the *Garbo* sketch. There's Billie's pleasant-faced good-naturedness juxtaposed against a slithery and not so kind version of *Miss Garbo*.

In Elstree the peaches are in blossom and pubs see toilers of the soil order tankards of ale. Pat and Renée join the talk at the bar. Renée plays a game of darts with her hubby. She joins a discussion about literature, describing the Rabelaisian book she's reading: about a quaint French village and the uproar that follows the building of a new *pissoir* bang in the centre of town.[1] Wouldn't Elstree love one of these! She likes a good joke does our Renée, and one time she has the studio's makeup team transform her into an authentic old hag, reprising her *widow* part from her *James Houston and Company* days, this time with a sophistication worthy of Lon Chaney. Then comes a series of *'widow'* pranks played on unsuspecting people. She's at her best aided and abetted. Pat obliges being the good old sport he is.

She loves sponteneity. She rejoices in the broken plate Alan's little friend owns up to and celebrates by shattering more crockery. She never seems to count costs. She's 'up' when stranded alone in a French town and walking along the railway track near Waterloo. Then she's quiet on her own sitting on a wall waiting for the pub to open. There's a ribbon in her hair. In awe, men stop and bow to her. She entertains ordinary folk on the train home, dispensing the old magic that leaves an entire audience spellbound. Can you imagine stars doing that now?

She has the fire. Polanski sees it. The alarm is enough that we listen and watch. In quirky pictures with plenty of parts for women Renée gives her best. *Petticoat Line* - long in coming is the right substitute for such a talent. *Coronation Street* might suffice. It's like a series of turns in a variety show but it fails to feature Miss H. Not many Glaswegians on The Street.

I'll buy that dream:

Renée and Donald put on the charm. They must in order to get work. They can't afford to stand outside the loop. Renée has the ear of producers and executives even if she's arousing sympathy more than pulling weight with them. The star that had helped unite us in laughter, that added saucy adlib into musical comedy in the 30s has to conform as an older performer. Privately they grumble. Donald writes to his mother about how he hasn't: 'received any gratitude or financial reward for loyalty in this business. It's become a rat race in latter years. I hate the attitude *I'm alright Jack the hell with you*. But that is the attitude of today so if you can't beat them join them.'[2] Renée and Don aren't seen at many social events where everyone's 'oh so nice' for the sake of it. Renée turns out one miniaturist performance after another in TV and films in parts hardly empowering. She does a run of film appearances to raise money to pay for medical care that Donald needs. He's her purpose, more so than receiving praise from fellow pros for her years of hard work.

The drink is there and it's a battle fought alone. That pressure to lead a 'dryer' lifestyle aided and abetted by public awareness is yet to come. Later in life actress Dora Bryan tells the press she missed out on the times her kids were having their tea after school when she had to leave. A life of stardom has a lot to answer for given its excesses. By 1997 a far simpler life appeals to Dora: 'I'm glad, in a way, that we haven't as much money as we used to have'[3] she says. For Renée, it's near impossible coping in isolation in the wake of Donald's death. Who would dream of removing that glass from her hand? Yet she surprises all by finally cutting out the whisky.

American Dream:

Over in the northern Sierra Nevada, Kathleen and Bob Gonzaga, Shirley and Hal Silander, Claire Rennie, and Renée's daughter Terry pose for a photo with the Alpine woodland of the Donner Pass stretching out behind them, and afterwards they're by the lake in the recreational area, seated, and taking food out of boxes. It's October 1980. Claire had never til now made the journey to the States but it wasn't the first time Shirley – last of the Houston Sisters - had gone west with faithful husband Hal. Terry has flown in all the way from Ohio and Alan and Tavy enjoy the grand family reunion.

Aren't dreams the sweetest things in life?

Over seventeen years pass and Tony Aherne is in the loo enacting a battle with his mother and Donald. Don interrupts him, insulting her. Tony turns on him: 'why don't you go back to your native *Pitts* burgh.' Every day in his diary Tony notes the outside temperature. He records what time he has brecca, what he eats for lunch and where, names of Latin trees and shrubs, literary works and science fiction he's reading, that he spoke to Alan, David, Tavy, a neighbour or an old friend, and how a small spider treks the ceiling. He adds poems, jokes, and phrases appealing to his writer's mind. He seeks recurring themes. Personal qualities that he admits to possessing sound strangely familiar. It's something cut from the same Houston tweed: an *egocentric* base cloth with herringbone to signify *feelings of omnipotence*.

> ... shyness disappears, the right words and gestures are suddenly there ... things become intensely interesting. Sensuality is pervasive; the desire to seduce and be seduced is irresistible. Your marrow is infused with unbelievable feelings ... omnipotence, euphoria ... you can do anything ... but somewhere all this changes ... later alone ... all that's left is l'esprit d'escalier.

Tony's a septuagenarian, walking alone in parks, and when he writes it all down he captures the minutiae of life as good as Virginia Woolf ever did. He follows winged insects, tiny caterpillars, throws a ball back to two players on the tennis courts, sits beside a pond watching a heron, and sees a little boy held and comforted by Daddy after falling from his tiny bike. He chuckles over the antics of toddlers. Awakening from a daydream, midway coming home from Hammersmith, he practically leaps off the bus, straight across the road into the Salvation Arms, and later it's the Duke of York, then the Mason's Arms. He can be breathless, nervous, even terrified, experiencing the reverse side of the senses he felt in the park. Another time he heads towards Acton Park but a lack of confidence makes him change direction via Churchfield Road. Later he criticizes himself for wasting money and having forgotten the words *'refocus and reframe.'* He writes some days he's free of the thrall of alcohol. For the generation or two later than Renée's this problem was recognizable and discussed.

Tony blames Pat and Renée saying: 'I never had a life, due to my bloody parents,'[4] although regret for not being able to seize the day in young adulthood might have been at least as significant. Watching university students mucking around and having fun, Tony envies the younger generations' freedoms. It was a more innocent and a narrower world he knew – where the price of not conforming was to live on the outskirts and attract town gossip. There was no place to hide or slip through the gaps. You obeyed the rules of a single community that everyone was part of. Meanwhile, people listened intently to the 'sincere' words of public figures like Renée Houston at local fêtes and Conservative rallies.

Tony contemplates whether or not to purchase a poster for sale in Cecil Court but the price is high so he puts it out of his mind. He sets himself the task in his diary to investigate old reviews by James Agate but it's easier said than done and he opts for 'Hunted' by James Herbert instead. He hadn't realized his mother and aunt Billie had ever billed themselves as the *Irresistibles* on playbills - not until 1997. He is knowledgeable about his family and early life in conversation. Alone, he reverts to amnesia. In the diary he seldom refers to his mum by name. Is it the old habit of not sharing her - afraid of a new intrusion into his home-life maybe? If only he had known about the times when things didn't go to plan for those *Irresistibles* fed to the lions in the Empires, Hippodromes and Palaces. They bore the shame of deathly atmospheres and took the flak. They were imprisoned in a family business with a name to live up to. Tony got away. Life rescued him.

He references Robb Wilton – his great uncle by marriage, and Auntie Joan Fontaine who he sees on television playing a ship saboteur who's eaten by a shark while dying of radiation. He finds the film 'a load of rubbish.'[5] On April 11, 2002, he visits his Mum's grave, and a week later notes that he loved his mother. His beloved Claire Rennie dies at the end of that month. By late October 2002, he writes how he's 'Unable to settle. Bad fantasies acting out a family drama in which I stab, kick and mutilate mum and Donald Stewart. Got so wrought up I got up.'[6] Two days pass, and he's back again reading Jim's and Mum's 'write up' from the old days. Ghosts return the next day and the toilet sees more dramatic scenes with dead relatives: Mum, Dad, Donald, and Lulu de Lacy Aherne. The garden at Stanmore had seen his rage:

Renée: Pat adores kids too. They made him angry a few weeks ago, though. He had a fine lot of peaches in the garden; he'd been nursing them for weeks and they were just getting nice and red. When we got home one night we found the kids had picked them all and used them for cricket balls, thinking they looked the right colour, size and shape.'[7]

One fruit was picked from the espalier, then another, and another until it became frenzied. The mess from all those smashed peaches is a means of expressing yourself and the air has the sweet smell of hypomania.

Niall's anniversaries are always recorded in Tony's diaries but never Renée's, although he once notes £1558.67 as the value of her earnings, eighteen years after her death, including the latest cheque from Pamela Simons. It seems so cheap a price for so much talent and wit.

I dream silently about the past:

Renée had appeared to the crowds at the rally in July 1940. She stood alongside Will Hay, who spoke about British humour as the resource that united us. I miss people of her generation, not just the famous entertainers but ordinary men and women who lived then. They were great tellers of stories, often blessed by wit. They inspired with the force of personality. I was lucky enough to know a few of them: folk who had fought in the war or survived the blitz. For them, the shared experience of being united in laughter was essential – it expressed humanity. The value of this way of life was obvious. Men would risk their lives to help defend it. Can you imagine a time when Londoners were considered a theatre-going public unlike the provinces that tended towards films?[8] Londoners lived in and out of a communal experience. Today, in our changed cities, current types of entertainment would startle our great grandparents. Much is by and by with the *Krankies* - last of the kiddy acts - for a while cast out and made to feel like social pariahs.[9] Alas, Netflix look inwards while CGI hasn't brought me closer to humanity or taught me to defend it. None give me pride in my town and country and I can't even get a job at WC Boggs these days.

Grumbles are valuable. When a household name has rubbed shoulders with old-time megastars, survived wars, supported charities for decades, and earned all kind of stripes, a cutting comment from them is one you listen to more than that of some whippersnapper. It's reassuring when a true pro graces the table – their mere presence enhancing a sociable gathering and creating magic wherever they go. Yet young unsociable stars scowl behind their Versace sunglasses. Could they learn from that world without implants when laughter alone lightened dissatisfaction and reality kept us on track?

A Fantastic Dream:

If Renée were around today, it would be natural for her to be vociferous and she would suit today's topical discussions on TV even if they do only go so far. On radio she would get away with a measure of independence and lay into us for being bored and blasé, urging us to speak our minds whilst remaining kind to others at the same time. To be too zipped-up would be a difficult prospect for one who enjoyed freedom of speech and hated cant. Smoke-free studios and drink-free dressing rooms would rankle too, and choice words would be reserved for today's smart Alec comics. She'd bear witness to her beliefs, sailing against the tide and defying corporate invasions into her comedy space. It feels like outspokenness has got nastier on all entertainment mediums. We still love a well-delivered line, eloquent in its punch, and you don't hear these so frequently now. Rare too, is to find a lady to laugh along to, whose style turns out to be matchless and whose sheer class is unparalleled.

There was none more Scotch in their welcome than Renée. It's true that some were never going to find olive branches dispensed down Walton way but she provided a sense of comfort to needy listeners and theatregoers. She had the theatrical magic that inspires and beckons you to follow your dream. Being the great laugh she was won her new fans instantly. Some were struck by her good nature and refreshing modesty. Others saw a spiritual quality and recognized the influence she had once had. What's gone is gone, and her thoughts about what she had done were modest. Her new fans didn't see her selfish side. 'It doesn't pay to think about what might have been,' the Little Mother said in a calm moment. I cried about my losses and dropped searching questions into the conversation. But her advice was to get rid of that idea now. There would definitely be a place for her now, if she could be so ageless. Laughter might bring peace I muse - thinking about a time the world was less violent. Renée would help matters by getting us laughing. We were foolish people and we did foolish things. Isn't this the only truthful way of looking at our lives, and the explanation that best serves?

THE END

Notes and Credits

Chapter 1
1. Evening Standard October 12, 1974 Page 9, as witnessed by Molly Parkin –Courtesy Independent Print Ltd
2. Radio Pictorial Magazine June 5, 1936 page 7, 'Girls Will Be Boys!' Nerina Shute – Courtesy British Library
3. The People's Journal, May 2, 1936 – Courtesy British Library
4. Lines from Old Bill And Son (1940) Quoted by kind permission of STUDIOCANAL Films Ltd
5. The Official Gracie Fields Website team tells me Gracie said this in a radio interview many years later.
6. The Scotch Comedians, Albert D. Mackie. Ramsay Head Press, Edinburgh 1973
7. A full page advert in The Stage, June 3, 1926 page 13, describes it as 'A Riot with the Houston Sisters and the Savoy Orpheans Band,' conducted by Ramon Newton.' Historians of the Savoy bands tell me the Sisters never actually recorded with the band - the ad a marketing ploy dreamt up by the publishing company.
8. Pub. Keith Prowse & Co. Ltd 1926. Reprinted by kind permission of estate of Leslie Sarony.
9. Recorded September 1926 on a double sided ACO label Gramophone record Reference: C16024/C8011
10. She did this at Fulham's Granville City of Varieties – then newly refurbished- a source for jokes.
11. The Daily Mail, August 23, 1926
12. The Era, October 3, 1928, M. Willson Disher – Courtesy British Library
13. The Era, May 25, 1927 – Courtesy British Library
14. The Observer, May 29, 1927, MWD – Courtesy Guardian News & Media
15. Script for variety routine by Renée Houston 1935 – Courtesy Aherne Family
16. Script for variety routine by Renée Houston 1935 – Courtesy Aherne Family
17. 'True to me: A domestic scene with piano' (FB 1307) was recorded on Columbia Records' 'FB' label - a special label for song and patter variety routines. The Columbia recording is dated 02.02.1936. The initial song is by the Kidd Brothers - Miss Houston's stage partners (before she teamed up with Donald Stewart).
18. Her father, fearing they might turn into Glesca keelies insisted his daughters take elocution lessons.
19. Excerpt of Houston Sisters dialogue from John Argyle's 'Variety - The Romance of the Music Halls'(1935)
20. Excerpt of Houston Sisters dialogue from British International Pictures 'Radio Parade'(1933)
21. The Stage, Jan 26, 1939, Page 3 describes Renée and Donald's appearance at The Grand, Clapham
22. Excerpt of Houston Sisters dialogue from John Argyle's 'Variety - The Romance of the Music Halls '(1935)
23. Excerpt of Houston Sisters dialogue from John Argyle's 'Variety - The Romance of the Music Halls'(1935)
24. People's Journal, Argyll & The Isles, Saturday February 29, 1936 – Courtesy British Library
25. The Daily Express, December 7, 1927 – Courtesy Express Newspapers/N&S Syndication
26. My Life of Music, by Sir Henry Wood Pub. Gollancz, 1938.
27. The Era, December 12, 1927 – Courtesy British Library
28. The Daily Mail, May 9, 1949 page 3 – Courtesy Solo Syndication
29. The Stage, January 10, 1929 Page 11 - Courtesy of The Stage
30. My thanks to Scottish Theatre Archive - Town Hall, Dingwall – October 22, 1956 (STA Fa 9/33)
31. An Actor and His Time - by John Gielgud. Pub. Sidgwick and Jackson 1979
32. This was to the sound of Debussy's 'Clair de Lune' and Percy Grainger's 'Shepherd's Hey'
33. MWD in The Observer, March 20, 1927 – Courtesy Guardian News & Media
34. The Era, May 19, 1926 page 16 – Courtesy Westminster Reference Library
35. 'Don't Fence Me In' by Renée Houston, 1974 – by kind permission of Pan Macmillan via PLSclear

Chapter 2
1. This owner avoided the fall-out from the Wall Street crash. He lived here until just after the war.
2. The Evening Standard, November 26, 1974, Maureen Cleave.
3. The current owners have developed this into a smart extension with glass patio doors.
4. The Evening Standard, November 26, 1974, Maureen Cleave.
5. The Guardian, February 11, 1980, 'Renée Houston 'Old trouper' of the stage dies.'
6. BBC WAC, R/19/2233, September 14, 1966 Memo Publicity Officer to RPI CC. BPO and John Cassels - 'Fresh Petticoats For The Line' about Autumn series starting October 6 © BBC.
7. He would blow the whistle on contestants during Just a Minute
8. The Evening Standard Page 9, October 12, 1974
9. Conversation with Bettine Le Beau: panellist on Petticoat Line 1967-76
10. BBC WAC, R/19/2233, December 23, 1966 Memo BSG Bumpus to John Cassels and letter of December 15, 1966 Capt ET MacMichael to Director-General of the BBC © BBC.
11. Letter Elana Aherne 20 Southover Street, to Aunt Eunice (early 1970s).
12. The Evening Standard October 12, 1974, Molly Parkin – Quoted courtesy of Independent Print Ltd
13. The Evening Standard October 12, 1974, Molly Parkin – Quoted courtesy of Independent Print Ltd
14. Based on R4 PETTICOAT LINE - 19 March 1975 18.15 Ref. SX 12989/2 by kind permission of the BBC
15. Based on R4 PETTICOAT LINE - 19 March 1975 18.15 Ref. SX 12989/2 by kind permission of the BBC
16. BBC WAC, R/19/2233, Audience Research Report on Petticoat Line, November 11, 1966.
17. The Evening Standard October 12, 1974 Page 9, Molly Parkin
18. Based on R4 PETTICOAT LINE - 11 November 1969 12.25 Ref. SX 29731/1 by kind permission of the BBC
19. BBC WAC, R/19/2233, Memo 'FAB' Girl Joins the Petticoat Line'- November 10, 1965 - Sarah Stoddart Publicity to RPI, John Cassels © BBC.
20. BBC WAC, R/19/2233, Memo January 25, 1967 John Cassels quotes 1 million listeners for 1967 © BBC.

21. Ian Messiter quotes 2 million viewing figure for 1974 (in Evening Standard October 12, 1974 Page 9)
22. Based on R4 PETTICOAT LINE - 11 November 1969 12.25 Ref. SX 29731/1 by kind permission of the BBC
23. Based on R4 PETTICOAT LINE - 11 November 1969 12.25 Ref. SX 29731/1 by kind permission of the BBC
24. The Daily Mirror, January 28, 1974 p15 'Renee's Word Game' - By kind permission of Trinity Mirror PLC.
25. The Evening Standard October 12, 1974, Molly Parkin
26. Based on short clip on BL SoundServer B3321/2: British Radio fun - episode 10 Cargill, Neil (director) 1988.09.30 by kind permission of the BBC
27. Based on R4 PETTICOAT LINE - 19 March 1975 18.15 Ref. SX 12989/2 by kind permission of the BBC
28. Based on R4 PETTICOAT LINE - 26 February 1975 18.15 Ref. SX 12989/1 by kind permission of the BBC
29. BBC WAC, R/19/2233, Audience Research Report on Petticoat Line, November 11, 1966 © BBC
30. Janet Hitchman 1916-1980 was the author of Such a Strange Lady.
31. BBC WAC, RCONT/15, March 8, 1976 memo Clare Lawson Dick about Petticoat Line, © BBC.
32. BBC WAC, RCONT/15, June 16, 1976. Letter Clare Lawson Dick to Anona Winn © BBC.
33. BBC WAC, RCONT/15, June 23, 1976. Letter Ian Messiter to Clare Lawson Dick © BBC.
34. BBC WAC, RCONT/15, June 23, 1976. Letter Anona Winn to Clare Lawson Dick © BBC.
35. BBC WAC, RCONT/15, October 8, 1976. Letter Janet Hitchman of Bury St Edmunds to Ian MacIntyre © BBC.

Chapter 3
1. The Sunday Mail, Sept 5, 1954, 'The Renee Houston Story' - Courtesy British Library
2. A playground and car park of the current infants' school now stands where her house was.
3. Reflections of a Clyde-Built Man by Jimmy Reid, Condor, 1976 – Courtesy of The Souvenir Press
4. 'Past Horizons', James Allan Rennie Jarrolds 1962
5. 'Don't Fence Me In,' Renée Houston, 1974, by permission of Pan Macmillan via PLSclear
6. The Gray family's Westmuir pits were once the biggest supply source of fuel to Glasgow.
7. 'Past Horizons', Jarrolds 1962 – With permission of the estate of JA Rennie
8. The Theatre, Music Hall and Cinema Blue Book 1917 tells me Alfred Butt presided over the Glasgow Alhambra and London's Victoria Palace. London's Met was in the hands of H. Tozer. J. Duff, and M. Ballantine directed Glasgow Pavilion. Tozer, Wells, and Payne: the London Pavilion.
9. Boy Life and Labour: the Manufacture of Inefficiency, Arnold Freeman, 1914.
10. Ted Ray was named by his agent - George Barclay.
11. The Burnley News, January 20, 1915 – Courtesy British Library
12. The Burnley Express, January 20, 1915 – Courtesy British Library
13. The Nottingham Evening Post - September 24, 1927 – Courtesy British Library
14. The Falkirk Herald, August 7, 1918 – Courtesy British Library
15. Information including Helen Crawfurd's memoirs: display at People's Palace, Glasgow
16. My thanks to John Lewis-Stempel's: 'Scotland the brave: Tough 'kilties' battled for Britain in WWI ' 2014.
17. The Era November 3, 1915 p15, H Chance Newton– Courtesy British Library
18. Essay: The Variety Year by EM Sansom – in The Stage Year Book, 1915 – V&A Museum
19. The Surrey Comet, May 10, 1916 – Courtesy British Library
20. The British Working Class and Enthusiasm for War, 1914-1916 by David Silbey
21. The Falkirk Herald, September 26,1914 – Courtesy British Library
22. The Stage, June 10, 1915 Page: 15 – Courtesy of The Stage Archive
23. Produced by Henry de Vries, its dialogue was 'unpolished' The Stage, May 27, 1915 Page 14
24. 'Past Horizons', James Allan Rennie Jarrolds, 1962 – With permission of the estate of JA Rennie
25. My thanks to turtlebunbury.com/history/history
26. Daily Express, Dublin August 5, 1914 – Courtesy British Library
27. The People's Journal, March 14, 1936 – Courtesy British Library

Chapter 4
1. Area bounded by Denbeck Street, Darleith Street, Old Shettleston Street and Fernan Street
2. Regular Recitals and choirs listed in The Glasgow Observer - a Catholic weekly illustrates this.
3. The People's Journal, Saturday April 4, 1936 – Courtesy British Library
4. Evening Standard, November 26, 1974, Maureen Cleave – Courtesy Independent Print Ltd
5. BBC Scotland, Spotlight, Produced by Ian MacFadyen April 1973. My thanks to BBC Scotland.
6. The People's Journal, Argyll & The Isles, February 29, 1936 – Courtesy British Library
7. 'Past Horizons', James Allan Rennie Jarrolds, 1962 – With permission of the estate of JA Rennie
8. The People's Journal, February 29, 1936 – Courtesy British Library
9. The latter plot was in The School by the Sea, Angela Brazil 1914
10. 'Past Horizons', by James Allan Rennie Jarrolds 1962
11. 'Don't Fence Me In' by Renée Houston, 1974 - with permission of Pan Macmillan via PLSclear
12. A Ragged Schooling, Robert Roberts, 1976. Pub. Mandolin
13. Across the Bridges, by A. Paterson, 1911
14. Reflections of a Clyde-Built Man, Jimmy Reid, 1976 - with permission of The Souvenir Press.
15. 'Laughter in the Roar,' Brian O'Gorman. Badger Press, 1998 -by kind permission of the author.
16. Study by Joyce Senders Pederson, in Carol Dyhouse's Girls going up in Victorian and Edwardian England Pub Routledge & Kegan Paul (1981) p57
17. Logbooks for Our Lady and St Francis School. My thanks to The Mitchell Library, Glasgow.
18. Document sent by Franciscan Sisters of Immaculate Conception. Charity No SC 006881 7109

Notes and Credits

19. Logbooks for Our Lady and St Francis School - My thanks to The Mitchell Library, Glasgow.
20. The Lincolnshire Chronicle Fri November 28, 1913– Courtesy British Library
21. The Stage, November 14, 1912 Page 12 – Courtesy of The Stage
22. The winner got a prize of £2 10s. There were 42 competitors ranging in age.
23. The People's Journal, March 7, 1936 – Courtesy British Library

Chapter 5
1. At East Ham (April 17, 1916), Kingston (May 10, 1916), Chelsea (May 14, 1916)
2. The People's Journal March 21, 1936 page 6 – Courtesy British Library
3. The Surrey Comet, May 10, 1916 – Courtesy British Library
4. The Sunday Mail, September 5, 1954 – Courtesy British Library
5. The People's Journal, March 21, 1936 – Courtesy British Library
6. In 'Those Variety Days - Memories of Scottish Variety Theatre' Ed. by F.Bruce, A.Foley and G. Gillespie pub. Scottish Music hall Society (1997)
7. Interview with May Moxon - by Jean Donald, Sunday Herald.
8. Music's Great Days in the Spas & Watering Places by Kenneth Young, 1968 Pub Macmillan.
9. Shoes were for Sunday Molly Weir London: Hutchinson, 1970
10. Music Hall Memories - by Jack House, Pub. Richard Drew Publishing, Glasgow, 1986.
11. Voices from the Hunger Marches: Personal Recollections by Scottish Hunger Marchers of the 1920s and 1930s by Ian Macdougall (Edinburgh 1990) with permission via PLSclear
12. People's Journal, March 28, 1936 – Courtesy British Library
13. Training Girls as Guides, Lady Baden Powell 1917 – Courtesy University of Kent Library
14. One was Galashiels Pavilion on October 2, 1921 - The Stage, Thursday, October 6, 1921 Page 4
15. The Fife Free Press, & Kirkaldy Guardian, December 14, 1918 – Courtesy British Library
16. The Falkirk Herald Stirlingshire, Scotland 23 Nov 1918 – Courtesy British Library
17. The Era November 3, 1915 page 15, H Chance Newton – Courtesy British Library
18. The Stage Year Book for 1917 – Courtesy V&A Museum, London, Theatre & Performance Collections
19. The Falkirk Herald Tuesday, December 3, 1919 – Courtesy British Library
20. The Aberdeen Journal Tuesday, December 16, 1919 – Courtesy British Library
21. The People's Journal, April 4, 1936 – Courtesy British Library
22. The Aberdeen Journal, December 16, 1919 – Courtesy British Library
23. The People's Journal March 21, 1936 – Courtesy British Library
24. Interview with Mavis Nicholson, Good Afternoon LWT Broadcast: 31/01/74
25. The People's Journal March 21, 1936 – Courtesy British Library

Chapter 6
1. Jimmie Houston talking about his daughters Renée and Billie.
2. My thanks to West Lothian Local History Library.
3. 'Make 'Em Laugh' by Eric Midwinter, Pub. George Allen & Unwin, 1979. By kind permission of the author.
4. Interview with Pete Davis for Spotlight, BBC Radio Scotland. My thanks to BBC Scotland.
5. May and her sister Ella Logan soon became part of Jack Short's 'Starlights' in the early 1920s before May and Jack developed their act as 'Pa and Ma Logan'.
6. The Fife Free Press, & Kirkaldy Guardian, 17 December 1921 – Courtesy British Library
7. 'Past Horizons', Jarrolds 1962. Quoted with the permission of the estate of James Allan Rennie.
8. The Burnley News Saturday September 30, 1922 – Courtesy British Library
9. The People's Journal, April 4, 1936 – Courtesy British Library
10. The People's Journal, May, 1936 – Courtesy British Library
11. The Era, May 10, 1922 page 5 – Courtesy British Library
12. Theatre Royal Programme for Wondering Jew, August 28, 1922 – found on Ebay
13. BBC Scotland, Spotlight, Produced by Ian MacFadyen April 1973
14. This is mentioned at the very end of 'Don't Fence Me In.'
15. This was on the Bostock tour, with dates in Motherwell and Aberdeen
16. The School Foundation paid George's fees - a legacy of Jinglin' Geordie George Heriot.
17. The Folkestone, Hythe, Sandgate and Cheriton Herald, July 21,1923 – Courtesy British Library
18. See Portable days: A Personal Account of Life in the Theatre, as told to Neil McNicholas, by Violet Godfrey Carr, Spredden Press 1991
19. 'Don't Fence Me In' by Renée Houston, 1974, with permission of Pan Macmillan via PLSclear
20. The Era November 10, 1926, GS Melvin – Courtesy British Library
21. The People's Journal Saturday April 4, 1936 – Courtesy British Library
22. The Sunday Post - February 22 1925 'Romantic Wedding of Glasgow Panto Artiste'
23. This was the cramped tenement they moved to after 71 Crail Street
24. Interview with Mavis Nicholson, Good Afternoon LWT Broadcast: 31/01/74
25. Mentioned in Renée's 1936 memoir in The People's Journal
26. The Aberdeen Journal, March 17, 1925 – Courtesy British Library
27. The Era October 10, 1919 – Courtesy Westminster Reference Library
28. The People's Journal, April 11, 1936– Courtesy British Library
29. Spotlight interview: Pete Davis. Interviewer Robin Russell. BBC Scotland. Produced by Ron Spencer, 1974

RENÉE HOUSTON: SPIRIT OF THE IRRESISTIBLES

30. The People's Journal, April 25, 1936 – Courtesy British Library
31. The Stage, January 11, 1973 Page 7, Georgie Wood Stage Man's Diary – Courtesy The Stage

Chapter 7
1. British Music Hall: An Illustrated History, by Richard Anthony Baker
2. 'Past Horizons', Jarrolds 1962. Quoted with the permission of the estate of James Allan Rennie.
3. Leslie Sarony conversation –My thanks to Stephen Dixon for information on his excellent website: www.voices-of-variety.com
4. The Pavilion had a company of actors headed by MD Waxman and held Yiddish seasons until 1935, after which the Grand Palais at 133 Commercial Road took over.
5. 'Past Horizons', Jarrolds 1962. Quoted with permission of the estate of James Allan Rennie.
6. Minstrelsy was an immensely popular genre at the dawn of the 20th Century. Eugene Stratton's 'inimitable coon scene' often featured a 'Drum Major' back in 1911.
7. Radio Pictorial, January 15, 1937, Howard Thomas – Courtesy British Library
8. Radio Pictorial, January 15, 1937, Howard Thomas – Courtesy British Library
9. BBC Scotland, Spotlight, Produced by Ian MacFadyen April 1973. My thanks to BBC Scotland.
10. The People's Journal, March 7, 1936 – Courtesy British Library
11. The Evening Standard, November 26, 1974, Maureen Cleave – Courtesy Independent Print Ltd
12. Some sources say Irish singer May Belfort was a sadistic bully. She sang this song in 1895.
13. The Stage, November 19, 1931 refers to a Palladium visit when the Sisters shared the bill with Will Hay, GS Melvin and Hutch. Singing 'Oh! Rosalita!' Renée, was described as 'a high blonde.'
14. Highly regarded, The Performer, or 'Official Organ of the Variety Artistes Federation' cost 3d.
15. The Performer, January 20 1926 p13 – Courtesy British Library
16. The Stage, January 21, 1926 Page: 13 – Courtesy British Library
17. The London Coliseum: The Story of London's Largest Theatre ENO Golden Jubilee Ed. Richard Jarman 1964
18. The People's Journal, February 29, 1936 – Courtesy British Library
19. See Voices from the Hunger Marches: Personal Recollections by Scottish Hunger Marchers of the 1920s and 1930s by Ian Macdougall, Edinburgh 1990 p118-181
20. In The Daily Sketch on April 26, 1926
21. Mosley and his wife continued to be popular speakers at miners' galas in the 20s. See - The Rules of the game 1896-1933 by Nicholas Mosley, London: Secker & Warburg, 1982
22. Sybil Thorndike: A Life in the Theatre by Sheridan Morley, Wiedenfield and Nicholson, 1977
23. The South London was based at 92 London Road, Lambeth.
24. 'Past Horizons', Jarrolds 1962. Quoted with permission of the estate of James Allan Rennie.
25. Memories of Joe O'Gorman - My thanks to Brian O'Gorman.
26. See For Ladies Only? Eve's Film Review Pathé Cinemagazine 1921-33, Jenny Hammerton 2001
27. Conversation with film historian Tony Fletcher
28. The Portsmouth Evening News May 28 1927 – Courtesy British Library
29. How Films Were Made and Shown: Some Aspects of the Technical Side of Motion Picture Film 1895-2015, By David Cleveland and Brian Pritchard 2015.
30. Pronounced 'Hot Knees'
31. My thanks to David Cleveland, Tony Fletcher and Paul Matthew St Pierre for information they kindly shared with me regarding Widgey Newman and the history of De Forest Phonofilms.

Chapter 8
1. North Cheshire Herald February 1, 1913, The Stage March 6, 1980
2. The Glasgow Herald, August 2, 1927
3. James M.Glover, The Music Box column in The Stage, January 19, 1928 Page: 17
4. Radio Pictorial, October 30, 1936 pages 11, 29 – Courtesy British Library
5. The Observer, July 2, 1920
6. The London Coliseum: The Story of London's Largest Theatre by Richard Jarman
7. David F. Cheshire, Music hall in Britain, 1974. Quoted by kind permission of FDU.
8. Vesta Tilley by Sara Maitland, Pub Virago, 1986
9. Vesta Tilley by Sara Maitland, Pub Virago, 1986
10. 'Masquerading as a man'-The charm of playing principal boy, The Era, 1926 (Westminster Ref. Library)
11. The People's Journal, March 7, 1936 – Courtesy British Library
12. Sunday Post, 22 February 1925 'Romantic Wedding of Glasgow Panto Artiste'– Courtesy British Library
13. Gloucester Citizen, November 7, 1922 – Courtesy British Library
14. 'How we became a double act' The Era August 4, 1926 – Courtesy Westminster Reference Library
15. The Performer, August 29, 1927 page 19 – Courtesy British Library
16. Sunday Post, 22 February 1925 'Romantic Wedding of Glasgow Panto Artiste'
17. The Era, May 23, 1928 – Courtesy Westminster Reference Library
18. From Dressing Up by Peter Ackroyd © 1979 by Peter Ackroyd. Reprinted by kind permission of Thames & Hudson Ltd., London.
19. The Stage, April 20, 1933 Page 3
20. Comœdia, September 24, 1929 with kind permission of BnF (Translated by M Gregoire)
21. Radio Pictorial, October 30, 1936 p11, 29 – Courtesy British Library

Notes and Credits

22. A book by George Sala from 1859 has the same title, with one chapter for each hour of the day, but that's about London in the 1850s.
23. The Daily Sketch's editor, A Curthoys was cashing in on fascination for the variety star.
24. The Era, April 10, 1935 – Courtesy British Library
25. Sheffield Independent, February 18, 1935 – Courtesy British Library
26. Quoted in Yorkshire Post and Leeds Advertiser, March 6, 1935 – Courtesy British Library
27. Twice Round the Clock - by Billie Houston, pub. Hutchinson, 1935. Page 49
28. Twice Round the Clock - by Billie Houston, pub. Hutchinson, 1935, Page 31
29. Another book 'Exit Aunt Susan' was apparently 75% written but never finished.
30. The Encore November 11, 1926 Page 6 – Courtesy British Library
31. The Encore: December 9, 1926 and December 30, 1926 – Courtesy British Library
32. From St Mark's Gospel
33. The Encore, March 24, 1927 Page 6 – Courtesy British Library
34. The Irish News and Belfast Morning News, November 29 and 30, 1926
35. The Encore December 9, 1926 Page 18 – Courtesy British Library
36. A youth troupe run by a Miss Terry 'a ferocious Jewish lady' that lasted until the 1960s. Kids joined at 12 and on tour had 2 'Aunties' looking after them.
37. The orphanage's location is unclear - possibly St. Joseph's Mother and Baby Home' at 107 Tulse Hill but Terry's orphanage was operated by the Southwark Catholic Rescue Society.
38. Those in the 'Company of Star Artistes' are unknown. Frank Boston & Betty, and Jack Barty were leads.
39. The Cape Argus, February 4 1938 – Courtesy British Library
40. There was an embargo on this whole topic in the Houston home.
41. In 1936 she revealed she had adopted Trevor. This was shortly before the Houston Sisters appeared together in a film in which their family was the storyline. This was the time to make a statement about it.

Chapter 9
1. West Lancashire Evening Gazette, July 23, 1929 – Courtesy British Library
2. The Era, July 16, 1924, 'Smoothing the Path of Theatrical Travel' by St John White
3. Main points of essay called 'The Variety Year' by EM Sansom in The Stage Year Book, 1926.
4. The Performer, June 30 1926 p14 and July 7, 1926 p14 – Courtesy British Library
5. The Performer, October 29, 1930 page 4 – Courtesy British Library
6. The Scotsman, March 5, 1935
7. Article in the Guardian July 2015 Younger Scots Losing Distinctive Burr Say Linguistic Experts
8. The Era 10.11.1926, 'Is Versatility a Handicap?-Where the Solo Artist Scores over the Man with Many Parts'
9. The Performer, September 10, 1930 records this night at the Coliseum.
10. The Stage, March 29, 1928 page 11
11. The Performer, May 31, 1928, page 10 reports on the Locality act – Courtesy British Library
12. By Raymond Wallace & Reginald Tabbush
13. By Harry Leon; Leo Towers; Horatio Nicholls
14. Funny Way to be a Hero, by John Fisher. Pub. Random House, 2013, p245
15. You Tube has the Mal Hallett's Orchestra version with squeaky falsettos in its vocal duet
16. By Harry Carlton
17. The Stage, April 4, 1929 page 13 details the Alhambra visit on April 1, 1929 – Courtesy The Stage
18. Daily Mail, August 6, 1929 page 10
19. The Performer February 29 1928 p10 praises Ivor Vintor: 'A big hand for the little chap.'
20. West Lancashire Evening Gazette, July 23 1929 – Courtesy British Library
21. The Stage, August 1, 1929 page 6 reviews variety at the Alhambra
22. V&A Museum, London, Theatre & Performance Collections, Programme B'ham Hipp. December 31, 1934
23. The Stage, December 31, 1925 Page 21
24. The Stage, August 26, 1926 Page 21
25. The Performer March 26 1930 p4
26. The Performer March 2, 1932 p10
27. 'Sisters Return' in Portsmouth Evening News, February 5 1952
28. The Stage Year Book 1926 – Courtesy V&A Museum, London, Theatre & Performance Collections
29. 'Better variety is answer - mediocrity is fatal,' The Performer May 13 1931 page7
30. The Performer No. 1105 June 1 1927 page 5 – Courtesy British Library
31. Daily Mail, June 24, 1927 page 17
32. Hannen Swaffer's Who's Who by Hannen Swaffer, 1929
33. 'If Variety is Dead, who has killed it? - Mistakes and the Future.' The Era February 1, 1928 –British Library
34. Stoll Picture Theatre To Change To All 'Talkie' Next Month,' The Performer, April 10 1929
35. British Films 1927-1939 - BFI Library Services edited by Linda Wood, 1986 – Courtesy BFI
36. 'Don't Fence Me In' by Renée Houston, 1974, reproduced with permission of Pan Macmillan via PLSclear
37. My thanks to www.radiorewind.co.uk
38. Radio Comedy 1938-1968, by Andy Foster and Steve Furst, Pub. Virgin Publishing 1996
39. The Golden Days - British Dance Bands TV Programme with Len Goodman commentary
40. 'Music Hall and Wireless - What Managements Should Do,' The Performer Apr 21, 1927 –British Library
41. 'If you broadcast - Federation Decision' The Performer October 31, 1928 – Courtesy British Library
42. 'Sir Oswald Stoll Replies: Artistes and Broadcasting,' The Performer, February 6 1929 page 11

43. The Performer, November 25 1931 page 7 – Courtesy British Library
44. 'Shortage of Variety - A Rejoinder to the BBC' The Performer May 28 1931 No. 1313 page 3
45. 'Radio costs theatre £10000 in one night' The Performer, January 18, 1933 p14 – Courtesy British Library
46. 'Romantic Wedding of Glasgow Panto Artiste, 'Sunday Post, February 22, 1925 – Courtesy British Library
47. 'How we became a double act' Houston Sisters Interview, The Era, August 4, 1926–Westminster Ref. Library
48. Picture Show, March 5, 1927 – Courtesy British Library
49. Just a Little Bit of String by Ellaline Terriss, pub. Hutchinson & Co 1955

Chapter 10
1. The Sphere September 11,1926 page 318. Herbert Vandyk – Courtesy British Library
2. Published by Philip Allan & Co. Ltd of Quality Court in 1926.
3. The verse is from one of his 'Stanzas for Music'
4. Beaton brought out his 'Book of Beauty' in 1930 and wrote books like 'The Glass of Fashion.'
5. The Stage, March 3, 1927 Page 23
6. Reference in article 'Just Think' by George Munro in The Era, September 13, 1938 – Courtesy British Library
7. As referenced by an article written by Maureen Cleave.
8. The Encore, January 21, 1926 page 5 – Courtesy British Library
9. Extracts from More First Nights by James Agate reprinted by permission of Peters Fraser & Dunlop (www.petersfraserdunlop.com) on behalf of the Estate of James Agate
10. Tom Driberg, Swaff: Life and Times of Hannen Swaffer. MacDonald, 1974
11. AC Astor in 'Just Jottings', The Stage, October 27, 1927, Page 21 – Courtesy The Stage
12. Variety, Cabaret, Film News September 27, 1934 page 8, 11
13. BBC Scotland, Spotlight, Produced by Ian MacFadyen April 1973. My thanks to BBC Scotland.
14. The People's Journal, April 11,1936
15. Ivan Patrick Gore's column, The Stage, July 25, 1929 Page 12 – Courtesy The Stage
16. 'Evelyn Laye talks to Alex Noel Watson,' Croydon Advertiser September 24, 1976.
17. The National Archives UK ref. B 9/1354 Proceedings under Bankruptcy Acts: Patrick de Lacy Aherne, 1940
18. Letter February 16, 1956 from Donald to Mrs FC Wintermute

Chapter 11
1. He had appeared in Growing Pains at the Ambassadors, Sons and Fathers and Mary's John with the RADA Players at Malet Street, and in The Squeaker - a Scotland Yard drama by Edgar Wallace at the Apollo.
2. A time and place is given: September 12-17, 1932 at 23 Alexandra Road, Edgbaston,
3. Scripted by Bill Lipscomb, Clive played at the Royal, Windsor then 3 West End theatres. The play, made into a film, got Lipscomb a Hollywood contract. He created the script for 'A Town Like Alice' later on.
4. Portsmouth Evening News, March 19 1935 – Courtesy British Library
5. 'Billie Houston Husband runs out to die' Daily Mirror, July 23, 1938 by kind permission Trinity Mirror plc.
6. Hull Daily Mail, July 25, 1938 – Courtesy British Library
7. Dundee Evening Telegraph, Saturday 23 July 1938 – Courtesy British Library
8. Daily Mirror, July 23, 1938 By kind permission of Trinity Mirror PLC.
9. The Encore: January 20, 1927 – Courtesy British Library
10. The Encore: January 14, 1926, March 11, 1926, June 10, 1926 – Courtesy British Library
11. The Encore: February 25, 1926 – Courtesy British Library
12. Jim's first office was at Wieland's Agency, Faraday House, 8 Charing Cross Road.
13. 'James Houston's New Venture' by WJ Bishop The Era, April 6 1932 describes the Cine-Variety Service
14. The Stage, March 28, 1929 page 22
15. 'Past Horizons', by James Allan Rennie Jarrolds 1962 with permission of the estate of James Allan Rennie.
16. The Encore, June 15, 1927 – Courtesy British Library
17. Evening News, August 8, 1959 – Bill Boorne's Close-up Article
18. See Olivier by Anthony Holden, Pub. Weidenfield and Nicolson, 1988
19. The Leader, April 22, 1930 – Courtesy British Library
20. Daily News, February 10, 1930: Cutting from Sybil Thorndike's scrapbook V&A Museum, London
21. Sybil's acting expressed 'the emotional beauty of old age'(The Era, February 19, 1930). While it praised the lighting and harp music, The Times thought the conversation was unrealistic.
22. V&A Museum, London, Theatre & Performance Collections, Cuttings:V&A Sybil Thorndike's scrapbook
23. 'Don't Fence Me In' by Renée Houston, 1974, reproduced with permission of Pan Macmillan via PLSclear
24. This was his parents' home at 43 Park Hill, Edgbaston.
25. They were here by Easter 1929, after 3 years in Kensington. In 1933 'Carntyne' became house number 31.
26. Daily Express November 22, 1930 'Not To Drive For 5 Years'
27. The Great British Picture Show by George Perry, 1985, Pavilion Books
28. 'Save The Theatre! By Oswald Stoll - See Westminster Archive, Coliseum Box.
29. 'How I Crashed In' - the breezy young Irish juvenile unloads the truth, The Picturegoer, June 1929.
30. Derby Daily Telegraph, 26 March 26, 1929. – Courtesy British Library
31. 'My Brother Brian Aherne' by Pat Aherne, Film Pictorial, March 12, 1937 – Courtesy British Library
32. The old school building, designed by Charles Barry - architect of the Houses of Parliament - is now sadly lost. Burne-Jones paintings once covered the walls. Pat and Brian were previously at Miss Green's Boarding School for Boys, Bastion House - a seaside preparatory school in Prestatyn, North Wales.

Notes and Credits

33. See Birmingham In The First World War, J P Lethbridge, Newgate Press.
34. 'Hollywood Interlude' in The Picturegoer March 25, 1933 - v2 n96 – Courtesy British Library
35. Hawks' 'A Girl In Every Port' and Stoloff's 'Goldie' retain the death leap spectacle.
36. A venue obliterated in the Second World War, apart from the rear entrance in Parker Street: leads you nowadays to a strip club, always looking for staff. A sign 'No Experience Necessary' is pinned to the door.
37. The screenplay based on John Buchan's book
38. Adapted from a story by Bai David, the film, directed by Thomas Bentley was made at Elstree and photography was by William Shenton. It was a remake of a 1919 picture Billy Wells had appeared in.
39. I have not yet been able to identify which film this was.
40. The Performer, June 18 1930 page 9 – Courtesy British Library
41. V&A Museum Theatre & Performance Collections, Alhambra Production Box, Cutting Dec. 6, 1929 -By CM.
42. Seen first at London's Coliseum on February 23, 1931, they took it to Camberwell Palace on September 14
43. The Performer, October 21, 1931 p11 – Courtesy British Library
44. 'Gem Frauds By Ex-Film Chief,' Daily Telegraph, April 21, 1954 – Courtesy British Film Institute
45. 'Ex-Film Chief Gaoled 3 Years Became £8 Clerk,' Telegraph, December 21, 1957 – Courtesy BFI
46. The Bioscope v90 n1330, March 30, 1932 – Courtesy British Film Institute
47. Kinematograph Weekly, March 31, 1932 page 41 – Courtesy British Library
48. Daily Mirror, Friday January 15, 1932.
49. Dundee Courier, November 29 1932 – Courtesy British Library
50. 'Hollywood Interlude,' The Picturegoer - v2 n96 March 25, 1933 – Courtesy British Library

Chapter 12
1. Knight at the Music Hall by Frank Granville Barker, Plays And Players, October 1957 – British Library
2. The Performer March 15 1933 page 3 – Courtesy British Library
3. Comœdia, September 24, 1929 with kind permission of BnF (Translated by M Gregoire)
4. The Dundee Telegraph, August 8, 1966 – Courtesy British Library
5. Comœdia, September 24, 1929 with kind permission of BnF (Translated by M Gregoire)
6. 'Don't Fence Me In' by Renée Houston, 1974, reproduced with permission of Pan Macmillan via PLSclear
7. The People's Journal, February 1936
8. Swiss-born Adrien Wettach
9. Bransby Williams, by Himself,' Hutchinson, London, 1954
10. Love, dears! Edited memoirs of Marjorie Graham by Clive Murphey Pub. Dennis Dobson, 1980
11. Article about Variety in The Evening Standard December 12, 1934
12. The Performer, January 25, 1933 page 4 – Courtesy British Library
13. 'A Music Hall Veteran Looks Back,' London Evening Standard, November 23, 1932 page 5
14. Article in Variety, Music, Stage and Film News, June 21, 1933 page 13.
15. The Reinsch Brothers from Olympia Circus were at the Coliseum in January 25, 1926
16. V&A Collection - Coliseum Programme, November 28, 1927
17. Nazimova in a playlet by Edgar Allen Woolf was at the Coliseum on May 30, 1927
18. Radio Comedy 1938-1968, by Andy Foster and Steve Furst, Pub. Virgin Publishing 1996
19. My thanks to The Alexandra Palace Television Society
20. The Performer, December 16, 1931 page 6 – Courtesy British Library
21. 'Why Star Comedians Are Scarce' The Era, 1924 – Courtesy Westminster Reference Library
22. The American Society of Recording Artists had started claiming compensation from the radio stations - 'Protecting Artistes' Rights' The Performer, August 23 1934 – Courtesy British Library
23. Britain was listening to Garbo's Talkie debut
24. 'Miss Renée Houston Objects' The Examiner, Launceston, Tas. November 18, 1935 page 8
25. The Stage, May 30, 1929 Page 5
26. At the Holborn Empire, The Performer November 23 1927 p11 – Courtesy British Library
27. At the Coliseum, The Stage, November 13, 1927 Page 13 – Courtesy The Stage
28. At the Prince Of Wales, Daily Mirror, April 14 1939
29. At the Alhambra, The Stage, April 11, 1929 Page 6
30. 'The Renée Houston I Know' by Herbert Harris, Radio Pictorial, September 9, 1938 –British Library
31. 'The Renée Houston I Know' by Herbert Harris, Radio Pictorial, September 9, 1938 page 15,39
32. 'Eve Dresses Up For The Mike' by Verity Clare, Radio Pictorial, September 25, 1936 –British Library

Chapter 13
1. Quoted by kind permission of STUDIOCANAL Films Ltd
2. Written by Robert Hargreaves, Stanley Danerell, and Harry Tilsley
3. Film Pictorial, June 3, 1933 page 20 – Courtesy British Library
4. The Picturegoer - v2 n96, March 25, 1933 – Courtesy British Library
5. He acquired Wardour Films in 1924 and Elstree's British National Studios in 1927
6. The theatre-renter-producer combine rebuilt Shepherd's Bush studios at a cost of £250,000.
7. 'British output for 1933' by PL Mannock, Kinematograph Weekly January 12, 1933 –British Library
8. NLA - Sydney Morning Herald. August 28, 1933
9. 'Hollywood Interlude,' The Picturegoer - v2 n96, March 25, 1933 – Courtesy British Library

10. The modernization was to satisfy the demands of a film quota established in 1927. There was even a plan to build a huge new studio at Stanmore for the European Sound Film Company.
11. Programme for Barrfields Pavilion, Largs, June 1933, Scottish Theatre Archive
12. The Nine Days Wonder revue was broadcast on August 22.
13. The London Pavilion had pillars that obstructed views. At times it was a cinema.
14. Falkirk Herald, April 13, 1935 – Courtesy British Library
15. Comœdia, September 24, 1929 with kind permission of BnF (Translated by M Gregoire)
16. People's Journal interview Feb-May 1936
17. Lancashire Evening Post, March 15, 1935 – Courtesy British Library
18. Hal Gordon, who plays Alf and Fuller sing the Legionnaires song we hear in the soundtrack.
19. Article about Variety in The Evening Standard, December 12, 1934
20. The Telegraph (Brisbane) December 12, 1935, page 20 – Courtesy National Libraries of Australia
21. Kinematograph Weekly February 28, 1935 page 21 – Courtesy British Library
22. BRUNEL Box 77, BFI Collections- Letter Adrian Brunel to Michael Balcon September 26, 1935.
23. 'World market can be had for British Films,' Kinematograph Weekly, December 20, 1934 p. 34 –B. Library
24. 'British and Unashamed,' by PL Mannock, Kinematograph Weekly, January 10, 1935 p133 –B. Library
25. The ten films in Butcher's Jubilee Programme included 'Danny Boy', 'Eventide', 'Broken Rosary', 'Barnacle Bill', 'The City of Beautiful Nonsense' and 'Cock o' the North'.
26. By 1937 'Variety' had been divided into shorts: No 1 (730 ft) featuring George Carney, Sherman Fishers, Billy Cotton, No 2 (812 ft) with Bertha Wilmott, the Can Can Dancers and RH and BH and No 3 (752 ft) with Harry Brunning, Anita Low and Olsen's Sea Lions.
27. *King Of UK Cinemas Poverty Row* by Pathé film expert Graham Newnham
28. Excerpt of Houston Sisters dialogue from John Argyle's 'Variety - Romance of the Music Halls '(1935)
29. The Era, August 21, 1935 – Courtesy British Library
30. 'Don't Fence Me In' by Renée Houston, 1974, reproduced with permission of Pan Macmillan via PLSclear
31. Val Guest, later a BAFTA winning director was a penniless songwriter cum copyist for Picturegoer and the London version of Hollywood Reporter at the time.
32. Based on a short extract of dialogue from Marcel Varnel's 'No Monkey Business'(1935)
33. 'Don't Fence Me In' Renée Houston, 1974, reproduced with permission of Pan Macmillan via PLSclear
34. 'British film production push,' Lancashire Evening Post, October 19, 1935 – Courtesy British Library
35. Kinematograph Weekly November 21, 1935 pages 6 and 26 – Courtesy British Library
36. Variety US December 4, 1935 – Courtesy British Library
37. Song - written by Robert Ganthony in 1894.
38. 'IDA BARR Your old favourite sings you The Coster's Honeymoon' is one example.
39. Viola produced children's plays at her sister's studio in Red Lion Square. She would appear on stage with Renée a year later as Lavinia Skindle in Certainly Sir.
40. 'Jane's Journal – Diary of a *Bright Young Thing*,' Daily Mirror, October 9, 1935 page 11
41. 'A Chat With the Houston Sisters,' Telegraph (Brisbane), December 12, 1935, page 20 – Courtesy NLA
42. 'Girls Will Be Boys by Nerina Shute, Radio Pictorial Magazine June 5, 1936 page 7 – Courtesy British Library
43. In Clarkson Rose's Peradventure column, The Stage, March 12, 1936 Page 2
44. Excerpt of Houston Sisters dialogue -Argyle Productions 'Happy Days Are Here Again'(1936)
45. Excerpt of Houston Sisters dialogue -Argyle Productions 'Happy Days Are Here Again'(1936)
46. See Tom Driberg, Swaff: Life and Times of Hannen Swaffer. MacDonald, 1974
47. Monthly Film Bulletin V3, n27, March 1936 page 41 – Courtesy British Film Institute
48. Tamworth Herald, March 14 1936 – Courtesy British Library
49. The reference for their gramophone record is COLUMBIA FB 1467
50. 'The Renée Houston I Know', Herbert Harris, Radio Pictorial, September 2,1938 page 10 –British Library
51. 'Renee Turns Dramatist by Margery Rowland' The Era, April 22, 1937 – Courtesy British Library
52. The Era, July 29, 1936. – Courtesy British Library
53. Radio Pictorial, September 25, 1936 'Eve Dresses Up For The mike' by Verity Clare –British Library
54. Letter January 26, 1935 from Donald to Mrs FC Wintermute 25 Sheldon Street W-B.
55. Char-A-Bang's score included 'Let's Keep on Drifting' and 'No One Ever Brings Me Flowers' by Robert Nesbitt and Dennis Van Thal.
56. Article about Income Tax, The Performer, August 22, 1928. – Courtesy British Library

Chapter 14
1. Portsmouth Evening News, April 25, 1935 – Courtesy British Library
2. Between January 21 and February 16, 1935
3. Her signings included one at Hills & Co, 17 Waterloo Place, Sunderland on February 28.
4. The Stage, December 24, 1935 Page 11
5. 'Star Writes Film,' Dundee Courier, April 12, 1935 – Courtesy British Library
6. The Evening Standard, April 10 1935 page 9
7. 'Houston Sisters' Future.' By 'Old Hand, Variety, Cabaret, Film News May 2 1935 page 5
8. Variety, July 17, 1935 reports how Lee Schubert, Jack Waller, Lew Leslie and several others are suddenly bidding hysterically for the service of Renée Houston
9. Variety, July 31, 1935
10. Notice: 'Signs For Three Pictures With British Lion,' Variety, February 26, 1936
11. The Era, October 9, 1935 – About Down in Forest at Birmingham – Courtesy British Library
12. The Stage, October 24, 1935 Page 8

Notes and Credits

13. Possibly a take on Miles Mander
14. Article by Alan Bott - The Tatler No. 1780, August 7, 1935 p250-251
15. 'Cupid and I by Renée Houston,' Radio Pictorial, October 23, 1936 – Courtesy British Library
16. The Stage, July 4, 1935 Page 9
17. Diary of Tony Aherne, 07.03.97
18. Diary of Tony Aherne, 30.11.97
19. 'Convicts In Comedy and Cinema Stars Satirized,' by Vernon Woodhouse, The Bystander, July 10, 1935 p50
20. Review signed I.B. in The Manchester Guardian, June 28, 1935
21. 'Renée Houston Makes a Hit' by WA Darlington, The Telegraph, June 28, 1935
22. The Sunday Times, June 30, 1935 - The Dramatic World – about Love Laughs
23. Her part in Love Laughs went to Marie Dayne for the tour
24. The Evening Standard, June 28, 1935 by SW
25. 'Renée Houston Makes a Hit' by WA Darlington, The Telegraph, June 28, 1935
26. People's Journal interview Feb-May 1936 – Courtesy British Library
27. Extracts from More First Nights by James Agate reprinted by permission of Peters Fraser & Dunlop (www.petersfraserdunlop.com) on behalf of the Estate of James Agate
28. 'Houston Sisters' Future.' Variety Gossip By 'Old Hand, Variety, Cabaret, Film News May 2 1935 page 5
29. Ivor Brown in The Manchester Guardian, February 22, 1936
30. V&A Museum, London, Theatre & Performance Collections - Programme for Babes in the Wood, Prince of Wales Theatre, Birmingham
31. As you were: Reminiscences by Douglas Byng, Pub. Duckworth, 1970
32. The Stage, January 23, 1936 Page 2
33. Based on Interview with Mavis Nicholson, Good Afternoon LWT Broadcast: 31/01/74
34. 'I Do - A Song Under Difficulties' is a Houston sketch with music composed by M & H Nesbitt. It features on Side 2 of double-sided gramophone record Columbia FB 1307 recorded: 02.02.1936. Pat Aherne provided dialogue only and someone else improvised *Nicky*'s tinkering on the piano as Pat couldn't play.
35. Script for variety routine by Renée Houston 1935 – Courtesy Aherne Family
36. Script for variety routine by Renée Houston 1935 – Courtesy Aherne Family
37. Script for variety routine by Renée Houston 1935 – Courtesy Aherne Family
38. 'Another Houston Sister Triumphs,' The Era, September 16 1936 –British Library
39. The Straits Times, 7 October 1936, Page 18
40. Film Pictorial October 13, 1934 page 26 – Courtesy British Library
41. 'Here's a Rival For Marlene,' Evening News, June 7, 1949 – Courtesy British Library
42. Interview with Mavis Nicholson, Good Afternoon LWT Broadcast: 31/01/74
43. Sunday Mail, September 5 1954 – Courtesy British Library
44. Radio Pictorial, September 25, 1936 'Eve Dresses Up For The mike' by Verity Clare –British Library
45. Derby Daily Telegraph, November 12, 1936 – Written by Joan in Derby and Joan column –British Library

Chapter 15
1. People's Journal, Feb-May 1936
2. The former King Edward's Theatre - today, it's Prince Edward Theatre on Old Compton Street.
3. Built by Sir Edward Moss on Nicholson Street
4. People's Journal Argyll & The Isles, May 2, 1936 – Courtesy British Library
5. In some reports the ransom demand was £25.
6. The People's Journal Argyll & The Isles, May 2 1936 – Courtesy British Library
7. Western Morning News, April 29 1936 – Courtesy British Library
8. 'Girls Will Be Boys! Studio Smalltalk by Nerina Shute, Radio Pictorial, June 5, 1936 page 7 –British Library
9. The Daily Sketch May 1, 1936 – Courtesy British Library
10. Western Morning News, April 29 1936 – Courtesy British Library
11. Leicester Square Looks Round moved to Lewisham Hippodrome. Helen Binnie took over Renée's part.
12. Parliamentary Archives, HC/Deb 05/May 1936/vol.311/cc1513-4
13. Drawn by Flotsam, for his Jetsam Jottings column.
14. Jetsam Jottings column in The Stage, May 21, 1936 – Courtesy The Stage
15. The Manchester Guardian, July 17, 1936 – Courtesy British Library
16. Supplement to the London Gazette, September 26, 1941 page 5591
17. 'Jane's Journal – The Diary of a *Bright Young Thing*,' The Daily Mirror, September 11, 1935
18. My thanks to Shoreham History Portal website for information from BBC Radio interviews and article 'Along the Beach at Bungalow Town' - by Nelson.
19. The site of 'Abbotswood' has been re-developed - today, the vicinity of 31 Uxbridge Road
20. Born in October 1917
21. Their headmistress was Mrs Mabel Hellen.
22. They wore royal blue blazers and caps with a badge bearing the letters 'AH'.
23. Letter Donald to Mickey (on board ship)- September 8, 1938
24. Letter From Renée, The Midland Hotel, Manchester - To Mickey (on board ship - to be given Saturday September 3, 1938)
25. NLA - The Argus (Melbourne) March 18, 1937 'Miss Merle Oberon in Motor-car Accident'
26. Broadcast at 20.41.00 that Wednesday

27. Letter From Renée at The Midland Hotel, Manchester - To Mickey (on board ship) – Jack Wintermute was Donald's older brother.

Chapter 16
1. Joyce Jeffreys in the Sunday Pictorial, July 30, 1939 writing about Renée's performance in 'A Girl Must Live'
2. Figures are from: 'The Story of the Music Hall XXXIII: Transition to New Variety' by Archibald Haddon, Variety, Cabaret, Film News, April 18, 1935 page 6.
3. Tax concessions keeping seats in theatres less than 6d to benefit the poor was the extent of help for theatres - Kinematograph Weekly No. 1458 March 28, 1935 page 1 – Courtesy British Library
4. The Era, January 13, 1937 – Courtesy British Library
5. Radio Pictorial Magazine, January 15, 1937 – Courtesy British Library
6. See article: transdiffusion.org/2005/05/01/howard2
7. My thanks to Mike Lang's excellent website and book 'Cine-Variety: Memories Of A Forgotten Era.'
8. Cutting Nov 2, 1937- Unknown newspaper. V&A Holborn Empire Production Box
9. The Billboard, November 13, 1937 – Courtesy British Library
10. Kinematograph Weekly, June 25, 1936. – Courtesy British Library
11. Renée Houston to sue,' Portsmouth Evening News, June 13, 1938 – Courtesy British Library
12. 'Don't Fence Me In' by Renée Houston, 1974, with permission of Pan Macmillan via PLSclear
13. 'Packing the Family Voices,' The Cape Argus, February 4 1938 – Courtesy British Library
14. 'A Good Cast', The Cape Argus, March 22, 1938, page 8 – Courtesy British Library
15. 'A full house welcomes "Bio-Vaudeville" The Cape Times, March 16, 1938
16. Letter Renée, Midland Hotel, Manchester -to 'Mickey Mouse' given on board ship, September 6, 1938
17. The Daily Mirror, March 29, 1938 By kind permission of Trinity Mirror plc.
18. Variety – US – Magazine, February 1, 1939 – Courtesy British Library
19. Harris Dean's Show News, Sunday Graphic London July 30, 1939 p19 – Courtesy British Library
20. See Prime Minister of Mirth by AE Wilson Pub Odhams Press, 1956
21. New Statesman July 29, 1939 – Courtesy British Library
22. 'Don't Fence Me In' by Renée Houston, 1974, reproduced with permission of Pan Macmillan via PLSclear
23. The Times, July 31, 1939.
24. Empire News Manchester, July 30, 1939 – Courtesy British Library
25. 'Up To Date Balzac,' The Cinema, by James Agate in The Tatler, August 16, 1939 My thanks to Condé Nast
26. Note from Mae Murray, Studio Publicity, BFI file for 'A Girl Must Live'
27. 'The nomad enjoys girls, gags and gold-diggers' - the set of 'A Girl Must Live'' Film Pictorial, December 1938
28. Sunday Pictorial, July 30, 1939 by Joyce Jeffreys – Courtesy British Library
29. Argyle TV Films USA
30. radiotimesarchive.co.uk RT-TV-1939.pdf
31. Hull Daily Mail, July 11, 1939 – Courtesy British Library
32. The Stage, January 4, 1940 Page 3 – Courtesy The Stage
33. 'Don't Fence Me In' by Renée Houston, 1974, with permission of Pan Macmillan via PLSclear
34. Revealed in the diary of Korda's production manager Sir David Cunynghame
35. May 17 entry in the diary of Sir David Cunynghame
36. Korda, Britain's Only Movie Mogul by Charles Drazin. Sidgwick and Jackson, 2002
37. Derbyshire Times and Chesterfield Herald, September 19, 1941
38. 'The Renée Houston I Know' by Herbert Harris, Radio Pictorial, September 16, 1938 page 11
39. Diary of Tony Aherne, 07.03.87
40. The Glasgow Herald, March 12, 1965
41. 'Ministry Give 15,000 People a Free Show.' Daily Express, July 22, 1940
42. Stratford-Upon-Avon Herald and South Warwickshire Advertiser. September 6, 1940 –British Library
43. Evening Despatch, September 11, 1940 – Courtesy British Library
44. Stratford-Upon-Avon Herald and South Warwickshire Advertiser, October 4, 1940 –British Library
45. 'Pat and Brian, the Brothers Aherne,' Daily Mail, July 27, 1940 – Courtesy British Library

Chapter 17
1. See Portable days: A Personal Account of Life in the Theatre as told to Neil McNicholas by Violet Godfrey Carr, Spredden Press 1991
2. Produced and conducted by Ernest Longstaffe
3. My thanks to the Scottish Theatre Archive - Programme: STA Fn 12/18f
4. Greasepaint and Cordite: How ENSA Entertained the Troops During World War II, by Andy Merriman. Aurum Press Ltd, 2013
5. The Stage, March 26, 1998 Page 14
6. The Stage, September 10, 1942 Page 1
7. Evening Standard, November 26, 1974, Maureen Cleave – Quoted courtesy of Independent Print Ltd
8. BBC WAC, R/30/2592, Renée Houston Script: Grand Celebrity Concert
9. Figures are from Paul Ford's blog at wyrleyblog.wordpress.com
10. The Evening Despatch October 11, 1943 – Courtesy British Library
11. The Mill House, Bourne End: It's place in Wartime History - by John Lunnon
12. An Autobiography of British Cinema, by Brian McFarlane, Methuen 1997 p299
13. The Sydney Morning Herald, July 24, 1946 – Courtesy NLA

Notes and Credits

14. Flora: An Appreciation of the Life and Works of Dame Flora Robson by Kenneth Barrow, Heinemann 1981.
15. Tragedy struck Betty in real life too, when she died in childbirth. This was her last film.
16. Launder and Gilliat, Bruce Babington, 2002 p72. Quoted by kind permission of Manchester University Press.
17. Diary of Tony Aherne, 04.11.2009
18. Based on R4 PETTICOAT LINE - 26 February 1975 18.15 Ref. SX 12989/1 – By kind permission of the BBC.
19. 'Don't Fence Me In' by Renée Houston, 1974, reproduced with permission of Pan Macmillan via PLSclear
20. Letter Elana Aherne to Aunt Eunice from 20 Southover St late 1970s
21. 'Noted Actor Dies in England at 55' in Wilkes-Barre's Times Leader, March 1966
22. The Stage, June 8, 1944 Page 5
23. Showmen's Trade Review, March 23, 1946 – Courtesy British Library
24. Hockley County Herald, December, 1946 – Courtesy Family of Terry Long
25. Aberdeen Journal, July 11, 1944 – Courtesy British Library
26. It was boarded up and abandoned for 12 years before then.

Chapter 18

1. Again and again they would appear in this programme. Over its lifetime Bill Worsley, John Ellison, John Foreman, Howard Lockhart, Bryan Sears, and Bill Gates were producers.
2. The Grades were based at Astoria House, 62 Shaftesbury Avenue.
3. This was broadcast to Forces stationed overseas
4. Diary of Tony Aherne 03.06.2003
5. Laughter in the Roar by Brian O'Gorman, Pub Badger Press, 1998. Quoted by kind permission of the author.
6. 'Renée Houston Lost Temper', Hull Daily Mail, July 21, 1947 – Courtesy British Library
7. Letter Donald to Mrs FC Wintermute c/o Miss Lois Wintermute 307 West 11th St NYC- April 5, 1950
8. Programme in V&A Production file for Finsbury Park Empire
9. The theatre had reverted to its old self after its 'Queensberry' years
10. The Stage, August 26, 1948
11. From Sherrie - Behind the Laughter p273. Reprinted by permission of HarperCollins Publishers Ltd © Sherrie Hewson, 2011
12. Their joint earnings for the forty-five weeks of 1948 were given as £2100 (about £48,000 today) compared to £5000 (£130,000 today) annually between 1943 and 1945.
13. The National Archives UK ref. B 9/1428 - Proceedings under the Bankruptcy Acts for Katherina Valorita Veronica Wintermute, 1948. Date of Filing Petition Aug 18 1948
14. Opportunity Knocked by Hughie Green – published by Frederick Muller. Reproduced by kind permission of The Random House Group Ltd © Hughie Green, 1965
15. Yorkshire Evening Post, October 2, 1948 – Courtesy British Library
16. Evening Standard, November 26, 1974, Maureen Cleave – Quoted courtesy of Independent Print Ltd
17. The Stage, December 9, 1948, page 5
18. 'Putting the Laughs into Radio' by Michael Standing. Radio Times, February 25, 1949
19. 'No Star's safe from the Townhead Terrors' Sunday Post, April 10, 1949 – Courtesy British Library
20. Transmitted on Saturday 22 January 1949 at 20.30 - the 'Seventh visit to Television's own Nightspot'.
21. BBC WAC, T/12/330, Renée Houston rejected script for 'Roof Top Rendezvous'- January 1949
22. BBC WAC, T/12/330, Renée Houston accepted script for 'Roof Top Rendezvous'- January 1949
23. As revealed in photographs the Alexandra Palace Television Society has kindly shown me.

Chapter 19

1. The Observer, May 8, 1949 by JC Trewin
2. One headline in The Daily Express, May 19, 1949 was entitled 'And Renée Provides the Sauce.'
3. Daily Mail Thursday May 9, 1949 p3 – Review of Sauce Tartare by Cecil Wilson
4. My thanks to Martin Milner for his super essay about Jean Bayless
5. Jessie Matthews – A Biography, by Michael Thornton, Pub. Hart-Davis, 1974
6. The Call Boy, Volume 52, No.4 - Interview with Jean Bayless by Geoff Bowden
7. When Victor Saville left for the USA in the late 30s she lost her finest collaborator.
8. Daily Express, March 6, 1950
9. The Stage, October 19, 1950 Page 3
10. Dundee Courier, December 19, 1951 – Courtesy British Library
11. Portsmouth Evening News, February 5, 1952 – Courtesy British Library
12. BBC WAC, RCONT/1, Internal memo October 18, 1950 Michael Standing, Head of Variety to Bryan Sears, Bill Worsley and Mr John Foreman © BBC.
13. BBC WAC, RCONT/1, Letter Renée to Michael Standing - November 24, 1950. After mailing the letter, somebody told her Standing had recently lost his mother. Renée instantly wrote apologizing for her 'distressing letter' aware his sorrows were greater. He replied telling Renée not to despair. He'd do his best.
14. BBC WAC, RCONT/1, Letter Renée to R. Waldman early 1951
15. Messiter received just a token - £50, and forwarded it to the BBC Benevolent Fund.
16. BBC WAC, RCONT/1, Letter Donald Stewart to Michael Standing - November 30 1951
17. BBC WAC, RCONT/1, Memo (handwritten) between Cecil McGivern and unknown person, © BBC.
18. BBC WAC, RCONT/1, Letter Renée to R. Waldman- March 21, 1952
19. 'Funny Way to be a Hero' John Fisher. Pub. Random House 2013. Quoted by kind permission of the author.

20. BBC WAC, RCONT/1, Letter Renée to R. Waldman - June 10 1952
21. BBC WAC, RCONT/1, Letter Renée to Michael Standing - June 11, 1952
22. Sunday Mail, September 5, 1954 – Courtesy British Library

Chapter 20
1. Letter June 23, 1952 From Renée at Hayes To Mickey at Wyoming Ave, Forty Fort, Penn
2. Letter Elana Aherne to Aunt Eunice January 31, 1974
3. BBC WAC, RCONT/1, Letter March 4, 1952 Renée to R. Waldman
4. BBC WAC, RCONT/1, Letter March 4, 1952 Renée to AE Boxhall
5. Letter March 23 1952 From Renée 26 Queens Rd - To Mickey at 354 Horton Street, W-B
6. Richmond and Twickenham Times, March 1, 1952 – Courtesy British Library
7. The stolen sewing machine worth £30 was sold to a Twickenham dealer for £10
8. Letter March 23 1952 From Renée 26 Queens Rd - To Mickey at 354 Horton Street, W-B
9. Letter March 23 1952 From Renée 26 Queens Rd - To Mickey at 354 Horton Street, W-B
10. Letter From Renée 38 E Ave Hayes - To Mickey at Wyoming Ave, Forty Fort, Penn
11. Letter September 18, 1952 from Renée to AE Boxhall
12. Letter December 17 1952 from Donald – to Mrs FC Wintermute at Wyoming Ave, Penn
13. Letter June 23 1952 from Renée To Mickey at Wyoming Ave, Forty Fort, Penn
14. BBC WAC, RCONT/1, Letter March 30, 1953 Renée to R. Waldman
15. He mentions them in 'Take It From Me' by J. Edwards Werner Laurie, 1953
16. BBC WAC, RCONT/1, Letter April 7, 1953. Renée to Michael Standing
17. BBC WAC, RCONT/1, Memo April 2, 1953 between Pat Hillyard and Bill Gates. Hillyard's latest attempt to help them got responses like 'too expensive with my small programme allocation' © BBC.
18. Letter March 23 1952 From Renée 26 Queens Rd - To Mickey at 354 Horton Street, W-B
19. Cutting from Dundee newspaper, late April 1953. It was enclosed in letter to Mickey.
20. Cutting from Leith Gazette, May 23 1953 sent to Mickey. Miss Houston looks like an artist.
21. Variety US June 3, 1953 – Courtesy British Library
22. Obituary for Renée by Bennitt, Daily Telegraph February 14, 1980
23. BBC WAC, RCONT/1, Letter October 5, 1953 Renée to P. Newman
24. BBC WAC, RCONT/1, Letter October 26,1953 Renée to Cecil McGivern.
25. BBC WAC, RCONT/1, Letter December 7, 1953 Renée to Frankie Howerd
26. So Much Love, by Beryl Reid and Eric Braun, Pub. Hutchinson, 1984 Reproduced by kind permission of The Random House Group Ltd © Beryl Reid, 1984
27. Sunderland Daily Echo and Shipping Gazette, March 9, 1952 'Mediocre Show' Angus Hunter –British Library
28. Some Sort of Life © Miriam Karlin, Jan Sargent 2007, p50-51. By kind permission of Oberon Books Ltd.
29. Letter October 19, 1954 from Donald at Norman Ave to Mrs FC Wintermute
30. From Tony Aherne's diary 08.03.96
31. Letter June 23 1952 from Renée in Hayes to Mickey at Wyoming Ave, Forty Fort, Penn

Chapter 21
1. Ballintian located on the outskirts of Cromer is pronounced 'bal-in-shee-an'
2. Courtesy of Harold Silander's excellent website www.talcy.com/talcy13/history.silmcw.htm
3. Sunday Mail, September 19 1954 – Courtesy British Library
4. The article was 'The Houstons Sing Again' in The Daily Mail, August 24, 1954
5. BBC WAC, RCONT/1, Letter August 25, 1954 Renée to R. Waldman about Limelight
6. BBC WAC, RCONT/1, Letter November, 1954 Renée to R. Waldman about Limelight
7. BBC WAC, RCONT/1, Letter May 5 1954 R. Waldman to Donald © BBC.
8. BBC WAC, RCONT/1, Letter June 9 1954 Renée to R. Waldman
9. Letter July 17 1953 From Donald - To Mickey
10. Letter July 23, 1971 Elana Aherne to Aunt Eunice.
11. Encyclopedia of Chess, by Anne Sunnucks - Pub. Robert Hale Ltd (1976) page 432.
12. Quoted by kind permission of STUDIOCANAL Films Ltd
13. The Stage –1994 article. David Howe recalls the 1954 BBC live broadcast from the Coliseum
14. Based on a line of dialogue from 'Track The Man Down' (1955). My thanks to Paramount Pictures.
15. BBC WAC, RCONT/1, Letter March 1, 1955 - P. Newman to Booking Manager, Scottish Programme Executive © BBC.
16. BBC WAC, RCONT/1, Memo -March 3 1955 - Scottish Programme Executive to London Variety Booking Manager Re. Jimmy Logan Show © BBC.
17. Arbroath Herald and Advertiser for the Montrose Burghs, November 25, 1955
18. Article April 29, 1955, in The Spectator by Joseph Hayes about Desperate Hours
19. BBC WAC, RCONT/1, Letter to Pat Hillyard from Renée April 24, 1955 © BBC.
20. Letter Apr 13, 1955 from Renée RH to Mrs FC Wintermute
21. The Advent of ITV & Television, Chris Hand, Journal of British Cinema and TV Vol 4 no.1 2007
22. An Autobiography of British Cinema, Brian McFarlane, Methuen 1997 p7
23. An Autobiography of British Cinema, Brian McFarlane, Methuen 1997 p357. Quoted by kind permission of the author.
24. The Stage, April 12, 1956 Page 5
25. Symson Harman at the pictures, The Evening News, March 1, 1956

Notes and Credits

26. Time And Tide, March 10, 1956 – Courtesy British Library
27. BBC WAC, RCONT/1, Letter October 1955 - from Renée to R. Waldman
28. BBC WAC, RCONT/1, Letter April 1, 1956 Renée to R. Waldman
29. The Stage, July 19, 1956
30. The Daily Mail, July 13, 1956
31. Programme in Glasgow University Special Collections GB 247 STA Fa 8/120
32. The Southport Visiter November, 1956 – Article
33. The Stage November 29, 1956, Page 10 referring to the future Mike Baldwin
34. BBC WAC, RCONT/1, Memo January 1, 1957 CF Meehan to Bill Worsley © BBC.
35. BBC WAC, RCONT/1, Reply January 2, 1957 Pat Hillyard to CF Meehan © BBC.
36. BBC WAC, RCONT/1, Memo January 2, 1957 Bill Worsley to Pat Hillyard and CF Meehan © BBC.
37. Letter January 31, 1957 from Donald to Mrs FC Wintermute
38. Part of the BBC's Sunday Night Theatre - shown February 24.
39. The Daily Express, February 25, 1957 p3
40. BBC WAC, RCONT/1, Letter April 1 1957 Stephen Harrison to Renée © BBC.
41. Letter April 26, 1957 from Renée to Mrs FC Wintermute
42. V&A Museum, Theatre & Performance Collections, Sir Michael Redgrave Archive, THM/31/7/4 Contract 84
43. Article by Carol Foreman about Filming in Europe, BFI press articles for The Key
44. Daily Express, November 6, 1957 page 12
45. The Stage, January 2, 1958 Page 18
46. BL, Sir Alec Guinness Archive, MS 89015/2/7/8
47. 'Big Momma Renée leaves The Cat', Daily Mail, January 23, 1958
48. The Stage, January 2, 1958 Page 18
49. Sunday Times, February 2, 1958
50. BFI - 'French Impressionists on View' Document in file on 'The Horse's Mouth'
51. Derek Hill article in The Tribune, February 13, 1959 – Courtesy British Library
52. The Times February 1, 1959
53. Nina Hibbins - The Daily Worker, February 3, 1959 – Courtesy British Library

Chapter 22

1. Alan believes that Trevor's wife Tricia later moved to the USA or tried to.
2. To Manchester's Playhouse or the Hulme Hippodrome, to record before a studio audience.
3. The cast included Tony Melody, Leonard Williams, Rosalie Williams and Judith Chalmers.
4. Reagan would soon serve his 7th presidency of the guild.
5. The Observer, June 1, 1958 – Courtesy British Library.
6. Evening Standard, May 29, 1958 – Courtesy British Library
7. Letter December 11, 1959 To Mrs FC Wintermute at Hanover St, W-B
8. Dundee Journal, August 27, 1966 – Courtesy British Library
9. Lesley Storm in BBC Scotland, Spotlight, April 1973. My thanks to BBC Scotland.
10. BBC Scotland, Spotlight, Produced by Ian MacFadyen April 1973. My thanks to BBC Scotland.
11. For three years, Barkworth - one of RADA's most respected teachers, had been teaching during the day and playing Bernard Taggart-Stuart in Roar in the evenings.
12. The first film made with the Eastman colour process.
13. Letter April 28, 1960 from Renée, Opera House, Manchester to Mrs FC Wintermute at Hanover St, W-B
14. Radio Times, September 26, 1963 Maigret article
15. BBC WAC, T/5/2166, Memo September 13, 1960 from Ronald Waldman Gen. Manager TV Promotions cc Andrew Osborn re. Maigret series © BBC.
16. BBC Scotland, Spotlight, Produced by Ian MacFadyen April 1973 – My thanks to BBC Scotland
17. TV Times May 1961 - Article by James Green about No Hiding Place
18. Letter November 10, 1960 from Donald to Mrs FC Wintermute, Wilkes-Barre, Penn
19. Film Notes by Patrick Gibbs, The Telegraph, August 12, 1961 – Courtesy British Library
20. Letter Apr 4, 1961 from Donald To Mrs FC Wintermute
21. The Stage, April 5, 1962 Page 11
22. Letters October 31, November 29 1960 and January 2, February 17, 1961 from Donald to Mrs FC Wintermute, Wilkes-Barre
23. Letter October 24, 1961 from Donald to Mrs FC Wintermute, Wilkes-Barre

Chapter 23

1. Letter December 8, 1961 from Donald to Mrs FC Wintermute, Wilkes-Barre, Penn
2. BBC WAC, RCONT/1, Letter May 9, 1961 Renée to AE Boxall
3. The cast included Eric Pohlman, Ina de la Haye, Peggy Marshall, Derek Benfield, Gordon Whiting, Peter Madden, Patrick Cargill and Moira Redmond.
4. Letter June 21 1962 from Renée to Mrs FC Wintermute, Wilkes-Barre, Penn
5. For 'Sword of Lancelot' (1963)
6. Alexander Walker, Evening Standard, June 7,1962
7. Derek Prowse, The Sunday Times, June 10, 1962
8. Aka 'Fog for a Killer'. Produced at Twickenham. Directed by Montgomery Tully.

9. Letter June 21, 1962 Donald to Mrs FC Wintermute, Wilkes-Barre, Penn
10. Letter January 14, 1963 from Donald to Mrs FC Wintermute, Wilkes-Barre, Penn
11. Letter February 21, 1963 Renée to Mickey, Wilkes-Barre, Penn
12. In his youth he'd acted with Sir Henry Irving and stated his film career in 1908. Cyril had first worked with Renée in 1933 for the Nine Days Wonder Radiolympia revue.
13. Bernard Levin, The Daily Mail, October 17, 1962 page 2
14. Starring Kenneth Williams and Maggie Smith.
15. Gentlemen Prefer Blondes had moved here.
16. Afternoon radio show (extending life of TV chat show *In Town Tonight*) that John Ellison hosted until 1960.
17. BBC WAC, RCONT/1, Letter October 26, 1962 Pam Simons to David Dore
18. Brett later became a member of an offbeat comedy band called the 'Temperance Seven.'
19. Tandy became a 1st Assistant Director on many blockbuster films.
20. Peter mentions the journey in his book Redhead with Fire in his Boots' Pub. Fonthill, 2014
21. Radio Times February 27, 1964 page 33 – Courtesy British Library.
22. BBC WAC, T/5/2469, Production notes for Z Cars 'Scare' undated © BBC.
23. She's in episode 16 Wonderful War and episode 25 Gentle Ladies in Season two of The Saint
24. Email from Sir Roger Moore via his office.
25. Interview with Anne Donaldson, The Glasgow Herald - March 12, 1965 – Courtesy British Library
26. Saved by a local Oatlands lady.
27. The Glasgow Herald, December 31, 1980 – Courtesy British Library
28. Interview with Gerhard Midding (1990) in Roman Polanski Interviews - Ed by Paul Cronin (2005) University Press of Mississippi. Reproduced by kind permission of Gerhard Midding.
29. Interview with Michel Ciment, Michel Perez and Roger Tailleur (1969) in Roman Polanski Interviews - Ed by Paul Cronin (2005) University Press of Mississippi
30. Played by ex-St Trinians's 4th former Catherine Feller.
31. Review of Marriage Brokers, Malcolm Rutherford, The Spectator, February 12, 1965 page 16
32. Iain Walker in the Scottish Daily Express, June 5, 1965
33. David Lilleker in The Scotsman, April 7, 1965 – Courtesy British Library
34. Winifred Bannister in Theatre World, July 1965
35. Iain Walker in the Scottish Daily Express, June 5, 1965
36. Programme in Glasgow University Special Collections - for the Jimmy Logan Theatre Hour - Special TV performance of Beneath the Wee Red Lums at the Metropole May 23 1965
37. 'Shoes were for Sunday' by Molly Weir Pub. Hutchinson, 1970.
38. Jim was asked to appear on the same radio programme on June 24, intriguing listeners with his travel tales of Canadian lumberjacks, Mounties, and telling the quick from the dead in Haiti.
39. Edith Evans and Peter Barkworth were also in Bagnold's play at the Globe Theatre directed by V. Matalon.

Chapter 24
1. Sunday Mail, September 26, 1954 – Courtesy British Library
2. Interview with Philip Haudiquet (1966) in Roman Polanski Interviews – Ed. Paul Cronin (2005) University Press of Mississippi.
3. Close Up by John Fraser Pub. Oberon Books, 2004
4. Transmission was in the higher-definition 625-line format - then used only by BBC2, hence the title.
5. It was broadcast on January 2, 1966.
6. BBC WAC, T/5/2031, Letter January 27, 1966 - John Mair to Controller of BBC2 © BBC.
7. Soon Robert would pen a controversial TWTWTW sketch: 'The Consumer's Guide To Religion'.
8. Memories of Robert Gillespie
9. Memories of Robert Gillespie
10. Pam Simons made sure there was a special clause in her contract that Renée would receive fourth billing. Hannah Gordon had a small part in The Dear Ones, broadcast on June 4.
11. TV Times, June 2, 1966 - Article by Sarah Snow about The Dear Ones.
12. March 1966 copy of Times Leader, Wilkes-Barre – Courtesy Wintermute Family
13. The Stage, March 24, 1966, Page 12
14. The Stage and Television Today Issue 4451 August 4, 1966
15. Dundee Journal, August 27, 1966 – Courtesy British Library
16. Joining them were Ronald Bain, Christopher Godwin and Patsy Mair.
17. Dundee Journal, August 27, 1966 – Courtesy British Library
18. Dundee Journal, August 27, 1966 – Courtesy British Library
19. Glasgow Herald, August 24, 1966
20. Courier and Advertiser, Dundee, Thursday August 25, 1966 – Courtesy British Library
21. BBC WAC, RCONT/12, Letter December 14, 1966 Joan Craft to Renée Houston © BBC.
22. The Stage, June 08, 1967 Page 12
23. Dorothy: *Revelations of a Rejected Soprano* by Dorothy Paul, Harper Collins, 1997
24. By Edward Percy, whose other success was The Shop at Sly Corner, and Reginald Denham
25. Memories of Michael Gaunt
26. Cutting from The Northern Times, May 25, 1968 – Courtesy Michael Gaunt
27. Tilly went on to find success in television, radio, as well as a great stage career at Manchester's Royal Exchange, The National Theatre and the West End.
28. Dundee Journal, August 27, 1966 – Courtesy British Library

Notes and Credits

29. 'Don't Fence Me In' by Renée Houston, 1974, reproduced with permission of Pan Macmillan via PLSclear
30. 'Don't Fence Me In' by Renée Houston, 1974, reproduced with permission of Pan Macmillan via PLSclear
31. Letter: from Elana to Aunt Eunice January 31, 1974
32. Letter from Elana to Aunt Eunice from 20 Southover St, July 23, 1971
33. The Secret of Staying Young: Pollen-B and how it can prolong your youth. By Neil Lyall and Robert Chapman – Pub. Pan Original (1976).
34. Pills developed by Wassen Developments (Walton, Surrey) were available between 1965 and 1978.
35. Based on London Weekend Television's *Doctor in the House*: Season 1, Episode 4 *'Peace and Quiet'* (Broadcast 2 Aug. 1969)
36. Recorded on October 6 at Television Centre's Studio 7. She had already begun the sixth *Petticoat Line*.
37. Article about Sailor Beware by JKM, The Glasgow Herald, Mar 10, 1970

Chapter 25
1. The Tablet, March 6, 1971, Page 18 – Courtesy British Library
2. The Tablet, March 6, 1971, Page 18 – looking back to the previous year's elected women
3. Written by Barry Cryer and produced by Bill Hitchcock for LWT
4. Article by Peter Lewis, Daily Mail, January 22, 1971 page 10
5. This Week In The Arts, The Tablet, February 6, 1971, Page 17
6. My thanks to carryon.org.uk/talbotrothwell.htm for a great article about the screenwriter.
7. Ken Cope and David Frost made a vinyl recording of this show
8. The Morning Star, December 17, 1971 – Courtesy British Film Institute
9. 'I warned BBC bosses about Jimmy Savile forty years ago' Article by Lucy Thornton, Daily Mirror, November 8, 2012 Reproduced with the permission of Trinity Mirror plc.
10. The Stage, June 29, 1972 Page 3
11. You Won't Remember Me was episode 11 of season 3's Special Branch broadcast on June 20, 1973.
12. Based on dialogue from Thames Television's Looks Familiar (Broadcast 23/07/73)
13. Based on dialogue from Thames Television's Looks Familiar (Broadcast 23/07/73)
14. His real name was James Montgomery Fife and like, he was born in Glasgow.
15. Based on Interview with Mavis Nicholson, Good Afternoon LWT Broadcast: 31/01/74

Chapter 26
1. Evening Standard, November 26, 1974, Maureen Cleave – Quoted courtesy of Independent Print Limited
2. My thanks to Matthew Coniam's excellent blog about Tyburn films
3. The Guardian October 23, 1975 - Review by Derek Malcolm
4. They made films in Britain with limited resources, when the industry was facing desolation.
5. Founder of the Devonshire Collection of Period Costume. The collection gave costume shows at Torquay's Singer Mansion.
6. Surrey Herald Kingston, February 14, 1980 – Courtesy British Library
7. Evening Standard, November 26, 1974, Maureen Cleave – Quoted courtesy of Independent Print Ltd
8. The royal couple divorced a few years later and the Roman Catholic Church granted a canonical annulment.
9. Diary of Tony Aherne, 30.12.97
10. The Surrey Herald and Middlesex News, February 21, 1980– Courtesy British Library
11. Surrey Herald, February 14, 1980 – Courtesy British Library
12. The Stage, February 5, 1981 Page 15

Chapter 27
1. Clochemerle, by Gabriel Chevallier (1934) was her favourite novel on *Desert Island Discs*.
2. Letter December 11, 1962, Donald - To Mrs FC Wintermute, 154 Hanover st, Wilkes-Barre.
3. Daily Mail, July 5, 1997 Article about Dora Bryan by Lynda Lee-Potter – Courtesy Solo Syndication
4. Diary of Tony Aherne 26.03.96
5. The film was 'Voyage to the bottom of the sea' - Diary of Tony Aherne, 31.05.98
6. Diary of Tony Aherne, 27.10.02
7. Renée in an interview for Radio Pictorial, October 23, 1936 'Cupid and I by Renée Houston' – British Library
8. As recalled by Jessie Matthews in an interview with John Kobal - Gotta Sing Gotta Dance: A Pictorial History of Film Musicals by John Kobal Pub The Hamlyn Publishing Group 1970.
9. In the 90s, the Krankies were thought 'seedy' by a newly elected panel of 'morality police' employed by TV companies – see Fan Dabi Dozi - The Krankees, Blake Publishing (2004).

Adventures of Robin Hood (TV), 467
A for Andromeda (TV), 486
A Girl Must Live (1939), 10, 216, 259, 316-326, 354, 367, 403-4,
A Matter Of Conscience (TV), 488
A Town Like Alice (1956), 211, 356, 429, 447-453, 497
Abbotswood (house), 294-296, 302, 329, 360, 560
Ace of Spades Roadhouse, 120, 208, 213
Advertising, 221, 266, 279, 282, 305, 306, 402, 501
Agate, James, 164, 271-4, 319, 559
Aherne, Alan, 4, 5, 18, 20,300-3,333, 338,343-4,348,350,353,365,375, 386,396,401-4; emigrates, 405; California, 436-7, 466,468; 486, 530, 541-3; 549, 556-8
Aherne, Brian, 195-9, 201, 203,209, 295, 298- 301, 338, 376-81, 433 437, 440,489, 498, 509, 541-3, 555
Aherne, David, 375, 408, 414, 425, 443, 509, 556
Aherne, Elana, 88, 135, 188, 195-6, 198-9, 201, 301, 339, 376-8, 414, 416, 441-2, 451, 529
Aherne, Lulu de Lacy, 194, 195, 203-4, 300, 339, 364
Aherne, Pat, 9, 88; early life, 194-7; Silent Films, 192-3; marriage to Renée, 208; Bankruptcy, 174,338; injury in bombing, 366; divorces Renée, 377 & 386; emigration to USA, 378; UK visit, 293, 509,529; death, 541; 137, 168, 174, 187-9, 192, 206, 231, 280, 285, 291, 299, 335, 359, 374-7, 391, 441, 468
Aherne, Tony; Birth,192;1,169, 178, 204, 207, 231, 269-70, 294-8, 302-3, 306-7, 331-3,360-1, 364-5, 377, 415-9, 440-3, 475, 529, 530, 555-6, 558-9
Aherne, William de Lacy, 195,203-4
Alhambra, The London, 6, 68,101-3, 108-111, 126,143, 146-7, 149-51, 155-6, 165, 175, 177, 190, 202-4
All Hands on Deck (comedy sketch), 126
All-Star Concert 1929 (theatre), 133, 135, 549
Alquin House (school), 296
Amalgamated Dairies(sketch), 400
An Evening of Old Time Music Hall (theatre), 502
And the Same To You (1958), 470
Anderson, Jean, 429, 450, 481

Andrews, Archie, 366, 377, 393
Andrews, Barbara, 553-4
Andy Stewart Show (TV), 550
Anna Christie (TV), 457
Annie's Lorry, 314-5
Argyle Theatre, Birkenhead, 48, 84, 85, 89, 190, 267
Argyle, John, 2, 240-1, 249, 256, 264
Armadale, 73
Arnold, Tom, 151, 296, 373
Artiste's Studio (comedy sketch), 147
Askey, Anthea, 1,26, 28, 449
Askey, Arthur, 64, 351, 411, 449, 540
Atlantic Spotlight (radio), 373
Auntie Mame (theatre), 469
Baber, Polly, 428
Babes in the Wood (theatre), 249,274
Bachelor's Walk Shooting, 50
Baird, John Logie, 6, 191, 522
Baddeley, Hermione, 427
Bader, Dave, 314-5
Bairnsfather, Bruce, 286, 328-9
Baker, Robert, 473, 475, 499
Balcon, Michael , 161, 241
Baldwin, Stanley, 106, 203
Balfour, Betty, 172,193, 198
Balfour, Michael, 445, 495, 506
Balharrie, George; marries Renée,84; divorce,207; death,323;14,81,84-8, 94, 106, 132-40,148,171-3,184-5, 190-2, 212-3, 236-7, 295, 347, 545
Balharrie, Trevor; Adoption, 131-8; conviction, 420; visit to Elana, 425; 106,231,237,249,292-5,333,337-8, 347, 357, 359, 364, 368, 386, 401, 419, 430, 466-7, 475-6, 480-6, 554
Balliol and Merton, 102, 133
Bamberger, Freddie, 333
Bankhead, Tallulah, 14,165, 170, 525
Bankruptcy (Renée & Don); 388-9, relinquishing possessions,390; Reasons, 391; 174, 392
Banks, Monty, 5,173, 238, 411
Barclay, George,89-90,94-6,104,171, 175-6, 202,207, 251, 296, 307,343
Bard, Wilkie, 89
Barkworth, Peter, 473
Barnes, Binnie, 226, 228
Barnett, Lady Isobel, 26, 34, 36
Barr, Ida, 150, 247, 250-3, 452
Barrat, Philip, 453
Barretts of Wimpole Street, 201
Barrfields Pavilion, 230
Barry, Joan, 167
Basil Dean, 168, 243
Bass, Alfie, 451, 456, 467
Bates, Nan, 238

Bathurst, Peter, 527
Battle, The (1934), 299
Battley, David, 535
Batty, Archibald, 534
Bayless, Jean, 400-402, 419, 430
Beach House (Santa Monica), 379-80, 530
Beatles, 496, 516
Beattie, James, 533
Beatty, Robert, 533
Becke, Shirley, 32
Bedtime Story (song), 148
Belfast Radio Exhibition, 290
Belita, 455, 457
Belles of St Trinian's (1954), 427-8, 460
Bells are Ringing (theatre), 458, 469
Beloved Enemy (1936), 298-9
Bendon, Bert, 48, 85, 88
Beneath The Wee Red Lums (theatre), 507,508
Bennett, Billy, 15, 111, 157, 162
Bentine, Michael, 385
Berens, Harold, 335, 452
Bertha Willmott, 240
Best Man (comedy sketch), 45-6
Betjeman, John, 264
Betty Stockfield, 169
Beverley Sisters, 518
Bickerton, FH, 240, 248-9, 252
Big Money (1956), 451-2
Billy Cotton's Band, 236, 240
Billy Merson, 104, 233
Black And Blue (theatre), 326-8
Black, Edward, 316, 328
Black, George, 158, 168, 217-8, 282, 322, 326-7, 421
Blake, Barbara, 32, 521
Blighty (1927), 15, 160-1, 200, 241, 316
Blinkeyes (1926), 198
Blood is Strong (TV), 452
Blower, Patsy, 551, 552
Bodie, Dr Walford, 174
Bond, Derek, 510, 533
Bonnet, Emery, 317
Book of Beauty (book), 163, 280
Booth, Harry, 519
Bouchier, Chili, 193-4, 249, 403
Bowlly, Al, 121, 342
Bowman, Sidney, 398
Box, Betty, 481-2
Boy Blue (theatre), 75
Boyle, Katie, 1, 26, 28
Braden, Bernard, 532
Brambell, Wilfred, 481

580

INDEX

Bramfield Road(home)442,447,466
Bray, Hazel, 347, 357-64, 419, 556
Bresslaw, Bernard, 237, 476, 537, 538, 551
Bridie, James, 272-3, 507, 534
Briggs, Johnny, 400, 453
Bright Spots (theatre), 88
Brighthampton(home)20,468,486-9
British International Pictures, 156, 200-3, 228, 232, 243, 256, 377
British Lion; Court Case, 310; 155, 258, 277, 309, 411
British National Film League, 168
British United Press, 180, 483-4
Britton, Tony, 532
Broadhurst Gdns (home) 190, 201
Brook, Faith, 472, 476
Brough, Peter, 367, 393
Brown, Teddy, 166, 305, 349, 350
Brunel, Adrian, 2, 11-12, 15-16, 155, 160, 202, 240-2, 250
Bryan Michie Discoveries, 217, 383
Bryan, Dora, 430, 493, 495, 562
Buchanan, Jack, 126, 160, 161, 174
Buckingham, Naida, 431, 433
Burke, Marie, 150
Burke, Patricia, 431, 435
Burns and Allen, 86, 97-8, 149, 223, 415
Butchers Film Service, 241,248, 467
Bygraves, Max, 460, 463, 483
Byng, Douglas, 256, 274-5, 401,418
Call My Bluff (TV) 532
Calvert, Phyllis, 354-357, 376
Calvin, Wyn, 5, 22, 216
Cameron, Anne, 522
Caprice Parisien (theatre), 325
Cardiff, Jack, 452
Careless Talk (theatre), 342
Carey, Joyce, 463, 481
Cargill, Patrick, 488
Carlisle, Elsie, 104, 148,171, 260
Carlyle Cousins, 223-4, 325
Carney, Kate, 93, 94, 324
Carr, Robert, 538, 539
Carr, Walter, 533
Carry On at Your Convenience (1971), 7, 318, 535-8
Carry On Cabby (1963), 497, 560
Carry On Spying (1964), 501
Carson, Violet, 402
Carstairs, John Paddy, 452, 470
Cartier, Rudolph, 477, 497
Cartland, Barbara, 29
Casani, Santos, 238
Cat on a Hot Tin Roof (theatre), 458-461

Catholic Stage Guild, 518
Catholic Woman of the Year, 3, 534
Catholicism: 40, 41, 49, 53, 56, 57, 87, 107, 132, 134, 135, 139, 165, 351, 359, 366, 376, 418, 484, 518, 534, 543
Cavanagh, Peter, 393
Cave, Rita, 246, 451, 454; death, 485;
Celebrity Squares (TV), 550
Certainly Sir (theatre), 278-9
Champion, Harry, 218, 323
Charles Hawtrey, 309, 535-538
Charlot, André, 260-1
Chetwynd-Talbot, Joan, Lady, 240
Chevalier, Maurice, 308, 463
Children's Film Foundation, 495, 519
Chinese Prime Minister (theatre), 509
Christie, Julie, 486
Chung Ling Soo, 142
Churchill, Sir Winston,107,334, 373, 392
Churchill's Club, 430, 447
Cilento, Diane, 457
Cine-variety, 44, 67-68, 112, 154, 156 184, 232, 312
Cinematograph Films Act 1927, 192
Citizens Theatre, 507
City of Play (1929), 194, 198, 201
Clapham and Dwyer, 145, 191, 231, 348
Clapham, Peter, 551, 552
Clare, Mary, 198, 317, 329
Clark Gable, 113, 353
Clark, Petula, 141, 444
Clark, PL (Auntie), 101, 146,275
Cleave, Maureen, 21, 350, 393, 546, 549-50, 552
Cliff, Laddie, 171, 228, 268-71
Clitheroe Kid (radio), 373, 466
Clogwallop (comedy sketch), 15
Closing at Sunrise (theatre), 273
Clyde, June, 245, 300, 307
Co-Optimists, 167, 170, 228, 268
Cochran, Charles, 193, 260, 272, 435
Cockles and Champagne (theatre); 15, 431, 433, Cockles strike, 435;
Cohen's Accident(comedy sketch), 161
Cole, George, 411, 428, 451, 533
Coliseum, London, 8, 14, 101, 102, 103, 104, 123, 549, 559
Colleano Family, 327
Colleano, Bonar, 328, 334, 467
Collins, Pauline, 510
Colman, Ronald, 209, 378, 380,437
Columbia Records, 148, 256
Come into my Parlour (1932), 206, 207, 258, 497

Comfort, Lance, 491-2
Comic, The (TV), 532
Coming home from the Club (comedy sketch), 44
Compton Group, 504, 510
Compton, Viola, 249
Connery, Sean, 457
Connolly, Cyril, 319
Cooper, Tommy, 470, 527
Cope, Kenneth, 491-2, 499, 535, 538
Coram and Gerry, 70, 208
Corbett, Harry H, 488
Corbett, Ronnie, 534, 542
Cornalla and Eddie, 142
Cornell, Katherine, 201
Cosmo Club, 104, 171
Countess Binoskha, 380, 436
Coward, Noël, 194, 235, 273,429
Cowper, Richard; 181, death; 178-9, 180, 183, 315
Cox, Jack, 320, 452
Cox, Ma, 200, 311
Crawford, Anne, 346
Crazy Gang, 146, 218, 310, 460
Cricklewood Studios, 193, 200, 241
Cronin, AJ, 42, 500
Cronkite, Walter, 349, 523
Crowther, Leslie, 532
Cul-de-Sac (1966), 504, 505, 511
Culver, Roland, 330
Cummings, Johnnie, 76-79
Cummings, William, 184, 426
Cushing, Peter, 473, 474, 546, 548
Customer is Always Right (comedy sketch), 152
Cutts, Graham, 244
Dalrymple, Ian, 329-30
Daly, Jack, 152, 273
Damn Yankees, 455
Daniels, Bebe, 98, 115, 202, 224, 415
Darcey, Françoise, 331
Dare, Patricia, 397, 400, 430
Darky Ragtime Octette, 58
Davies, Geoffrey, 531-2
Davies, Marion, 195, 208
Davies, Rupert, 458, 478
Davis, Bette, 412, 424
Davis, Dabber, 98, 126, 337-8, 347, 365-6, 391, 398,404,407, 439, 556
Davis, Pete, 75, 78, 90-92, 96, 230
Day, Vera, 467, 470, 481, 498
De Bear, Archie, 228, 321
De Forest, Lee, 114, 115
De Havilland, Olivia, 300
Deanna of the Dairies (comedy sketch), 15, 399

Dear Ones (TV), 514
Delfont, Bernard, 412
Denham Studios: 328, 343, 349
Denville, Alfred, MP, 287, 304
Desert Island Discs (radio), 517
Desmond, Florence, 29, 309, 323, 355, 469, 540, 541
Desperate Hours (theatre), 447
Devil at Four O' Clock (1961), 471
Devitt, Nina, 231, 224, 305
Dietrich, Marlene, 209, 243-4, 541
Dinner with the Family (TV), 485
Dixon Of Dock Green (TV), 515
Doctor in the House (TV), 531
Dodd, Ken, 392, 466
Does the Team Think (radio), 468
Dolin, Anton, 14, 16, 165, 550
Dollie and Billie, 117
Dolly Sisters, 117, 182
Don Ross, 15
Don't Fence Me In (book), 17, 311, 542, 543, 545
Donat, Robert, 185
Doolittle, General, 353
Dorleac, Françoise, 512
Dors, Diana, 452
Douglas Fairbanks Jr Presents (TV), 448
Dowager Fairy Queen (comedy sketch), 152
Down in the Forest (theatre), 267, 314
Down Melody Lane (1943), 241
Down on the Farm (comedy sketch), 188
Dr Finlay's Casebook (TV), 499, 500, 517
Dr Knock - BBC2 Theatre 625 (TV), 512
Dr Knock - Schools Production for BBC (TV), 481
Driver, Betty, 366
Du Boulay, Shirley, 509
Duchess of York (HRH Queen Elizabeth the Queen Mother), 226, 463
Dudan, Pierre, 431
Duffell, Bee, 461
Duke of York (HRH King George VI), 168, 226, 282
Dulcie (Landlady), 99, 173
Dunbar, Philip, 516
Eaker, Brigadeer, 352-3
Eddington, Paul, 467, 479
Edwards, Jimmy, 410, 413, 422
Elliot, Eleanor; case against Renée, 384; satirized, 385; 465, 370, 390

Elliott, GH, 150, 216, 452-3
Ellis, Vivian, 232, 262, 330
Ellison, John, 392
Elsham Road (home), 105, 109, 132
Elstree Studios: 138, 168, 193, 201, 205, 208, 226, 229, 230, 232, 448, 463, 495, 514, 550, 561
Elvey, Maurice, 205, 309
Elwell, Cyril, 98, 114
Emery, Dick, 520
Emney, Fred, 322, 518
ENSA, 11, 346-348, 366
Equity, 107, 195, 402, 435, 461, 535
Esmé, 36, 557
Evans, Barry, 531-2
Eve, Paul; marriage to Billie, 303; 178, 180-3, 303, 344, 367, 476, 483-4, 541
Eve, Ruby, 180, 182, 348
Eve's Week (theatre), 123
Fase, Berkeley, 398
Faye, Janina, 551-2
Fellner, Herman, 243-6, 265, 277, 310
Field, Sid, 282-3, 315, 427
Fielding, Fenella, 15, 211, 430-435
Fields, Betty, 238, 306
Fields, Gracie; 4, 5, 68, 86,105, 148,158, 161,165, 173, 190, 204, 220-2, 242, 248,256, 271, 291, 374, 411, 449; estate in Capri, 175, 411;
Finch, Peter, 449-50
Fine Feathers (1937), 258, 259, 260, 290, 291, 305, 309
Finlay, Alec, 230, 342, 507-8
Finlay, Frank, 401
Finney, Albert, 468
Fireside Sodgers (comedy sketch), 47
First A Girl (1935), 261
Flanagan and Allan, 166, 205, 217, 444
Flash Soap Powder commercial, 501
Flesh And The Fiends (1959), 445, 473-4
Flittin, The (comedy sketch), 46-47, 58, 61, 62, 197,
Flotsam and Jetsam, 231, 277, 334
Flower, Sir Archie, 338
Flying Flacoris, 142
Flying Fortress (1942), 344-5
Flynn, Errol, 380
Fontaine, Joan, 301, 560
Forde, Florrie, 292, 323
Forde, Walter, 345-6, 367
Foreman, Carl, 457
Formby, George, 239, 394
Fosse, Bob, 455, 458
Fox, Roy, 220
Franceska Juveniles, 370
Francis, Freddie, 500, 456-7

Francis, Kevin, 546
Francis, Raymond, 479
Frank Tinney, 89-90
Frankau, Ronald, 256, 348, 399
Fraser, Eddie, 446, 507
Fraser, Liz, 481
French, Valerie, 432
Freud, Clement, 520, 550
Frost, David, 499, 536
Froth (theatre), 79
Fuller, Leslie, 237-8
Fuller, Loïe, 102
Fulton, Rikki, 64
Furber, Douglas, 152, 279, 323,
Furie, Sidney J, 479
Fyfe and Fyfe, 65, 67
Fyffe, Will, 17, 64, 72, 144, 173, 205, 221, 305, 308, 323, 335
Gable, Clark, 353
Gail, Zoë, 397, 399
Gainsborough Contract, 310, 354
Gainsborough Studios: 160, 193, 194, 249, 316, 320, 328, 357
Gallacher, Tom, 8,10,17-18,88,136,273
Gallery First Nighters' Club, 163
Garbo, Greta; Pat Aherne friendship, 380; 379
Garden, Graeme, 531
Garrison Theatre, 446
Gates, Bill, 381
Gaumont-British: 171, 200, 205, 209, 228, 244, 262, 354
Gaunt, Michael, 212, 521, 546
Gay, Noel, 204, 271
General Strike 1926, 107
Gentlemen Prefer Blondes (theatre), 493
George White's Scandals (theatre), 263
George, Muriel, (and Ernest Butcher), 191
Gerrard, Gene, 244-6
Gielgud, Sir John, 16, 167, 401
Gifford, Dennis, 531
Gillespie, Robert, 506, 512-3
Gilliat, Sidney, 10, 411
Gilling, John, 474
Glasgow Exhibition 1911, 53
Glaze, Peter, 531
Glendale Avenue (home) 138, 222, 231,269; Burglary, 277; 294, 359
Glenville, Peter, 471
Glover, Peter, 397
Godfrey Carr, Violet, 82, 343
Gone Talkie (comedy sketch), 204-5
Gonella, Nat, 257, 502
Goodsir Smith, Alexandar, 521

INDEX

Goodwin, Dennis, 439
Grace Mary Teresa Barry, 133-4
Grade, Lew and Leslie, 370-3, 421, 467
Graham, Morland, 329
Grandmother's Hundredth Birthday (comedy sketch),145-6
Grant Sisters, Lena and Cherry, 424
Grant, Cary, 379, 380, 437, 490
Green Trees (home), 20,39, 374-8, 549
Green, Harry, 167, 456
Green, Hughie, 309, 392
Greene, Richard, 345, 467
Greenstreet, Sidney, 376
Gregson, John, 491, 540
Greta Garbo burlesque (comedy sketch), 222, 255, 561
Gribben Trio, 44
Grieve, John, 507-8
Griffith, Hugh, 547-8
Grock, 201, 216
Guest, Val, 245, 451, 479
Guinness, Sir Alec, 211, 459-464
Gullan, Campbell, 268, 273
Gulliver, Charles, 98, 157-8
Gutowski, Gene, 504
Haimann, Julius, 244
Hakim, Eric, 205-6
Hale, Sonnie, 151, 261, 403
Hall, Henry, 231
Hall, Sir Peter, 18, 455, 459, 460
; discipline of Renée, 461; 462, 464
Handl, Irene, 402, 427, 458
Handley, Tommy, 305, 343, 508
Happy Days Are Here Again (1936) ;*Taming of the Shrew*, 210 & 252; 2, 109, 247,248-9, 251, 252, 253, 255, 256, 264, 266, 280, 336, 510
Harris, Air Chief Marshall, 352
Harris, Herbert, 225, 256, 279,331
Harris, Marion, 170-1
Harrison, Kathleen, 317
Harrison, Rex, 300, 318
Harrison, Stephen, 455
Harry Hughes, 228
Harry McKelvie, 78
Harte, Bret, 76, 78
Hartnell, William, 345-6, 470,492
Harvey, Peter, 496
Hawdon, Robin, 472-3
Hawkins, Jack, 195, 335
Hawtrey, Charles, 308,497,535-8
Hay, Will, 70, 161,166, 236, 245, 323, 334, 354, 561

Hayes, Melvyn, 474
Hayes, Patricia, 7, 494, 505
Hays, Bill, 528
Hayter, James, 490
Hazel Ellis Girls, 370-71
Hearne, Richard, 245-6, 322
Hempseed (Pearson), Ella, 70, 81, 424
Henderson, Dick, 13, 110,114, 166, 220, 460
Henderson, Lorna, 428, 429, 460, 461
Henry Hall's Guest Night, 381
Henry, Charles, 421, 461
Henshall, William, 282, 284, 315
Henson, Leslie, 234, 323
Hepburn, Audrey, 280, 397-9, 400, 402 405,430,432; at Alan's party, 404; appeal for Broadway work, 422;
Hepburn, Katherine, 379
Hermione Baddeley, 167
Hewer, John, 430, 434
Heyhoe-Flint, Rachael, 27, 36
Hibbin, Nina, 464, 539
Hicks, Seymour, Sir, 105, 167, 194, 309
Hickson, Joan, 485, 539
Hill, Benny, 422, 429
Hill, George Joshua, 368, 466
Hill, Ronnie, 174, 224, 260, 290, 305, 307, 326,434
Hillyard, Pat, 427, 447, 454
Hinds, Tony, 489, 547
Hird, Thora, 349, 354, 356
Hiscott, Leslie, 257, 260
Hitchcock, Alfred, 201, 380, 437
Hitchman, Janet, 36, 37, 363
Holden, William, 430, 457
Holloway, Stanley, 24, 151, 171, 325
Home From School (comedy sketch), 151
Home This Afternoon, 527
Hooray! We're Here (theatre), 69, 70, 552
Hope, Bob, 2, 119, 161, 263, 353
Horne, Kenneth, 412
Horse's Mouth, The (1958), 459, 463-4, 470
Housewives Choice (radio), 448
Houston Household, The (radio), 415
Houston Sisters, 7, 8, 12, 17, 72, 92, ; material, 97; 101, 102; Top Ten venues, 111; De Forest Phonofilm, 99, 114-5; musicality, 147-9; salary, 152; radio career, 156-7; failure to tour America, 159-160,214; reunion, 406-7; separation, 264-6; Isle Saint-Louis performance, 484-5; 122, 143, 175, 178, 206, 212, 223, 232, 414, 441, 542, 559

Houston, Billie, 19, 54, 60, 65,
; childhood touring 60-61; stage character, 118-122, 124; 126-7; early marriages, 177-8; back injury, 77, 267 & 406; 311, 385, 421, 438, 439, 442-3, 472, 483, 526, 530; death, 541, 554
Houston, Granny, 38,39,41,72,60,85, 111,138, 145, 184, 237, 274, 332, 350, 353, 373, 375-6; death, 384;
Houston, Jimmie, 40-53, 236, 290, 360, 419, 558, 561; death, 328;
Houston, Lizzi,38,40-52, 58, 61-2,62 69,72,81,85-6,105,109,112,123, 137,172, 237, 274,290,328; death, 350; 419,360, 438, 517, 550, 561
Houston, Shirley, 62, 92, 152, 179, 191, 216, 218, 236, 273, 293, 341, 372, 383, 421, 425, 435, 501, 551, 558
Houston, Terry; adoption, 133-5 & 358-9; 294, 326, 341, 358; escapes Shibden, 363; first marriage, 368; emigrates to US, 376; 382, 466, 549, 558
Howard, Jenny, 221
Howard, Trevor, 457
Howerd, Frankie, 426, 481, 483
Howes, Bobbie, 232
Hudson, Rock, 430
Hughie's Full House (TV), 551
Hulbert, Claude, 226, 227, 228, 229, 399, 400, 405
Hulbert, Jack, 167, 541, 544
Hulme, Benita, 378
Huntingtower (1927), 159, 199
Hutch, 126, 205, 299, 353
I'll Get You For This (1951), 409
Imperial Airways Flight, 129, 177
Inverclyde, Alan, Lord, 91, 230-1, 235
It's a Wonderful World (1956), 451
Jack and Jill (theatre), 80
Jackson, Sir Barry, 188, 194, 196, 198
Jacob, Pat, 27, 29, 35
David Jacobs, 470, 520
Jacques, Hattie, 373, 537-8
James Houston and Company, 45, 47, 62, 197, 276, 561
James, Sid, 411, 448-9, 467-8, 470, 497, 514, 535, 537, 540
Janni, Joe, 447, 452
Jaye, Bobby, 531
Jeffries, Lionel, 516
Jewel and Warriss, 392, 444
Jimfy, 22, 476, 494, 552-4

Jimmy Logan Show (TV), 446
Jimmy Logan Theatre Hour
  (TV), 508
Johns, Glynis, 455
Johns, Stratford, 497
Johnson, Pauline, 433
June, 262
June Rose Ball, 167, 191
Kaempfert, Bert, 22, 517
Kaplan, Syd, 305
Karlin, Miriam, 30, 430-3, 481
Karno, Fred, 68
Katherine Cornell, 196
Kazan, Elia, 459
Kearns, Allan, 269
Kelly, Grace (Princess Grace of
  Monaco), 541, 555
Kemble, Charlie, 65-6, 385
Kemp-Welch, Joan, 452
Kemp, Harry, 89, 111
Kendall, Kay, 411
Kendall, Marie, 251, 256
Kenney, Horace, 231, 274, 413
Kent, Jean, 356
Kester, Max, 415
Key, The (1957), 457, 479
Kidd Brothers, 249, 277, 283,
  286, 293, 296, 503
Kidnapping by students
  ; ID parade, 284, 286; trial
  defence, 288; testimonies, 288;
  stage profession's reaction &
  Parliamentary Questions, 287;
  trial prosecution & public
  reaction, 289;
King Edward VI School, 338
King George's Fund, 509
King, Hetty, 118-120, 124-5,
  247-8, 292, 412, 443, 452-3
Klinger, Michael, 504
Kocsis, Anne, 436
Komeda, Krzysztof, 512
Korda, Alexander, 226, 299, 329-30
Krankees, 116, 562
Kunz, Charlie, 325
Kydd, Sam, 532, 481
La Rue, Danny, 68, 417, 447, 540
Ladies In Retirement, (theatre),
  521-526
Lady Godiva Rides Again (1951),
  411
Lady Ratlings, 287, 406-7, 411, 443
Lambert, Verity, 527
Lanchester, Elsa, 167, 208,
  300, 468-9
Landeau, Cecil, 397-8, 405, 429
  430, 435-6, 447

Lane, Lupino, 231
Lang, Matheson, 78, 522
Lauder, Sir Harry, 41, 74, 82, 85,
  159, 173, 199, 365, 517
Laughton, Charles, 208, 211, 299,
  300, 404, 450, 468, 469
Launder, Frank, 10, 316, 354-7,
  411, 427-9, 483
Laurie, John, 452, 514
Lawson Dick, Clare, 36
Laye, Evelyn, 166, 322, 401-3, 517
Layton and Johnstone, 103,
  148, 174, 236
Le Beau, Bettine, 28-29
Le Mesurier, John, 512
Lee, Belinda, 428, 452
Lee, Jack, 447, 450
Lee, Norman, 245, 248-250
Legend of the Werewolf (1975),
  546-548
Leicester Square Looks Round
  (theatre), 282
Leigh, Vivien, 300, 301, 401
Lesley, Carole, 479
Let Loose (theatre), 346-7, 419
Let Me Do the Talking (TV), 520
Life With Cooper (TV), 527
Life With The Lyons (radio & TV),
  412, 415, 508
Lillie, Bea, 165, 221, 257, 469
Lime Grove Studios: 200, 205,
  354, 364, 439, 455, 469, 481
Lister, Lance, 152, 418
Little Tich, 55, 222, 224,
Little Women (theatre), 551
Littler, Emile, 273
Lloyd George, David, 44, 89, 203
Lloyd, Marie, 48, 49, 103, 159, 167
Lockhart, Howard, 426, 506,
  508, 533
Lockwood, Margaret, 309,
  310, 317, 355
Loftus, Marie, 292
Logan, Buddy, 424
Logan, Jimmy, 67, 424, 496,
  503, 506, 507, 528, 533
Logan, May, 75, 424
Löhr, Marie, 449-450
Lom, Herbert, 490
London Music Hall, 93-4
Long Jr, John, 466
Longden, John, 194, 205-7, 497
Loobs, The, 56
Looks Familiar (TV), 544
Loose Women (TV), 23, 31-2
Loren, Sophia, 281, 457-8
Lorne, Tommy, 64, 79, 84

Losey, Joseph, 456
Loss, Joe, 416, 540, 544
Lost In The Legion (1934),
  237, 238, 239, 501
Love Laughs (theatre), 243-4,
  264-6, 268-273, 527
Lownes, Victor, 504
Loxley Lily, 340-41, 351
Lubicz, Christina, 430
Luzita, Sara, 398
Lyall, Helen, 441
Lyall, Niall, 440-3, 460, 474-5,
  529-30, 555, 563
Lynn, Vera, 221, 298, 367, 407, 416, 540
Lyon, Ben, 98, 224, 309, 336, 415
Mabel Constanduros, 156
MacDonald, Aimi, 35, 550
MacDonald, Murray, 472, 452
MacDonald, Ramsay, 166
MacFadyen, Iain, 503, 542
MacLeod, Tex, 133, 167, 224, 308, 323,
Macmillan, Harold, 499
Madden, Father Robert, 21,
  539, 540, 556-7
Maigret (TV), 476, 478-9
Main Wilson, Dennis, 494
Male Impersonation, 124-5
Malleson, Miles, 470
Man of the World (TV), 489
Mander, Miles, 114
Mannix, Eddie, 437
Mannix, Toni, 437
Mannock, PL, 228, 241, 321
Mansfield, Jayne, 468
Mantovani, 416, 540
March, Elspeth, 528
Marlana, 397, 399
Marriage Brokers (theatre), 506
Marriot, Moore, 17, 300, 318, 321
Martin Harvey, Sir John, 195
Martin, Millicent, 499, 503
Massie, Paul, 459
Matthews, Jessie, 17, 151, 159, 172, 224,
  249, 261, 330; 402-4, rows with Renée;
Maxwell, Charles, 410, 425, 468
Maxwell, John, 156, 200, 202, 228
Maxwell, Lois, 457
May We Introduce (theatre),
  343, 348
May, Charmian, 516
Maynard, Bill, 210, 216-7, 383, 391-2
Mayne, Clarice, 145, 171, 453
McBride, Sally, 174, 247-9, 260,
  278, 305, 426
McCallum, David, 452
McCallum, John, 472
McGivern, Cecil, 410, 412, 426, 427

584

INDEX

McGovern, John - MP, 286-7
McGowan, Cathy, 29
McGuire, Patricia, Mary and sisters, 180, 181, 326
McIntyre, Thea, 11, 216, 347
McKenna, Virginia, 449, 450
McKern, Leo, 457, 459
McLaglen, Cyril, 200, 201, 205, 230, 380
McLaglen, Victor, 200
McLeod, Tex, 134, 167, 308, 324
McNaughton, Gus, 228-9
McQueen, Jimmy, 63
Meehan, CF, 343, 454
Meeting at Night (theatre), 534-5
Melody and Romance (1937), 309-10
Melvin, GS, 82,97,144,145,174, 305
Merrier We Shall Be (theatre), 373
Merrily We Go (theatre), 304-5, 307, 349, 371
Merson, Billy, 151, 234, 236
Merton, Jessica, 102, 134, 173, 287
Messiter, Ian, 23-25, 27-29, 34, 37, 275, 362, 412-3
Meyrick, Kate, 183
Michie, Bryan, 290
Miles, Lord Bernard, 349, 506
Miller, Arnold Louis, 510
Miller, Glenn, 353
Miller, Max, 126, 151-2, 158, 168, 170, 220, 229, 305, 388,535; Appreciation Society, 216;
Mills, Annette, 405
Mills, John, 329,330, 349
Mills, Juliet, 331, 482, 488, 490
Mills, Nat and Bobbie, 316
Mister Cinders (1934), 232-234, 560
Moffat, John, 506
Mollison, Clifford, 232-3, 550
Monkhouse, Bob, 1, 398, 405, 439, 544, 550
Monks, Diana, 397, 405, 430, 434
Montagu, Ivor, 160
Moodie, Douglas, 520
Moody, Ron, 548
Moore, Richard, 506
Moore, Sir Roger, 499
More Dam Things (theatre), 144, 151, 152, 179, 267, 283
More, Kenneth, 468
Mosley, Oswald, 172
Moss Empires, 43, 304, 335
Movie Actor's Home, Woodland Hills, 541

Moxon, May, 63
Mrs Beatty's Home Perms (comedy sketch), 435
Mrs Marchbanks (comedy sketch), 435
Mrs Pat (boat), 291-3
Muir, Frank, 23, 410, 532
Mullard, Arthur, 550
Mullen, Barbara, 499, 500
Murdoch, Richard, 541, 544
Murphy, Greta, 270, 294
Murphy, Kathleen, 294-5, 360, 368, 558
Murray, Chic, 17, 426, 496, 503
Murray, Pete, 476, 531, 533, 545
Musical Medley No. 5 (1932), 115
Mycroft, Walter, 160, 228
Nairn,Binkie,59,60,133,171,301,436
Naughton and Gold,74,146, 168,217
Navy Mixture (radio), 366, 410
Nazimova, 219
Neame, Ronald, 459, 463
Neilson-Terry, Phyllis, 146, 431, 433-4
Nervo and Knox, 115, 171, 217
Nettlefold Studios, 193, 345, 446, 467, 470,
Nevern Road (home), 430, 443
New Metropole theatre, 507, 533
Newman, Patrick, 410, 427, 446, 451
Newman, Widgey, 115
Newmeyer, Fred, 237
Nichols, Joy, 410, 422, 425
Nicholson, Mavis, 70, 87, 276, 281,544-5
Nicholson, Nicky, 355
Nicholson, Nora, 450
Nicolson, Harold, 334
Nimmo, Derek, 521
Niven, David, 298-9, 379, 380
No Hiding Place (TV), 479, 490
No Monkey Business (1935), 187, 243-247
No My Darling Daughter (1961), 481-483
No, That's Me Over Here (TV), 534
Noble, Trisha, 533
Nolan, Margaret, 537-9
Noni, 151, 324
Norbrooke (home), 364
Norden, Dennis, 23, 410, 544
Norman Road (home), 438
Northwick Circle (home), 138, 190, 359
Nurse on Wheels (1963), 490, 491
O' Callaghan, Richard, 7, 536

O' Farrell, Talbot, 124,146, 323,396
O' Flynn, Philip, 499
O' Gorman Brothers, 97, 174,219, 222-3, 308, 323, 342, 381
O' Gorman, Brian,186, 223,381,435
O' Gorman, Joe; 44, 68, 186
O' Shea, Tessie, 278, 343, 373, 396
O' Neil, Zelma, 232
Oberon, Merle, 298-300, 306, 380
Old Bill And Son (1941), 5, 329, 331, 330
Old Vicarage, Alveston (home), 333
Oliver, Vic, 166, 305, 326, 444
Olivier, Sir Lawrence, 167, 186, 188, 210, 300, 401, 404, 458, 459, 483
Olsen's sea lions, 188
On Stage Coliseum (radio), 444
One Exciting Night (1944), 367
One Minute Please (radio), 412, 414
One O'Clock Gang (TV), 503, 520
Open House (radio), 534, 552
Optimists of Nine Elms (1973), 548
Orde, Beryl, 221
Ormerod, James, 488
Osborn, Andrew, 477, 479, 500
Ostrer Brothers, 158, 354, 356-7
Our Lady and St Francis (school), 56-58, 62, 212, 234
Out of the Fog (1962), 488, 490
Over My Dead Body (TV), 517
Owen, Bill, 476, 498
Palmer, Lilli, 317, 319
Paris Exhibition 1937, 308
Parnell, Val, 385, 421, 449
Parsons Family, 117
Parsons, Geoffrey, 398, 418
Parsons, Nicholas, 22, 342, 521
Party, The (theatre), 468-9
Pathé films of celebrities, 291
Pathéscope' prints, 259
Paul, Dorothy, 503, 520
Peers, Donald, 230, 286, 373, 407
Penfold, Patricia, 371
Perfect Harmony (comedy sketch), 152
Pertwee, Michael, 317, 432
Peterville Diamond (1942), 345-6
Petrie, Daniel, 516
Petticoat Line: 1, 3, 22-37, 98, 362, 505-6, 508, 514, 517, 523, 528, 531,539-40, 542, 544, 546, 548, 550-1, 558, 562
Phantom of the Opera, The (1962), 488-9, 547
Phillips, Leslie, 452

Phoenix, Pat, 503, 533
Phonofilms, 98-99, 114-5
Pilgrim Players, 194
Pinewood Studios: 343, 447, 450, 452, 489, 490, 535, 547-8
Piper, Jackie, 281, 536
Pitt, Archie, 68, 86
Plaisance, The (home), 195
Pleasance, Donald, 473, 511, 543
Plomley, Roy, 412, 517
Plough Pub, Elstree, 560
Pola, Eddie, 240, 255, 300, 321-2, 327
Polanski, Roman, 504-5, 511-2
Pollen-B supplement, 529, 555
Pons, Lily, 262
Pope John XXIII, 484
Potter, Gillie, 104, 305, 351
Pounds Sisters, 116
Powell, Dilys, 554
Powell, Eleanor, 263, 394
Powell, Enoch, 197
Powell, Margaret, 32-3
Price, Vincent, 437, 498
Priestley, JB, 335
Prince of Wales, The (King Edward VIII), 14, 107, 120, 166, 168, 169, 304, 311
Prince Paul of Greece, 169
Princess Margaret, 463
Programmes Seller (comedy sketch), 434
Proops, Marjorie, 33, 505
Purcell, Noel, 499
Puzzle Corner, 440
Queens of Sport (comedy sketch), 434
Radio Luxembourg, 306-7
Radio Parade (1933), 2, 12, 228-9, 249
Radio Pictorial, 135, 219, 220, 403
Radiolympia (theatre & radio) 24, 231
Raft, George, 410
Rainbow, Lynn, 522
Raitt, Ann, 507-8
Raki, Laya, 435
Ramsbottom Rides Again (1956), 449
Randall & Hopkirk Deceased (TV), 536
Randle, Frank, 78, 413
Rappaport Always Pays (TV), 456
Ray, René, 331
Ray, Ted, 2,7, 45, 93, 102, 290, 381, 406-7, 412, 444, 454, 535, 544

Reader, Ralph, 275, 278, 443
Reagan, Ronald, 468
Real Thing (comedy sketch), 400
Redgrave, Sir Michael, 211, 404, 455, 456, 482
Redistribution of film shorts, 248, 259
Redman, Joyce, 468
Reed, Carol,10,316-7, 320,403, 458
Reeve, Ada, 24, 118, 444
Reeves, George, 437
Rehearsing a Drama (comedy sketch), 145
Reid, Beryl, 33-36, 427, 428, 551
Reid, Jimmy, 40, 56
Reinsch Brothers, 219
Reith, John, 156
Rennie, Claire,134-5,138,184-5,236 316, 365,438, 475, 532, 558,560
Rennie, James Alan,41-3,49,53-6, 112,172, 183, 185, 191, 316, 365, 424, 438, 475, 508; death, 532;
Rent Strikes 1915, 46
Repulsion (1965), 504-5, 511
Rescue Squad (1963), 495
Restaurant (comedy sketch), 234
Return of Bulldog Drummond (1934), 200
Revnell and West, 117, 444, 541
Richard, Sir Cliff, 479,480, 496, 524, 532, 540
Richards, Shelagh, 488
Richardson, Ralph, 200, 401
Richmond, June, 388
Riddle of Rainbow Mountain (book), 56
Riding Lesson (comedy sketch), 152
Ripley, Heather, 516
River Rivals (1967), 519
Riviera Club, 171
Road To Rome(comedy sketch),432
Roar Like A Dove (theatre) ; Phoenix Theatre, 186 & 471; 211, 475, 480, 485, 496, 498, Dundee Rep, 516; 533
Robey, George,103, 234, 278-9,291, 308, 318, 320-1, 232,381, 412
Robins, Phyllis, 223-4, 334
Robinson Crusoe 1922(theatre),78
Robinson Crusoe 1945 (theatre), 370, 373
Robson, Flora, 356, 357, 401, 472
Roc, Pat, 356
Rock A Bye Sailor (theatre), 7, 494
Rock n' Roll Murder (theatre), 453
Rogers, Eric, 538-9

Rogers, Peter,489, 491,497, 514
Roly Polys, 11
Rooftop Rendezvous (TV), 394-5, 409
Rose, George, 445-6, 473
Rose, Julian, 231, 235
Ross, Don, 15, 393, 502
Ross, Julian, 65, 67
Rossiter, Leonard, 512
Rothwell, Talbot, 535, 539
Rowe, Ronnie, 302
Rowlands, Patsy, 535
Rowley, 387, 422, 424
Royal Performance 1926 (theatre), 14, 109, 157, 215
Royal Performance 1938 (theatre), 323
Ruby Eve, 180, 182-3, 348
Rudy Vallée, 263
Rushton, William, 499, 550
Russell, Billy, 333
Russell, Robin, 23, 52, 72, 385, 479, 542
Ryder, Sue, 534
Sailor Beware (theatre), 533
Salberg, Derek, 324
Salomon, AH (Doc), 345, 367
Sanders, George, 436, 541
Sarony, Leslie, 7, 93, 94, 95, 166
Sauce Piquante (theatre), 405
Sauce Tartare (theatre) ;Renée's speech, 461; 397, 404, 417, 422, 434
Savile, Jimmy, 540-1
Saville, Philip, 457
Savoy Hill Studios (radio), 224
Schubert, Lee, 257, 265
Scotch Broth (theatre), 90, 91, 113
Scott-Johnson, Alistair, 25, 426
Scott, George Urie, 44
Scott, Terry, 470, 541
Seal, Elizabeth, 211-12, 432, 455
Searle, Ronald, 429
Sears, Heather, 490
Secombe, Sir Harry, 460,540, 543
Secrets of a Windmill Girl (1966), 510
See You Later (theatre), 76, 77, 122, 267
Sellars, Elizabeth, 528
Sellers, Peter, 463, 548
Serle, Christopher, 25
Sewell, Gladdy, 151, 155
Shadwell, Charles, 224, 290
Shakespeare Memorial Theatre (theatre), 335-7, 339, 549

INDEX

Shand, Jimmy, 503
Sharman, John, 306, 338, 415
Shaver, Buster, 393
Shaw, George Bernard, 160, 194
Shaw, Robert, 491
Sheila Tracy, 25
Sheldon, Horace, 13, 202, 205, 241
Shelton, Ann, 350, 383, 416
Shenton, William, 205
Shepherd's Bush Studios, 448
Sheriff of Fractured Jaw(58), 468
Sherman Fisher Girls, 240, 305
Sherrin, Ned, 476, 499
Shibden (home),344,347-8,351,374
Shields, Ella, 89, 117-9, 123, 396
Shrewsbury, Lord, 235, 239
Shurey, Dinah, 193
Silander, Hal, 333,340, 376, 372, 376, 383, 501, 558
Silander, Herbert, 184
Silander, Marion, 184, 235, 236, 350, 351, 466 - death
Silver Lining (1927), 200, 205
Sim, Alistair, 309, 411, 427, 428
Simons, Pam, 485, 488, 495, 505, 542, 543, 554, 556, 563
Sims, Joan, 427, 481, 489
Sinatra, Frank, 471
Sinclair, Hugh, 317-8
Sinclair, Peter, 425, 467, 502
Sinden, Donald, 489
Singapore Chess Federation Championship, 442
Sir William Borlase (school), 375
Sirk, Douglas, 429
Skating Nelsons, 142
Slater, John, 469
Smeedon, Enid, 397, 405
Smith, Cyril, 231, 494
Smith, Julia, 500
Smith, Liz, 550
Smith, Mildred, 431
Snagge, John, 300
So This is Hollywood (comedy sketch), 256
Society Reporter (comedy sketch), 145
Somlo, Josef, 244, 329, 331
Shepperton Studios: 250, 428-9, 464, 489, 519,
Sounds Familiar (radio), 531
South Africa Trip, 311-314
Southwark Catholic Rescue Society, 134-5
Speakeasy (radio), 540
Special Branch (TV), 543
Spotlight BBC (radio),91,542

Springsteen, Bob, 445
Spy with a Cold Nose (1966), 516
St Anne's Catholic Settlement, 540
St Erconwalds, 539, 556
St John, Earl, 384
St Mark's School, 53
St Paul's School, 348, 364
Stage costumes, 225, 260, 281, 283, 323
Stander, Lionel, 511
Standing, Michael, 393, 409, 410, 412, 452
Stanford, Jack, 186, 305
Stanley, Kim, 459
Starlight (radio), 306, 308
Step-By-Step To Stardom (People's Journal series), 266
Stepham, Renée, 521
Stevens, Maureen, 432
Stewart, Andy, 64,426,430,446,448
Stewart, Donald, early life, 262-3; act with Renée, 17, 159, 174, 211, 265 & 280 & 307-8, 316,323-7, 336-7, 346-7, 350-352, 366-372, 382, 394-5, 436, 448, 453; with Renée's family, 294-6 & 298 & 305-6; foreign Status, 297, 337, 369; injuries, 342, 370; letters, 325, 440, 480; film career, 345-6; 367-8, 468, 489; marries Renée, 387; as husband, 333, 375-8, 421-4, 438-41, 475-6; West End, 447, 455, 458, 469, 472, 493; marquetry 404 & 423; hospital treatments, 456 & 486 & 495; death; convalescence, 503; death 514-5;
Stocks, Baroness, Mary 1, 28, 29
Stoll, Sir Oswald, 8, 10, 43, 101, 103, 157, 174, 192, 463, 550
Storm, Lesley, 211, 455, 471, 472, 475, 542
Stroud, Pauline, 411
Summerfield, Eleanor, 469
Summerskill, Baroness, 33
Sumner, David, 490
Sunday Night at the Palladium (TV), 449
Sunny Days (theatre), 178, 230
Sutton, Randolph, 346-8, 444, 452
Swaffer, Hannen, 155, 164, 254-5
Swinley, Ion, 252
Taggart, Alice, 425
Takaki, Tenji, 450, 497
Take It From Here (radio), 410, 425

Talk Yourself Out Of This (radio), 402, 409
Tapfer, Sydney, 535
Tarakanova, Nina, 398,400,430
Tarri, Suzette, 323, 469
Tate, Harry, 93, 174, 223, 323
Tate, Sharon, 530
Tax Issues, 174-5, 265, 476
Taxi (TV), 497
Taylor, Gil, 504
Taylor, Kent, 444
Teds attack Renée Houston, 476-7
Teddington Studios: 344-5, 367-8, 409, 527,
Tell the Truth (TV), 470
Temple, Claude, 197, 292, 295
Tenser, Tony, 504
Terriss, Ellaline, 160
Terry's Juveniles, 134
That Was The Week That Was (TV), 499, 536
Thatcher, Margaret, 33, 389, 539
Theatrical digs, 186, 212, 213
Theatrical travel, 141
Their Night Out (1933), 2, 226, 228-230, 271, 317, 443, 463
Them Nice Americans (1958), 467
Theobald, Terrence, 397, 430-1
Thomas, Gerald, 489, 497, 502, 536, 539
Thomas, Howard,97-8,113,224,306
Thomas, Ralph, 481-3
Thomsett, Sally, 519
Thorndike Theatre, 526
Thorndike, Dame Sybil, 107, 186, 188-9, 211, 401
Thorne, Kenneth, 490
Three Bears (comedy sketch), 15, 143
Three Beauty Queens (comedy sketch), 400
Three Fat Women of Antibes (TV), 527-8
Three on a Spree (1961), 479
Thripp, Alfred, 388
Thunderbird Ranch (home), 378
Tiller Girls, 133
Tilley, Vesta, 10, 54, 104, 117, 118-121, 141, 159, 167, 173
Time Of My Life, The (radio), 527
Time Without Pity (1957), 454-6, 492
Titheradge, Peter Dion, 326-7
To Meet The King (theatre), 188-9
Todd, Ann, 177, 457
Todd, Richard, 463, 533, 536

Todman, John, 552
Togare, 187-8
Tom, Tom the Piper's Son (theatre), 83-4
Tomorrow At Ten (1963), 491-2
Tomorrow Mountain (comedy sketch), 432
Took, Barry, 531
Topsy Turvy (theatre), 80-3
Tossell, Henry, 335-6
Tower Holme, 195
Townsend, Peter, 435
Toy Drum Major(song)93,95-6,102
Track The Man Down (1955),444-6
Tracy, Spencer, 471
Travers, Susan, 490
Tremayne, Tilly, 522, 523, 526
Triad Films, 473
Trinder, Tommy, 2, 168, 399, 414, 443, 449, 469, 518
Triumph Theatre Productions, 533
Trix Sisters, 116
Trowlock Island, 425
Tucker, Sophie, 103, 146, 164, 167, 170, 219, 234, 309, 394
Twice Round The Clock, 129, 130, 179, 181, 264
Twice Round the Daffodils (1962), 489
Twickenham Studios, 228
Two Leslies, 323, 365
Two Thousand Women (1944), 10, 245, 328, 353-356, 363-4, 404
Tyburn Productions, 546, 548, 556
Underground (1929), 196, 201
United Press International, 484
United Service Overseas shows, 348, 353, 365-6
United States Army Air Forces, 352
Urry, Leonard, 171, 343, 373
Valentine, Dickie, 444, 448
Van Damm, Sheila, 33
Van Dock, 92, 167
Vandyk, Herbert, 163
Variety (1935), 2, 12, 13, 102, 121, 240-3, 246, 251, 264
Variety Artistes Federation, 44, 47-8, 80, 143, 155, 157-8, 192
Varnel, Marcel, 245
Vaughan, Frankie, 408, 448, 463
Ventriloquist (comedy sketch), 12, 93, 337, 408, 485
Vietnam War, 523

Vintor, Ivor, 150-1
W Plan, The (1930) 196, 299
Wakefield, Oliver, 345
Waldegrave Park (home), 386, 401, 420, 439
Waldman, Ronnie, 394, 409, 422, 439, 440
Walker, Bruce, 453
Walker, Jimmy, 119
Walker, Syd, 270
Wall, Max, 48, 205
Wallace, Edgar, 309, 312
Wallace, Nellie, 6, 68, 70, 146, 192, 220, 240,291, 393
Waller, Jack, 265, 278, 291
Walsh, Kay, 459, 463-4
Ward, Dorothy, 231, 471
Ward, Mackenzie, 278
Warner Brothers UK, 345
Warner, Jack, 64, 117, 334, 515
Warrender, Harold, 409
Watch It, Sailor! (1961), 481
Water Rats, 177, 406, 443, 502
Waters, Elsie and Doris, 117, 232, 322-3, 346, 444, 539
Watling, Jack, 479
Watt, John, 231, 290, 388
Watt, Sylvia, 65
Wayne, Naunton, 64, 126, 150, 317, 320
Weavers, Mark, 547
Weir, Molly, 64, 415, 501, 507-8
Weissmuller, Johnny, 541
Weisweiller, Pamela, 534
Welch, Elizabeth, 324
Welcome Mr Washington (1944), 489
Well End Lodge (home), 137, 230
Welland, Colin, 497
Wells, Billy, 199, 292
Whitehouse, Mary, 34
Whitelaw, Billie, 456, 474, 488
Whitelock, Trafford, 23, 527
Whitley, Clifford, 268
Wilding, April, 510
Williams, Bransby, 49, 94, 110 142, 146, 156-7, 174, 192, 204, 216, 323
Williams, Kenneth, 37, 489, 535
Williams, Tennessee, 455, 458-9
Willis, Dave, 90-92, 392, 425,446, 453, 502
Willis, Ted, 497, 514-5
Wilson, Harold, 515

Wilton-Smith, Bob, 177-8, 183, 305, 349
Wilton, Robb, 14, 93, 102, 110, 144, 173, 177-9, 191, 223, 257, 258, 310, 323, 348-9, 560
Windsor, Dame Barbara, 501
Winn, Anona, 1, 23-8, 30, 32,34-37, 98, 231, 324, 239, 362, 505, 517, 527, 542, 544
Winstone, Eric, 347, 364
Wintermute, Janice, 262, 297, 311, 486
Wintermute, Lois, 324, 387, 401, 419, 421, 486
Wintermute, Mrs Jessie (Mickey), 261-2, 297, 313, 345, 387, 421, 468, 476, 487-8, 513
Wisdom, Norman, 411
Wise, Ernie, 223
Wise, Herbert, 512-13
Woman's Hour (radio), 509, 550
Wonderful War - The Saint (TV), 498
Wood, Georgie, 62, 97, 98, 133, 134, 191, 303, 373, 396, 412, 527, 549, 550
Wood, Sir Henry, 14, 121
Woodward, Hubert, 521
Woolf, CM, 158, 243, 246, 329-30
Worker's Playtime (radio), 373, 380-83, 390, 409,412,452
World War One Bombings; Longbridge Works, 197;
World War Two bombings; Battle of Britain, 334; Coventry, 340 & 342; Thousand Bomber Raid, 343; Ilford, 370-372; Sheffield, 342; V1s, 367;
World's Workers (comedy sketch), 434
Worsley, Bill, 454
Wrigg, Ann, 522
Wright, Lawrence, 95-6, 108, 173, 255, 488
Wylie, Julian, 78, 151
Wymark, Patrick, 514
Wynne, Maie, 90
Yates, Marjorie, 548
Young, Dan, 76, 78
Young, Paul, 533
Z Cars (TV), 496-7
Zandona, Chi Chi, 544-5
Zarina, Manya, 335
Zelnik, Friedrich, 232,243